The European Union

and Histo

Second Edition

The European Union

Economics, Policies and History

Second Edition

Susan Senior Nello

*The **McGraw·Hill** Companies*

London Boston Burr Ridge, IL Dubuque, IA Madison, WI New York San Francisco
St. Louis Bangkok Bogotá Caracas Kuala Lumpur Lisbon Madrid Mexico City
Milan Montreal New Delhi Santiago Seoul Singapore Sydney Taipei Toronto

The European Union: Economics, Policies and History, 2nd Edition
Susan Senior Nello
ISBN-13 978-0-07-711813-6
ISBN-10 0-07-711813-8

McGraw-Hill
Higher Education

Published by McGraw-Hill Education
Shoppenhangers Road
Maidenhead
Berkshire
SL6 2QL
Telephone: 44 (0) 1628 502 500
Fax: 44 (0) 1628 770 224
Website: www.mcgraw-hill.co.uk

British Library Cataloguing in Publication Data
A catalogue record for this book is available from the British Library

Library of Congress Cataloging in Publication Data
The Library of Congress data for this book has been applied for from the Library of Congress

Acquisitions Editor: Natalie Jacobs
Development Editor: Thomas Hill
Marketing Manager: Vanessa Boddington
Senior Production Editor: James Bishop

Cover design by Adam Renvoize
Printed and bound in Great Britain by Bell & Bain Ltd, Glasgow

ISBN-13 978-0-07-711813-6
ISBN-10 0-07-711813-8

The McGraw-Hill Companies

Dedication

This book is inevitably dedicated to Paolo, Matteo and Caterina, and to the many friends I have made throughout Europe and elsewhere while studying and teaching EU integration.

Brief Table of Contents

Detailed Table of Contents

Guided Tour

Learning Objectives

Each chapter opens with a set of learning objectives, helping readers to quickly grasp the essentials to be learned in the chapter

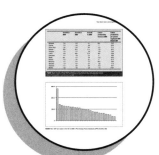

Key Terms

These are highlighted in the relevant chapters providing ease of reference

Figures and Tables

Each chapter provides a number of figures and tables to help illustrate and summarize important concepts.

Summary of Key Concepts

Summary of Key Concepts

- The **1969 Hague Summit** envisaged
  the monetary instability of the 1970s.
- The **'snake in the tunnel'** was created
  of currencies linked to the D-mark ag
- The **European Monetary System** was
  mechanism, introduction of the ECU
  The ECU was the forerunner of the
  the institutional basis on which t
- The operation of EMS can be
  the 1992 crisis and after. F
  15 per cent.

This briefly reviews and reinforces the main topics you have covered
in each chapter to ensure you have acquired a solid understanding
of the key topics.

Questions for Study and Review

Questions for study a.

1 Describe the static and dynamic e
2 Compare the effects of non-discrim
   arrangement or customs union.
3 What explanations have been given
   agreements to non-discrimination?
4 Under what conditions is a customs
5 What are the main approaches use
   integration?
6 Does regional integration prom
7 Exercise on trade creation
   cts of formation

These questions encourage you to review and apply the knowledge
you have acquired from each chapter and can be undertaken to test
your understanding.

Appendices

Appendix 1

EU–Turkish Relations

Turkey became a member of the OECD
1952. It applied for Associate Membersh
following the coup in 1960, talks were sus
   In 1963 Turkey signed an Association
Since being European is one of the con
President of the European Commission,
was 'part of Europe'. However, debate
and the implications for EU membersh
   An Additional Protocol modifie
reation of a customs union by 1
us crisis and the Greek
in Europ

Relevant chapters end with an Appendix that aims to expand on
themes explored in the chapter.

Technology to enhance learning and teaching

Visit **www.mcgraw-hill.co.uk/textbooks/senior** today

Online Learning Centre (OLC)

After completing each chapter, log on to the supporting Online Learning Centre website. Take advantage of the study tools offered to reinforce the material you have read in the text, and to develop your knowledge of psychology in a fun and effective way.

Resources for students include:

- *Learning Outcomes*
- *Useful Weblinks*
- *Topical Essays*
- *Guide Answers to Exercises*

Also available for lecturers:

- *Lecture Outlines*
- *PowerPoint presentations.*

Custom Publishing Solutions: let us help make our **content** your **solution**

Custom Publishing Solutions: Let us help make our **content** your **solution**

At McGraw-Hill Education our aim is to help lecturers to find the most suitable content for their needs delivered to their students in the most appropriate way. Our **custom publishing solutions** offer the ideal combination of content delivered in the way which best suits lecturer and students.

Our custom publishing programme offers lecturers the opportunity to select just the chapters or sections of material they wish to deliver to their students from a database called Primis at www. primisonline.com

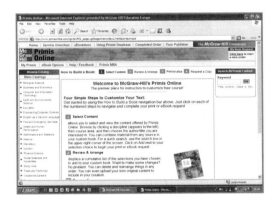

Primis contains over two million pages of content from:

- textbooks
- professional books
- case books – Harvard Articles, Insead, Ivey, Darden, Thunderbird and BusinessWeek
- Taking Sides – debate materials

Across the following imprints:

- McGraw-Hill Education
- Open University Press
- Harvard Business School Press
- US and European material

There is also the option to include additional material authored by lecturers in the custom product – this does not necessarily have to be in English.

We will take care of everything from start to finish in the process of developing and delivering a custom product to ensure that lecturers and students receive exactly the material needed in the most suitable way.

With a Custom Publishing Solution, students enjoy the best selection of material deemed to be the most suitable for learning everything they need for their courses – something of real value to support their learning. Teachers are able to use exactly the material they want, in the way they want, to support their teaching on the course.

Please contact your local McGraw-Hill representative with any questions or alternatively contact Warren Eels e: warren_eels@mcgraw-hill.com.

Preface

Many years ago when studying European integration at the College of Europe in Bruges, one of the professors organized a trip to the battlefields of Flanders of the First World War. The day seemed a little like a school outing, but with the relentless rain falling in the former trenches, the lesson was well taken. One of the main aims of integration was to render war in Europe not only inconceivable, but 'materially impossible'. Today, despite tensions in certain areas, in the EU we tend to take this success almost for granted. One of the aims now is to extend this achievement to other less stable areas of Europe such as the former Yugoslavia.

Of the many experts working on East-West studies, few predicted the collapse of Communism in 1989. Right from the start of transition the Central and Eastern European countries wanted to join the integration process. At first the European Community seemed rather unprepared and overwhelmed at the prospect, but after a long and difficult process of preparation, between 2004 and 2007 much of Europe was again 'reunified'.

In 2007 there were celebrations of fifty years of European integration and under the then German Presidency of the EU, Angela Merkel singled out environmental policy as a way of re-launching the integration process, announcing that the EU was at the vanguard of the battle against climate change. In recent years increased priority has also been given to increasing competitiveness, improving 'employability' and encouraging the adaptability of businesses in the EU.

European integration has a strong political impetus, but the method of implementation has been primarily economic. The first successful initiative was the European Coal and Steel Community created in 1951, while in the early years of the European Economic Community (EEC) the main progress was in trade and agriculture (though the policy mechanisms chosen for the latter can be criticized). Numerous studies show that the Single Market Programme introduced from 1985, and bolstered in many member states by the euro, has fostered trade and other closer economic ties between countries.

The book is aimed mainly at students of economics, European studies, business, political science and international relations. Though the approach is grounded in economics, the aim is to provide a multidisciplinary account of EU integration. The debate about whether the EU is primarily an economic or political entity is of long standing, but the view here is that in order to understand the process of integration a combination of economics, politics and history is necessary. The textbook is intended to have a strong policy orientation.

The objective has also been to organize the material in a flexible way so it can be directed at different audiences. For this reason the theory has been concentrated in Chapters 4 and 5 and in separate sections in other chapters. Omitting Chapters 4 and 5, and the theoretical sections, the book can and has been used in various courses where the students have little or no economics background. The aim has also been to write chapters that stand individually, and can be used independently from the rest of the book. A basic introduction to the EU could cover Chapters 1–3, Chapters 6–11 and Chapter 20. Those interested in individual policies can select from Chapters 12 to 16. A course on the external relations of the European Union could use Chapters 17 to 20. The intention has been to permit the use of different combinations of chapters depending on the needs or interests of the reader.

The EU is evolving constantly, and though every effort has been made to ensure that the text is up to date, more recent developments are necessarily covered by the online learning centre (OLC) of this book.

Because each chapter has been written so that it can stand independently, the aim is also to provide a text that can be consulted by researchers or policy makers. For this purpose each chapter sets out references for further reading and relevant websites.

Acknowledgements

Our thanks go to the following reviewers for their comments at various stages in the new edition's development:*

Annette Bongardt, Universidade Moderna, Lisbon
Etienne Bresch, London Metropolitan University
Sean Byrne, Dublin Institute of Technology
Jim Campbell, Glasgow Caledonian University
Tom Craven, University of Ulster
Stephen Kinsella, University of Limerick
Paul Roosens, University Antwerp
Colin Simpson, University of Gloucestershire
Barbara Timms, Napier University
Francisco Torres, IEE, Universidade Católica Portuguesa, Lisbon
Stefan Weishaar, Maastricht University

*Thanks again to those who reviewed the first edition

Few would be foolhardy enough to sit down and begin writing a textbook on the European Union these days. This book was never actually planned, but emerged as a result of teaching various aspects of EU integration over the years. As many of the courses were repeated, it seemed a good idea to keep a written record, and gradually the book emerged. My first thanks therefore go to the many students on whom (often inadvertently) the material was tried out. These include the students of the Faculty of Economics 'Richard Goodwin' and the Faculty of Political Science of the University of Siena, the Scuola Superiore Sant'Anna of Pisa, the California State University Florence Program and Cornell College, Iowa.

University work is invariably a combination of teaching and research, and this book has grown out of many years of research into European integration. I would therefore like to thank the many colleagues, in particular those at Siena University, the European University Institute and the European Commission, for offering opportunities for discussion of topics related to the book, including seminars, summer schools and conferences. Though I was helped by too many people to thank them all individually, I would like to mention the late Secondo Tarditi who provided help and advice over the years. I am also grateful to Alberto Chilosi, Pompeo della Posta, Mario Nuti, Milica Uvalic, Massimo di Matteo, Alessandro Vercelli and Amy Verdun. Much of the second edition was written during my time as a visiting fellow at the Robert Schuman Centre for Advanced Studies in Florence, and I would like to thank Helen Wallace and Stefano Bartolini for making this possible.

Recognizing that it would be difficult to pull together a final version of this text I hesitated some time before presenting the manuscript. The various members on the publishing team were invaluable in helping me to complete this final step. I am very grateful to those who helped with both the first and second editions for their encouragement and assistance, in particular in organizing numerous reviews by the referees. These reviews have radically shaped the final version of this book, but any eventual mistakes that remain are, of course, my responsibility.

I would like to thank the following organizations and publishers for permission to reproduce material in this book:

Agricultural Policy Studies (APS)
CABI Publishing
Carocci editore, Roma
Harper Collins
IFPRI
IMD International World Competitiveness Centre
OECD
Official Publications Office of the European Communities
Oxford University Press
Palgrave MacMillan
Pearson Education
W.W. Norton & Company
Taylor and Francis, incorporating Routledge
UNHCR
John Wiley & Sons Inc.
World Bank

Every effort has been made to to trace and acknowledge copyright and to obtain permissions to reproduce material in the text. The publishers would be pleased to make arrangements to clear permission with any copyright holders it has not been possible to contact.

List of Abbreviations

AC	average cost
ACED	Action Committee for Democracy
ACP	African, Caribbean and Pacific countries covered by the Lomé Conventions and the Cotonou Agreement
ACTS	Advanced Communications Technology and Services
AENEAS	financial and technical assistance to third countries in the area of migration and asylum
AGEA	Agenzia per le Erogazioni in Agricoltura
AGOA	African Growth and Opportunity Act
AII	Adriatic-Ionian Initiative
AIMA	Azienda Italiana per i Mercati Agricoli
AR	average revenue
ASEAN	Association of South-East Asian Nations
ASEM	Asia–Europe Meeting
BRITE/EURAM	Basic Research in Industrial Technologies for Europe/Advanced Materials for Europe
BSE	bovine spongiform encephalopathy
BSEC	Black Sea Economic Co-operation
CAP	Common Agricultural Policy
CARDS	Community Assistance for Reconstruction, Development and Stabilization
CARE	Climate Action and Renewable Energy
CCP	Common Commercial Policy
CEEC	Central and Eastern European country
CEFTA	Central European Free Trade Area
CEN	Centre Européen de Normalisation
CENELEC	Centre Européen de Normalisation Electrotechnique
CFC	chlorofluorocarbon gases
CFP	Common Fisheries Policy
CFSP	Common Foreign and Security Policy
CGE	computable general equilibrium
CJDv	Creutzfeldt-Jakob variant
CMEA	Council for Mutual Economic Assistance
COPA	Comité des Organizations des Producteurs Agricoles
Coreper	Committee of Permanent Representatives
CSCE	Conference on Security and Co-operation in Europe
CSE	Consumer Support Estimate
DAC	Development Assistance Committee
DDA	Doha Development Agenda
DG	Directorate-General
DRC	Development Research Centre on Migration, Globalisation and Poverty
DSM	Disputes Settlement Mechanism
EAFRD	European Agricultural Fund for Rural Development

EAGGF or FEOGA	European Agricultural Guidance and Guarantee Fund
EAP	Environmental Action Programme
EBA	Everything but arms
EBRD	European Bank for Reconstruction and Development
EC	European Communities
ECB	European Central Bank
ECCP	Europe Climate Change Programme
ECHO	European Community Humanitarian Office
ECN	European Competition Network
Ecofin	Council of Economic and Finance Ministers
ECRE	European Council on Refugees and Exiles
ECSC	European Coal and Steel Community
ECU	European currency unit
EDC	European Defence Community
EDF	European Development Fund
EEA	European Economic Area
EEC	European Economic Community
EES	European Employment Strategy
EESC (Ecosoc)	European Economic and Social Committee
EEA	European Environmental Agency
EFF	European Fisheries' Fund
EFTA	European Free Trade Association
EGTC	European Grouping for Territorial Co-operation
EIB	European Investment Bank
Eionet	European Environmental Information and Observation Network
EIT	European Institute of Technology
EJ	Court of Justice
EMAS	Environmental Management and Audit Scheme
EMCF	European Monetary Co-operation Fund
EMI	European Monetary Institute
EMS	European Monetary System
EMU	Economic and Monetary Union
ENP	European Neighbourhood Policy
EP	European Parliament
EPA	Economic Partnership Agreement
EPC	European Political Co-operation
EQUAL	Community Initiative on transnational co-operation to combat all kinds of discrimination and inequalities in the labour market
ERA	European Research Area
ERASMUS	European Community Action Scheme for the Mobility of University Students
ERDF	European Regional Development Fund
ERM	Exchange Rate Mechanism
ESCB	European System of Central Banks
ESDP	European Security and Defence Policy
ESF	European Social Fund
ESPRIT	European Strategic Programme for Research and Development in Information Technologies
ESTI	European Telecommunications Standards Institute

ETS	Emissions Trading Scheme
ETUC	European Trades Union Conference
EU	European Union
Euratom	European Atomic Energy Community
Eureka	European Research Co-ordination Agency
EURES	European Employment Services Network
Eurogroup	Group of Economic and Finance Ministers of the euro area
EUSF	European Union Solidarity fund
FAO	Food and Agricultural Organisation
FDI	foreign direct investment
FEOGA	European Agricultural Guidance and Guarantee Fund
FIFG	Financial Instrument for Fisheries Guidance
FRG	Federal Republic of Germany
FRONTEX	the EU agency responsible for managing operational co-operation at the EU's external borders
FSA	Financial Services Action Plan
FTAA	Free Trade Area of the Americas
GAERC	General Affairs and External Relations Council
GATS	General Agreement on Trade in Services
GATT	General Agreement on Tariffs and Trade
GCC	Gulf Co-operation Council
GDP	gross domestic product
GMO	genetically modified organism
GNI	gross national income
GNP	gross national product
GSP	Generalised System of Preferences
ICES	International Council for Exploration of the Seas
ICT	information and communication technologies
ICTY	International Criminal Tribunal on the former Yugoslavia
IDA Ireland	Industrial Development Agency Ireland
IEA	International Energy Agency
IFI	international financial institution
IFPRI	International Food Policy Research Institute
IGC	Intergovernmental Conference
IMF	International Monetary Fund
INTERREG II	Community Initiative on cross-border, transnational and interregional co-operation
IPA	Instrument for Pre-Accession Assistance
IPCC	Intergovernmental Panel on Climate Change
ISPA	Instrument for Structural Policies Pre-Accession
ITO	International Trade Organization
LDCs	Least Developed Countries
JET	Joint European Torus on thermonuclear fusion
JHA	Justice and Home Affairs
LEADER	Community Initiative on rural development
LINGUA	programme for the learning and teaching of European languages
MAGP	Multi-Annual Guidance Plan
MC	marginal cost
MCAs	monetary compensatory amounts

MDGs	Millennium Development Goals
MEC	marginal external cost
MEP	Member of the European Parliament
MFA	Multifibre Agreement
MFN	most favoured nation
MGQ	maximum guaranteed quantity
MIFID	Markets in Financial Instruments Directive
MNPB	marginal net private benefit
MR	marginal revenue
MRS	marginal rate of substitution
NAFTA	North American Free Trade Agreement
NAMA	non-agricultural market access
NATO	North Atlantic Treaty Organization
NCB	national central bank
NGO	non-governmental organization
NIEO	New International Economic Order
NIS	Newly Independent States (of the ex-USSR)
NPAA	National Programme for the Adoption of the Acquis
NRAs	New Regulatory Agencies
NTA	New Transatlantic Agenda
NTB	non-tariff barrier
OCA	optimum currency area
OCTs	Overseas Countries and Territories
ODA	official development aid
OECD	Organization for Economic Co-operation and Development
OEEC	Organization for European Economic Co-operation
OLAF	European Anti-Fraud Office
OMA	Orderly Marketing Arrangement
OPEC	Organization of the Petroleum Exporting Countries
OSCE	Organization for Security and Co-operation in Europe
PCA	Partnership and Co-operation Agreement
PHARE	Poland/Hungary Aid for Economic Reconstruction
PJCCM	Police and Justice Co-operation on Criminal Matters
PPF	production possibility frontier
PPS	purchasing power standards
PROGRESS	Community Programme for Employment and Social Solidarity
PSE	Producer Support Estimate
QMV	qualified majority vote
RAC	Regional Advisory Council
RACE	Research in Advanced Communications in Europe
R&D	research and development
REACH	Registration, Evaluation, Authorisation and Restriction of Chemical Substances
RTAs	regional trade arrangements
SAA	Stabilisation and Association Agreement
SAARC	South-Asian Association for Regional Co-operation
SAPARD	Special Accession Programme for Agriculture and Rural Development
SDT	Special and Differential Treatment
SEA	Single European Act

SEE	South-Eastern Europe
SEECP	South East Europe Co-operation Process
SEM	Single European Market
SFP	Single Farm Payment
SICA	Central American Integration System
SIS	Schengen Information System
SITC	Standard International Trade Classification
SOLVIT	the redress system for implementation of Internal Market rules
SME	small and medium enterprise
STEFC	Scientific, Technical, Economic Fisheries Committee
TABD	Transatlantic Business Dialogue
TAC	total allowable catches
TACIS	Technical Assistance for the Commonwealth of Independent States
TEC	Treaty establishing the European Community
TEN	Trans-European Network
TEP	Transatlantic Economic Partnership
TEU	Treaty on the European Union
TMT	technology, media and telecoms
TRIM	trade-related investment measure
TRIP	trade-related intellectual property rights
UNCTAD	United Nations Conference on Trade and Development
UNDP	United Nations Development Programme
UNECE	United Nations Economic Commission for Europe
UNFCCC	United Nation Framework Convention on Climate Change
UNFICYP	United Nations Peacekeeping Force in Cyprus
UNHCR	United Nations High Commissioner on Refugees
UNSCR	United Nations Security Resolution
UNMIK	United Nations Mission in Kosovo
URAA	Uruguay Round Agreement on Agriculture
URBAN	Community Initiative on economic and social regeneration of cities and urban neighbourhoods
VER	voluntary export restraint
WEU	Western European Union
WHO	World Health Organisation
WTO	World Trade Organization

An Introduction to European Integration: Definitions and Terminology

❖ LEARNING OBJECTIVES

By the end of this chapter you should be able to understand:

❖ The difference between the terms 'European Economic Community', 'European Community' and 'European Union';

❖ How the membership of the European Union has changed over the years;

❖ What we mean by integration, and its various stages;

❖ What is the *acquis communautaire*;

❖ What we mean by the term 'subsidiarity';

❖ The importance of the EU in the world economy.

Questions of terminology[1]

The term 'European Economic Community' (EEC) dates from the Treaty of Rome (which was signed in 1957 and came into force 1 January 1958). It was one of the then three European Communities, the others being the European Coal and Steel Community or ECSC (1951) and Euratom (1958). The institutions of the three Communities were fused from 1967.[2] In July 2002 the ECSC was formally wound up, and its assets and liabilities were transferred to the European Union (EU).

The widespread use of the term 'European Community' dates from a resolution of the European Parliament of 1975 when it was decided to drop the term 'economic' because the Community was considered to have extended its activities beyond the purely economic sphere. This term was confirmed formally with the Maastricht Treaty.

In the Treaty of Rome the founders of the original EEC laid the foundations for working towards 'an ever closer union'. According to the opening words of the Treaty of Maastricht (signed in 1992 and came into force in 1993) this objective had been reached: 'By this Treaty, the High Contracting Parties establish among themselves a European Union, hereinafter called

---

[1] There is a great deal of jargon associated with the European Union. For explanations of the various terms see the Europa Glossary of the EU: http://europa.eu/scadplus/glossary, the site of the European Convention at keywords www.european-convention.eu.int/glossary or the website of Baldwin and Wyplosz (2006) at www.mcgraw-hill.co.uk/textbooks/baldwin

[2] When the 1965 Merger Treaty came into force.

"the Union".' With the Treaty of Maastricht the European Community was reinforced and flanked by two other 'pillars': the Common Foreign and Security Policy (CFSP) and Justice and Home Affairs (JHA). As a result of the Treaty of Amsterdam (signed in 1997 and came into force in 1999), many aspects of JHA were brought under the Community pillar (which covers areas such as the Common Agricultural Policy, the Common Commercial Policy, the Single Market, Competition Policy and Economic and Monetary Union), and the name of the third pillar was changed to reflect its residual competences: Police and Justice Co-operation in Criminal Matters (PJCCM). The three together form the EU (see Fig. 1.1). If ratified by all the member states, the Lisbon Treaty (see Chapter 3) would abolish the pillar structure and absorb the European Community into the EU.

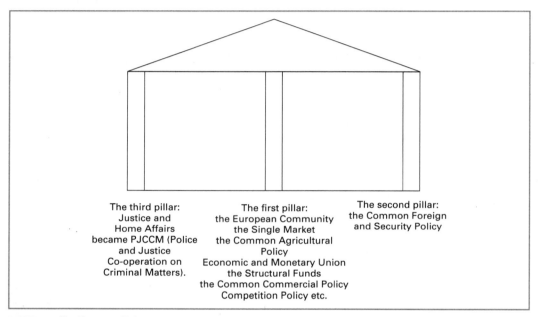

The third pillar:
Justice and
Home Affairs
became PJCCM (Police
and Justice
Co-operation on
Criminal Matters).

The first pillar:
the European Community
the Single Market
the Common Agricultural
Policy
Economic and Monetary Union
the Structural Funds
the Common Commercial Policy
Competition Policy etc.

The second pillar:
the Common Foreign
and Security Policy

FIGURE 1.1 The European Union

The reason for creating the pillar structure was that, at least initially on some sensitive issues, the member states were reluctant to give up responsibility and preferred to take decisions in these spheres using a form of inter-governmental co-operation, which implies that initiatives are reached by direct negotiation between governments and as a general rule require unanimity in decision-making procedures. In contrast decisions under the Community pillar are taken by the 'Community method', which *inter alia* envisages member states giving up their right of veto and taking decisions on the basis of some form of majority voting.[3]

---

[3] As described in Chapter 3, decision-making under the Community method assigns specific roles to the various EU institutions. Strictly speaking the method used for the second and third pillars is similar to the so-called 'intergovernmental method', with the difference that the Commission shares its right of initiative with the Member States, the European Parliament is informed and consulted, the Council may adopt binding acts, and as a general rule, the Council acts unanimously. These institutions are described in Chapter 3.

The Common Foreign and Security Policy

The Common Foreign and Security Policy (CFSP) covers what its name suggests and is one of the external relations instruments of the EU. The EU pursues the CFSP by means of: common positions (which require the member states to implement national policies in line with the position defined by the EU on a particular issue), joint actions and common strategies in areas where the member states have important interests in common. In 1992 at a meeting in Petersberg near Bonn the role of the EU was defined in what became known as the Petersberg tasks: humanitarian and rescue missions, peacekeeping and crisis management. In 1999 the EU agreed on the development of a common European Security and Defence Policy (ESDP). The Online Learning Centre of this book describes the historical process of trying to develop the CFSP and the ESDP.

In terms of economic power the EU is already a heavyweight international actor. The Common Commercial Policy was one of the first Community policies to be implemented (see Chapter 2), and the EU is a major trading bloc and generally (but not always) presents a united front towards the rest of the world on economic issues (see Chapter 19). However, the frequent criticism is that in practice the EU is essentially a civil power, and while it acts as an economic giant, the EU remains a political pygmy. The EU member states have extreme difficulty in evolving common positions on foreign policy and defence issues, let alone imposing them. Differences between the member states on such matters frequently erupt, and countries often act unilaterally with little or no consultation. Despite some common initiatives – such as administration in Bosnia (see Chapter 20) and missions to the Congo – the EU proved largely ineffectual in halting the horrors on its doorstep that accompanied the disintegration of Yugoslavia. Difficulties were encountered in reaching common positions with regard to sending a mission to Chad, recognition of the independence of Kosovo (see Chapter 20), Iraq and the ongoing tensions in the Middle East. The evolution of the EU on the international stage therefore appears lop-sided. Margaret Thatcher in her famous 1988 Bruges speech argued that 'On many great issues Europe should try to speak with a single voice. Europe is stronger when we do so whether it be in trade, in defence, or in our relationship with the world.'

Part of the co-ordination difficulty arises because the various member states arrived at the integration process with very different historical baggage in terms of traditional alliances, geographical situation, perceived cultural interests and so on. Some member states (Austria, Denmark, Finland, Ireland and Sweden) have a tradition of neutrality. Britain emphasizes its 'special relationship' with the USA and until the late 1990s was reluctant to see the Community develop as a forum for foreign policy and defence issues. For many years French attitudes were shaped by the decision to leave the military structure of NATO in 1966, and until recently Germany was hesitant to participate in military initiatives. Many of the new member states felt the legacy of the Cold War. As Hill (1993) argues, there also appears to be a capability-expectations gap: not only does the EU often lack a common front on foreign policy questions but it also frequently seems unwilling or unable to supply the necessary means to deliver what is expected.[4]

From Justice and Home Affairs to 'Freedom Security and Justice' and Police and Justice Co-operation on Criminal Matters

With increasing tendency towards abolition of border controls between member states (see Chapter 6), there was a growing awareness of a need for more co-operation in combating

---

[4] Not surprisingly the head of the US Senate's Foreign Relations Committee, Jesse Helms, was reputed to have said that the EU could not fight itself out of a wet paper bag.

transnational phenomena such as terrorism, organized crime and migration. The view was that freedom of movement of people within the Community should not be allowed to take place to the detriment of the security of the population, public order and civil liberties. Over time national solutions to resolve such questions appeared increasingly inadequate. The collapse of the Soviet Union, the increase in immigration pressures and the events of 11 September 2001 added a new urgency to the question.

However, governments are reluctant to sacrifice sovereignty on such sensitive issues, so common EU policies were slow to develop, and co-operation covers a heterogeneous collection of policies, with decision-making procedures that are complex and in flux.

As set out in the Maastricht Treaty, Justice and Home Affairs involved co-operation between the police, judicial, immigration and customs authorities of the member states in order to jointly prevent and combat crime (Articles 29 and 30, Treaty on European Union, or TEU). The areas of co-operation cover both civil and criminal law, and include:

■ Combating terrorism;
■ Fighting drugs and the illicit arms trade;
■ Combating racism and xenophobia;
■ Fighting organized crime;
■ Preventing criminal acts against children and trafficking in human beings;
■ Immigration, asylum and visas;
■ Preventing corruption and fraud (and taking common measures against money-laundering); and
■ Customs administration.

The Maastricht Treaty also aimed at promotion of a European citizenship. This entails four special rights:

1 Freedom to move and take up residence anywhere in the EU;
2 Any EU citizen living in another member state has the right to vote or stand in local and European elections;
3 Any EU citizen can use the diplomatic and consular activities of another EU country in any part of the world where their own country is not represented;
4 A Community ombudsman was to be attached to the European Parliament in order to address alleged cases of maladministration by EU institutions.

The Treaty of Amsterdam called for the development of the EU as an area of 'Freedom, Security and Justice'. This entailed a number of issues, including visas, asylum, immigration and other policies relating to the free movement of people being 'communitized' or brought under the first (or Community) pillar. The Tampere European Council of October 1999 took key decisions on rendering this area of 'Freedom, Security and Justice' operational, calling for:

■ A common immigration and asylum policy;
■ Minimum rights for the victims of crime; and
■ Re-enforced efforts to combat cross-border crime.

In 2004 the EU agreed the Hague Programme, which sets out the objectives to be implemented in the area of Freedom, Security and Justice in the period 2005–2010.

Chapter 8 deals with problems connected to the free movement of labour in the EU, and the Online Learning Centre of this book describes key features of the evolution of the EU as an area of 'Freedom, Security and Justice' and of the operation of the third pillar of Police and Justice Co-operation on Criminal Matters.

The changing membership of the EU

There were six original members of the EEC, the ECSC, and Euratom: Belgium, France, Germany, Italy, Luxembourg and the Netherlands. The various enlargements of the EU entailed the following countries joining:

- Denmark, Ireland and the UK in 1973;
- Greece in 1981;
- Spain and Portugal in 1986;
- Austria, Finland and Sweden in 1995;
- Ten new member states in May 2004: Cyprus, the Czech Republic, Estonia, Hungary, Latvia, Lithuania, Malta, Poland, Slovakia, and Slovenia;
- Bulgaria and Romania in 2007.

As described in Chapter 20, Turkey, Croatia, and the Former Yugoslav Republic of Macedonia are candidate countries.

The definition of integration

Economic integration can be defined as the elimination of barriers to the movement of products and factors of production between a group of countries and the introduction of common policies.[5] Tinbergen (1954) made the distinction between negative integration (the removal of barriers to trade) and positive integration – the introduction of common policies, and building of common institutions. However, this distinction only remains clear when a state's intervention is limited to measures taken at the border, such as tariffs, import quotas and so on. If a state's more active role in the economy is considered, many measures with 'domestic' objectives will have repercussions for trade. For example, subsidies to domestic production in a particular country (e.g. by the Italian government to Fiat) could constitute a barrier for foreign firms. As a result, in a modern, mixed economy with wide-scale state intervention, the effective elimination of barriers may require common policies.

The stages of integration

Following the pioneering work of Balassa (1961), the traditional literature on integration refers to different 'stages' in the process.[6] As explained below, these stages are: a free trade area, a customs

---

[5] Examples of definitions of political integration include those by Deutsch (1968) who is associated with the so-called transactional theory of integration and refers to integration as 'the attainment within a territory of a sense of a community'. Haas (1958) defines integration as a 'shift of loyalties', expectations and political activities to a new centre whose institutions possess or demand jurisdiction over pre-existing nation states. Lindberg (1963) calls integration a process whereby nations seek to take joint decisions or to delegate decision-making to a new central organ.

[6] See Chapter 19 for examples of integration initiatives, many of which also involve developing countries.

union, a common market, economic and monetary union and political union. However, if the more active role of the state in the economy is taken into account, these should not be regarded as steps in an ascending scale since even complete realization of one of the 'lower stages' may require full economic, monetary and political union. None the less, the classification remains useful to indicate different forms of integration.

Free trade areas

The member states remove all barriers on trade between themselves but retain the freedom to implement different commercial policies towards third countries. In order to get around the problem of importing for re-exporting, free trade areas require rules of origin. In other words, when a good is traded it has to be accompanied by documentation stating where it was made. Rules of origin may be complex to administer, and the regulatory uncertainty to which they give rise means that market access is conditional.

An example of a free trade area is the EFTA (the European Free Trade Association), which was set up in 1960 by seven European countries as an alternative to joining the EEC (see Chapter 2).[7] A further example is NAFTA (the North American Free Trade Agreement), which came into operation between the USA, Canada and Mexico in 1994.[8]

Customs unions

The member states remove all barriers on trade between themselves and introduce a common external commercial policy (for instance a common external tariff) towards the rest of the world.

Examples of customs unions include the EEC, which had created a customs union by 1968 (see Chapter 2), and that between the EU and Turkey which came into operation from 1995, but which largely excluded agricultural products.

Common markets

These are customs unions, which also allow for free factor mobility. In other words, a common market entails the so-called four freedoms: freedom of movement of goods, services, labour and capital. During the early years the Community was sometimes called the 'common market', although this description was not very accurate as the then EEC was more like a customs union with certain sectoral policies (notably the Common Agricultural Policy) financed largely through a Community budget.

Economic and monetary union

An economic and monetary union should include the following elements: a common market; co-ordination or central control of monetary and fiscal policies; a common money or complete convertibility among national currencies with no possibility of exchange-rate adjustments; and a common authority which acts as a central bank. As will be seen in Chapter 9, in the case of the EU it was decided to introduce a single monetary unit (the euro), a common monetary policy, co-ordination of fiscal policy and a European Central Bank in Frankfurt.

---

[7] The UK, Norway, Sweden, Denmark, Austria, Switzerland and Portugal.

[8] Work is going on to create a Free Trade Area of the Americas, which would cover cover countries in North and South America.

Political union

The definition of this term in the literature is often imprecise and ambiguous, reflecting different conceptions of what it entails. In very general terms, political union involves a central authority that has supranational powers similar to those of a nation's government over various policy areas including, for example, foreign policy and security matters, and is responsible to a directly elected central parliament.

Early views of approaches to integration

As will be shown in Chapter 2, early views about approaches or strategies to integration were influential in shaping the formation of the Community. The aim here is not to provide a comprehensive survey of these theories, but to indicate a few of the views of particular importance in influencing the early development of integration.[9]

The **federalist** approach calls for the immediate creation of a political union with transfer of many of the sovereign rights and obligations of the member states to a supranational federal authority.[10] Early US history offers many examples of the federalist approach. For instance, the Constitutional Convention of 1787 was concerned with wresting powers from the individual states in a way that was palatable to them. The various states had distinct histories, often dating back nearly two centuries, and were reluctant to relinquish their autonomy to an untried central authority.

Functionalists such as Mitrany (1966) advocated a form of integration that was pragmatic, flexible and technocratic. The functionalist approach maintains that in the modern world, technical, economic and social forces lead to interdependencies and shared problems for nation states. Individual countries acting in isolation cannot decide on issues such as the environment, the control of multinational enterprises, telecommunications and information technology. International co-operation is needed to deal with such matters. The potential gains of economic, functional and technical co-operation could be used to build international organizations. The function in question was to determine the appropriate level of integration (such as postal services at a global level, shipping at an intercontinental level and so on), regardless of national or political boundaries. The goal was not to create a 'super state' above the member states, and Mitrany opposed European federalism considering that this would only change the arena or level of conflict and not avoid it. International integration between states would acquire its own internal dynamic as the benefits achieved would attract the loyalty of citizens and create mutual dependencies, making war unfeasible.

In contrast the **neo-functional approach** developed, in particular, by Haas (1958) and by Lindberg (1963) brought the functionalism of Mitrany down from international spheres to the more concrete case of regional integration between a group of neighbouring countries. At the centre of the neo-functionalist approach is the idea of functional spill-over, i.e. that integration in one sector will generate impetus for integration in other sectors. For example, integration of the defence effort will require democratic control, thus creating a spill-over leading to integration in the political sphere. In this way, according to the approach, it should become possible to proceed with a strategy of 'integration by sector'.

---

[9] For a more complete view of the various theories about approaches to integration (including later theories) see Wallace et al. (2005), or Pollack (2005).

[10] For early exponents of this theory see, for instance, Coudenhove-Kalergi (1926) or Spinelli (1972).

George (1991) identifies another aspect of neo-functionalism as 'political' spill-over, whereby both supranational actors such as the European Commission, and subnational actors such as interest groups become the drivers of integration. At the subnational level interest groups in an integrated sector have to deal with the international organization responsible for their sector. The groups would therefore gradually transfer their activities and loyalties away from national governments towards the supranational authority. At the supranational level, organizations such as the Commission encourage such transfers of activities and loyalties. Clearly, this view was influenced the early experience of the Community with, for instance, the Common Agricultural Policy. As a result of sectoral and political spill-overs the neo-functionalists predicted that the integration process would be self-sustaining. The neo-functionalist approach envisages a federal authority as the final stage in an ongoing process, whereas the federalist approach favours introducing that stage directly.

In contrast the **intergovernmental** approach maintains that the member states should retain their sovereignty, but should co-operate to achieve certain economic or political objectives, such as trade liberalization.[11] This is the idea of a *Europe des patries*, based on intergovernmental co-operation rather than transfer of power to a supranational authority.

The *acquis communautaire*

The *acquis communautaire* is literally 'what the Community has achieved'. It consists of the body (sometimes called 'patrimony') of EU legislation, practices, principles and objectives accepted by the member states. It is composed of:[12]

- The treaties, especially the Treaties of Rome (signed in 1957 and came into force in 1958), the Single European Act (signed in 1986 and entered into force in 1987), the Maastricht Treaty (signed in 1992 and came into force in 1993), the Treaty of Amsterdam (signed in 1997 and entered into force in 1999) and the Treaty of Nice (signed in 2001 and came into force in 2003).[13] This is referred to as primary legislation;
- Legislation enacted at the EU level and judgments of the European Court of Justice (secondary legislation);
- Other acts, legally binding or not, adopted within the EU framework, such as resolutions, declarations, statements, recommendations and guidelines;
- The second (CFSP) and third pillars (PJCCM); and
- Treaties of the EU with third countries.

Progress in EU accession negotiations depends to a large extent on the speed with which the candidate countries can take on and implement the *acquis communautaire*.

The *acquis* has been accumulating over the years and now amounts to about 12 000 legislative acts, and in 2007 debate exploded as to how long the *acquis* is. According to Open Europe, a UK organization sceptical of the integration process, the *acquis* had reached 170 000 pages, but a Commission working group maintained that this also contained judgements of the Court of Justice, and that in effect there were 94 484 pages of which 3000 were international treaties.

---

[11]A basis for this approach was the claim by Hoffman (1966) that the nation state far from being obsolete had proven 'obstinate'.

[12]See the Commission website www.ec.europa.eu/enlargement, or Chapter 20 for a breakdown of the *acquis* by chapter.

[13]Unless otherwise stated, elsewhere in this book the dates given refer to when the treaties entered into force.

The Commission working group also maintained that, as part of the attempt to cut red tape, the *acquis* would be cut by 40 000 pages.[14]

Subsidiarity

In practice difficulties may arise in deciding which is the appropriate level of government to take decisions on various policy areas. In other words, is a particular issue best decided at the EU, national, state, regional or local level? Subsidiarity is the principle that decisions should be taken at the lowest level that permits effective action.[15] The idea of subsidiarity is linked to that of taking decisions 'as closely as possible to the citizens'. It is also maintained that by limiting action at the Community level to where it is really necessary, the quality of EC legislation could be improved.[16]

In the EU context the word 'subsidiarity' first appeared in the EC Commission's submission to the 1975 Tindemans Report on European Union and the steps to be taken to create a more united Europe, closer to the citizens. However, the principle was not taken up in the final version of the report, partly because the proposals were less far reaching than the Commission had suggested, so there was less need to reassure those member states fearing a loss of their sovereignty.

Since the late 1980s the term has frequently been used by the EC member states and regions wanting to limit the powers of the Community, in particular Britain, Denmark and the German Länder. It was largely to assuage the fears of these countries that a subsidiarity clause was introduced in Article 3b of the Treaty of Maastricht. A protocol to the Amsterdam Treaty confirms that Community actions should not exceed what is necessary to realize the objectives of the Treaty, and this has become known as the 'principle of proportionality'.[17] Article 5 of the Treaty establishing the European Community (TEC) indicates the main aspects of subsidiarity:[18]

- 'The Community shall act within the limits of powers conferred upon it by this Treaty and of the objectives assigned to it therein.

- In areas which do not fall within its exclusive competence the Community shall take action, in a accordance with the principle of subsidiarity, only if and so far as the objectives of the proposed action cannot be sufficiently achieved by the Member States and can there-

---

[14]*Financial Times*, 20 February 2007.

[15]The first reference to the principle was in the Papal Encyclical, *Rerum Novarum* of 1891, and it was again taken up in the 1931 Encyclical, *Quadragesimo Anno*. In this context the principle warned against the ever-increasing powers of the state (Bainbridge, 2002).

[16]As Jacques Santer, a former president of the Commission, stated in a speech to the European Parliament of 17 January 1995: 'I have a different notion of subsidiarity: it means not harmonizing every last nut and bolt, but stepping up our co-operation wherever this is really worth it. We should take as our motto "Less action, but better action".'

[17]The principle of proportionality seeks to set within specific bounds the action taken by the institutions of the EU. The extent of action must be in keeping with the aim pursued. When various forms of intervention are possible to achieve the same effect, the EU must opt for the approach that leaves greatest freedom to the member states and citizens.

Another principle with relevance to the delimitation of activities between the EU and member states is that of additionality. Additionality aims at ensuring that EU allocations are additional to national financing, and do not simply replace national measures (see, for instance, the discussion of EU economic and social cohesion in Chapter 15).

[18]This is part of the Nice Treaty, which applies until the Lisbon Treaty is ratified and comes into force.

fore, by reason of the scale or the effects of the proposed action be better achieved by the Community.

- Any action by the Community shall not go beyond what is necessary to achieve the objectives of the Treaty.'

In practice it is difficult to establish which measures should be centralized, and to what extent.[19] Eurobarometer (2006) carried out a survey to assess which decisions EU citizens felt were best carried out at the national level and which at the EU level. Not surprisingly, according to the survey, EU decisions were preferred in areas such as fighting terrorism, scientific research, protecting the environment, defence and foreign affairs, energy, fighting crime, support for regions facing economic difficulties and immigration. The policy areas where national decisions were favoured included pensions, taxation, health and social welfare, the education system and fighting unemployment.

The competences of the EU

The **principle of conferral** is a fundamental principle of European Union law, according to which the EU is a union of member states, and all its competences are conferred on it by its member states. The EU has no competences by right, and thus any areas of policy not explicitly agreed in treaties remain the domain of the member states. The treaties may allow for an extension of EU tasks if this is necessary to realize the objectives of the Treaty establishing the European Community.[20] Over the years there has been a tendency towards 'competence creep', or an increase in the sphere of activities of the EU.

As shown in Table 1.1, the Lisbon Treaty (which still has to be ratified by all the member states) classifies the policy areas of the EU according to:

- Exclusive competence, where the EU has exclusive competence for legislation, or to conclude international agreements;
- Shared competence, where the competence to legislate is divided between the EU and member states; and
- Supporting competence, where the EU carries out actions to support, co-ordinate or supplement the actions of the member states.

The EU in the world

The success of the EU as an integrated bloc has meant that it has emerged as one of the main partners in world trade and investment, as shown in Figures 1.2 and 1.3 and Table 1.2. If intra-EU trade is also taken into account the share of the EU in world trade is much higher. In 2006 intra EU(27) exports amounted to €2494 billion while imports were €2415 billion. In the same

---

[19]So much so that in a speech to the European Parliament Jacques Delors, then president of the European Commission, offered a job and ECU 200 000 to anyone who could define subsidiarity in one page!

[20]According to Article 308 (ex Article 235) of the Treaty establishing the European Community (TEC): 'If action by the Community should prove necessary to attain, in the course of the operation of the common market, one of the objectives of the Community and this Treaty has not provided the necessary powers, the Council shall, acting unanimously on a proposal from the Commission and after consulting the European Parliament, take the appropriate measures.'

Exclusive competence	Shared competence	Supporting competence
Customs union	Internal Market	Protection and improvement of human health
The Common Commercial Policy	Social Policy, for the aspects defined in the Treaty	Industry
Establishing the competition rules necessary for functioning of the Internal Market	Economic, social and territorial cohesion	Culture
Monetary policy for euro countries	Agriculture and fisheries (excluding the conservation of marine biological resources)	Tourism
The conservation of marine biological resources under the common fisheries policy	Environment	Education, youth, sport, and vocational training
	Consumer protection	Civil protection
	Transport	Administrative co-operation.
	Trans-European networks	
	Energy	
	The area of Freedom, Security and Justice	
	Common safety concerns in public health matters for aspects defined in the Treaty.	

TABLE 1.1 Division of competences between the EU and member states

year extra EU(27) exports were €1165 billion and imports amounted to €1361 billion.[21] In 2006 the upward trend in foreign direct investment (FDI) outflows of the EU(25) to the rest of the world (which started in 2002) continued, and reached €202 billion. Foreign direct investment inflows to the EU(25) from extra-EU(25) countries rose in 2005 and 2006, reaching €145 billion in 2006.

Table 1.3 presents comparative statistics for EU economic weight and performance *vis-à-vis* the USA, Japan and China. Its weight in the world economy and the repercussions of EU policies for other countries imply a growing need for the EU to adopt a more active and responsible role for the international economy, a topic that is taken up in more detail in Chapters 18 to 20.

The functions of the GATT (General Agreement on Tariffs and Trade) and its replacement, the WTO (the World Trade Organization), are discussed in some detail in Chapter 18, but it is useful at this point to give a brief indication of their roles. The GATT came into operation in 1948 in order to provide a framework for international trade negotiations in an attempt to regulate world trade. The GATT aimed at setting out regulations governing the conduct of international trade by making provisions for the settlements of disputes and retaliatory actions, and providing the

---

[21] Despite the high share of intra-EU trade in total EU trade, Delgrado (2006) argues that intra-EU trade integration is less than might be expected in an integrated economic area.

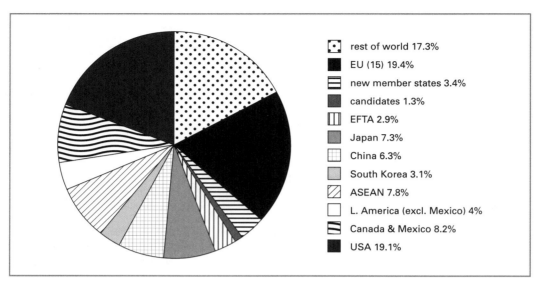

FIGURE 1.2 Share in world exports (2005)
Source: Elaboration on the basis of Eurostat data, © European Communities, 2008.

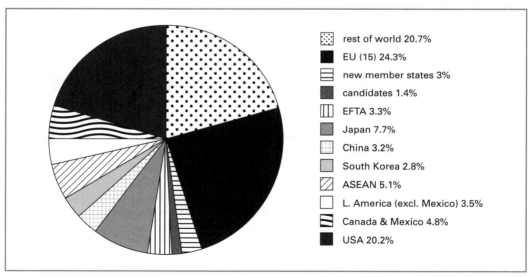

FIGURE 1.3 Share in world imports (2005)
Source: Elaboration on the basis of Eurostat data, © European Communities, 2008.

	2006		2006
Outward flows to extra EU(25)	202.2	Inward flows to extra EU(25)	145.0
From EU(15)	196.9	to EU(15)	139.4
From 10 new member states	5.3	To 10 new member states	5.6
Of which, to		Of which, from	
Switzerland	19.4	Switzerland	5.8
Russian Federation	4.3	Russian Federation	0.0
Canada	21.7	Canada	5.0
USA	71.2	USA	47.7
Brazil	5.3	Brazil	1.4
China	8.0	China	1.0
Of which, Hong Kong	4.3	Of which, Hong Kong	−1.1
Japan	−3.5	Japan	10.5
India	−1.6	India	0.1

TABLE 1.2 Foreign direct investment flows to and from the EU (2006) in billion euro
Source: Eurostat data, © European Communities, 2008.

framework for multilateral negotiations to liberalize world trade. In 1995 the WTO replaced the GATT, and differs from its predecessor in having full institutional status, a legal personality and reinforced powers to settle trade disputes. In 2008, 153 countries were members of the WTO.

	Population 1 January 2005 (millions)	Area (thousand sq km)	Total GNI USA $ b using current PPP*	Inflation Rate**	Unemployment Rate**		Growth 2006
					Male	female	
EU(27)	479	4333	14625**	2.2	7.9	9.8	3.0
Japan	128	378	4020	−0.3	4.6	4.2	2.9
US	294	6929	12449	−3.4	4.1	5.1	2.2
China*	1312	9598	8858	2.9	4.2	n/a	10.7

TABLE 1.3 Key EU indicators (2005)
* World Bank data
Elaboration on the basis of World Bank data
** EU(25)
Source: Unless otherwise stated the statistics are taken from Eurostat, © European Communities, 2008.

Summary of Key Concepts

◆ The term '**European Economic Community**' dates from the Treaty of Rome of 1958. The widespread use of '**European Community**' dates from a resolution of the European Parliament of 1975 when it was decided to drop the word 'economic'. With the Maastricht Treaty the European Community was reinforced and flanked by two other 'pillars': Justice and Home Affairs, and the Common Foreign and Security policy. The three together form the '**European Union**'. As a result of the Amsterdam Treaty, many aspects of Justice and Home Affairs were brought under the Community pillar, and the name of the third pillar was changed to reflect its residual competences: Police and Justice Co-operation in Criminal Matters. If ratified by all the member states, the Lisbon Treaty would abolish the pillar structure, and absorb the European Community into the European Union.

◆ There were six original members of the European Economic Community: Belgium, France, Germany, Italy, Luxembourg, and the Netherlands. Denmark, Ireland and the UK joined in 1973, Greece in 1981, Spain and Portugal in 1986 and Austria, Finland and Sweden in 1995. Ten countries joined the EU in 2004: Cyprus, Malta, the Czech Republic, Estonia, Hungary, Latvia, Lithuania, Poland, Slovakia and Slovenia. Bulgaria and Romania joined in 2007. Turkey and Croatia, and the Former Yugoslav Republic of Macedonia are candidate countries.

◆ Economic integration can be defined as the elimination of barriers to the movement of products and factors of production between a group of countries (**negative integration**) and the introduction of common policies (**positive integration**).

◆ The **stages of integration** are: a free trade area, a customs union, a common market, economic and monetary union, and political union.

◆ The *acquis communautaire* is the body of EU legislation, practices, principles and objectives accepted by the member states.

◆ **Subsidiarity** is the principle that decisions should be taken at the lowest level that permits effective action.

◆ The **principle of conferral** is a fundamental principle of European Union law, according to which the EU is a union of member states, and all its competences are voluntarily conferred on it by its member states.

◆ The EU has become one of the major global actors in terms of trade and FDI.

Questions for study and review

1 *Define integration and indicate the different stages of integration.*

2 *What are the different approaches to integration?*

3 *What do we mean by the term 'acquis communautaire'?*

4 *What do we mean by the term 'subsidiarity'? What policies do you think should be the responsibility of the EU?*

5 *Describe the economic weight of the EU in the world.*

References

Bainbridge, T. (2002) The *Penguin Companion to European Union*, 3rd edn, Penguin Books, London.

Balassa, B. (1961) *The Theory of Economic Integration*, Irwin, Homewood, IL.

Coudenhove-Kalergi, R.N. (1926*) Pan-Europe*, Knopf, New York.

Delgrado, J. (2006) *Single Market Trails Home Bias*, Breugel Policy Brief 5, www.breugel.org

Deutsch, K.W. (1968) *The Analysis of International Relations*, Prentice Hall, Englewood Cliffs, New Jersey.

Eurobarometer (2006) *Public Opinion in the EU, No. 66*, Autumn, www.ec.europa.eu/public_opinion

George, S. (1991) *Politics in the European Union*, Oxford University Press, Oxford.

Haas, E.B. (1958) *The Uniting of Europe*, Stanford University Press, Stanford, CA.

Hill, C. (1993) 'The capability-expectations gap, or conceptualising Europe's international role', *Journal of Common Market Studie*s, Vol. 31, No. 3, pp. 305–28.

Hoffman, S. (1966) 'Obstinate or obsolete? The fate of the nation-state and the case of Western Europe', *Daedalus*, 95/3, pp. 862–915.

Lindberg, L.N. (1963) *The Politics of European Economic Integration*, Stanford University Press, Stanford, California.

Mitrany, D. (1966) *A Working Peace System,* Quadrangle Books, Chicago.

Pollack, M.A. (2005) 'Theorizing the European Union: international organization, domestic polity, or experiment in new governance?' *Annual Review of Political Science*, Vol. 8, pp. 357–98.

Spinelli, A. (1972) 'The growth of the European movement since the Second World War', in Hodges, M. (ed.) *European Integration,* Penguin, Harmondsworth.

Tinbergen, J. (1954) *International Economic Integration*, Elsevier, Amsterdam.

Wallace, H., Wallace, W. and Pollack, M.A. (2005) *Policy-Making in the European Union*, Oxford University Press, Oxford.

Useful websites

There is a great deal of jargon associated with the European Union. For glossaries of the various terms see the Europa Glossary of the EU:
http://europa.eu/scadplus/glossary

The site of the European Conventions:
www. european-convention.eu.int

or the website of Baldwin and Wyplosz at:
www.mcgraw-hill.co.uk/textbooks/baldwin

The website of the European Union:
www.europa.eu

For the treaties and EU legislation see:
eur-lex.europa.eu/en/index.htm
www.europa.eu.scadplus/lex

The OECD and the WTO provide statistics and analysis of the world economy:
www.oecd.org
www.wto.org

The IMF provides reports and international financial statistics:
www.imf.org

The World Bank is mainly concerned with development issues, but publishes numerous studies on the world economy:
www.worldbank.org

A Brief History of European Integration

❖ LEARNING OBJECTIVES

By the end of this chapter you should be able to understand:

❖ The initial failure to create a supranational organization in Europe after the Second World War;

❖ The purpose of setting up the European Coal and Steel Community (ECSC);

❖ The failure of early attempts to promote European co-operation on defence and to set up a common policy on agriculture;

❖ Why the integration process gained a new impetus in the mid-1950s;

❖ The principal objectives and policies set out in the Treaty of Rome;

❖ The main elements of the European Economic Community (EEC) in the 1960s: trade and agriculture;

❖ The 1969 Hague Summit: deepening, widening and completion of the integration process;

❖ The years of eurosclerosis in the 1970s;

❖ The main events in the development of the European Union (EU) (the Single Market Project; the Maastricht Treaty and economic and monetary union; the enlargement process; the Mediterranean Programme and the European Neighbourhood Policy (ENP); the Lisbon Strategy, and the lengthy process leading to the Reform or Lisbon Treaty).

Introduction

The main aim of this chapter is to provide a brief overview of the chief events leading to the creation of the EEC in 1958, and the most important developments in its subsequent history. Discussion of almost all of these later developments is taken up in more detail in later chapters. The Appendix to this chapter provides a brief chronology of the process of European integration.

The origins of European integration

The idea of a united Europe dates back several centuries, but in the years following the Second World War it acquired a greater urgency.[1] The aim was to make another war in Europe materially impossible, and to co-operate in the post-war reconstruction process. At the same time, the creation of the Eastern bloc and the perceived Soviet threat left Western Europe feeling divided and vulnerable. After the war the USA and the USSR emerged as the two superpowers (an international scenario to last until the 1990s), and it became increasingly evident that only a united Europe would carry weight at an international level.

During the early years, most of the initiatives to carry forward the integration process came from France, usually backed by Germany and the Benelux countries. Despite widespread popular belief in the European ideal, the position of the other 'large' founder-member of the Community, Italy, often appeared confused and contradictory, possibly reflecting the overriding concern with the internal political situation.

British ambivalence towards the integration process soon became apparent. Britain had emerged victorious from the war, participating in meetings such as Yalta to create a new world order. Great importance was attached to the 'special relationship' with the United States. In addition, much trade was still carried out with former members of the Empire rather than with continental Europe.

Background to the integration process: the 1940s

The first European organization to be created after the war was the **UNECE** (United Nations' Economic Commission for Europe), which was set up as a regional organization of the UN in Geneva in 1947. Its initial aim was to carry out economic reconstruction and encourage co-operation among all the states of Europe: East, West and Central. Soon after creation of this organization, the East–West division of Europe became a reality and the USSR feared Western influence on its satellites. The UNECE was to prove the last pan-European organization for many years. It remained in operation as a useful research centre for East–West studies, and subsequently for analysis of the transition of countries in Central and East Europe and the former Soviet Republics into market economies and functioning democracies.

The European integration process gained a new impetus in 1947 with the introduction of the **Marshall Plan.** A bad harvest in 1946 increased food prices, and the severe winter of 1947/8 led to a fuel crisis. The continental European countries faced an acute shortage of foreign reserves as the result of a combination of huge import requirements and limited exports. US General George Marshall proposed a programme to aid Europe. It was initially suggested that the programme would be administered through the UNECE, but this was opposed by the USSR, which feared an increase of Western influence on its satellites. The Marshall Plan involved US and Canadian aid to 16 European countries. The aid was to be conditional on the European countries dismantling barriers to trade among themselves, and co-operating in the creation of a European organization to administer the aid programme.

In 1948 this led to the creation of the OEEC (Organization for European Economic Co-operation). There was a difference of opinion between Britain and France as to whether this

---

[1] See Swann (2000), Milward (1984 and 1999) and Craig and De Burca (2007) for more detailed accounts of the historical background. For glossaries of the various terms used in this chapter see the site of the European Convention at keywords www. european-convention.eu.int/glossary or the website of Baldwin and Wyplosz (2006) at www.mcgraw-hill.co.uk/textbooks/baldwin

organization should be based on inter-governmental co-operation, or whether a supranational element should be injected, as favoured by the French (with US support). The French pushed for an international secretariat that could take initiatives on major issues, but in the end the British view prevailed. The OEEC led to the setting up of the European Payments Union in 1950, and was the forum in which the six founding members of the EEC began the discussions that led to the Treaty of Rome. After the winding up of Marshall aid, in 1961 this organization was transformed and became the **OECD** (Organization for Economic Co-operation and Development) (see Box 2.1).[2]

Box 2.1: *The OECD (Organization for Economic Co-operation and Development)*

Based in Paris, the OECD unites major industrial countries and plays an important role in international economic co-operation. Its main functions include the co-ordination of development aid, the promotion of trade liberalization and economic growth, and the analysis of economic performance, including international trade questions. It is well known for its statistics, and for its publications that include country surveys and reviews.

The economic division of Europe was formalized in 1949 with the creation of the **Comecon or CMEA** (Council for Mutual Economic Assistance).[3] In addition to the USSR and smaller Central–East European countries, Cuba, Mongolia and Vietnam were also CMEA members. The founding of the CMEA was largely a political response to the Marshall Plan, but the organization really only became active after the signing of the Treaty of Rome in 1957. Though the CMEA never became a supranational body like the Community, Soviet hegemony implied a certain degree of political integration. The CMEA was formally dissolved in September 1991.

In 1948 pro-European statesmen (including Churchill) rallied at a Congress of Europe in The Hague and called for progress towards economic and political union in Europe, if necessary by sacrificing some national sovereignty. It was decided to create the **Council of Europe**, but again attempts to create a supranational European organization failed, largely due to opposition from Britain and the Scandinavian countries, who were among the founder-members. The French and Belgians were in favour of a European parliamentary assembly which could use majority voting, but the powers finally agreed for the first Consultative Assembly were so limited that its first president, the Belgian, Paul-Henri Spaak, resigned.

Set up in Strasbourg in 1949, the Council of Europe is *not* an institution of the European Community. Though the Council of Europe disappointed the federalists, it provided the seat for various debates and initiatives in the European integration process, and continues to play an important role in the field of human rights, rule of law and democracy (see Boxes 2.2 and 2.3).

---

[2] Following the EEC/EFTA division, see below.

[3] For many years the term 'Comecon' was generally avoided in Central–East Europe as it was considered reminiscent of the cold war.

Box 2.2: *The Council of Europe*

The Council of Europe deals with areas such as culture, education, the environment, control of the international drugs trade and medical ethics. Since 1989 it has been active in promoting constitutional and institutional reforms to assist democratic consolidation in Central and Eastern Europe and certain former Soviet Republics.

In 1950 a European Convention on Human Rights was also drawn up, and in 1995 a Framework Convention for the Protection of National Minorities was also signed. The organs of the Council of Europe include a parliamentary assembly, a committee of foreign ministers and, probably the best known and most effective of its institutions, the Court of Human Rights. Previously separate, two of the organs of the Council of Europe, the European Commission of Human Rights and the Court of Human Rights, were merged in 1998.

In theory membership of the Council of Europe is only for those countries able and willing to sign and implement its treaties, but in practice tensions may arise. It is frequently argued that the Council is in a stronger position to influence countries if they are members. At the time of their accession there was much controversy about countries such as Russia and Croatia, which were considered to have shortcomings with regard to freedom of expression and the rule of law. When Georgia joined in 1999 it was given a list of needed reforms and deadlines for introducing them. Other countries, such as Belarus, have been excluded on the grounds that they are undemocratic and fail to respect human rights.

The Council of Europe can play an important role for countries outside the EU as membership may provide evidence that they belong to Europe, as well as giving such countries some say in a pan-European organization.

Box 2.3: *The OSCE (Organization for Security and Co-operation in Europe)*

There is a certain overlap of functions between the Council of Europe and the OSCE. Created in 1975 during the era of détente, the aim of what was then known as the CSCE (Conference on Security and Co-operation in Europe) was to promote East–West dialogue. The 'final act' of the CSCE was signed in Helsinki and was primarily of interest to Western countries as a means of improving human rights in the Eastern bloc, while the Eastern partners were mainly concerned with economic and technological co-operation. The final act set out four Helsinki 'baskets': security and disarmament; economic and technological co-operation and protection of the environment; co-operation in humanitarian and other fields; and the commitments of the signatory states. Following the collapse of communism, this organization was transformed into the OSCE, and became focused on an ongoing process of ensuring that commitments were being implemented. The main function of the OSCE is to provide a forum for its members to discuss and co-operate on security issues, and to ensure the operation of democratic practices (in particular, free and fair elections). It is active in early warning, conflict prevention, crisis management and post-conflict rehabilitation. OSCE membership includes most European countries, the USA, Canada and various former Soviet Republics. At least in theory, the Council of Europe is responsible for codifying and upholding legal rules, while the obligations of the OSCE are only politically binding; its main function is to encourage improved practices in areas of tension.

Integration by sector

The failure of federalist attempts to create a supranational European architecture in both the OEEC and Council of Europe brought about a change in tactics, with subsequent proposed initiatives in European integration adopting a more neo-functionalist approach. It was felt that less ambitious plans to co-operate in specific economic sectors might provide experience in working together, and could also induce spill-over into increased political co-operation.

The ECSC (European Coal and Steel Community)

The combination of US aid and the determination of the German people soon led to post-war recovery of the German economy. The question became how to allow Germany to regain her powerful position in what were then the strategic industries of iron, steel and coal production without endangering peace in Europe. At the time a large majority of all energy needs in Europe were met by coal. Moreover, it was realized that Allied control of coal and steel production in the Ruhr could not continue indefinitely.

The proposed solution was the Schuman Plan which was elaborated by Jean Monnet (then in charge of the French *Commissariat du Plan*; see Box 2.4), and put forward by the French foreign minister, Robert Schuman (Box 2.5). The Schuman Plan aimed at making war in Europe not only 'unthinkable, but materially impossible' through the creation of a common market for iron, steel and coal in Europe. For Germany this offered a passport to international respectability, and an end to Allied occupation and checks on economic recovery (Swann, 2000). For France the plan provided a means of concluding French occupation of the Saarland, since handing the Saarland back to Germany would be more acceptable if Germany formed part of a common market in coal and steel. The plan was also attractive to the federalists, who were disappointed by the failure to transform the OEEC into a supranational organization.

Box 2.4: *Jean Monnet (1888–1979)*

Jean Monnet* was a French economist and diplomat, at times called the 'Father of Europe'. As director of the post-war planning commission in France, he was the initiator of the Monnet Plan (1947–53) for the modernization and re-equipment of French industry. Monnet was instigator of the Schuman Plan in 1950, and first president of the European Coal and Steel Community. In 1950 he also fostered the eventually unsuccessful plan to create a European Defence Community.

During the war Monnet turned down an invitation to join de Gaulle's government-in-exile in London. In the summer of 1940 he persuaded Churchill to make an offer of Franco-British Union. He was convinced of the importance of US support for the war effort, and for several years was technically a senior British civil servant in Washington with his French passport personally endorsed by Churchill. In some French circles Monnet's vision, which led him to work so closely with the USA and Britain, was criticized. An interesting account of his life is provided in his memoirs (Monnet, 1978).

*Not to be confused with the French painter Claude Monet!

Box 2.5: *Robert Schuman (1886–1963)*

Although born in Luxembourg, Schuman's family came from Lorraine and he grew up in Metz while it was under German rule. A prominent statesman in post-war years, Schuman always emphasized the importance of Franco-German rapprochement.

Schuman entered politics when Lorraine was returned to France, becoming prime minister (1947–48) and foreign minister (1948–53) in the Fourth Republic. He was a member of the Mouvement Républicain Populaire (MRP), a centrist, Christian Democrat party.

The 9th May, which is the day on which Schuman announced the plan for setting up the ECSC, is still celebrated as a holiday in EU institutions.

According to the Schuman Plan, production of steel and coal should be 'pooled' (the famous 'black pool') and placed under a supranational High Authority. The aim was to eliminate trade barriers and increase competition, but since in such highly regulated sectors many exceptions had to be allowed, the approach was essentially that of 'regulated competition'. The High Authority could levy taxes, influence investment and fix minimum prices and production quotas in times of 'imminent' and 'manifest' crisis.

Abhorring the transfer of sovereignty to an authority that was 'utterly undemocratic and responsible to nobody' (Attlee, speaking in the House of Commons[4]) the UK remained out of the initiative. France, Germany, Italy and the Benelux countries (who were to become the founder members of the EEC) went ahead and signed the Treaty of Paris, establishing the ECSC in 1951. The new Community was to lay the foundations for Franco-German post-war reconciliation, which was to prove the cornerstone and driving force in the integration process.

Attempts at co-operation in defence

Given the aim of rendering war in Europe impossible, and the fear of the perceived Soviet threat, it was to be expected that a common defence policy would be one of the main aims of the European integration process. As a first response to creation of the Eastern Bloc, in 1948 France, the UK and the Benelux signed the Treaty of Brussels which provided for a system of mutual assistance in the event of attack. Western defence efforts acquired an Atlantic flavour from 1949 when these countries joined with the USA, Canada, Denmark, Italy, Norway, Portugal and Iceland to form **NATO (North Atlantic Treaty Organization).**

With the outbreak of the Korean War in 1950, the USA and the UK were in favour of German rearmament. France was against this idea and also opposed Germany becoming a member of NATO, instead proposing the creation of a European army with West German participation (the Pleven Plan). The UK was not opposed to such an initiative but was against being directly involved, partly because of the 'special relation' with the USA and partly because the French proposal contained supranational elements.

Negotiations among the six future founding members of the EC went ahead with a view to creating a **European Defence Community (EDC).** The institutional structure of the Community was to be similar to that of the ECSC, with a Joint Defence Commission, a Council of Ministers, a Parliamentary Assembly and a Court of Justice. There was to be a combined army with a

---

[4] Quoted in Swann (2000).

single uniform and flag, and its own budget. In order to ensure control of the European army, political integration was also to be strengthened, and in 1953 a draft proposal for the creation of a European Political Community was also presented. It was envisaged that after a transitional period, the institutions of the ECSC, the EDC and the European Political Community would be fused.

In 1952 the Treaty on the EDC was signed, but required ratification by the six participating states. In 1954 the French parliament refused to ratify the Treaty (though the other five countries involved had done so). There was reaction to the supranational element of the proposal, with the French Right objecting to the creation of an army under European control,[5] especially as the UK was not involved. At the same time the French Left feared German rearmament.

The solution to this impasse was the creation of the **Western European Union** (WEU) in 1955. This is a traditional inter-governmental organization whose founding members were the original European Communities (EC; 6) plus the UK. Its aim was to provide a European framework in which Germany could be rearmed and enter NATO, and in which the last vestiges of Allied occupation of Germany could be removed. The WEU remained relatively ineffective for almost 30 years before the question of an EU security initiative was revived (as described in the Online Learning Centre for this book).

Agriculture: Towards the creation of the Common Agricultural Policy

For many years the Common Agricultural Policy (CAP) was considered the cornerstone of the integration process.[6] In the immediate post-war period there were strong reasons for creating a common market for agricultural products:

- The initial deal is frequently regarded as an exchange of interests between France who was seeking markets for her agricultural exports, and Germany who was anxious to reduce tariffs in order to ensure outlets for her industrial exports. Germany had a tradition of heavy protection and substantial income support for the agricultural sector, and was also keen to transfer part of the burden of such policies to the Community level. Italy and the Netherlands also considered that a common agricultural market would provide opportunities for developing their typical forms of production (Mediterranean, and dairy products and vegetables respectively), though in the event the latter was more successful in realizing this objective.

- At the time agriculture was extremely important economically, socially and politically. In 1958 agriculture accounted for 20 per cent of the labour force in the original EC (6) countries and generally incomes were lower than in non-agricultural sectors. In some countries and areas the farm vote was a strong force to be reckoned with.

- The farm policies in the original EC (6) countries were very different and had to be harmonized; otherwise, differences in agricultural price levels and support measures would cause distortions in intra-EC trade.

- The introduction of a common market for agriculture would encourage competition and specialization according to the principle of comparative advantage (see Chapter 4), thereby increasing the productivity of the sector. Insofar as this resulted in lower food prices, there might be less pressure for wage increases.

---

[5] News that the Treaty had failed ratification led to a rendering of the 'Marseillaise' in the French parliament.

[6] See Tracy (1989) for a more detailed account of the foundation of the CAP.

■ The harmonization of agricultural prices was envisaged as the first step towards harmonization of wage levels, which was considered necessary for the creation of a common market in industrial products and services.

The proposed 'green pool'

In 1950 in response to a French initiative, the Special Committee of the Council of Europe agreed to consider the prospects for agricultural integration in Europe. The French presented a proposal, known as the Charpentier Plan, to create a 'green pool' in Europe similar to the 'black pool' of the ECSC. This would entail:

■ Common agricultural prices;

■ The elimination of trade barriers between the member states;

■ Preference for the producers of the member states, i.e. they could sell at lower prices on the domestic market than producers from third countries; and

■ A High Authority with supranational powers.

Although the UK and Denmark were strongly opposed to the supranational element of the Charpentier Plan, the Special Committee of the Council of Europe accepted the proposals, and it was agreed to prepare a draft treaty along the lines of the plan.

In 1951 the main elements of the proposal were presented formally in the Pfimlin Plan (taking the name of the French agricultural minister), and they were discussed at the Paris Conferences of 1952 and 1954, which enabled the positions of the various countries to become more precisely defined. However, during these years little progress towards an agreement on agricultural integration was made as France was distracted by the turbulent internal politics of the last days of the Fourth Republic.

Towards the Treaties of Rome

By 1955 the rift between the European countries who wanted to limit integration to intergovernmental co-operation and those who preferred the creation of a supranational authority could no longer be breached. The UK and the Scandinavian countries were in favour of the creation of a free trade area and co-operation on agricultural questions within the OEEC framework. In this context any supranational initiative could be blocked as each of the member states had the power of veto.

The 'Six' founding members of the EEC were not satisfied with this arrangement and in 1955 the Benelux countries presented a Memorandum. This called for the creation of a common market, and specific action in the areas of energy and transport. Though political union was recognized as an ultimate aim, the practical difficulties encountered in its implementation suggested that it was preferable to concentrate on more specific, concrete aims of economic integration.[7] It was considered that the experience gained in working together would then pave the way for political integration. The aim was to: 'work for the establishment of a United Europe by the development of common institutions, the progressive fusion of national economies, the creation of a common market and the progressive harmonization of social policies' (1955 Memorandum).

---

[7] See Swann (2000).

The foreign ministers of the Six at the Messina Conference considered the ideas of the Memorandum, and it was agreed to set up an intergovernmental committee under the Belgian foreign minister, Paul-Henri Spaak, which would study the problems and prepare the treaties necessary for establishing a common market and energy pool. Initially the UK (as a member of the WEU and associate of the ECSC) participated in the activities of the Spaak Committee, but withdrew in 1955 because the UK remained in favour of simply strengthening the OEEC framework, and preferred a free trade arrangement to the creation of a customs union.

In Venice in 1956 the foreign ministers of the Six accepted the results of the Spaak Committee, and work began on the drafting of the two treaties establishing the European Economic Committee and Euratom. These were signed in Rome in March 1957, and entered into force from January 1958.

Two external events help to explain the speed with which the Six worked towards agreeing the Rome Treaties: Suez and the Soviet invasion of Hungary. In 1956 as a reaction to Egyptian raids across the border, Israel invaded Egypt and was subsequently supported by an Anglo-French force. France and Britain opposed Nasser's nationalization of the Suez Canal in which they held shares. Fearing Soviet intervention, the USA exerted diplomatic and economic pressures, which led to the withdrawal of the Anglo-French troops. British and French relations with the USA became very strained, and it was again demonstrated that a weak and divided Europe would have no hope of standing up to the superpowers.

The same lesson emerged from the example of Hungary. In 1953 the Nagy government was permitted to introduce certain reforms such as the freeing of political prisoners, the relaxing of political and economic controls and the ending of collectivization. In less than two years Rakosi replaced Nagy, but in the face of wide-scale demonstrations, he was allowed to return to power in 1956. Nagy then declared Hungarian neutrality and the withdrawal from the Warsaw Pact, and released Cardinal Mindszenty, the Primate of Hungary, from prison. In 1956 despite fierce resistance, Soviet troops occupied Hungary and Nagy was executed, and the West European countries were left feeling weak and vulnerable.

Faced with the decision of the Six to proceed with more ambitious forms of integration, in 1960 the European countries that then preferred intergovernmental co-operation decided to create EFTA (European Free Trade Association). The founder members of EFTA were the UK, Norway, Sweden, Denmark, Austria, Switzerland and Portugal. Subsequently Iceland (in 1970), Finland (in 1986) and Liechtenstein (in 1991) joined. As its name suggests, EFTA involved the creation of a free trade association for industrial products. Agricultural products were largely excluded from this arrangement.

The Treaties of Rome

The Treaties of Rome (signed in 1957 and entered into force in 1958) provide the legal basis for establishment of the EEC and the Euratom. The former is of greater concern here, with Euratom being created mainly in response to a French request, and subsequently shelved, again largely thanks to France. The Treaties are among the most fundamental elements of the *acquis communautaire*.

The Treaty of Rome establishing the EEC consists of 248 Articles. Article 2 sets out the main objectives:

- 'Harmonious development;
- Continuous and balanced expansion;
- Increased stability;

■ Ever more rapid growth in living standards;

■ Closer links between the member states.'

This short list has been the subject of considerable debate and controversy. The Treaty left open the fixing of priorities and the question of how possible conflicts between objectives were to be resolved. In particular, the list raises the fundamental economic question of how to reconcile equity ('harmonious development' and 'balanced expansion') with efficiency ('ever more rapid growth in living standards').

Subsequent treaties added new priorities so that in the Treaty Establishing the European Communities (TEC) Article 2 reads:[8]

> to promote throughout the Community a harmonious, balanced and sustainable development of economic activities, a high level of employment and of social protection, equality between men and women, sustainable and non-inflationary growth, a high degree of competitiveness and convergence of economic performance, a high level of protection and improvement of the quality of the environment, the raising of the standard of living and quality of life, and economic and social cohesion and solidarity among Member States.

Article 3 of the Treaty of Rome lists the mechanisms by which the objectives were to be realized. A 12-year transition period from 1958 until 1969[9] was envisaged for their implementation. These measures include:

■ The abolition of tariffs, and of quantitative and qualitative restrictions in intra-EC trade;

■ The creation of a common external policy and, in particular, a common external tariff;

■ The elimination of obstacles to the free movement of people, capital, goods and services;

■ A common agricultural policy;

■ A common transport policy;

■ The introduction of means to ensure fair competition;

■ The co-ordination of the economic policies of the member states to avoid balance-of-payments disequilibria;

■ The creation of a European Social Fund (ESF) to improve employment opportunities and raise living standards for workers;

■ The creation of a European Investment Bank (EIB) to help reduce regional disparities;

■ Special trade and development arrangements for colonies and former colonies.

Progress in implementing these measures has been very uneven. The elimination of tariffs on intra-EC trade and the introduction of the common external tariff were largely completed by mid-1968, 18 months ahead of schedule.

However, despite many proposals, only limited steps were taken to remove non-tariff barriers and to free factor movements within the Community. As a result, these objectives had to be relaunched many years later in the programme to complete the Single Market from 1993. Linguistic and cultural differences partially account for the relatively limited increases in the movement of people, and similarly for the slow progress in the recognition of qualifications and

---

[8] As amended by the Nice Treaty. See also Chapter 3 for a discussion of the Lisbon Treaty. The new Article 3 of the Treaty on the European Union sets out the objectives of the Union, while Articles 2–6 of the Treaty on the Functioning of the Union (replacing the Treaty Establishing the European Community) deal with delimitation of the competences of the EU (see Chapter 1).

[9] Divided into three four-year periods.

in obtaining social security benefits in other member states. The Treaty called for liberalization of capital movements only insofar as this was necessary for the creation of a common market. The main instruments of the CAP were in operation from 1967. Already during the 1960s and 1970s some steps were taken in applying competition policy to limit the abuse of dominant position by private firms and against restrictive business practices.

According to Swann (2000), three main factors account for the inclusion of a common transport policy among the objectives of the Treaty of Rome:

1 Transport costs could act as a trade barrier, and measures to promote a cheap, efficient transport system in the Community could help to stimulate trade.

2 Transport has traditionally always been a heavily regulated sector and failure to harmonize policies could lead to distortions (as the experience of the ECSC showed).

3 The Treaty of Rome was a compromise, balancing the national interests of the founding countries, and the Netherlands in particular was anxious to include transport policy as part of the deal. Transport, especially through Rotterdam and along the Rhine, makes an important contribution to Dutch GDP.

Although envisaged as one of the first three common policies by the Treaty of Rome, embedded national interests meant that progress in introducing common measures on transport policy was slow. The Treaty was remarkably unencumbered with details concerning the implementation of a common policy. As late as 1985 there was a judgment of the European Court of Justice against the Council for failing to introduce a common transport policy, and calling for the situation to be remedied as soon as possible.[10]

Despite the mention of co-ordination of economic policies, the Treaty contains no specific commitment to macroeconomic co-ordination or to economic and monetary union. Various considerations (Tsoukalis, 1997) help to account for the reticence of the Treaty on this point:

■ The importance of the dollar in the international monetary system at the time meant that there was little need or purpose to establish a regional monetary arrangement in Europe;

■ Reasons of political feasibility (quite enough was already being taken on with the creation of the common market);

■ Differences among the member states;

■ In the golden age of Keynesian demand management (which entailed active intervention in an attempt to regulate economic activity) member states were reluctant to sacrifice autonomy of fiscal and monetary policies.

The ESF and EIB envisaged by the Treaty were operational at an early stage. With the exception of the Italian Mezzogiorno, regional disparities among the original Six were relatively limited and the EIB was conceived essentially as an instrument to assist the Mezzogiorno.

At the time of the Treaty, the prevailing view appears to have been that the transfers to and from the Community budget by the member states should roughly balance. Despite the references to 'harmonious' development and 'balanced expansion' in Article 2, extensive redistributional policies were not foreseen by the Treaty. Though various Community structural (social and regional) measures were introduced over the years, the spending involved was fairly limited, at least until 1988 when the Structural Funds were doubled (see Chapter 15).

The provision for special trade and aid arrangements with colonies and former colonies was a concession to France who wanted to maintain her links, but with the other EC members (and Germany in particular) helping to foot the bill. Trade preferences to these countries were

---

[10]See Chapter 6 for a more detailed discussion of EC transport policy.

extended throughout the Community, and aid was granted through the European Development Fund (EDF). From the 1960s many of these countries gained independence, and in 1963 (renewed in 1969) the Yaoundé agreements covering trade and aid arrangements were signed between the EC and former French colonies in Africa.

The entry of the UK into the Community in 1973 led to a reappraisal of development policy, resulting in the first Lomé Convention of 1975. Subsequent agreements followed in 1980, 1985 and 1990 (which was extended to cover a ten-year period) and the Cotonou Agreement of 2000. The Cotonou Agreement (see Chapter 19) covers 79 ACP (African, Caribbean and Pacific) countries.

The European Community in the 1960s

The 12-year transitional period in which the provisions of the Treaty of Rome were to be implemented coincided with a particularly favourable international economic climate. Growth was rapid and employment in the EEC countries reached unprecedented levels, while inflation was rising but had not reached dangerous levels (see Tables 2.1–2.3). In general the economic performance of the Six outshone that of the USA and the UK.

It was in this climate that the tariffs and quantitative restrictions on intra-EC trade were dismantled and the common external tariff was introduced (by mid-1968). Internal developments in EC commercial policy were linked to external events as the Six prepared common positions to negotiate as a single actor in the GATT (General Agreement on Tariffs and Trade) Kennedy Round over the 1964–7 period.[11] A precondition for agreeing tariff reductions for third countries was that the common external tariff should be in place. During the 1960s trade and, in particular, intra-EC trade grew faster than output, and a 'virtuous circle' of trade liberalization and rapid growth seemed to be in operation. Growth eased the adjustment process rendering the reduction or elimination of trade barriers less painful.[12]

The emergence of the EEC Six as a single actor and their successful economic performance encouraged the UK to apply for membership in 1961 and 1967, but on both occasions De Gaulle vetoed the application. The opposition of de Gaulle to any transfer of French sovereignty to the Community also meant that agreement on financing of the EC budget had to wait until 1970 (see Chapter 11), and an initiative to strengthen European political integration was blocked.

The 1960s also marked the birth of the CAP, which was then regarded by many as the greatest achievement in integration (see Chapter 12). In 1962 agreement was reached on the mechanisms for agricultural support, with the decision on the level of the common prices for agricultural products following in 1964 and being applied from 1967. The Mansholt Plan was presented in 1968 with radical proposals for restructuring EC agriculture in order to raise incomes and efficiency.

---

[11] The GATT is described in Chapter 18.

[12] Important legal developments relate to the two leading cases of van Gent and Loos (Case number 26 of 1962) and Costa vs. ENEL (Case number 6 of 1964). In these cases the Court of Justice expounded its doctrine concerning the 'direct effect' of certain provisions of the Treaty of Rome. This entails that where provisions of the Treaty impose on the member states clear and unconditional obligations, and the implementation or effectiveness of the provisions is not dependent on any further action of state, Community law not only imposes obligations on individuals, but also confers rights on them, which are enforceable in the courts of the member states.

	1960–69	1970–1980	1980–1990	1991–2000	2006
Belgium	4.8	3.3	2.3	2.2	2.8
France	5.5	3.3	2.2	1.9	2.0
Germany	4.5	2.7	2.1	1.5	2.9
Italy	5.7	3.6	2.5	1.6	1.9
Lux.	3.6	2.6	3.3	5.5	6.1
NL	4.4	2.9	1.9	2.9	3.0
Denmark	4.8	2.2	1.8	2.4	3.5
Ireland	4.3	4.7	3.0	7.3	5.7
UK	2.9	1.9	4.4	2.4	2.8
Greece	7.6	4.7	1.6	2.4	4.3
Portugal	6.1	4.7	3.1	2.8	1.3
Spain	7.7	3.5	3.0	2.7	3.9
USA	4.3	3.1	2.7	3.1	2.9
Japan	10.4	4.4	4.2	1.5	2.2

TABLE 2.1 The economic growth of the EU(12), the USA and Japan (average percentage change in real GDP at constant prices)
Source: OECD and own calculations on the basis of OECD for the decade averages, and Eurostat (© European Communities, 2008) for 2006.

	1960–67*	1974–1979*	1980–1990	1991–2000	2006
Belgium	2.1	5.7	10.9	8.5	8.1
France	1.5	4.5	9.1	10.9	9.2
FRG	0.8	3.5	6.8	7.8	9.8
Italy	4.9	6.6	10.1	10.6	6.8
Lux.	0.0	0.6	2.5	2.5	4.7
NL	0.7	4.9	9.6	5.1	3.9
Denmark	1.6	–	7.8	6.6	3.9
Ireland	4.9	7.6	14.4	11.1	4.4
UK	1.5	4.2	9.2	7.9	5.3
Greece	5.2	1.9	6.8	9.9**	8.9
Portugal	2.4	6.0	7.1	5.6	7.7
Spain	2.3	5.3	17.5	16.0	8.5
USA	5.0	6.7	6.9	5.6	4.6
Japan	1.3	1.9	2.5	3.3	4.1

TABLE 2.2 Unemployment in the EU(12), the USA and Japan (average of annual rates, percentage of labour force)
* This column is taken from Table 2.2 from *The New Economy Revisited 2/e* by Tsoukalis, Loucas. By permission of Oxford University Press.
**Commonly used definitions of unemployment rather than standardized rates.
Source: OECD and own calculations based on OECD data. for the decade averages, and Eurostat (© European Communities, 2008) for 2006.

	1961–70	1974–1979*	1980–1990	1991–2000	2006
Belgium	2.8	8.5	4.5	1.9	2.2
France	4.0	10.7	6.7	1.8	1.9
FRG	2.5	4.7	2.8	2.3	1.8
Italy	4.0	16.1	10.4	3.8	2.2
Lux.	2.3	7.4	4.4	2.2	3.0
NL	4.2	7.2	2.7	2.1	1.7
Denmark	5.2	10.8	6.3	2.1	1.9
Ireland	4.8	15.0	8.3	2.6	2.7
UK	3.7	15.6	7.3	3.3	2.3
Greece	2.2	16.1	19.4	9.2	3.3
Portugal	3.7	23.7	16.7	4.7	3.0
Spain	5.8	18.3	9.7	3.9	3.6
USA	2.5	8.5	5.4	2.8	3.4**
Japan	5.7	9.9	2.5	0.8	−0.3**

TABLE 2.3 Inflation in OECD countries: consumer price index (average annual percentage change)

* This column is taken from Table 2.3 from *The New Economy Revisited* 2/e by Tsoukalis, Loucas. By permission of Oxford University Press.

** 2005

Source: OECD and own calculations based on OECD data for the decade averages, and Eurostat (© European Communities, 2008) for 2006.

The 1969 Hague Summit

With the end of the transition period due in 1970, the search was on for new ways of relaunching the integration process. This gained new impetus in 1969 when Pompidou replaced de Gaulle. At the Hague Summit of 1969 a package was presented, which was described by Pompidou as containing three main elements: completion, deepening and enlargement.

The completion of the integration process referred essentially to placing the financing of the CAP on sounder footing. This entailed agreement on the own resources for the EC budget, and a slight increase in the budgetary powers of the European Parliament. The deepening process was to consist of gradual progress towards the creation of an Economic and Monetary Union (EMU) by 1980, and the introduction of European Political Co-operation (EPC). The first EMU programme met with little success (also because of the difficult economic situation following the 1973 oil crisis), though in 1979 the EMS (European Monetary System) was introduced.

At the Hague Summit, it was agreed to study the best way of implementing European Political Co-operation (EPC), and a report was presented in 1970.[13] The basis for EPC was to be inter-governmental co-operation, and member states would attempt to work out common positions and agree on common actions. However, progress in developing common positions on foreign policy issues was slow before the 1990s. With de Gaulle no longer on the political scene, the path to further enlargement of the Community was now open. This occurred in 1973 when the UK, Ireland and Denmark became members, while Norway (not for the last time) voted against membership in a referendum.

---

[13] Though the membership was to be the same, the EPC was to be separate from EC institutions. There was to be no majority voting (qualified or otherwise), and member states were not obliged to agree.

The Community in the 1970s: the years of Eurosclerosis

After the successes of the first 12 years, the Community entered a long period of stagnation when little progress was made in integration. Particularly after the 1973 oil crisis, the EC economy entered a phase of slower growth, higher unemployment, more rapid inflation and falling competitiveness (see Tables 2.1–2.3). The process of trade liberalization wavered, and non-tariff barriers were applied on trade both within the EC and with third countries in what became known as the 'new protectionism'.

Divergence in the economic policies and performance of the EC member states, and the more unstable international monetary situation meant that the first programme to introduce monetary union had to be shelved. The main energies of the EC member states seemed concentrated on the seemingly endless squabbles about the level of agricultural price support and the EC budgetary mechanisms. As Tsoukalis (1997) notes, the energy expended on these debates would seem excessive given that the sums involved accounted for such a tiny fraction (then less than 1 per cent) of the Community's GDP.

These are often called 'the years of Eurosclerosis or Europessimism', but none the less a few successes must be noted (see the Appendix to this Chapter): the 1973 enlargement; the creation (albeit on a small scale) of the European Regional Development Fund in 1975; the establishment of the European Monetary System; the introduction of direct elections to the Parliament in 1979, and the entry of Greece in 1981. The path was also prepared for Spanish and Portuguese accession in 1986.

The relaunching of integration: the Internal Market Programme

By the mid-1980s there was growing discontent in the Community about poor economic performance and loss of competitiveness, particularly when compared with rivals such as Japan and the USA. Some governments of the EC member states, such as those of Thatcher, Kohl and even Mitterand, were committed to deregulation as a means of stimulating output and trade.

Against a background of increasing frustration with the slow pace of integration, Jacques Delors became President of the Commission in 1985. The strategy chosen to revive the integration process was the completion of the internal market. The objective was to eliminate barriers at the frontiers between member states and promote the freedom of movement of labour, capital, goods and services. In 1985 France, Germany and the Benelux countries signed the Schengen Agreement, which aimed at the removal of checks on people at borders. Schengen was incorporated into the Amsterdam Treaty (signed in 1997 and entered into force in 1999), and its membership was gradually extended (see Chapter 6).

Freedom of movement of goods and services entailed eliminating the remaining non-tariff barriers on trade between the member states, one of the most important of which was differences in standards. A key element of the Community's strategy in tackling differences in standards was to rely as far as possible on the principle of mutual recognition. This was defined in the much-cited *Cassis de Dijon* case of 1979 when the European Court of Justice established the general principle that all goods lawfully manufactured and marketed in one member state should also be accepted in other member countries. Certain exceptions were allowed if they were necessary to protect public health, the fairness of commercial transactions and the defence of the consumer.

The introduction of the Single or Internal Market Programme had the effect of launching a new phase in the integration process, spilling over into renewed efforts in institutional reform, reinforced EC social, regional and competition policies, and economic and monetary union. Reform of the Community decision-making process was necessary to ensure that all the legislation could be introduced in time to meet the January 1993 deadline for introduction of the Single Market. The programme was initially presented as an exercise in deregulation and received wholehearted support from the EC member states and business community. However, the weaker countries and regions of the Community feared that they might not be able to meet the increased competitive pressure implied by the Single Market, and that as a result regional disparities might worsen. To assuage these fears, in 1988 it was agreed to double the Community Structural Funds and to reform the way in which they operated (see Chapter 15). The Single Market Programme spurred a spate of mergers in the Community and led to a tightening of competition policy (see Chapter 17). Introduction of a single currency could be regarded as a further step in completing the Single Market (see Chapters 9 and 10).

The Maastricht Treaty and Economic and Monetary Union

In addition to creating the European Union, the Maastricht Treaty (signed in 1992 and entered into force in 1993) envisaged a strengthening of the Community. This would consist of EMU, greater economic and social cohesion, some institutional reform (including increased powers for the European Parliament, see Chapter 3), the creation of European citizenship and the extension of EU competence to new areas.

The Treaty of Maastricht set out the three stages in the process of implementing EMU, fixing dates and describing the objectives to be reached in each stage. In addition, it presented criteria to be satisfied before member states could participate in EMU and allowed for certain countries to opt out. The third stage of economic and monetary union began on 1 January 1999 with 11 countries as full participants; Greece also subsequently joined, Denmark and the UK chose to opt out, and Sweden decided not to participate and remained out on technical grounds. Slovenia adopted the euro in 2007, and Malta and Cyprus joined in 2008.

The objective of greater economic and social cohesion in the Treaty was translated into an increase in transfers through the Structural Funds to the poorer regions of the Community. The Treaty was also accompanied by a separate protocol known as 'the Social Chapter', which aimed at improving living and working conditions (see Chapter 16). Initially the Social Chapter was accepted by only 11 of the then member states and had to wait for the advent of the Blair government to be adopted by the UK. The new areas of competence introduced by the Treaty of Maastricht refer to an increased role for the Community in education, culture, public health and the environment. In addition, there were to be the development of trans-European networks in transport and energy.

EU enlargement

In part because they feared that with the Single Market Programme their industries would lose relative competitiveness, the EFTA countries began to negotiate the creation of a European Economic Area (EEA). This would enable the EFTA countries to participate in a unified market but imposed strong limits on their ability to participate in decision-making. In the event, three of the EFTA countries (Austria, Sweden and Finland) opted for EU accession, joining in 1995 (see Table 2.4, the comparable data for countries joining the EU in 2004 and 2007 in Table 2.5, and for the present candidate countries, Table 20.1 in Chapter 20). In a referendum Norway

	Growth 1991–2000	2006	Unemployment 1991–2000	2006	Inflation 1991–2000	2006
Austria	2.4	3.3	5.2*	4.7	1.9	1.7
Finland	2.0	5.0	12.5	7.7	2.1	1.3
Sweden	2.0	4.1	7.6	7.1	2.6	1.5

TABLE 2.4 Selected economic indicators for Austria, Sweden and Finland (per cent)
*Commonly used definitions of unemployment rather than standardized rates.
Source: Own elaborations based on OECD data for 1991–2000, Eurostat (© European Communities, 2008) for 2006.

	Growth	Unemployment	Inflation	GDP per capita in PPS#
BG	6.1	9.0	7.4	37.1
CZ	6.4	7.1	2.1	79.3
EE	11.2	5.9	4.4	67.9
CY	3.8	4.6	2.2	93.4
LT	11.9	6.8	6.6	55.8
LI	7.7	5.6	3.8	57.7
HU	3.9	7.5	4.0	65.3
MA	3.2	7.3	2.6	75.5
PL	6.1	13.8	1.3	52.9
RO	7.7	7.3	6.6	37.6 (f)
SL	5.7	6.0	2.5	91.7 (f)
SK	8.5	13.4	4.3	67.6 (f)
EU(27)	3.0	8.1	2.2*	100.0

TABLE 2.5 Selected economic indicators for 2006 for the member states that joined the EU in 2004 and 2007 (per cent)
*EU(25)
# purchasing power standards EU(27) = 100
f = forecast
Source: Eurostat (© European Communities, 2008) www.epp.eurostat.ec.europa.eu

again decided against EU membership, while the Swiss voted even against participation in the EEA. When the EEA came into operation from January 1994, the EFTA members were limited to Norway, Iceland and Liechtenstein.

Following the fall of communism in 1989, the smaller Central and East European countries wanted tighter links and eventual membership of the EC. The Community responded first by offering trade and co-operation agreements to these countries, but was slow to offer them an accession strategy. The 1993 Copenhagen European Council set out the conditions that the applicant countries have to fulfil in order to join the EU. Between 1994 and 1996 ten Central and Eastern European countries (CEECs) applied for EU membership. All these countries signed association agreements with the EU and all were participants in the EU pre-accession strategy to help prepare them for membership.

In July 1997 the EC Commission published the document Agenda 2000, which analysed the steps needed to prepare both the EU and accession countries for enlargement, and included

'Opinions' on the readiness of each of the applicant countries to join the EU. At the Luxembourg Summit[14] of December 1997 it was decided to open accession negotiations with Cyprus and five CEECs: the Czech Republic, Estonia, Hungary, Poland, Romania and Slovenia. These negotiations began in March 1998.

At the Helsinki Summit it was also decided to begin negotiations for accession with six further candidates: Bulgaria, Latvia, Lithuania, Malta, Romania and Slovakia, and to declare Turkey a candidate. Malta's application had lapsed in 1993 but was subsequently resumed in 1998. Negotiations with these six countries began in February 2000.

The Gothenburg Summit of June 2001 set the objective of trying to complete negotiations with the first applicant countries by the end of 2002 so they could participate in the European Parliament elections of 2004. The Copenhagen European Council of December 2002 confirmed this timetable and ten new member states joined the EU in May 2004, while Bulgaria and Romania joined in 2007 (see Table 2.5).

In October 2005 the EU decided to begin negotiations for membership with Croatia and Turkey. The negotiations with Turkey are likely to prove lengthy, with 2015 being mentioned as the earliest expected date for accession (see Chapter 20). In December 2006 EU foreign ministers decided Turkey had not met the request to open ports and airports to Greek Cypriots, so suspended negotiations on eight chapters of the *acquis*, which were considered to be related this issue. Negotiations on other chapters of the *acquis* continued, and in 2007 three new chapters were opened.

In December 2005 the Former Yugoslav Republic of Macedonia was declared a candidate country. In 1999 the EU introduced the Stabilization and Association process, which offered eligible West Balkan countries the possibility of signing Stabilization and Association Agreements and eventual EU membership. The EU is considering the possibility of further enlargements to countries in the Western Balkans, which could eventually include Bosnia and Herzegovina, Serbia, Montenegro and Albania.

From the Mediterranean Policy to the European Neighbourhood Policy

There was an attempt to counterbalance the eastward developments of the EU with a strengthening of the EU Mediterranean Policy. This is strongly favoured by the present southern members of the Union, partly as a means of stemming the growing flow of immigration across the Mediterranean, but also to increase security in the area. At the Barcelona Summit of 1995 it was agreed to set up the Euromed Programme to increase aid and create a free trade area in the Mediterranean area by 2010 (see Chapter 19).

In March 2003 the European Commission launched the ENP to deal with relations between an enlarged EU and its eastern and southern neighbours. The aim is to prevent new dividing lines emerging between the EU and its neighbours, and to enhance security and narrow the prosperity gap on the new external borders of the EU. The ENP offers EU neighbours greater political, security, economic and cultural co-operation. The ENP is for countries with no immediate prospect of EU membership and covers Ukraine, Moldova and other ex-Soviet Republics, and southern Mediterranean countries, but not the Western Balkans (given the possibility of accession to the EU by these countries).

The ENP was launched in 2003 also with Russia specifically in mind, but was rejected by Russia as inadequate (see Chapter 19). The EU has a Partnership and Co-operation Agreement

---

[14] These summits, or European Councils, are attended by heads of state and of the government of the EU member states (see Chapter 3).

with Russia, and in 2003 agreed to reinforce co-operation by setting up four common spaces covering economic relations; Freedom, Security and Justice; external security; and research and education, including cultural aspects. The EU is heavily dependent on Russia for energy imports, but at times, in particular after the 2004 enlargement, relations have been tense.

Employment, productivity and the Lisbon Strategy

In 1997 the Luxembourg Process, or European Employment Strategy (EES), was set up (see Chapter 16). This aimed at improving 'employability' and encouraging the adaptability of businesses and their employees. Concerns with relatively low EU productivity led in March 2000 to the decision of the Lisbon European Council to launch a 'new strategic goal' for the following ten years aimed at creating a knowledge-based economy focusing on better use of information science and research and development, and more flexible labour markets (see Chapter 7).

The Lisbon Strategy was confirmed at the March 2002 Barcelona European Council, which called for measures to guarantee EU competitiveness, promote sustainable development and improve employment across skills and geographical areas (also by increasing labour mobility). To date, however, it is difficult not to conclude that the process has produced a great deal of rhetoric and rather less concrete change.

From the Amsterdam to the Lisbon Treaty

The prospect of enlargement gave a new urgency to the question of institutional reform of the EU as it was necessary to ensure that the decision-making process could function with a growing number of members. The Treaty of Amsterdam (signed in 1997 and came into force in 1999) was intended to resolve these questions but fell well short of expectations. For that reason there was a further attempt to tackle the question of institutional reform with the Nice Treaty (signed in 2001 and came into force in 2003), and in 2001 EU leaders meeting at Laeken in Belgium agreed on the creation of a Constitutional Convention aimed at drawing up a Constitutional Treaty (see Chapter 3). The results of the work of the Convention were presented in July 2003. EU leaders failed to agree on the proposals at a summit in December 2003 in Brussels, but subsequently reached agreement in June 2004 during the Irish Presidency. The Constitutional Treaty was signed in a ceremony in Rome in October 2004, but required ratification to come into operation. In May 2005 France rejected the Constitutional Treaty in a referendum, and three days later it was also rejected in a Dutch referendum. A 'period of reflection' on the future of Europe was subsequently launched.

In 2007 at the celebrations of the 50th anniversary of the Treaty of Rome, EU leaders agreed to the Berlin Declaration, which aimed at working towards a new Treaty for the EU before the elections to the European Parliament in 2009. In June 2007 the EU leaders agreed on the outline of a draft Reform Treaty to replace the Constitutional Treaty, and the text of this Reform Treaty was agreed in a summit in Lisbon in October 2007. What became known as the Lisbon Treaty was signed at a special meeting of the European Council in Lisbon in December 2007. In order to come into force it has to be ratified by all the member states, and the initial aim was to complete this process in time for the Treaty to enter into force by January 2009, though following rejection of the Treaty in an Irish referendum of June 2008, this seems unlikely.

Summary of Key Concepts

- After the **unsuccessful efforts to set up a supranational organization** in Europe, there was a change in tactics. In line with the neo-functionalist approach, there were various attempts at integration by sector.

- The **European Coal and Steel Community** (or 'black pool') was set up in 1951 with the aim of making war in Europe 'materially impossible'.

- Attempts to set up a **European Defence Community and a 'green pool' for agriculture** failed, largely because of France.

- Article 2 of the **Treaty of Rome** sets out the main objectives of the EEC, while Article 3 sets out the mechanisms by which these were to be realized. Progress in implementing the measures was very uneven, but a common commercial policy and the Common Agricultural Policy were soon operating.

- **The 1969 Hague Summit** called for widening (enlargement), deepening (economic and monetary union) and completion (a settlement to the budgetary question) of the Community.

- The 1970s and early 1980s were the years of **Eurosclerosis or Europessimism**, when much of the energy of the Community was spent on quarrels over the budget and agricultural spending.

- When Jacques Delors became president of the Commission in 1985, his strategy to relaunch the integration process was the completion of the **Single Market**.

- In addition to creating the European Union, the Maastricht Treaty set out the steps for establishing **economic and monetary union.**

- The **EFTA** countries began to negotiate the creation of an EEA which would enable them to participate in the Single Market but which limited their ability to participate in decision-making. In the event, three of the EFTA countries (Austria, Sweden and Finland) opted for EU accession in 1995. In a referendum Norway again decided against EU membership, while the Swiss even voted against participation in the EEA.

- In 2004 ten new countries joined the EU, and Bulgaria and Romania joined in 2007.

- In October 2005 the EU decided to begin negotiations for membership with **Croatia and Turkey**, but the negotiations with Turkey are likely to prove lengthy.

- In December 2005 the Former **Yugoslav Republic of Macedonia** was declared a candidate country. The EU is considering the possibility of further enlargements to countries in the Western Balkans.

- At the Barcelona Summit of 1995 it was agreed to set up the **Euromed Programme** to increase aid and create a free trade area in the Mediterranean area by 2010. In 2003 the **European Neighbourhood Policy** was established to provide closer co-operation with EU neighbours that have no prospect of EU accession.

- In 1997 the Luxembourg Process, or **European Employment Strategy (EES),** was launched.

- In March 2000 the **Lisbon Strategy** was introduced to create a knowledge-based economy in ten years.

- The Treaties of Amsterdam and of Nice, and the proposed Constitutional Treaty, were intended to introduce the necessary **institutional changes** for an enlarged EU.

- Following the rejection of the Constitutional Treaty in referenda in France and the Netherlands and reflection period, agreement on the Reform or **Lisbon Treaty** was finally reached in 2007.

- The aim is to complete the ratification process so the Lisbon Treaty can come into operation by January 2009, but this seems unlikely with Irish rejection of the Treaty in a 2008 referendum.

Questions for study and review

1 How far do the federalist and neo-functionalist approaches to integration help to explain the initiatives of the 1940s and 1950s?

2 Describe the main functions of the OECD.

3 What are the main differences between the Council of Europe and the OSCE?

4 Describe the main objectives of the Treaty of Rome, and the mechanisms by which these objectives were to be realized.

5 How was the Community been successful in implementing the policies envisaged by Article 3 of the Treaty of Rome?

6 What strategy was used to overcome the years of Europessimism or Eurosclerosis?

7 What were the main European integration initiatives in the 1990s?

8 Describe the enlargement process of the EU.

9 What attempts have been made to reform the EU decision-making process since the late 1990s?

Appendix

Key dates in the history of European integration

1950

In a speech inspired by Jean Monnet, Robert Schuman proposed the pooling of coal and steel resources between France and Germany, and any other European country that wished to join them.

1951

The Six (France, Germany, Italy and the Benelux countries) signed the Paris Treaty establishing the European Coal and Steel Community.

1952

The Treaty establishing the European Defence Community (EDC) was signed in Paris.

1954

The French parliament rejected the EDC Treaty.

1955

The Western European Union (WEU) was created.

At Messina the foreign ministers of the Six decided to launch a new integration initiative aimed at the creation of a common market, and common policies for agriculture, transport and the civilian use of nuclear energy.

1958

The Treaties of Rome entered into force, and the EEC and Euratom were created.

1960

The European Free Trade Association (EFTA) was set up.

1962

Key decisions on the Common Agricultural Policy (CAP) were taken. The decision on common prices was not reached until 1964 and came into operation from 1967.

1963

De Gaulle vetoed UK application to join the EC. A second veto followed in 1967.

1966

The Luxembourg compromise entered into force, with France resuming its seat in the Council in return for use of the unanimity rule when any country deems an issue to be of 'vital national interest'.

1967

The Treaty merging the EEC, the European Coal and Steel Community (ECSC) and Euratom entered into force.

1968

Remaining customs duties in intra-EC trade in manufactured goods were removed 18 months ahead of schedule, and the Common External Tariff was introduced.

1969

The Hague Summit agreed on proposals to deepen (EMU by 1980), widen (allow Denmark, Ireland and the UK to join) and complete (by introducing own resources) the Community.

1973

Denmark, Ireland and the UK joined the Community.

1975

The European Regional Development Fund was established.
The Treaty giving the European Parliament wider budgetary powers and establishing the Court of Auditors was signed and entered into force in 1997.
The first Lomé Convention was signed between the Community and developing ACP (African, Caribbean and Pacific) countries. Later Lomé Conventions entered into force in 1980, 1985 and 1990 and from 2000 there was the Cotonou Agreement.

1979

European Monetary System (EMS) started to operate.
The first direct elections to the European Parliament were held.

1981

Greece joined the EC.

1985

Jacques Delors was appointed president of the Commission and announced the Single Market Programme.
France, Germany and the Benelux countries signed the Schengen Agreement, committing themselves to the gradual removal of checks on people at borders. The Amsterdam Treaty that came into force in 1999 incorporated the Schengen Agreement, which was extended to all EU countries except the UK and Ireland, while Denmark has a partial opt-out, reserving its position on all questions except visas.

1986

Spain and Portugal became members of the Community.

1987
The Single European Act entered into force.
Turkey applied to join the EU.

1988
The financial perspective covering EC expenditure and resources for the 1988–92 period was agreed and included a reform of the Structural Funds.

1989
June: elections to the European Parliament.
November: the fall of the Berlin Wall.

1990
October: German unification.

1991
Agreement was reached on setting up a European Economic Area (EEA).
December: the Maastricht European Council reaches agreement on the Treaty on European Union.

1992
The MacSharry Reform of the CAP was agreed.
The Edinburgh European Council decided the financial perspective for 1993–99 ('Delors 2' or the bill for Maastricht), and on further reform of the Structural Funds with the introduction of the Cohesion Fund.

1993
1 January: introduction of the Single Market.
November: the Maastricht Treaty entered into force.

1994
April: the GATT Uruguay Round was signed at Marrakech.
June: elections to the European Parliament.

1995
Austria, Finland and Sweden joined the EU. Norway remained out after a referendum that rejected EU membership.
January: a new European Commission with Jacques Santer as President.
The Barcelona European Summit decided to create Euromed, a free trade area involving Mediterranean countries, by 2010.

1997
July: Agenda 2000.
The Amsterdam Treaty was signed.
The Luxembourg Process, or European Employment Strategy (EES), was launched.
The Luxembourg European Council decided to open enlargement negotiations with the Czech Republic, Estonia, Hungary, Poland, Slovenia and Cyprus.

1998
March: accession negotiations started with five countries of Central and Eastern Europe and Cyprus.
May: the Brussels Summit decided to set up the European Central Bank and on member states ready to enter the third stage of EMU.

1999
1 January: beginning of third stage of EMU.
Berlin Agreement (March) on Agenda 2000 (including financial perspective for the period 2000–06).
The Amsterdam Treaty entered into force.
June: direct elections to the European Parliament.
September: new European Commission with Romano Prodi as President.
October: the Tampere European Council decides to make the EU an area of Freedom, Security and Justice.
December: the Helsinki European Council took the decision to open accession negotiations with Malta and the other five CEECs that had applied for membership and to treat Turkey as a candidate.
Agreement to create an EU rapid-reaction force to assist peacekeeping.

2000
February: accession negotiations began with Bulgaria, Latvia, Lithuania, Malta, Romania and Slovakia.
The Lisbon European Council set the creation of a 'knowledge-based economy' as a priority for the EU.
December: the Nice European Council reaches agreement on the text of a new Treaty.

2001
The Gothenberg European Council reaffirmed the objective to complete negotiations with a first wave of candidate countries so they could join the EU in time for the European Parliament elections of 2004.
June: ratification of the Nice Treaty was rejected by the Irish in a first referendum, but passed in a second referendum in October.
December: the Laeken European Council decided to set up the European Convention to work on drafting a Constitutional Treaty.

2002
1 January: euro notes and coins came into circulation. Coins and notes in national currencies were withdrawn in the euro countries.
December: Copenhagen European Council confirmed the deadline of 2004 for accession of ten applicant countries and indicated 2007 as a possible date for Bulgarian and Romanian accession. A decision on Turkey was to be taken in December 2004.

2003
March: as part of the Common Foreign and Security Policy the EU took part in peace-keeping missions in the Balkans replacing NATO, first in the Former Yugoslav Republic of Macedonia, and then in Bosnia and Herzegovina.
March: the European Commission launches the European Neighbourhood Policy (ENP) to deal with relations between an enlarged EU and its eastern and southern neighbours.
July: the European Convention completes its work on the draft Constitutional Treaty.
October: the Intergovernmental Conference to draw up the Constitutional Treaty begins.
December: the Brussels European Council failed to reach agreement on the Constitutional Treaty.

2004
May: ten new member states joined the EU.
June: elections to the European Parliament.

June: the European Council agreed on the Constitutional Treaty.
November: a new European Commission takes office with Barroso as its President.

2005
May 29: the Constitutional Treaty is rejected in a referendum in France.
June 1: the Constitutional Treaty is rejected in a referendum in the Netherlands. Following the referenda a period of reflection on the future of Europe was launched.
October: accession negotiations begin with Croatia and Turkey.
December 2005: EU leaders agree on the financial perspective setting out EU expenditure and revenue for the 2007–2013 period.
December: the Former Yugoslav Republic of Macedonia was declared a candidate country.

2006
May: an Interinstitutional Agreement between the European Parliament, the Council and the Commission formalized the financial perspective setting out EU expenditure and revenue for the 2007–2013 period.

2007
January: Bulgaria and Romania joined the EU.
January: Slovenia adopted the euro.
June 2007: under the German Presidency the EU agrees to work towards a new Treaty.
October: the European Council in Lisbon agrees on the text of the Reform Treaty.
December: EU leaders sign the Reform Treaty in Lisbon.

2008
January: Cyprus and Malta adopt the euro.
June: the Lisbon Treaty is rejected in a referendum in Ireland.

References

Craig, P. and De Burca, G. (2007) *EU Law: Text Cases and Material*, 4th edn, Oxford University Press, Oxford.
Milward, A.S. (1984) *The Reconstruction of Western Europe 1945–1951*, Methuen, London.
Milward, A.S. (1999) The *European Rescue of the Nation State*, 2nd edn, Routledge, London.
Monnet, J. (1978) *Memoirs*, Collins, London.
Swann, D. (2000) *The Economics of Europe: From Common Market to European Union*, 2nd edn, Penguin Business Library, London.
Tracy, M. (1989) *Government and Agriculture in Western Europe 1880–1988*, Harvester Wheatsheaf, London.
Tsoukalis, L. (1997) *The New European Economy Revisited*, 3rd edn, Oxford University Press, Oxford.

Useful websites

There is a great deal of jargon associated with the EU. For glossaries of the various terms see the Europa Glossary of the EU:
http://europa.eu/scadplus/glossary

The site of the European Convention:
www. european-convention.eu.int

The website of Baldwin and Wyplosz at:
www.mcgraw-hill.co.uk/textbooks/baldwin

The OECD (Organization for Economic Co-operation and Development):
www.oecd.org

The OSCE Organization for Co-operation and Security in Europe:
www.osce.org

The UNECE United Nations Economic Commission for Europe:
www.unece.org

The Council of Europe:
www.coe.int

The European Union:
www.europa.eu

The Decision-Making Institutions of the European Union

❖ LEARNING OBJECTIVES

By the end of this chapter you should be able to understand:

- ❖ The main changes that would be introduced by the Reform or Lisbon Treaty;
- ❖ What are the main decision-making institutions of the Community;
- ❖ The structure and functions of the European Commission;
- ❖ The role of the Council of Ministers and of the European Council;
- ❖ The system of voting in the Council of Ministers;
- ❖ The organization and role of the European Parliament;
- ❖ The role of the Court of Justice;
- ❖ The main features of the Court of Auditors;
- ❖ The decision-making procedure of the European Community;
- ❖ What we mean by 'differentiated integration';
- ❖ The debate on the future architecture of Europe.

Introduction

One of the main difficulties of the European Union (EU) is that of accommodating its institutional structure to a growing membership, at the same time ensuring that decision-making respects democratic principles and is 'as close to the citizens as possible'. An increasing membership adds to the difficulty of ensuring 'efficiency', or what is usually defined in the EU context as ability to take decisions. Respect for democratic principles generally entails legitimacy of the decision-making process, but there has been growing criticism of EU institutions as not being answerable to the preferences of its citizens. The European initiative has been driven mainly by political elites, and opinion polls and referendums often reveal a disturbing lack of confidence in the EU on the part of the public. As will be shown in this chapter, the EU is accused of having a 'democratic deficit' in that the practices and operation of its decision-making institutions are said to fall short of democratic principles, and in recent years there have been various attempts to meet this criticism through reform of EU decision-making.

Difficulties arise in analysing EU decision-making because the EU is neither a country nor a 'traditional' international organization. The institutions of the EU appear messy and complex, and are very different from those of a country such as the USA, which are based on the distinction between legislature, executive and judiciary. European Union institutions have been evolving over time and reflect successive compromises to balance various (and varying) interests.[1]

In the next section recent steps in the process of reform of EU decision-making institutions, and in particular, the debate about the Lisbon Treaty will be described. There then follows an introduction of EU decision-making institutions, each of which is subsequently analysed in more detail. The issue of 'differentiated integration' or allowing those member states, which are willing and/or able to proceed more rapidly with integration is then addressed, before discussing the future architecture of Europe in the final section.

Towards the Lisbon Treaty

Following the unsuccessful attempts in the Amsterdam and Nice Treaties to prepare EU institutions for enlargement (see Box 3.1), in 2001 an EU summit at Laeken in Belgium agreed on the creation of a Constitutional Convention to draw up a Constitutional Treaty aimed at making EU decision-making more democratic, transparent and efficient.[2] The draft Constitutional Treaty was signed in Rome in 2004, but before coming into operation had to be ratified by all the member states, either by a vote in the national parliament or by a referendum. In May 2005 France rejected the Constitutional Treaty in a referendum, and this was followed by a negative outcome in a Dutch referendum of 1 June 2005. A 'period of reflection' on the future of Europe was subsequently launched.[3]

Meeting in Berlin in March 2007 at the celebrations of the fiftieth anniversary of the Treaty of Rome, EU leaders agreed to the Berlin Declaration, which aimed at working towards a new treaty for the EU before the elections to the European Parliament in 2009. In June 2007 under the German Presidency (thanks also to the efforts of Angela Merkel) the EU leaders agreed on the outline of a draft Reform Treaty to replace the Constitutional Treaty. An Intergovernmental Conference (IGC) began work in July. Intergovernmental conferences are necessary for revisions of the treaties (in contrast the Constitutional Treaty would have replaced earlier treaties), and have been frequent since the mid-1980s. Intergovernmental conferences entail regular meetings between national representatives at various levels to prepare the drafts of treaty changes, or new treaties.

European Union heads of state and of government accepted the text of this Reform Treaty

---

[1] For more detailed accounts of these institutional aspects see CEPS et al (2007), Hix (2005), Nugent (2006), Peterson and Shackleton (2006), Schmitter (2000), Wallace et al. (2005), and Westlake (2001). There is a great deal of jargon associated with the European Union. For explanations of the various terms see the Europa Glossary of the EU: http://europa.eu/scadplus/glossary, the site of the European Convention at keywords www.european-convention.eu.int/glossary or the website of Baldwin and Wyplosz (2006) at www.mcgraw-hill.co.uk/textbooks/baldwin

[2] The EU Convention was composed of representatives of the governments of member states and of the candidate countries, the European Parliament, Commission and Council, and of national parliaments. Giscard D'Estaing was chosen as president of the Convention, with two vice-presidents, Amato and Dehaene (former prime ministers of Italy and Belgium, respectively). Both the name and the rhetoric deliberately echoed the 1787 Philadelphia Constitutional Convention, whose role had been to mould a federation out of the 13 original US states.

[3] During this time the Amato Group, or Action Committee for Democracy (ACED) backed by the Barroso Commission worked unofficially on a new draft treaty.

Box 3.1: *Key dates in the evolution of the Reform Treaty*

1997 The Amsterdam Treaty was agreed (and came into operation in 1999) but fell well short of expectations that it would prepare EU institutions for enlargement.

December 2000 The Nice Summit agreed to reform EU decision-making, but the compromise was complex and not very transparent. A Declaration annexed to the Treaty of Nice refers to the need to prepare the institutional structure for decision-making in an enlarged EU.

December 2001 The Laeken Summit agreed to set up the European Convention.

July 2003 The European Convention completes its work on the draft Constitutional Treaty.

December 2003 An attempt to agree the text of the Constitutional Treaty at the Brussels Summit failed.

June 2004 the Brussels European Council agreed on the Constitutional Treaty during the Irish Presidency.

October 2004 The Constitutional Treaty was signed in Rome.

May 2005 France rejected the Constitutional Treaty in a referendum.

1 June 2005 The Netherlands also rejected the Constitutional Treaty in a referendum.

A period of reflection on the future of Europe was launched.

March 2007 at the celebrations of the 50th anniversary of the Treaty of Rome, EU leaders agreed to the Berlin Declaration, which aimed at working towards a new treaty for the EU before the elections to the European Parliament in 2009.

June 2007 Under the German Presidency the EU agreed to work towards a new treaty.

July 2007 The Intergovernmental Conference (see text) began work.

October 2007 The European Council in Lisbon agreed on the Treaty text.

December 2007 EU leaders signed the Treaty in Lisbon.

June 2008 Ireland rejects the Lisbon Treaty in a referendum.

---

in a summit in Lisbon in October 2007.[4] What then became known as the Lisbon Treaty was signed at a special meeting of the European Council in Lisbon in December 2007.[5] In order to come into force it has to be ratified by all the member states, and the aim was to complete this process by January 2009 so the Treaty could come into operation by January 2009 before the next European Parliament elections. By its constitution as interpreted by its Supreme Court,

---

[4] Several concessions were necessary to reach agreement including an extra member of the European Parliament for Italy, and stronger blocking powers for minority groups of states (see Box 3.2). A nomination for an additional Advocate General (whose numbers are to increase from 8 to 11) was granted as a concession to Poland following a highly controversial intervention in which the Prime Minister Kaczynski argued that Poland would have had a substantially larger population had it not been for the Second World War.

[5] The formal title is 'Treaty of Lisbon amending the Treaty on European Union and the Treaty establishing the European Community'. The European Council is described below.

Box 3.2: *Main changes implied by the Lisbon Treaty*

- A single legal personality for the EU replacing the pillar structure;

- A European Council President holding office for two and a half years renewable once will replace the present 6-month Presidency;

- A new High Representative of the Union for Foreign Affairs and Security Policy. Due to British reservations, the term 'EU Foreign Minister' was dropped;

- A reduction in the number of the Commissioners to 2/3 of the number of member states from 2014, and direct election of the President of the Commission by the European Parliament;

- A 'double-majority' voting rule is to be introduced in the Council of Ministers, with 55 per cent of member states and 65 per cent of the population necessary to pass a measure by qualified majority vote. A third rule would in fact apply in that a blocking minority would require a minimum of four states. To meet Polish requests the new system will apply from 2014, with a transitional period until 2017 during which time additional provisions will apply to render it easier to block legislation. These provisions allow a minority of member states to delay key decisions taken in the Council by qualified majority voting for 'a reasonable time', and this is known as the Ioannina Clause.[6]

- Extending qualified majority voting to over 40 policy areas, including immigration and asylum policy, and judicial and police co-operation in criminal matters;

- The number of members of the European Parliament is to be fixed at a maximum of 750, with a minimum of 6, and a maximum of 96 per country. Italy managed to gain an extra seat. The 750-plus-one formula assumes that the President of the European Parliament will not vote;

- Strengthening the national parliaments by giving them the right to raise objections to proposed EU legislation (the so-called orange card), and to reinforce the principle of subsidiarity;

- Reference to new challenges such as climate change and energy solidarity;

- The European Security and Defence Policy would be called the Common Security and Defence Policy with an extension of its missions through a 'solidarity clause' and a mutual defence commitment, both with substantial qualifications and provisos (Articles 27 and 28). According to the Lisbon Treaty, such changes would not affect the responsibility of member states for the formulation and conduct of their foreign policy and defence and security policy (Articles 30 and 31), and the primary responsibility of the UN Security Council for maintaining international peace and security.

- The possibility of exit of a member state from the EU.[7]

---

[6] The Clause is included in a Declaration, and there is a stipulation that amendment requires consensus in Protocol 9 of the Treaty, which means that amendment is possible without undergoing the cumbersome process of treaty change.

[7] The only withdrawal to date has been that of Greenland, whose status was renegotiated in 1994. Greenland remains associated with the EU and has an agreement covering fisheries. With the Lisbon Treaty change in the status of an overseas territory of France, Denmark or the Netherlands no longer requires a Treaty revision. This provision was requested by the Netherlands, which is reviewing the status of Netherlands Antilles and Aruba.

Ireland had to hold a referendum, but all other member states are committed to ratification by their national parliaments. In June 2008 the Irish rejected the Lisbon Treaty in a referendum.

The UK had promised a referendum on the Constitutional Treaty. Both Tony Blair and Gordon Brown maintained that a referendum on the new Treaty would not be necessary as certain 'red lines' had not been crossed since the UK is to maintain its veto over foreign policy, common law (so the Charter of Fundamental Human Rights would be without legal effect in the UK, see Box 3.3), and social security and tax laws.[8] Many observers (including the European Scrutiny Committee of the House of Commons) argued that the Lisbon Treaty was substantially the same as the Constitutional Treaty, a position denied by the British Foreign Affairs Minister, David Miliband.

Box 3.2 illustrates the main elements of the Lisbon Treaty, and Box 3.3 sets out some of its differences from the Constitutional Treaty.[9] The Lisbon Treaty dropped reference to constitutional terminology and to certain symbols of the EU such as the flag and anthem.[10] The 'Treaty on Establishing the European Communities' (TEC) would be renamed the 'Treaty on the Functioning of the European Union' and its articles would be renumbered. However, it would not be merged with the Treaty on the European Union (TEU) as the Constitutional Treaty had proposed. The three-pillar structure of the EU would be replaced, with increased competence of

---

Box 3.3: *Differences Between the Constitutional Treaty and The Lisbon Treaty*

- The references to the symbols such as the EU flag and anthem were dropped.

- The 'constitutional' label was abandoned, and the Lisbon Treaty returns to the traditional method of treaty change through amendment, rather than replacing existing treaties as the Constitutional Treaty would have done.

- The full text of the Charter of Fundamental Human Rights is not to be integrated into the Treaty, but is to be indicated by a short cross-reference with the same legal value. The Charter sets out political, social and economic rights of citizens and aims at ensuring that EU legislation does not contradict the European Convention of Human Rights, which has been ratified by all EU member states. The Charter would only be legally binding in the UK, and Poland to the extent that it confirms rights or principles already recognized in those countries.[11]

- The reference to 'free and undistorted competition' in the treaties was removed at the request of France.[12]

---

[8] Critics maintained that the UK veto on foreign policy was undermined by the strengthening of EU competence in this area implied by the Treaty.

[9] The changes proposed are discussed below in the context of the various EU institutions. See CEPS et al. (2007) for a more detailed discussion of this issue.

[10] Sixteen member states declared their allegiance to these symbols, but the declaration annexed to the Lisbon Treaty is not legally binding.

[11] According to Protocol No. 7, Article 1 of the Treaty, 'The Charter does not extend the liability of the Court of Justice of the European Union, or any court or tribunal of Poland or of the United Kingdom, to find that laws, regulations or administrative provisions, practices or actions of Poland or the United Kingdom are inconsistent with the fundamental rights, freedoms and principles that it reaffirms ...'.

[12] Article 3 of the Nice Treaty states that 'The Union shall establish an Internal Market where competition is free and undistorted'. French President, Nicolas Sarkozy, argued that competition was not an end in itself.

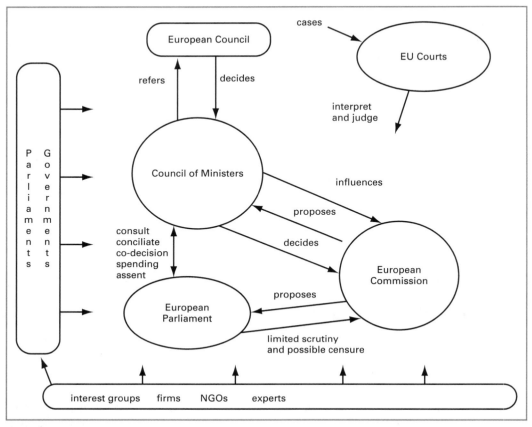

FIGURE 3.1 An overview of EU decision-making institutions
Source: Adapted from Wallace (2005) by permission of Oxford University Press

the EU over Common Foreign and Security Policy (CFSP), and Police and Judicial Co-operation on Criminal Matters (PJCCM). In general the Treaty allows member states to opt out of EU policies in the areas of police and criminal law. The UK would not be obliged to co-operate on PJCCM and will maintain its veto on foreign policy and defence issues.

The decision-making institutions of the EU

The main decision-making institutions of the EU are:[13]

- The European Commission;

---

[13] This list does not include the other institutions of the EU, and, for example, the financial institutions such as the ECB (European Central Bank), the ESCB (European System of Central Banks), the EMI (European Monetary Institute), etc. that are discussed in Chapter 10.

- The Council of Ministers;
- The European Council;
- The European Parliament (EP);
- The European Economic and Social Committee (EESC);
- The Committee of Regions;
- The Court of Justice (EJ); and
- The Court of Auditors.

Figure 3.1 sets out the key interconnections between the main EU decision-making institutions (for simplicity the EESC and the Committee of the Regions have been left out). In general the European Commission proposes new legislation, while the Council and Parliament pass the laws (and these three together are sometimes known as the 'institutional triangle' producing the policies and laws that apply throughout the EU). The following sections of this chapter explain the roles of the various institutions.

The European Commission

With the Lisbon Treaty the term 'European Commission' (already widely used) would replace 'the Commission of the European Communities'. In a strict sense the 'European Commission' is made up of the one Commissioner from each of the member states (described below), but more generally the term is used to refer to all the officials (*fonctionnaires*) working for the institution. Roughly the language staff takes up 15 per cent of this full-time, permanent bureaucracy (see Box 3.4). The working languages are usually English, French and German.

Box 3.4: *The Berlaymont*

For many years the Commission was housed in the famous Berlaymont Building in Brussels. It was extremely easy to get lost in the curved corridors of a building shaped like a cross and 13 floors high. Considered the symbol of the Commission, and appearing on the news nearly every time Brussels was mentioned, the Berlaymont was riddled with asbestos, and was evacuated for 10 years while the asbestos was removed. During that time white protective sheeting shrouded the building, provoking the inevitable comment that it looked like a work by the Bulgarian-born artist Christo.

The Commissioners at the head of the Commission are responsible for one or more areas of policy and required to act independently of national interests. Many come from prominent political careers in their own countries. A President heads the Commission and can play an important role in influencing the image of the Commission and determining the pace of integration. For instance, the personal role of Commission President Jacques Delors (from 1985 to 1995) was fundamental for the introduction of the Single Market Project and economic and monetary union. In 2004 the Portuguese José Manuel Barroso became President of the Commission. The Commissioners generally try to take decisions by consensus on a 'collegial basis',[14] and a small cabinet backs each. One or more vice-presidents assist the President.

---

[14]The Barroso Commission generally operates on a collegial basis, though the Nice Treaty (Article 219, TEC) envisages the Commission taking decisions by simple majority.

France, Germany, Italy, Spain and the UK had two Commissioners prior to the 2004 enlargement, but then gave up their second Commissioner. According to the Protocol on Enlargement annexed to the Nice Treaty, when the EU reaches 27 members the number of commissioners 'shall be less than the number of member states and will be agreed by the Council acting unanimously'. A future rotation system based on 'the principle of equality' will have to be agreed. During the debate on the Nice package deal various smaller member states expressed serious misgivings on this point. The Lisbon Treaty envisages a smaller Commission from 2014, with commissioners being sent only from two-thirds of the member states on the basis of equal rotation, unless the European Council acting unanimously decides to alter this number. The Lisbon Treaty therefore defers the decision on the size of the Commission by five years, but if the Treaty is not ratified, a unanimous agreement will have to be reached on the rotation system by 2009.

It is argued that a smaller Commission would be less cumbersome and more efficient and would be freer from national ties. However, the full participation of each member state in the Commission is felt to increase its public acceptability and to ensure that the interests of each member state are taken into account. Moreover, the Commission often relies on support from the member states to push forward its initiatives, and if a member state lacks a Commissioner this support may be less forthcoming. Media visibility is also likely to be lower. In September 2006, while still candidate for the French Presidency, Nicolas Sarkozy voiced the possibility of the Commission President choosing his or her team of Commissioners.[15]

The commissioners are chosen for a five-year period. After consulting the European Parliament, the governments of the member states nominate the president of the Commission and, according to the Nice Treaty, this was to be by a qualified majority rather than the earlier requirement of 'common accord'. The nominee president then has to be approved by the European Parliament, and in 1995 this almost resulted in the rejection of Jacques Santer. The Lisbon Treaty proposes election of the new president by the European Parliament based on nominations by the heads of state and of government of the EU countries, taking into account the election results of the European Parliament. This is likely to lead to increased politicization, and a tighter link between the President and the ideological majority in the EP.[16]

The Commissioners are appointed by their national governments after consultation with the European Parliament and the new president of the Commission. Once chosen, the Commissioners are subject to a vote of approval by the European Parliament.[17] Until 2003 the 'collegial' nature of the Commission (which implies collective responsibility) meant that the European Parliament could only dismiss it as a whole. There were calls for dismissal of the Commission 1997 over the treatment of the 'mad cow disease' and again over the 1999 scandal (see Box 3.5). Since the Nice Treaty, the president can force a member of the Commission to resign after obtaining the approval of the whole Commission.

When a new Commission comes into office, a complex and controversial process of deciding the allocation of portfolios begins. Each commissioner is responsible for one or more portfolios, or policy areas, and balancing the relative importance of the portfolio(s) given to each Commissioner is a delicate process.

Each Commissioner also takes charge of at least one of the Directorates-General (DGs) into which the Commission is divided. Each DG covers a main policy area such as external affairs or agriculture (the largest DG of all). The system of vertical hierarchies means that at times there is

[15] As reported in CEPS et al. (2007).

[16] Already in 2004 the political affiliation of Barroso corresponded to that of the European Parliament.

[17] Leading, notably, to the call on Italy to retract the candidacy of Rocco Buttiglione in 2004 allegedly because he maintained that homosexuality was a sin but not a crime.

Box 3.5: *The 1999 Scandal*

The events of 1999 constitute one of the most profound institutional crises in the history of the EU, and a milestone in the shift in the balance of power between the Commission and the European Parliament. The starting point was the reluctance of the European Parliament to approve the accounts relating to the 1996 budget, accusing the Commission of mismanagement, cronyism and fraud. In January 1999 a motion of censure against the Commission was tabled, but in the event the European Parliament voted in favour of a compromise measure consisting of an independent inquiry into allegations against the Commission. The results of this inquiry were published in March 1999, and accused the Commission on a number of counts. Irregularities were found in programmes relating to humanitarian aid (with the discovery of fictitious contracts supposedly granting aid to Rwanda and former Yugoslavia), tourism and educational and training programmes. There was said to be evidence of nepotism, and of bending staff rules to appoint acquaintances, in particular in the case of Edith Cresson, the commissioner responsible for health and educational programmes. The most famous attack was against the appointment of a 70-year-old dentist from her home town as a 'scientific adviser', on a salary said to be $4,500 a month, with his son also receiving a consultancy contract (*The Economist*, 6 March 1999). The Security Office, which was directly responsible to the president, was accused of operating as a regulation-free zone granting 'small favours' to colleagues such as the cancellation of parking fines, practising dubious recruitment practices (so that it appeared like a private club for retired Belgian policemen) and permitting irregularities such as the disappearance of office furniture and equipment. The president of the Commission, Santer, was said to have lost control of the institution he was supposedly running, allowing a 'culture of complacency' to arise. The immediate reaction was a press release in which Santer announced that he was 'whiter than white' and protested that it was misleading and distorting to judge the output of the Commission on the basis of a few cases of fraud. A code of conduct was drawn up for those working in the Commission, but the damage was done and in March 1999 the Santer Commission resigned.

insufficient co-ordination between the various DGs. Following the 1999 scandal (see Box 3.5), various reforms in the organization of the Commission were introduced, including the substitution of names for numbers of the various DGs, so that, for example, DGVI was to be called the Agriculture DG.

The functions of the European Commission

In the literature, the phrase 'The Commission proposes and disposes' is frequently used to describe its functions, but a more complete list would include the following:

- The Commission has the right of initiative and is involved at each stage in the EU legislative process. According to the Lisbon Treaty, Article 9d, the Commission shall 'promote the general interest of the Union and take appropriate initiatives to that end' Commission proposals are not drawn out of thin air but are generally the result of a lengthy process of consultation involving interest groups, national civil servants, politicians and so on. Over the years the European Council (see below) and the European Parliament have played an increasing role in proposing policy initiatives.[18]

- The Commission has to 'exercise the powers conferred on it by the Council [of Ministers] for the implementation of rules laid down by the latter'.[19] This 'management' role of the Commission is important in the day-to-day running of policies such as the Common Agricultural Policy and Common Commercial Policy.

- The Commission has certain autonomous powers in areas such as competition policy, and negotiates for the Community on some policy issues including foreign trade. It represents the EU in international organizations such as the Organization for Economic Cooperation and Development (OECD), the United Nations and the World Trade Organization (WTO).

- The Commission prepares the annual preliminary draft Budget for the Community and is responsible for implementing the Budget and submitting accounts at the end of each financial year. Most actual spending is done by national and local authorities, but is subject to the supervision of the Commission and Court of Auditors (see below).

- The Commission acts as Guardian (or 'Watchdog') of the Treaties. Article 211, TEC states that the Commission must 'ensure that the provisions of this Treaty and the measures pursuit thereto are applied'. If a firm, institution or member state is found to be acting contrary to the treaties, the Commission may issue a reasoned Opinion, impose a fine or even refer the matter to the Court of Justice.

- The Commission makes recommendations or opinions on matters related to the treaties (see Box 3.6).

- The Commission may publish formal presentations (White and Green Papers) on specific policy areas in order to make the position of the Commission known and obtain reactions before the start of the legislative procedure. Green Papers present broader, initial ideas of the Commission, while White Papers set out more detailed guidelines for policy proposals.

The fact that the Commission is not elected (but rather is composed of technocrats) and is not directly answerable to the public is one aspect of the problem of the 'democratic deficit'.[20] The Commission derives its legitimacy from its independence from national interests and its expertise on EU matters, but its lack of accountability and transparency are frequently called into question.

In the shifting balance of power between EU institutions, the Commission appears to have been losing power. Successive reforms of EU institutions have strengthened the European Parliament, while the European Council has increasingly gained responsibility for setting priorities and establishing the policy agenda. This tendency is likely to be reinforced by the creation of a longer-term President of the European Council (see below), who could act as a rival to the Commission President. The Commission does not have a monopoly of proposing legislation with respect to the second (CFSP) and third pillars (PJCCM). The Lisbon Treaty would formalize the extension of the Commission's power over the third pillar, but refrains from giving it substantial competences on the Common and Foreign Security Policy or macroeconomic affairs.

---

[18]The Maastricht Treaty introduced the 'request clause', which permits the Parliament to 'request' the Commission to submit any proposal where the EP decides by absolute majority that new legislation is needed.

[19]TEC, Article 211.

[20]This type of complaint was raised as early as the 1960s with, for instance, de Gaulle describing the Commission in his inimitable words as 'an embryo technocracy, for the most part foreign' (Bainbridge, 2002).

Box 3.6: *EU legislative instruments*

According to the Treaty Establishing the European Communities (Article 249), a **Regulation** is directly binding in all EC member states.

A **Directive** fixes an objective, which is binding, but leaves the choice of method to achieve that aim to the member states. Unlike a Regulation, a Directive therefore has to be transposed into national legislation before entering into force. In practice the distinction between regulations and directives is less clear-cut as regulations generally also require some transposition into national legislation, while directives are rarely a simple statement of objectives.

Decisions deal with specific problems and are binding on those to whom they are addressed, which may include member states, companies or individuals.

In contrast, **Recommendations** and **Opinions** have no binding force.

The proposal of the draft Constitutional Treaty that regulations should be called 'European laws' and directives should be called 'European framework laws' was dropped in the Lisbon Treaty.

The Council of the European Union or Council of Ministers

The Council of the European Union would become known as the 'Council of Ministers' or 'Council' in the Lisbon Treaty, recognizing the more commonly used terms. The Council is the principal decision-making institution of the EU, but since the Maastricht Treaty it has increasingly legislated jointly with the European Parliament, and can be overridden in certain cases by the EP's veto. It is also the only EU institution that directly represents the member states, and is sometimes referred to as the 'brake on European integration', reflecting the (rather simplistic) view that Commission proposals presenting the EU position have been checked by national interests in the Council.

The Council is composed of representatives of each of the member states at the ministerial level, plus a representative of the Commission. The composition of the Council varies according to the question considered, so there is a Council of Economic and Finance Ministers ('Ecofin'); a Council of Foreign Ministers (known as the General Affairs and External Relations Council or GAERC, sometimes referred to as 'the Gurk'); a Council of Agriculture and Fisheries Ministers; a Council of Transport, Telecommunications and Energy Ministers, and so on. In 1998 there were 23 councils of this type, but by 2007 the number had fallen to 9. With so many specialized councils, consistency and unity of operation may be difficult to achieve.

The main functions of the Council are:

- To pass European laws – jointly with the EP in many policy areas;
- To co-ordinate the broad economic policies of the member states;
- To conclude international agreements between the EU and other countries or international organizations;
- To approve the budget of the EU, jointly with the EP;
- To develop the Common Foreign and Security Policy of the EU, based on guidelines set by the European Council;
- To co-ordinate co-operation between the national courts and police forces in criminal matters.

The Council is assisted in its work by the Committee of Permanent Representatives (**Coreper**), which is composed of ambassadors of the delegations of the member states in Brussels. The Coreper helps to prepare Council meetings, and may take decisions on issues that are not controversial. On agricultural questions the Special Committee for Agriculture carries out this role. It is estimated that some 90 per cent of all Council decisions are taken by Coreper and the Special Committee on Agriculture, or in working groups of national officials before the Council of Ministers even meets, though the 10 per cent that remains almost invariably concerns the more controversial questions. The Council generally meets in Brussels where there is a Council Secretariat served by a staff.

The European Council

The Council of heads of state and of government is known as the **European Council**.[21] Though the summits of heads of state date from 1961, the European Council only received formal recognition as a Community institution in the Single European Act of 1987. The summits of the European Council should take place 'at least twice a year' (SEA, Article 2), though in practice they are more frequent. The European Council plays an important role in providing overall political direction to the Union, defining goals and strategies, and in resolving problems that have proved intractable at the Council of Ministers level.[22] The European Council takes decisions on an intergovernmental basis, and implementation of the measures is left to the other EU institutions.

The **Presidency** of the Council of Ministers and the European Council rotates among the EU member states in six-month terms. Up until 1998 the sequence followed the alphabetical order of the names of member states in their own languages, but subsequently this was changed to ensure a better balance between countries (see Box 3.7).

The Presidency may allow a particular member state to press for policy decisions and initiatives in which it is particularly interested. To date European Council meetings have generally been held in the country holding the Presidency, though it has been proposed that more summits should be held in Brussels to reduce expense and (at times) inconvenience. The country holding the Presidency has the power to represent the Council in dealings with other institutions and non-member countries; set the agenda; draft compromises; play the role of honest broker in negotiations, and ensure the continuity and consistency of policy-making. For instance, a priority of the German Presidency in 2007 was to launch a new initiative on environmental policy and reach agreement on constitutional reform. The subsequent Portuguese Presidency succeeded in brokering an agreement on the Lisbon Treaty.

In order to provide continuity, and assist smaller countries holding the Presidency, in the 1980s the **Troika** was introduced and entailed that countries immediately preceding and following flank the current holder of the Presidency, but difficulties remain with the shortness of the mandate. The interval between successive presidencies may lead to a lack of experience, and encourage countries to exploit the presidency for domestic interests.

The Lisbon Treaty proposes introducing a President of the European Council who would

---

[21] The term 'heads of state and of government' is used because France reserves the right to send both.

[22] The Nice Treaty establishes that the European Council should 'provide the Union with the necessary impetus for its development and shall define the general political guidelines thereof ' (Article 4, TEU), discuss the conclusions of 'broad guidelines of the economic policies of the member states and of the Community' (Article 99, TEC) and should 'define the principles and the general guidelines for the Common Foreign and Security Policy' (Article 13, TEU).

Box 3.7: *The order of the Presidency*

	January–June	July–December
2007	Germany	Portugal
2008	Slovenia	France
2009	Czech republic	Sweden
2010	Spain	Belgium
2011	Hungary	Poland
2012	Denmark	Cyprus
2013	Ireland	Lithuania
2014	Greece	Italy
2015	Latvia	Luxembourg
2016	The Netherlands	Slovakia
2017	Malta	The UK
2018	Estonia	Bulgaria
2019	Austria	Romania
2020	Finland	

hold office for two and a half years, renewable for a following term. The President would be elected by a qualified majority of members of the European Council and, unlike the President of the Commission, would not be subject to approval by the European Parliament. The President would have functions similar to those of the present Presidency, co-ordinating the work of the European Council, but is also likely to play a role in external representation of the EU. With the exception of the General Affairs Council the present system of six-month rotating presidency would continue for the other Council formations, within a troika of pre-established groups of three countries for 18 months. The Foreign Affairs Council would be separate from the General Affairs Council.

The Lisbon Treaty also envisages creating a High Representative for Foreign Affairs and Security Policy to replace the European Commissioner for External Relations and the European Neighbourhood Policy, and the High Representative for the Common Foreign and Security Policy ('Mr CFSP' or Javier Solana). The High Representative would become a Commission Vice-President and would be backed by a European External Action Service.

The proposal to have a longer presidency of the European Council is aimed at providing continuity and answering Kissinger's famous question of 'Who should I call if I want to phone Europe?'. However, the proposed solution seems likely to lead to rivalries and overlapping responsibilities, for instance, between the European Council President, Commission President, the High Representative, and government of the country holding the rotating presidency of other Council formations.

The weighting of votes and the threshold for qualified majority voting

The Council of Ministers may take decisions by **unanimity, simple majority or qualified majority voting (QMV).** According to the treaties, unless otherwise specified, simple majority will be the rule.[23] However, almost invariably the treaties specify that QMV or unanimity voting should be used.

Qualified majority voting is the most widely used system of voting in the Council (and could be used for about 80 per cent of Council decisions), although in practice attempts are generally made to reach consensus (Hayes-Renshaw et al., 2005). Each of the ministers in the Council is allocated a certain number of votes (very roughly) reflecting the population of the country of origin. With each enlargement of the European Union adjustments have been necessary in the allocation of votes and the number of votes necessary to block a proposal. Table 3.1 illustrates the weights of each of the EU(27).

From 2007, the QMV rule for passing a measure in the EU(27) required:

- 255 out of a total of 345 votes, or 73.9 per cent of the votes;
- a majority of member states (a 2/3 majority in some cases); and
- a member of the Council may request verification that the qualified majority represents at least 62 per cent of the EU population, and if that condition is not met the decision will not be adopted.

The requirement that a majority of states should back a measure was introduced to favour the interests of smaller member states, while the population requirement reflected the interests of larger countries. The second and third voting rules were introduced with the Treaty of Nice, and though the introduction of additional voting rules renders decision-making more complex and less transparent, the aim was to increase legitimacy in an attempt to reconcile two views of the EU. The EU can be regarded either as a union of states or as a union of people. In the case of a union of states equality of power (or the ability to influence decisions) would require each state to have equal voting power. For a union of people each citizen should have the same voting power. The hybrid nature of the EU requires some compromise between the two. Prior to enlargement this was achieved through over-weighting the votes of the smaller member states in QMV. The Treaty of Nice increased the weight of larger countries in QMV, implying a shift of the compromise away from of the union-of-states concept.[24] This is to some extent corrected by the requirement that at least 50 per cent of member states support a measure. The introduction of the second and third rules above renders this dual nature of the EU more explicit.

One of the aims of the Nice Treaty was to increase the efficiency of EU decision-making, or the ability to pass legislation. This can be defined as 'passage probability', or the chances of reaching a majority on an issue given a particular voting rule. Baldwin and Wyplosz (2006) found that compared with applying the status quo in either an EU of 15 or 27, the Nice Treaty actually reduced the passage possibility of QMV in the Council.[25] However, at least in the first years after the 2004 and 2007 enlargements the feared paralysis of decision-making failed to occur and EU institutions seemed to demonstrate a certain resilience and capacity to adapt.

---

[23] For a theoretical analysis of different voting rules using the New Political Economy approach (explained in Chapter 4) see Buchanan and Tullock (1962). For an application of this type of approach to EU decision-making in the case of the Common Agricultural Policy see Senior Nello (1997).

[24] See Laruelle and Widgren (1998), and Baldwin and Wyplosz (2006) for more detailed analyses of this issue.

[25] 'Passage possibility' is defined as the number of all possible winning coalitions divided by the number of all possible coalitions.

EU(15)	Population million 2006	Vote in the Council after Nice	New member states	Population 2006	Vote in the Council
Germany	82.4	29	Poland	38.1	27
France	63.0	29	Romania	21.6	14
UK	60.4	29	Czech Rep.	10.3	12
Italy	58.8	29	Hungary	10.1	12
Spain	43.8	27	Bulgaria	7.7	10
NL	16.3	13	Slovakia	5.4	7
Greece	11.1	12	Lithuania	3.4	7
Portugal	10.6	12	Latvia	2.3	4
Belgium	10.5	12	Slovenia	2.0	4
Sweden	9.0	10	Estonia	1.3	4
Austria	8.3	10	Cyprus	0.7	4
Denmark	5.4	7	Malta	0.4	3
Finland	5.3	7			
Ireland	4.2	7			
Lux.	0.5	4			

TABLE 3.1 Weights in the Council of Ministers
Source: Protocol on the enlargement of the European Union, annexed to the Nice Treaty.

The debates about the relative weights of countries have been heated and acrimonious in successive attempts to reform the treaties. This is because weights in the Council are generally assumed to reflect the power of a member state to influence the outcome of the decision-making process. Various empirical studies have been carried out to test this hypothesis. Baldwin et al. (2001) find a close correlation between the number of votes of the poorer member states and spending on what is now called economic and social cohesion.[26] Kandogan (2000) finds a similar result both for such measures and for the link between the number of member states with a strong interest in agriculture and agricultural spending. On the basis of the experience of successive enlargements Kandogan concludes that the allocation of voting power in the Council is more important than the initial budgetary deal for the new member state, as voting power will determine successive budgetary outcomes.

Given the complexity of the solution agreed at Nice, the Lisbon Treaty entails a simpler system based on a dual majority, so that 55 per cent of member states representing at least 65 per cent of the EU population would be required to pass a measure from November 2014.[27] In order to avoid a situation where only three large member states could block legislation, a blocking minority would require at least four member states. Between 2014 and 2017 new voting rules will apply, but the Nice voting weights can be applied if a proposal is of political sensitivity for a member state. In response to Polish request, from 2014 a new version of the Ioannina Compromise applies, allowing small minorities of EU member states more scope to call for deferral and re-examination of EU decisions.[28]

---

[26]See Chapter 15.

[27]When the Council is not acting on a proposal of the Commission the necessary majority of member states increases to 72 per cent, representing 65 per cent of the EU population. Strangely, there are no formal legal specifications on how to report population statistics.

[28]The Ioannina compromise was first introduced in 1994 with the enlargement of the EU to 15 states. In the

The voting rules used in the Council of Ministers

During the early years of the Community (1958–65) unanimity voting was generally used. In 1965 the Commission (under the aegis of its then president, Hallstein) put forward proposals for the financing of the Common Agricultural Policy (CAP), the introduction of own resources for the Community Budget and increased powers for the EP, which were also aimed at ensuring democratic control of Community spending. At the same time, the third phase of the transitional period for introducing the Community was due to begin in 1966, and the Commission called for implementation of the Treaty of Rome with respect to the use of the qualified majority vote.

The French President, de Gaulle,[29] fiercely contested these proposals, and instructed his ministers to boycott meetings of the Council of Ministers. The non-participation of France in Council meetings became known as the 'Empty Chair' crisis, and had the effect of paralysing EC decision-making for six months. The crisis coincided with presidential elections in France, and following the failure of de Gaulle to win outright in the first ballot of December 1965, he let it be known that a more conciliatory tone would be adopted towards the Community. As an important agricultural producer, France was also concerned to ensure adequate financing for the CAP, which then absorbed about 90 per cent of EC spending.

Following de Gaulle's success in the second ballot, negotiations with the Community were resumed, leading to the Luxembourg compromise in early 1966. This entailed that whenever any member state declared that a measure affected a 'vital national interest', the Council would endeavour to reach solutions within a reasonable time that could be adopted by unanimity. Though in practice during the following years the Luxembourg compromise was seldom invoked, unanimity became the rule, and majority voting was rarely used, except occasionally on details of agricultural policy or budgetary matters.

It was only with the Single European Act (SEA) that this situation changed, with the number of areas subject to the QMV rule being substantially extended. The SEA specified that all measures relating to completion of the Single Market were to be decided on the basis of QMV, which was probably the only way of ensuring that the 1993 deadline could be reached. The Maastricht and Amsterdam Treaties brought limited extensions of the areas where QMV was to be used, but unanimity continued to be used in many areas.

The fact that so many areas remained under the unanimity-voting rule (with any member state able to threaten use of a veto) raised a spectre of even greater risk of deadlock and the breakdown of decision-making in an enlarged EU. To meet this problem the Nice Summit aimed at increasing the use of qualified majority voting in the Council, and in the event it was agreed that QMV would be extended to 29 of the 70 Treaty articles, that were still subject to unanimity. However, national sensibilities meant that the right of veto in the Council was maintained in many crucial areas. For instance, the UK managed to ensure that unanimity remained for tax questions and social security. Spain insisted on keeping unanimity for decisions relating to the

---

Lisbon Treaty version of the clause member states representing 3/4 of either the population or number of states necessary to form a blocking minority can request the Council to continue its work to find an agreement with broader support. The deferral of the decision must take place 'within a reasonable time without prejudicing obligatory limits laid down by Union law'. European Union decision laws generally require a Council agreement within three months of a Commission proposal or Parliament opinion. Initially the Polish government argued that they had been promised a deferral period of up to two years, but in the final compromise no time limit is mentioned in the Declaration.

[29] According to de Gaulle, the provisions for QMV in the Treaty of Rome had been negotiated during the IV Republic when France was politically weak, and he was in favour of 'taking our destiny back into our own hands' as it was unacceptable that 'a foreign majority can constrain recalcitrant nations' (quoted in Bainbridge, 2002).

Cohesion Fund,[30] while Germany demanded it for movement of professionals. France was able to block an extension of qualified majority voting for trade in audiovisual services, culture, education, health and social services. Denmark and Greece obtained exceptions from the QMV for maritime transport.

The Lisbon Treaty proposes that QMV be extended to 21 new legal areas and 23 policy areas currently under unanimity. Unanimity would be limited to areas such as those relating to constitutional issues, the EU Budget, taxation, treaty revision, defence, foreign policy, and some aspects of social policy.

The European Parliament

For many years the European Parliament (EP) was primarily a consultative body, but its legislative powers have been increasing. It is elected every five years, and since 1979 a system of direct election has been used. The EP is the only directly elected EU institution, but the elections tend to be fought mainly on national issues. The elections often seem to be a vote of confidence about the incumbent national government. As Figures 3.2–3.4 indicate, the low turnout in some member states illustrates how the EP has failed to secure a hold over public opinion.

The Amsterdam Treaty set a ceiling of 700 on the future size of the EP, but this was happily exceeded. Following the accession of Bulgaria and Romania, in 2007 the EP had 785 members (see also Table 3.2). The seats are apportioned roughly according to the populations of the member states (though again there is a bias to ensure adequate representation of the smaller member states). The Lisbon Treaty proposes a maximum of 750 Members of the European Parliament (MEPs), and a digressively proportional rule for representation with a minimum of 6 seats and a maximum of 96 per member states.[31]

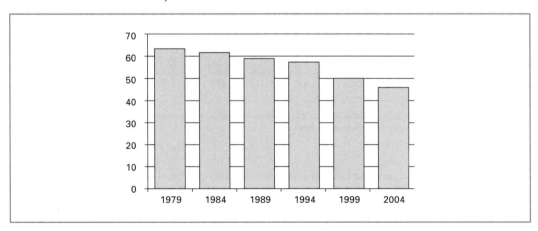

FIGURE 3.2 Percentage turnout in successive European Parliament elections
Source: www.elections2004.eu.int, © European Communities, 2004.

---

[30]See Chapter 15.

[31]Under the Lisbon Treaty the new composition of the EP would be decided by the European Council acting by unanimity on the basis of Parliament's proposal and after obtaining its consent. The October 2007 European Council decided on the 750-plus-one formula, which assumes that the President of the EP will not vote, in order to give an extra MEP to Italy. The composition of the EP will require further changes to take account of demographic changes and/or future enlargements of the EU.

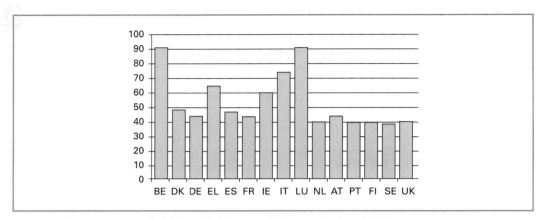

FIGURE 3.3 Percentage turnout in the June 2004* European Parliament elections EU(15)
*The data for Italy, Luxembourg and the UK are provisional. The division of countries between Figures 3.2 and 3.3 was simply for reasons of space.
Source: www.elections2004.eu.int, © European Communities, 2004.

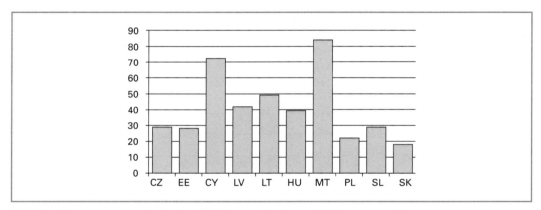

FIGURE 3.4 Percentage turnout in the June 2004 European Parliament elections: new member states
Source: www.elections2004.eu.int, © European Communities, 2004.

The MEPs are organized into large groupings that reflect political leaning rather than nationality. In 2007 the largest of these was the European People's Party (Christian Democrats) and European Democrats (284 MEPs), the Party of European Socialists, (215 MEPs), the Alliance of Liberals and Democrats for Europe (103 MEPS), Union of Europe of the Nations (44 MEPs), Greens/European Free Alliance (42 MEPs), European United Left-Nordic Green Left (41 MEPs), the Independence/Democracy (24 MEPS), and the non-attached (32). Many MEPs were initially national politicians, or in the media and sport (see also Box 3.8).[32]

---

[32]On one famous occasion the Italian MEPs included a famous porno-star, 'Cicciolina'.

EU(15)	Population (millions) 2006	European Parliament allocation of seats in the 2004–9 EP	Inhabitants per MEP (1000) in the 2004–2009 EP	New member states	Population (millions) 2006	European Parliament allocation of seats in the 2004–2009 EP	Inhabitants per MEP (1000) in the 2004–2009 EP
Germany	82.4	99	832	Poland	38.1	50	762
France	63.0	72	875	Romania	21.6	33	655
UK	60.4	72	839	Czech Rep.	10.3	20	515
Italy	58.8	72	817	Hungary	10.1	20	505
Spain	43.8	50	876	Bulgaria	7.7	17	453
NL	16.3	25	652	Slovakia	5.4	13	415
Greece	11.1	22	505	Lithuania	3.4	12	283
Portugal	10.6	22	482	Latvia	2.3	8	287
Belgium	10.5	22	477	Slovenia	2.0	7	286
Sweden	9.0	18	500	Estonia	1.3	6	217
Austria	8.3	17	488	Cyprus	0.7	6	117
Denmark	5.4	13	415	Malta	0.4	5	80
Finland	5.3	13	408				
Ireland	4.2	12	350				
Lux.	0.5	6	83				

TABLE 3.2 Representation in the European Parliament
Source: Protocol on the enlargement of the EU, annexed to the Nice Treaty, and own elaborations on the basis of Eurostat data, © European Communities, 2008.

Box 3.8: *Reform of the European Parliament*

During the debate on the European Convention, one of the proposed reforms of the EP entailed setting up a second chamber drawn from representatives of national parliaments. Elections to the EP have been contested largely on the basis of national issues in the various member states, and the Italian experience suggests a further drawback of the proposed reform. Many of the Italian members of the EP are also national politicians. In March 1999 a survey carried out by the French *Journal du Dimanche* found that on average Italian MEPs had been absent from 41.6 per cent of the plenary sessions of the EP, followed by the Danes (35.7 per cent) and the French (30 per cent). An article in the Italian newspaper *La Repubblica* of 8 March 1999 confirmed that party secretaries who are also MEPs rarely attended the EP. For instance, the head of the Northern League, Umberto Bossi, attended only 6 per cent of the sessions, and Gianfranco Fini of the National Alliance attended 11 per cent.

The Italian MEPs were also the most highly paid in the EU (at about €11,000 a month compared with a salary of €800 for MEPs from the Baltic States in 2005). In 2002 a coalition including Italians, Spanish and Germans blocked efforts to introduce the same salary for all MEPs. The salary of German MEPs would have increased to the average, but the German government was against such a measure at a time of fiscal austerity.

There was also a decade-long debate in the EP about whether to introduce a system to ensure that receipts backed expenses. MEPs are entitled to club class travel, but many fly economy and pocket the difference as they are only required to produce a boarding card to claim expenses.

In 2005 agreement was finally reached on introducing an obligation to back travel expenses with receipts, and to introduce a common salary, but only from the next EP elected in 2009.

The party relationships of members of these broad groups tend to be loose, but advantages such as increased possibility of obtaining places on committees or other official positions can be derived from membership. Most of the detailed work takes place in committees dealing with different policy areas.

The EP makes use of the 23 languages (see also Box 3.9) of the EU(27). A consequence of using so many languages is that debates tend to be dull, with little scope for repartee.

Box 3.9: *The problem of languages in the EU*

In 2005 the Directorate General for Translation translated 1 324 231 pages, while the Directorate General for Interpretation provided interpreters for more that 11 000 meetings. For many years French was the dominant language of the Community, but English and German are more widely spoken in the countries that joined the EU in 1995, and in 2004. According to the *Financial Times* (28 November 2003), an analysis of candidates from the new member states for Commission posts found that 83 per cent spoke English, 34 per cent German and 24 per cent French.

One of the proposals to meet the problem of languages with enlargement was to charge member states for using their native language. The proposal would not apply to ministerial meetings where full interpreting services would be provided, but it was suggested for working groups. In 2004 the Commissioner then responsible for administrative reform, Neil Kinnock, also called for Commission reports to be shorter, and not exceed 15 pages.

On one occasion Ernest-Antoine Seillière, the head of the employers association, BusinessEurope, spoke to EU leaders at a Brussels summit in English. The then French President, Chirac, walked out in protest.

The official seat of the European Parliament is Strasbourg, but its committee meetings take place in Brussels, and its secretariat is divided between Luxembourg and Brussels; hence the famous trunks in the corridors to accommodate the various moves of personnel.

The functions of the European Parliament

The EP has powers relating to legislation, the EU Budget, the conclusion of international agreements and supervision. With the Lisbon Treaty the EP would exercise jointly with the Council legislative and budgetary functions, as well as political control, consultation and the power to elect the Commission President.

With regard to **legislation,** in policy areas now covered by the consultation procedure (see below) such as agriculture, economic policy, immigration and asylum, the Parliament has the right to be consulted during the legislative process. The co-decision process (first introduced by the Maastricht Treaty, as described below) now covers most areas of legislation and places the Council and Parliament on equal footing. With the Lisbon Treaty use of the co-decision procedure would increase, and it would become the ordinary legislative procedure. This would imply changes, in particular, for the area of Freedom, Security and Justice, agriculture, and the Common Commercial Policy. However, an 'emergency brake' would allow a member state that considers proposed legislation to affect fundamental aspects of its legal system to refer the matter to the European Council and so suspend the co-decision procedure. According to CEPS et al. (2007) the increase in the use of co-decision might require reform of EP procedures to ensure efficiency, in particular, in committees.

The Parliament examines the annual work programme of the Commission in order to consider what new legislation is appropriate and ask the Commission to put forward proposals. The Commission is also required to inform the EP on a regular basis of its committee proceedings.

The Lisbon Treaty would also increase the role of the EP in treaty reform.

The Parliament has **budgetary powers**, and may adopt or reject the whole EU Budget. The European Parliament's committee on budgetary expenditure is responsible for monitoring expenditure. Parliament makes an annual assessment of the management of the budget before

---

Box 3.10: *The difference between compulsory and non-compulsory expenditure in the EU Budget*

Compulsory expenditure is defined as spending 'necessarily resulting from this Treaty or from acts adopted in accordance therewith' (Article 272 TEC). Compulsory spending is said to have a priority claim as it is considered necessary for the Community to meet its internal and external obligations. Most compulsory spending relates to agricultural price support and certain forms of foreign aid to third countries. The underlying logic was that when, for example, the level of common agricultural prices was decided, this became Community law, and the necessary financing should be forthcoming (and consequently not subject to possible cuts by the EP). The EP can only propose modifications of compulsory expenditure to the Council.

In contrast non-compulsory expenditure does not emanate from the commitments of the treaties, or the conventions and contracts signed by the EU. The largest component of non-compulsory expenditure is spending on social and economic cohesion (see Chapter 15). Other categories of non-compulsory expenditure include internal policies (education, the internal market, research and the environment), external programmes and administrative expenditure.

If the Parliament proposes an increase in non-compulsory expenditure, this will only come into effect if backed by a vote of the Council using QMV. Ceilings set by the Commission on the growth of that expenditure may further limit the power of the EP over non-compulsory expenditure. Moreover, some types of expenditure (for example, that of the European Development Fund which gives assistance to developing countries) are excluded from the budget completely.

The division between compulsory and non-compulsory expenditure is essentially political and relates to the balance of power between the EU institutions. As described above, in the 1960s the Commission and federalists envisaged a Community with its own resources subject to control by the EP as an important step in the creation of a federalist Europe. In contrast, France objected to transfers of sovereignty to the Community, but wanted to ensure adequate financing for the CAP. The compromise, involving the division of types expenditure and the inclusion of agricultural support under compulsory spending, ensured that the Council had the final say on most EC agricultural spending. This, together with the use of unanimity voting after the Luxembourg compromise, offered a guarantee that the interests of French farmers would not be overridden.

approving the accounts and granting 'discharge' to the Commission on the basis of the Annual Report of the Court of Auditors. The EP can propose amendments over what is called non-compulsory expenditure (see Box 3.10). The Lisbon Treaty would give the EP the budgetary powers over all types of spending, and abolish the distinction between compulsory and non-compulsory expenditure. However, the final word on financial perspectives (which set out expenditure and payment ceilings for a number of years; (see Chapter 11) would rest with the Council, though the EP can influence the decision.

Parliamentary assent (see below) is necessary before important agreements can be concluded with third countries or international organizations, and, in particular, its assent is necessary for treaties of accession or association. Assent is also necessary on decisions regarding the objectives of cohesion policy (see Chapter 15) and the functions of the ECB. The EP has no power to amend decisions under this procedure, but it can comment on them.

The EP has **supervisory powers** over the work of the Commission. It has to be consulted when a new Commission president and Commission are being chosen, and their appointment is also subject to a vote of approval by the Parliament. It can dismiss the whole Commission, and since the Treaty of Nice can also dismiss individual Commissioners. The Lisbon Treaty proposes that the EP elect the new Commission president on a proposal of the European Council. Parliament also regularly examines reports sent by the Commission (such as the Annual General Report) and can question the Commission. The Parliament also monitors the work of the Council.

The Maastricht Treaty gave the EP the power to investigate alleged contraventions of Community law and to appoint an **ombudsman**[33] to receive complaints from any EU citizen about suspected maladministration on the part of any EU institution.[34] The ombudsman may take the initiative in making investigations. The results of any inquiry are sent to the EP and to the institution concerned, but the ombudsman has no right of sanction. The first ombudsman, elected for the 1995–2000 period, and again from 2000, was a Finn, Jacob Magnus Soderman, who had previously acted as Parliamentary ombudsman in Finland. In the Parliament elected in 2004 the ombudsman was the Greek, P. Nikoforos Diamandouros.

The EP is an important **forum for discussion.** The Parliament sets its own agenda for discussions, invites important outside speakers and can send out delegations and fact-finding missions.

The role of national parliaments

During the debate on the Reform/Lisbon Treaty, the Prime Minister of the Netherlands, Balkenende, insisted on an increased contribution of national parliaments to the functioning of the EU as a 'red-line' issue.

With the Lisbon Treaty national parliaments would be given a greater role with regard to:

■ Reform of the EU Treaty (Article 33);

■ Responding to new applications for EU membership (Article 34);

■ Vetoing measures furthering judicial co-operation; and

■ Monitoring the proper application of the subsidiarity principle. National Parliaments would have eight weeks to study legislative proposals of the Commission to decide whether to send a reasoned opinion stating why the national parliament considers the proposal to be

---

[33] The ombudsman is an institution of Scandinavian origin, and the first ombudsman was appointed in Sweden in 1809.

[34] The term 'maladministration' is used to cover both incompetence and deliberate wrongdoing.

incompatible with subsidiarity. National Parliaments could also vote to have the proposal reviewed.[35]

Despite the additional complication of the proposed new measures, the reform may have the advantage of developing networks, and tightening the links between the EU and national levels, stimulating debate and awareness of EU issues.

The European Economic and Social Committee

The European Economic and Social Committee (also known as Ecosoc or the EESC) has its origins in the French notion of including the 'social partners' (and, in particular, trade unions and employers) in social dialogue; this entails consulting them on proposed legislation. In practice, the representatives from each member state in the Ecosoc are drawn from three categories: trade unions, employers and 'other interests'. The Ecosoc represents the various economic and social components of the European Union, including 'producers, farmers, carriers, workers, dealers, craftsmen, professional occupations, consumers and the general interest' (Article 257, TEC). Based in Brussels, following the 2007 enlargement the Ecosoc had 344 members.[36]

According to the Treaty of Rome, the EESC has to be consulted during the legislative process, but there is no obligation for the Council to take its Opinions into account. The EESC can also prepare Opinions on its own initiative. Though its influence on the legislative process is less than that envisaged in the Treaty of Rome, the expertise of the Ecosoc can prove a useful source of information and is valued in many circles, including the EP and Commission. The EESC has emerged as an important institutional forum for social partners to engage in key discussions of different aspects of integration. Many items raised by the social partners in the EESC have found their way into the proposals of the European Commission.

The Committee of the Regions

Since the Maastricht Treaty the EESC shares its secretariat with the **Committee of the Regions**. The latter consists of regional and local representatives appointed for four-year terms, whose function is to advise the Council and Commission on regional problems and policies. The Committee of the Regions has the same number of representatives per member state as Ecosoc. It must be consulted on matters affecting regional interests; it can also issue opinions on its own initiative but suffers from a relatively low profile.[37]

---

[35] If one third (or one quarter for Freedom, Justice and Security issues) of votes are in favour of review, the Commission will have to review the proposal, or give a reasoned opinion why it considers the measure compatible with subsidiarity.

[36] The four largest EU Member States each have 24 members; Spain and Poland have 21; Romania has 15; Belgium, Bulgaria, Greece, the Netherlands, Austria, Portugal, Sweden, Hungary and the Czech Republic have 12; Denmark, Ireland, Finland Lithuania and Slovakia have 9; Latvia, Slovenia and Estonia have 7; Luxembourg and Cyprus have 6, and 5 for Malta.

[37] In 2003 the Committee of the Regions was involved in a financial scandal when the Court of Justice forced its most senior civil servant to resign over severe irregularities. The Committee of the Regions was accused of travel expense fraud, and falsification of records to claim expenses by, for example, arranging 'fake' meetings on the eve of official meetings (*Financial Times*, 14 April 2003 and 19 September 2003).

The Court of Justice

The Court of Justice of the European Communities (EJ) would become known as the Court of Justice of the European Union with the Lisbon Treaty. The Court is composed of one judge from each member state, assisted by eight advocates-general.[38] All appointments are for six-year renewable terms, and the judges choose a president every three years. For the sake of efficiency the Court rarely sits with all 27 judges, but rather as a 'Grand Chamber' of 13, or smaller chambers of three or five judges.

In 1989, in order to speed up procedures, a Court of First Instance was created, which is also composed of one judge from each member state. The Court of First Instance has powers to hear direct actions and deliver preliminary rulings in certain areas. A European Civil Service Tribunal has been set up to adjudicate in cases between the EU and its civil service.

The European Court of Justice is responsible for interpreting Community law and adjudicating on disputes arising from the interpretation of the treaties and the legislation based upon them. If national law and EU law conflict, the latter takes precedence: in other words the EJ may overrule both national courts and governments. The Court of Justice is the highest court to which disputes on EC law can be taken, and national courts must abide by its judgments. Since the Maastricht Treaty the Court can impose fines on recalcitrant countries.[39] The Court cannot initiate cases, but makes judgments on cases referred to it by EU institutions, national governments and courts, corporate bodies and individuals. The Court can only act within the powers given by the treaties.

Despite being handicapped by a relatively small staff, the Court has played a 'discrete but substantial role in furthering the objectives laid down in the Treaties' (Bainbridge, 2002). Some of its rulings have established important principles, in particular in fields such as competition policy and equal pay.[40] The ruling in the famous 1979 *Cassis de Dijon* case formed the basis for mutual recognition of each other's standards by EU member states. This role of the Court in carrying forward the integration process has frequently been criticized, and certain member states have accused the Court of being the unguarded back door through which national sovereignty is being carried away.

The Court has, however, been criticized for not being sufficiently transparent and being too slow in its procedures. On average in 2000 it took 30 months for cases to come to judgement (Jones, 2001), but this is still less than in certain member states. The delays are largely due to the overload of work of the Court, and the Nice Treaty aimed at reducing the burden on the Court by delegating more work to lower levels.

---

[38] At Polish request, the number would rise to 11 with the Lisbon Treaty. A system of rotation is used for the smaller countries.

[39] Fines have been imposed on Italy, for example, for non-application of the milk quotas (see Chapter 12).

[40] This was also the case for the two leading cases of van Gent and Loos (Case number 26 of 1962) and Costa vs. ENEL (Case number 6 of 1964). In these cases the Court of Justice expounded its doctrine concerning the 'direct effect' of certain provisions of the Treaty of Rome. This entails that where provisions of the Treaty impose on the member states clear and unconditional obligations, and the implementation or effectiveness of the provisions is not dependent on any further action of state, Community law not only imposes obligations on individuals, but also confer rights on them, which are enforceable in the courts of the member states.

The Court of Auditors

The expenditure of all the EU institutions is subject to internal control by the Commission, and since 1977 to external control by the Court of Auditors. The Court's authority also extends to all institutions (including those in third countries) receiving or handling EU funds.

The Court is responsible for ensuring that all expenditure corresponds to the legal provisions, that correct accounting practices have been used, and financial objectives have been met. In practice, it has mainly been concerned with checking on fraud and the proper use of funds. The findings of the Court are published in an annual report, and other reports on specific topics may also be produced. Initially the Court could simply bring irregularities to the notice of the authorities responsible for the institution concerned (and its findings were frequently ignored), but since the Treaty of Maastricht it can refer cases to the EJ.

For the 12 successive years up until 2007 the Court refused to sign off EU accounts, maintaining that they could not verify a large share of the funds.

The decision-making procedures of the EU

Until the Single European Act, the EC legislative procedure was based on what is known as the **consultation procedure.** As shown in Figure 3.5, this consisted essentially of a Commission proposal being passed to the European Parliament and Economic and Social Committee, and,

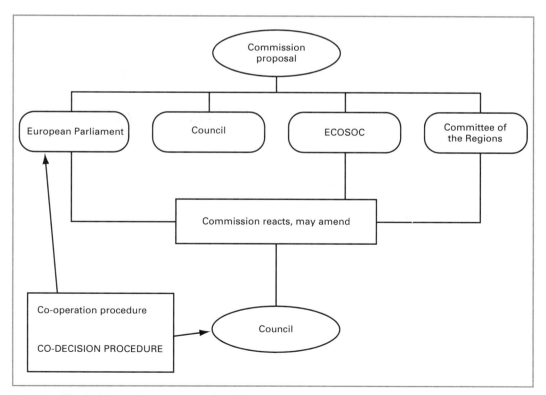

FIGURE 3.5 The decision-making procedures of the EU

since the Maastricht Treaty, to the Committee of the Regions for 'consultation'. The significant feature of this procedure was that there was only one reading by the EP. The Council would take the final decision, using the appropriate voting rule. It is important to note that neither the Commission nor the Council were bound to accept eventual amendments proposed by the EP.

The 1987 Single European Act introduced the **co-operation procedure** as a means of strengthening the role of the EP in the legislative process. The procedure allowed the EP to amend legislation. This required two readings by the EP. This procedure is now hardly ever used, and the Treaty of Amsterdam transferred most of the areas formerly dealt with under this procedure to the co-decision procedure.

The Maastricht Treaty introduced **the co-decision procedure**, and both the Amsterdam and Nice Treaties entailed an extension of its use so that it now covers about 80 per cent of Community legislation. The Lisbon Treaty proposes near generalization of the co-decision procedure, which would become known as the ordinary legislative procedure. The aim of wider use of the co-decision procedure was to reinforce the power of the EP in the legislative process and shift the balance of power away from the Commission. The main innovations of this procedure were:

1 to allow the EP to veto legislation in certain cases;
2 to add the possibility of a third reading of legislative proposals for the EP; and
3 the creation of a Conciliation Committee to help the Parliament and Council to reach agreement.

As mentioned above, the **assent procedure** applies to important international agreements, decisions concerning the objectives of cohesion policy, and the functions of the ECB. According to this procedure, the EP can give or withhold its assent to a legislative proposal, but it does not have the power to amend it.

'Flexibility' or 'enhanced co-operation'

The number of policy areas dealt with by the EU is growing, and so too is its membership. There is increasing concern about the efficiency of EU decision-making and the need to ensure that progress in integration is not limited to the pace of the slowest. The widening membership of the EU is bringing growing diversity, and with it the idea that more 'flexibility' or 'differentiated integration' will be necessary. Flexibility or differentiated integration allows those countries that are willing and/or able to proceed faster in some areas of integration.

One mechanism of flexibility is 'enhanced co-operation', by which the Council authorizes a group of member states to move ahead while remaining within the EU framework. The Amsterdam Treaty first introduced 'enhanced co-operation' (where it was called 'close co-operation'), and required it to:

- respect the treaties and objectives of the EU;
- involve a majority of member states;
- not affect the rights and obligations of states not participating;
- allow any other member state to join at a later stage;
- be introduced as a last resort;
- not impede the operation of the *acquis*; and

- be allowed to be vetoed by any single country that feels that vital interests are being threatened.

It was soon realized that these conditions were too restrictive to realize in practice. The Nice Treaty aimed at rendering flexibility easier, in particular, by removing the simple right of any member state to veto the process. According to the Amsterdam Treaty, enhanced co-operation required a majority of states, but this was modified to participation by eight member states in the Nice Treaty (at the time the 'critical mass' of eight corresponded to a majority of member states). The Lisbon Treaty attempted to render use of the enhanced co-operation easier. The last-resort condition was downgraded, the initial authorizing decision by the Council was to be by qualified majority, conditions for joining the initiative were to be laid down (to test the good will of participants), and the minimum number was to be nine member states. The Lisbon Treaty also envisages a passerelle system whereby participating member states can amend the procedures they use for implementing enhanced co-operation (e.g. by switching from unanimity to qualified majority voting).[41]

Though there was much debate about the formulation of the enhanced co-operation mechanism in the Amsterdam and successive treaties, to date it has never been triggered. The use of enhanced co-operation has been considered on a number of occasions, as, for example, for minimum taxation of energy products, a statute for EU companies, an EU arrest warrant and a common consolidated basis for taxation of company profits (CEPS et al., 2007).

The failure to use enhanced co-operation to date is partly because alternative mechanisms have been developed such as intergovernmental co-operation outside the EU (as in the CFSP and JPCCM pillars), but also because the treaties envisage other forms of flexibility, which often seem more appropriate and simpler to implement than the enhanced co-operation.

For instance, transitional periods may be used before countries are able to sign up fully for certain policies. This is sometimes referred to as a 'multi-speed' Europe, though the precise definition of this term varies in the literature. A multi-speed EU generally assumes that all member states will arrive at the same destination but require different speeds to do so. It implies that the goal for all member states would be that of membership in all aspects of the Union, but that member states (or the EU as a whole) may need more time to prepare for such membership. For instance, there was a delay before Greece could adopt the euro. In the case of the new central and eastern European member states, long transitional periods were also applied in areas such as labour movement, the CAP, land ownership and environmental regulations.

In contrast, in what is often referred to as a variable geometry EU, or Europe *à la carte*, all the member states can pick and choose whether to participate in different policies on the basis of preference rather than ability. In contrast to a multi-speed EU, it is not assumed that all member states will arrive at the same destination. Member states can choose voluntarily to remain outside certain policies or co-operation frameworks. There are various precedents for this such as the UK opt-out of the Social Charter in 1989 and Social Chapter in 1993 (see Chapter 16); the UK and Danish opt-outs of full participation in the third stage of the EMU, and the UK, Irish and partial Danish opt-outs of Schengen (see Chapter 6). However, here there is a risk that a 'hard core' of member states, having all signed up for the same policies, would decide to proceed with even deeper integration, and other member states would find that their options of eventually joining the hard core are excluded.

---

[41] 'Passerelle' or bridging clauses allow a switch from unanimity to qualified majority voting in the Council. They already exist for specific issues, but under the Lisbon Treaty their application would be extended to most areas except defence and CFSP decisions with military implications. A unanimous decision by the European Council, absence of opposition from member state parliaments, and consent of the EP are required.

Traditionally the notion of a 'core group' of EU countries proceeding more rapidly with integration generally rotated around the concept of the Franco-German relationship (often backed by the Benelux countries) as being the driving force of integration. Although the Franco-German alliance had long provided the momentum for many of the initiatives in European integration, there was a growing feeling that it might prove inadequate to propel the EU after enlargement. The misgivings were reinforced because at times co-operation between the two countries seemed increasingly geared to furthering national rather than EU interests, as in the October 2003 agreement on the CAP (see Chapter 12), or the 2004 controversy over the Stability and Growth Pact (see Chapter 10).

If the EU fails to permit sufficient possibilities for differentiated integration within its structures, there is a risk of flexibility by default with initiatives taking place outside the EU. The problem becomes one of finding a middle road, with some variable geometry to allow flexibility within EU structures, while at the same time avoiding excessive variable geometry that might undermine the cohesion and common core of the EU.

Evaluation

For many years the energies of the EU were absorbed by the question of institutional reform. The Amsterdam Treaty was patently inadequate to meet the challenges of enlargement, and though the Nice Treaty resolved some of the 'Amsterdam leftovers', and announced that the EU had 'completed the institutional changes necessary for the accession of new member states' in an annexed Declaration of the Future of Europe, that same Declaration launched a new round of debate on reform. The prolonged discussion in the Constitutional Convention and over the Constitutional Treaty led in the end to agreement on the Lisbon Treaty. This too has to be ratified by all the member states before it can come into operation, but with the exception of Ireland (where a referendum is required by the constitution) other member states have opted for the less risky option of ratification by the national parliament.

The Constitutional Treaty aimed at simplifying, clarifying and rendering more transparent the legal basis of the EU by replacing earlier treaties. This objective was certainly not achieved by the Lisbon Treaty, which returns to the traditional method of treaty revision and maintains two Treaties and numerous protocols. The question that arises is how different the Lisbon Treaty is from its predecessor, and if the two are not so different, whether countries that had promised a referendum on the Constitutional Treaty are justified in slipping the same measures in through the back door by parliamentary ratification of the Lisbon Treaty.

Many of the features of the Lisbon and Constitutional Treaty are similar: the longer-term President of the European Council, the smaller Commission, election of the Commission President, and the new voting rules in the Council (despite concessions on when and how they are to operate). Some changes are cosmetic: changing the name of EU Foreign Minister to High Representative of the EU for Foreign Affairs and Security Policy, and dropping all reference to EU symbols such as the flag or the anthem (as these will continue to be used by EU institutions and most member states anyway). However, the final compromise was such that EU member states appeared satisfied they could sell the deal to their domestic public. Britain ensured that certain 'red lines' were not crossed by maintaining its veto in various policy areas. The Dutch 'red line' was respected by increasing the role of national parliaments, while Poland obtained concessions over the application of the new voting rules in the Council.

Nonetheless in recent years the debate about the 'democratic deficit' in the EU has continued. Commissioners are not elected, and are said to be technocrats yielding more power than is justified by their limited democratic mandate. The system is said to be executive-dominated, with limited control by the EP or national parliaments. Elections to the EP are fought mainly over national issues. The Council is said to lack transparency, meeting in secret with no requirement to subject its decisions to public scrutiny. The supremacy by which EU law overrides national law has been challenged, and the Court of Justice has been accused of acquiring powers for itself and EU law not formally given by any treaty. The EU is accused of being too distant from its citizens, while its decision-making process is complex for them to understand. On various occasions when EU decision-makers have appealed to their citizens for approval (such as on the Nice and Lisbon Treaties in Ireland, or the Constitutional Treaty in France and the Netherlands), the outcome has not been what they expected. European integration has been confirmed as a process carried forward by elites.

Against this, it is argued that successive treaties have strengthened the role of the EP and, also in response to criticism, the EU decision-making process has been rendered more transparent and accessible. Most decisions are taken by consensus and the process by which this is reached may also lead to greater understanding, co-operation and convergence of views.[42] Moravcsik (1998) maintains that the EU has made executives more accountable to their citizens as the actions of government ministers are no longer scrutinized just at home, but also at the EU level, while governments do not simply have to account for their domestic record, but also what they have achieved in Brussels.

How far are the measures proposed by the Lisbon Treaty likely to render EU decision-making more democratic, transparent and efficient? The introduction of a smaller Commission could render it more difficult for member states without a Commissioner to justify EU policies back home, and could deprive the Commission President of important allies within the Commission in pushing initiatives. Election of a Commission President by the EP on the basis of a nomination by the European Council taking into account the composition of the parliament is likely to politicize the role. Already with Barroso in 2004 the tighter link with the majority in the EP became apparent, though subsequently he seemed concerned to establish his impartiality. A longer-term European Council President could contribute to continuity and a higher profile for the EU, but there may also be overlapping of responsibility and rivalry with other figures such as the Commission President or High Representative. The new voting rules in the Council would be more straightforward, but in practice the tradition of trying to reach consensus seems likely to continue, and the spectre of deadlock in an enlarged EU has not been completely removed. The increase in its legislative and budgetary powers would add to the legitimacy of the EP, but aspects of its gravy train image still need to be tackled. The more active role of national parliaments would be an additional complication, but seems likely to add to awareness and links between the EU and national levels.

Assuming that the Lisbon treaty is ratified, it still remains to be seen how many of these changes will operate in practice, so the debate about the future architecture of the EU seems set to continue in the years to come.

---

[42]See Chapters 9 and 10 for examples of how this may occur in the case of economic and monetary union (EMU).

Summary of Key Concepts

- Following the rejection of the Constitutional Treaty in referenda in France and the Netherlands, in 2007 EU leaders agreed on the **Lisbon Treaty**. This has to be ratified before it comes into operation, but aims at rendering EU decision-making more efficient and legitimate through changes such as a smaller Commission, an elected Commission President, simpler voting rules in the Council, a longer-term European Council President, increased legislative and budgetary powers for the EP, a High Representative for Foreign Affairs and Security Policy, and more involvement of national parliaments.

- **The main decision-making institutions** of the European Union are: the European Commission; the Council of Ministers; the European Parliament; the Economic and Social Committee; the Committee of Regions; the Court of Justice and the Court of Auditors.

- The functions of the **Commission** are: to present legislative proposals; to implement decisions; to exercise certain autonomous powers in areas such as competition policy and trade negotiations; to prepare the annual preliminary draft budget for the Community; to act as Guardian (or 'Watchdog') of the treaties; to make recommendations or opinions on matters related to the treaties, and to present White and Green Papers on specific policy areas.

- The **Council of Ministers** is the principal decision-making institution of the European Union, though since the Maastricht Treaty it can be overridden in certain cases by a veto of the European Parliament. The composition of the Council varies according to the question considered.

- The Council of heads of state and of government is known as the **European Council.** The European Council plays an important role in providing overall political direction to the Union and in resolving problems that have proved intractable at a lower level.

- The **Presidency** of the Council of Ministers and the European Council rotates among the EU member states in six-month terms. The country holding the Presidency has the power to set the agenda and further policy objectives in which it has a particular interest.

- The Council of Ministers may take decisions by **unanimity, simple majority or qualified majority voting.** Successive treaties have increased the number of policy areas subject to QMV. In practice there are usually attempts to reach consensus.

- The **European Parliament** was traditionally a consultative body, but over the years its legislative powers have increased. Since 1979 a system of direct election every five years has been used. The functions of the Parliament are: to be consulted during the legislative process and to use the power of amendment and veto in certain circumstances; to adopt or reject the whole EU Budget; to exercise budgetary powers over non-compulsory expenditure; to grant assent to important agreements with third countries or international organizations; to exercise supervisory powers over the work of the Commission; to investigate alleged contraventions of Community law and to appoint an ombudsman, and to act as a forum for discussion.

- The **European Economic and Social Committee and the Committee of the Regions** are consulted during the legislative process.

- The **European Court of Justice** is responsible for interpreting Community law and adjudicating on disputes arising from the interpretation of the treaties and the legislation based upon them.

- The expenditure of all the EU institutions is subject to control by the Commission and European Parliament, and since 1977 to external control by the **Court of Auditors**.
- The **decision-making procedures** of the European Community are the consultation procedure, the co-operation procedure, the co-decision procedure and the assent procedure. Eighty per cent of legislation is passed by the co-decision procedure, and this would increase with the Lisbon Treaty.
- The question of allowing **flexibility or differentiated integration** is rendered more urgent as the increasing membership of the EU is bringing growing diversity. To date the 'enhanced co-operation' clause in the treaties has not been applied, but other forms of flexibility such as intergovernmental co-operation outside the EU framework, transitional periods before fully applying policies and opt outs have been widely used.

Questions for study and review

1 Describe the organization and functioning of the European Commission. What are the main criticisms levelled against the Commission?

2 Why was it necessary to reform the system of voting in the Council of Ministers? What system of voting do you consider appropriate for the EU?

3 Why does the system of Presidency of the Council of Ministers need to change, and what reforms would you consider most effective?

4 Describe the European Parliament and indicate its main functions. What reforms are necessary to increase the democratic accountability of the European Parliament?

5 How would you resolve the problem of languages in the European Union?

6 Describe and criticize the reforms entailed by the Lisbon Treaty.

7 What are the dilemmas posed by flexibility or differentiated integration?

8 What measures could be taken to tackle the democratic deficit?

9 How do you envisage the future architecture of Europe?

References

Bainbridge, T. (2002) *The Penguin Companion to European Union*, 3rd edn, Penguin Books, London.

Baldwin, R., Berglof, E., Giavazzi, F. and Widgren, M. (2001) *EU Reforms for Tomorrow's Europe*, CEPR, London.

Baldwin, R. and Wyplosz, C. (2006) *The Economics of European Integration*, 2nd edn, McGraw-Hill Education, Maidenhead, UK.

Buchanan, J. M. and Tullock, G. (1962) *The Calculus of Consent*, University of Michigan Press, Ann Arbor.

CEPS, EGMONT and EPC Joint Study (2007) *The Treaty of Lisbon: Implementing Institutional Innovations*, http://shop.ceps.eu

Hayes-Renshaw, F., van Aken, W. and Wallace, H. (2005) *When and Why the Council of Ministers of the EU Votes Explicitly*, EUI Working Papers RSCAS No.2005/25, Robert Schuman Centre for Advanced Studies, European University Institute, Florence.

Hix, S. (2005) *The Political System of the European Union*, 2nd edn, Palgrave, London.

Jones, R.A. (2001) *The Politics and Economics of the European Union. An Introductory Text*, 2nd edn, Edward Elgar, Cheltenham, UK.

Kandogan, Y. (2000) 'Political economy of eastern enlargement of the European Union: Budgetary costs and reforms in voting rules', *European Journal of Political Economy*, Vol. 16.

Laruelle, A. and Widgren, M. (1998) 'Is the allocation of voting power among the EU member states fair?', Public Choice, Vol. 94.

Moravcsik, A. (1998) *The choice for Europe: Social Purpose and State Power from Messina to Maastricht*, Cornell University Press, Ithaca.

Nugent, N. (2006) *The Government and Politics of the European Union*, 6th edn, Palgrave MacMillan, Houndmills.

Peterson, J. and Shackleton, M. (2006) *The Institutions of the European Union*, 2nd edn, Oxford University Press, Oxford.

Schmitter, Philippe C. (2000) *How to Democratize the European Union – and Why Bother?* Rowman & Littlefield, Lanham, MD.

Senior Nello, S.M. (1997) *Applying the New Political Economy Approach to Agricultural Policy Formation in the European Union*, EUI Working Papers RSC No.97/21, Robert Schuman Centre for Advanced Studies, Florence.

Wallace, H. (2005) 'An institutional anatomy and five policy modes', in Wallace, H., Wallace, W. and Pollack, M.A., *Policy-making in the European Union*, 5th edn, Oxford University Press, Oxford and New York

Wallace, H., Wallace, W. and Pollack, M.A. (2005) *Policy-making in the European Union*, 5th edn, Oxford University Press, Oxford and New York.

Westlake, M. (2001) *The Council of the European Union*, 3rd edn, John Harper Publishers, London.

Useful websites

There is a great deal of jargon associated with the EU. For glossaries of the various terms see the Europa Glossary of the EU:

http://europa.eu/scadplus/glossary

The site of the European Convention:

www. european-convention.eu.int

The website of Baldwin and Wyplosz at:

www.mcgraw-hill.co.uk/textbooks/baldwin

See the European Union website for a description of 'The EU and its institutions' at:

http://europa.eu/institutions/inst/index_en.htm

The Centre for Economic Policy Research has carried out extensive research on EU institutions and voting rules:

www.cepr.org

Committee of the Regions:
www.cor.europa.eu

Economic and Social Committee:
www.eesc.europa.eu

The European Commission:
www.ec.europa.eu

The European Council:
www.consilium.europa.eu

European Court of Auditors:
www.eca.europa.eu

European Court of Justice:
www.curia.europa.eu

The European Parliament and, in particular its factsheets provide information on institutions and decision-making procedures:
www.europarl.europa.eu

Information on EU law is available from the Commission at Scadplus:
www.europa.eu/scadplus

04

The Theory of Trade and the EU

Introduction

The aim of this chapter is to introduce the different concepts used in the theory of trade, which will be used in the following chapter to explain integration. Integration is generally advocated for motives that are a mixture of politics and economics, and can perhaps be summarized as the desire to spread 'peace and prosperity' though other aims have also always played a role. The idea of using integration to avoid further wars in Europe ('peace') emerged clearly in the process of constructing the European Community in the years after the Second World War (see Chapter 2). Prosperity is generally associated with the benefits to be obtained by removing barriers to trade, and by permitting freedom of movement of goods, services, labour and capital.

In order to explain how integration is expected to lead to prosperity, it is first necessary to indicate the main arguments in favour of free trade. After a review of the classical concepts of absolute and comparative advantage, there is a brief discussion of the Heckscher-Ohlin-Samuelson framework. The second half of the chapter deals with protectionism, and, in particular, a description of the most commonly adopted obstacles to trade and the main arguments used to justify their introduction. Then follows a brief review of some political economy explanations of the prevalence of protectionist measures. Those who are already familiar with international economics can skip this chapter and move straight to the analysis of integration in Chapter 5.

The main arguments in favour of free trade

Many of our arguments in favour of free trade still owe much to the work of the classical economists Adam Smith and David Ricardo.[1] These writers illustrated that trade between two countries could be mutually beneficial (a 'win-win' game, to use more recent terminology) thanks to the specialization of production. These theories were based on restrictive assumptions, and when relaxed, as the section on globalization in chapter 7 discusses, a wide literature suggests that while trade liberalization leads to overall gains, there may be winners and losers in the process. The evolution of the new trade theory essentially involves relaxing of various of the assumptions.

Absolute advantage

Adam Smith illustrated the principle of absolute advantage, arguing that 'what is prudent in the conduct of every private family can scarce be folly in that of a great kingdom. A family will not make at home what it costs less to buy from outside. A taylor [sic] will not make his own shoes, but will buy them from a shoemaker.'

With two nations, if one country is more efficient in the production of one good, and less efficient in the production of the other, then each country should specialize in the production of the good where it has an absolute advantage. Part of the output of that country can be exchanged for the good for which it has an absolute disadvantage. In this way resources will be used in the most efficient way possible. For instance, according to this principle, in trade between the two countries, Ecuador should specialize in the export of bananas and Argentina in that of beef.

Comparative advantage

In practice Smith's concept of absolute advantage explains only a small share of international trade. From this point of view, the concept of comparative advantage developed by David Ricardo is much more useful. According to the principle of comparative advantage, even when one country is less efficient in the production of both goods there is a basis for mutually beneficial trade. An example frequently given in the textbooks is that of Justice Holmes of the US Supreme Court. Justice Holmes was, apparently, a very speedy typist, and could type twice as fast as his secretary. She could earn $10 an hour with the amount she typed, but he could earn $20. However, he would receive $100 an hour from his legal activity, so it was in his interest to concentrate on that. With every hour he spent typing he would earn $20 but would forgo $100, so the net loss would be $80.

According to the principle of comparative advantage, even if one country has an absolute disadvantage in the production of both goods, it should specialize in the production and export of the good where its absolute disadvantage is smaller and import the product where its absolute disadvantage is greater. The country with an absolute advantage in the production in both goods should specialize in the production and export of the product where its absolute advantage is greater, and import the good for which its absolute advantage is smaller. Thus, for example, if the USA has an absolute advantage in the production of grain and clothing compared with the

[1] Smith's *Wealth of Nations* was published in 1776, while Ricardo's *Principles of Political Economy and Taxation* was published in 1817. See also the contribution of economists such as Petty, Law or Quesnay.

	USA	EU
Wheat (tonnes produced in a man-hour)	6	1
Wine (litres produced in a man-hour)	4	2

TABLE 4.1 Comparative advantage

EU, but its absolute advantage is greater for grain, it should specialize in grain production, and export grain in exchange for clothing.

Comparative advantage still remains an important element of the toolkit in explaining the advantages of free trade, so it useful to provide an example of how this principle works in practice. Ricardo based his approach on the labour theory of value, by which the price of a product is said to depend exclusively on the amount of labour used in its production. This theory requires:

- either that labour is the only factor used in making products, or that the ratio between labour and other factors such as land or capital is constant; and

- that labour is homogeneous and there are no differences in skills between people.

Clearly, these are extremely restrictive assumptions, and have been eliminated in most later evolutions of the theory.[2]

To illustrate the principle of comparative advantage it is useful to take a simple example with only two partners involved in trade, the EU and the USA, and two products, wheat and wine. It is assumed that with one hour of work the USA can produce 6 units (tonnes) of wheat, or 4 units (litres) of wine. With one hour of work an EU labourer can produce 1 unit of wheat or 2 units of wine (quality differences are ignored in this highly simplified model). The USA has an absolute advantage in the production of both goods, but its advantage is greater in the production of wheat. Similarly, the EU has a disadvantage in the production of both goods, but the disadvantage is less in the production of wine (see Table 4.1). In the USA, 6 units of wheat can be exchanged for 4 units of wine. If in international trade more than 4 units of wine can be obtained for 6 units of wheat, it is to the advantage of the USA. In the EU 2 units of wine can be exchanged for 1 unit of wheat. If more wheat could be obtained, it would be to the advantage of the EU.

Assume that with the opening of trade between the EU and USA it is possible to exchange 6 units of wine for 6 units of wheat. The EU will gain, because before the opening of trade 12 units of wine had to be given for 6 units of wheat and now only 6, so there is a saving of three man-hours. The USA will also gain, as before 6 units of wheat could only be exchanged for 4 units of wine, and now it can obtain 6 units of wine, so there is a saving of 2 units of wine (30 minutes of labour).[3] If the EU is less efficient than the USA in the production of both goods, how can it export to the USA? The answer is that wages are lower in the EU, so that when the prices of the two products are expressed in the same currency, wine will be cheaper in the EU, and grain will cost less in the USA.

If the wage in the USA is $6 an hour, 1 unit of grain will cost $1 and 1 unit of wine will cost $1.50. If the wage in the EU is €2 per hour, then the price of a litre of wine is €1, and that of a

---

[2] See, for example, Salvatore (2007) for a discussion of this point.

[3] The only exception is the unlikely case in which the absolute disadvantage that one country has with respect to the other is the same for the two products. This would occur in the above example if the EU could produce 3 units of grain with one man-hour.

tonne of grain is €2. With an exchange rate of $1 = 1 euro, then the prices in the EU will be $1 for a unit of wine, and $2 for a unit of grain. Traders will have an incentive to buy wine in the EU and trade it for grain in the USA. With an exchange rate of $0.5 per euro, then the EU price would be $1 for grain and $0.5 for wine. There would be very strong pressure to sell EU wine in the USA, but no incentive to sell US grain in the EU. The value of the dollar against the euro would have to fall.

With an exchange rate of $2 = €1, then the EU price would be $4 for grain, and $2 for wine. There would be very strong pressure to buy grain in the USA, but it would be impossible to sell EU wine to the USA, and so the euro rate against the dollar would have to fall.

The Heckscher–Ohlin Theorem

Classical economists such as Ricardo explain the advantages of international trade on the basis of specialization according to comparative advantage, but fail to analyse in any detail what determines the comparative advantage of a country. Later developments in trade theory, and in particular, the Heckscher–Ohlin theorem, try to explain the pattern of comparative advantage between countries. In other words, why does a country have a comparative advantage in the production of a particular good? According to this approach, trade can be explained by the pattern of endowment of countries with different factors of production.

For purposes of simplification, the Heckscher–Ohlin theorem can be presented using a highly simplified case of two countries (1 and 2), two products (X and Y) and two factors (labour (L) and capital (C)). A country is said to have an abundance of a certain factor if the ratio of the total amount of one factor, say labour to capital, is higher than in the other country, and if the cost of labour relative to capital is less than in the other country.[4] If the production of one of the goods, say X, requires more labour relative to capital than the other good, then product X is said to be labour-intensive. According to the Heckscher–Ohlin theorem, a country will export the commodity whose production is intensive of the factor in which the country is relatively abundant.

For example, if China has an abundance of cheap labour, and the production of clothing is labour-intensive, China will tend to export clothing. In contrast, if the USA has a factor abundance of capital (or skilled labour), and computers are intensive of capital (or skilled labour), China will specialize in textiles and import computers, while the USA will specialize in computers and import textiles.

This explanation works rather well in accounting for trade between countries with different endowments of factors of production such as land, labour or capital. For example, it may explain certain trade flows between developing and industrialized countries. However, it works less well for trade between similar countries, such as most of those of Western Europe.

Figure 4.1 can be used to illustrate the Heckscher–Ohlin theorem. Country 1 is assumed abundant in labour, while country 2 has an abundance of capital. Product X is assumed intensive of labour, while product Y is intensive of capital. In Figure 4.1 quantities of product X are indicated on the horizontal axis, and quantities of product Y are indicated on the vertical axis.

The model is based on various simplifying assumptions.[5] The two countries are assumed to have the same technology and to be operating under conditions of perfect competition. They

---

[4] In case of conflict between the two criteria, the second is decisive.

[5] See Salvatore (2004) for a discussion of these assumptions and what happens when they are relaxed.

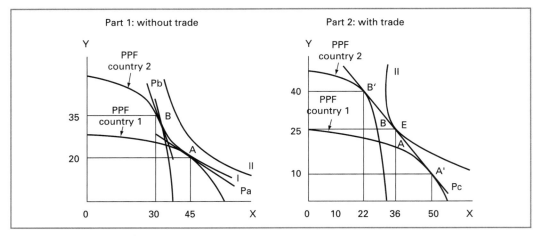

FIGURE 4.1 The Heckscher–Ohlin Theorem
Source: From *International Economics* by Dominick Salvatore, Copyright © 2007, John Wiley & Sons, Inc. This material is used by permission of John Wiley & Sons, Inc.

are also assumed to produce some of both goods X and Y, and production of both goods takes place with constant returns to scale. This implies that if the amount of inputs is increased in the production of a good, the amount of the good produced will increase by a proportional amount. The preferences of consumers are assumed to be identical in the two countries. All resources are used in each country (i.e. there is no unemployment in the factors of production). It is assumed that there is perfect mobility of factors of production within a country, but no mobility between countries. There are no transport costs or barriers to trade, such as tariffs. The exports and imports between the two countries are assumed to balance.

The production possibility frontier (PPF) shows the alternative combinations of the two products that a country can produce by fully utilizing its resources and making use of the best technology available. Each country must be on the production possibility curve to be in equilibrium, since points below the curve are inefficient, while points above cannot be reached. The slope of the production possibility curve in absolute terms indicates the opportunity cost of X, or the amount of Y which has to be given up to release enough resources to produce one additional unit of X. Under conditions of perfect competition each country will produce a combination of the two goods such that opportunity cost is equal to the ratio between prices of X and Y (Px/Py).

As shown in the diagram, the PPF for country 1 is flatter and wider than that of country 2. This is because country 1 has an abundance of labour, and product X is intensive of labour, so country 1 can produce a greater quantity of X than country 2.

The curves I and II are community indifference curves which show the various combinations of the two products that yield the same level of satisfaction or utility to a country.[6] Higher indifference curves indicate higher levels of satisfaction. For simplicity, in the example here, preferences of consumers in the two countries are assumed identical so the same collective indifference curves can be used for each.

The marginal rate of substitution (MRS) is the amount of good Y that the country has to give up in order to consume an additional unit of X while remaining on the same indifference curve.

---

[6] A discussion of the well-known problems with collective indifference curves is beyond the scope of the analysis here.

The MRS is given by the slope of an indifference curve in absolute terms at the point of consumption of the two goods. Moving down along the indifference curves shown in Figure 4.1, the MRS will decrease because of diminishing marginal utility. This implies that after a certain point increasing quantities of a good consumed yield smaller and smaller increases in utility.

In the absence of trade the equilibrium of each country is at the point where its production possibility curve is tangent to the highest collective indifference curve possible. This occurs at A for country 1 and B for country 2. Country 1 will produce and consume 45 X and 20 Y, while country 2 will produce and consume 30 X and 35 Y. The tangent of the PPF and highest indifference curve at point A indicate the relative price –Px/Py of the two goods, or Pa, in country 1. Similarly the relative price of the two goods in country 2 is Pb. In country 1 the relative price of X is lower (Pa is less than Pb in absolute terms) than in country 2 and Country 1 has a comparative advantage in the production of X, while country 2 has a comparative advantage in the production of Y.

With trade (see Part II of Figure 4.1) it will be to the benefit of country 1 to export good X to country 2 in exchange for good Y. Country 1 will therefore specialize in the production of X, moving along down its production possibility curve to the right. As it does so, the increasing slope of the production possibility curve implies that the opportunity cost of X will rise, and the price of X relative to Y will increase.

Without trade the price of Y relative to X in country 2 is lower than in country 1. With trade country 2 has an advantage in specializing in the production of Y moving up along its production curve and selling Y to country 1 in exchange for X. In this case the price of X relative to Y will fall (or, in other words, the price of Y relative to X will rise) in country 2.

This process of specialization will continue until the relative price Px/Py is the same in both countries. This occurs when production of the two goods reaches A' in country 1 and B' in country 2. At this point country 1 produces 50 X and 10 Y. Country 2 produces 22 X and 40Y. At the relative price Pc country 1 will export 14 X in exchange for 15 Y from country 2. In this way both countries reach equilibrium at E in Part II of the diagram, where they consume 36 X and 25Y. Both countries benefit from trade since they can reach the higher indifference curve II.

The Heckscher–Ohlin–Samuelson Theorem

According to the Heckscher–Ohlin–Samuelson theorem, the liberalization of trade will bring about the equalization of relative and absolute returns to the factors of production between countries or regions. This theorem is a corollary of the Heckscher–Ohlin theorem explained above and is based on the same restrictive assumptions.

Returning to the model used above, as Country 1 (China) specializes in the production of X (which is labour intensive) and reduces the production of Y (which is capital intensive), the demand for labour relative to capital will rise. This will cause the price of labour (w, or wages) relative to that of capital (r, or the interest rate) to rise. Country 1 is labour abundant, so initially the price of labour relative to capital was lower than in Country 2, but with trade the relative price for labour will rise in Country 1. The opposite will occur in Country 2 (the USA). As Country 2 specializes in the production of Y the demand for capital relative to labour will rise and so too will r relative to w. Trade will continue until the relative prices of the two factors are the same in the two countries.

Figure 4.2 can be used to illustrate this process. The vertical axis indicates the price of product X relative to product Y (Px/Py). The horizontal axis shows the price of labour relative to

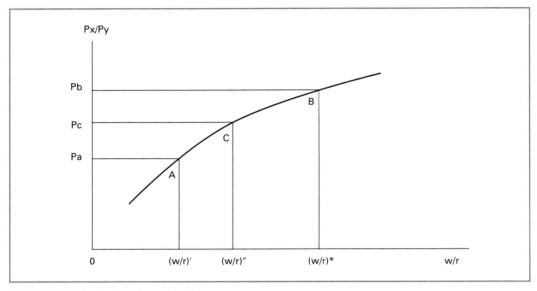

FIGURE 4.2 Relative factor–price equalization

Source: From *International Economics* by Dominick Salvatore, Copyright © 2007, John Wiley & Sons, Inc. This material is used by permission of John Wiley & Sons, Inc.

the price of capital (w/r). It is assumed that there is perfect competition, and that both countries use the same technology, so each value of Px/Py is associated with one and only one value of w/r.

Before trade Country 1 is at point A, with w/r = (w/r)′, and Px/Py= Pa. Country 2 is at B with Px/Py = Pb and w/r = (w/r)″.With trade Country 1 specializes in the production of X, causing Px/Py and w/r to rise. Country 2 specializes in Y, causing Px/Py (which is the inverse of Py/Px) to fall, so causing a reduction in w/r. The process will contine until both countries are at C, where Px/Py = Pc and w/r = (w/r)*.

So far what has been demonstrated is how trade leads to equalization of the relative price for the two factors in the two countries. Given the assumptions of the model (perfect competition in the product and factor markets, constant returns to scale and that both countries use the same technology), trade will also lead to the equalization of absolute factor prices. In other words, the real wage and the real rate of interest will be the same in the two countries.

Trade can therefore be said to act as a substitute for the international mobility of factors.With perfect mobility labour would move from where wages were lower to where they are higher until wages were the same in both countries. Similarly, capital would move from where interest rates were lower to where they were higher until interest rates were the same in both countries. There is, however, a difference between trade and factor mobility. Trade acts on the demand for factors of production, while factor mobility acts on their supply.

New trade theories

Given the very restrictive assumption of the traditional framework, there is now a rapidly expanding literature on the 'new trade theory', which tries to go beyond the efficiency gains from reallocating resources according to comparative advantage. These theories are more eclectic than the elegant traditional framework and incorporate a wide variety of elements. For instance, though the discussion here cannot be exhaustive, different strands of this literature attempt to accommodate aspects such as:

- imperfect competition and product differentiation (see below);
- political economy arguments (see the discussions at the end of this Chapter and in Chapter 5);
- new growth theory (see Chapter 5);
- the new economic geography (see Chapter 15); and
- open-economy macroeconomics (see Chapter 10).

Intra-industry trade and product differentiation

A large percentage (70–80 per cent in many cases) of trade between EU countries consists of exports and imports of the same product or group of products. For instance Italy exports Fiat, and imports BMW from Germany and Renault from France. This is known as **intra-industry trade** and arises when products are substitutes for each other but are slightly different (see Box 4.1). This kind of **product differentiation** means that a firm or plant can specialize in a few varieties of the product, making use of longer production runs, more specialized machinery and labour, and so on. Other varieties of the product can be imported. As a result consumers may have a wider range of products available at lower prices. The products are differentiated but similar and therefore substitutes.[7]

Box 4.1: *The Grubel–Lloyd index*

One of the most widely used measures of intra-industry trade is the Grubel–Lloyd index:

$$T = 1 - \frac{|Xi - Mi|}{[Xi + Mi]}$$

where X and M represent respectively the exports and imports of a particular commodity group i. The straight-line parenthesis indicates value in absolute terms. T may take values between 0 and 1. If T is zero there is no intra-industry trade, and the countries are specialized in different product categories indicating inter-industry trade. If T is 1 all trade is intra-industry, and the countries are specialized in the same product categories.

The index is frequently calculated using the Standard International Trade Classification (SITC). This breaks trade down by product category, and the number of digits indicates the level of disaggregation (00, 001, 0015 etc.). One of the difficulties in using the Grubel–Lloyd index is that the results may reflect the level of disaggregation of the statistics used.

A further shortcoming of the index is that products within the same classification group may be very different in terms of quality. Distinction is therefore sometimes made between vertical intra-industry trade (reflecting quality differences) and horizontal intra-industry trade in products of similar quality.

---

[7] Models of monopolistic competition are frequently used to analyse this type of market.

Static economies of scale

Static economies of scale occur when an increase in the use of inputs results in a more than proportional increase in output. In other words, the unit costs of production fall as the scale of production rises. This may arise, for example, from the use of more specialized machinery, or from the division of labour with workers specializing in the tasks they perform. A classic example is the assembly-line production introduced by Henry Ford.

Figure 4.3 can be used to illustrate how mutually beneficial trade between countries can arise from economies of scale.[8] The same highly simplified model is based on two countries, 1 and 2, and two products, X and Y, and two factors of production are used. In Figure 4.3 quantities of product X are indicated on the horizontal axis, and quantities of product Y are indicated on the vertical axis. The two countries are assumed to be identical in all respects so the same PPF B'B in Figure 4.3 can be used for both of them. In the case of economies of scale, the production possibility curve is convex to the origin. The two countries are assumed identical, so the same indifference curves can be used for both.

The equilibrium position before trade, A, will therefore be identical for both countries. At A each country is at the point where the production possibility curve is tangent to the highest collective indifference curve possible. At A both countries can produce and consume 40 units of X and 40 units of Y. The equilibrium point before trade A is not stable since if for any reason one of the countries, say country 1, increased its production of X, the price of X relative to Y would fall, and the country would move along its production curve until it became fully specialized in the production of X (i.e. producing only X and no Y) at point B. In the same way, if for some reason country 2 increased its production of Y, it would continue moving up and left along

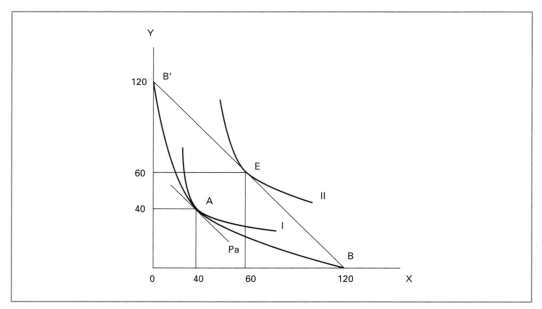

FIGURE 4.3 Static economies of scale

Source: From *International Economics* by Dominick Salvatore, Copyright © 2007, John Wiley & Sons, Inc. This material is used by permission of John Wiley & Sons, Inc.

---

[8] The analysis here is based on Salvatore (2007).

its PPF until it became fully specialized in the production of Y at B'. As the two countries are assumed identical, it is purely a matter of accident which country specializes in the production of which good.

At the equilibrium point B, country 1 produces 120 units of X, while at B' country 2 produces 120 units of Y. With trade country 1 could exchange 60 units of X for 60 units of Y and move to the new equilibrium point E that is on the higher collective indifference curve II. Similarly country 2 could sell 60 Y for 60 X and also move to E. As a result of specialization based on economies of scale and trade, both countries gain 20 X and 20 Y compared to the equilibrium point A. This is a highly simplified model, and in practice the two countries do not have to be identical to draw mutual benefit from trade based on economies of scale.

The learning process

Dynamic economies of scale are associated with the learning process. This process entails that a firm will have a unit cost advantage because of the experience it acquires through cumulative production of goods and services. The fall in cost may be due to technological improvements, better organizational structures and/or performance of workers. For example, the experience gained by McDonald's in producing hamburgers (how many billion sold?) enables it to compete against new firms attempting to enter the market and facing much higher initial costs. In contrast to static economies of scale, these dynamic economies of scale are independent of the degree of capacity utilization of the firm and accrue in function of cumulative output. The firm that first moves down the 'learning' curve of a strategic industry will gain a cost advantage over its competitors. The existence of these experience economies may render it difficult for new entrants to enter the market. According to strategic trade theory (see below), there may be a case for subsidizing or protecting strategic industries to help domestic firms move down the learning curve first. Economic policy should also ensure that markets are on an adequate scale to allow such learning effects to be exploited. Figure 4.4 illustrates a learning or experience curve, where Cn is the cost of the nth unit produced.[9]

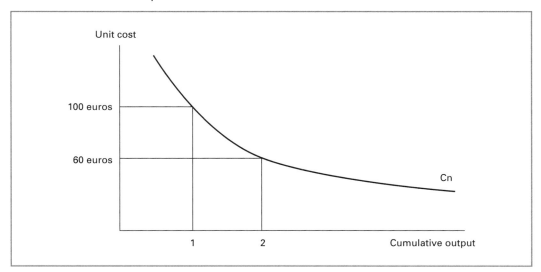

FIGURE 4.4 Dynamic economies of sale
Source: Figure 1.7 (p. 37) from *The Economics of the New Europe* (1995) by Healey, N.M. By permission of Taylor & Francis incorporating Routledge.

[9] This example is taken from Healey (1995).

Tariffs

In most economic textbooks the discussion of the theory of trade policies begins with an analysis of tariffs.[10] This is because at least up until the First World War it was widely accepted that if trade barriers were introduced for protectionist purposes they should be confined to tariffs (see Box 4.2). In the GATT/WTO context tariffs are considered the 'lesser evil' compared with other trade barriers because they are more transparent.[11] The GATT/WTO favours the conversion of other non-tariff barriers (NTBs) into tariffs.

An import tariff is a tax or duty levied on a product when it is imported into a country. Tariffs can be *ad valorem,* specific or compound. An *ad valorem* tariff entails a percentage increase in the price of the imported product. If, for example, p is the price of the good before the tariff, when a tariff rate t is applied the price will become $(1 + t)p$. A 10 per cent tariff on a bicycle worth 100 euros would increase the price of the bicycle in the importing country to €110. *Ad valorem* tariffs are the type most frequently used by the EU. A specific tariff is a fixed lump sum levied on an import. For instance, a specific tariff of €5 would increase the price of the bicycle to €105. The USA uses both *ad valorem* and specific tariffs. A compound tariff combines an *ad valorem* and a specific tariff. With a 10 per cent *ad valorem* tariff, and a specific tariff of €5, the price of the imported bicycle would rise to 115 euros.

Box 4.2: *Tariff levels*

As explained in Chapter 2, the Treaty of Rome envisaged the elimination of tariffs on trade between member states, and the EU met this objective six months ahead of schedule in 1968. The EU continues to apply tariffs (the common external tariff) on trade with third countries, but over time the level of these tariffs has shrunk as a consequence of the various GATT rounds.

Though difficult to measure in practice, the average level of world tariffs fell from roughly 40 per cent in 1948 to about 3 per cent by the early 2000s. Problems arise in calculating average tariff rates for a number of reasons: actual tariffs are often lower than the rates 'bound' by GATT agreements; in order to calculate averages, account has to be taken of weights of the good in trade; in practice there are likely to be exceptions to nondiscrimination (i.e. to most favoured nation treatment; see Chapter 18); if tariffs are too high they are prohibitive and no trade will take place, and tariffs change over time.

The economic effects of introducing a tariff in a 'small nation'

In order to analyse the economic effects of a tariff on imports, it is useful to make certain simplifying assumptions. The analysis here is partial equilibrium in that it only considers the market of the good on which the tariff is levied, ignoring the implications for other economic sectors or

---

[10]The discussion here is restricted to tariffs on imports. With the food shortages and high agricultural prices in 2008 many developing countries also used tariffs on exports. See Chapter 12 for a similar type of analysis of the economic effects of export subsidies.

[11]See Chapter 18 for a discussion of the GATT/WTO.

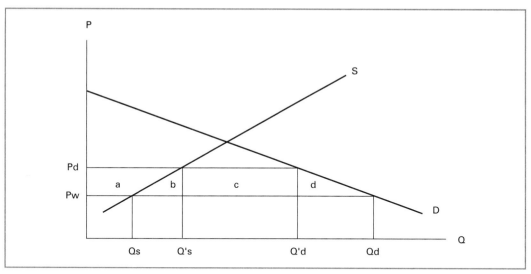

FIGURE 4.5 A tariff in a small nation

for factor markets. It is assumed that there are no stocks of the product, and transport costs or possible externalities are not taken into account.

For simplicity, the discussion here relates to an *ad valorem* tariff so, if p is the price of the good before the tariff, when a tariff rate t is applied, the price will become $(1 + t)p$. Initially it is assumed that the country is a 'small nation', so that any changes in its supply or demand for that product will have no impact on the international terms of trade or world price level for that product.

The demand and supply curves (assumed linear for simplicity) of a country for the traded good in question are shown in Figure 4.5. Prior to the introduction of the tariff, the domestic price of the product in the country is assumed equal to the world price Pw. At this price the country will produce Qs and demand Qd of the product. The country will therefore import Qd – Qs (equivalent to the excess demand) of the product.

With the introduction of the tariff t the domestic price for the product will rise to $(1 + t)$Pw, or Pd in the diagram. Assuming a small nation, the world price will remain unchanged at Pw. The new higher internal price will be Pd. The introduction of the tariff will entail the following effects on demand, supply and foreign trade:

- The quantity demanded will decline from Qd to Q'd.
- The quantity supplied will increase from Qs to Q's.
- The quantity imported will fall from (Qd – Qs) to (Q'd – Q's).

The tariff will also have the following 'financial' effects:

- Consumer expenditure on the product will change from QdPw before introduction of the tariff to Q'dPd with the tariff.
- Producer revenue will increase from QsPw before the tariff to Q'sPd after the tariff is introduced.
- The trade balance (or, in this case, the amount spent on imports) will improve from (Qs – Qd)Pw to (Q's – Q'd)Pw.

Introduction of the tariff will redistribute welfare between the three main groups in society: tax-payers, consumers and producers. In order to assess these effects, it is first necessary to introduce two concepts: consumer and producer surplus.

Consumer rent or **surplus** is defined as the difference between the price a consumer is prepared to pay for a certain quantity of a product and the price that is effectively paid for that quantity. This concept may be applied to an individual consumer or to the overall demand curve in a particular market. As shown in Figure 4.6, with a demand curve D and price OA, consumer surplus is indicated by the triangle ABC.

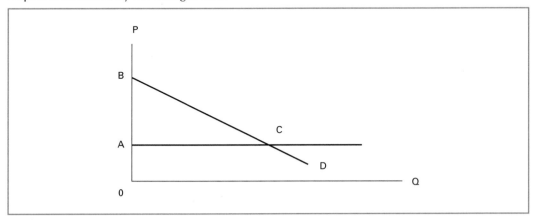

FIGURE 4.6 Consumer surplus

Producer rent is the difference between the total revenue and total cost of the producer and can be considered as the profits of the producer. Ignoring fixed costs, the total cost of producing a certain quantity is given by the area under the marginal cost curve (which coincides with the supply curve). As mentioned above, producer revenue is given by the price received by the producer multiplied by the quantity produced. In Figure 4.7, with a supply curve S, and price OF, producer revenue is equal to OFGQ and total cost is OHGQ, so that producer rent is indicated by the triangle HFG.

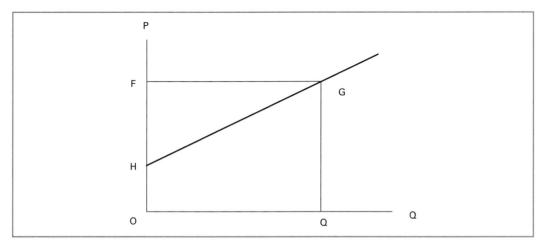

FIGURE 4.7 Producer surplus

The introduction of the tariff will alter consumer and producer surplus and the income of taxpayers. The tariff entails an increase in the price received by producers so, as Figure 4.4 above shows, there is an increase in producer surplus equivalent to area a. The consumers also have to pay a higher price for the product, so there will be a reduction in consumer surplus equivalent to area a + b + c + d. There is an increase in government revenue of area c.

The tariff is a source of revenue for the government budget.[12] The total revenue for the budget will be equal to the unit value of the tariff (Pd – Pw) multiplied by the quantity imported after introduction of the tariff (Q'd – Q's). In the diagram this corresponds to the area of the rectangle c, or (Pd – Pw) × (Q'd – Q's). If this revenue is used in a socially useful way, it represents a welfare benefit to the country. This benefit could be considered an increase in the income of taxpayers in that, *ceteris paribus*, in the absence of the tariff the government would have to impose higher taxes to obtain the same amount of revenue. It is, however, possible that the revenue from the tariff is not used in a socially useful way. For instance, a share of the revenue may be used to cover the administrative costs of levying the duty, and government funds spent in this way represent a net welfare loss to the community.

In order to calculate the overall net welfare effect of the tariff, it is necessary to assume that value of each euro lost by any individual is the same as that of any euro gained, regardless of who undergoes the loss or gain. With this assumption it can be seen that only part of the loss in consumer surplus is compensated by the gain in producer rent and the increase in government revenue. The net welfare cost of the tariff is indicated by the two triangles b and d.

Triangle b represents the net economic cost on the production side. It reflects the worsening in the allocation of resources as a result of introduction of the tariff. Triangle d represents the net welfare cost on the consumption side, because the tariff raises the price of the good relative to other products, causing a distortion in consumption. A numerical example of the effects of introducing a tariff in a small nation is included in Appendix 1.

The effect of introducing a production subsidy

Subsidies on domestic production may also distort competition and act as a barrier to trade. The difference between a tariff and a producer subsidy can be seen from Figure 4.8. The main difference between a tariff and a producer subsidy is that the introduction of producer subsidies leaves the domestic price unchanged for consumers. As Figure 4.8 shows, with the producer subsidy the domestic price to producers rises to Pd, while the price paid by consumers remains Pw. Producer surplus rises by area a, the cost of the surplus to budget contributors is area a + b (i.e. the unit cost of the subsidy, Pd – Pw times the new quantity of output Q's). The net welfare loss is triangle b.

The effect of introducing a tariff in a 'large nation'

In Figure 4.5 it was assumed that introducing a tariff would leave the world price for the product unchanged. However, it is possible that the introduction of a tariff will lower the world price for a product. The tariff raises the domestic price for that product, increasing production and reducing consumption. The country will therefore import less after the tariff is introduced, reducing the demand for that product on world markets. The *ceteris paribus* clause implies that

---

[12] See the discussion on the sources of revenue of the EU Budget in Chapter 11.

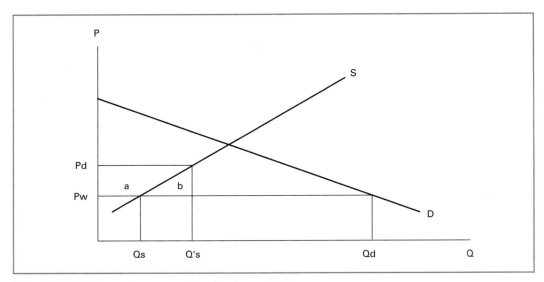

FIGURE 4.8 The difference between a tariff and producer subsidy

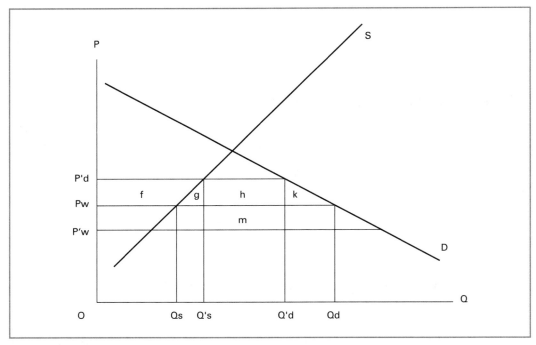

FIGURE 4.9 The introduction of a tariff in a large nation

supply on world markets remains unchanged. If that country accounts for a large share of world trade, the reduction in net imports for the product, with supply on world markets unchanged, will reduce the price on world markets. The assumption that the country is a 'large nation' implies that the introduction (or removal) of a policy such as a tariff will affect the price for that product on world markets or, in other words, that country's terms of trade.

If, as in the case being considered here, the country is a net importer, the reduction in world price will constitute a net welfare gain for that country. In other words there will be a transfer from exporters in the rest of the world to that country. This situation is shown in Figure 4.9. In the diagram, the introduction of a tariff leads to a reduction in the world price level to P'w. As a result, the internal price after introduction of the tariff will be P'd, or $(1 + t)$P'w, which is less than $(1 + t)$Pw.

In this case the reduction in consumer surplus is indicated by area $f + g + h + k$; the increase in producer rent is area f. The increase in government revenue is area h, which represents a transfer from internal consumers (because of the higher domestic price now paid) and area m, which consists of a transfer from producers in the rest of the world (because of the lower world price which they now receive).

The net welfare effect for the country introducing the tariff now consists of: the net welfare cost on the consumption side, triangle k; the net welfare cost on the production side, triangle g, and a net welfare gain, rectangle m, which represents transfers from the rest of the world.

It is possible that the net welfare gain represented by rectangle m outweighs the net welfare loss represented by the two triangles g and k. In this case the introduction of a tariff entails an increase in net welfare for the country. This has encouraged countries to seek the so-called optimal tariff, which leads to the maximum increase in net welfare possible for the country imposing a tariff (see below). A numerical example of the effects of introducing a tariff in a large nation is included in Appendix 1.

The effects of introducing a tariff on the exporting country

It is useful to show the effects of introducing a tariff by the home country on an exporting country.[13] For simplicity it is assumed that there is only one foreign country (called 'foreign'). The two countries are assumed to be small nations and have increasing production costs.[14] Figure 4.10a illustrates the demand and supply curves in the home country, and Figure 4.10b illustrates MDh, or the home import demand for X. At price P' home supply equals home demand and there is no import demand for X. At price P" home demand exceeds home supply of X by HJ, and this is equal to import demand OM.

Figure 4.11a illustrates the supply and demand curves for X of the foreign country that are used to derive the export supply of X by the foreign country XSf in part (b) of the figure. At price P' demand and supply are in equilibrium on the foreign market, and foreign export supply is zero. At price P" foreign supply exceeds foreign demand by amount FG of product X, and foreign export supply OH is equal to FG. In the simple two-country model, foreign export supply XSf is equal to home import supply, so can be labelled MSh.

The left part of Figure 4.12 shows the export supply of X by the foreign country, while the right part of Figure 4.12 combines the import demand and import supply for X in the home country and shows the effect of the tariff T on home imports and foreign exports. The tariff raises

---

[13] The discussion here follows Baldwin and Wyplosz (2006).

[14] The analysis is extended to the case of a large nation in Chapter 5.

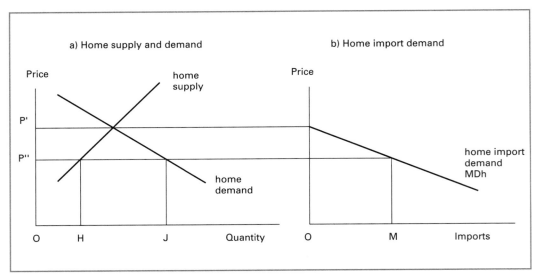

FIGURE 4.10 The import demand of the home country
Source: Baldwin and Wyplosz (2006).

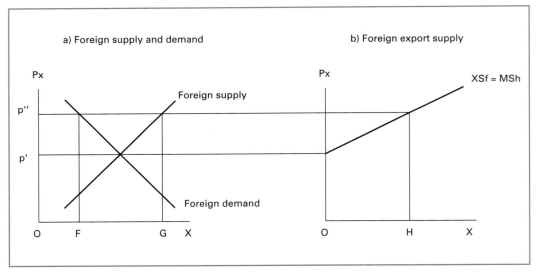

FIGURE 4.11 The import supply of the home country, or the export supply of the foreign country
Source: Baldwin and Wyplosz (2006).

the price faced by home consumers and producers from Pft to P'. The border price or the price received by foreigners falls to P' – T. The volume of imports falls from Mft (or Xft exports where ft stands for free trade) to M' (which is equal to X').

The welfare loss from the tariff to the foreign country is rectangle b (because of the lower price received) and triangle c (because of loss of sales). The home country receives a welfare

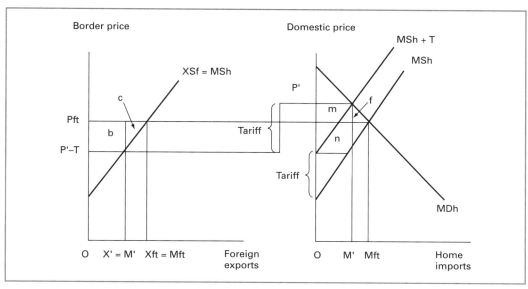

FIGURE 4.12 The effect of a tariff on the home and foreign countries
Source: Baldwin and Wyplosz (2006).

gain from tariff revenue equal to the unit value of the tariff (t) times the volume of imports M′, indicated by rectangles m and n. The loss in private surplus (i.e. the sum of changes in consumer and producer surplus) is equal to areas f and m. The overall impact on welfare for the home country is therefore area n minus area f. In terms of the analysis of the effects of a tariff above, triangle f is equal to the sum of triangles b and d in Figure 4.5.

Non-tariff barriers and the 'New Protectionism'

Despite the success of the GATT in reducing tariffs, from the 1970s international trade became increasingly subject to NTBs, in what is referred to as the 'new protectionism'. In particular, the Uruguay Round attempted to extend the jurisdiction of GATT regulations to cover these NTBs. The following list includes some of the main NTBs, but does not pretend to be exhaustive:[15]

- quotas on imports;
- voluntary export restraint agreements (VERs);
- cartels;
- anti-dumping duties;
- export subsidies;
- differences in standards and technical specifications, and administrative measures;
- discrimination in public procurement.

A **quota on imports** is a quantitative restriction imposed by the state on imports of a particular

---

[15]For reasons of space a formal analysis of these various measures based on the use of diagrams is not included here. For a study of this type see, for example, Salvatore (2007) or Krugman and Obstfeld (1997).

product. The quota may entail a limit on all imports of a particular product (or group of products) or it may relate to imports of a product from a particular country or group of countries. In general, a system of import quotas is implemented through the granting of import licences. In principle the GATT forbids quotas on imports, but in practice various exceptions have been allowed (see Box 4.3).

Box 4.3: *EU Quotas*

The EU applies seasonal quotas to the imports of some agricultural products. Quotas on the imports of certain textiles and clothing were applied under the Multifibre Agreement, though these had to be phased out by January 2005 in line with the GATT Uruguay Round Agreement (see Chapter 18), though in some cases they were replaced with anti-dumping measures. Another exception permitted by GATT/WTO is on imports from non-market economies, so the Community applied quotas on the imports of certain goods (such as footwear, glass products, some agricultural goods and so on) from the former centrally planned countries of Central and Eastern Europe. These were eliminated as part of the trade concessions granted from 1989 on.[16]

The economic effects of a quota on imports can be analysed using Figure 4.13. In the absence of the quota on imports it is assumed that a particular country imports quantity Qd-Qs at world price Pw. If the state introduces a quota limiting the quantity of imports to Q'd-Q's, the domestic price will rise to Pd because there is excess domestic demand for the product. Assuming perfect competition, the effect of the quota on the domestic price, quantity produced, quantity demanded and level of imports will therefore be the same as that of a tariff that increases the domestic price level from Pw to Pd (see Figure 4.5).

If the assumption of perfect competition is relaxed, there is a possibility that the introduction of an import quota converts a potential monopoly into an actual monopoly. The quota will have the effect of protecting the domestic firm(s) from foreign competition. In the case of a tariff domestic producers cannot raise prices above Pw without losing their market share because domestic consumers will prefer to buy imports.

One of the main differences between a quota on imports and a tariff relates to government revenue. In the case of a tariff, which raises the domestic price to Pd, the state benefits from the customs duties indicated by rectangle c (see also Figure 4.5 above). For a quota those holding import licences can generally appropriate the benefits indicated by rectangle c.

It is also possible that the state can acquire part of the revenue from the quota by organizing an auction of the import licences. With perfect competition, and an efficient auction the revenue to the state from an import quota Q'd-Q's and a tariff Pd-Pw would be the same. However, while such a result is theoretically possible, in practice it is unlikely to occur.

In the case of a shift of the demand curve from D to D', the quota limiting imports to amount Qd'-Qs' (or g-f) would cause an increase of the domestic price to Pd', with imports of Qd''-Qs'' (equal to g'-f' or Qd-Qs') . In contrast, with a shift of the demand curve from D to D' and a tariff that increases domestic prices from Pw to Pd the amount of imports would increase to h-f (or Qd*-Qs'), while the domestic price would remain Pd.

The question that inevitably arises is why a government should introduce a quota rather than

---

[16]See Senior Nello (1991) for a description of how these quotas operated, and their elimination.

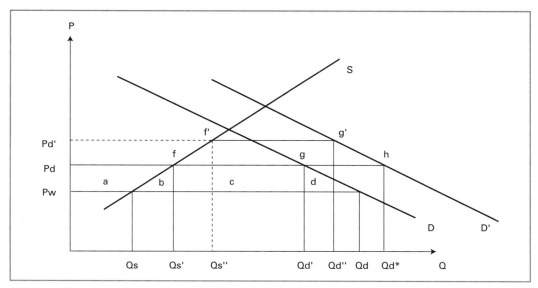

FIGURE 4.13 The effect of an import quota

Source: From *International Economics* by Domimick Salvatore, copyright © 2007, John Wiley & Sons Inc. This material is used by permission of John Wiley & Sons, Inc.

a tariff when it stands to lose a source of revenue? The reply probably lies in the fact that the quota on imports offers a better guarantee that the quantity of imports will be limited. Though in theory the same restriction in imports could be achieved through a tariff, this requires knowledge of the position and slope of the demand and supply curves for the product. In practice such knowledge is rarely forthcoming, and moreover the demand and supply curves are subject to frequent shifts.

Voluntary export restraint agreements (VERs) entail an export restriction which in formal terms was imposed unilaterally by the exporting country, but in practice was usually introduced in response to pressure from the government or industry in the importing country (see Box 4.4).[17] VERs were essentially bilaterally negotiated agreements. The export restraint involved could operate through quotas and/or minimum export prices. Although these arrangements appear to be an improvement on the autonomous setting of policy, it must be questioned how far they were in fact 'voluntary'. Often the exporter had to accept the demands made by the importing country, or risk the unilateral imposition of a tariff, quota or anti-dumping measures against its products. According to the GATT Uruguay Round Agreement, VERs were to be phased out by 1999.[18]

---

[17]Orderly marketing arrangements (OMAs) were a sub-category of VERs involving government-to-government arrangements. VERs also included agreements with the direct participation of industry.

[18]Figure 4.4 that was used to illustrate the effects of a tariff can also be applied to the case of a voluntary export restriction. The example again is of an importing country, which is assumed to be a small nation. Prior to introduction of the VER, at the world price level of Pw, imports amount to Qd-Qs. With the VER the quantity imported is reduced to Q'd-Q's, and the price in the importing country rises to Pd. Both in the case of a tariff and of a quota rectangle c represents a benefit for the importing country (for the state in the case of a tariff and for the holders of import licences for a quota). In contrast in the case of a VER rectangle c represents a benefit for the exporting country. This is one of the reasons why an exporting country generally preferred VER to a tariff or quota.

Box 4.4: *VERs*

VERs were used by the EU and US to limit exports of steel, electronic products, automobiles and other products, in particular from Japan, Central and Eastern Europe and Korea. Following the 1973 oil crisis there was a sharp drop in the demand for steel, and the Community threatened its major suppliers with anti-dumping measures unless they signed VERs. The Community applied VERs on steel, textiles and some agricultural products from most of the smaller Central and Eastern European countries during the 1970s and 1980s.

VERs were probably less effective than quotas in limiting the quantity of imports, as exporters were generally reluctant to cut their market share. Voluntary export restraints also tended to lead to a continual upgrading of products since the limit on quantity encouraged exporters to supply products of higher quality and price. As the VER usually applied to the main supplier, at times there was a tendency to switch to other exporters, or even for the main supplier to redirect exports through other countries.

An international **cartel** is an agreement between suppliers in different countries to restrict production and exports in order to increase their prices and profits. The most famous example of a cartel is that of OPEC (Organization of Petroleum Exporting Countries; see Box 4.5). The USA prohibits cartels between national producers but, as explained in Chapter 17, in the EU they are simply heavily regulated.[19]

Box 4.5: *The OPEC*

The OPEC is probably the most famous example of an international cartel. The OPEC was founded in Iraq in 1960, and meets regularly to discuss prices and, since 1982, to set crude oil production quotas. Original OPEC members were Iran, Iraq, Kuwait, Saudi Arabia, and Venezuela. Subsequently, the organisation expanded to include Qatar (1961), Indonesia (1962), Libya (1962), the United Arab Emirates (1967), Algeria (1969), and Nigeria (1971). Ecuador and Gabon were members of OPEC, but Ecuador withdrew in 1992, and Gabon left in 1995. Although Iraq remains a member of OPEC, Iraqi production has not been a part of any OPEC quota agreements since March 1998.

In March 2008 the OPEC decided that the market for oil was well supplied and decided to maintain existing production levels. However, OPEC noted that crude oil prices were being strongly influenced by the weakness in the US dollar, rising inflation and significant flow of funds into the commodities market.

A further difference between VERs and quotas arises in that the application of the VER may cause producers in the exporting country to form a cartel This may occur if, for example, the government leaves responsibility for the allocation of export quotas to the sector in question. The formation of a monopoly cartel may lead to producers in the exporting country exporting less at a higher price than the quantitative restriction fixed by the VER. Under such circumstances the VER offers a higher level of protection for the importing country (a smaller quantity of imports at higher prices) than an import quota applying the same quantitative limit as the VER.

[19]Chapter 17 also contains a formal analysis of the effects of a cartel.

Dumping consists essentially in the practice of international price discrimination, when the price charged by an exporter to a foreign market is lower than the domestic price for that product. Distinction is frequently made between sporadic, predatory and persistent dumping.

As the name suggests, sporadic dumping occurs occasionally when, because of a change in the pattern of demand or an error in production plans, a firm finds itself with an unsold surplus. Rather than risking disruption of the domestic market, the firm will sell this surplus at a low price abroad. In this case below-cost sales may occur. Predatory dumping is aimed at eliminating competing firms from international markets. The firm will charge low prices in order to drive its competitor(s) out of the market. Even though this may entail setting prices below costs for a time, the firm will be able to raise prices again once the competitor has been eliminated. Persistent dumping is practised by a producer with monopoly power who attempts to use price discrimination between different markets in order to maximize profits. This price discrimination is only possible if the markets are separate, for instance as a result of incomplete information, transport costs, trade barriers and so on. In other words retrading between the individual markets is impossible.

If dumping is found to cause injury or threat of injury to domestic producers, the WTO regulations permit a country to impose an **anti-dumping duty** (see Box 4.6). A frequent complaint is that countries may use anti-dumping duties as an instrument of protectionism.

Box 4.6: *EU Anti-dumping*

EU anti-dumping legislation is a sphere where authority is very much in the hands of the Community rather than its member states. The legislation draws heavily on the GATT/WTO Articles relating to dumping. According to EC legislation, dumping is said to occur when the price of an export to the EC is lower than its 'normal value'. The Commission acting on its own initiative never opens EC anti-dumping procedures; it is always at the request of one or more producer who represents the 'Community industry'. If dumping is found to cause injury or threat of injury, and the 'interest of the Community' so requires, the EC Commission may impose an anti-dumping duty, though in most cases it simply insists on a price undertaking from the exporting country involved.

The total number of EU anti-dumping investigations opened was 86 in 1999, reflecting worldwide difficulties in the steel industry in the wake of the Russian and Asian crises, but had fallen to 29 in 2004, 24 in 2005 and 35 in 2006. In 2006 13 new investigations were in chemicals and allied products, nine in metals other than iron and steel, and five were in electronics products. In 2006, 12 of the new cases opened were against China, with three each for Taiwan and the Ukraine, and two for Russia, the USA, Thailand, Malaysia, India and Kazakhstan.

Export subsidies may involve giving direct payments, tax breaks or low interest loans to exporters, subsidized loans to foreign purchasers, and assistance in export promotion (through advertising, trade fairs, meetings and so on). Though export subsidies are subject to a general ban by the WTO, in practice there are many exceptions to this rule. These include the agricultural export subsidies for which the EU is highly criticized by its trading partners (see Chapter 12). The WTO permits the granting of credits to clients by exporting firms and government-backed guarantees for certain risks to foreign direct investment, though the Organization for Economic

Co-operation and Development (OECD) tries to ensure that these are not used to promote domestic firms in an unfair way.[20] Countries sometimes use tax breaks to promote exports, but the WTO ruled against the system of Foreign Sales Corporations used by the USA (see the OLC website of this book).

Technical restrictions and standards and other administrative regulations may act as barriers to trade. These include safety regulations (for instance for electrical equipment), health regulations (in particular for food products) and labelling requirements. **Differences in standards and technical barriers** probably represent the main barrier in trade between developed countries. Firms also frequently complain about **customs formalities**, which may cause delays, additional costs, and even block trade. Differences in tax systems may also have to be offset at the border. The Single Market Project aimed at removing these barriers between EC member states (see Chapter 6), and there have been attempts to reduce their impact on trade with third countries (see Box 4.7).

Box 4.7: *Standards, technical restrictions and other administrative regulations in EU–USA trade*

A major objective of the Single Market Programme is to prevent differences in standards, technical restrictions and other administrative regulations from acting as barriers to intra-EU trade, but the problem also arises in trade between the EU and other countries such as the USA. Annual publications such as the US Trade Review or the European Commission's Report on United States Barriers to Trade and Investment describe many of these barriers.

For example, the EU Report for 2007[21] complains of excessive invoicing requirements on exports to the USA; of failure to recognize that the EU is a customs union, and of regulatory and technical barriers. The Agreement on Mutual Recognition in force since 1998 is said not been fully implemented and, for example, EU exports of electrical and electronic equipment, including telecommunications equipment, encounter obstacles. The document also complains that the lack of a clear definition of 'national security' seems to have led to an overly wide interpretation of the term by the US, and expressed fears that excessive use of the concept could be interpreted as a disguised form of protectionism.

Lack of transparency in **government procurement** may also act as a barrier to trade since local, regional and national authorities tend to buy from firms of their own country (see Chapter 6).

The main arguments presented in favour of protection

Protectionism may be advocated for **non-economic reasons,** such as for defence, national pride or to further foreign policy objectives. For instance, the need to ensure sufficiency of supply in

---

[20] Export credit subsidies and foreign investment guarantees are generally granted by special government-backed agencies. In France for example there is the Banque Française pour le Commerce Extérieur, and in Britain, the Export Credit Guarantee Department. In certain other countries the loan is granted by commercial banks, but interest rate payments are subsidized by a transfer from the government to the bank.

[21] European Commission (2008).

times of war has frequently been advanced to justify protection in sectors such as agriculture, shipbuilding, energy, steel production and so on. However, such explanations seem incomplete as an account of the behaviour of Western industrialized countries and are difficult to apply to some of the sectors most affected by protectionism.

The **infant industry** case is probably the oldest and best-known argument advanced in favour of protection. When an industry is first set up it may need time to acquire experience or competence (in terms of managerial resources, networks of suppliers, financial capabilities, etc.), or to reach a sufficient size to benefit from economies of scale. A new industry will therefore not be able to compete with a foreign industry that is already well established. According to this argument, the new industry should therefore be protected, for instance by a tariff, until it is large enough to compete with foreign firms.

However, for this argument to be valid the industry must eventually succeed in becoming competitive with foreign industry at the free trade world price; moreover the eventual benefit from the industry must exceed the cost of protection. Protection initially increases the price consumers have to pay, and for this to be justified it must be offset by the lower costs and prices that consumers will pay when the industry is established. Even if these two conditions are satisfied, it would be preferable to use a production subsidy rather than a tariff since subsidies are more transparent, less distorting and also tend to be easier to remove.

The practical implementation of protection of infant industries also encounters difficulties. For instance, how is the decision concerning which industries to be protected taken? And is there a risk of this selection process becoming politicized? When is the industry to be weaned, and is there likely to be pressure to prevent the protection ending? Even where protection helps an industry to become established, could this have occurred even without the protection? Clearly a general answer cannot be given to such questions and the outcome will depend on the particular case in question.

Another argument in favour of protectionism that has a long history is that of the **optimal tariff**. John Stuart Mill noted that if Britain introduced a tariff on a good widely used, consumption would decline causing the world price to fall. As a result, foreign producers would bear part of the cost of the tariff. This argument only applies in the case of a large nation that is able to influence the level of world prices.[22] The risk of introducing a tariff for this reason is that of retaliation on the part of other countries.

The **senescent industry** argument is frequently used, and maintains that protectionist measures may be necessary to avoid unemployment. However, the probable impact of such measures is simply to delay adjustment, and it is likely that the jobs saved in the declining sectors will be less numerous and will have less favourable prospects than those lost or foregone in non-subsidized sectors.

Second best

The traditional theory advocating free trade according to the principle of comparative advantage is based on some extremely restrictive assumptions, and in particular that there is perfect competition in factor and product markets both at national and international levels. This assumption is violated at a national level by cases of monopoly, oligopoly and imperfect competition, while at an international level the assumption appears even more heroic.

---

[22] For the country to benefit from introduction of the optimal tariff, it is also necessary that the transfer from the rest of the world following introduction of a tariff exceeds the net welfare loss to domestic producers and consumers.

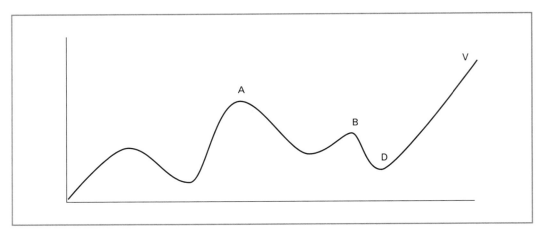

FIGURE 4.14 An illustration of second best
Source: Elaborated by Grandolfo, 1994, on the basis of Meade (1962).

If the conditions of perfect competition are not verified, then we are in a situation of **second best**. Second best implies that if the conditions of perfect competition are violated in some part of the economy, it need not be optimal for the rest of the economy to attain a perfectly competitive equilibrium. In other words, it is not possible to know whether the introduction of an additional distortion will increase (while still remaining in a suboptimal situation) or reduce total welfare. The situation may actually be improved by violating further conditions of perfect competition. In the context of the debate on protectionism this implies that it is impossible to say a priori whether a move towards free trade will improve the situation, or that the introduction of a protectionist measure will worsen it. Under such conditions it is necessary to examine the specific case in question to decide on the most appropriate policy.

Meade (1962) provided a useful analogy for understanding the concept of second best. Let us consider a person trying to reach the highest possible peak in a group of mountains. Going towards the highest peak, the mountaineer will at times have to climb smaller mountains and descend the other side: the path to the highest peak is not always upwards. Assume, for example, in Figure 4.14 the mountaineer has reached B, but discovers that there is a deep gorge at D over which it is impossible to cross. If the climber wants to reach the highest peak possible under the circumstances, he should not remain at B, nor move to D in order to try and reach V, but should return to A.

More recent arguments in favour of protection: strategic trade theory

Given the shortcomings of the traditional theory, there have been numerous attempts to develop new approaches to the study of international trade, which no longer rely on the assumption of perfect competition. The differences among authors are such that it is difficult to present a synthesis of this type of approach. What emerges from the literature, however, is an emphasis on dynamic phenomena that may influence the productive conditions of a firm. In this world, technology, and both static and dynamic economies of scale, may play a crucial role. These phenomena may enable a firm to gain a competitive advantage regardless of the initial endowments of factors of production in that country. This implies that comparative advantage may in some sense be created and may be of a temporary nature.

Box 4.8: *The political economy of protectionism*

The work by Olson (1965) provides a key in identifying the elements of success in pressure group activities. Olson explains the decision to join and participate in the activities of a pressure group in terms of expected benefits and costs. In the case of lobbying, the benefits relate to the probability of obtaining a favourable policy outcome, and the size of the per capita transfer to the beneficiary group.

The costs of pressure group activities include the costs of signalling preferences, organization and administration of the group and lobbying. According to Olson, the costs of organization and co-ordination may be higher, and the group may be rendered less effective with numerous members, each of whom feels that, whether they participate in the activities of the group or not, will not be noticed.[23] In other words there is a tendency for the members to 'free ride'. Olson argues that one way of overcoming free riding is by offering selective incentives to ensure membership or participation in the activities of a group. Alternatively, Olson maintains that the problem of free riding can be avoided in the case of what he calls a 'privileged group'. This involves one or more members of the group whose size or interest in having the goal of collective action is sufficient to induce them to take on the task of obtaining the common goal.

Downs (1957) provides an explanation of how, in a 'democratic system', a policy can serve the interests of a special group rather than those of the public as a whole. According to Downs, politicians are assumed to maximize their chances of re-election by competing for votes. They will adopt or reject a proposal on the basis of how many votes are expected to support or oppose it. However, voters will only reveal their preference if there is some advantage in doing so, such as action by the politician in favour of the voter. Information and signalling costs are involved in forming and expressing a preference. The rational voter will only undertake these costs if there is some incentive to do so. The fundamental theoretical insight of Downs is to illustrate why taxpayers and consumers may be 'rationally ignorant'.

This view underlies **strategic trade theory**, which advocates an active government trade policy and protectionism. According to this approach, a government may create a competitive advantage for its firms in high-technology industries through temporary protection, subsidies and tax breaks. Strategies to promote investment in infrastructure, people and research and development may also play an important role. Unfortunately, this approach shares many of the shortcomings of the infant industry argument: choosing which sectors will be future winners is as difficult as betting on horses, and too much government intervention may invite similar measures by major competitors.

The political economy of protectionism

The effect of trade protection for a particular product, say steel, is to raise domestic steel prices. Steel producers in that country will benefit, while consumers will have to pay higher prices. However, the benefits to the producers can be very high, while the cost to consumers is spread.

---

[23] Olson refers to this type of group as a 'latent' group.

The expected benefits to producers from protection may be sufficient to induce them to take on the costs of lobbying governments to introduce protectionist measures. The costs of lobbying may include the time, effort and expense needed to obtain information, organize a pressure group, signal preferences and carry out lobbying activities (see Box 4.8). The cost to consumers of the higher steel prices may be insufficiently high to induce them to organize any kind of protest. The government may have an incentive to give in to the requests of the steel lobby, knowing that consumers will be unlikely to organize any kind of effective resistance.

This type of political economy argument is very powerful in explaining the pervasiveness of protectionist measures. In the EU and USA, aside from steel, protection tends to be high in agriculture, textiles and clothing, and the automobile industry.

Summary of Key Concepts

- Many of our arguments in favour of free trade still owe much to the pioneering work of the classical economists **Adam Smith and David Ricardo** who illustrated that trade between two countries could be mutually beneficial thanks to the specialization of their production.

- The **Heckscher-Ohlin theorem** explains patterns of trade in terms of the endowments of factors of production of countries. For example, a country which has an abundance of cheap labour will specialize in the production of labour-intensive goods.

- According to the **Heckscher-Ohlin-Samuelson theorem**, under certain very restrictive assumptions, the liberalization of trade will bring about the equalization of relative and absolute returns to the factors of production between countries.

- '**New trade theories**' take into account aspects such as: imperfect competition; political economy arguments; new growth theory; the new economic geography, and open-economy macroeconomics.

- Much trade between EU countries consists of **intra-industry trade**. This arises from product differentiation and means each country (or producer) can specialize in a few varieties of the product and exploit economies of scale.

- **Static economies of scale** occur when the unit costs of production fall as the scale of production rises. Dynamic economies of scale are associated with the **learning process**.

- An import **tariff** is a tax or duty levied on a product when it is imported into a country. Tariffs can be *ad valorem*, specific or compound.

- Among the main **non-tariff barriers** are: quotas; voluntary export restraints (VERs); cartels; anti-dumping measures; trade facilitation measures (including customs procedures, measures to promote exports and so on); differences in standards and technical specifications; and lack of transparency in government procurement.

- **The effect of trade protection** for a particular product is to raise domestic prices. Producers in that country will benefit, while consumers will have to pay higher prices. However, the benefits to the producers can be very high, while the cost to consumers is diffused. Producers may have an incentive to lobby government to introduce protection in their favour, while it may not be worth their while for the consumers to object.

Questions for study and review

1 *What are the main arguments in favour of free trade?*

2 *What are the main obstacles to trade and how are they used in the EU (see also Chapters 12, 18 and 19)?*

3 *Why are protectionist measures so diffuse?*

4 *Illustrate how political economy reasons may help to explain the high levels of protection in sectors such as agriculture, steel or textiles.*

5 *Exercise on the effects of a tariff in a small nation (see Appendix 1 for an example of how to carry out the exercise). The quantity of a commodity supplied in a country is 24 tonnes, the quantity demanded (Qd) is 60 tonnes, and the world price (Pw) is €6/tonne. A tariff is introduced which raises the domestic price (Pd) to €7/tonne. The elasticity of demand is –0.3 and the elasticity of supply is 0.5. Calculate the effects of the tariff on: producer revenue, consumer expenditure, the trade balance and total welfare.[24]*

6 *Exercise on the effects of introducing a tariff in a large nation (see Appendix 1 for an example of how to carry out the exercise). It is assumed initially that in conditions of free trade the quantity supplied (Qs) by a country is 200 tonnes, the quantity demanded (Qd) is 400 tonnes, and the world price (Pw) is €4/tonne. A tariff is introduced which raises the domestic price (Pd) to €5/tonne and as a result the world price Pw falls to €3.5/tonne. The elasticity of demand is –0.5 and the elasticity of supply is 0.4. Calculate the effects of the tariff on: producer revenue, consumer expenditure, the trade balance and total welfare.*

Appendix 1

A numerical example of the introduction of a tariff in a small nation[25]

A simple numerical example can be used to calculate the effects of introducing a tariff. It is assumed initially that the quantity supplied (Qs) by the country is 8 tonnes, the quantity demanded (Qd) is 30 tonnes, and the world price (Pw) is €2/tonne. A tariff is introduced which raises the domestic price (Pd) to €3/tonne (see Figure A4.1).

The elasticity of supply with respect to price can be defined as the ratio of the proportional change in the quantity supplied to the proportional change in price that brought it about. In symbols we have:

---

[24]As a tip, calculate the total welfare effects using both approaches to ensure that they coincide. The country is a small nation, and for simplicity the demand and supply functions are assumed to be linear. It is also assumed that there are no stocks of the product or externalities. The approach used is partial equilibrium.

[25]The exercises presented here are a slightly different version of those developed by Prof. Secondo Tarditi in 1992 in an unpublished manuscript 'Esercitazioni' at the Faculty of Economics 'Richard Goodwin' of the University of Siena.

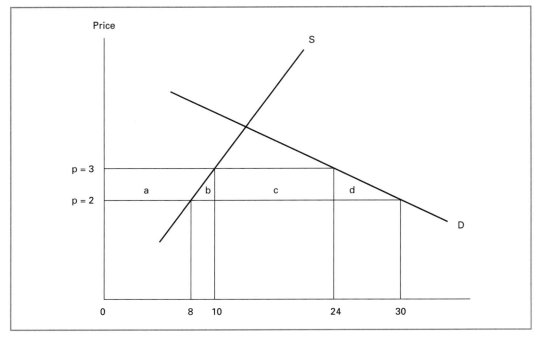

FIGURE A4.1 A tariff in a small nation: a numerical example

$$Es = \frac{\frac{\Delta Qs}{Qs}}{\frac{\Delta P}{P}}$$

Which can be rewritten as:

$$\frac{\Delta Qs}{Qs} = Es \frac{\Delta P}{P}$$

Assuming an elasticity of supply of 0.5 we can now calculate the new quantity supplied (Qs) after introduction of the tariff.

$$\Delta Qs = Qs \, Es \frac{(\Delta P)}{P} = 8 \frac{(0.5 \times 1)}{2} = 2$$

$$Q's = 10$$

In the same way the new quantity demanded (Q'd) can be calculated. The elasticity of demand with respect to price can be defined as the ratio of the proportional change in the quantity demanded to the proportional change in price that brought it about. In symbols we have:

$$Ed = \frac{\frac{\Delta Qd}{Qd}}{\frac{\Delta P}{P}}$$

Which can be rewritten as:

$$\frac{\Delta Qd}{Qd} = Ed \frac{\Delta P}{P}$$

Assuming a price elasticity of demand of –0.4 (in general the price elasticity of demand is negative since in most cases an increase in price provokes a reduction in the quantity demanded).

$$\Delta Q = Qd \, (Ed \, \tfrac{\Delta P}{P}) \quad \Delta Q = 30 \, \frac{(-0.4 \times 1)}{2} = -6$$

$$Q'd = 30 - 6 = 24$$

Before introduction of the tariff, producer revenue is:

$$Q's(Pw) = 8 \times 2 = 16$$

With the tariff it becomes:

$$Q's(Pd) = 10 \times 3 = 30$$

Before the introduction of the tariff, consumer expenditure is:

$$Qd(Pw) = 30 \times 2 = 60$$

After the introduction of the tariff it becomes:

$$Q'd \, (Pd) = 24 \times 3 = 72$$

Before the introduction of the tariff, the trade balance is:

$$(Qs - Qd)Pw = (8 - 30) \, 2 = -44$$

With the tariff it becomes:

$$(Q's - Q'd) \, Pw = (10 - 24)2 = -28$$

n.b. The world price is used to calculate the trade balance, but the domestic price is used to calculate producer revenue and consumer expenditure.

The loss in consumer surplus is given by:

$$-0.5 \, (Pd - Pw) \, (Qd + Q'd) = -27$$

The increase in producer surplus is given by:

$$0.5 \, (Pd - Pw) \, (Qs + Q's) = 9$$

The impact on the government budget (or the income of taxpayers) is:

$$(Pd - Pw)(Q'd - Q's) = 14$$

The total effect of introducing the tariff on welfare is given by:
loss in consumer surplus, plus the increase in producer surplus and the increase in government revenue:

$$-27 + 9 + 14 = -4$$

Alternatively, the effect of introducing the tariff on total welfare can be calculated using the net welfare effects:
triangle d is the net loss of welfare on the consumer side:

$$= -0.5 \, (Pd - Pw) \, (Qd - Q'd)$$

$$= -0.5 \, (3 - 2) \, (30 - 24)$$

$$= -3$$

Triangle b is the net loss of welfare on the production side (reflecting the worsening in the allocation of resources):

$$= -0.5 \ (Pd - Pw) \ (Q's - Qs)$$

$$= -0.5 \ (3 - 2) \ (10 - 8)$$

$$= -1$$

The total effect on welfare is the sum of the two net effects −4

Clearly the result must be the same as the total welfare effect calculated using the alternative method above.

Appendix 2

A simple numerical example of the effects of introducing a tariff in a large nation (see Figure A4.2)

Before the tariff is introduced it is assumed that:

$Pw = 40$ euro/t

$Qd = 1400t$

$Qs = 800t$

$Ed = -0.5$

$Es = 0.6$

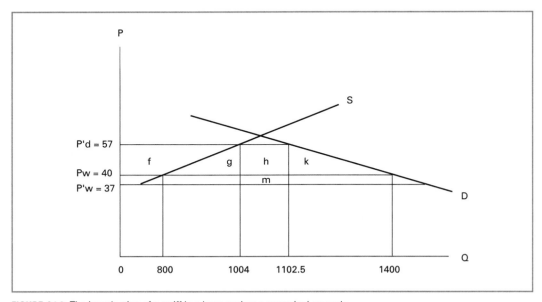

FIGURE A4.2 The introduction of a tariff in a large nation: a numerical example

Assume that a tariff of €20/t is then introduced causing the world price to fall to 37. The new domestic price will be 57.

Recalling the formula for the elasticity of supply with respect to price, it is possible to calculate the new quantity supplied (Q's) after introduction of the tariff:

$$Es = \frac{\frac{\Delta Qs}{Qs}}{\frac{\Delta P}{P}}$$

Which can be rewritten as:

$$\frac{\Delta Qs}{Qs} = Es\, \frac{\Delta P}{P}$$

$$\Delta Qs = \frac{Qs\, Es\, (\Delta P)}{P} = \frac{800\ (0.6(17))}{40} = 204$$

$$Q's = 800 + 204 = 1004$$

Similarly, the formula for elasticity of demand can be used to calculate the new quantity demanded (Q'd):

$$Ed = \frac{\frac{\Delta Qd}{Qd}}{\frac{\Delta P}{P}}$$

Which can be rewritten as:

$$\frac{\Delta Qd}{Qd} = Ed\, \frac{\Delta P}{P}$$

$$\Delta Q = Qd\ (Ed\, \frac{\Delta P}{P}) \quad \Delta Q = 1400\ (-0.5\ (\frac{17}{40})) = -297.5$$

$$Q'd = 1400 - 297.5 = 1102.5$$

Foreign trade without the tariff (i.e. net imports) is given by:

$$Qs - Qd = 800 - 1400 = -600\ t$$

With the tariff it becomes:

$$Q's - Q'd = 1004 - 1102.5 = -98.5$$

Before introduction of the tariff producer revenue is:

$$Qs(Pw) = 800 \times 40 = 32\ 000$$

With the tariff it becomes:

$$Q's(Pd) = 1004 \times 57 = 57\ 228$$

Before the introduction of the tariff consumer expenditure is:

$$Qd(Pw) = 1400 \times 40 = 56\ 000$$

After the introduction of the tariff it becomes:

$$Q'd\ (Pd) = 62\ 842.5$$

Before the introduction of the tariff the trade balance is:

$(Qs - Qd)Pw = -24\,000$

With the tariff it becomes:

$(Q's - Q'd)\, P'w = -36\,445$

n.b. The world price is used to calculate the trade balance, but the domestic price is used to calculate producer revenue and consumer expenditure.

The loss in consumer surplus is given by:

$-0.5\,(Pd - Pw)\,(Qd + Q'd) = -21\,271.25$

The increase in producer surplus is given by:

$0.5\,(Pd - Pw)\,(Qs + Q's) = 15\,334$

The impact on the government budget (or the income of taxpayers) is:

$(Pd - P'w)(Q'd - Q's) = 1970$

The total effect of introducing the tariff on welfare is given by:
loss in consumer surplus, plus the increase in producer surplus and the increase in government revenue:

$-21\,271.25 + 15\,334 + 1970 = -3967.25$

Alternatively, the effect of introducing the tariff on total welfare can be calculated using the net welfare effects:
triangle k is the net loss of welfare on the consumer side:

$= -0.5\,(Pd - Pw)\,(Qd - Q'd)$

$= -0.5\,(57 - 40)\,(1400 - 1102.5)$

$= -2528.75$

Triangle g is the net loss of welfare on the production side (reflecting the worsening in the allocation of resources):

$= -0.5\,(Pd - Pw)\,(Q's - Qs)$

$= -0.5\,(57 - 40)\,(1004 - 800)$

$= -1734$

Rectangle m represents the transfers from producers in the rest of the world to consumers in that country (a reduction in world prices is a welfare gain for an importing country).

$(Pw - P'w)\,(Q'd - Q's) = 295.5$

The total effect on welfare is the sum of the three net effects:

$-2528.75 - 1734 + 295.5 = -3967.25$

Clearly the result must be the same as the total welfare effect calculated using the alternative method above.

References

Baldwin, R. and Wyplosz, C. (2006) *The Economics of European Integration*, 2nd edn, McGraw-Hill Education, Maidenhead, UK.

Downs, A. (1957) *An Economic Theory of Democracy*, Harper & Row, New York.

European Commission (2008) 'Report on United States barriers to trade and investment', www.ec.europa.eu

Gandolfo, G. (1994) *Corso di economia internazionale. Volume primo: La teoria pura del commercio internazionale*, 2nd edn, UTET Libreria, Torino.

Healey, N.M. (1995) 'From the Treaty of Rome to Maastricht: The theory and practice of European integration', in Healey, N.M. (ed.) *The Economics of the New Europe*, Routledge, London and New York.

Krugman, P. and Obstfeld, M. (1997) *International Economics. Theory and Policy*, Addison Wesley Longman Inc., Reading, MA.

Meade, J.E. (1962) *The Theory of International Economic Policy, Vol. 2: Trade and Welfare*, Oxford University Press, Oxford.

Olson, M. jr. (1965) *The Logic of Collective Action: Public Goods and the Theory of Groups*, Harvard University Press, Cambridge, MA.

Salvatore, D. (2007) *International Economics*, 9th edn, John Wiley & Sons, New York.

Senior Nello, S.M. (1991) *The New Europe: Changing Economic Relations between East and West*, Harvester Wheatsheaf, Hemel Hempstead, UK.

Tarditi, S. (1992) 'Esercitazioni', unpublished manuscript, Facoltà di Economia 'Richard Goodwin', University of Siena.

Useful websites

Statements of the EU position and studies of various trade issues are provided by the European Commission:

www.ec.europa.eu

International trade statistics are available from Eurostat (www.eurostat.org) the Organization for Economic Co-operation and Development (www.oecd.org) and the United Nations (www.un.org).

Studies of US positions on trade and international monetary issues include: the US Department of Commerce, International Trade Administration (www.ita.doc.gov); the US Trade Representative (www.ustr.gov) and the US International Trade Commission (www.usitc.gov). The Institute for International Economics in the USA also produces numerous studies of international economic issues (www.iie.com).

Oxfam generally presents a critical position on trade issues, taking the side of developing countries:

www.oxfam.org.uk

The World Bank generally concentrates on development issues but also publishes reports on the state of the world economy and trade:

www.worldbank.org

The World Trade Organization provides statistics, analysis of trade issues and information about the state of negotiations:

www.wto.org

The Economics of Integration

Introduction

The early economic analysis of integration relies heavily on what is known as 'customs union theory'. One of the questions to arise was why preferential arrangements should be preferred to unilateral trade liberalization. Traditionally, 'customs union theory' attempted to address this question and assess the effects of customs unions using instruments based on the concepts of welfare economics. More recent analysis has taken into account the dynamic effects of integration and phenomena such as economies of scale, increased competition and better opportunities for more rapid technology transfer. According to empirical studies, these dynamic effects of integration seem far more important than the static welfare effects.

The costs and benefits of integration

The early literature on integration used customs union theory to analyse the so-called **static effects** of integration on welfare, making use of the distinction made by Viner (1953) between trade creation and trade diversion.[1] **Trade creation** arises when domestic production is replaced by cheaper imports from a partner country. **Trade diversion** involves low-cost imports from suppliers in third countries being replaced by more expensive imports from a partner country. It was generally assumed that integration would lead to a welfare gain because the positive effect of trade creation would exceed the possible negative effects of trade diversion.[2]

Viner considered the costs and benefits of forming a customs union only from the point of view of production, and assumed that products were always consumed in the same proportion. Lipsey (1957) pointed out that the customs union is also likely to have an effect on the consumption side. It is also ambiguous as to whether the terms 'trade creation' and 'trade diversion' refer to trade flows or welfare effects, but Pelkmans and Gremmen (1983) have illustrated that changes in trade flows can be a misleading indicator of welfare changes.

Trade creation

The 'static' effect of a customs union can be illustrated with the help of a diagram similar to that of Figure 4.4 in Chapter 4. Figure 5.1 shows the domestic demand (Dx) and supply (Sx) curves for product X of a country that imports that product, say Belgium. Assume that the free trade price of a commodity is Px = €1 in country 1 (say Germany), and Pw = €2 in country 2 (or the rest of the world). For simplicity Belgium is assumed to be a 'small nation' in the sense that its economy is too small to affect the prices in Germany or the rest of the world. Assume initially that Belgium imposes a non-discriminatory *ad valorem* tariff of 100 per cent on imports from all sources. S1 represents the perfectly elastic supply curve of Germany with free trade, and S1 + T is the tariff-inclusive German supply curve. Belgium will import commodity X from Germany at a price of Pd = €2, reflecting the effect of the tariff. It will not import from the rest of the world, since after the tariff the price in Belgium would be €4.

If Belgium now forms a customs union with country 1 (Germany), the tariffs will be removed on German imports but not on those from the rest of the world. Belgium can now import at Px = €1 from Germany, and at this price Belgium will produce 10 million units of X, consume 65 million units, and import 55 million units.

The increase in consumer surplus as a result of creation of the customs union is area a + b + c + d. The loss in producer surplus is indicated by area a. Belgium loses its tariff revenue on imports from Germany (rectangle c). The net positive impact on welfare as a result of the customs union is therefore comprised of triangles b and d. Triangle b represents the welfare gain on the production side as a result of improved allocation of resources with the shift in the production of 10 million X from less efficient domestic producers to lower cost producers in the partner country Germany. Triangle d represents the welfare gain on the consumption side from creation of the customs union. With the lower prices in the customs union, Belgian consumption

---

[1] In the subsequent literature there was further refinement of the different effects of integration. For example, external trade creation was said to arise when the faster growth of the integration unit led to higher imports from the rest of the world. Trade suppression may arise when creation of the customs union leads to production in one of the partners stopping and production shifting to the other partner, which had previously imported from the rest of the world.

[2] The rules of the GATT/WTO were aimed at ensuring that this is the case (see Chapter 18).

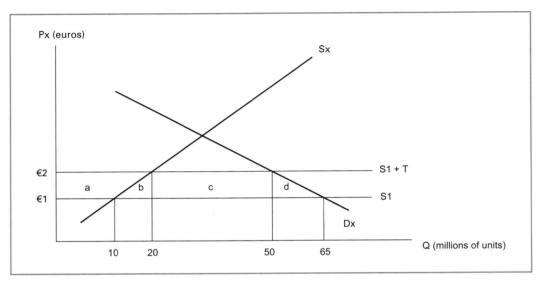

FIGURE 5.1 Trade creation (million units of product X)

will increase by 15 million units. Together, triangles b and d illustrate the net increase in welfare as a result of establishing the customs union.

A strict application of Viner's term 'trade creation' would refer simply to the production side and the effect of replacement of the more expensive domestic production of 10 million X by imports from the partner country, Germany. Many economists use the term 'trade creation' to cover the total net increases in welfare on both the production and the consumption sides, i.e. triangles b and d in the diagram. It is probably more precise to refer to triangle b as the trade-creation effect, and triangle d as the consumption effect of forming a customs union.

Trade diversion

Figure 5.2 illustrates the case of trade diversion.[3] Again Dx and Sx are domestic demand and supply of commodity X in the country in question (Belgium). S2 and S3 are the free trade, perfectly elastic supply curves of commodity X in country 2 (say the USA) and country 3 (say France) respectively. With a 100 per cent non-discriminatory tariff, the home country (Belgium) will import from country 2 (the USA) at a price of €2. At this price Belgium will produce 35 million units and consume 60 million, so 25 million units are imported from country 2 (the USA). There will be no imports from France as the price inclusive of tariff is €3.

Assume that Belgium now forms a customs union with country 3 (France) but not with country 2 (the USA). As a result tariffs are removed on imports from France, but the 100 per cent tariff remains on imports from the USA. After formation of the customs union Belgium will import from France at price €1.50. At this new price Belgium will produce 30 million units, and consume 70 million, importing 40 million units from country 3 (France).

With the customs union the imports of Belgium have been diverted from more efficient producers in country 2 (the USA) to less efficient producers in country 3 (France), so there is

---

[3] This type of analysis was first used by Kindleberger (1973).

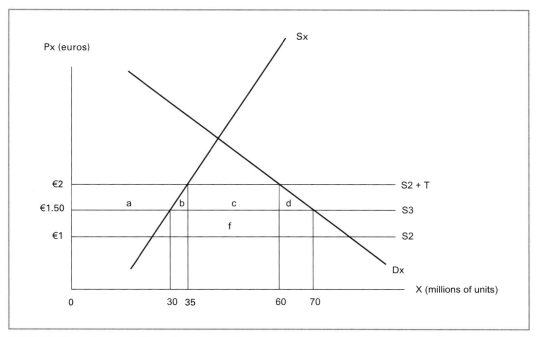

FIGURE 5.2 Trade diversion (million units of product X)

a worsening in the allocation of resources. Five million units of X (35 − 30 million) are now imported from the partner country, France, rather than being produced at home in Belgium, while 25 million units (60 − 35 million) that were previously imported from the USA are now imported from France.

Belgium will no longer receive tariff revenue. The welfare loss from trade diversion is indicated by the area of rectangle f. The 25 million units that were previously imported from more efficient country 2 (the USA) whose free trade price is €1 per unit are now imported from country 3 (France) with a free trade price of €1.50. In this case the welfare loss will be €12.5 million.

Triangles b and d reflect the welfare gain from the customs union as more expensive production in Belgium is now replaced with cheaper imports from France. The welfare gain on the production side due to trade creation (triangle b) is equal to €1.25 million, while that on the consumption side (triangle d) is €2.5 million.

The total impact on welfare as a result of formation of the customs union is given by the sum of the areas of the two triangles (b and d), representing a welfare gain due to the trade creation and consumption effects, minus the area of the rectangle (f) representing welfare loss due to trade diversion. In this case the total effect on welfare is equal to −8.75 million euros (2.5 million +1.25 million −12.5 million), so creation of the customs union causes a net welfare loss.

If the sum of the areas of the two triangles representing welfare gain is greater than the area of the rectangle representing the welfare loss due to trade diversion, formation of the customs union will cause a net welfare gain for the home country. The idea that a customs union is either 'trade creating or 'trade distorting' is misleading; Figure 5.2 illustrates that a customs union may give rise to both effects.

The effect of a customs union on the partner country

The analysis can be extended to consider the effect of forming a customs union on the partner country. Figure 5.3a illustrates the demand and supply curves for product X in the partner country, while Figure 5.3b illustrates the demand and supply curves for the home country. The two countries are assumed to be small and have increasing production costs. The costs of production are assumed to be higher in the home country, and for simplicity it is assumed that at the initial level of protection the partner country is just self-sufficient at the perfectly elastic world price Pw.[4] The partner country therefore does not need to protect its industry from world competition. Before creation of the customs union, the home country applies a tariff that raises its domestic price to Ph. With the creation of the customs union trade is liberalized between the home and partner country, and they introduce a common external tariff in trade with the rest of the world. The price including the common external tariff is indicated by Pcu in Figure 5.3.

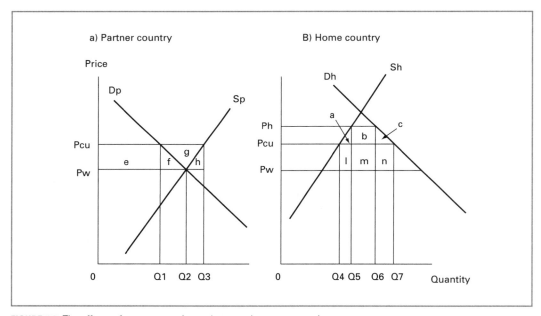

FIGURE 5.3 The effects of a customs union on home and partner countries

In the home country the reduction in the apparent price of imports will lead to a welfare gain of a on the production side due to trade creation, a welfare gain on the consumption side of c, and a welfare loss of m due to the diversion of imports from the rest of the world.

In the partner country prices will rise because of increased protection. Equilibrium occurs in the customs union when the combined supply of the two countries equals their combined demand (and Q1Q3 = Q4Q7). The increase in price from Pw to Pcu in the partner country causes an increase in producer surplus of e + f + g and a reduction in consumer surplus of e + f. The partner country is able to increase its exports to the home country to Q1Q3 and obtain a net welfare gain of area g.

In the example the net welfare benefit of the partner country rises. This is sometimes called

---

[4] The simplifying assumption of initial self-sufficiency of the partner country is taken from Robson (1984).

'trade creation'. However, more accurately this is an income transfer from the home country to the partner country. The home could have imported quantity Q4Q7 from the rest of the world, rather than from the partner country at Pcu. In this way the home country would have received revenue of l + m + n from the common external tariff. Instead, this passed to the partner country with areas f + g representing profit, while area h is the additional cost of production compared with the lower world price Pw.

In this example there is a net welfare loss for the home country (rectangle m is greater than the sum of triangles a and c) and a net welfare gain for the partner country of triangle g. There will be a net welfare loss for the rest of the world whose exports are replaced by exports from the partner country.

The difference between non-discriminatory tariffs and preferential arrangements

The analysis based on import demand and supply curves shown in Chapter 4 is also useful to illustrate the difference between non-discriminatory tariffs and preferential arrangements.[5] As explained in Chapter 17, non-discriminatory tariffs could be, for example, those extended to all WTO members on the basis of the most-favoured-nation clause (MFN).

Figure 5.4 illustrates the effect of the home country introducing an MFN tariff on the partner country and the rest of the world. XSrow indicates the export supply of the rest of the world, and XSp shows the export supply of the partner country. Prior to introducing the tariff, at the free trade world price Pft the home country will import a total of M of product X of which Xp comes from the partner country and Xr comes from the rest of the world. MS shows the import supply

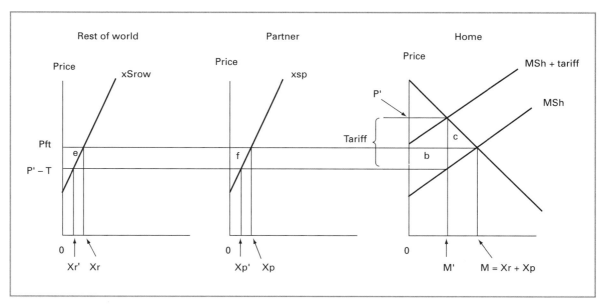

FIGURE 5.4 The effect of a non-discriminatory tariff on the partner country and the rest of the world
Source: Baldwin and Wyplosz (2006).

---

[5] The analysis in this section follows Baldwin and Wyplosz (2006).

of the home country in a situation of free trade. With the tariff the import supply curve in the home country becomes MSh + tariff, and the domestic price in the home country rises to P'. The border price (i.e. the price received by exporters) falls to P' – T in both the partner country and the rest of the world. As a result home imports fall to M', of which Xp' comes from the partner country and Xr' from the rest of the world. The home country receives a welfare gain of b and a welfare loss of c, while the partner receives a welfare loss of f and the rest of the world suffers a welfare loss of e (see Chapter 4 for an explanation of these effects).

A customs union involves all members eliminating trade barriers with their partners and introducing a common external tariff towards the rest of the world. In the interests of simplification, before analysing the effect of a customs union on the partner country, it is useful to consider the effect of just one country introducing a unilateral preferential trade arrangement.

In Figure 5.5 MSmfn shows the supply of imports of product X in the home country with a non-discriminatory (or MFN) tariff, and MSh shows the import supply in a situation of free trade. MSpta shows the import supply in the home country with a preferential trade arrangement. As the trade liberalization is preferential, MSpta is assumed to be lower than MSmfn. In this simple model with two exporters, a partner and the rest of the world, preferential trade liberalization applies only to the partner, and MSpta can be assumed to lie halfway between MSh and MSmfn. However, the rest of the world cannot supply the home market at a price less than Pa, which represents their zero export supply price (p') plus the tariff T. Up to Pa only firms from the partner country will supply imports. The import supply curve MSpta with a preferential trade arrangement therefore takes the form shown in Figure 5.5.

With a non-discriminatory tariff, the import supply curve MSmfn and the import demand curve in the home country intersect at price P'. The border price received by exporters in both the rest of the world and the future partner country is P' – T.

With the preferential trade arrangement the new domestic price becomes P'', and this is also the border price in the partner country joining the preferential arrangement. The border price

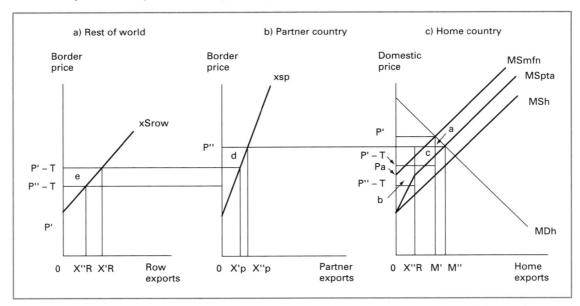

FIGURE 5.5 The impact of introducing a preferential trade arrangement on the home country, the partner and the rest of the world
Source: Baldwin and Wyplosz (2006).

in the partner country therefore rises from P' – T to P'' as a result of creating the preferential trade arrangement. In contrast, following the introduction of the preferential trade arrangement, the border price in the rest of the world falls from P' – T to P'' – T. The exports from the partner country rise from X'p to X''p, while those of the rest of the world fall from X'R to X''R.

The welfare effects of introducing the preferential trade arrangement can also be shown in the diagram. The partner country gains area d because it can sell a larger quantity at a higher price. The rest of the world has a welfare loss of e since it sells a smaller quantity at a lower price.

Following the introduction of the preferential trade arrangement home imports increase from M' to M'', with X''r of the latter coming from the rest of the world and M'' – X''r coming from the partner country. The increase in total imports from M' to M'' leads to a welfare gain due to the increased volume of imports equal to area a and the lower price of imports from the rest of the world leads to a welfare gain equal to rectangle b (the price difference (P' – T) – (P'' – T) times the imports from the rest of the world X''r). The higher price of imports from the partner implies a welfare loss equal to the area of the rectangle c or the price difference (P'') – (P' – T) multiplied by the quantity of imports (M' – X''r). The effect of the price difference does not apply on the extra amount of imports M'' – M' as initially the home country did not import this quantity. The total net welfare effect on the home country as a result of formation of the preferential trade agreement is: a + b – c.

In the case of a customs union, the partner country will also eliminate tariffs on its imports from the home country but not on those from the rest of the world. For simplicity, to illustrate the case of a customs union it can be assumed that the home country imports good X from the partner country and exports good Y to the partner country. The rest of the world exports product X to the home country, and product Y to the partner country. The home, the partner and the rest

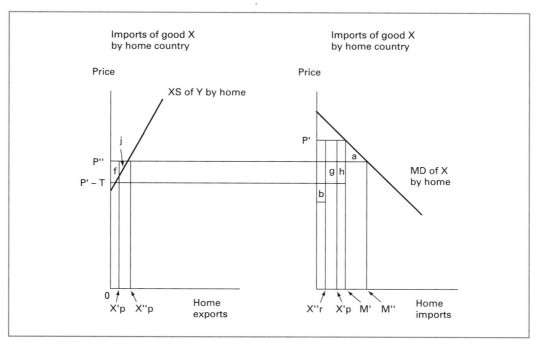

FIGURE 5.6 The welfare effects of forming a customs union on the home country
Source: Baldwin and Wyplosz (2006).

of the world are also assumed symmetric in all aspects, including the tariffs initially applied on imports.

Figure 5.5 can also be used to analyse the effect of the partner eliminating the barrier on imports of Y from the home country. This simply requires inverting the partner and home countries as parts (b) and (c) of Figure 5.5 (which is possible due to the symmetry assumption). The partner country then becomes the importing country (of Y), and the home country is an exporter (of Y).

The total welfare effects of forming a customs union for the home country are shown in Figure 5.6. To explain the welfare effects more precisely, area c of Figure 5.5 is divided into areas g and h, and area d is broken down into f and j. On the import market for product X the home country gains areas a and b and loses areas g and h (g + h are equal to area c in Figure 5.5), while on its export market for product Y it gains areas f and j (area d in Figure 5.5). The welfare loss of areas h and g to the home country is the result of paying the higher price after the tariff cut on imports from the partner. Part of this loss, area h simply represents a transfer to the partner country who receives higher prices for its exports. Area h is equal to area f. The home country's loss of area h on its imports of product X will be offset by a gain of area f for the partner country's exports of X. Similarly for product Y (because of the assumption of symmetry) the loss of area h on the partner country's imports of Y will be equal to the home country's gain of f on its exports of Y.

In contrast, area g represents trade diversion because of switching from cheaper exports from the rest of the world to exports from the higher-cost partner country. The size of this welfare loss is given by the quantity of supply switching X'p – X"r multiplied by the price difference P" – (P' – T). Given that h = f, the total net welfare effect on the home country from formation of the customs union is a + b+ j – g.

The conditions under which a customs union is likely to increase welfare

From the analysis here it emerges that the net effect of forming a customs union on the welfare of the home country may be positive, negative or zero. This is known as 'Viner's ambiguity'. *Ex ante* general predictions of the welfare effects of introducing customs unions cannot be given as they will depend on the case in question. The analysis of the introduction of a customs union is a case of second best in which a shift from one sub-optimal situation to another does not permit generalizations about the overall effect on welfare.

However, even from this simplified analysis, certain principles about the effect of introducing a customs union on welfare can be deduced and, in general, the benefits are likely to be higher:

- The higher the original level of the tariff before forming the customs union;[6]
- The lower the common external tariff towards the rest of the world;[7]
- The higher the number of countries joining a customs union, and the greater their size. Under these circumstances there is more likelihood of low cost producers within the customs union;

---

[6] This can be seen by using Figure 5.2 or 5.5 to consider the effect of a higher initial tariff.

[7] To verify, consider the effect of applying a lower common external tariff in Figure 5.3 or 5.5.

- The smaller the differences in costs of production between the members of the customs union and third countries;[8]
- The closer the countries are geographically, as transport costs will be lower;
- The more competitive (producing the same goods) rather than complementary (producing a different range of goods) the economies of the member states are. In this way there will be more opportunities for specialization;
- The greater the trade flows and economic relations between the countries before forming the customs union.

Terms of trade effects

The traditional static analysis assesses the overall impact of a customs union by comparing the situation before and after creation of the customs union. However, Cooper and Massell (1965) challenged this approach, arguing that the comparison should be made between discriminatory reduction of tariffs, as in the case of a customs union, and a non-discriminatory elimination of tariffs.[9] They argue that a non-discriminatory removal of tariffs would not involve trade diversion and would be superior. The question then becomes: why do countries create customs unions (or preferential trade liberalization) rather than use non-discriminatory trade arrangements?

One reason given is the possible terms-of-trade loss from unilateral trade liberalization, and the possible terms-of-trade gain that may arise for the customs union as a whole as result of discrimination against the rest of the world.[10] The individual member states may be too small to affect their external terms of trade individually, but together they are able to affect the terms of trade with third countries. Given the weight of the EU in world trade, this argument could be quite important. However, some countries in the rest of the world are also large nations (such as the USA or Japan) so, as indicated in Chapter 4 in the context of the optimal tariff argument, the customs union could risk retaliatory measures from other countries.

The dynamic effects of integration

Over time attempts to assess the effects of integration and explain why countries opt for preferential trade arrangements rather than multilateral liberalization, has entailed a shift in emphasis towards the so-called dynamic effects of integration. These have evolved in parallel with the development of new trade theories described in Chapter 4. Among the most comprehensive studies of these dynamic effects were those carried out in the context of the Single Market Programme (see Chapter 6). Studies such as the Cecchini Report and Emerson et al. (1989) argued that the benefits from these dynamic effects could be as much as five or six times as large as the static effects of integration. As indicated below, the extent to which the various dynamic effects of integration have actually come to fruition in the EU is taken up in later chapters. The dynamic effects of integration include:

---

[8] Again Figures 5.2 or 5.3 can be used to see this effect.

[9] The approach used in Figures 5.5 and 5.6 provides a toolkit for carrying out this type of comparison.

[10]See the discussion of Figure 4.7 for an explanation of the terms of trade effect.

- **increased competition**

  By bringing down the barriers integration should lead to reductions in costs and prices and encourage the restructuring of industry (see Figure 6.1 in Chapter 6).

- **economies of scale**

  With integration, firms operate in a larger market and have more opportunities for exploiting economies of scale (see Chapter 4). The issue then becomes whether there is more scope for exploiting economies of scale at the EU rather than the national or international level (see Chapter 6).

- **technology and knowledge transfers**

  It is frequently argued that economic integration also contributes to technological progress. This is increasingly a global rather than a regional phenomenon though; as explained in Chapter 15, location counts.

- **political economy arguments**

  Sectoral interests may explain why a country prefers a regional trade bloc to multilateralism (see below), and it may be easier to deal with the adverse effects of lobbying in a larger integration unit.

- **increased bargaining power at an international level**

  By presenting a more united front, a regional bloc such as the EU would be able to carry more weight vis-à-vis its main trading partners.

- **more rapid growth**

  The link between growth and integration is taken up in more detail in the next section.

Growth and integration

According to orthodox neo-classical growth theory (based on the pioneering work of the Nobel laureate, Solow, 1956), the key determinant of growth is capital accumulation. As more capital is added to a fixed amount of labour, output per worker increases, but by a progressively smaller amount for each additional unit of capital due to diminishing returns. The basic assumption of the Solow model is that since people save and invest a certain percentage of their income each year, the inflow of investment is a fixed fraction of output per worker. If y is output per worker, the curve sy in Figure 5.7 shows investment per worker (which is equal to savings per worker). The shape of the sy curve reflects diminishing returns.

The ratio of capital to labour in an economy will depend on investment, but also on depreciation, since old capital has to be replaced and repaired. A constant fraction of stock capital n is assumed to depreciate each year. The straight line n(k/l) shows the depreciation per worker that increases in proportion with the amount of capital per worker. At E investment is sufficient to keep capital per person constant. At E the inflow of investment just equals depreciation. At this point the capital/ labour ratio reaches its equilibrium k/l*, or steady state. Below E investment exceeds depreciation and capital per worker will rise. Above E depreciation exceeds investment so capital per worker will fall. Accumulation of capital cannot be an ongoing source of long-run growth.

In order to explain ongoing rates of growth other elements have to be introduced into the Solow model. If, for instance, technological progress is introduced, this will lead to increased output per worker, thus raising investment and the capital/labour ratio. Technological progress

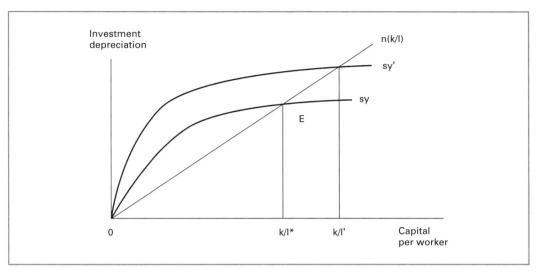

FIGURE 5.7 The Solow growth model

causes the sy curve to rotate upwards each year. Figure 5.7 shows the effect of one such rotation in which the sy curve is translated to sy', and the new capital/labour ratio becomes k/l'.

Endogenous growth theory as developed by Romer (1986) provides other explanations of long-term growth. Continual growth of output per person in the long run requires ceaseless accumulation of factors of production. In order to endogenize growth, it is necessary to endogenize investment. The decision to accumulate factors of production will depend on the costs and benefits of investment. Continual accumulation therefore requires that the return on investment does not fall as capital stock rises.

Various accounts of how this may occur have been advanced. Much of the literature relies on the concept of productivity-boosting knowledge capital. For example, a firm may invest in knowledge to increase its advantage *vis-à-vis* other firms. The additional profits from exploiting this knowledge represent the return on investment in knowledge capital for the firm. However, the investment will have a spill-over effect in increasing the stock of knowledge in the economy. It is assumed that this spill-over will increase the productivity of resources used in innovating.

The model developed by Lucas (1988) focuses on the role played by human capital in contributing to growth.[11] Individuals will invest in skills because they expect that there will be adequate capital for their higher skills to be reflected in higher salaries. Firms invest in capital as they anticipate that there will be sufficient skilled workers for the firm to earn a profit. There is a positive spill-over as those investing in human capital do not consider the output-boosting effect that their investment will have.

The elimination of barriers implied by integration may facilitate international flows of knowledge. This could reduce the cost of innovation, thereby increasing the private return on research and development (R&D) and encouraging more resources to be drawn into innovation. At the same time, the creation of a larger market could increase the profitability of innovation.

According to this approach, integration could also have a positive effect on financial markets, thereby leading to higher levels of investment and long-term growth. In particular, greater com-

---

[11]This could be regarded as a special case of the knowledge capital argument.

petition might encourage more efficiency in financial markets, enabling a reduction in the spread between the return earned by savers and the costs of funds to investors (Baldwin, 1994).

A lesson from approaches based on the new growth theory is that public intervention can contribute to growth by encouraging R&D and rendering the appropriation of new technology easier. The message for the EU is therefore that in order to foster growth, measures to promote R&D, improvements in human capital and more efficient financial markets are necessary.

As Deardorff and Stern (2002) maintain, empirical estimates of the impact of European integration on growth run into difficulties since it is difficult to isolate integration from other variables influencing growth. None the less Baldwin (1989) and Italianer (1994) found substantial growth effects from the Single Market Programme (see Chapter 6).

Political economy arguments to explain why countries may prefer regional trade blocs to multilateral liberalization

Johnson (1965) introduces political economy arguments to maintain that countries with a strong preference for industrial production that are (or feel themselves to be) at a comparative disadvantage *vis-à-vis* the rest of the world may favour the creation of a customs union or preferential trade arrangements.[12] According to this view, governments use tariffs to achieve certain non-economic objectives. Countries are assumed to have a preference for industrial production, so consumers are prepared to expand industrial production beyond what would occur in a free trade scenario. Governments are assumed to respond rationally to the demands of the electorate and will use protection to expand industrial production. Tariffs are the usual instrument used, since most types of export subsidy are ruled out by the WTO, and domestic political considerations lead to a preference for tariffs rather than production subsidies because of the burden posed by the latter on domestic taxpayers.

El-Agraa (2007) modifies Johnson's model by considering industrial production not as a single aggregate but as a variety of products for which countries have varying degrees of comparative advantage. In this way countries can be both exporters and importers of industrial products.

Considering a simplified case with only two countries, one will be a net exporter and the other a net importer of any industrial product. For each country the prospective gain from tariff reduction lies in the expansion of industrial production. With non-discriminatory trade liberalization the reduction of the home country's tariff is considered a source of loss that must be compensated by tariff reductions on the part of the other country.

With a customs union, trade creation is not considered as a means of replacing higher cost production with cheaper imports but is regarded as the price to be paid for expanding export markets. Trade diversion offers a chance for increasing production within the customs union by replacing imports from the rest of the world with imports from the partner. As a result trade diversion is preferable to trade creation for the home country since no sacrifice of domestic production is necessary. Stress is also placed on the gains to domestic industry from economies of scale, increased competition and the growth potential of a larger market area as a result of establishing the customs union. Preferential trade liberalization gives rise to chances for expanding industrial production to an extent not possible through non-discriminatory liberalization.

The choice for a country then becomes whether to form or join a customs union. According to Johnson's model as refined by the El-Agraa assumption, a country will join a customs union only if it considers that its comparative advantage in some forms of industrial production is

---

[12]The argument is easily extended to countries having a preference for agricultural production.

strong enough for its industrial production to increase (or for any loss in industrial production to be compensated by greater efficiency). Other member states will only allow the country to join if they think that there is no threat of the new member increasing its industrial production at the expense of their own. As a result, customs unions are likely to be negotiated between countries with a similar preference for industrial production and a similar degree of comparative advantage in industrial production (or, in other words, a similar level of economic development).

As Johnson argues, this approach helps to explain why the Treaty of Rome attempted to ensure that each of the member states maintained a 'fair share of production', even if this required additional mechanisms such as the measures to promote growth in Southern Italy.

Grossman and Helpman (1995) developed the political economy argument, explaining policy formation as the outcome of lobbying and competition among industries. In this framework free trade negotiations become a process of providing a sufficient balance between the interest groups of a country.

Baldwin (2006) makes use of new trade theories to introduce also the 'juggernaut' approach to trade liberalization. New trade theories allow for differences in firm size and efficiency to explain why the largest and most efficient firms export, while small and medium firms tend to sell domestically. Large firms want access to foreign markets to expand exports, but the price to pay is a lowering of tariffs and expansion of imports. This will add to the competitive pressures on small and medium firms that sell locally. Some of the smaller firms may be forced out of the market, but larger firms can compensate increased competition at home with expanded foreign markets. Introducing political economy arguments, the larger exporting firms may be more effective at lobbying governments, also because they are less numerous, so have less costs of organizing interest group activities (and overcoming the problem of free-riding indicated by Olson, see Chapter 4).

Empirical research on the effects of integration

Many of the early empirical studies of the formation and successive enlargements of the EC were based on customs union theory. This type of approach generally involves an attempt to measure the effects of passing from free trade to a customs union. Over time customs union theory became somewhat anachronistic, as in later enlargements most countries joining the EU already had a free trade area or customs union with the Community. For instance, thanks to the Europe Agreements the new Central and East European member states had a free trade area for manufactures and passed to a single market (with some derogations) with enlargement. Turkey already has a customs union with the EU, though agricultural goods are largely excluded.

Early empirical research based on the customs union approach (i.e. attempting to measure trade creation and trade diversion) found the effects of integration surprisingly small. Though there are considerable variations in the results, in general the gains from creation of the Community were found to be in the order of 1–2 per cent of gross domestic product (GDP) (Harrop, 2000, p. 65). This was partly because trade was generally a rather small share of GDP, and most of the studies concentrated on tariff reductions, but tariffs were already relatively low. The reward seemed remarkably small for all the effort of creating the Community, so led to questioning of the approach, and the emergence of the view that integration probably also involved dynamic effects (see above).

The aim here is not to present a comprehensive overview of the research on integration effects, but an indication of some of the approaches used may be useful (see, for example, Baldwin and Venables, 1995, for a survey).

A first distinction can be made between **ex-ante** and *ex-post* analyses of the effects of integration. An *ex-ante* analysis attempts to estimate the future effects of setting up an integration bloc, or enlargement to new members. In this case information is available concerning the present, pre-integration situation, but predictions have to be made about the likely impact of beginning or extending the integration process.

Ex-post analyses of the effects of integration take place after the process has been in operation for some time. In this case data are available on what has occurred with integration, but the difficulty lies in attempting to assess what would have happened in its absence. In other words it is necessary to assess likely developments in economic variables such as trade, production and consumption if there had been no integration. This entails constructing an **anti-monde** or fictitious world in which the integration bloc is absent or the country in question remains outside it. The *anti-monde* is then compared with actual developments in order to assess the integration effect. As the approach is based on an unknowable *anti-monde* that cannot be tested against experience, ultimately the evaluation of estimates based on this type of approach is largely a matter of judgement about the plausibility of the simplifying assumptions made about the *anti-monde*.

Most of the early studies concentrated on the trade effects of integration, attempting to impute hypothetical trade flows from existing trade flows by various methods such as:

- extrapolating developments existing prior to the creation or extension of the integration process;
- comparing developments in the integration bloc with what was happening in third-party countries.

An early survey of empirical estimates of the trade effects of the EC using extrapolation is provided in Mayes (1978). The survey suggests that there was evidence for trade creation in the 1970s and 1980s, and though trade diversion was estimated to be much lower scale, it appeared to be substantial in the agricultural sector. Among the best-known studies of this type for the EEC are those by Truman (1969), Sellekaerts (1973) and Balassa (1967, 1974 and 1975). A more recent application of this type of approach was carried out by Bojnec and Ferto (2007) to assess the impact of the 2004 and 2007 enlargements on food and agricultural trade and found evidence of trade creation.

Balassa (1967, 1974) proposed a method that uses the *ex-post* income elasticity for imports, and assumes that this would have remained constant in the absence of integration. The *ex-post* income elasticity of demand is defined as the ratio of the average annual rate of change in imports to that of GDP, both expressed in constant prices. The method consists of comparing the elasticities for intra-EC trade and extra-EC trade for periods before and after integration. Under *ceteris paribus* conditions, a decline in the income elasticity of demand for extra-EC imports indicates trade diversion. Alternatively, according to Balassa, a rise in this elasticity for intra-EC imports indicates gross trade creation, while an increase in these elasticities from all sources indicates overall trade creation. Balassa compared the pre-integration period (1953–59) with two post-integration periods (1959–65 and 1965–70) and found evidence for overall trade creation, though there appeared to have been trade diversion for foodstuffs.

There are, however, certain drawbacks to the approach and, in particular, that of defining the *anti-monde* and assuming that all, and only, integration effects are picked up in changes in the income elasticity of demand for imports. Moreover the results of the approach depend on the choice of base period, and supply-side effects are ignored.

Kreinen (1972) carried out a comparison of EEC performance with that of third countries such as the USA, the UK and other industrial countries outside Europe. Clearly, the results depend heavily on the country chosen as a control group to 'normalize' trade shares. Kreinen's results suggested that trade creation was far more substantial than trade diversion.

In the more recent literature on empirical assessments of the effects of integration two approaches that figure prominently are gravity models and computable general equilibrium models (see Burfisher et al., 2004, for a review of this literature).

The **gravity model** approach involves attempting to predict the level of bilateral trade flows on the basis of variables such as gross national product (GNP), population, geographical distance, and preferential trading arrangements. Gravity models are often relatively successful in predicting trade flows between countries but have been criticized for lacking theoretical underpinnings. The estimated coefficients of the model may reflect unrelated developments occurring at the same time rather than integration effects. Gravity models were developed by Tinbergen (1952), and have been applied to the EC by Verdoorn and Schwartz (1972), Aitken (1973) and, more recently, Frankel (1997), Soloaga and Winters (1999) and Kandogan (2005). Other studies (Frankel and Rose, 2000; Rose, 2000 and 2002) have used gravity models to show how introducing a common currency appears to have encouraged trade growth (see Chapter 9).

Following the collapse of communism in Central and Eastern Europe in 1989, various authors used gravity models to assess the 'normal' level of trade with the EC, i.e. what trade would have been had communism never been introduced in those countries. Among the most well-known studies of this type are those of Wang and Winters (1992), Hamilton and Winters (1991), Baldwin (1994), Faini and Portes (1995) and various studies of the European Bank for Reconstruction and Development.[13]

Wilhelmsson (2006) used a gravity model to assess the impact of the 2004 enlargement on trade between the EU(15) and the new Central and Eastern European member states, and found evidence for significant trade creation and limited trade diversion.

Computable general equilibrium models (CGE) attempt to take into account the repercussions of trade liberalization on the whole of the domestic economy and on trading partners. The aim of a CGE model is to specify the conditions for equilibrium in all markets and countries. As described in Chapter 6, models of this type were used to assess the impact of the Single Market programme and, as shown in Chapter 15, the evolution of regional disparities in the EU. In a review of the CGE literature, Robinson and Thierfelder (2002) find that, according to most studies, integration increases the welfare of participants, trade creation tends to be larger on aggregate than trade diversion, and welfare effects are generally larger if features of new trade theory are considered and if there is an enlargement of membership. Schiff and Winters (2003) have criticized the use of CGE models in this way as they are generally based on the assumption that products are differentiated by country of origin, so all countries appear to have some market power. As a result, it is argued that these models tend to overestimate the terms of trade effects of integration.

Regionalism versus multilateralism

One of the more recent developments in the theory and practice of integration has been the emergence of a new wave of regionalism in the sense of a proliferation of regional trade blocs (see also Chapter 19), which has been accompanied by a revived debate in the literature on the virtues or otherwise of regional co-operation.

---

[13] See European Bank for Reconstruction and Development, Transition Report, various years. For a discussion of the application of gravity models to the Central and Eastern European countries (CEECs) see Senior Nello (2002).

The explosion of regional blocs since the 1990s follows the first wave of regional trade agreements mainly between developed countries in the 1950s and 1960s.[14] There could be about 400 regional blocs by 2010, according to the Director General of the WTO, Pascal Lamy.[15] About half the value of international trade is now covered by such agreements (Josling, 2007). Ethier (1998a and b) has identified some main features of this new proliferation of regional trade arrangements (RTAs):[16]

- Recent RTAs typically involve at least one developing country linking to more developed countries.

- Membership generally follows a significant unilateral liberalization – for instance, by the Central and East European countries in the case of the EU, and by Mexico for North American Free Trade Agreement (NAFTA);

- RTAs are rarely restricted to trade aspects.

- Developing countries tend to make bigger concessions in RTAs, often because the tariffs of developed countries are already low.

According to Ethier (1998a and b), regionalism is the means by which new countries enter the multilateral system and attempt to attract foreign direct investment (FDI).

Parallel to this growth in the number of regional trade blocs, a theoretical toolkit on regional co-operation has emerged since the 1990s. This approach places the issue of regional integration in the wider context of multilateral trade liberalization. The literature attempts to address the question of whether regional co-operation acts as a stumbling block to or a building block for multilateral trade liberalization (Bhagwati et al., 1998) and to identify the conditions for successful regional initiatives. Bhagwati and Panagariya (1996) define building blocks as RTAs that either further multilateral negotiations, or continue adding new members until the bloc converges on global free trade. In contrast, stumbling blocks are defined as giving rise to trade diversion and protectionism, and as being closed to expansion.

As the traditional Heckscher-Ohlin-Samuelson framework, and static customs union theory centred on the notions of trade creation, trade diversion and terms of trade effects was inadequate to analyse the new RTAs, the literature increasingly made use of the new trade theories described in Chapter 4.

Important contributions to the regionalism vs. multilateralism debate include that of Baldwin (1993), who introduces the domino effect in favour of the argument that regional integration promotes world-wide trade liberalization. According to this model, the preferential lowering of some trade barriers causes new pressures for outsiders to join, and as the trade bloc grows, the pressures to join become bigger. Outsiders want to become insiders, increasing the incentives to add members to the integration bloc. This enlarges the market, causing other countries to be pulled in as well.

Not all the literature is so confident of the proliferation of regionalism promoting multilateral trade liberalization. Regional trade blocs may follow a hub-and-spoke pattern, being organized around one or more large country, and this may place the smaller member states at a disadvantage with regard to bargaining power. Bhagwati et al. (1998) refer to the 'spaghetti bowl' phenomenon caused by the overlapping of complex systems of trade concessions. This may help to explain why the EU has often preferred free trade associations to customs unions with the

---

[14]See Baldwin (2006) for a description of this first wave of regionalism.

[15]Speech of 17/1/2007, Bangalore, India, www.wto.org.

[16]The term here is in a wide sense to cover arrangements at the various stages of integration described in Chapter 1.

applicant countries (with the notable exception of Turkey, where the motives were political as much as economic). Bhagwati and Panagariya (1996) also express fears that RTAs may be trade distorting, though, as illustrated above, this is an empirical question, depending on the case in question.

The new regionalism approach may also help to identify the characteristics that are likely to lead to success (or failure) of a regional bloc. A study by the World Bank (2000) argues that a strong liberalizing arrangement with the right partner (preferably rich, large and open) may lead to a virtuous circle of increased credibility, investment, growth and political stability. This may help to explain the interest of Mexico in NAFTA and of the successive waves of applicant countries in joining the EU.

Regionalism is here to stay and dealing with it could provide a means for the WTO to reinvent its role. The WTO could provide research and information of the likely consequences of the proliferation of bilateral and regional deals, and create a negotiating forum for the co-ordination and harmonization of rules of origin. Though the WTO has begun work on this task, so far little progress has been made. For instance, the WTO created the Regional Trade Agreements Committee in 1996 to monitor whether such agreements are consistent with WTO obligations, but no examination report of the Committee has been finalized since then. In order to correct a possible increase in power asymmetry in a hub-and-spoke system of regional blocs, the WTO could also provide a forum for the smaller and/or economically weaker spoke countries to co-ordinate their positions and increase their bargaining power.

Summary of Key Concepts

- Viner introduced the concepts of **trade creation and trade diversion** on which customs union theory is based. Trade creation arises when domestic production is replaced by cheaper imports from a partner country. Trade diversion results from low-cost imports from suppliers in third countries being replaced by more expensive imports from a partner country. Usually these concepts are taken to refer to welfare effects rather than trade flows. The welfare effects of forming a customs union on the consumption side also have to be taken into account

- The net effect of forming a customs union on the welfare of the home country may be positive, negative or zero. This is known as **Viner's ambiguity**.

- The **benefits of forming a customs union** are likely to be higher: (1) the higher the original level of the tariff before forming the customs union; (2) the lower the common external tariff towards the rest of the world; (3) the higher the number of countries joining a customs union and the greater their size; (4) the smaller the differences in costs of production between the members of the customs union and third countries; (5) the closer the countries are geographically; and (6) the more competitive (producing the same goods) rather than complementary (producing a different range of goods) the economies of the member states are.

- In order to explain **why a country should prefer a customs union to non-discriminatory trade liberalization** the early literature advanced arguments such as terms-of-trade effects and economies of scale. Johnson argued that the political economy argument – that governments may have a preference for industrial production – can be used to explain why they favour preferential trade arrangements.

- **Early empirical research** based on the customs union approach found the effects of integration surprisingly small.

- **The dynamic effects of integration** are: economies of scale, increased competition, specialization, increased bargaining power at an international level and technological progress. These effects are generally considered to be greater than the traditional static integration effects.

- Integration may contribute to long-term **growth** by encouraging R&D, technology diffusion, improved human capital and more efficient financial markets. In practice empirical studies may encounter difficulties in isolating integration from the other variables having an impact on growth.

- There has been much recent debate as to whether **regional co-operation** helps or hinders multilateral trade liberalization.

Questions for study and review

1 Describe the static and dynamic effects of integration.

2 Compare the effects of non-discriminatory trade liberalization with a preferential trade arrangement or customs union.

3 What explanations have been given of why countries may prefer preferential trade agreements to non-discrimination?

4 Under what conditions is a customs union likely to lead to an increase in welfare?

5 What are the main approaches used in empirical studies to assess the effect of integration?

6 Does regional integration promote multilateral trade liberalization?

7 Exercise on trade creation. Use the example of trade creation in the text to calculate the effects of formation of a customs union on: producer revenue, consumer expenditure, the trade balance and total welfare in Belgium (see also the Appendices to Chapter 4 for examples of how to calculate these effects).

8 Exercise on trade diversion. Assume that the free trade price of commodity X is equivalent to €2 in the USA, and €3 in Luxembourg. Initially Belgium applies a 100 per cent tariff on all imports, and produces 60 million units of X and consumes 80 million units. Belgium then forms a customs union with Luxembourg, but maintains the 100 per cent tariff with the USA. After formation of the customs union Belgium produces 50 million units of X, consumes 100 million X and imports 50 million X. Calculate the net impact on welfare as a result of formation of the customs union.

References

Aitken, N.D. (1973) 'The effects of the EEC and EFTA on European trade: A temporal cross-section analysis', *American Economic Review*, Vol. 68.

Balassa, B. (1967) 'Trade creation and trade diversion in the European common market', *Economic Journal*, Vol. 77.

Balassa, B. (1974) 'Trade creation and trade diversion in the European Common Market: An appraisal of the evidence', *Manchester School*, Vol. 42.

Balassa, B. (ed.) (1975) *European Economic Integration*, North-Holland, Amsterdam.

Baldwin, R. (1989) 'The growth effects of 1992', *Economic Policy*, Vol. 2, pp. 247–81.

Baldwin, R. (1993) A domino theory of regionalism, CEPR Working Paper No. 857, London.

Baldwin, R. (1994) *Towards an Integrated Europe*, Centre for Economic Policy Research, London.

Baldwin, R. (2006) *Multilateralising Regionalism: Spagetti bowls and building blocs on the path to global free trade*, Centre for Economic Policy Research Discussion Paper No. 5775, www. cepr.org

Baldwin, R. and Venables, A. (1995) 'Regional Economic Integration' in Grossman, G.M. and Rogoff, K. (eds) *Handbook of International Economics*, Vol. 3, North Holland Press, Amsterdam.

Baldwin, R. and Wyplosz, C. (2006) *The Economics of European Integration*, 2nd edn. McGraw-Hill Education, Maidenhead, UK.

Bhagwati, J., Greenaway, D. and Panagariya, A. (1998) 'Trading preferentially: Theory and policy', *The Economic Journal*, Vol. 108, pp. 1128–48.

Bhagwati, J. and Panagariya, A. (1996) 'Preferential trading areas and multilateralism: Strangers, friends or foes?' in Bhagwati, J. and Panagariya, A. (eds) *The Economics of Preferential Trading Arrangements*, AEI Press, Washington DC.

Bojnec, S. and Ferto, I. (2007) *European Enlargement, Trade Creation and Dynamics in Agro-food Trade*, www.econ.core.hu

Burfisher, M.E., Robinson, R. and Thierfelder, K. (2004) 'Regionalism: Old and new, theory and practice' in Anania, G., Bohman, M.E., Carter, C.A. and McCalla, A.F. (eds) *Agricultural Policy Reform and the WTO: Where are we Heading?* Edward Elgar Publishing, Cheltenham, UK.

Cooper, C.A. and Massell, B.F. (1965) 'A new look at customs union theory', *Economic Journal*, Vol. 75, pp. 742–75.

Deardorff, A. and Stern, R. (2002) *EU Expansion and EU Growth*, Ford School of Public Policy Working Paper No. 487, University of Michigan, Ann Arbor.

El-Agraa, A.M. (2007) 'The theory of economic integration', in El-Agraa, A.M. (ed.) *The European Union: Economics and Policies*, 8th edn, Cambridge University Press, Cambridge.

Emerson, E, Aujean, M., Catinat, M., Goybet, P. and Jacquemin, A. (1989) *The Economics of 1992: The EC Commission's Assessment of the Economic Effects of Completing the Single Market*, Oxford University Press, Oxford.

Ethier, W.J. (1998a) 'The new regionalism', *The Economic Journal*, Vol. 108, pp. 1149–61.

Ethier, W.J. (1998b) 'Regionalism in a multilateral world', *Journal of Political Economy*, Vol. 106, No.6.

European Bank for Reconstruction and Development (various years) *Transition Report*.

Faini, R. and Portes, R. (eds) (1995) *European Union Trade with Eastern Europe: Adjustment and Opportunities*, Centre for Economic Policy (CEPR), London.

Frankel, J.A. (1997) *Regional Trading Blocs in the World Trading System*, Institute for International Economics, Washington DC.

Frankel, J.A. and Rose, A. (2000) *Estimating the Effect of Currency Unions on Trade and Output*, National Bureau of Economic Research Working Paper 7857, Cambridge, MA.

Grossman, G.M. and Helpman, E. (1995) 'The Politics of free trade agreements', *American Economic Review*, Vol. 84, No.4.

Hamilton, C.B. and Winters, L.A. (1992) 'Opening up international trade with Eastern Europe,' *Economic Policy*, No. 14.

Harrop, J. (2000) *The Political Economy of Integration in the European Union*, 3rd edn, Edward Elgar, Cheltenham, UK.

Italianer, A. (1994) 'Whither the gains from European integration?' *Revue Economique*, Vol. xx, pp. 689–702.

Johnson, H.G. (1965) 'An economic theory of protectionism, tariff bargaining and the formation of customs unions', *Journal of Political Economy*, Vol. 73, pp. 256–83.

Josling, T. (2007) 'The WTO: What next?', *Eurochoices*, Vol. 6, No. 2.

Kandogan, Y. (2005) Trade creation and diversion effects of Europe's liberalisation agreements, William Davison Institute Working Paper, No. 746, www.wdi.umich.edu

Kindleberger, C.P. (1973) *International Economics*, 5th edn, Irwin-Dorsey, Homewood, IL.

Kreinen, M.E. (1972) 'Effects of the EEC on imports of manufactures', *Economic Journal*, Vol. 82.

Lipsey, R.G. (1957) 'The theory of customs unions: Trade diversion and welfare', *Economica*, Vol. 24.

Lucas, R.E. (1988) 'On the mechanics of economic development', *Journal of Economic Literature*, Vol. 22.

Mayes, D. (1978) 'The effects of economic integration on trade', *Journal of Common Market Studies*, Vol. 17, No. 1, pp. 1–25.

Pelkmans, J. and Gemmen, H. (1983) 'The empirical measurement of static customs union effects', *Rivista Internazionale di Scienze Economiche e Commerciali*, Vol. 30, 7 July.

Robinson, S. and Thierfelder, K. (2002) 'Trade liberalisation and regional integration: The search for large numbers,' *Australian Journal of Agricultural and Resource Economics*, Vol. 46, pp. 585–604.

Robson, P. (1984) *The Economics of International Integration*, 2nd edn, Allen & Unwin, London.

Romer, P. (1986) 'Increasing returns and long run growth', *Journal of Political Economy*, Vol. 94 .

Rose, A. (2000) 'One money, one market: The effect of common currencies on trade', *Economic Policy*, Vol. 30, pp. 7–33.

Rose, A. (2002) 'The effect of common currencies on international trade: Where do we stand?', unpublished manuscript available at http://faculty.hass.berkeley.edu/arose/RecRes.htm

Salvatore, D. (2007) *International Economics*, 9th edn, John Wiley & Sons, New York.

Schiff, M. and Winters, L.A. (2003) *Regional Integration and Development*, World Bank, Washington DC, www.worldbank.org

Sellekaerts, W. (1973) 'How meaningful are empirical studies on trade creation and trade diversion?', *Weltwirtschaftliches Archiv*, Vol. 109, pp. 519–51.

Senior Nello, S.M. (2002) 'Progress in preparing for EU enlargement: The tensions between economic and political integration', *International Political Science Review*, Vol. 23, No. 3, July.

Soloaga, I. and Winters, L.A. (1999) *How has regionalism in the 1990s affected trade?* World Bank Policy Research Working Paper No. 2156, www.worldbank.org

Solow, R. (1956) 'A contribution to the theory of growth', *Quarterly Journal of Economics*, February.

Tinbergen, J. (1952) *On the Theory of Economic Policy*, North-Holland, Amsterdam.

Truman, E.M. (1969) 'The European Economic Community: Trade creation and trade diversion', *Yale Economic Essays*, Spring.

Verdoorn, P.J. and Schwartz, A.N.R. (1972) 'Two alternative estimates of the effects of the EEC and EFTA on the pattern of trade', *European Economic Review*, Vol. 3.

Viner, J. (1953) *The Customs Union Issue*, The Carnegie Endowment for International Peace, New York.

Wang, Z.H. and Winters, L.A. (1991) *The Trading Potential of Eastern Europe*. CEPR Discussion Paper No. 610. Centre for Economic Policy Research, London.

Wilhelmsson, F. (2006*) Trade creation, diversion and displacement of the EU enlargement process*, www.nek.lu.se/NEKFWI

World Bank (2000) 'The road to stability and prosperity in South Eastern Europe: A regional strategy paper', World Bank, Washington DC.

Useful websites

Studies of various trade and integration issues are provided by the European Commission: www.ec.europa.eu

See also the WTO site for rules covering preferential trade arrangements: www.wto.org

For an example of a free trade area see the NAFTA website: www.nafta-sec-alena.org

CHAPTER

06

The Single Market

❖ LEARNING OBJECTIVES

By the end of this chapter you should be able to understand:

❖ How much specialization of industry is there in the EU;

❖ The main forms of non-tariff barrier still applied in the EU;

❖ What advantages were expected from the Single European Market (SEM) Programme;

❖ What were the main steps in introducing the SEM;

❖ How important the Single European Act (SEA) was in the integration process;

❖ The difficulties encountered in the liberalization of services in the EU, in particular, in areas such as financial markets and transport;

❖ What were the estimated effects of the SEM on the European economy;

❖ What progress has been made in realizing the SEM, and what aspects are not yet complete.

Introduction: Background to the Single Market Programme

Following the 1979 increase in oil prices, the European economy experienced a prolonged recession with stagnating output, rising unemployment and declining world export shares. During these years the terms 'Eurosclerosis' and 'Europessimism' were coined to describe the flagging process of integration. The main energies of the Community appeared absorbed by budgetary squabbles and the annual marathons to fix agricultural prices.

The EC member states were becoming increasingly concerned about the growing lag between their economic performance and that of countries such as Japan and the USA, especially in high technology sectors.[1] The Community was not only losing its world market share in industries such as automobiles and industrial machinery but also in rapidly growing sectors such as information technology and electronics. Moreover EC markets were increasingly being penetrated in these sectors by foreign firms.

In searching for the explanation for this lack of competitiveness, European industrialists and policy makers laid the blame on the fragmentation of the EC market. The EC business lobby

---

[1] Where possible, in this chapter the terms 'EC' or 'Community' have been used when reference is prior to implementation of the Maastricht Treaty, and the term 'EU' is used subsequently.

	Germany	Italy	Midwest	South
Textiles	3.7	9.1	0.3	11.7
Apparel	2.6	5.6	2.4	10.6
Machinery	15.8	12.9	15.0	7.1
Transport equipment	13.2	10.4	12.8	5.9
Automobiles	38.4	17.6	66.3	25.4

TABLE 6.1 Industrial specialization (share of manufacturing employment) in Germany, Italy and the USA (%)
Source: Krugman (1991)

soon began to press for EC initiatives to overcome this disadvantage, and the initial response of the Community was to introduce a series of measures to promote co-operation in research and development among European firms.

Theoretical studies, such as that of Krugman (1991), also provided evidence of the fragmentation of the EC market. Krugman argued that the four large countries of the EC were comparable in size and population to the four great regions of the USA: the North-East (New England and the mid-Atlantic), the Midwest (the north-central and western north-central states), the West and the South. Examining industrial specialization as measured by share of manufacturing employment, Krugman found that the level of specialization in the USA was higher than in the EC, even though the distances were greater. The Midwest could be compared to Germany in that both were centres of heavy, traditional industry, while the South was similar to Italy with light, labour-intensive industry. However, while there was almost no textile production in the Midwest, Germany still accounted for a substantial share. As shown in Table 6.1, Italy had a far higher share of machinery and auto production than the South. Krugman attributed the lower level of specialization in the EU to the continued existence of non-tariff barriers.[2]

In 1985, when Jacques Delors became president of the Commission, the Single or Internal Market Programme was announced as a strategy to raise EC competitiveness.[3] The idea was to return to and complete the original objectives set out in the Treaty of Rome. The removal of tariffs on intra-EC trade was considered a major factor contributing to the quadrupling of that trade in the first decade of the Community, with intra-EC trade growing twice as fast as world trade over that period. If the Community could now eliminate non-tariff barriers between its members, the earlier success of the Community could perhaps be repeated.

The main non-tariff barriers identified were:

- frontier controls;
- differences in technical specifications and standards;
- restrictions on competition for public purchases;
- restrictions on providing certain services (in particular financial and transport services) in other EC countries;
- differences in national tax systems.

The Commission divided these barriers into three somewhat arbitrary categories: physical barriers, fiscal barriers and technical barriers (all the rest). The third category lumps together

---

[2] In the literature various indices to measure specialization have been developed. For an overview of these indices see Coombes and Overman (2004).

[3] The term 'Internal Market' is generally adopted by the Commission and is used in the Lisbon Treaty.

measures such as differences in technical specifications and public procurement procedures with institutional restrictions on the free movement of people and capital, etc.

The choice of completion of the SEM to re-launch the integration effort represented a major strategic decision on the part of Delors and the Commission. Following the Hague Summit of 1969, economic and monetary union was the main integration objective of the 1970s. The difficulties encountered and limited success realized help to explain the search for an alternative.

Expected advantages of the SEM

The EC Commission sponsored what was probably the most extensive single assessment of the likely effects of an economic policy ever carried out. The results were published in 16 volumes and are known as the Cecchini Report, or 'Costs of non-Europe'.[4] As will be shown below, many of the results of the study have been subject to heavy criticism, but the description of the various approaches used in the analysis is interesting both as a guide to many of the prevailing theories on integration at the time and as an insight into the views of the Commission.

Traditionally, in order to assess the impact of economic integration, customs union theory made use of the 'static' concepts of trade creation and trade diversion (see Chapter 5). However, empirical studies of integration effects increasingly pointed to the gap between the traditional theory and real issues and stressed the need to take dynamic effects such as increased competition, growth and the scope for exploiting economies of scale into account.[5] As will be shown below, dynamic effects figure strongly in the analysis of expected benefits of the SEM.

Studies such as the Cecchini Report emphasize the impact that the SEM was likely to have in reducing prices and costs. Prior to the 1993 Programme large price differences existed between EC states,[6] and these were taken as an indication of the degree of market fragmentation.

Figure 6.1 provides a useful shorthand illustration of the expected effect of the SEM on costs and prices. The elimination of barriers would enable firms from other EC member states to sell at lower prices in a particular EC country, say Italy. The increased competition from other EC firms selling at lower prices on the Italian market would first induce Italian firms to reduce excess profits and wages and eliminate inefficiencies within the firms. Subsequently, the increased demand resulting from lower prices would encourage restructuring and attempts to exploit economies of scale, both through mergers and new investment.

It was argued that these processes would free resources for alternative productive uses, so raising the levels of investment and consumption sustainable in the Community. The rationalization of production and distribution would increase productivity, thereby reducing prices and costs.

In the case of public procurement, the cost savings would release resources enabling governments either to cut taxes or carry out other growth-inducing activities. The liberalization of financial services was of particular importance to the programme since the reduced cost of credit would stimulate increased consumer demand and investment. It was estimated that these

---

[4] Cecchini (1988).

[5] See Chapters 4 and 5.

[6] According to Emerson et al. (1989), the average variation from EC mean price without indirect taxes in 1985 across countries was 15 per cent for consumer goods and 12 per cent for capital products (taking the EC-9 members prior to 1981 as 100). In the service sectors these variations were even greater, amounting to 28 per cent for road and rail transport, 29 per cent for financial services, 50 per cent for telephone and telegram services and 42 per cent for electrical repairs.

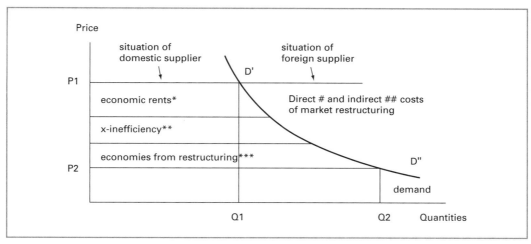

FIGURE 6.1 The effects of eliminating cost-increasing trade barriers

*Economic rents consist of the margin of excess profit or wage rates that result from market protection.

** X-inefficiency consists of, for example, the costs of over-staffing, excess overhead costs and excess inventories (i.e. inefficiencies not related to the production technology of the firm's investments). Because the firm is not operating in a competitive environment, there is inadequate pressure to cut these costs.

***Economies from restructuring include, for example, greater economies of scale, or the benefits obtained when inefficient production capacity is eliminated and new investments are made.

Direct costs include delays at the frontier and the cost of differing technical regulations, which would immediately fall if market barriers were eliminated.

Indirect costs are those that would fall as foreign suppliers adjust to the more competitive situation with more efficient production and marketing.

Source: Figure 2.2 (p. 26) from *The Economics of 1992* (1989) by Emerson, Michael et al. By permission of Oxford University Press.

benefits would be apparent after a period of 5–6 years (see the section on the achievements of the SEM Programme below).

The timetable for the introduction of the SEM

In March 1985 the new president of the Commission, Jacques Delors, presented his programme for the SEM to the European Parliament. Later that year the Cockfield White Paper, 'Completing the Internal Market', was presented at the European Council in Milan. This called for the elimination of barriers between EC countries by the end of 1992 and set out 282 measures necessary to achieve this aim.

Many of these measures had been around as draft proposals for many years, and although the completion of the SEM was not a new idea, it now acquired a new impetus. The way in which the Programme was presented represents a major marketing success: the timetable set out deadlines that represented precise targets, and focused the attention of politicians and business. The Commission, and in particular Delors, were largely responsible for introducing what was to become a self-fulfilling prophecy. The personal style of Lord Cockfield, Commissioner for the Internal Market, who emphasized the technical and low-key nature of the programme, also contributed to its success (Tsoukalis, 1997).

The emphasis on deregulation meant that the programme coincided with the economic doctrine being advocated at the time by politicians such as Thatcher and Reagan. Initially the programme seemed to be concerned with rules, not money, so did not appear a threat to national governments. However, it was soon to emerge that the programme would have to be flanked by redistributive measures to compensate the weakest regions and sections of the population.

The Milan Summit also had to decide on the intergovernmental conferences to prepare the necessary revision to the existing treaties. Initially the UK, Denmark and Greece were opposed to the proposed institutional reforms that would increase the use of majority voting in the Council, strengthen the European Parliament and extend the use of European Political Co-operation. The decision of the Italian Presidency to go ahead on a majority vote was 'unexpected and without precedent' (Tsoukalis, 1997).

The three governments that had initially opposed institutional reform soon overcame their misgivings. In part this reflected a fear of being excluded and not being able to influence the decision-making process. However, in the case of the UK in particular, institutional reform was seen as the necessary price to pay for the SEM, which was an objective strongly favoured by national politicians and businessmen.

The Single European Act (SEA)

The SEA sets out the formal procedure necessary to implement the 1993 programme. It also modified the EC decision-making process and called for a revived integration effort in other fields such as technology and in monetary, social, regional and external policies. The SEA defined the SEM as 'an area without internal frontiers in which the free movement of goods, persons, services and capital is ensured'.

The SEA represented the first major revision to the treaties, but at the time its importance was underestimated. With the benefit of hindsight it can be argued that the SEA launched a new phase in the integration process, spilling over into renewed efforts in political union, institutional reform, economic and monetary union, and reinforced EC social, regional and competition policies. The way in which the SEM Programme pushed the integration process forward in other areas lends itself well to interpretation according to the neo-functionalist approach (see Chapter 1).

With regard to institutional reform, qualified majority voting was to be used in the Council for the harmonization of national rules and regulations.[7] Unanimity voting was still to be used in the Council for questions relating to fiscal policy, the free movement of persons, and the rights and interests of employees. This was because these were sensitive issues on which the EC member states held divergent views.

The SEA stipulates that any institutional change in economic and monetary policy would require a new revision of the treaties, a prospect that seemed unlikely at the time. However, the SEA contains formal recognition of the European Monetary System (EMS) and the role of the European Currency Unit (ECU). As discussed in Chapter 9, economic and monetary union (EMU) is linked to completion of the internal market as exchange rate uncertainty between currencies can be regarded as another obstacle to trade. The introduction of a single monetary unit would confirm the reality of the SEM, but this in turn would push the integration process further. Democratic control of the new European Central Bank would require further steps in the direction of political union.

---

[7] This voting rule was also extended to the liberalization of capital movements and of sea and air transport. The *quid pro quo* for wider use of majority voting was a safeguard clause that would allow member states to continue to apply national provisions after the introduction of new EC rules in certain circumstances. This was to ensure that standards for the protection of the environment or working conditions would not deteriorate.

Title V of the Single European Act deals with 'economic and social cohesion' to ensure harmonious development and the reduction of regional disparities. The weaker regions, and in particular the periphery of the Community, feared that they would not be able to withstand the increased competition implied by the SEM and that there would be a worsening of regional and sectoral imbalances. In response to their requests, Article 130d of the SEA calls for effective co-ordination and rationalization of the Structural Funds.

Certain derogations and special provisions were permitted in order to take account of the heterogeneity and different levels of development of EC member states, but the outcome was far from permitting a multi-speed Europe.

The Treaty also called for increased Community responsibility for social policy, in particular on questions relating to the health and safety of workers. In 1988 the idea of a 'Social Europe' was launched, which entailed identifying the regions and industries most likely to be negatively affected by the 1993 programme and offering some measures of compensation. It was also argued that social policy measures were necessary in order to ensure a 'level playing field' and prevent the Internal Market being undermined by the phenomenon of 'social dumping'.

Social dumping refers to fear that employment will be lost in member states where better social standards are reflected in higher labour costs. There may be downward pressure on wages, social security conditions and minimum health and safety regulations in those countries in order to prevent loss of market share. This phenomenon is attributed to 'unfair competition' from countries in which labour laws are less restrictive. A major aim of both the 1989 Social Charter and the Social Chapter of the Maastricht Treaty was to prevent this type of 'social dumping'.

One of the immediate effects of announcement of the SEM Programme was to induce a rapid increase in the number of cross-border mergers of EC firms, which rose from 200 in 1985 to some 2000 in 1989 (Tsoukalis, 1997). This led to a tightening of EC competition policy and, in particular, the introduction of *ex ante* Community authority over mergers from 1989 (see Chapter 17).

Implementation of the SEM Programme

At the EC level rapid progress was made in passing the necessary measures for the Internal Market Programme and, according to the Commission, by 31 December 1992 95 per cent of the legislative programme set out in 1985 was complete.[8] The transposition of EC measures into national legislation was to prove a slightly more lengthy process, but the real difficulties arose in implementation of the measures and the granting of temporary derogations.

Subsequently, the European Commission attempted to tighten up on enforcement and implementation procedures. The 1997 Amsterdam European Council endorsed an Action Plan that entails the Commission drawing up a 'Single Market Scoreboard' every six months. The Scoreboards indicate whether member states meet the objectives of:

- an average deficit of transposition into national law of less than 1.5 per cent;
- Zero tolerance for legislation not transposed after 2 years or more;
- Reducing the number of cases of infringement.

According to the Single Market Scoreboard of July 2007 the transposition deficit was 1.6 per cent for the EU(25) in mid-2007, or 1.8 per cent if Bulgaria and Romania were also considered (though these countries had the huge task of transposing the whole *acquis*). The countries with

---

[8] The main exceptions related to company legislation, fiscal harmonization and intellectual property rights.

the highest transposition deficits were Portugal, Luxembourg, Italy, Greece, and the Czech Republic. Those with the lowest were Lithuania, Latvia, Slovakia and Denmark.

According to the Scoreboard, Luxembourg, the Czech Republic, Spain, Portugal and Belgium had the most long outstanding directives (legislation not transposed after 2 years or more) in mid-2007.

Italy, Spain, France, Greece, Germany and Portugal were the countries with most infringements according to the July 2007 Scoreboard. The sectors in which most infringements occurred were the environment, taxation and the customs union, and energy and transport.

Since 1987 there have been 'package meetings' of experts from the member states and the Commission to discuss a 'package' of cases under examination by the Commission for violation of Community law. The aim is to solve cases without the need for further legal action, and in recent years the use of these meetings has increased, and reached 16 between July 2005 and July 2006.

In 2002 the redress system for implementation of Internal Market rules (SOLVIT) was introduced in order to improve implementation of Internal Market rules (see Box 6.1). Previously victims of failure to apply rules (such as non-recognition of a valid diploma or denied market access for a product) had to appeal to national courts or to the Commission. Under the new system the victim can refer the case by Internet or telephone to the SOLVIT office in their own member state, and the office will raise the case with the country in which the misapplication has occurred. In 2006 SOLVIT dealt with 467 cases, but in the first half of 2007 there was an increase in cases by 50 per cent following the introduction of an online complaint form. The SOLVIT centres of Spain, Portugal, France and the Czech Republic resolve about 90 per cent of the cases presented to them. However, in about half the member states the SOLVIT offices suffer from a shortage of staff and in many countries a low priority is attached to SOLVIT activities. The cases dealt with most often relate to social security, taxation issues and recognition of professional qualifications.

Box 6.1: *SOLVIT Cases*

A Portuguese breakdown vehicle was transporting a damaged Portuguese car from Belgium to Portugal and was fined €600 by the Spanish police because the breakdown vehicle was not fitted with tachograph equipment. The Portuguese SOLVIT office pointed out that breakdown vehicles were not required to have this equipment by EU regulations, and the fine was refunded.

A Danish citizen was registered as an EU job seeker in the Netherlands, but the Dutch authorities only granted her Mexican husband the same status after intervention by the Dutch SOLVIT office.

Source: Internal Market Scoreboard No. 12 of May 2003, © European Communities, 2003. www.ec.europa.eu/internal_market

---

The European Commission maintains that differences in the price of a single model of new car between member states may reflect fragmentation of markets and lack of competition and so serve as evidence that the Internal Market is not working in this sector (see Box 6.2). According to European Commission (2007a) increased market integration has accelerated price convergence overall among the EU member states. Prices in the high income EU(15) have converged downwards to the EU average (due to increased price transparency, cheaper imports and the monetary policy of the European Central Bank), while those in the new member states and lower income EU(15) have converged upwards.

Box 6.2: *Car prices in the EU*

Every six months since 1992 the Commission has carried out a survey of price differences of new cars net of taxes between the member states. There appears to be some price convergence for the 100 best-selling models, with average price dispersion at a historical low in May 2007 (a standard deviation of 6.5 per cent for the EU(27)). The cheapest countries were Denmark, Lithuania and Finland. The most expensive countries were Slovakia and the Czech Republic, while Germany was the most expensive eurozone country. Of the 10 best-selling cars in the EU in 2006, the widest price difference in the euro zone was for the Peugeot 307, which costs 31 per cent more in France than in Finland, a potential saving of €4700 (including VAT).*

*European Commission Car Price Report of 1 May 2007, © European Communities, 2007. www.ec.europa.eu/comm/competition/sectors/motor_vehicles/prices/report/html

---

The main elements of the SEM Programme: the Schengen Agreement and other aspects of the removal of frontier controls

A key aim of the removal of frontier controls is to facilitate free movement of people within the Community. In 1985 Benelux, Germany and France formed the Schengen Group with the aim of eliminating border controls between each other as rapidly as possible.[9] Subsequently other countries joined the group, though the UK and Ireland opted out (though they participate in police co-operation), and Denmark has a partial opt-out, reserving its position on all questions except visas. Iceland and Norway signed association agreements in 1996, and Switzerland will participate in Schengen from November 2008. In December 2007 Schengen was enlarged to include 24 member states.[10]

Schengen implies the removal of all controls on people (whether they are citizens of the EU or of third countries) when they cross frontiers between member states, though a safeguard clause allows a country to reinstate controls in the event of a serious threat to public policy, public health or public security. Schengen also involves developing a common visa policy, and introducing measures to enable the lifting of internal borders (and, in particular, police and judicial co-operation on criminal matters).

In 1990 the Schengen countries agreed a Convention on Application of the Agreement, which entered into force from 1995,[11] and was incorporated into a protocol Annex to the Amsterdam Treaty in 1999. In addition to a mechanism for settling disputes, this set out a series

---

[9] The name 'Schengen' derives from the town near the Luxembourg, French and German borders.

[10] The new members joining were: Poland, the Czech Republic, Hungary, Estonia, Latvia, Lithuania, Slovakia, Slovenia and Malta.

[11] 1997 for Italy, Austria and Greece.

of provisions on issues such as extradition, drugs, firearms, asylum and transmission of personal data. The provisions included:

- Establishing the institutional framework for the abolition of border controls between Schengen countries;
- Setting up the Schengen Information System (SIS), a computer network for the exchange of information between national police forces. This was to act as a joint automated search system and involved setting up and maintaining data files on persons and certain objects (firearms, stolen or lost vehicles, bank notes, official documents and so on);
- Common rules and procedures for checks at the external borders;
- More co-operation on extradition;
- Harmonization of legislation governing firearms;
- Measures to facilitate cross-border transport of goods, including increased co-operation between customs authorities;
- Common lists of countries requiring visas and a common model of visas;
- Increased co-operation between national police forces, including the establishment of Europol.[12]

Some aspects of Schengen have been challenged on grounds of privacy and accountability. For instance, it has been claimed that the SIS may run counter to national legislation on data protection and could therefore infringe civil liberties.

Box 6.3: *Football integration*

One of the effects of the SEM was to encourage integration of soccer. Football integration has paralleled the overall integration process. In 1956 the first European Cup was played and, as in the case of the EEC, initially the UK failed to participate.* With the SEM objective of free movement of labour it was no longer legal for EU teams to limit the number of citizens they had from other EU states. At about the same time the European Court decided that footballers were free to move anywhere after the end of their contract without their club demanding a transfer fee. Wages and transfers increased, and the Champions League emerged.

1958 marked not only the entry into force of the Treaty of Rome, but also the debut of Manchester United as the first English club to enter the European Cup. To celebrate in March 2007, Commission President Barroso decided to hold a match between Manchester United and the EU.** The EU team was coached by Marcello Lippi, and included players such as David Beckham, Steven Gerrard, Gianluca Zambrotta, Carles Puyol, Grégory Coupet, and the Brazilian Ronaldinho (who had applied for Spanish citizenship). The EU strip was not blue with yellow stars, but white with blue trim.

* *Economist*, 31 May 2003.

** *Financial Times*, 2 March 2007.

---

[12]See the OLC for this book for a description of Europol. The Schengen Agreement also envisages cross-border surveillance and cross-border pursuit of suspects by police officers.

Other aspects of the elimination of border controls required by the Internal Market include the abolition of customs formalities, veterinary and road safety checks at frontiers. In addition, quantitative restrictions could no longer be applied at the national level by EC member states and had to be replaced by EC measures.[13] The Cecchini Report estimated that industry would save €8 billion a year, and government would save €1 billion per year if frontier controls were removed.

A series of measures was introduced to facilitate the right to work in other member states (see Box 6.3) and to develop exchange programmes, including EU Programmes such as:

- ERASMUS (university exchanges);
- Leonardo da Vinci (training and vocational education); and
- LINGUA (promotion of language teaching and learning).

Between its creation in 1987 and 2007 an estimated 1.2 million students participated in the ERASMUS Programme.[14] The Programme also extends to the three countries of the European Economic Area (Iceland, Liechtenstein and Norway), and Turkey. There has also been a renewed effort to encourage recognition of university diplomas and other professional qualifications in respective member states. Though legislation permitting the residence of EU workers and their families in other member states had existed for some time, measures to promote easier residence for other categories, such as pensioners and students, were also passed. The European Employment Services (EURES) network was established to provide information on job opportunities in EU states.

Differences in national rules and regulations

According to Mattera (1988), at the time when the SEM programme was launched differences in standards and technical barriers accounted for some 80 per cent of the remaining barriers to intra-EC trade. Though the words are sometimes used interchangeably, technical regulations refer to legally binding rules relating to the health and safety of consumers, while 'standards' are voluntary and aim to provide adequate information and ensure the quality of a product.

Barriers, supposedly on 'health' grounds, were levied, for example, on chocolate and French mineral water by the FRG, and by Italy on imports of pasta not using durum wheat. In some cases differences in technical regulations prevented cross-border trade, while in others it added to the costs of firms that had to modify their products to meet the requirements of other EC countries.

Article 30 of the Treaty of Rome prohibits quantitative restrictions on intra-EC trade and 'all measures having an equivalent effect'. In the 1974 Dassonville ruling of the European Court of Justice, it was argued that 'measures having an equivalent effect' included 'all trading rules enacted by member states which are capable of hindering directly or indirectly, actually or potentially intra-EC trade'.

One way of eliminating these barriers to trade between EC member states is by harmonizing the national standards and technical regulations of member states. This 'old approach' has

---

[13] This had important implications for the quotas on textile products permitted by the MFA Multifibre Agreement (MFA), and entailed abolition of the monetary compensatory amounts of the Common Agricultural Policy (a system of taxes and subsidies levied at the border to cushion the impact of exchange rate changes on the system of price support). The SEM Programme and the transition of Central and Eastern Europe from 1989 also account for the elimination of the different quotas applied by the member states on imports from the former CEEC 'non-market economies'.

[14] European Commission, www.ec.europe.eu/education/programmes/llp/erasmus

proved slow and inefficient as the detailed, technical legislation involved is complex and costly. It also runs the risk of excessive uniformity and bureaucratic interference. The topic is one on which feelings run high, with complaints that 'Eurocrats' are concerned with 'measuring the size of sausages', 'shape of cucumbers', or determined to bring about the demise of rare breeds and crops. Against this, however, excessive deregulation runs the risk of inadequate protection for consumers.

The solution reached by the Community was to rely as far as possible on the principle of mutual recognition, which was defined in the much-cited *Cassis de Dijon* case of 1979. In this case the European Court of Justice ruled against a German prohibition of imports of a French liqueur on the grounds that it did not conform to German rules and regulations, and established the general principle that all goods lawfully manufactured and marketed in one member state should be accepted also in other member countries. At the same time, the Court recognized the need for some exceptions relating to public health, the fairness of commercial transactions and the defence of the consumer. According to European Commission (2007a), the mutual recognition principle covered about 20 per cent of EU industrial production and 26 per cent of intra-EU manufacturing trade. It has also been extended to some dealings with third countries, including the USA.

Surveys carried out by the Commission suggest that mutual recognition works well for relatively simple products but less so for more complex goods.[15] When a product is denied access to a country there is no clear procedure for a company to challenge a negative decision so the company is forced to modify the product or abandon that market. According to European Commission (2007a), an impact assessment was being carried out by the Commission to examine policy options to improve the functioning of the mutual recognition principle.

To speed up the process of harmonization, in 1985 a 'new approach' was developed. Wherever harmonization of rules at the EC level was deemed necessary, it was decided that this should be limited to essential objectives and requirements. Directives cover large groups of products and/or hazards, and specify the essential safety or other requirements the product must meet. The manufacturers are free to choose between applying either the appropriate EU standard (see below), or any other technical specifications that meet these essential requirements. Any product conforming to the requirements can circulate freely in all the member states. By 2007 it was estimated that the trading volume of products covered by the new approach exceeded some €1500 billion a year.[16]

The task of defining technical specifications was left to private standardization bodies. At EC level standardization bodies included the CEN (Centre Européen de Normalisation), the CENELEC (Centre Européen de Normalisation Electrotechnique) and the ETSI (European Telecommunications Standards Institute). The membership of these organizations consists of national standardization bodies.

According to the European Commission,[17] the new approach has proved relatively successful, but needs improved conformity assessment procedures, increased administrative co-operation and better market surveillance to ensure that effective action is taken when products fail to meet essential requirements. A product manufactured according to EU standards can carry the mark 'CE' if it conforms to the basic safety requirements laid out in the relevant directive. Compliance is voluntary and manufacturers may choose not to observe Community standards, but the onus is on them to prove that their product is safe.

---

[15] European Commission (2002a).

[16] European Commission (2007a).

[17] European Commission (2003b).

The average time needed to adopt an EU standard increased from 4.5 years in 1995 to 8 years in 2001, and the European Commission called for measures to speed up this process and ensure uniform quality in the production and application of standards.[18]

The Community and, in particular, the DG for Consumer Affairs of the Commission are also active in the field of protecting consumer rights, and its initiatives can be divided into four main categories:

1 Actions for the protection of consumer health and safety. These include rules on the testing and registration of pharmaceutical, medical and cosmetic products, measures to ensure the safety of toys, health controls, labelling for food and agricultural products and so on.

2 Protection of the economic interests of consumers by, for instance, measures against unfair contracts and misleading advertising.

3 Actions to ensure that consumers have comparative information, through rules on packaging and labelling, and support for consumer organizations.

4 Measures to ensure the right of consumers to redress, with simple clear procedures.

The Commission set out a Consumer Policy Strategy and Programme for the 2007–2013 period which is focused on three main objectives: empowering EU consumers; enhancing their welfare in terms of price, choice, quality, diversity, affordability and safety; and protecting consumers effectively from the serious risks and threats that they cannot tackle as individuals.[19]

Fiscal harmonization

Differences in national tax systems represented a barrier to completion of the internal market in two ways. In the first place, tax differences may cause price distortions and so undermine the competitive process. Secondly, differences in national taxation have to be adjusted at the border, thereby necessitating controls at the frontier. Moreover, operating with different tax systems adds to the cost and complexity of doing business in other EU countries.

The Community has made slow progress in introducing fiscal harmonization, partly because this is one of the areas where unanimity voting is required in the Council of Ministers since taxation raises sensitive issues. The power to tax is central to the sovereignty of a country, and differences in tax systems frequently reflect underlying differences in culture and tradition.

Article 99 of the Treaty of Rome called for harmonization of indirect taxes, but the Treaty is rather vague on what is meant by harmonization (Ardy and El-Agraa, 2007). Article 100, for example, states only that 'laws should be approximated'.[20] Although the Single European Act (Article 17) called for 'harmonization of legislation concerning turnover taxes, excise duties and other forms of indirect tax', to date the approach adopted has been that of approximation rather than harmonization of taxes. The emphasis on indirect taxation reflects the assumption that goods and capital are more mobile than labour, and so more sensitive to differences in national tax systems. It probably also reflects political feasibility as agreement of the member states on issues relating to direct taxes seems even more difficult to reach.

At the time of the Treaty of Rome the system of indirect taxation adopted by the member

---

[18] European Commission (2003b).

[19] European Commission (2007b).

[20] Harmonization entails introducing common legislation, while approximation involves bringing national laws more in line with each other.

Country	Standard 1991/2	Reduced 1991/2	Increased 1991/2	Standard 2007	Reduced 2007	Country	Standard 2007	Reduced 2007
Belgium	19.5	1, 6 and 12	—	21	6	Austria	20	10
Denmark	25	—	—	25	—	Finland	22	7/8
FRG	15	7	—	19	7	Sweden	25	6/12
Spain	15	6	28	16	4/7	Bulgaria	20	7
France	18.6	2.1 and 5.5	—	19.6	2.1/5.5	Czech Republic	19	5
Greece	18	4 and 8	—	19	4.5/9	Estonia	18	5
Italy	19	4, 9 and 12	38	20	4/10	Cyprus	15	5/8
Ireland	21	0, 2.7, 10.0, 12,5 16	—	21	4.8/13.5	Latvia	18	5
Lux.	15	3 and 6	—	15	3/6	Lithuania	18	5/9
NL	18.5	6	—	19	6	Hungary	20	5
Portugal	16	5	—	21	5/12	Malta	18	5
UK	17.5	0	—	17.5	5	Poland	22	3/7
						Romania	19	9
						Slovenia	20	8.5
						Slovakia	19	10

TABLE 6.2 VAT rates in the member states in 1991/2 and May 2007 (per cent)
Source: European Commission (2007c), © European Communities, 2007 and (for the 1991/2 rates) Hitiris, T. (1994) *European Union Economics*, 3rd edition. Prentice Hall: Harlow, UK © Pearson Education.

states varied considerably.[21] One of the main achievements of the Community was to introduce a common system of turnover tax from 1967, based on the French VAT (value added tax).[22] This was considered necessary as a percentage of VAT returns constituted one of the own resources of the Community Budget (see Chapter 11).

VAT accounts for some 10–20 per cent of the total tax revenue of the member states (Molle, 2006). Although the EC members agreed on a uniform method for calculating VAT in 1979, its application differs greatly from country to country. Differences relate to tax coverage (i.e. which products are liable to tax), the number of VAT rates and their levels. As shown in Table 6.2, Denmark applied only one VAT rate in 1991/2, while Ireland applied six. The standard rate applied varied from 15 per cent in Spain, the FRG and Luxembourg to 25 per cent in Denmark. Differences also arose as to which products were subject to reduced rates either to compensate for the regressive nature of VAT, or for merit goods, such as books and cultural services. For example the UK applied zero rating for foodstuffs, gas and electricity.

The 1985 White Paper called for the reduction or elimination of fiscal barriers, and in 1987 the Commission produced detailed proposals of how to reach this objective in the case of VAT. The negotiations were heated and prolonged. Higher rate countries such as Ireland, France and Denmark feared the loss of VAT revenue. Low rate countries such as Germany feared that increased VAT could add to inflationary pressures. The UK and Ireland wanted to maintain zero rating on 'social necessities' such as foodstuffs to offset the regressive nature of VAT.

---

[21] With the exception of France, the other original EC members applied a cascade system. This was a multi-stage tax levied on the gross value of output at each stage of the production process. At each stage the tax was levied on selling price, and this price might reflect tax paid at an early stage. The system was therefore cumulative and provided an incentive to vertical integration. In contrast, VAT is neutral towards vertical integration and has the advantage that it is self-policing since the purchasing firm has an interest in obtaining an invoice from suppliers showing that taxes on inputs have been paid.

[22] VAT is paid at each stage in the productive process (including marketing) on the value added at that stage.

A compromise was eventually reached, which entailed a standard minimum rate of VAT of 15 per cent and a list of products (food, pharmaceuticals, energy, water, hotels, passenger transport, etc.) on which a reduced rate of 5 per cent could be applied. Subsequently a band of 15–25 per cent was introduced for the standard rate. Existing zero rates could be continued but not extended. In 2003 the Commission proposed measures to simplify the VAT regime, which included abolishing the zero VAT rating on children's clothes in Britain and Ireland. The UK and Irish governments fiercely opposed the proposal, but, according to the Commission, the exemption was not necessarily passed on as lower prices.

As can be seen from Table 6.2, over time convergence has been minimal. In a 2004 survey (European Commission, 2006a) 86.1 per cent of large businesses quoted cross-border payment or refund of VAT as a major difficulty, and 53.5 per cent of large firms have not requested refunding at some point because of complexity of procedures.

Box 6.4: *Excise duties in the SEM*

According to Commons (2002), the duty on a pint of beer was 30p in the UK, 5p in France, 3p in Germany and 7p in the Netherlands. Duty on a 70cl bottle of spirits was £5.48 in the UK, £2.51 in France and £1.19 in Spain. Duty on a 75cl bottle of wine was £1.16 in the UK, 2p in France and zero in Spain. Total excise duty on a packet of cigarettes was £2.80 in the UK, £1.22 in France, £1.00 in the Netherlands and 99p in Belgium.

The price differences had narrowed little by 2007. Duty on a litre of wine varied from the equivalent of €2.6 in the UK, €2.7 in Ireland, €2.4 in Sweden and €2.1 in Finland to zero in countries such as Greece, Italy, Spain, Portugal, Malta, Bulgaria, Romania, Slovenia, Slovakia, the Czech Republic, Cyprus, Hungary, Austria, and Luxembourg. In 2007 the excise duty on a litre of beer ranged from 20 cents in Ireland and Hungary, to 0.7 of a cent in Romania. The excise duty on spirits (on a litre of pure alcohol) was the equivalent of €28.9 in the UK, €53.7 in Sweden, €39.25 in Ireland, but only €8.0 in Italy and €5.6 in Bulgaria.

Under the Single Market, the quantity of products subject to excise duty that could be taken from one country to another for 'personal consumption' initially amounted to 800 cigarettes, 10 litres of alcohol, 90 litres of wine, 110 litres of beer etc. For private individuals going to another member state this was subsequently increased to an 'unlimited quantity' of goods for personal use transported by the traveller himself or herself on which excise had been paid. Differences in excise duties between the member states were sufficient to stimulate a lively trade exploiting these personal allowances, creating significant losses of revenue for some of the member states (notably the UK). From 2004 transitional measures were permitted on imports from new member states where excise duties were below EU(15) levels.

Sweden and Finland were initially allowed to maintain state monopolies on retailing alcohol and, together with Denmark, tighter limits on how much alcohol travellers could bring back from other EU states, though subsequently they were required to adopt EU-wide limits. In June 2007 the European Court of Justice ruled that the Swedish alcohol monopoly was not compatible with EU law as it was against the principle of movement of free goods. The Swedish Health Minister, Maria Larsson, confirmed that the alcohol monopoly would stay in place and that the Swedish government would work for restrictive alcohol policies within the EU.

*European Commission (2007d).

Traditionally VAT in the Community was applied according to the principle of destination, in other words it was paid in the country of consumption. If a product were traded between two EU countries, the tax would be paid in the importing country, and VAT paid in the exporting country would be refunded. This may be complex and costly for firms as businesspeople may not be acquainted with the legislation and language of the country to which they are exporting. The Commission proposed that with the introduction of the Single Market, the destination system should be replaced by a system based on the principle of origin (also known as the 'common market' principle). In practice little progress has been made in this direction, and reform of the system remains a long-term goal.

Excise duty accounts for about 6–12 per cent of the total tax revenue of the member states (Molle, 2006). There are also considerable differences in the level and coverage of excise duties (on petrol, alcohol, cigarettes, wine, beer, etc.) in the various EC countries (see Box 6.4). These reflect differences in social customs, public health considerations and the revenue requirements of governments of the member states. In some cases decisions are also influenced by the existence of state monopolies (for example tobacco for many years in Italy).

Little progress has been made in reducing differences in national systems of excise duties in the Community. The member states have adopted common lists of products on which excise duties apply, and these are divided into alcoholic, tobacco and petroleum products. The 1993 programme simply entailed minimum rates of duty for alcohol,[23] tobacco, cigarettes and mineral oil, and an imprecise commitment to harmonization in the medium term. In the meantime goods could circulate an interconnected circuit of customs deposits and were subject to duty only when and where they left that circuit.

There was an increase in the quantity and value of products subject to excise duty that could be taken from one country to another for 'personal consumption' (see Box 6.4). It is likely that the increased mobility of products in the SEM will force governments into further measures of market-induced harmonization.

Duty-free sales have no place in an internal market, but their abolition entailed a serious loss of revenue for airports and ferry companies. It was eventually decided to allow sales of duty-free on intra-EU trips to continue until 1999 when, despite protests by certain member states (the UK, France and Germany), they were abolished.

Though the Commission has presented various proposals, little progress has been made in harmonizing direct taxes, also because a unanimity vote is required. Top personal income taxes range from a minimum of 16 per cent in Romania to a maximum of 59 per cent in Denmark, with the new member states in general having lower top rates (European Commission, 2007e).

The fear of 'tax competition' again came to the fore from the late 1990s. It was argued that removal of the barriers, with capital and labour becoming more mobile, would lead workers and investment to move to low-tax destinations. Ireland, for example, was accused of setting its taxes on profits low, helping to contribute to high levels of inward foreign direct investment. New member states were warned that if they attempted to emulate the successful Irish model (see also Chapter 15), they would not be permitted to introduce what were considered as unfair tax concessions. However, since the second half of the 1990s corporate income tax has been cut substantially (European Commission, 2007e). For instance, on accession to the EU Bulgaria cut its tax rate by a third and became the second member state, with Cyprus, to levy a 10 per cent rate on corporate income (compared with the highest EU rate of 38.7 per cent in Denmark).

The principle of mutual recognition has been applied to corporation taxes. In 2001 the European Commission presented proposals for reform of company taxation in the EU,[24] and rec-

---

[23] The minimum rate on wine is zero, because of its importance for the Mediterranean countries.

[24] Document COM(2001)582.

ommended that in the long run the member states should agree on a single consolidated base for computing tax on their EU-wide profits. The Commissioner for taxation, Kovacs, has pushed hard for agreement on a consolidated corporation tax base in the face of opposition for countries such as the UK and Ireland, and some of the new member states who might be required to raise taxes by the new system. The Commissioner even voiced the possibility of proceeding by enhanced co-operation if consensus could not be reached.[25]

In 1999 a heated dispute arose over a Commission proposal to introduce a withholding tax on incomes from cross-border, non-resident savings. Germany and the Scandinavian countries were in favour of such a measure, claiming that they forgo a large share of tax revenue because their wealthier citizens transfer savings to non-resident accounts. The UK and Luxembourg were thought to be the prime beneficiaries of such flows. The UK was strongly opposed to such a measure since it would hit the London-based eurobond market and encourage investors to place their holdings outside the EU.

In June 2003 agreement was reached among 12 of the member states to start exchanging information from 2005 on non-residents' savings so that each country could tax its citizens on such savings.[26] Austria, Belgium and Luxembourg are exempt from exchanging information and will levy a withholding tax instead. Three-quarters of the proceeds from this tax will go to the saver's own country with the rest remaining with the three countries. The tax rate will rise from 15 per cent in 2005 to 35 per cent in 2010. The aim is to ensure that non-EU tax havens such as Switzerland and the Channel Islands also apply the withdrawing tax. In 2005 taxes on savings in Switzerland (€100 million) and Luxembourg (€48 million) were surprisingly low, leading the European Commission to call for a review of the situation.

The liberalization of public procurement

Public orders account for about 16 per cent of EU gross domestic product (GDP) (European Commission, 2007a). According to the Cecchini Report, only one public procurement contract out of 50 was granted to a firm from another country, and the Report maintained that governments were overspending by the equivalent of 22 billion euro, often paying 25 per cent more than their private counterparts.[27] Only part of public purchases (public procurement) is subject to tender or formal contract (7–10 per cent of GDP). The aim was to introduce common rules and greater transparency in tenders.

A series of Directives was introduced relating to public procurement in the sectors of telecommunications, water, energy and transport. Measures have been taken to assist small and medium enterprises in competing for public procurement and to provide legal remedies to firms that feel they have been unfairly excluded from contracts. However, in practice public procurement has proved one of the most difficult markets to open. According to European Commission (2007a), cross-border procurement accounts for only 3 per cent of the total number of bids, though indirect public procurement made by the local subsidiaries of foreign firms amounts to 30 per cent. Some sectors such as defence are subject to special rules, and only 22 per cent of public procurement is published and hence open to competition.

---

[25] *Financial Times*, 6 October, 2007.

[26] Italy threatened to veto the agreement until the question of the fines on Italian milk farmers not respecting their quotas was resolved (see Chapter 12).

[27] European Commission (2003a).

Liberalization of the service industries

The advantages of liberalizing services are said to be similar to those of the international goods market, and are based on the improved allocation of resources with international specialization and the opportunities for exploiting economies of scale.

However, traditionally countries tend to apply restrictions on trade in services. These are said to be necessary, for example, to protect consumers, to ensure safety and minimum standards (medical services), and financial solidarity (the banking system). Alternatively, restrictions are said to be justified to protect national industries,[28] for instance for strategic or prestige reasons (air transport), to control key technologies (information science or telecommunications), for regional, social or environmental reasons (rail transport) or for cultural reasons (audiovisual services).

Restrictions on free trade in services may take various forms:[29]

- Authorization procedures;
- Quantitative restrictions;
- Reserving a certain share of the market for home producers;
- Government procurement;
- Requirements with regard to labour qualifications;
- Technical requirements and standards;
- Exchange controls;
- Subsidies.

The Treaty of Rome (Article 50) defined services as 'all those activities normally provided for remuneration insofar as they are not governed by the provisions relating to the freedom of movement of goods, capital and persons'. The Treaty called for two types of freedom in this context:

1 To provide services: any company of a member state can provide services in other member states without having to set up an office there (Article 49); and

2 To set up an establishment (Article 43): companies (or persons) from one member state may set up an establishment in another member state on the same conditions as nationals of the other member state (the principle of national treatment).

The new Lisbon Treaty would include a Protocol on services of general interest annexed to the Treaty. Services of general interest range from the so-called network services (such as energy, telecommunications and transport) to education, waste management, health and social services. The Protocol will stress the joint responsibility of the EU and member states, and establish the legal basis for EU action.

Progress in liberalizing the EU service sector in the Community has been slow. By 2006 services accounted for 60–70 per cent of economic activity in the EU (25), but only 20 per cent of intra EU cross-border trade.[30] The Lisbon Summit of 2000 called for liberalization of services and in 2002 the Commission published 'State of the Internal Market for Services' setting out the legal, administrative and practical obstacles to the movement of services in the EU.

---

[28]See also Chapter 17.

[29]This list is a modified version of that in Molle (2006).

[30]European Commission (2007a).

The Services Directive

In January 2004 the then Internal Market Commissioner, Frits Bolkenstein, proposed a directive to create an effective SEM for services. The directive aimed at removing a large number of barriers that prevent or discourage cross-border trade in services. *Inter alia* the initial proposed directive envisaged applying the country of origin principle, which would mean that if a service operator were operating legally in one member state (i.e. following home-state legislation), it could offer its services freely in others. There were widespread protests that the directive would lead to unfair competition (the 'Polish plumber' was considered the personification of the fear that there would be a huge influx of low-paid workers from Central-East Europe,[31] and in some circles there was reference to the 'Frankenstein' Directive).

In April 2006 the Commission presented a revised proposal, which was adopted by the European Parliament and the Council of Ministers in December 2006.[32] The Directive will have to be transposed into national legislation by 2009. Under the new Directive it will be easier for businesses to establish anywhere in the EU and to provide services across borders, but the country of origin principle has been removed. Businesses would be able to complete all formalities online with a single point of contact. However, member states would be able to apply restrictions that are non-discriminatory, necessary and proportionate if this were required to protect public safety, social security, health and the environment. Member states would be obliged to remove unnecessary obstacles (such as the need to open a national office or register with the local authorities).

Service providers were to be supervised by 'mutual assistance', i.e. under enhanced provisions for co-operation between national authorities, backed up by an electronic information system allowing authorities to exchange information. There is to be limited harmonization of rules including rights for recipients of services (consumers and other businesses), and information requirements.

The new service Directive would cover:

- Business services such as management consultancy, advertising, certification and testing, facilities management including office maintenance, and the services of commercial agents;
- Services provided to businesses and consumers such as real estate services, estate agents and letting services, construction architects, distributive trades and the organization of trade fairs;
- Consumer services, such as tourism, amusement parks, plumbers and electricians.

Financial services, telecommunications, transport services, broadcasting and recognition of professional qualifications were already covered by specific legislation so were excluded from the Directive.

In line with the EP's amendments the revised proposal does not affect labour law (such as collective agreements and domestic legislation on working hours and minimum wages), posted workers (for which there is separate legislation, see below), healthcare, social services relating to social housing, childcare, support of families and persons in need, activities related to the exercise of official authority, temporary work agencies, private security services, gambling and audiovisual services.

---

[31] See http://en.wikipedia.org/wiki/Polish_plumber for a picture of the original poster of the Polish plumber.

[32] It was adopted as Directive 2006/123/EC.

The posting of workers

The issue of posting of workers has also proved controversial in the EU. Posted workers are employed by a firm and, for a time, work in a member state other than the country in which work is normally carried out. A Directive of 1996 requires firms to guarantee a central core of mandatory protective legislation (e.g. covering certain conditions of work and employment) in the country where the work is carried out. None the less, in the host country there may be fears that local firms cannot match the competition of posted workers subject to less restrictive regulations in their home country, with the risk of pressure to relax legislation and instigate a 'race to the bottom'.

To meet these fears transitional measures were introduced after the 2004 enlargement. In order to avoid disruption in certain vulnerable sectors member states can limit the temporary movement of workers providing services provided they respect the general transitional arrangements to free movement of labour (see Chapter 8). Measures of this type were introduced by Germany and Austria. In response, reciprocal measures were applied by Hungary, Poland and Slovenia.

In an attempt to meet this dissatisfaction, in 2006 the Commission published 'Guidance on the Posting of Workers in the Framework of the Provision of Services'.[33] Businesses providing services should encounter less bureaucracy, quicker procedures and fewer obstacles (such as no obligation to have a permanent representative or to obtain prior authorisation in the host country, though some service companies may have to obtain a general authorisation). Member states must make it clear what they require of companies when they post workers, and can ask for a declaration on the posting of workers prior to the beginning of work. Companies must have better information regarding wages and working conditions. Service providers must keep social documents such as those relating to health and safety at work. The Commission is to help the exchange of information and administrative co-operation between member states.

The liberalization of individual service industries

The liberalization of services is rendered complicated by the fact that the various service industries have very different characteristics. For instance, services can be provided across the border (Internet services), by the customer moving to the producer (such as in tourism), or by the producer moving to the customer (for instance in the construction trade). Given this diversity, most of the discussion here is limited to financial services, transport, telecommunications, and postal services (see Box 6.5).[34] Energy is dealt with in Chapter 14. Water is not discussed here, but was singled out by the European Commission as an area where EU initiatives could prove beneficial.[35]

Financial services

According to the Cecchini Report, roughly one-third of the gains from completion of the Internal Market were to come from liberalization of financial services. The 1985 White Paper identified the main barriers in this sector as controls on capital movements and different regulatory

---

[33] European Commission (2006b).

[34] See the Single Market News (various issues) for case studies in these and other sectors, online at http:// ec.europa.eu/internal_market/smn/index_en.htm

[35] European Commission (2003b).

Box 6.5: *Postal services*

After a year-long deadlock with heated opposition being expressed by countries such as France and Luxembourg, in October 2007 agreement was reached on liberalizing the EU postal market from 2011 (compared with the initial Commission proposal of 2009). This implies that national operators will no longer have a monopoly on mail below a certain weight (currently 50 gm) known as the 'reserved area', though it seems likely that many incumbents will retain this business.

frameworks for banks and other financial institutions. Liberalization was to be based on mutual recognition, with harmonization being limited to essential legislation such as the taxation of savings and incomes from investment.

Freedom of movement of capital is generally advocated because it improves efficiency by increasing the supply of capital (additional savings will be mobilized if the prospects for investing them are better) and by enabling entrepreneurs in need of capital to raise greater amounts more tailored to their needs.

The Treaty of Rome was very cautious with regard to liberalization of capital movements, requiring liberty of movement only 'to the extent necessary to ensure proper functioning of the Common Market'. In part this reflected a fear of potential instability in capital markets, but capital controls were also considered a means of maintaining autonomy of monetary policy and of securing some exchange rate stability.[36] The Treaty allowed restrictions on capital movements, which were permitted in certain circumstances such as if movements of capital would cause disturbances in the capital market or for balance-of-payments reasons.

Essentially the Treaty of Rome was a framework agreement to be padded out by later legislation. Directives were introduced for this purpose in 1960 and 1962, and distinguished various types of transaction according to the degree of liberalization of capital movements.[37]

Until the mid-1980s, despite various proposals, there were few Community initiatives to liberalize capital movements. Some of the member states, such as Germany, the UK, the Netherlands and Belgium also proceeded with liberalization in transactions with countries outside the Community (Molle, 2006). However, France, Italy and the three new Mediterranean member states continued to make use of capital restrictions.

By the 1980s there was growing world-wide support for deregulation and liberalization of capital movements. Increasingly capital controls were felt to be ineffective on a number of grounds, in particular because:

---

[36] A theoretical justification for this kind of position was provided by the Mundell-Fleming model presented in the Appendix to Chapter 10. According to the model, autonomous monetary policy is incompatible with fixed exchange rates and free capital movements.

[37] Three categories were introduced for capital movements:
- *Fully free.* This included foreign direct investment, the purchase of real estate, short-term export credits, personal transactions such as the repatriation of earnings and former investments, and the purchase of quoted stocks in another member state.
- *Partly free.* These were: the issue of shares on the stock market of another member state, the purchase of non-quoted shares or shares in an investment fund by non-residents of that country and long-term trade credits.
- *No obligation to liberalize.* This category included short-term treasury bonds and other capital stocks, and the opening of bank accounts by non-residents of that country.

- Technological innovations, such as the use of computers and telecommunications, increased the ease and speed of capital movements, rendering it simpler to evade controls.

- Unregulated offshore financial centres provided a means of avoiding restrictions.

- Innovations in financial instruments, and the emergence of new and larger actors (such as financial conglomerates), rendered the task of regulation more complex.

Following a first modest step in 1986, in 1988 a Directive called for complete elimination of controls on capital movements both between EC member states and with third countries. This was achieved from July 1990, with the later deadlines of 1992 for Ireland and Spain, and 1996 for Greece and Portugal, though Portugal liberalized all capital controls in 1992.[38]

With regard to the **banking system**, the main obstacles to establishing banks in other EC member states included authorization procedures, capital endowment requirements and restrictions on foreign acquisitions. In 1988 the average market share of foreign banks in member states was only 1 per cent.[39] According to the White Paper, liberalization was to proceed through mutual recognition and harmonization of essential legislation and also on the basis of control by the home country.

In 1989 three Directives were passed which formed the basis for liberalization of the banking sector and a model for liberalization of other financial services. Of particular importance was the Second Banking Directive,[40] which established a single banking licence. Any bank that has received authorization by the appropriate authority in any EC state can provide services over the border and can open branches in any other EC state without the need for further authorization. The home country has main responsibility for control of the bank's activities, while the host country shares responsibility for supervision of the liquidity of branches in their own territory, as well as for measures related to the implementation of national monetary policy. Similar systems of single licences were subsequently introduced for insurance and investment services.

The division of responsibility for supervision between the home and host countries was blurred from the outset and reflects reluctance on the part of the member states to give up their authority. The immediate response of the banking system to the liberalization process was to embark on a spate of mergers and co-operation agreements.

By the mid-1990s progress was still slow in liberalizing financial services. According to the Monti Report (Monti, 1996), regulatory and other barriers had prevented the emergence of pan-European provision of services, and there was limited consolidation of the financial services industry.

To remedy this situation in 1999 **a Financial Services Action Plan (FSAP)** was launched. The Commission argued that EU financial markets had difficulty competing on an international scale and that an integrated EU capital market was important to ensure sustainable investment-driven growth and employment.

According to Commission estimates, integrated EU financial markets would increase EU GDP by at least 1.1 per cent, or €130 billion, in 2002 prices over about a decade. Total employ-

---

[38] A safeguard clause permitted the reintroduction of certain controls when the monetary or exchange rate policy of a member state was threatened. However, such controls could only be applied on capital movements liberalized under the 1988 Directive, were limited to a maximum of six months and required approval of the Commission.

[39] European Commission (2003a).

[40] The other Directives established principles and definitions regarding bank capital and the establishment of a minimum solvency ratio of 8 per cent.

ment would increase by 0.5 per cent, while the cost of equity capital would decrease by 0.5 per cent and that of bond finance by 0.4 per cent.[41]

The legislation for the FSAP at the EU level was largely in place by 2005, and its aim was to:

- create a single wholesale financial market to allow firms to raise capital on an EU-wide basis;
- complete a single EU retail market;
- ensure state-of-the-art prudential rules and supervision;
- eliminate tax obstacles to financial market integration.

Measures introduced include the Directives on: taxation of savings income (see above in the section on fiscal harmonization), insider dealing and market manipulation, pension funds and market abuse (see Chapter 17). High priority was given to improved arrangements for the effective supervision of financial institutions and the management of financial crises with a cross-border dimension (see, for instance, the 2005 White and Green Papers on Financial Services 2005–2010). In May 2007 the Commission also published a Green Paper recommending further liberalization of retail financial services (bank accounts, loans, insurance, mortgages, investment and insurance provided to individual consumers).

When the FSAP was introduced, the Commissioner for the Internal Market, Charlie McCreevy, was anxious to allay fears of excessive regulation. There was much debate as to whether regulation of the EU securities market should be carried out on the basis of co-operation and mutual recognition among the national authorities of the member states (as favoured by many in the City of London), or whether there should be a single central regulator. A single supervisor would require cross-border enforcement, and it is difficult to see how this could operate in practice in the EU where there are substantial differences in criminal and civil law among member states.

A Committee of Wise Men chaired by Alexandre Lamfalussy (a former Belgian banker) was set up to examine these questions and in 2001 presented its report. In what has become known as the 'Lamfalussy procedure' the EU is responsible for passing broad framework laws, while committees of experts work out the technical details. The procedure involved four levels:

- Level 1 deals with high-level framework legislation proposed by the Commission and voted on by the European Parliament and Council of Ministers.
- Level 2 comprises committees to advise on technical details and how measures should be implemented.
- Level 3 entails representatives of national security agencies working through a series of committees to assist the Commission as it prepares Level 2 legislation. Committees were set up for banking supervisors, insurance and occupational pensions, asset management, and securities regulators.
- Level 4 deals with compliance and enforcement of legislation.

The aim of the procedure was to permit flexibility and effective regulation of a fast-changing sector and ensure adequate consultation of market professionals. One of the difficulties is that the framework leaves the member states to fill in the details of what is a very complex legislation. In 2007 the Commission called for measures to improve the functioning of the procedure, in particular at level 3, in order to enhance supervisory convergence and co-operation. This became

---

[41] European Commission (2003c), www.europa.eu.int/comm/internal_market/en/finances/actionplan. The Commission estimates were based on a background study by the CEPR (Centre for Economic Policy Research).

more urgent following the turmoil of financial markets in the wake of the US subprime mortgage crisis from 2007. In December 2007 a proposal presented by Italy's then Finance Minister, Padoa-Schioppa, called for common standards for supervising financial institutions across the EU, but Ecofin rejected this in favour of a roadmap for more cautious step-by-step reform. The roadmap would involve a series of experts' studies to analyse the need to increase transparency, set higher valuation standards for complex financial instruments, enforce tight prudential rules and improve risk management techniques.

The tension between introducing common rules, while limiting interference and allowing sufficient flexibility to meet differing national situations was also evident in the long and confused process of introducing the MIFID, or Markets in Financial Instruments Directive. The Directive, which entered into force in November 2007 covers wholesale and retail trading in securities, including shares, bonds and derivatives. According to the 'single passport', financial firms with the approval of their home authorities will be able to operate throughout the EU. However, this also requires harmonization of investor protection rules in areas such as investment advice and the handling of orders. The Directive sets out principles rather than detailed prescriptions (also because this was the only way agreement could be reached between member states). Commissioner McCreevy maintained that this meant less regulation, but the member states encountered difficulties in transposing the legislation, while business and regulators were unsure how the new system would operate in practice.

From 2007 international financial turbulence lent new urgency to the debate in the EU about how best to ensure adequate regulation and supervision of financial markets.

Transport

Transport plays an essential role in the EU economy, accounting for about 7 per cent of GDP and 5 per cent of employment in 2006.[42] The transport system was responsible for about 71 per cent of EU oil consumption, of which 60 per cent was for road transport and 9 per cent was for air transport. Transport caused about 21 per cent of all EU carbon dioxide emissions, and emissions have risen by about 23 per cent since 1990. Road congestion has escalated and costs about 1 per cent of EU GDP.

Articles 3 and 74–84 of the Treaty of Rome (now Articles 70–80 of the TEC) envisaged the creation of a common transport policy.[43] The common transport policy was to be based on non-discrimination, different regimes for different modes of transport, and the right of establishment but not freedom of services (access to other EC markets was dependent on EC provisions). This rather contradictory list already showed the difficulty in reaching common positions. The Treaty of Rome lacked details about how the common transport policy was to operate, and the actual design of the common policy was left to the Council.

Progress in introducing common transport measures proved slow and controversial because of different attitudes about the form that intervention in transport should take, and conflicts of interest among the member states.

In 1961 the Commission presented its proposals for the general principles of the common transport policy in a document known as the 'Schaus Memorandum' after the first commissioner responsible for transport, Lambert Schaus. The purpose of the Schaus Memorandum was

---

[42] The statistics in this paragraph are taken from European Commission (2006d).

[43] Article 71 (Formerly Article 75) sets out the main features of the common transport policy, which include common rules applicable to the internal transport of member states, the conditions for operating in other member states, and measures to improve safety. According to Article 80, the common transport policy applies to rail, road and inland waterways, but the Treaty envisages the Council extending its provisions to sea and air transport, and an amendment to this effect was included in the Single European Act.

to begin discussion of the basic principles underlying the common policy. According to the Commission, this would involve an attempt to 'create healthy competition of the widest scope'. National transport policies were to be replaced by a common policy based on competition. Measures would be introduced to eliminate discrimination, to liberalize the provision of services and to harmonize measures such as the weights and dimensions of vehicles, the conditions of work in road transport and the taxation of vehicles. The emphasis of the Commission's proposals was therefore on deregulation. The proposals were bound to create controversy given the highly regulated nature of transport policy in the member states at that time.

Though Ecosoc and the European Parliament accepted the principles of the Commission's recommendations, the Council took little action to implement the proposals. In 1962 the Commission presented an Action Programme setting out the measures that the Commission thought necessary to implement the common transport policy. The emphasis was still on competition and liberalization, and the Commission also proposed extending these principles to national transport systems. Again the Commission's proposals met with opposition from the member states. It was argued that 'excessive' competition would cause safety standards to be undermined, lead to bankruptcies and render railways incapable of competing with road haulage (Swann, 2000).

Following the first enlargement of the Community in 1973, the Commission attempted a change in strategy and called for harmonization of national policies as a first step in introducing a common policy. A revised version of the Action Plan was presented in 1973. After a substantial delay, the Council called on the Commission to define its priorities. Over the next few years the Commission presented various proposals, but the Council failed to agree on the necessary steps for their implementation. Eventually, in 1982 the European Parliament decided to take the Council to the Court of Justice for failing to respect its obligation to introduce the common transport policy set out in the Treaty of Rome.

Since 1985 progress in introducing common transport measures has been more rapid for a number of reasons:

- Transport was an integral part of the 1993 Programme.
- In 1985 the European Court ruled that the Council should adopt measures to liberalize transport 'within a reasonable time'.
- There was an international trend towards the liberalization of transport that was particularly evident in the United States during the Reagan years.
- In 1986 in the Nouvelles Frontières case the European Court of Justice ruled in favour of a French firm that had been charging prices below those fixed by the French authorities. This ruling gave leeway to the EC Commission to overrule national agreements.

In 1992 the EC Commission published a White Paper, 'The future development of the common transport policy', aimed at liberalizing transport markets. With the exception of the rail sector, considerable progress was made in the following decade in realizing the basic aim of the White Paper to open up the transport market.

Given the difficulties in introducing common measures on transport in the early years of the Community, the Maastricht Treaty reinforced the legal, decision-making and financial bases of the common transport policy. The Treaty also laid the basis for TENs, or trans-European networks, to improve transport, energy and telecommunications infrastructure with the help of Community financing.

However, difficulties arose because the modal split between different forms of transport was increasingly biased towards road and air transport (see also Box 6.6), inducing additional problems of congestion and pollution. Infrastructure (for example, for rail freight transport) remained inadequate, and attempts to improve the situation through programmes such as the TENs suffered from inadequate financing, bureaucratic delays and complexities of co-ordination. New and different traffic patterns as a result of EU enlargement exacerbated the problems.

Box 6.6: *Ryanair subsidies*

Ryanair became the EU's leading low-cost airline by cutting out the frills, using one type of aircraft, flying its aircraft more frequently and concentrating on smaller regional airports to cut costs and shorten turnaround times. In February 2004 the European Commission ruled against airport subsidies granted by Charleroi (the airport used for Brussels) to Ryanair. The owner of Charleroi, the Walloon regional government, had given a 50 per cent reduction in landing fees to Ryanair, and contributed in money or kind to Ryanair's local hotel, office, training and marketing costs. According to the EU Commission such assistance was discriminatory and ran counter to EU legislation on state aids.

In 2007 a Commission ruling blocked a Ryanair takeover bid for Irish flag-carrying airline Aer Lingus. The head of RyanAir, Michael O'Leary, not known for his understatement, referred to the chief anti-trust regulator of the EU as an 'evil empire' among various other expletives reported in the popular press.

In 1998 the Cardiff European Council called for strategies with regard to sustainable development, also in transport, and this objective was also taken up in the Amsterdam Treaty and the Gothenburg European Council of 2001.

In 2001 the European Commission published a White Paper, 'European transport policy for 2010: Time to decide' setting out 60 measures to be introduced, an Action programme extending until 2010, and a monitoring process (European Commission, 2001). In 2006 a mid-term review of the programme (European Commission, 2006d) assessed progress and reorganized the objectives into four main pillars:

1 **Mobility of people and businesses throughout the union.** Measures were to include common rules relating to professional qualifications and working conditions for road transport; extending the liberalization of international rail transport also to passenger transport; creating a single European sky, increasing airport capacity and tackling the environmental consequences of air travel, and the creation of an internal shipping space and greater port capacity for maritime transport.

2 **Environmental protection, the security of energy supply, promoting minimum labour standards, and protecting passengers and citizens.** In addition to environmental measures there was to be more training and job creation in the transport sector, and the promotion of higher levels with regard to passenger rights, safety, security and urban transport.

3 **Innovation to make the sector more efficient and more sustainable.** This would involve measures to improve energy efficiency, also by promoting new technologies, and increased investment in infrastructure, also through the encouragement of co-financing with private sponsors. Galileo, Europe's satellite radionavigation system would be used to improve measures of communication, navigation and automation.

4 **Action on the world stage so other countries can share the objectives.** Increased co-operation is necessary because regulation of transport is becoming an increasingly international

matter, but international rules sometimes take insufficient account of environmental protection or safety considerations.

Telecommunications

The telecommunication and information sectors were traditionally characterized by national monopolies in the provision of equipment and services. It was considered that with more than one supplier costly networks would be duplicated, leading to an overall loss in welfare. The Cecchini Report found price differences in telephone and telegraph services of as much as 50 per cent among EC member states prior to the introduction of the SEM.

With the rapid technological progress in the information and telecommunications industry, the argument in favour of natural monopolies was undermined. There was strong pressure to liberalize both from corporate users of telecommunication services, and at the international level.

A 1988 Directive was aimed at the ending of national monopolies on equipment, and a further Directive of 1990 called for liberalization of the provision of services (except basic telephone services). New Regulatory Agencies (NRAs), which were to be independent from both government and operators, were set up in all the member states to implement EU regulations.

The EU has launched programmes such as RACE (Research in Advanced Communications for Europe) and ESPRIT (European Strategic Programme for Research and Development in Information Technologies) and BRITE/EURAM (Basic Research in Industrial Technologies for Europe/Raw Materials and Advanced Materials) to help Community firms develop new technologies.

In 2007 the EC presented proposals for an overhaul of telecommunications, a key sector in efforts to render the EU economy more competitive. This would entail a pan-European regulator to open the telecoms market to competition and ensure regulatory consistency. National telecoms watchdogs would be allowed to split the service and network businesses of large operators in order to allow access to rivals. The EC would have powers of intervention if national telecoms authorities failed to address problems. The proposal seems likely to encounter opposition from established operators such as France Telecom, and Deutsche Telecom, and some member states may be reluctant to give up regulatory powers.

Agreement was also reached on a regulation to limit the costs of roaming (making and receiving mobile phone calls) charges from summer 2007.

The Internal Market Strategy for the twenty-first century

In May 2003 the European Commission published a 10-point plan to improve the working of the Internal Market. The priorities of the plan were to improve the implementation and enforcement of Internal Market legislation, encourage the free movement of services, remove the remaining barriers to trade in goods and create a free market for public procurement.[44]

Box 6.7 sets out the 10 points of the Strategy. Many of the proposed initiatives have been discussed above in the context of the various barriers to be removed by the Internal Market Project (services, taxes etc.) and the difficulties of implementation. In order to improve the conditions for business, the Commission aimed at fostering innovation and entrepreneurship, building in particular on the European Charter for Small Enterprises endorsed by the Feira Council of 2000.

---

[44]European Commission (2003b).

Box 6.7: *The 10-point plan to improve the working of the Internal Market*

- enforcing the rules
- integrating service markets
- improving the free movement of goods
- meeting the demographic challenge
- improving essential services
- improving conditions for business
- simplifying the regulatory environment
- reducing tax obstacles
- introducing more open public procurement markets
- providing better information

In 2007 the Commission carried out a review of initiatives of the previous 20 years related to the SEM, assessing its achievements (see next section) and indicating ways in which it could be adapted better to meet the needs of the twenty-first century (European Commission 2007f). The study indicated a number of priorities including:

- more attention to the needs of citizens, consumers and small and medium enterprises;
- further integration of the EU economy;
- development of a knowledge society;
- improved regulation;
- a more sustainable EU;
- a market more responsive to the global context; and
- improved monitoring, and better communication.

The achievements of the SEM Programme

The Cecchini Report

As stated above, at the time when the SEM Programme was launched the most extensive analysis of its likely effects was the Cecchini Report, which was based on the following methods of evaluation:

- **Opinion surveys of business.** These were based on questionnaires about the costs of given barriers and likely responses to their removal.
- **Industry case studies** of the cost structure of enterprises and the likely market barriers they face, including attempts to estimate the possible impact of restructuring the industry branch in response to increased competitive pressures.

■ **Micro- and macroeconomic analyses** of the expected effects.[45]

The most discussed and controversial estimates were those based on a macroeconomic approach, which suggested that in the case of passive macroeconomic policies, the overall impact (after an estimated 5–6 years) of the SEM Programme could be a 4.5 per cent increase in GDP, a 6 per cent reduction in the price level and the creation of about 2 million jobs. With a more active macroeconomic policy (reflecting the improved economic performance), there would be a 7 per cent increase in GDP, a 4.5 per cent reduction in inflation and the creation of 5 million jobs.[46]

With the benefit of hindsight, various criticisms of the Cecchini predictions of the Internal Market effects can be made. The analysis of the economic consequences of the Internal Market Programme shares the difficulty of all empirical analysis of integration in that it is almost impossible to separate the integration effect from overall economic developments.

In the Report the estimates of direct benefits from reduced controls at the border were relatively small, while the estimates of secondary dynamic effects (economies of scale, restructuring, increased competition) were large. It is difficult to produce more than 'guestimates' or 'speculative ranges' concerning the size of such dynamic effects. In fact, the more important the effects are said to be, the more vague and less precise the Commission's analysis appeared.

Too much emphasis was placed on economies of scale in the Cecchini analysis. It had to be shown they are only possible in a European rather than a national market and that they promote efficiency. Too little account was taken of the costs of adjustment or of the impact on regional disparities. The approach tended to emphasize the supply rather than the demand side, and the results were very sensitive to changes in the economic environment.

One of the criticisms of the Cecchini study to attract most attention at the time was that of Baldwin (1989), who argued that the expected gains from the SEM Programme might be far larger than those estimated in the Cecchini Report. The Cecchini study attempted to estimate how the SEM Programme would increase the level of output rather than the rate of growth. In other words, according to Baldwin, the Cecchini Report was considering a one-off rather than a continuing effect.

---

[45]Various approaches were used, including:
A static, partial equilibrium approach, which uses information obtained from the industry studies and other surveys to assess the net welfare effects on producers, consumers and government spending. The analysis is 'partial' equilibrium in the sense that each barrier and each economic sector is considered one at a time and then the results are aggregated. The approach ignores the extent to which barriers overlap and markets are interconnected. In other words, no account is taken of the consequences of changes in factor prices or in the relative prices of products as a result of reducing the barriers.
A general equilibrium microeconomics approach which attempts to take into account the interactions between different sectors.
The use of macroeconomic models in an attempt to show the evolution of costs, prices, income and other macroeconomic variables (including policy) as a result of introduction of the Single Market. The emphasis here is on what happens during the adjustment period, considering questions such as how quickly workers made redundant by the restructuring process can find work elsewhere.
Estimates of dynamic effects were carried out, attempting to estimate how market conditions affect the rate of technological progress, innovations and the strategic reactions of business (through the learning process and so on).

[46]The results of the general equilibrium microeconomic approach suggest possible gains of 2.5 per cent of GDP (or 70 billion ECU) for a narrow conception of the gains from removing barriers, to a range of 4.5–6.5 per cent (125–90 billion ECU) for a more competitive, integrated market.

Assessments of the SEM Programme by the European Commission

In an extensive review of the SEM carried out by the European Commission in 2007,[47] various achievements were indicated:

- Between 1992 and 2006 the estimated gains of the Internal Market amounted to 2.15 per cent of GDP and 2.75 million extra jobs.
- Intra-EU trade rose by 30 per cent between 1995 and 2005.
- Cross-border investments increased, with the share of total foreign direct investment flows in the former EU(15) originating in other EU(15) countries rising from 53 per cent in 1995 to 78 per cent in 2005.
- As a result of more open public procurement rules there have been savings to governments of 10–30 per cent.

However, another study by the European Commission in the same year suggested that the effect of the SEM was slowing down, citing various developments:[48]

- The ratio of intra-EU trade to GDP increased in the second half of the 1990s but stabilized in 2000.
- Foreign direct investment (FDI; mainly by EU firms) grew rapidly in the 1990s, but has fallen as a share of EU GDP since 2001.
- Despite rapid convergence of prices in the EU(25), price divergence remained stable in the EU(15) in recent years. Introduction of the euro appears to have boosted trade, FDI and cross-border mergers but not price convergence in the euro area.
- The largest EU firms earnt 2/3 of revenue outside their home country in 2005 (1/2 in 1997), but the average consumer spent 86 per cent of income on goods made or provided at home.

In 2006 an extensive public consultation on the SEM was carried out,[49] and on the basis of its results, the European Commission indicated various benefits of the Internal Market for EU citizens (see Box 6.8).[50] Despite the broad agreement emerging from the consultation that the SEM has brought benefits, some (consumer organizations and small and medium enterprises) questioned how far the benefits have gone to consumers and small businesses. The survey suggested that gaps needed to be addressed in services (including retail financial services, insurance and transport), energy, taxation, free movement of workers and intellectual property. It was also felt that there were problems with implementation and enforcement, and some of those responding called for the development of the 'social dimension' of the SEM (see Chapter 16).

---

[47] European Commission (2007f).

[48] European Commission (2007a).

[49] European Commission, 2006c. The consultation received 1514 replies from the public sector, individual businesses, citizens, academia and so on, though there were relatively few replies from the new member states and from regional and local authorities. See also Special Eurobarometer 254, and Flash Eurobarometer 180 and 190 of 2006.

[50] European Commission (2007f).

Box 6.8: *The public consultation on the SEM of 2006*

- 84 per cent of EU citizens considered the opportunity to study abroad positive.

- 72 per cent of citizens find that travelling in the EU is easier than 10 years ago.

- Despite the restrictions after the 2004 and 2007 enlargements (see Chapter 8), 70 per cent of EU citizens consider the possibility of working in another member state positive, and some 15 million EU citizens work or are retired in other member states.

- 73 per cent of citizens think that the Internal Market has improved the range and quality of products being sold.

- Prices are perceived as lower, and consumer rights better protected as a result of the Single market.

- Most citizens favour further liberalization in areas such as transport, telecommunications, banking and insurance.

The study by the Commission also summarized the benefits for business:

- A single market of almost 500 million people permitting economies of scale and linked by improved networks for transport, telecommunications and electricity;

- Easier cross-border trade with the elimination of border bureaucracy and the spread of the euro;

- The average cost of setting up a new business fell from €813 in 2002 to €554 in 2007, with the average time for registering a company also down from 24 days in 2002 to 12 in 2007;

- The spread of EU standards and labels;

- New sources of financing, contracts and funding;

- Improved cross-border co-operation and technology transfer.

The impact of the SEM project on third countries

Emerson et al. (1989) estimated that the completion of the Internal Market would increase the competitiveness of EC industry, leading to a decline in imports from the rest of the world by as much as 10 per cent.[51] Fear of loss of relative competitiveness was a major factor in causing the European Free Trade Association (EFTA) countries to negotiate the European Economic Area, and this in turn led to EU accession by Austria, Sweden and Finland.

Countries such as Japan and the USA feared the prospect of a 'Fortress Europe' and attempted to ensure a foothold within the fortress through increased foreign direct investment. The rapid increase in Japanese firms operating in the Community led to a tightening of 'screwdriver' legislation in 1987 aimed at ensuring a minimum EC share of components in goods produced in the Community.

At the time the Commission argued that this possible negative effect of increased EC com-

---

[51] Emerson et al. (1989, p. 182) also estimate the possible percentage changes in extra-EC imports for various sectors. These range from 0 for agriculture, −5.8 for textiles and clothing to −30.9 for communications, and −61.3 for credit and insurance.

petitiveness in reducing imports from the rest of the world would be offset insofar as higher GDP would lead to increased demand for imports.[52] Dealing with EU or mutually recognized standards, and EU rather than national quotas, also simplifies procedures for producers in third countries. It is difficult to isolate Internal Market effects from other developments, but the more buoyant EU economy indicated by the Commission studies discussed above could be reflected in greater confidence at a world level, rendering the EU more willing to improve access to its markets. This could prove important in facing the growing turbulence of international markets from 2007, and the likely failure of the WTO Doha Round.

Evaluation

The SEM Programme was an important stimulus to restructuring of the EU economy, and in its absence there would probably have been slower growth and less job creation in Europe. The Internal Market Programme has also been important for its spill-over into other areas of integration, including EMU, institutional reform, the 1995 enlargement, regional and social measures and competition policy.

However, following the economic success of the Community until the mid-1970s, the SEM Programme failed to stem the growing gap in GDP and productivity compared with the USA (see also the next chapter). Various explanations for this shortcoming have been advanced:

- The SEM Programme is incomplete, in particular, in areas such as services, public procurement and taxes.

- The SEM Programme was mainly restricted to product and capital markets, excluding liberalization of labour markets, which remained largely the prerogative of member states. More recent analysis, such as the Sapir Report (Sapir et al., 2004) maintained that without greater labour market reform, liberalization of product markets would prove inadequate to trigger the reallocation of resources necessary to promote more rapid growth.

- The diagnosis at the time of the SEM Programme, that the poor economic performance of the Community was due to fragmentation of markets and inability to exploit economies of scale, seemed increasingly dated in an environment characterized by the need to meet the challenges of globalization, knowledge-based economies and information and communication technologies (ICT).

To address these shortcomings of the SEM Programme, as explained in Chapter 7, in 2000 the Lisbon Strategy of 'economic, social and environmental renewal' was launched. As explained in Chapter 7, the Lisbon Strategy suffers from weaknesses, but is intended to flank the ongoing task of completion of the SEM.

---

[52] It has also been argued that the SEM Programme could lead to changes in trade distribution, or the substitution of one third-country supplier for another. This may occur, for instance, because the removal of national restrictions involving preferences for a particular third country, or group of countries, or because some countries are better able to adjust to the new situation than others.

Summary of Key Concepts

- During the 1970s and early 1980s the EC member states were becoming increasingly concerned about the growing lag between their economic performance and that of countries such as Japan and the USA, especially in high-technology sectors. The explanation given was the **fragmentation of the EC market**.

- Krugman (1991) found that the level of specialization in the USA was higher than in the EC, even though the distances were greater.

- In 1985 Jacques Delors launched the SEM Programme as a strategy to raise EC competitiveness.

- **The main non-tariff barriers** that the SEM Programme aimed at removing were: frontier controls; differences in technical specifications and standards; differences in national tax systems; and restrictions on competition for public purchases and restrictions on providing certain services (in particular financial and transport services) in other EC countries.

- The **Cockfield White Paper**, 'Completing the Internal Market', of 1985 called for the elimination of barriers between EC countries by the end of 1992 and set out 282 measures necessary to achieve this aim.

- The **Single European Act of 1987** set out the formal steps necessary to introduce the SEM.

- In practice **incomplete implementation** of the measures and the granting of temporary derogations have undermined the effectiveness of the SEM.

- One of the main aims of removing **frontier controls** is to permit the free movement of people, as described in Chapter 8.

- **Standards and technical restrictions** may act as barriers to trade but may be needed to protect consumer interests.

- The Community has made slow progress in bringing the national **tax systems** of the member states in line with each other.

- Little progress has been made in opening up **public procurement** to foreign firms.

- In 2006 agreement was reached on a revised version of a Directive to create an effective SEM for **services.**

- With the SEM programme the movement of capital between member states was liberalized. With regard to **financial services**, any bank that has received authorization by the appropriate authority in any EC state can provide services over the border and can open branches in any other EC state without the need for further authorization. The FSAP (Financial Services Action Programme) entailed the introduction of 42 measures to liberalize financial markets.

- Difficulties in interpreting the Treaty of Rome, and different interests of the member states, meant that progress in introducing a common **transport** policy was slow. The SEM Programme, and the deregulation prevalent from the mid-1980s, lent a new emphasis to introducing common transport measures.

- The White Paper published by the Commission in 2001 set out the main objectives of EU transport policy until 2010, and this was updated with a mid-term review in 2006. The objectives are divided into four main pillars: mobility of people and businesses; environmental measures and protection; innovation; and action on the world stage.

- The SEM programme ended national monopolies of telecommunications and information services, and will entail liberalization of postal services by 2011.
- The **Cecchini Report** suggested that if macroeconomic policies remained unchanged, the overall impact (after an estimated 5–6 years) of the SEM Programme could be a 4.5 per cent increase in GDP, and a 6 per cent reduction in the price levels. A later Commission study estimated the increase in GDP at about 2.2 per cent in 2006, and the creation of jobs at 2.75 million compared with the situation without the 1993 Programme.
- Possibly the most **lasting effects** of the SEM Programme are the kick-start it gave to the deregulation process and the spill-over effect into other areas of integration such as institutional reform, the restructuring of EU firms through mergers and acquisitions, EMU and social and regional measures.

Questions for study and review

1 Describe the main barriers causing fragmentation of the European market.

2 What were the expected advantages of the SEM Programme?

3 Indicate the main steps in introducing the SEM Programme.

4 What was the significance of the Single European Act in the integration process?

5 Describe, with examples, the areas where implementation of the SEM Programme has been particularly slow.

6 What measures are necessary to introduce an SEM for financial services?

7 Why was it so difficult to introduce a common transport policy?

8 What developments from the mid-1980s led to acceleration in introducing common transport measures?

9 What measures do you consider necessary for the improvement of the EU transport system, and how far is the EU introducing such measures?

10 In practice the effects of the SEM Programme were different from those initially predicted. Explain why you think that this was the case.

11 Why is it probable that the SEM will never be achieved?

Research tasks

1 Choose a specific EU industry; examine the role of the EU Commission in promoting the achievement of the SEM in that industry; the expected benefits that would come from the SEM in the sector considered and the potential obstacles (short-term and long-term) remaining to completing the SEM in that industry.

2 Analyse the activities of the SOLVIT Office in your country, using case studies.

References

Ardy, B. and El-Agraa, A. (2007) 'Tax harmonisation' in El-Agraa, A., *The European Union: Economics and Policies*, 8th edn. Cambridge University Press, Cambridge, UK.

Baldwin, R. (1989) 'The growth effects of 1992', *Economic Policy*, Vol. 2, pp. 247–81.

Cecchini, P. (1988) *The European Challenge: The Benefits of a Single Market*, Wildwood House, Aldershot.

Commons (2002) 'Crossborder shopping and smuggling', *House of Commons Library*, Research paper 02/40, London.

Coombes, P. and Overman, H. (2004) 'The special distribution of economic activity in the EU' in Henderson, V. and Thisse, J.F. (eds) *Handbook of Regional and Urban Economics*, Vol. 4, Elsevier, Amsterdam.

Emerson, E., Aujean, M., Catinat, M., Goybet, P. and Jacquemin, A. (1989) *The Economics of 1992: The EC Commission's Assessment of the Economic Effects of Completing the Single Market*, Oxford University Press, Oxford.

European Commission (2001) *European transport policy for 2010: Time to decide*, COM (2001) 370 final, www.europa.eu/scadplus/leg

European Commission (2002a) *Second Biennial Report on the application of the principle of mutual recognition in the Single Market*, COM(2002) 419 final.

European Commission (2003a) *The Internal Market: Ten years without frontiers*, www.europa.eu.int/comm/internal_market

European Commission (2003b) *Internal Market strategy. Priorities 2003–2006*, COM (2003) 238 final, www.europa.eu.int/comm/internal_market

European Commission (2003c) *Financial services. Ninth report, November*, www.europa.eu.int/comm/internal_market/en/finances/actionplan

European Commission (2006a) *Survey on a Future Single Market Policy*, SEC(2006).

European Commission (2006b) *Guidance on the Posting of Workers in the Framework of the Provision of Service*s, COM(2006) 159 final.

European Commission (2006c) *Public Consultation on a Future Single Market Policy,* SEC(2006) 1215/2.

European Commission (2006d) *Keep Europe Moving – Sustainable mobility for our Continent. Mid-term review of the Transport White Paper published in 2001 by the European Commission*, COM (2006) 314 final, www.europa.eu/scadplus/leg

European Commission (2007a) 'Steps towards a deeper economic integration: The internal market in the 21st Century. A contribution to the Single Market Review', *European Economy*, No. 272, January.

European Commission (2007b) *Consumer policy strategy 2007–2013: Empowering consumers, enhancing their welfare, effectively protecting them*, COM(2007) 99 final, www.ec.europa.eu./consumers

European Commission (2007c) *VAT rates applied in the member states of the European Community*, Doc/2137/2007, www.ec.europa.eu/taxation_customs

European Commission (2007d) *Excise duty tables*, www.ec.europa.eu/taxation_customs

European Commission (2007e) *Taxation Trends in the EU: Main Results*, www.ec.europa.eu/taxation_customs

European Commission (2007f) *A Single Market for 21st Century Europe*, COM(2007)724, www.ec.europa.eu/internal_market

Hitiris, T. (1994) *European Community Economics*, 3rd edn, Prentice Hall, Harlow, UK.

Krugman, P. (1991) *Geography and Trade*, Leuven University Press, Leuven and The MIT Press, Cambridge, MA.

Mattera, A. (1988) *Marché unique européen: Ses règles, son fonctionnement*, Jupiter, Paris.

Molle, W. (2006*) The Economics of European Integration. Theory, Practice, Policy*, 5th edn, Ashgate, Aldershot.

Monti, M. (1996) *The Single Market and Tomorrow's Europe: A Progress Report from The European Commission*, Kogan Page, London.

Sapir, A., Aghion, P., Bertóla, G. et al. (2004) *An Agenda for a Growing Europe: The Sapir Report*, Oxford University Press, Oxford.

Swann, D. (2000) *The Economics of Europe: From Common Market to European Union*, 2nd edn, Penguin Business Library, London.

Tsoukalis, L. (1997) *The New European Economy Revisited*, 3rd edn, Oxford University Press, Oxford.

Useful websites

Studies of various trade issues are provided by the European Commission: www.ec.europa.eu/internal_market

The Directorate-General Energy and Transport of the European Commission: www.ec.europa.eu/dgs/energy_transport

Other international organizations that deal with standards are:

The United Nations Economic Commission for Europe (UNECE), www.unece.org

World Intellectual Property Organization, www.wipo.org

World Trade Organization, www.wto.org

CHAPTER 07

The Lisbon Strategy and Beyond

❖ LEARNING OBJECTIVES

By the end of this chapter you should be able to understand:

❖ Some of the possible effects of globalization on EU countries;

❖ How the Lisbon Summit of 2000 aimed to improve EU economic performance through the creation of a 'knowledge-based economy', and an EU education and training system of 'world quality reference' by 2010;

❖ The main criticisms made of the Lisbon Strategy;

❖ How the Commission attempted (with limited success) to revise the Lisbon Strategy and introduce an 'Agenda for a Growing Europe'.

Introduction

Years after the 1993 Internal Market deadline the EU continued to lag behind the USA in terms of competitiveness and productivity. Though it can be argued that the Single Market Project is still not complete, the assumption that all the shortcomings of the European economy could be attributed to market fragmentation became increasingly questionable. Subsequently, low EU productivity has been more frequently explained in terms of factors such as labour market rigidities, inadequate investment in education and training, and a technology gap, in particular with regard to information science.

In addition to the gap compared with US economic performance, there was also growing concern regarding the challenge posed by Asia, with China emerging as a major economic actor, and India becoming an increasingly important location for outsourcing. As will be described in the first part of this chapter, the opening up of such countries, and the acceleration of globalization, have lent a new urgency to the task of increasing EU competitiveness.

In March 2000 the Lisbon European Council decided to launch a 'new strategic goal' aimed at economic, social and environmental renewal in the following 10 years. The objective was to transform the EU into the 'most dynamic competitive knowledge-based economy in the world' by 2010. EU training and education systems were to become a 'world quality reference'. The second part of this chapter deals with the main aspects of the Lisbon agenda and its criticisms, revision and outlook.

The diagnosis: lagging growth and productivity

As a result of the economic success of the early years of the Community, with growth and employment reaching unprecedented levels (see Chapter 2), the GDP per capita of the Community rose to about 70 per cent of the US level by the mid-1970s. Subsequently this gap has failed to narrow (see Table 7.1). In both 1997 and 2006 labour productivity per person employed in the USA was 139 per cent of that of the EU(27). An ongoing query since the aftermath of the 1979 oil crisis is to explain why the EU has failed to close this gap, and what remedy could reverse the process.

The need for faster EU growth is advocated on a number of counts: to facilitate the catching up of the new member states; to preserve the European model (combining economic, social and environmental objectives – see Chapters 14 and 16) in the face of demographic ageing, or because slow growth makes the process of reform more difficult and may render the political influence of the EU negligible (Alesina and Giavazzi, 2006).

As shown in Table 7.2, according to two of the best-known indices of competitiveness the USA still ranked higher than almost all the EU economies in 2006.[1] This may change following

	EU(27)	EU(25)	USA
GDP per capita (PPS*, EU(27)=100)	100	103.9	151.1 (f)
Labour productivity per person employed (PPS, EU(27)=100)	100	103.9	140.3
Employment rate (%)	64.4 (p)	64.7 (p)	72.0
Employment rate females (%)	57.3	57.6	66.1
Employment rate of older workers (%)	43.5	43.6	61.8
Comparative price levels (EU(27)=100)	100	101.1	102.5 (2003)
Greenhouse gas emissions (index base year =100)# #2005	92.1	n/a	116.3
Energy intensity of the economy**	208.5	n/a	308.6 (2005)
Volume of freight transport relative to GDP 1995 = 100	106.7	106.2	94.1 (2004)

TABLE 7.1 Selected structural indicators of the EU and USA (2006 unless otherwise indicated)#

Source: *Eurostat*, © European Communities, 2008 www.epp.eurostat.ec.europa.eu.

#These are some of the standard indicators published on a regular basis by Eurostat to assess progress in realizing the Lisbon Strategy.

In general 1990, but 1995 for HFC, PFC and SF6 (see Chapter 14).

* purchasing power standards

**Gross inland consumption of energy divided by GDP (kilogram of oil equivalent per euro).

f: forecast

p: provisional

n/a: not available

---

[1] The IMD in Switzerland carries out annual studies of competitiveness taking into account more than 300 variables. These reflect current economic performance, business surveys and factors such as infrastructure and innovation. The rankings of the World Economic Forum are calculated from both publicly available data and an annual opinion survey conducted by the World Economic Forum together with its network of partner institutes (research institutes and business organizations). In 2007 over 11 000 business leaders were polled in 131 countries.

Overall ranking International Institute for Management Development (IMD) 2006.		Overall ranking World Economic Forum 2007/8 (2006 ranking in brackets)*	
	Rank	Country	Rank
USA	1	USA (1)	1
Hong Kong	2	Switzerland (4)	2
Singapore	3	Denmark (3)	3
Iceland	4	Sweden (9)	4
Denmark	5	Germany (7)	5
Australia	6	Finland (6)	6
Canada	7	Singapore (8)	7
Switzerland	8	Japan (5)	8
Luxembourg	9	UK (2)	9
Finland	10	Netherlands (11)	10

TABLE 7.2 World competitiveness

* Part of the change of ranking between 2006 and 2007 reflects a change in methodology. For instance, a measure of the exchange rate was removed from the index on the grounds that although a weak currency makes exports more competitive, it also adds to import costs. The statistics on world competitiveness ranking of the World Economic Forum in 2006 and 2007 are reproduced with permission of Palgrave MacMillan 2006 data is reproduced with the permission of IMD International, Switzerland, World Competitiveness Center www.imd.ch/wcc.

the fallout from the crisis in the US sub-prime mortgage market in 2007, and both the EU and the USA have to face the challenge of a more turbulent international environment.[2]

In 2006 the increase in the gap in growth and labour productivity that had been observed for a decade came to a halt. In 2006 growth of the EU GDP was 3 per cent, and the 2.6 per cent growth rate of GDP per capita in the EU(27) was higher than that of the USA (2.3 per cent).[3] Gross domestic product per capita growth is determined by changes in population, employment and labour productivity. In 2006 EU employment growth rose to 1.6 per cent, and the increase of EU productivity per worker was 1.5 per cent, outstripping that of the USA (1.4 per cent). According to the 2007 Competition Report of the European Commission, the upturn was cyclical, but there was also a structural component linked to structural reforms in the member states, in particular in labour markets.[4]

When expressed as GDP per hour worked the productivity gap between the EU and USA is lower at 26 per cent in 2005. Productivity per hour worked depends on capital intensity, labour quality and total factor productivity. Capital intensity indicates the capital stock per hour worked. The quality of labour can be measured by the educational attainment of those employed. Total factor productivity is a residual between total hourly labour productivity and the other two components, and indicates the impact of technological progress, knowledge and organizational changes. According to the European Commission (2007) most of the labour productivity gap

---

[2] The rise in international economic uncertainty already began earlier. A major setback in terms of promoting the creation of a fully-fledged 'knowledge-based economy' was the series of technology, media and telecoms (TMT) stock crashes that occurred between March 2000 (days after the Lisbon Summit) and late 2002, and impacted massively on investors' confidence around the world. Add to this the string of accounting scandals (Worldcom, Enron, AA …) and the resulting stringent regulatory environment in major countries. The overall impact was to undermine confidence in the robustness of western economies.

[3] The statistics in this paragraph are taken from European Commission (2007).

[4] European Commission (2007).

between the EU and USA is to be explained by total factor productivity, with labour quality also being lower (though it improved in the EU in 2006). Capital intensity is higher in the EU than USA, but further analysis would be necessary to assess whether there is a gap in the quality of capital relative to the USA. The policy implication is that to close the gap the EU should give priority to policies increasing total factor productivity such as information and communication technology (ICT), research, innovation, competition and better regulation, as well as measures to improve human capital.

According to European Commission (2007), at a sectoral level, in the EU GDP growth tends to be concentrated in a few sectors, in particular, services. Among manufacturing sectors only electrical and optical equipment, and chemicals make a substantial contribution to growth. The labour productivity gap between the EU and USA did not appear to be due to the sectoral composition (or industry mix) of the EU economy.

The challenges of globalization for the EU

Recent years have witnessed an intense process of globalization (understood here as increasing worldwide economic integration), with trade in goods and services and cross-border capital flows rising substantially relative to GDP. In the case of trade this has led to global merchandise exports amounting to over 20 per cent of world gross national product in 2007 compared with 8 per cent in 1913 at the end of the last era of globalization (from 1870 and ending with the start of the First World War).[5] Financial integration has also proceeded rapidly. The sum of stocks of foreign assets and liabilities as a share of GDP increased fivefold since the 1980s and rose by more than 130 per cent between 1995 and 2005.[6]

Various studies indicate that recent globalization has increased living standards worldwide, but not for everybody: there have been winners and losers from globalization (della Posta et al., forthcoming); World Bank, 2007; IMF, 2007). Empirical evidence suggests that developing countries that experienced substantial poverty reduction have generally been those most integrated into the global economy through trade and foreign direct investment. However, though beyond the scope of the present discussion, studies such as World Bank (2007) point to the share of world income falling for countries less well able to participate in the process of globalization such as sub-Saharan Africa.

The international financial turbulence following the crisis of the US subprime mortgage market also illustrates how the globalization of international capital movements has added a new urgency to the need for adequate supervision and regulation of financial markets (see Chapter 6), and appropriate macroeconomic policies.

Schumpeter refers to the process of 'creative destruction' and in the context of the challenge of globalization it implies the shift of EU production away from traditional, low-skilled tasks and sectors towards new competitive activities and specializations. According to economic theory,[7] when developed countries compete with low-wage economies such as China and India there will be downward pressure on wages, in particular, for unskilled work, and there may also be adjustment costs and/or increased unemployment if there are labour market rigidities. In what is

---

[5] www.worldbank.org

[6] Giovannetti (forthcoming).

[7] According to the process of factor price equalization of the Heckscher–Ohlin–Samuelson theorem described in Chapter 2.

known as the Australian case for protection (Irwin, 2002) unskilled workers in developed countries may lose their jobs and experience difficulty in finding a new occupation.

According to IMF (2007), globalization has reduced the share of national income going to workers in advanced economies, but has left them better off overall. On balance these workers have benefited from globalization because it has increased productivity and reduced the price of traded goods (consumers are the great beneficiaries from globalization). Many authors also attribute the falling share of workers in the national income of advanced economies to other factors such as labour-saving technology or tax systems.

A related issue is the impact of outsourcing on employment and wages in developed countries. Outsourcing (sometimes called offshore outsourcing or offshoring) is the international fragmentation of production, which entails previously integrated production activities being segmented and spread over an international network of production sites (Baldone et al., 2003). In other words, there is trade in tasks within manufacturing and services. The digital revolution permits the unbundling of production to an unprecedented extent, rendering obsolete the idea that all services were non-tradable. The rapid growth of information technology services being produced in India is an example of this phenomenon. The number of tasks that can be outsourced is changing over time.

There are attenuating arguments to the presages of the dire consequences of outsourcing for the wages and jobs of workers in developed countries. As Venables (2006) and Krugman (1991, see also Chapter 15) point out, there are still advantages arising from the agglomeration of economic activities, with firms finding gains from locating in proximity to concentrations of business. An example of this is the dominance of a few large cities in the world of international finance. Moreover, as Grossman and Rossi-Hansberg (2006) suggest, outsourcing has the effect of raising productivity, improving terms of trade (as export prices rise relative to imports), and releasing labour from previous tasks, so the overall impact on workers in developed countries may be more complex than is sometimes supposed.

The internationalization of production through outsourcing means that EU competitiveness has to be addressed in a new way, by looking at tasks within the supply chain. The issue becomes how far the EU is able to hold on to core competences and activities that add most value.[8]

The challenge for the EU is to provide an institutional framework capable of stimulating the competitiveness of tasks and of sectors, and of fostering flexible adjustment, and this is the aim of the Lisbon Strategy. Flexible adjustment means 'learning how to learn' (Baldwin, 2006) so requires attention to labour market, social and education policies, as well as emphasis on research and innovation. At the same time on equity grounds there may be a case for compensation for the losers from globalization. Various options are possible: subsidies for retraining or to raise the wages of the unskilled, or longer term policies aimed at employability such as improving education and training. An initiative of this type is the European Globalisation Adjustment Fund to provide additional support for workers who have suffered as a result of major structural changes in the pattern of world trade (see Chapter 11).

---

[8] See, for instance, the articles by Bongardt and Torres (2007) and Giovannetti in della Posta et al. (forthcoming). Giovannetti describes how successful firms in Italy in sectors such as textiles and clothing facing high levels of international competition adopted a mix of strategies including outsourcing low-valued tasks, increasing average skills, innovation and cutting costs and sought new markets and adopted new marketing strategies.

The original Lisbon Strategy

In 2000 the Lisbon European Council argued that a 'radical transformation of the European Economy' was necessary to meet the challenges of globalization and the need to create a knowledge-driven economy based on ICT. Various goals were indicated:[9]

- better policies for the information society and research and development (R&D). This includes measures to create closer links between research institutes and industry, to develop conditions favourable to R&D, to improve access to finance and know-how and to encourage new business ventures;

- making EU training and education systems a 'world quality reference' by 2010;

- stepping up 'the process of structural reform for competitiveness and innovation by completing the internal market';

- ensuring full employment, by emphasizing the need to open employment opportunities, to increase productivity at work and to promote life-long learning;

- ensuring an inclusive labour market in which unemployment is reduced and social and regional disparities are narrowed by 'modernizing the European social model, investing in people and combating social exclusion';

- connecting Europe, in particular through closer integration, and by improving transport, telecommunications and energy networks;

- sustaining 'the healthy economic outlook and favourable growth prospects by applying an appropriate macro-policy mix'; and

- protecting the environment (this objective was added at the Gothenburg European Council of 2001).[10]

The Strategy relied on a new 'open method of co-ordination' for implementation. According to the Presidency conclusions of the Lisbon Council, this entailed guidelines with specific timetables for reaching goals; establishing, where appropriate, quantitative and qualitative indicators and benchmarks against the best in the world; adapting these guidelines to national and regional policies by setting specific targets, and periodic monitoring, evaluation and peer review.

In 2002 a Competitiveness Council was created with the aim of re-launching the competitive drive of the EU. The role of the Competitiveness Council was to give an opinion on all matters affecting competitiveness, and in this way it was hoped to co-ordinate the efforts of different policies such as the Internal Market, industrial policy, competition policy and research and development.

Better policies for the information society and research and development

In order to build a knowledge-based society *inter alia* the Lisbon Strategy calls for:

- the creation of an information society by defining a regulatory framework for electronic communications, and encouraging the spread of information and communication technologies;

---

[9] The Presidency conclusions of the 2000 Lisbon European Council, www.europa.eu

[10] Environmental and energy aspects of globalization will be discussed in Chapter 13.

	Educational attainment (20–4) % population having completed at least secondary education	Gross domestic expenditure on R&D as % GDP	Business investment as % GDP
BE	82.4	1.9	19.1
BG	80.5	0.5	22.2
CZ	91.3	1.5	19.6
DK	77.4	2.4	20.5
DE	71.6 (p)	2.5	16.6
EE	82.0	1.4	29.6
IE	85.7	1.3 (p)	22.6
EL	81.0 (p)	0.6 (p)	20.3 (f)
ES	61.6	1.1 (p)	26.6
FR	82.1 (p)	2.1 (p)	17.1
IT	75.5	1.1 (2005)	18.5
CY	83.7 (p)	0.4	16.9
LT	81.0	0.7	30.1
LI	88.2	0.8	20.6
LU	69.3	1.6 (2005 p)	14.4
HU	82.9	1.0	17.4
MA	50.4	0.6 (p)	15.1
NL	74.7	1.7 (p)	16.4
AU	85.8	2.5	19.5
PL	91.7	0.6	16.0
PT	49.6	0.8 (2005)	18.6
RO	77.2	0.5	21.8
SL	89.4	1.6	22.6
SK	91.5	0.5	24.1
FI	84.7	3.5	16.7
SW	86.5	3.8	14.8
UK	78.8	1.8 (2005)	16.1
EU(27)	77.8	1.8	18.2

TABLE 7.3 Relative performance of the member states according to selected indicators relating to creation of a knowledge-based economy (2003)

Source: *Eurostat*, © European Communities, 2008, www.epp.eurostat.ec.europa.eu.
f: forecast
p: provisional

- measures to encourage research by boosting R&D spending to 3 per cent of GDP (of which, private investment should account for 2 per cent of GDP), making the EU more attractive for its best brains, and promoting new technologies;
- improved education and human capital by halving the number of early school leavers, fostering lifelong learning and facilitating mobility.

As can be seen from Table 7.3, the reality is still rather distant from these objectives. Moreover, Gros (2007) argues that in addition to the quantitative lag of the EU behind the USA in R&D spending, there is also a qualitative or efficiency lag. This relates to the rate at which R&D spending generates commercially exploitable ideas as measured by the number of patent applications filed per worker. On this basis US knowledge workers emerge as twice as productive on average than their EU counterparts. The relative inefficiency of European R&D is attributed to the segmentation of public research efforts, the overlapping of competing research programmes, and consequently the under-utilization of available human resources.

Increasing employment

EU unemployment has been consistently higher than that of the USA since the mid-1970s, while participation rates in the labour force have been lower (see Tables 7.1 and 7.3). Prescott (2004) argues that the lower utilization of labour in the EU is largely due to differences in the tax systems, while Blanchard (2004) maintains that it is due to a higher preference for leisure (with shorter working hours and a lower rate of participation in the labour force in the EU). However,

	Total	Males	Women
BE	61.0	67.9	54.0
BG	58.6	62.8	54.6
CZ	65.3	73.7	56.8
DK	77.4	81.2	73.4
DE	67.5 (p)	72.8 (p)	62.2 (p)
EE	68.1	71.0	65.3
IE	68.6	77.7	59.3
EL	61.0	74.6	47.4
ES	64.8	76.1	53.2
FR	63.0 (p)	68.5 (p)	57.7 (p)
IT	58.4	70.5	46.3
CY	69.6	79.4	60.3
LT	66.3	70.4	62.4
LI	63.6	66.3	61.0
LU	63.6	72.6	54.6
HU	57.3	63.8	51.1
MA	54.8	74.5	34.9
NL	74.3	80.9	67.7
AU	70.2	76.9	63.5
PL	54.5	60.9	48.2
PT	67.9	73.9	62.0
RO	58.8	64.6	53.0
SL	66.6	71.1	61.8
SK	59.4	67.0	51.9
FI	69.3	71.4	67.3
SW	73.1	75.5	70.7
UK	71.5	77.3	65.8
EU(27)	64.4 (p)	71.6 (p)	57.2 (p)
EU (15)	66.0 (p)	73.5 (p)	58.6 (p)

TABLE 7.4 Employment rates of men and women in the EU member states (per cent of labour force 2006)
Source: *Eurostat*, © European Communities, 2008, www.epp.eurostat.ec.europa.eu.
f: forecast
p: provisional

developments in demography may force changes in pension systems leading to changes in choices about leisure.

A major ongoing debate is how far the higher level of participation in the USA is the result of greater labour market flexibility. The dilemma for the EU is how to reconcile a relatively high level of social protection with international competitiveness. The question that arises is to whether competitiveness should remain a primary goal of the EU or whether it might threaten the European 'social model' (see Chapter 15).[11]

The aims of the Lisbon Strategy include achieving higher employment rates (rather than lower unemployment rates), increasing the rate of participation in the labour force to 70 per cent by 2010 (60 per cent for women). The interim target was 67 per cent for total employment and 57 per cent for women in 2005. Eurostat calculates the employment rate by dividing the number of persons aged 15 to 64 by employment in the total population of the same age group. As Table 7.4 shows, in 2006 the employment rates were still below these targets (see also Chapter 16). Major challenges also included addressing skill shortages and improving the quality of work (through 'more and better jobs'). Part of proposed answer to the demographic challenge entails keeping older workers in employment longer, but this measure has encountered limited success.

The Sapir Report

One of the criticisms made of the Lisbon Strategy was that it lacked an intellectual basis, unlike the Single Market Programme, which relied on the Cecchini Report, or Economic and Monetary Union (EMU), which drew on the Commission Report, *One Market, One Money* (see Chapter 9). To meet this gap the President of the European Commission set up an independent high-level study group, which presented its results in 2003 in what became known as the Sapir Report (Sapir et al., 2004). The Report carried out a comprehensive analysis of the growth and catching-up problem of the EU, pointing out that both labour utilization and productivity had fallen in absolute terms and relative to the USA since the mid-1970s.

The Sapir Report agreed that the objectives of the Lisbon Strategy were rightly ambitious, but maintained that it rested on an excessive number of targets and a weak method. To meet these drawbacks the Sapir Report recommended focusing on growth (reflected in the title *An Agenda for a Growing Europe*), and called for coherence between EU policies and instruments on the one hand, and between decision-makers at the EU and national levels at the other.

In order to meet the challenges of globalization and external competition, the Sapir Report put forward a 6-point agenda for reforms:

- **Making the Single Market more dynamic.** This would include completing the Single Market for services and network industries, and encouraging labour mobility.

- **Boosting investment in knowledge.** EU funding for research and innovation and increased spending on higher education should make important contributions here.

- **Improving the macroeconomic policy framework.** After the success in maintaining price

---

[11]For example, in an article in the *Financial Times* of 8 October 2004, the famous professor of political science at Princeton University, Andrew Moravcsik, praises the European role model, which he maintains is more egalitarian, more communitarian and more cosmopolitan than the USA. Egalitarianism is evident in a welfare state that guarantees a certain minimum living standard, not only in cash, but also through healthcare, pensions and unemployment insurance. Europeans tend to be more committed to culturally diverse communal traditions and less convinced by the work ethic (a major reason behind the disparity in per capita income). At an international level Europeans seem more committed to conflict resolution through peaceful means.

stability, EMU should also focus on growth, and the monetary and fiscal framework of EMU should be rendered more symmetrical over the cycle.

■ **Redesigning policies for convergence and restructuring.** EU funding should promote restructuring and should target institution-building in the new member states.

■ **Achieving effectiveness.** The EU should have more power to oversee Single Market rules, there should be increased use of qualified majority voting on economic matters, and, where necessary, independent EU bodies should be created for specific policy areas.

■ **Refocusing the EU budget.** The financial perspectives should act in unison with national budgets and should better reflect the priorities of the Lisbon Strategy.

The Sapir Report stimulated a wide-reaching debate on the economic future of the EU. It shaped the Commission proposals for the 2007–2013 financial perspective, though, as explained in Chapter 11, in the final Inter-institutional Agreement of 2006, spending on increasing competitiveness was scaled back and the fundamental debate on the EU budget was postponed until 2008/9.

The Sapir Report was influential in the debate leading to reform of the Growth and Stability Pact in 2005),[12] and in the creation of a Globalization Adjustment Fund.[13] It was also instrumental in creating the European Research Council to encourage scientific research in the EU.

The KOK Report

The European Commission regularly publishes documents assessing progress in realizing the Lisbon Strategy, and in November 2004 a high-level group led by the former Prime Minister of the Netherlands, Wim Kok, also presented a report. The picture that emerged from these stock-taking efforts is rather negative. Kok himself announced that the Strategy risked becoming 'a synonym for missed objectives and failed promises'. According to the Kok Report the blame lies with national leaders, and four reasons for the poor EU performance were given:

1 an overloaded agenda;
2 poor co-ordination;
3 conflicting priorities; and
4 lack of determined political action.

The diagnosis presented by the Kok Report was better than the therapy it proposed. The Kok Report rephrased the goal of overtaking the USA as the world's most competitive economy, referring instead to making Europe 'a single, competitive, dynamic, knowledge-based economy that is among the best in the world'. The Kok Report proposed focusing on growth and employment. However, it still favoured maintaining too many priorities. Assessment of progress in the Lisbon Strategy had been based on over one hundred indicators. The Kok Report (2004) proposed reducing these to 14.[14] This is not exactly a reduced agenda. If member states are faced with too many targets attention is not focused and they can gener-

---

[12] See Chapter 10.

[13] See Chapter 11.

[14] These are the indicators shown in Tables 7.1 and 7.3 here plus the at-risk-of-poverty rate, the long-term employment rate and the dispersion of regional employment rates.

ally claim that progress has been made in some areas and ignore the rest. The Kok Report also proposed benchmarking the progress of individual countries, but this has been tried in various fields with limited success, and was in any case opposed by the member states. The Report called on national governments to draw up national action plans with roadmaps and targets setting out how Lisbon targets are to be realized. In order to increase involvement and awareness of the Lisbon Strategy, the Report called for debate on the action plans with national parliaments and the social partners. The Report suggested that the European Commission publish annual league tables indicating the progress of each of the member states according to the key indicators of the Lisbon Strategy. The Commission would praise countries that have done well, and castigate those falling behind. The Report also called for reshaping of the EU budget to reflect Lisbon priorities, with financial incentives to induce progress.

The European Council of November 2004 did not accept the proposal of benchmarking, with 'naming and shaming' of those member states making slow progress. The German Chancellor, Gerhard Schroeder, argued that member states needed to adapt reforms to national circumstances. The scoreboards published on progress of the member states in implementing the Internal Market (see Chapter 6) seem to have a limited impact, and proposing increased supervision by the European Commission was a sensitive issue at a time when there was differences over the division of responsibility for the Growth and Stability Pact (see Chapter 10).

The revised Lisbon Agenda

The Commission accepted the recommendations of the Kok Report, and in a speech to the European Parliament of 2 February 2005, President Barroso stated that it was necessary to 'give a new and stronger focus to the Lisbon Strategy' and 'deliver jobs and growth'. In the same year the Commission presented the communication, *Working Together for Growth and Jobs: A New Start to the Lisbon Strategy*,[15] which indicated four main objectives:

1 making the internal market work better;
2 more and better jobs
3 knowledge and innovation;
4 improved implementation.

The steps necessary indicated as necessary to complete the Single Market include liberalization in areas such as services, network industries and labour mobility (see Chapter 6). The goal of more and better jobs was to be advanced in the context of the European Employment Strategy (EES) launched in 1997, which aims at full employment, improved quality and productivity of work and increased social cohesion (see Chapter 16). The social agenda of the Commission included:

- building prosperity and reducing the risks of social exclusion;
- national reforms to modernize labour and social policies;
- the launch of a broad debate on the impact of the ageing of population;
- pushing up employment, which means equipping people with skills and 'ensuring that our tax and benefit systems help people into the workplace'.

---

[15]European Commission (2005).

With regard to knowledge and innovation, a number of priorities were indicated:

- Member States must speed up efforts to meet the 3 per cent target of spending on research.
- Member States and regional and local actors should look at new ways of supporting research and innovation, particularly by small and medium enterprises, and through the creation of 'Innovation Poles'.
- European Union universities should become a world reference.
- A 'European Institute of Technology' (EIT) should be created. The creation of the EIT was initially rejected by the member states as duplicating existing structures, but was eventually agreed by the Competitiveness Council in November 2007.
- Efforts to promote eco-innovation should be stepped up.

The Commission also attempted to address the problems of too many targets, lack of political commitment and ownership of programmes, and to introduce a new system of Lisbon governance. While it was admitted that major responsibility lies with the member states, there were calls to get 'all European and national actors working together', and reach 'beyond national capitals' to involve also the social partners (i.e. firms and trade unions). There was also stress on the need to 'explain what Lisbon is and why it is important'. The emphasis was therefore on co-operation with the member states and peer pressure rather than 'naming and shaming' and formal sanctions.

Bongardt and Torres (2007) argue that working together in the EU has conditioned the economic policy framework and set in motion new governance patterns. From this point of view the Lisbon Strategy can be regarded as an exercise in policy co-ordination with a view to stimulating interdependencies and policy learning. The effort to meet the Lisbon goals has required co-ordination of policies at the EU and member state levels and this has triggered improvements in governance methods.

Evaluation

Despite the renewed efforts of the Commission, and the improved economic performance of the EU from 2006, the Lisbon Strategy continues to have difficulties in overcoming its shortcomings. As explained above, the Commission proposals received various setbacks from the European Council, and spending on competitiveness and growth was less than initially envisaged in the 2007–2013 financial perspective. Although governance has improved, at times the Lisbon Strategy still receives little more than lip service from the governments of the EU member states and has failed to capture the imagination of the European public. In many member states additional funds for education, training and R&D failed to materialize, and job creation projects were on a relatively limited scale.

Many Lisbon objectives are covered by other programmes and would probably be better addressed separately. For instance, it seems superfluous to include the objective of completing the Internal Market under the Lisbon Strategy. Labour market measures and attempts to adapt the European social model and eradicate poverty can be tackled under Social Policy and the European Employment Strategy (see Chapter 16). European Union environmental measures are covered by the Environmental Action Programmes and by efforts to combat climate change (see Chapter 14).

Even if these other objectives are hived off, and creation of the knowledge society is left as the remaining core target, the Lisbon Strategy as revised in 2005 is still in need of restored credibility. Increasing EU competitiveness and promoting growth are crucial, but the Lisbon Strategy as it stands does not seem the best framework for realizing these aims.

Summary of Key Concepts

- Globalization has led to overall gains, but there have been winners and losers in the process. There are fears that workers in developed countries will suffer from downward pressure on wages and/or higher unemployment.

- The GDP per capita of the Community rose to about 70 per cent of the US level by the mid-1970s, but subsequently this gap failed to narrow.

- In addition to the gap compared with US economic performance, there was also growing concern regarding the challenge posed by Asia, with China emerging as a major economic actor, and India becoming an increasingly important location for outsourcing.

- The **Lisbon European Council** of 2000 attributed poor EU economic performance to lack of completion of the Single Market, labour market rigidities, insufficient investment in education and training, and a technology gap between the EU and USA, in particular, with regard to information science. It indicated goals and a new method of co-ordination to overcome these shortcomings.

- **The Sapir Report** agreed that the objectives of the Lisbon Strategy were rightly ambitious, but maintained that it rested on an excessive number of targets and a weak method. To meet these drawbacks the Sapir Report recommended focusing on growth, and improving governance of the Strategy.

- **The Kok Report** also criticized the Lisbon Strategy for an overloaded agenda and insufficient political commitment. It proposed focusing on growth and employment, but still favoured maintaining too many priorities. The Kok Report also proposed benchmarking to assess progress of individual member states in realizing the strategy.

- The Barroso Commission attempted to **revise the Lisbon Strategy in 2005**, focusing on completion of the Single Market, more and better jobs, knowledge and innovation, and improved implementation.

- The European Council cut back the Commission's proposal for spending on competitiveness in the Financial Perspective, postponed the debate on EU budget priorities until 2008/9, and only agreed on the proposal to create a European Institute of Technology in 2007. It also rejected the Kok proposal of benchmarking of Lisbon Strategy progress.

- The **shortcomings of the Lisbon Strategy** such as excessive targets, lack of political will and insufficient co-ordination do not appear to have been overcome.

Questions for study and review

1 *What criticisms can be made of globalization?*

2 *What are the main objectives of the Lisbon Strategy?*

3 *What criticisms have been made of the Lisbon Strategy?*

4 *How did the Commission attempt to revise the Lisbon Strategy?*

5 *What measures do you think should be introduced to promote growth and the increased competitiveness of the EU?*

6 *Do you consider GDP an adequate measure for international comparisons between countries?*

References

Alesina, A. and Giavazzi, F. (2006) *The Future of Europe: Reform or Decline*, MIT Press, Cambridge, MA.

Baldone, S., Sdogati, F. and Tajoli, L. (2003) 'Patterns and Determinants of International Fragmentation of Production. Evidence from Outward-processing Trade between the EU and Central-Eastern European Countries', *Weltwirtschaftliches Archiv*.

Baldwin, R. (2006) *Globalisation: The Great Unbundling*, www.hei.unige.ch/baldwin

Blanchard, O. (2004) 'The economic future of Europe', *Journal of Economic Perspectives*, Vol. 18, pp. 3–26.

Bongardt, A. and Torres, F. (2007) 'Is the European Model viable in a globalised world?', NIPE WP 20/2007, www.eeg.uminho.pt

Della Posta, P., Uvalic, M. and Verdun, A. (eds) (in press) *Globalization, Development and Integration*, Palgrave MacMillan, Basingstoke, UK.

European Commission (2005) *Working Together for Growth and Jobs: A New Start to the Lisbon Strategy*, www.ec.europa.eu/internal_market

European Commission (2007) *Raising productivity growth: Key messages from the European Competitiveness Report*, COM(2007)666 final, www.ec.europa.eu

Giovannetti, G. (forthcoming) 'An overview of current globalisation, opportunities and threats', in della Posta, P., Uvalic, M. and Verdun, A. (eds) *Interpreting Globalisation: A European Perspective*, Palgrave MacMillan, Basingstoke, UK.

Gros, D. (2007) *How to Make European Research more Competitive*, Centre for European Policy Studies, www.ceps.be

Grossman, G.M. and Rossi-Hansberg, E. (2006) *The Rise of Offshoring: It's not Wine for Cloth Any More*, paper presented at the annual economic symposium organized by the Federal Reserve Bank of Kansas at Jackson Hole, www:KansasCityFed.org

IMF (2007) *World Economic Outlook,* www.imf.org

Irwin, D. (2002) 'Interpreting the Tariff-Growth Correlation in the Late Nineteenth Century', *American Economic Review Papers and Proceedings*.

The Kok Report (2004) *Facing the Challenge. The Lisbon Strategy for Growth and Employment*, Report from the High Level Group chaired by Wim Kok, www.ec.europa.eu

Krugman, P.R. (1991) *Geography and Trade*, Leuven University Press, Leuven and The MIT Press, Cambridge, MA.

Prescott, E. (2004) 'Why do Americans work so much more that Europeans?', *Federal Reserve Bank of Minneapolis Quarterly Review*, Vol. 28, pp. 2–13.

Sapir, A., Aghion, P., Bertola, G., et al. (2004) *An Agenda for a Growing Europe: The Sapir Report*, Oxford University Press, Oxford.

Sapir, A. (2007) 'European strategies for growth', in Artis, M. and Nixson, F. (eds) *The Economics of the European Union*, Oxford University Press, Oxford.

Venables, A. (2006) *Shifts in Economic Geography and their Causes*, paper presented at the annual economic symposium organized by the Federal Reserve Bank of Kansas at Jackson Hole, www:KansasCityFed.org

World Bank (2007) *Global Economic Prospects: Managing the Next Wave of Globalisation,* www.worldbank.org

Useful websites

The website of the European Commission:
www.ec.europa.eu

The Eurostat website:
www.ec.europa.eu/eurostat

The IMD International, Switzerland, World Competitiveness Center:
www.imd.ch/wcc

Movement of Labour, Immigration and Asylum

By the end of this chapter you should be able to understand:

❖ The main advantages said to arise from freedom of labour movement;

❖ The most frequent justifications given for introducing restrictions on immigration;

❖ The main factors influencing the decision to migrate;

❖ How migration may influence wage levels and unemployment;

❖ The most common forms of immigration;

❖ The barriers to freedom of movement of labour in the EU;

❖ The difficulties in establishing a common EU policy with regard to immigration and asylum;

❖ How the pattern of immigration has changed in the EU over time.

Introduction

Ensuring freedom of labour movement within the Community was one of the main objectives of the Treaty of Rome, subsequently reinforced by the 1993 Single Market Programme. In practice barriers to labour movement remain within the EU, and this has been even more the case since the 2004 and 2007 enlargements. Over the years immigration from third countries to the EU has acquired new forms and dimensions, and urgently requires co-ordination of the positions of EU member states and/or the introduction of common policies. However, geographical, historical and cultural differences between the member states have rendered the creation of a common EU policy towards immigration and asylum difficult.[1]

The aim of this chapter is first to provide a brief account of some of the theoretical aspects of

---

[1] The issue is further complicated in that allowing free movement of people involves a trade-off – control of international crime, terrorism, drug trafficking and migration becomes more difficult. European Union policy has gradually shifted towards increased co-operation on home affairs, and police and judicial matters. As described on the online learning centre for this book, labour movement and immigration policy are intrinsically linked to the evolution of the EU as an area of Freedom, Security and Justice. The online learning centre for this book (OLC) provides an account of the changes in the third pillar of the EU over time.

labour movement. Then follows a description of the evolution of EU policies, before outlining the main developments in migratory flows within the EU and from third countries.

The effects of migration

Freedom of movement of labour on an international scale is generally advocated because the removal of restrictions is said to increase efficiency and improve the allocation of resources. Workers will have higher chances of using their qualifications in the best possible way. Employers will be able to overcome possible labour shortages and increase their possibilities of finding labour with the skills required.

More specific arguments are also advanced in favour of immigration. For example, in the country of destination it is sometimes claimed that the inflow of young workers can be used to offset possible negative effects of ageing of the population, or immigrants can be used to cover a skill shortage. Labour-exporting countries may favour emigration so that the balance of payments can benefit from workers' remittances (which in some countries are larger than foreign aid or inward investment), though these often tend to be invested in housing and consumption and may have limited lasting positive effect on the home economy.

The effects of migration can be analysed using a simple model. It is assumed that there are two factors of production, capital C and labour L; two countries, home and foreign; that both countries produce one good and that there is perfect competition. The marginal product of labour shows how the output of a product increases when one additional unit of labour is used. Diminishing returns means that as additional units of labour are added to a given amount of capital, output will increase but by ever smaller amounts for each additional unit of labour.

Figure 8.1 shows the marginal product of labour in the home country MPLh. With the stock of home labour Lh, the equilibrium wage in the home country is Wh. Total earnings by home labour are given by the wage Wh multiplied by the amount of labour Lh. Under perfect competition the payments to the two factors of production will just equal the value of total production.

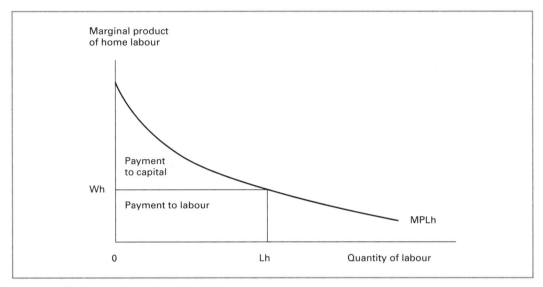

FIGURE 8.1 The income shares of capital and labour

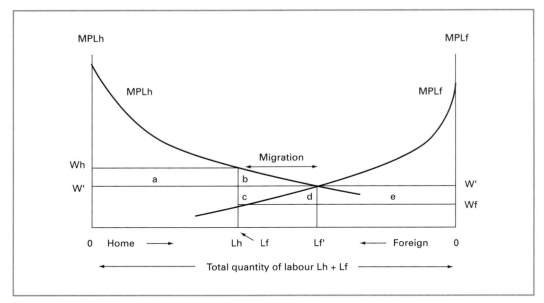

FIGURE 8.2 The causes and effects of immigration
Source: Adapted from Baldwin and Wyplosz (2006).

The area under the curve indicates the total output of the home country. The payment to capital is therefore given by the area under the MPLh curve minus the payment to labour.

In order to show the effects of migration the marginal product of labour curves for both the home and foreign countries can be shown in a single graph. Assume initially that immigration is not allowed. Figure 8.2 reproduces the MPLh curve for home labour from Figure 8.1 but adds a second vertical axis and shows the marginal product of labour curve for the foreign country running right to left. The total horizontal distance between the two axes indicates the total amount of labour in the two countries (Lh + Lf).

With stock of labour Lf (total labour minus Lh), the equilibrium wage in the foreign country will be Wf. As can be seen from the graph, the equilibrium wage Wh in the home country is higher than Wf, so if migration is now allowed, there will be an incentive for workers to move from the foreign country to the home country to earn higher wages. The immigration will cause the wage at home to fall, and the wage in the foreign country to rise until they reach the same level W'. Equilibrium is reached when Lf'Lf workers have moved from the foreign country to the home country.

The welfare effects of migration can also be seen from Figure 8.2:

- Home labour loses earnings of area a.
- Home capital gains earnings of a + b.
- The total gain to the home country is therefore b.
- Payments to labour remaining in the foreign county rise by e.
- Earning by capital in the foreign country fall by d + e.
- If foreigners now working in the home country are also taken into account, the earnings to foreign workers rise by c + d + e, the earnings of foreign capital fall by d + e, so there is a net gain of c.

Various effects of migration are, therefore, shown by this simple model:

- There is convergence of wages in the two countries with wages falling at home and rising in the foreign country.
- Total world output, which is given by the area under the two curves MPLh and MPLf, rises. This is because migration has the effect of increasing efficiency.
- There are winners and losers from the migration.

The causes of migration

The simple model above attributes migration to wage differences, but in practice various factors influence the decision to migrate (and pattern of migration), so the list becomes:

1 The wage gap between the home and host country;
2 Political and ethnic disturbances (which emerge as the main cause of major large-scale migration flows in Europe);
3 The employment possibilities in both countries;[2]
4 Economic expectations;
5 The geographical proximity of the two countries;
6 Emigration traditions;
7 Ethnic and family networks;
8 Cultural and linguistic factors.

Migration involves economic and psychological costs to the person involved. Individuals have a preference for living in their own country for social, cultural and linguistic reasons. Migration entails costs of travel, finding a house, job and so on. An individual will only undertake migration when the expected benefit is large enough to offset the costs of migration.[3]

Restrictions on migration

In practice most countries use restrictions on immigration, and as Boeri and Brücker (2005) state, international migration is the 'great absentee' in the era of globalization, as barriers to trade and international capital movements have been reduced substantially. Restrictions on immigration generally consist of border controls and work or residence permits, but may also take other forms such as limited access to certain jobs and professions, or financial disincentives such as limits on access to social security benefits, long and/or difficult administrative procedures for admission, or unfavourable tax treatment. Other factors such as inability to find housing may also inhibit migration.

In the case of countries receiving immigrants the most frequently cited negative effects are:[4]

- Increased government expenditure in order to provide the necessary social provisions for

---

[2] Faini (1995) also argues that, *ceteris paribus*, countries with a large informal sector tend to be attractive to immigrants because lower skills are generally required for employment.

[3] As Faini and Venturini (1994) argue, migration is an 'inferior' good, and staying at home is the 'normal' good.

[4] This list is taken from Molle (2006).

foreigners. Empirical studies such as Boeri and Brücker (2005) find that the income of natives in countries receiving immigrants will fall as the level of welfare benefits available also to immigrants rises, but conclude that the effect is relatively limited;

- Societal disruption due to cultural differences and so on;
- Increased regional disparities as the foreign workers tend to be attracted to urban agglomerations where jobs are more readily available. Against this, where internal labour mobility in a country is low, immigration may 'grease the wheels' in reducing regional disparities as immigrants move to richer regions and may exert downward pressure on wages and higher unemployment of native workers in those areas;
- A worsening of the balance of payments as foreign workers send their earnings home;
- The downward pressure on wages (see next section);
- Increased unemployment (see next section).

In practice the importance of the political effects of immigration often outweigh the economic impact, because populist and nationalist political parties may exploit societal tensions, as has been the case in various EU countries.

In countries of emigration the most frequent justification for restrictions is that they are said to be necessary to avoid the possible negative effects of migration. These include the loss of human capital necessary for the development of the country as in general the younger, most dynamic and better skilled workers tend to leave (the so-called 'brain drain').

The impact of migration on wages and employment

One of the main debates about migratory flows relates to their impact on wages. Neo-classical economic theory argues that freedom of labour movement will lead to convergence of wages, as suggested by the model above. If costs of migration are also taken into account, the migratory flow will continue until the difference in wages between the two countries just matches the costs of migration.

According to the neo-classical view a similar mechanism is in operation for unemployment, and in the long run unemployment rates are likely to be independent of the size of the labour force. In the short run an increase in migration may lead to an increase in unemployment in the receiving country. As unemployment rises in the country of destination, this puts downward pressure on wages, inducing firms to take on more labour, and eventually unemployment will revert to its original level. The difficulty lies in assessing how long this process of adjustment will take.

However, the view that migration will lead to wage convergence and will not influence the long-run level of employment is based on some rather restrictive assumptions. Institutional barriers, such as restrictions on labour movement, may prevent adjustment from taking place. For example, trade unions or employee associations may prevent access to certain jobs, or employers may discriminate against certain types of workers on grounds of race or gender. Moreover, in practice the adjustment process may take some time, and in the meantime immigration may lead to lower wages and higher unemployment.

The impact of migration on wages and unemployment therefore becomes a question for empirical research. Boeri and Brücker (2005), for instance, estimated that, assuming labour markets are clearing, immigration equivalent to one per cent of the population increases GDP by 0.3 per cent.[5] However, most of the gains accrue to migrants whose incomes rise between 130 and 150 per cent. In the receiving countries the wages of manual and non-manual workers decline from 0.04 to 0.56 per cent, depending on the assumptions made about the skill composition of the migrants. There are gains for labour in the source country of the migrants. If labour market rigidities are assumed, the gains to GDP from migration drop to 0.19 to 0.28 per cent. Depending the extent of rigidities assumed, the unemployment rate in the receiving countries may increase by between 0.12 and 0.3 per cent, while the post-tax wages for manual workers drop by 0.5 per cent, and those of non-manual workers fall by between 0.2 and 0.3 per cent. Aggregate income of natives in the receiving country falls between 0.06 and 0.2 per cent.

The issue of whether immigrants are high-skilled or low-skilled labour is crucial to the analysis of the impact of immigration on the economy of the recipient country. As Baldwin and Wyplosz (2006) point out, the issue is one of complementarity versus substitutability. In many West European countries there is a shortage of unskilled workers. In Italy, for instance, unskilled immigrant labour is essential during the harvest and in helping in restaurants and bars during the tourist season. The unskilled work of immigrants therefore complements the skilled work of the Italian owners and managers of hotels, farms and so on. High-skilled labour can be regarded as a form of human capital, and so could be included as part of capital in Figure 8.2. Immigration of high skilled labour to a country can therefore be seen as an increase in human capital, which tends to increase the marginal product (and hence wages) of low-skilled labour.

Types of immigration

Various categories of immigrants are generally distinguished:

- economic immigrants seeking permanent residence to improve their living standards;
- asylum seekers looking for refuge from war or oppression;
- illegal immigrants;
- seasonal or temporary workers.

As it is becoming ever more difficult to enter the EU from a third country as a long-term economic immigrant, there has been a growing tendency to seek other forms of access. The 1951 Geneva Convention provided a definition of refugees as those who are fleeing persecution for 'reasons of race, religion, nationality, membership of a social group or political opinion'. However, in practice it is very difficult to distinguish whether refugees are fleeing poverty rather than persecution. The number of those seeking asylum remained fairly stable in the 1980s but increased dramatically following the collapse of communism and the Balkan wars.

The treatment of requests for asylum varies considerably among the EU member states both with regard to percentage of asylum cases accepted, and the treatment of applicants while procedures are being carried out. From 1993 Germany became more restrictive in accepting

---

[5] These results are similar to those of an earlier study by Boeri and Brücker et al. (2000) on the impact of immigration from the 10 Central and East European countries (CEECs), which suggests that a 1 per cent increase in the share of foreign workers from these countries would lead to a fall in wages by 0.25 per cent in Austria and by 0.6 per cent in Germany, and to an increase in the risk of dismissal by 0.8 per cent in Austria and 1.6 per cent in Germany. According to Boeri and Brücker et al. (2000) the negative employment and wage effects from CEEC immigrants would be concentrated on less qualified, blue-collar workers. Initially immigrants from Central and East Europe were considered to be relatively well qualified, but a closer analysis revealed that, in particular, the skills obtained in vocational schools under the old regime were often not suited to operating in a market economy.

requests for asylum,[6] but few refugees were sent home. In 1997 the UN High Commissioner on Refugees (UNHCR) estimated that Germany was harbouring about 1.3 million people who had requested asylum, creating a form of covert immigration. When Germany became more restrictive about asylum, the number of requests in the UK and Ireland rose (see Table 8.2, page 193) as these were considered countries with a higher record of accepting claims, but they in their turn tightened restrictions.

To prevent asylum-seekers 'shopping around' the 1990 Dublin Convention requires asylum-seekers to apply for asylum in the first EU country they enter.[7] As will be discussed below, the EU is committed to evolving a common asylum system.

Temporary immigration generally involves a fixed-term contract, usually of less than one year. As permanent immigration to the EU has become more difficult, there has been a considerable increase in temporary immigration, which may take various forms:[8]

- Guest-workers;
- Seasonal workers;
- Project-tied workers;
- Border-commuters;
- Exchanges of trainees.

With the economic boom in Germany, from 1961 *Gastarbeiter* or temporary guest workers were recruited from Turkey and the former Yugoslavia. Many of these Turkish workers, in particular, failed to return home and were joined by their families, and it is estimated that there are still some 2 million people of Turkish origin in Germany.

Seasonal workers are mainly employed in agriculture and tourism. They are generally taken on at times of the year when extra labour in necessary, for example during the harvest, so the employment of these workers tends to have complementary effects on the incomes of workers in the host country.

Tied-project programmes permit firms in the host country to subcontract parts of a project to foreign firms that employ workers with the wages and social security conditions of their own country, and are covered by the Posted-Workers Directive described in Chapter 6.

Border commuting was frequent in countries such as Poland, the Czech Republic and Hungary, and the main countries of destination tend to be Germany and Austria (Boeri and Brücker et al., 2000).

Labour movement in the EU in theory and practice

Distinction must be made between freedom of movement of labour, which constitutes (at least in theory) one of the four fundamental freedoms of the Single Market, and common EU policies with regard to immigration and asylum from the rest of the world (discussed in the next section).

The free movement of workers within the Community was one of the main objectives set out in the Treaty of Rome. The Treaty makes the distinction between workers and self-employed or independent persons:

---

[6] Between 1989 and 1994 some 2 million ethnic Germans or Aussiedlers, mainly from Russia, Poland and Romania, benefited from the provisions of the German constitution to move to Germany. In 1993 Germany introduced quotas of some 222 000 of such persons per year.

[7] The Dublin Convention was extended and replaced by Regulation No. 343/2003 of February 2003.

[8] Boeri and Brücker et al. (2000).

- Articles 48–51 of the Treaty of Rome refer to the free movement of workers that should entail the abolition of any discrimination based on nationality between workers from member states with regard to employment, remuneration and other conditions of work.

- Articles 52–58 deal with the freedom of establishment, or the right of self-employed or independent citizens of Community member states to set up businesses (including agencies, branches and subsidiaries) in other member states.

Both the free movement of labour and the freedom of establishment were to be based on the principle of national treatment, which entails the same conditions for citizens of other EU member states and the nationals of that country. The Treaty of Rome (Articles 117–28) also included references to social policy, including the improvement of working conditions, equal pay for men and women, and paid holidays (see Chapter 16). The European Social Fund was to be set up with the aim of 'rendering the employment of workers easier and increasing their geographical and occupational mobility' (Article 123).

The legislation covering freedom of movement of workers was completed in 1968 (at the same time as the legal basis of the customs union), and extended to the European Economic Area in 1994. The 1993 Single Market Project (see Chapter 6) gave a new impetus to the task of eliminating frontier controls and permitting the free movement of people (notably through the Schengen Agreement).

Under Article 39 of the Treaty Establishing the European Community (Article 48 of the Treaty of Rome) freedom of movement of workers entails the right to move freely and to stay in a member state for the purposes of employment, subject to limitations on grounds of public policy, public security or public health. However, as explained below, fears that the 2004 and 2007 enlargements would lead to wide scale immigration to the EU(15) from the new Central and East European member states led to derogations of up to 7 years on the movement of labour from these countries.

Numerous measures have also been introduced aimed at eliminating intra-EU barriers to movement of people, relating *inter alia* to the aggregation of social security rights (including pensions), the recognition of qualifications, harmonization of regulation relating to residence permits, working conditions and so on, and providing information about job opportunities and working conditions in the various member states.

Despite these various EU initiatives, differences in labour market regulations and social security systems among the member states remain a major factor continuing to discourage labour movement within the EU. These regulations include laws on minimum wages, collective contracting, hiring and firing, the duration of the working week, flexible labour contracts and so on. Given the diversity and complexity of these laws, workers often have inadequate information to assess the various opportunities and risks in other member states. Together with natural barriers to labour mobility such as language, social and cultural differences between member states, and the ageing of the work force (younger workers tend to be more mobile) these factors explain why labour mobility within the Community has been relatively low (see the statistics below).

The development of EU policies with regard to immigration and asylum from the rest of the world

The policies of the member states on asylum and immigration from third countries have generally evolved separately, and reaching common EU positions has not proved easy. As a result national policies continue to play a predominant role in this policy area.

As Boeri and Brücker (2005) argue, economic theory suggests strong reasons for policy co-ordination in this field relating to spillovers from national jurisdictions (with the fear that tightening of restrictions in a neighbouring country could lead to a diversion of flows of migration), economies of scale and potential free-riding in the enforcement of border controls. Various factors may explain the different attitudes of the member states to immigration policy, and the extent to which they consider that common EU policies are opportune:

- Geographical differences between the member states (with, for instance porous external borders of countries such as Spain, Italy and Malta, which are the main destinations of thousands of illegal immigrants on perilous boat journeys);
- Cultural and historical factors may shape national attitudes to immigration;
- National politicians may prefer to maintain jurisdiction for immigration policy as it is often a highly emotive issue, and has at times been exploited for populist motives.

Given the rise in number of legal and illegal immigrants (including asylum-seekers), and the role that immigrant workers could play in meeting the demographic challenge in the EU, in 1999 the European Council at Tampere in Finland agreed on the basic elements for creating a common EU immigration policy, namely:

- A comprehensive approach to management of migratory flows so as to find a balance between humanitarian and economic admission;
- Fair treatment for third-country nationals;
- The creation of partnerships with countries of origin, including policies of co-development.

Legislation to implement the Tampere Programme included a directive on family reunification of 2003;[9] a directive on long-term resident status;[10] and directives on the admission of students and researchers from third countries.[11] The Commission is to present proposals on a general framework defining the basic rights of immigrant workers in the EU and for a directive on the conditions of entry and residence of highly skilled immigrants. In 2007 The Commission proposed to introduce a blue-card system, similar to the US green cards to offer skilled immigrants a fast-track procedure for obtaining work permits (see Box 8.1). Other measures include: networks to facilitate integration of immigrants; an action plan on illegal immigration agreed in 2002, and readmission agreements with various countries. Mainstreaming of immigration was introduced, by which it is taken into account in all EU policies. A programme for financial and technical assistance to third countries in the area of migration and asylum (AENEAS) covers the 2004-2008 period with a budget of €250 million.

FRONTEX was set up as an EU agency responsible for managing operational co-operation at the external borders of the EU. In 2008 the capacities and functions of FRONTEX are to be extended to networking of sea-border controls and the implementation of a European surveillance system aimed at helping member states to deal with the growing numbers of illegal immigrants. The budget of FRONTEX for 2008 is €10.9 million. Concerns have been expressed about the transparency and democratic accountability of this agency.

The approach to EU immigration policy is that of 'unity in diversity', based on co-operation and exchange of best practice of member states. In 2004 the Council agreed on Common Basic Principles for Immigration Integration Policy, and in 2005 the Commission proposed a Common

[9] Council Directive 2003/86/EC.

[10] Council Directive 2003/109/EC.

[11] Council Directives 2003/109/EC and 2005/72/EC.

Box 8.1: *The blue card system*

In October 2007 the European Commission proposed introducing a blue card system similar to the US green card, aimed at attracting high-skilled labour to the EU. High-skilled foreigners account for about 10 per cent of the workforce in Australia, over 7 per cent in Canada and over 3 per cent in the USA. The equivalent figure for the EU is 1.7 per cent or about 70,000 highly skilled workers.* Not only does the EU suffer a shortage of high-skilled engineers, technicians and so on, but many of those who are qualified emigrate. Commission President Barroso maintained that the EU needed to attract more high-skilled workers to increase competitiveness and growth, and tackle the demographic challenge.

The blue card is a special residence and work permit. The system is demand-driven and offers fast-track procedures to skilled workers with job offers. It respects the principle of Community preference, and the jurisdiction of the member states to decide on the numbers of persons admitted. The system offers a series of socio-economic rights including easier family reunification and facilitated access to other jobs.

Franco Frattini, Vice-President of the Commission, who was then responsible for Freedom, Security and Justice, expressed hopes that the scheme would increase the number of highly skilled foreign workers in the EU to more than 100 000.

*These statistics are taken from *The Economist*, 27 October 2007.

Agenda for Integration aimed at providing a framework for the integration of third-country nationals into the EU. However, decision-making powers on immigration remain largely the responsibility of member states, and in recent years policies have diverged (with, for example, France increasing expulsions of illegal immigrants at a time when Spain and Italy were giving legal status to many illegal entrants).

The 1999 Tampere European Council also agreed on the principles of a common EU asylum policy. A scoreboard was drawn up to spell out the respective responsibilities of the member states, the Commission and the Council. The aim in the long term was to establish a common asylum procedure and uniform status for those granting asylum throughout the EU.

In January 2003 the EU, Iceland and Norway launched Eurodac, a system to fingerprint all asylum-seekers and exchange information. This will enable member states to determine whether an individual has already applied for asylum in another EU country or whether that person was apprehended for attempting to enter the EU illegally.

In November 2004 the European Council agreed on the Hague Programme aimed at creating a common European Asylum System, with common procedures and uniform status for those granted asylum by 2010. This is to be established by practical co-operation (including exchange of information) between member states within a framework of rules set by the EU. Regional Protection Programmes would be developed to increase the capacity for protection in the country of origin, and to permit resettlement. In 2006 the Commission presented a Communication on Strengthened Practical Co-operation on asylum, setting out proposals of how the member states should work towards a fully harmonized system. In addition to AENEAS (see above), financial support was to be available through a European Refugee Fund.

Statistics on EU migration

It is notoriously difficult to find accurate statistics on migration. Collection practices vary between countries, and illegal immigration poses a challenge. For this reason work was begun on an international bilateral migration stock database (see Box 8.2), with the support of the University of Sussex and World Bank, and some of the findings of this database are presented in Table 8.1. The EU is also committed to improving its data on immigration.

	Countries of immigration*			Countries of emigration*		
	Number (million)	**As % population**			**Number (million)**	**As % population**
USA	34.63	12.48	Mexico		10.10	10.01
Germany	9.14	11.15	India		8.96	0.87
France	6.28	10.55	Bangladesh		6.64	5.03
India	6.27	0.61	China		5.79	0.46
Canada	5.72	18.30	UK		4.19	7.08
Saudi Arabia	5.25	23.03	Germany		4.05	4.94
UK	4.87	8.21	Pakistan		3.39	2.39
Pakistan	4.07	3.00	Philippines		3.39	4.26
Australia	4.07	20.97	Italy		3.28	5.71
Hong Kong	2.70	37.74	Turkey		3.00	4.53
Côte d'Ivoire	2.34	15.38	Afghanistan		2.70	9.86
Iran	2.32	3.57	Morocco		2.61	8.96
Total	87.84	:	Total		58.10	

TABLE 8.1 Principal recipient and origin countries of world migration ('around 2000')
*Excludes former USSR countries
: not available
Source: Winters (2007) CEPR Policy Insight No. 17 and World Bank.

Box 8.2: *A global database on migrant stocks*

Anybody who has done research on migration is only too aware of the difficulty of finding accurate statistics. One of the best attempts to date to meet this challenge, is that of the Development Research Centre (DRC) on Migration, Globalisation and Poverty based at the University of Sussex. The DRC was set up in 2003 with the aim of constructing a global database on migrant stocks in order to facilitate analysis of the complex link between migration and poverty. The database consists of a 226x226 matrix of origin-destination stocks, and was created by disaggregating the information on migrant stock in each destination country or economy as given in its census. The reference period is the 2000 round of population censuses, so the data do not refer to precisely the same time period. Four versions of the database are available, giving increasing levels of completeness, but decreasing levels of accuracy as the missing data are added by assumption and interpolation with each successive version. The Migration DRC database extends the basic stock data on international migration that is published by the United Nations (http://www.un.org/esa/population/ publications/ migstock/2003TrendsMigstock.pdf).

Statistics from the database and a World Migration Map are available on www.migrationdrc. org. For a description of the database see Winters (2007), or Parsons et al. (2007).

	Migrant stock 2005		Refugees end-2006
	Number 1000	% population	
EU(27)	39593	8.3	
BE	719	6.9	16820
BG	104	1.3	4504
CZ	453	4.4	1887
DK	389	7.2	36659
DE	10144	12.3	605406
EE	202	15.2	5
EL	974	8.8	2289
ES	4790	11.1	5275
FR	6471	10.7	145996
IE	585	14.1	7917
IT	2519	4.3	26875
CY	:	:	924
LV	449	19.5	21
LT	165	4.8	531
LU	174	37.4	2206
HU	316	3.1	8075
MT	11	2.7	2404
NL	1638	10.1	100574
AT	1234	15.1	25486
PL	703	1.8	6790
PT	764	7.3	333
RO	113	0.6	1658
SL	167	8.5	254
SK	124	2.3	248
FI	156	3.0	11827
SE	1117	12.4	79913
UK	5408	9.1	301556

TABLE 8.2 Migrant stocks in the EU(27)
Source: European Commission (2007b) and UNHCR (United Nations High Commissioner on Refugees) for statistics on refugees.
: not available

According to the European Commission (2007a), in January 2006 there were about 18.5 million third-country nationals residing in the EU, amounting to about 3.8 per cent of the EU population. Net migration ranged between 0.5 and 1 million a year during most of the 1990s, but rose to levels between 1.5 and 2 million between 2002 and 2005.

The typology of immigration varies between member states. Family reunification was important in countries such as Austria, France and Sweden. In other member states such as Ireland, Spain, Portugal and the UK, a high percentage of immigration was work-related.

According to European Commission (2007a), the most numerous groups of third-country nationals in the EU were from Turkey (2.3 million), Morocco (1.7 million), Albania (0.8 million) and Algeria (0.6 million). However, in some countries (such as France, Sweden, the Netherlands and the UK) many immigrants acquired nationality, so the number of foreign-born citizens is higher than the number of third-country nationals.

	Recorded immigration 2001	Recorded emigration 2001	Net migration 2000–2005, number 1000	Net migration 2006, number 1000
BE	77469	42125	13	53
BG	:	:		0
CZ	12912	21469	10	35
DK	55984	43980	12	10
DE	882279	607282	220	26
EE	:	:	−2	0
EL	:	:	36	69
ES	213340	14539	405	40
FR	:	:	60	60
IE	59000	26200	39	90
IT	236292	66821	120	377
CY	:	:	:	9
LV	2591	1779	−2	−2
LT	:	:	−4	−5
LU	12135	8824	4	5
HU	:	:	10	21
MT	1002	75	1	2
NL	133404	82566	30	−26
AT	89928	72654	20	29
PL	6625	23368	−16	−36
PT	18729	20582	50	26
RO	:	:	−30	−6
SL	7803	4811	2	6
SK	2023	1011	1	4
FI	18955	13153	8	11
SE	60795	32141	31	51
UK	479600	307700	137	214

TABLE 8.3 Net migration in the EU
: not available
Source: Eurostat, © European Communities, 2008.

Also taking intra-EU migration into account the UN estimated that there were almost 40 million migrants in the EU(27) in 2005 (see also Tables 8.2, 8.3 and 8.4).[12] About 3 per cent of these migrants were refugees. In 10 member states the share of foreign-born population was estimated as being over 10 per cent. Net migration into the EU reached a peak in 2003/4, but the statistics were heavily influenced by the decisions of Spain and Italy (accounting for almost two-thirds of the total) to regularize illegal immigrants at that time.

Statistics from the database and a World Migration Map are available on www.migrationdrc. org. For a description of the database see Winters (2007), or Parsons et al. (2007).

---

[12] The statistics in this paragraph are taken from European Commission (2007a).

	Maximum estimated number of irregular migrants (thousands, 2003)	Average % of total migrants
Greece	320	59.87
Portugal	100	42.96
Italy	500	30.59
UK	1,000	24.82
Spain	280	22.24
Belgium	150	17.06
Germany	1,000	13.61
Netherlands	163	8.72
France	400	6.37
Ireland	10	3.23
Finland	1	0.75
Poland	600*	28.73
Czech Rep.	40	16.98
Slovakia	8**	15.69
Lithuania	2#	0.59

TABLE 8.4 Estimated irregular migrants
*2000
** 1998
#1997
Source: World Bank (2007). The statistics in this table are not always consistent with the other data presented in this chapter.

The changing pattern of immigration over the years

The 1958–73 Period

As described above, a major aim of the Treaty of Rome was to remove obstacles to the mobility of labour by 1970 when the transitional period would come to an end. During the first years of the Community, growth was rapid and, with the exception of Italy, the labour markets of the member states tended to be tight. During the 1958–73 period the only substantial migration flow within the Community was from Italy to Northern Europe.

In contrast there were large-scale migrations from third countries to the Community. Between 1960 and 1973 the number of foreign workers doubled from 3 per cent to 6 per cent of the workforce.[13] In particular there was immigration from:

- Turkey and the former Yugoslavia as guest workers to Germany;[14]

- the Mediterranean countries then outside the EC to Northern Europe. These included flows from Franco's Spain (mainly to France, Germany and Switzerland), Greece (to Germany and to a lesser extent the UK) and Portugal (mainly to France);[15]

- From colonies of EC countries which gained independence, and in particular, France and the UK, which granted relatively open access to citizens of former colonies.

---

[13] Hall (2000).

[14] Hall (2000) estimates that in the 25 years following 1960 the number of foreigners (nearly half Turks) rose by 4 million.

[15] www.cnn.com

The 1973–89 Period

Over time with the growth of the Italian economy, and the process of catching up with the other member states, the number of Italians migrating to Northern Europe dwindled. Italian emigration shrank still further after the 1973 oil crisis when employment opportunities in Northern Europe became scarce. The subsequent revival of the EC economy failed to bring about a corresponding return to earlier levels of migration and, indeed, many Italians, Spanish and Portuguese returned home. This suggests that when income and employment conditions at home reach a certain minimum threshold, most workers are unwilling to undertake the costs of migration.

During this period other main categories of intra-EC migration included those working in multinational and international organizations, and Irish working in the UK. In 1973 these two categories, together with Italian emigrants in other EC states, amounted to some 3 million persons (Molle, 2006), so the degree of labour movement within the Community was relatively limited.

Between 1973 and 1989 the main trends in migration from third countries included:

- migration from Spain, Greece and Portugal, though this dropped drastically with EC membership, and many immigrants returned home;
- immigration from North Africa, Turkey and, to a lesser extent, Yugoslavia, also as a result of residence permits granted for family reinification;
- continuing immigration from other former colonies.

Since 1989

From 1989 immigration from third countries increased, in particular from:

- the Mediterranean basin;
- the Middle East, Asia, sub-Saharan Africa and Latin America, where immigrants were at times subject to unscrupulous human trafficking, as for example in the case of June 2000 when 58 Chinese were found dead in a lorry at the UK port of Dover;
- Central and Eastern Europe, and the former Soviet Republics.

After 1989 some experts predicted large migration flows from CEECs to Western Europe as a result of lower levels of income in those countries, and the newfound freedom of citizens of those countries to travel abroad.[16] These fears grew as the prospect of EU enlargement drew closer.

The end of the Cold War was also marked by a rise in the number of ethnic conflicts, including those in the former Soviet Union and ex-Yugoslavia (in particular Bosnia and Kosovo) with an increase in the number of people fleeing from conflict at home.

Many EU member states were worried about the phenomenon of transit immigrants (i.e. immigrants whose ultimate aim is elsewhere) passing through Central and East Europe to other EU countries, in particular, after the extension of Schengen (see Chapter 6). Even before enlargement the EU declared the Central East European states bordering the Community 'safe countries' and forced them to accept readmission agreements to take back unwanted migrants even if the migrant came from elsewhere. With the prospect of EU membership these countries had little choice but to comply and were transformed into the EU's 'reluctant gatekeepers' (Vachudova, 2000). In their turn the Central and East European countries declared neighbouring countries to be 'safe' and triggered a chain of readmission agreements for illegal immigrants and asylum-

---

[16]Many Roma also left Bulgaria and Romania after 1989, and the Czech Republic and Slovakia subsequently. Racial discrimination, poverty and nomadic traditions all contributed to the exodus from the East.

	year	Residents from CEEC(10)	As % population	As % total CEEC(10) migrants
Austria	2001	78886	1.0	7.3
Belgium	2001	13208	0.1	1.2
Denmark	2004	11596	0.2	1.1
Finland	2001	13639	0.3	1.3
France	1999	51942	0.1	4.8
Germany	2003	614094	0.7	57.0
Greece	2001	71742	0.7	6.7
Ireland*	2002	12235	0.4	1.1
Italy**	2001	102105	0.2	9.5
Luxembourg	2001	1547	0.3	0.1
Netherlands	2004	17538	0.1	1.6
Portugal	2001	963	0.0	0.1
Spain#	2003	17104	0.0	1.6
Sweden	2003	24295	0.3	2.3
UK	2001	45858	0.1	4.3
EU(15)		1076752	0.3	100.0

TABLE 8.5 Regional break-down of migrants from the CEEC(10) across the EU(15) before enlargement
*Only Latvia, Lithuania, Poland and Romania,
**Only Poland and Romania
#Only Bulgaria and Romania.
Source: Boeri and Brücker (2005), © European Communities, 2005.

seekers ever further to the east and south. This successive deportation of migrants at times placed human rights at risk and was criticized by both the European Council on Refugees and Exiles (ECRE) and by the UNHCR.

Various studies attempted to estimate the long-run effect of migration from the CEECs. Many of these studies estimated the long-run migration potential from the CEECs to the EU(15) as being between 3 and 4 per cent of the CEEC population (see for example, Layard et al., 1992, or Boeri and Brücker et al., 2000, updated subsequently as Alvarez-Plata et al., 2003, and Boeri and Brücker, 2005) and, therefore, manageable.

According to Boeri and Brücker et al. (2005), before enlargement there were little more than a million CEEC residents in the EU(15), most of whom were concentrated in Germany, Italy and Austria (see Table 8.5).

Boeri and Brücker et al. (2005) predicted that with freedom of movement of labour initial net migration from the new member states would be 270000 in 2004 and about 300000 the following year. The long-term migration potential was estimated at about 3 million thirty years later.[17] The study predicted migration diversion from countries with restrictions on immigration to those without if (as happened) only some of the EU(15) opened their labour markets to the new member states.

Although emigration from the CEEC(10) was expected to be limited, transitional periods of up to 7 years were introduced after the 2004 and 2007 enlargements, which permit restrictions on freedom of labour movement under certain conditions. Under these transitional arrangements a

[17] The earlier Boeri and Brücker et al. study of 2000 estimated that by 2030, the total number of CEEC residents in the EU could rise to 3.9 million, or roughly 1 per cent of the EU population, and 4 per cent of that of the CEECs. In an updated version of the research (Alvarez-Plata et al., 2003), this estimate was revised down slightly to 3.8 million by 2030.

formula of two years, plus three years plus two years was introduced for the new CEEC members states.[18] For the first two years following the 2004 and 2007 enlargements the national law and policy of countries that were EU member states before the respective enlargements governs access of CEEC workers to their labour markets. National measures may be extended for a further three years. Subsequently, a member state applying the national measures may be authorized to continue such measures for a further two years, but only if serious disturbances on its labour market are experienced.

During the first two-year phase after the 2004 enlargement only Ireland, Sweden and the UK liberalized access to their labour markets under national law. However, the UK adopted a mandatory Worker's Registration Scheme, and both Ireland and the UK applied two-year residency restrictions before access to social welfare. The remaining member states of the EU(15) maintained work permit systems, in some cases with modifications, and some countries also applied quota systems.[19] Austria and Germany applied restrictions on the posting of workers (see Chapter 6) in certain sensitive sectors. Poland, Slovenia and Hungary applied reciprocity to EU(15) member states implementing restrictions.

During the second phase a further seven member states joined Ireland, Sweden and the UK in opening their labour markets: Spain, Italy Finland, Greece, Portugal, the Netherlands and Luxembourg. Hungary (but not Poland or Slovenia) continued to apply reciprocal measures.

Following the 2007 enlargement, 10 of the EU(25) countries liberalized access of Romanian and Bulgarian workers to their labour markets under national law.[20] Of these, Cyprus, Finland and Slovenia required that employment must be registered for monitoring purposes. The remaining member states (including the UK and Ireland who had liberalized after the 2004 enlargement) maintained work permits, although frequently with modifications and simplified procedures. Germany and Austria also apply restrictions on posting of workers. Bulgaria and Romania decided against applying reciprocal measures.

According to the European Commission, by the end of 2005 nearly 300 000 from the CEEC new member states had applied to work in Britain and 160 000 had moved to Ireland and 8 000 to Sweden.[21] Ninety-two thousand migrants from the new member states came to Britain in 2006, of which almost three-quarters were from Poland.[22] This compares with the estimate of the UK Government of migration of between 5000 and 13 000 from the countries that acceded to the EU in 2004. This suggests that some migration diversion had taken place and following the 2007 enlargement the UK and Ireland were among to countries to maintain restrictions.

Table 8.6 illustrates the results of a Eurostat labour survey breaking down resident population by nationality. Data are not presented for Italy, but statistics of the Italian government and the charity Caritas suggested that in 2007 the resident foreign population was 3.69 million, of whom 556 000 were Romanian.[23] Seven hundred thousand were expected to arrive in Italy in 2007. It was estimated that some 2 million Romanians were working abroad, mainly in Spain and Italy (with linguistic reasons probably influencing the choice of destination).

---

[18]Cyprus and Malta have labour shortages so Cyprus was excluded from these arrangements and for Malta there is only the possibility of invoking a safeguard clause. See www.ec.europa.eu/employment_social/free_ movement/enlargement for a description of these arrangements.

[19]Quota systems were applied by Austria, Denmark, Italy, the Netherlands and Portugal.

[20]The Czech Republic, Estonia, Cyprus, Latvia, Lithuania, Poland, Slovenia, Slovakia, Finland and Sweden.

[21]www.ec.europa.eu/employment_social

[22]As reported in the *Financial Times* of 16 November 2006.

[23]The statistics here were reported in the *Financial Times* of 7 November 2007.

	National	EU(15)	EU(10)	Non-EU
BE	91.3	5.8	0.2	2.8
DK	96.4	1.1	:	2.4
DE	89.5	2.8	0.7	7.0
EL	94.0	0.3	0.4	5.3
ES	90.5	1.2	0.2	8.1
FR	94.4	1.9	0.1	3.6
IE	92.3	3.0	2.0	2.8
LU	57.9	37.6	0.3	4.2
NL	95.7	1.4	0.1	2.8
AT	89.2	1.9	0.4	7.5
PT	97.0	0.4	:	2.6
FI	98.3	0.4	0.3	1.0
SE	94.8	2.3	0.2	2.7
UK	93.8	1.7	0.4	4.1

TABLE 8.6 Resident population by nationality, 2005

Italy is excluded as it does not disaggregate by nationality.

: signifies data not reliable due to small sample size.

Source: European Commission (2007a), © European Communities, 2007 based on a Eurostat labour force survey, Q1 (Ireland Q2) for working age population.

Evaluation

Economic theory tells us that freedom of labour movement leads to increased efficiency, but in practice all countries apply restrictions on access to their labour markets. Empirical studies suggest that immigration could have negative effects on the wages of less-skilled blue-collar workers, unemployment in the receiving country, and on the bill for welfare payments, although these effects are probably on a limited scale and may be temporary.

Although freedom of labour movement is one of the fundamental freedoms of the EU, in practice there are various barriers to the movement of labour within the EU. In part these are because of language, social and cultural factors, but they are also due to differences in labour market regulations and social security systems among the member states, and to the derogations on labour movement after the 2004 and 2007 enlargements.

In recent years there has been a tendency towards tightening of the immigration and asylum policies of the member states, also as a consequence of increased security concerns following 9/11. Though there is a strong case for co-ordinating these policies (to avoid unwanted spillovers between jurisdictions), in practice the evolution of a common EU immigration and asylum policy as envisaged by the Tampere and Hague Programmes has proved slow and piecemeal. Geographical, historical and cultural factors may explain why member states wish to retain responsibility for immigration policy, but the interests of populist politicians may also play a role.

Summary of Key Concepts

- Freedom of movement of labour on an international scale is generally advocated because it is said to lead to increased efficiency. More specific arguments are also advanced such as to offset possible negative effects of ageing of the population or skill shortages.

- **Restrictions on immigration** include border controls and work or residence permits, limited access to certain jobs and professions, inability to find housing, financial disincentives, limits on access to social security benefits, or unfavourable tax treatment.

- Various factors influence **the decision to migrate**: the income gap between the home and host country; employment possibilities in both countries; the geographical proximity of the two countries; emigration traditions; ethnic and family networks; political and ethnic disturbances; cultural and linguistic factors; and economic expectations.

- The impact of migration on wages and unemployment is a question for empirical research. Some studies suggest that in the receiving countries the wages of manual and non-manual workers may fall, unemployment may rise and the cost of welfare benefits may increase, though these effects are likely to be on a limited scale.

- **The different kinds of immigrant** are: economic immigrants, asylum-seekers, illegal immigrants and seasonal or temporary workers.

- To prevent asylum-seekers 'shopping around', the Dublin Convention requires them to apply for asylum in the first EU country they enter.

- **Temporary immigration** may take various forms: guest workers, seasonal workers, project-tied workers, border-commuters and exchanges of trainees.

- Articles 48–51 of the Treaty of Rome refer to the **free movement of workers**, and Articles 52–58 deal with the **freedom of establishment**.

- In practice there are barriers to the movement of labour in the EU as a result of the derogations after the 2004 and 2007 enlargements, and because of differences in social security systems and labour-market regulations of the member states.

- In 1999 the European Council at Tampere in Finland agreed on the basic elements for creating a common EU immigration policy. At Tampere and at the Hague in 2004 it was agreed to work towards a common EU asylum policy. The aim is to co-ordinate the policies of the member states within a framework of EU legislation.

- During **the 1958–73 period** the only substantial migration flow within the Community was from Italy to Northern Europe, but there were large-scale migrations from third countries to the Community. **Between 1973 and 1989** the degree of labour movement within the Community was relatively low, but immigration from third countries continued. **After 1989** immigration within the EU continued to be on a rather limited scale, but immigration from third countries increased substantially.

- Member states applied **different policies with regard restrictions on workers from the new member states** after the 2004 and 2007 enlargements, and this appears to have caused immigration diversion, with inflows from the CEECs higher that expected in the UK and Ireland.

Questions for study and review

1 What are the main arguments in favour of freedom of labour movement?

2 What are the main arguments used by governments to justify restrictions on immigration? To what extent do you consider that these arguments are justified?

3 What is the effect of immigration on wages?

4 How does immigration affect unemployment?

5 Describe the main forms of immigration.

6 What are the remaining barriers to freedom of labour movement in the EU?

7 What common policies do you consider that the EU should introduce with regard to immigration and asylum? Why is it so difficult to agree on common policies?

8 How has the pattern of immigration changed in the EU over the years?

9 What changes in the policy towards movement of labour in the EU were expected with enlargement?

10 Why do human rights organizations criticize policies in the EU with regard to immigration? Do you consider these criticisms justified?

References

Alvarez-Plata, P., Brücker, H. and Siliverstovs, B. (2003) *Potential Migration from Central and Eastern Europe into the EU–15 – An Update*, Report for the European Commission DG Employment and Social Affairs, http://europa.eu.int/comm/employment_social

Baldwin, R. and Wyplosz, C. (2006) *The Economics of European Integration*, 2nd edn, McGraw-Hill Education, Maidenhead, UK.

Boeri, T. and Brücker, H. (2005) *Migration, Co-ordination Failures and EU Enlargement*, Discussion paper 481, DIW (Deutsches Institut für Wirtschafts forschung, Berlin, www.diw.de/deutsch/produkte/publikationen/discussionpapiere/docs/papers/dp481.pdf

Boeri, T., Brücker, H., et al. (2000) *The Impact of Eastern Enlargement on Employment and Wages in the EU Member States*, Report for the European Commission, http://europa.eu.int/comm/employment_social

European Commission (2007a) 'The Third Annual Report on Migration and Integration', COM(2007)512.

European Commission (2007b) 'Europe's demographic future: Facts and figures', SEC(2007)638.

Faini, R. (1995) 'Migration in the integrated EU', in Baldwin, R., Haaparanta, P. and Klander, J. (eds) *Expanding Membership of the European Community*, Cambridge University Press, Cambridge.

Faini, R. and Venturini, A. (1994) 'Migration and growth: The experience of Southern Europe', CEPR Discussion Paper no. 964, Centre for Economic Policy Research, London.

Hall, B. (2000) 'Immigration in the European Union: Problem or Solution?', *OECD Observer*, No. 221–2.

Krugman, P. and Obstfeld, M. (1997) *International Economics. Theory and Policy*, Addison Wesley Longman Inc., Reading, MA.

Layard, R., Blanchard, O., Dornbusch, R. and Krugman, P. (1992) *East–West Migration: The Alternatives*, MIT Press, Cambridge, MA.

Molle, W. (2006) *The Economics of European Integration Theory, Practice, Policy*, 5th edn, Ashgate, Aldershot.

Parsons, C.R., Skeldon, R., Walmsley, T.L. and Winters, L.A. (2007) 'Quantifying international migration: a database of bilateral migrant stocks', in Ozden, C. and Sciff, M. (eds) *International Migration, Economic Development and Policy*, Palgrave and the World Bank, pp.17–58.

Vachudova, M.A. (2000) 'Eastern Europe as gatekeeper: The immigration and asylum policies of an enlarging European Union' in Andreas, P. and Snyder, T. (eds) *The Wall around the West: State Borders and Immigration Control in North America and Europe*, Rowman & Littlefield, Lanham, MD.

Winters, L.A. (2007) 'Introducing a Global Database on Migrant Stocks. American in Paris – But How Many Are There?', *Centre for Economic Policy Research (CEPR), Policy Insight* No. 17, www.cepr.org

World Bank (2007) 'Overview of Migration Trends in Europe and Central Asia, 1990–2004', www.worldbank.org

Useful websites

Information on EU policies on labour movement and immigration are available from:
The European Commission
www.ec.europa.eu/justice_home

The European Parliament
www.europarl.europa.eu

The EU Council of Ministers
www.consilium.europa.eu/pol/justice

Statistics on immigration can be obtained from:
International Organization for Immigration
www.iom.int

Organization for Economic Co-operation and Development
www.oecd.org

United Nations Development Programme
www.undp.org

The World Bank for a description of the database of global migrant stocks:
http://econ.worldbank.org/external

Discussion of asylum and human rights issues is provided by:
Cable News Network (CNN)
www.cnn.com

European Council on Refugees and Exiles
www.ecre.org

Human Rights Watch
www.hrw.org

Inter-governmental Consultations
www.igc.ch

The Organization for Security and Co-operation in Europe
www.osce.org

United Nations High Commission on Refugees
www.unhcr.ch

The United Nations for basic stock data on international migration:
http://www.un.org/esa/population/ publications/migstock/2003TrendsMigstock.pdf

CHAPTER 09

The Theory of Economic and Monetary Union

❖ LEARNING OBJECTIVES

By the end of this chapter you should be able to understand:

❖ What we mean by an optimum currency area (OCA);

❖ The main expected costs and benefits of introducing the euro;

❖ What we mean by an asymmetric shock;

❖ How the exchange rate mechanism may be used to address the problem of asymmetric shocks;

❖ Whether the likelihood of asymmetric shocks increases or decreases as the level of integration rises;

❖ What other instruments can be used to address asymmetric shocks;

❖ What the conditions are for joining an optimum currency area;

❖ What the difference is between the 'monetarist', and 'economist' views of economic and monetary union (EMU);

❖ Whether the EU constitutes an OCA;

❖ What the conditions are for Britain to join the euro;

❖ Whether the EU could become an OCA.

Introduction

From 1 January 2002 12 EU countries replaced their national currencies with euro notes and coins. Only three of the then EU member states remained out of what became known as the 'eurozone' or 'euro area': the UK, Denmark and Sweden. In May 1998 the decision concerning which countries could join the euro was taken (later for Greece which became a member from 1 January 2001) and, as will be shown, the verdict on which countries were ready to join was ultimately political. In June 1998 the European Central Bank (ECB) came into operation in Frankfurt. Slovenia joined from January 2007, and Cyprus and Malta from 2008. The countries of the eurozone adopted a common interest rate and close co-ordination of their fiscal policies.

What were the expected advantages of adopting a single currency, and what were the possible costs of giving up exchange rate changes? Which countries and when were ready to adopt the euro? This chapter presents the theory used in attempting to address these questions.

The theory of optimum currency areas

Early theoretical assessments of whether countries should join together to form an economic and monetary union generally make use of the concept of an optimum currency area (OCA).[1] A currency area may be defined as either a group of countries that maintain their separate currencies but fix the exchange rates between themselves permanently. They also maintain full convertibility among their currencies and flexible exchange rates towards third countries. Alternatively, the member states may adopt a common currency, which floats against third currencies. The problem then becomes determining the optimum size of the currency area and, more specifically, deciding whether it is to the advantage of a particular country to enter or remain in a currency area.

The early literature in this field concentrates on finding individual criteria that are necessary and sufficient to identify optimum currency areas. This involves indicating alternatives which could act as substitutes for exchange rate policies *vis-à-vis* other member countries, or which would render exchange rate adjustment within the area unnecessary. Possible candidates include trade integration, international factor mobility, financial integration, the diversification of production, convergence of inflation rates and integration of economic policies. As can be seen, most of these also indicate the degree of integration between the member countries.

Cost/benefit analyses of economic and monetary union

Later authors adopt the traditional optimal currency area approach as a starting point but attempt to evolve a global framework that takes the various criteria into account. This involves using cost/benefit analysis to assess whether a country or group of countries should form an EMU. In order to decide whether membership is advantageous or not, it is necessary to identify the different costs and benefits involved and attach weights to each of these. The evaluation of whether countries should form an EMU will depend on the weight attributed to the various costs and benefits, and this can be very subjective as in practice some of these costs and benefits are extremely difficult to quantify.

According to Krugman (1990), the benefits of forming an EMU will increase, and the costs will decline, as the level of integration rises. The level of integration can be measured by, for example, the ratio of intra-EU trade to GDP.[2]

It is useful at this stage to identify the various possible costs and benefits of EMU.

The benefits of economic and monetary union

- ■ In changing from one currency to another, not only does a customer have to pay a commission but the price paid for buying a currency is higher than that received for selling at any given time. According to European Commission (1990), if a citizen changed a certain sum of money successively into each of the former currencies of the EU, at the end less than half the money would remain.[3] The 'transaction costs' of changing money reflect the fact

---

[1] This concept was introduced by Mundell in 1961, and developed by McKinnon (1963) and Kenen (1969).

[2] This issue is taken up again below when costs and benefits are compared.

[3] The example given was of 10 000 ECU in Belgian francs being changed into the then other ten currencies of member states and back into Belgian francs.

that real resources are used up in the provision of foreign exchange services. The bank, or *bureau de change*, has to pay the overheads for maintaining an office, the salaries of staff and so on. The benefit from elimination of transaction costs rises with the level of integration, as the savings will tend to be greater as the level of trade increases. According to the EC Commission (1990), the reduction in foreign exchange transactions as a result of EMU could amount to some €13-20 billion, or between 0.25 and 0.5 of GDP each year.

■ Economic and monetary union would represent a further step towards completion of the Single Market. Quoting all prices in a single currency could provide a further stimulus to price convergence in the EU (see Chapter 6).[4] However, it seems likely that in Europe differences in tastes, habits, culture and language will prevent the eurozone from becoming a single homogeneous market (see Box 9.1). In part price differences between countries may also be because much of the retail trade is organized on a national basis.

Box 9.1: *Product differences in the EU*

Even in the case of multinational firms, surprisingly few homogeneous products are sold from one end of Europe to another. For instance, in the USA the same brands of soap powder are sold throughout the country, but in the EU even detergents are different from country to country to suit local conditions. As a representative from Henkel maintains, stains in the Scandinavian countries are different from those in Southern Europe because of 'the special challenges of olive oil and tomatoes'.*

* As reported in the *Financial Times*, 5/6 January 2002.

■ Introduction of the single currency could encourage the creation of a deeper, wider, more liquid capital market. Portes and Rey (1998) describe a circular mechanism by which this might come about. As euro markets for money and securities become more integrated and liquid, transaction costs will fall, rendering euro-denominated assets more attractive. Increased holdings of euro-denominated assets, and use of the euro as a vehicle currency, make the EU financial market deeper, broader and more liquid and so on. The shortcoming in this argument is that one of the main European financial centres, the City of London, remains outside the euro area, but even here trading in euros has been expanding rapidly (ECB, 2007b).

■ Following the pioneering work by Andrew Rose (Rose, 2000 and 2002; Frenkel and Rose, 2000), various studies have shown how introducing a common currency encourages trade growth. Rose (2000) found that countries with the same legal tender have trade flows between each other on average 100 per cent higher than those between pairs of countries that are not members of a monetary union.[5] This result spawned a vast and growing literature. Rose (2002) considers 24 recent studies of the impact of currency unions on trade, and

---

[4] According to European Commission (2007a) there has been rapid convergence in the EU(25), but less in the eurozone in recent years. Engel and Rogers (2004) analysed price convergence for 100 identical products in 18 cities in the eurozone between 1990 and 2003. They found that most convergence took place before 1999, and then stopped.

[5] The Rose (2000) analysis was based on a cross-country dataset covering bilateral trade between 186 economic systems at five-year intervals, using a linear gravity model. One of the surprising outcomes of Rose's study is that exchange rate volatility plays little significant role in the picture.

despite the differences in approach and coverage of the studies, all seem to confirm that currency unions have a positive impact on trade. In a review of the literature on the Rose finding, Baldwin (2005) found an effect of 50 per cent or more for smaller countries, which was lower than the initial results, but still substantial.

■ The euro is likely to become an international reserve currency, and be able to reap some benefits of seigniorage as some of the printed money will end up as international reserves.[6] In so far as non-euro countries hold euros, they will also have to pay some of the costs of seigniorage. However, the benefits of having an international currency are relatively small. Over half of the US dollars issued by the Federal Reserve were held outside the USA, but the seigniorage earnt was only about 3 per cent of gross domestic product (GDP) (Baldwin and Wyplosz, 2006).

■ A monetary union would entail the introduction of a common monetary policy, which according to some was a benefit, and to others a cost (see below). Some studies presented the likely reduction of inflation and interest rates as one of the main advantages of a monetary union. This argument in favour of EMU rests on the assumption that the ECB is committed to low inflation (which seemed even excessively the case in the first years of the euro), and that inflation-prone countries are incapable of pursuing the policies necessary to keep inflation low outside the EMU. A distinction can be made between the political and credibility constraints on governments in this context (see, for example, Torres, 2008). Political constraints arise as a result of differences over ultimate policy goals. Credibility constraints arise because of the temptation of governments to deviate from pre-announced plans (because for instance, of the pressures of interest groups the risk of manipulation of economic policies for electoral purposes).[7] Torres (2006) argues that the experience of co-operation in the creation and operation of EMU has led to a process of convergence of preferences with regards to political goals. Moreover, in the EU context a common monetary policy allowed other EU countries more say than was the case in the 'German policy leadership' model of the European Monetary System up until 1992 (see Chapter 10). With regard to credibility constraints, a common monetary policy might be considered an advantage in providing external discipline and 'borrowed' credibility for inflation-prone countries (see the discussion of the monetarist view below).[8]

---

[6] Seigniorage refers to the capacity of governments to increase their budget receipts as a result of their right to print money The term seigniorage derives from the benefits to the *seigneur* or lord of the manor in issuing coins. The gold content of such coins was generally less than their face value. In other words, if there were confidence in holding such coins, the *seigneur* could 'clip' part of their gold content.

A government may cover a budget deficit by printing money. The question that then arises is why the public is prepared to hold a greater stock of money, or even a stock of money that is increasing in size year after year. In part this willingness of the public may be the consequence of real growth of the economy, but it is generally also the result of inflation. Assuming that there is no real growth in an economy, the public will want to hold a constant stock of money in real terms. However, with inflation the purchasing power of a given nominal stock of money will decline. In order to maintain the real value of money holdings unchanged, the public will have to hold an increasing stock of nominal money to compensate for the inflation rate. Inflation can therefore be regarded as a type of tax insofar as the public can only spend a smaller share of its income and has to pay the difference to the government in exchange for money. In other words, if the government sector is financing its deficit by printing money, and the public is prepared to hold this extra money to maintain the real value of its money holdings constant, the government is imposing a kind of 'inflation tax'.

[7] See Mueller (2003) for a review of the literature on these issues. The seminal work by Barro and Gordon (1983) indicates the role that can be played by rules and reputation.

[8] If governments take advantage of the temporary trade-off between inflation and unemployment and raise inflation to reduce unemployment, agents will come to expect them to do so and will predict a higher level of inflation. What is needed is a way of making commitment to lower inflation credible, and an independent

■ Exchange rate uncertainty is taken into account by firms in their location decisions. If this uncertainty is removed, firms are likely to have better long-run information about future prices, rendering decisions about investment and production easier. Firms will be able to locate where their unit costs are lowest, and where they can best exploit economies of scale. This is another reason why the benefits curve is assumed to slope up to the right as the level of integration increases.

More generally, the impact of exchange rate uncertainty on the revenue of firms is less clear. Risk-averse firms will prefer less uncertainty, but exchange rate changes may create opportunities for making profits.

■ According to the neo-functionalist approach, introducing an EMU might further the integration process through spillover into other policy areas. For instance, the need for democratic control of a central bank could lead to institutional reform and further steps towards political union.[9]

■ It seems likely that members of a monetary union will carry more weight at a world level in their dealings with third countries.

The main costs of economic and monetary union

■ Joining an economic and monetary union entails loss of an autonomous monetary policy, which also implies that a country loses the power to change the value of its currency and of the exchange rate mechanism.

A single interest rate may be unsuited to the differing economic situation in individual member states, being too tight for some and too loose for others. In 1998, for example, the business cycles of countries joining the euro were evidently not synchronized. Countries such as Finland and Portugal were growing faster than Italy or Germany, and in Ireland and Spain there was a risk of overheating. However, some economists have argued that the experience of participating together in EMU will bring the business cycles of the euro countries more in line with each other and so reduce this problem of 'one size fits all'.

According to economic textbooks, the role of the exchange rate mechanism is to act as a shock absorber in the event of asymmetric shocks, i.e. disturbances that affect the countries involved in different ways. Asymmetric shocks arise because countries are different in some important ways, often relating to their legal or political systems, or to differences in national labour market legislation and organization.

Differences between countries may also mean that the same, identical shock has asymmetric effects in different countries. For instance, a rise in oil prices will affect countries differently according to their oil dependency. Similarly, a single action by the ECB may have differing effects in various euro countries depending on their banking systems, financial markets or the size of firms and their ability to borrow. The analysis of asymmetric shocks here can also be applied to the asymmetric effects of a symmetric shock.[10]

It is useful to take an example to consider the effects of an asymmetric shock. For instance, if it is assumed that France is relatively intensive in the production of wine, and

---

ECB committed to curbing inflation may perform this function and bring about a lower rate of inflation. In this way the inflation-prone country may 'borrow' credibility.

[9] See the discussion on the independence and accountability of the ECB in the next chapter.

[10] For example, Dornbusch et al. (1998) estimate that the initial impact of a rise in short-term interest rates is twice as high in Italy as in Germany.

Germany is relatively intensive in the production of beer, an asymmetric shock could take the form of a health scare concerning wine that causes consumers to start drinking beer in place of wine. Output declines in France and rises in Germany, and this is likely to lead to increased unemployment in France, and lower unemployment in Germany. There will be an incentive for French workers to move to Germany. To meet this situation France could try and increase competitiveness by reducing prices and wages. If this is not possible, before introduction of the euro France could have devalued the franc against the German D-mark, rendering French output cheaper relative to German output. As a result people will again start drinking more wine and less beer, so it should therefore be possible to use the devaluation to return to the original situation in each country.[11] The Appendix at the end of the chapter provides a more formal treatment of this question.

- The introduction of a new, single currency is likely to involve psychological costs. A survey carried out by Eurobarometer suggested that in November 1997 the share of public opinion opposed to introducing a single money was highest in Finland, Denmark, Britain and Sweden. The countries with the largest share of public opinion in favour of the single money initially were Italy, Ireland, Luxembourg and Spain. This situation was soon to change and according to a survey carried out by Cetelem,[12] 59 per cent of 5000 people surveyed in 2003 said they were worried about the effects of the euro, compared with a third in 1999. Italians were the most critical with 78 per cent expressing concern, probably because of the widespread conviction that the euro added to inflation (see Box 9.1 and Tables 9.1 and 9.2). Later Eurobarometer surveys confirm a decreasing trend in enthusiasm for the euro and a general belief that the euro had a negative impact on prices.

Country	Advantageous overall	Euro added to the increase of prices
Ireland	75	71
Finland	65	91
Luxembourg	64	90
Austria	62	88
Belgium	58	88
Spain	55	97
France	51	96
EU (12)	48	93
Germany	46	90
Portugal	43	86
Italy	41	96
Netherlands	38	91
Greece	38	97

TABLE 9.1 Attitudes to the euro in 2006 (per cent)
Source: Eurobarometer (2006), © European Communities, 2006.

[11] Alternatively, in a country with a flexible exchange rate such as the UK, the country can manipulate the interest rate to achieve the same objective (see the analysis in the Appendix to this Chapter).

[12] As reported in the *Financial Times*, 8 January 2004.

Box 9.2: *The euro and inflation in Italy*

In all eurozone countries and Italy, in particular, introduction of the euro was believed to have caused large price increases. A first reaction of the Italian authorities was to deny such charges, and then the official consumer price index was adjusted, bringing the basket on which it was based up to date, but the increase in the consumer price index was only 2.6 per cent for 2002.[13] A common complaint of the public was that what had cost 10,000 lira, now cost €10 (i.e. roughly 20,000 lira). As Table 9.2 illustrates, Italian food prices certainly increased substantially in the year the euro was introduced. However, the Italian authorities maintained that the weight of food in the consumption of households was low so this had little impact on the rate of inflation.

Although the price elasticity of demand for food is low, food is generally sold in competitive markets so its is difficult for retailers to exploit this low elasticity by raising price. A price rise requires simultaneous action by all suppliers, but in general it is difficult to reach agreement on this type of collective action. The introduction of the euro provided a window of opportunity, lowering the costs of collective action so all could raise the price together (De Grauwe, 2007). This was not simply the rounding up of prices that economists expected.

There has been much speculation about Italy leaving the lira after the then Italian Minister of Welfare, Roberto Maroni, voiced the possibility in June 2005. The idea was to return to the lira and use devaluation as an instrument for regaining competitiveness. However, much of Italy's large public debt is in euro, and leaving the common currency would probably lead to higher interest rates adding substantially to the burden of debt.

On 3 March 2006 Leggo, an Italian newspaper distributed free, ran the headline 'About turn: From June 1st the lira will return!' According to the hoax article, Italy's request to leave the euro had been agreed by the Ecofin, while the UK, France and Germany were threatening to leave the EU.

Breakfast items (bread, snacks)	23.3%
Pasta, bread, rice	20.1%
Beverages	32.9%
Meat, eggs and fresh fish	22.1%
Cold cuts	27.5%
Canned food	30.9%
Fruit and vegetables	50.8%
Frozen food	23.6%
Average	29.2%

TABLE 9.2 Price increases of food products in Italy between November 2001 and November 2002
Source: De Grauwe (2007), Table B5.1, p.68.

[13] Eurostat data.

Box 9.3: *What happened to the notes and coins not traded in?*

It was estimated that central banks and governments in the eurozone were likely to collect a windfall of up to €15 billion from old currency notes and coins not handed in after introduction of the euro (*Financial Times*, 20 December 2001).

The euro area central banks are responsible for the physical issuing of euros. The introduction of the euro required old coins to be rounded up and eventually melted down so their metal could be recycled. In order to guard against theft, a German firm, Eurocoin, introduced a machine known as the 'decoiner' which squashes and corrugates higher denomination coins, rendering them useless to thieves (*Financial Times*, 4 December 2001). Eurocoin provides coin blanks for the euro and also for other currencies like the Thai baht and Malaysian ringgit.

■ The transition to the new system involves 'technical' costs such as the printing of new money (see also Box 9.3), the adjustment of slot machines, changes in accountancy etc.

■ Monetary union entailed a loss of seigniorage for some EU member states. On 9 December 2001 the European Central Bank indicated how the estimated €13 billion seigniorage was to be allocated among the central banks of the euro members. The allocation was based on each central bank's share in the capital of the European Central Bank, with France, Greece and Finland standing to gain most from the new system, while Germany, Spain and Italy were the greatest losers.[14]

Seigniorage may be an important source of revenue in countries with a high level of inflation. If inflation is brought down, seigniorage revenues will probably have to be replaced by taxes. During the 1980s revenues from seigniorage accounted for about 2–3 per cent of GNP in countries such as Greece, Portugal, Spain and Italy, but declined substantially in the 1990s due to lower inflation (De Grauwe, 2007). As a result there was little need to replace seigniorage revenues with tax when EMU was introduced, but this could be a problem for some of the Central and East European member states.

How effective is the exchange rate mechanism in correcting asymmetric shocks?

The effectiveness of the exchange rate mechanism in correcting asymmetric shocks has been questioned (see also the Appendix to this Chapter). Even if French domestic prices remain the same, the devaluation will increase the franc price of German beer bought by French workers. If there is a high level of integration between the French and German economies, a large share of products in France will be imported from Germany. This means that a French devaluation will have a substantial effect in raising consumer prices in France.

These higher prices reduce real wages, and may lead to requests by French workers to increase nominal wages. There is even a risk that repeated devaluations lead to a wage–price–devaluation spiral. With a higher level of integration, an exchange rate change is more likely

---

[14] *Financial Times*, 20 December 2001. France stood to gain most: although the franc accounted for only 12 per cent of issuance across the euro area, under the capital key the economic size and population of France entailed an estimated share of 20 per cent.

to alter consumer prices and lead to this kind of price–wage reaction. The higher the level of integration, the less is the cost of forgoing the exchange rate mechanism.

This observation was the basis of the important contribution of McKinnon (1962) to the theory of optimal currency areas. The effect of an exchange rate change on the aggregate price level will be greater in a small open economy than in a relatively closed one.[15] This is a major reason that the cost curve of monetary union with respect to trade integration is assumed to slope down to the right. For instance a 10 per cent devaluation is likely to have more impact on a country that exports 90 per cent of its output, than one that exports only 10 per cent. A small open economy has little power to change the price on international markets so the cost of giving up the currency is less. Similarly, if the country has a high level of import dependency a devaluation is likely to lead to a larger increase in prices.

Although this type of price–wage reaction reduces the effectiveness of the exchange rate instrument, few economists would argue that it loses all its effectiveness. The reactions may not be immediate, so that devaluation can give governments a breathing space while other policies are introduced.

In the more recent literature the view has emerged that rather than neutralizing asymmetric shocks, exchange rate changes might actually cause them. For instance, Buiter (2000: 236) maintains that with very high international financial capital mobility, market-determined exchange rates are primarily a source of shocks and instability, arguing: 'The potential advantages of nominal exchange rate flexibility as an effective adjustment mechanism or shock absorber are bundled with the undoubted disadvantages of excessive noise and unwarranted movements in the exchange rate, inflicting unnecessary real adjustments on the rest of the economy'.[16]

Does the likelihood of asymmetric shocks increase or decrease as the level of integration rises?

A further question that arises is whether a higher level of integration makes the likelihood of asymmetric shocks greater or less. It seems likely that a higher level of integration will lead to some convergence of consumer tastes and preferences. If this were the case, on the demand side the shocks would be more likely to affect all the partners, reducing the role for a shock absorber such as adjustment of exchange rates between the member states.

The implications for the production side are less clear. If integration leads to specialization,[17] the economies of the member states will become less similar and more vulnerable to asymmetric shocks. Against this, most trade within the EU is intra-industry and is usually explained in terms of economies of scale and imperfect competition.[18] If this is the case it seems likely that shocks would be more likely to affect all the member states. If, however, as Krugman (1990 and 1993) argues, integration implies centrifugal forces leading to the concentration of industry, asymmetric shocks may affect the poles of development.[19] However, these agglomerations may not necessarily respect national boundaries, and may transgress one or more border.

---

[15] In terms of the aggregate demand and aggregate supply analysis of the Appendix of this chapter, a devaluation is likely to lead to a larger shift in the aggregate demand and supply curves.

[16] Mundell (1973) also made the point about exchange rates being a source of instability.

[17] In terms of international trade theories, this would be the case with specialization according to a Ricardian concept of comparative advantage.

[18] See Chapter 4 for a description of these effects.

[19] These agglomeration effects are discussed in Chapter 15.

Kenen (1969) proposed that a criterion for a country to join an OCA was that the production and exports of member states should be diversified and of a similar structure. If countries are specialized in the production of a narrow range of products they are more vulnerable to asymmetric shocks.

Some authors (see, for example, Torres, 2006 and Bongardt and Torres, 2007) stress the importance of institutional factors, arguing that the ongoing negotiation and discussion of economic policies at the EU, national and regional levels and the repeated confronting of positions has led to a convergence of preferences so tending to reduce the likelihood of asymmetric shocks as a result of differences in policies and market structures.

The issue of how increased integration affects asymmetric shocks is essentially an empirical question. Frankel and Rose (1998) found that more trade integration is strongly associated with more correlated economic activities between countries. Artis and Zhang (1995) also found that as European countries became more integrated, their business cycles became more synchronized. If this is the case, forming a currency union can help to create the conditions for its functioning.

However, it seems unlikely that the problem of asymmetric shocks will disappear in the EU, also because member states are responsible for many areas of economic policy, and this may be a source of such shocks. Taxation and spending decisions are taken largely by national authorities and may give rise to asymmetric shocks. The issue of fiscal policy in a monetary union is taken up in the next chapter. Wage bargaining also differs and may create asymmetric disturbances, while differences in legal systems mean that shocks may have asymmetric effects on financial markets between countries. Some economists have therefore called for political union as a solution to the problem of asymmetric shocks.

Alternative mechanisms to the exchange rate instrument

The cost of forgoing the exchange rate mechanism will also be less if it can be replaced by alternative mechanisms. These could include:

- wage–price flexibility;
- factor mobility;[20]
- transfers from the EU budget to compensate regions or countries that have been adversely affected.

Wage–price flexibility implies that in the case of a permanent adverse asymmetric shock the real wages and relative prices in that country (or region, if the production is concentrated in a particular area) will fall. There will be a strong incentive for workers to move to other regions or countries where real wages are higher. Similarly, if there is sufficient capital mobility among the member states, in the example above there will be a reduced incentive to invest in the French wine industry and a tendency towards increased investment in German beer production. If factors of production were sufficiently mobile, this process would continue until differences in the remuneration of factors in different regions were eliminated. Although much progress has been made in increasing factor mobility in the EU, as the discussion in Chapter 8 shows, this process is far from complete, particularly

---

[20]The role of labour mobility was stressed by Mundell (1961).

in the case of labour.[21] If labour is not mobile in a currency area, it is likely that in the event of asymmetric shocks employment will have to take more of the burden.

In the case of a single country, if the demand for a good whose production is concentrated in a particular region falls, transfers from the government budget may be used to compensate producers in that region for the loss of income. This may, however, give rise to moral hazard by encouraging people in the region to assume that they will be bailed out, thereby reducing the incentive for adjustment. The compensation should therefore be used for temporary shocks, or in a temporary way for permanent shocks to avoid hindering the adjustment process.

In the case of the USA, at times individual states have experienced asymmetric shocks as, for example, Texas with the fall in oil prices in the mid-1980s, or the collapse of the defence industry in California in the late 1980s and early 1990s. In the USA not only do people tend to be more mobile, and willing to change state, but transfers from the federal government play an important role. Any fall in the income of a state will lead to higher benefits received from the federal authorities and lower taxes paid to them. According to Sachs and Sala-i-Martin (1992) for every $1 decline in state income the Federal budget transferred back 40 cents, though subsequent studies suggest that this figure should be revised downwards and may be in the order of 10–40 per cent (Baldwin and Wyplosz, 2006).

At least in theory EU regional or budgetary policies could be used in a similar way to offset the repercussions of asymmetric shocks among the member states.[22] However, the scale of the EU budget is too limited to enable the Community to carry out this kind of stabilizing role between member states effectively.[23]

A comparison of costs and benefits

As argued above, it is difficult to quantify and give relative weights to the various costs and benefits of EMU. None the less is it useful here to attempt to compare the costs and benefits, which have been identified.

Figure 9.1 illustrates the relationship between costs and benefits of monetary union and the openness of a country as measured by trade as a percentage of GDP. As the level of trade integration increases so too will the gains from elimination of transaction costs and the reduction in decision errors by firms and consumers as a result of exchange rate uncertainty, so the benefit line is assumed to slope up to the right. In line with the McKinnon (1962) view explained above, with more trade openness the cost of giving up an independent currency is less, so the cost line is assumed to slope down to the right. At the point of intersection between the cost and benefit lines it becomes worthwhile for a country to join a currency area.

The shape and position of the cost curve will depend on views about the effectiveness of monetary policy, including exchange rate policies.[24] At one extreme, according to the 'mon-

---

[21] Baldwin and Wyplosz (2006) argue that one reason why currency areas often coincide with nation states is that labour mobility is likely to be higher within a country for reasons of language, culture, information and so on.

[22] The 1977 MacDougall Report advocated an increase in the Community budget to 7 per cent of GDP to enable it to perform this stabilizing role. Some more recent work such as that by Danson et al. (2000) has suggested that a dedicated budget function may be significantly less costly, however.

[23] Moreover, as explained in Chapter 10, the need to meet the Maastricht criteria and the constraints imposed by the Stability and Growth Pact reduced the leeway for national budgetary spending or for increased contributions to the EU budget.

[24] The account here is based on De Grauwe (2007).

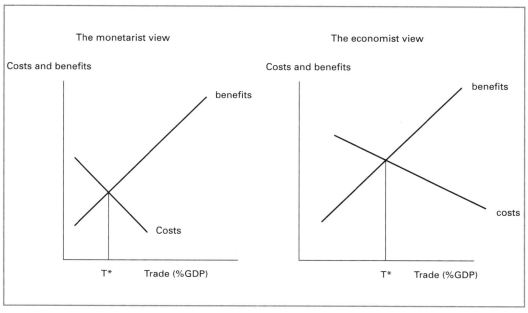

FIGURE 9.1 Costs and benefits of monetary union
Source: Figure 4.2 (p. 82) from *The Economics of Monetary Union* (2007) by De Grauwe, Paul. By permission of Oxford University Press.

etarist' view, the exchange rate is an ineffective corrective for different developments between countries, and the cost curve is close to the origin (see Figure 9.1). Monetary integration is considered the best way to commit national governments to taking the necessary steps to reduce inflation (for instance by cutting the budget deficit or curbing the wage claims of trade unions). It is assumed that once a monetary union is formed, past expectations are irrelevant and inflation is not sticky. The credibility of the common central bank will shape expectations and will deliver low inflation to all member states. As a result the cost of reducing inflation is assumed to be high before joining the monetary union, but almost negligible afterwards. According to this view many countries would gain by giving up their national currencies and joining a monetary union. As a result the emphasis should be on building strong institutions rather than having demanding criteria and a lengthy convergence period before creating EMU. In the long debate about introducing EMU (see Chapter 10) countries such as France, Belgium, Italy and Luxembourg generally held monetarist views.

In contrast, the 'economist' view maintains that a higher level of co-ordination of economic policies and integration is necessary before creating a monetary union.[25] This view stresses rigidities (of wages and prices, and labour is considered immobile), arguing that the exchange rate is an effective instrument. The assumption that inflation is sticky means that countries with a history of high inflation will not support tight monetary policy once they have a representative in the common central bank. Moreover, as these high-inflation countries see nominal interest rates decline, the low (or even negative) real interest rate that results might fuel demand causing

[25]Wyplosz (2006) calls the use of the two terms 'economists' and 'monetarists' bizarre and questions the reasons behind them. Torres (2008) criticizes the mistaken tendency at times in the literature to identify the 'economist' view with the Keynesian approach, pointing out that the FRG (namely the Bundesbank) did not have a Keynesian perspective of macroeconomics, but simply wanted clearly defined rules before embarking on monetary union.

further inflationary pressures. Low-inflation countries may import higher inflation from non-converged countries. This view is sometimes called the coronation theory as monetary union is regarded as the final step in a long process, occurring only when monetary policies have become fully aligned and national currencies are indistinguishable. The cost and benefit curves are considered to intersect a long way from the origin, implying that it would be in the interests of relatively few countries to join a monetary union. Typically countries such as FRG and the Netherlands maintained 'economist' views.

According to Wyplosz (2006: 217) the Maastricht Treaty reflects the 'economists' or German view, and all the monetarists obtained was a timetable for introducing EMU, but in practice in 1998 when the initial decision was taken on which countries could join the euro 'the monetarists carried the day on the ground'.

Is the EU an optimal currency area?

There is a large and growing literature on which European countries form part of an OCA. Although the results of different studies vary, there seems to be a certain consensus among economists that neither the EU(15) nor the EU(25 or, presumably, 27) should form a monetary union.[26] However, in general from empirical studies a 'core' group of countries emerges for which it was easy to recommend EMU membership. In general these include Germany, Austria and the Benelux countries. In contrast there is another group of countries, the 'periphery', for which membership was less easy to recommend, but the list of countries that fall into the category of periphery varies considerably between different studies. The distinction between core and periphery failed to correspond to the initial participation or not in the euro because in many cases the latter was ultimately decided on a political basis (see Chapter 10).

The first articulated study of the optimal currency approach was carried out by the Commission document 'One Market, One Money' (European Commission, 1991). However, the theory was not sufficiently developed to render the approach operational, and, as explained in Chapter 10, played little role in the early stages of adopting the euro, though later it became more important in monitoring the progress of the EMU project.

Bayoumi and Eichengreen (1997) developed an OCA index based on the question of how far, given past experience, countries would have adjusted their exchange rate against the D-mark to deal with asymmetric shocks. The countries that emerge as most suitable to join are Belgium, the Netherlands, Austria (long linked to the German D-Mark), Ireland and Switzerland (not even an EU member). The group with little convergence consists of the UK, Finland, Norway, Denmark and, rather surprisingly, France.

Korhonen and Fidrmuc (2001) examine the correlation of demand and supply shocks between the new Central and East European member states and the euro area during the 1990s. Hungary and Estonia emerge as the countries most suited to join the euro area.

As argued above, one of the main criteria in deciding whether a country forms part of a currency area is openness. Figure 9.2 uses trade as a percentage of GDP to measure openness, and illustrates that openness varies considerably between EU member states.

As stated above, Kenen (1969) maintains that asymmetric shocks are less likely among countries that share a similar production and export structure. Bayoumi and Eichengreen (1997) construct a trade dissimilarity index compared with Germany, and find greatest dissimilarity for Norway (whose trade is dominated by oil and fish), Greece, Netherlands (with a large component of energy products) and Denmark.

---

[26]See De Grauwe (2007) for a review of the literature.

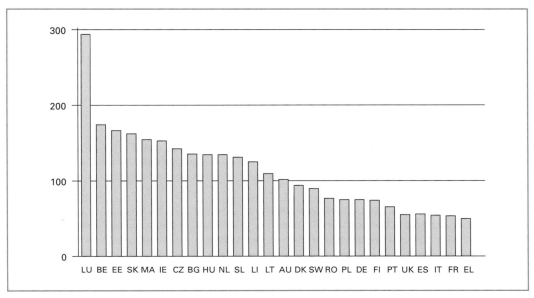

FIGURE 9.2 Openness: Trade as a percentage GDP in 2005
Source: World Bank World Development Indicators database. Statistics were not available for Cyprus.

The creation of an optimum currency area is facilitated by the existence of alternative adjustment mechanisms such as labour movement or the possibility of transfers through the common budget, but as argued above, the EU fares badly on both these counts.

Among the benefits of EMU for high inflation countries such as Greece or Italy was the possibility of gaining credibility rendering it easier to reduce inflation. As explained in Chapter 10, the European Central Bank is strongly committed to price stability and the Stability and Growth Pact is aimed at limiting the size of public deficits. None the less preferences with regard to inflation still appear to differ between member states and could be a source of tension in the future.

Evaluation

The theory of OCAs has attracted much attention and debate, but is difficult to apply in practice. The theory would suggest that the choice of countries to join the euro should be made on the basis of real convergence as measured by criteria such as openness and similarity of the structure of production and exports, but as explained in Chapter 10, the Maastricht criteria relate to nominal variables such as inflation and public deficits.[27] The choice of initial countries to join the third phase of EMU was essentially political.

Most economists agree that the EU(15) or EU(27) do not constitute an optimal currency area. But they generally disagree over the division of countries into the core and periphery categories.

Though the EU is not now an OCA, the mere creation of EMU could help progress in this direction. Joining a monetary union encourages rapid growth of trade, speeding up the integra-

---

[27] In contrast, as will be shown in Chapter 10, the British assessment was based more closely on the optimal currency approach.

tion process. Authors such as Frankel and Rose (1998) and Artis and Zhang (1995) have found empirical evidence for increased integration reducing the likelihood of asymmetric shocks, though there is debate about this issue. The decision to join a monetary union may therefore lower the costs relative to the benefits, so it is possible that the criteria for joining an OCA assume an endogenous nature.

Summary of Key Concepts

- Most theoretical assessments of whether countries should join together to form an economic and monetary union (EMU) take the traditional optimal currency area approach as a starting point but attempt to assess the various costs and benefits.

- The main **benefits** of EMU are: a saving in transaction costs; increased transparency in comparing prices; encouraging the creation of deeper and wider capital markets; increased trade; the use of the euro as an international reserve could yield seigniorage; the introduction of a common monetary policy which may permit countries to 'borrow credibility'; improved location of industry; neo-functionalist spillover into other integration areas; and increased weight of the member countries at a world level.

- The main **costs** of EMU are: loss of monetary policy autonomy, including the possibility of exchange rate changes among the member states; the psychological cost of losing a national currency; the technical costs of changeover, and loss of seignorage for some member states.

- The role of the exchange rate mechanism is to compensate **asymmetric shocks**, i.e. shocks that affect the countries involved in different ways.

- When a country is small and open to trade, the effect of exchange rate movements will be higher price variations. This is a major reason that the cost curve of monetary union is assumed to slope down to the right.

- The cost of forgoing the exchange rate mechanism will be less if other instruments such as **wage/price flexibility and/or factor movements, or budget transfers** can replace it.

- In general it is assumed that the costs of forming an EMU will fall, and the benefits will rise as the level of integration increases. At the point of intersection between the cost and benefit lines it becomes worthwhile for a country to join a currency area.

- The shape and position of the cost curve will depend on views about the effectiveness of monetary policy, including exchange rate policies. At one extreme, according to the **'monetarist' view**, the exchange rate is an ineffective corrective for different developments between countries, and the cost curve is close to the origin. The **'economist' view** maintains that a higher level of co-ordination of economic policies and integration is necessary before creating a monetary union. The Maastricht Treaty reflects the 'economists' or German view, and all the monetarists obtained was a timetable for introducing EMU, but the initial decision in 1998 on which countries could join the euro largely reflected the monetarist view.

- The main criteria in deciding whether a country should form part of a currency area include: openness; the degree of similarity of the structure of production and trade; existence of alternative adjustment mechanisms such as labour movement or the possibility of transfers; and the extent to which high inflation countries can borrow credibility. The results of different studies vary, but there seems to be a certain consensus among economists that **neither the EU(15) nor the EU(25) should form a monetary union.**

■ Though the EU is not now an OCA, the mere creation of EMU could help progress in this direction. Joining a monetary union encourages rapid growth of trade, speeding up the integration process. Some authors have found empirical evidence that increased integration reduces the likelihood of asymmetric shocks so facilitating the creation of a currency union.

Questions for study and review

1 What do you consider the main costs and benefits of introducing a single currency?

2 How effective is the exchange rate instrument in correcting asymmetric shocks? What other instruments could be used?

3 Does the likelihood of asymmetric shocks increase or decrease as the level of integration rises?

4 What are the conditions for forming an optimal currency area?

5 Is the eurozone an optimal currency area?

6 Should the UK adopt the euro?

7 Could the EU become an optimal currency area?

Appendix

An illustration of the role of the exchange rate mechanism using aggregate demand and supply curves

The role of the exchange rate as a shock absorber can be analysed using the concepts of aggregate demand and aggregate supply.[28] For simplicity, initially it is assumed that nominal wages are fixed. Figure A9.1 presents the aggregate demand and supply curves for two countries, say France and Germany prior to EMU.

The aggregate demand curve slopes down from left to right. This is because with lower prices the economy is more competitive, increasing the demand for domestic products, with a tendency to raise exports and reduce imports. At the same time, for a given money stock, lower prices will increase the value of real money balances, leading to an excess supply of money and an excess demand for bonds. This will raise the price of bonds and reduce the interest rate, leading to increased investment and a higher level of production.

The aggregate supply curve is assumed to slope upwards to the right. A possible explanation is that as prices rise, real wage costs fall and firms will take on more labour, increasing output. According to this view, the upward sloping curve is based on the assumption that there is some money illusion on the labour supply side. This implies that an increase in money wages is perceived as an increase in real wages so more labour is offered. If prices rise, but money wages rise less quickly, there will still be an increase in the labour supply.

[28]The analysis here is based on the standard forms of aggregate supply and demand curves explained in any basic Macroeconomic textbook (see, for example, Dornbusch et al., 2004, or Blanchard, 2006).

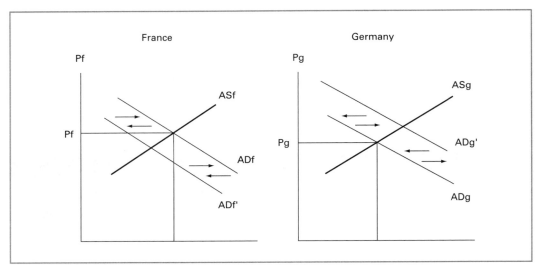

FIGURE A9.1 The aggregate demand and supply curves for France and Germany

Assume that the initial position of the aggregate demand curves in France and Germany are ADf and ADg respectively.[29] An asymmetric shock then takes place because consumers' preferences change, possibly in response to a health scare. For instance, it is assumed that France is relatively intensive in the production of wine, and Germany is relatively intensive in the production of beer. As a result of a health scare concerning wine, consumers may start drinking beer in place of wine. This will shift the aggregate demand curve in France downwards to the left to ADf', and that in Germany up to the right to ADg', as shown in Figure A9.1.

Prior to introduction of the euro, to meet this situation the French franc might be devalued against the German D-mark, rendering French output cheaper relative to German output. This will have the effect of moving the French aggregate demand curve out to the right and the German curve in to the left. According to textbook analysis, it should therefore be possible to use the devaluation to return to the original situation in each country, ADf and ADg.

Alternatively, if France and Germany had flexible exchange rates, France could have lowered its interest rate thereby simulating aggregate demand, while Germany would have raised its interest reducing domestic demand. It is probable that these changes in monetary policy would have led to a depreciation of the French franc and an appreciation of the German D-mark. These changes would make German products sold in France more expensive. The effect would again be to raise aggregate demand in France and to lower aggregate demand in Germany.

However, the price levels so far considered are the domestic price levels in France and Germany (Pf and Pg respectively). Workers are not interested in the prices of domestically produced goods, but in the consumer price index, and this is also based on the price of imported goods. For instance, even if French domestic prices remain the same, the devaluation will increase the franc price of German beer bought by French workers. The French consumer price index PcF can be expressed by the following formula:

---

[29]The example here is taken from Artis (1994), and owes much to the work of Mundell (1961). Source: pp. 351–52 from *The Economics of the European Union* (1994) by Artis, M. and Lee, N. By permission of Oxford University Press.

$$PcF = aPf + (1 - a)e\ Pg$$

where e is the exchange rate for converting D-marks into francs, a is the share of domestic products, and (1 − a) is the share of imported goods.

Even if Pf and Pg remain unchanged, a devaluation of the franc will increase PcF. If there is a high level of integration between the French and German economies, a large share of French products will be imported from Germany. This means that (1 − a) will be high, and a French devaluation will have a substantial effect in raising consumer prices in France.

These higher prices reduce real wages and may lead to requests by French workers to increase nominal wages. If these are granted, the aggregate supply curve will shift to the left offsetting part of the effect of the devaluation. Prices will be higher and French output has not returned to its original level. There is even a risk that repeated devaluations lead to a wage–price–devaluation spiral.

With a higher level of integration, an exchange rate change is more likely to alter consumer prices and lead to this kind of price–wage reaction. The cost of forgoing the exchange rate mechanism is less the higher the level of integration, and this is is a major reason that the cost curve of monetary union is assumed to slope down to the right.

References

Artis, M. (1994) 'European Monetary Union', in Artis, M. and Lee, N. (eds) *The Economics of the European Union: Policy and Analysis*, Oxford University Press, Oxford.

Artis, M. and Lee, N. (eds) *The Economics of the European: Policy and Analysis*, Oxford University Press, Oxford.

Artis, M. and Zhang, W. (1995) *International business cycles and the ERM: Is there a European business cycle?* CEPR Discussion Paper No. 1191.

Baldwin, R. (2005) *The Euro's Trade Effect*, www.hei.unige.ch/-baldwin

Baldwin, R. and Wyplosz, C. (2006) *The Economics of European Integration*, 2nd edn, McGraw-Hill Education, Maidenhead, UK.

Barro, R. and Gordon, D. (1983) 'Rules, Discretion and Reputation in a Model of Monetary Policy', *Journal of Monetary Economics*, Vol. 12, pp. 101–21.

Bayoumi, T. and Eichengreen, B. (1997) 'Ever Close to Heaven. An Optimum Currency Area Index for European Countries', *European Economic Review*, Vol. 41 (3–5), pp. 761–70.

Blanchard, O. (2006) *Macroeconomics*, 4th edn, Prentice Hall, New Jersey.

Bongardt, A. and Torres, F. (2007) 'Institutions, governance and economic growth in the EU: is there a role for the Lisbon Strategy?', *Intereconomics: Review of European Economic Policy*, Vol. 42, No. 1, pp. 32–42.

Buiter, W.H. (2000) 'Optimal currency areas. Scottish Economic Society/Royal Bank of Scotland Annual Lecture', *Scottish Journal of Political Economy*, Vol. 47, No. 3, August.

Danson, M., Halker, H. and Cameron, G. (2000) *Second Report on Economic and Social Cohesion*, European Commission, Brussels.

De Grauwe, P. (2007) *The Economics of Monetary Union*, 7th edn, Oxford University Press, Oxford.

Dornbusch, R., Favero, C. and Giavazzi, F. (1998) 'Immediate challenges for the European Central Bank', *Economic Policy*, Vol. 26.

Dornbusch, R., Fischer, S. and Startz, R. (2004) *Macroeconomics*, 9th edn, McGraw Hill, Maidenhead.

Engel, C.and Rogers, J. (2004) 'European product market integration after the euro', *Economic Policy*, CEPR and CESifo, July.

Eurobarometer (2006) *The Eurozone Five Years After the Introduction of the Euro Coins and Banknotes*, Flash EB No. 193, www.ec.europa.eu

European Central Bank (2007) *Review of the International Role of the Euro*, June, www.ecb. europa.eu

European Commission (1990) 'One market, one money', *European Economy*, Vol. 44.

European Commission (2007a) 'Steps towards a deeper economic integration: The internal market in the 21st Century. A contribution to the Single Market Review', *European Economy*, No. 272, January.

Frankel, J.A. and Rose, A. (1998) 'The endogeneity of the optimum currency area criteria', *Economic Journal*, Vol. 108, No. 441, pp. 1009–25.

Frankel, J.A. and Rose, A. (2000) 'Estimating the effect of currency unions on trade and output', National Bureau of Economic Research Working Paper 7857, Cambridge, MA.

IMF (1998) *World Economic and Social Survey*, Washington DC.

Kenen, R. (1969) 'The theory of Optimum Currency Areas: An Eclectic View', in Mundell, R. and Swoboda, A. (eds) *Monetary Problems of the International Economy*, University of Chicago Press, Chicago.

Korhonen, I. and Fidrmuc, J. (2001) 'Similarity of Supply and Demand Shocks between the Euro Area and the Accession Countries', *Focus on Transition*, Austrian National Bank, Vienna, www.oenb.at/en/geldp_volksw/zentral_osteuropa/ eu_enlargement/2001_korhonenfidrmuc

Krugman, P.R. (1990) 'Policy problems of monetary unions' in De Grauwe, P. and Papademos, L. (eds) *The European Monetary System in the 1990s*, Longman, London.

Krugman, P.R. (1993) 'Lessons of Massachusetts for EMU' in Giavazzi, F. and Torres, T. (eds) *Adjustment and Growth in the European Monetary Union*, Cambridge University Press, Cambridge.

McKinnon, R. (1962) 'Optimum Currency Areas', *American Economic Review*, Vol. 53, pp. 717–25.

Mueller, D.C. (2003) *Public Choice III*, Cambridge University Press, Cambridge.

Mundell, R. (1961) 'A theory of optimum currency areas', *American Economic Review*, Vol. 51.

Mundell, R. (1973) 'Uncommon Arguments for Common Currencies', in Johnson, H.G. and Swoboda, A.K. (eds) *The Economics of Common Currencies*, Allen and Unwin, London, pp. 114–32.

Portes, R. and Rey, H. (1998) 'Euro vs dollar: Will the euro replace the dollar as the world currency?', *Economic Policy*, April.

Rose, A. (2000) 'One money, one market: The effect of common currencies on trade', *Economic Policy*, Vol. 30, pp. 7–33.

Rose, A. (2002) 'The effect of common currencies on international trade: Where do we stand?', unpublished manuscript available at http://faculty.hass.berkeley.edu/arose/RecRes. htm

Sachs, J. and Sala-i-Martin, X (1992) 'Fiscal Federalism and Optimum Currency Areas: Evidence for Europe from the United States', in Canzoneri, M., Masson, P. and Grilli,

V. *Establishing a Central Bank: Issues in Europe and Lessons from the US*, Cambridge University Press.

Torres, F. (2006) 'On the efficiency-legitimacy trade-off in EMU', in Torres, F., Verdun, A. and Zimmermann, H. (eds) *EMU Rules: The Political and Economic Consequences of European Monetary Integration*, Nomos Verlagsgesellschaft, Baden-Baden.

Torres, F. (2008) 'The long road to EMU: The economic and political reasoning behind Maastricht' in Baroncelli, S., Spagnolo, C. and Talani, L.S. (eds) *After Maastricht: The Legacy of the Maastricht Treaty for European Integration*, Cambridge Scholars Publishers, Cambridge.

Wyplosz, C. (2006) 'EMU: The dark sides of a major success', *Economic Policy,* April, pp. 207–16.

Useful websites

The British Treasury has carried out extensive research into the issues of exchange rates and EMU, much of which is available on:
www.hm-treasury.gov.uk

The European Central Bank for statistics, reports and analysis:
www.ecb.int

The website on Economic and Monetary Affairs of the EU:
www.europa.eu/emu

The EU and EC treaties available on:
www.europa.eu/scadplus

The Long Road to Economic and Monetary Union

By the end of this chapter you should be able to understand:

❖ Why the aim of the 1969 Hague Summit to introduce economic and monetary union (EMU) failed;

❖ What we mean by the 'snake in the tunnel';

❖ What the main features of the European Monetary System (EMS) were;

❖ What we mean by the 'impossible trinity';

❖ How the Maastricht Treaty set out the conditions for joining the single currency, the timing of its introduction and its main institutional features;

❖ The arrangements used for EU countries outside the euro area;

❖ What the tasks of the Eurosystem are, and the main issues in the debate about independence and accountability of the European Central Bank (ECB);

❖ How successful the early record of the eurosystem was;

❖ The debate about the role of fiscal policy in a monetary union;

❖ What problems the Stability and Growth Pact has encountered;

❖ How the role of the euro in the international financial system is evolving.

Introduction

Although there was no precise commitment to EMU in the Treaty of Rome, subsequently various initiatives were taken in this direction. For many years these initiatives met with mixed success, but they created a framework of institutions and arrangements on which EMU could eventually be built. This first part of this chapter therefore adopts a historical approach in discussing the long road to EMU. The objective of EMU was revived during the 1980s and, following the collapse of Communism, was carried out with a surprising momentum so that theory could hardly keep pace with the political developments. Though little initial use was made of the optimum currency area theory (also because it was still in a fairly rudimentary stage), subsequently the approach was used to assess progress in the EMU project.

The second part of the chapter deals with the institutional structure of EMU, indicating the main features of the Eurosystem (ECB and national central banks of the euro area countries), and the difficulty in reconciling the objectives of independence and accountability of the ECB. Then follows a brief assessment of the early record of EMU and of the problem of ongoing inflation differentials between euro countries. The debate about the necessity or desirability of fiscal co-ordination in a monetary union is then described before illustrating the vicissitudes of the Stability and Growth Pact. Finally, the increasing role of the euro in the international financial system is assessed.

The international monetary system in the early years of the Community

As described in Chapter 3, the Treaty of Rome contains no specific commitment to EMU, partly because of the importance of the dollar in the international monetary system at the time. During the late 1950s and 1960s international monetary arrangements were still based on the agreement reached at the 1944 Bretton Woods Conference. This entailed that members decided to make their currencies convertible into other currencies and gold at fixed exchange rates, and agreed not to impose import controls without permission of the International Monetary Fund (IMF, which was also set up as a result of Bretton Woods).

Gold continued to play an important role in the international monetary system in the 1950s and 1960s, and was used in settlement of imbalances. The price of gold remained fixed for many years at $35 per ounce, but the supply of gold was not rising fast enough to keep pace with the rapid increase in world trade.

After the Second World War the dollar became increasingly important as the main reserve currency. During the 1950s and 1960s the USA ran large and persistent payments deficits, thereby increasing dollar balances, since surplus countries were prepared to hold short-run debt in dollars. The US deficits therefore had the effect of increasing international liquidity as long as foreigners were prepared to hold dollars.

In 1970 and 1971 the US balance-of-payments deficit reached record levels partly because of large-scale investment by US firms abroad but also because of financing of the Vietnam War. At home the fiscal deficit was also growing, in part because of Lyndon B. Johnson's 'War on Poverty'. There was widespread speculation against the dollar, and pressure on the 'stronger' EC currencies, the D-mark and the Dutch guilder.

The Hague Summit: 'EMU by 1980'

One of the most optimistic beliefs of the founding fathers of the Common Agricultural Policy (CAP) was that the introduction of a common system of prices for agricultural products (see Chapter 12) would render exchange rate adjustments between the EC currencies impossible. Theoretical support for this view was drawn from the neo-functionalist approach to integration: progress in harmonizing agricultural policy would spill over into the economic and monetary sphere. The optimism was to prove short-lived: common agricultural prices began to operate from 1967, and by 1969, with the French devaluation and the German revaluation, exchange rate instability had arrived in the Community.

In order to resolve this situation in 1969 the European Commission submitted the Barre Plan to create a distinct monetary identity in the Community. As part of the package for 'completion, deepening and enlargement' of the EC, at the 1969 Hague Summit the Community announced its intention to proceed towards EMU as a long-term objective.

Differences of opinion were soon to emerge: in particular, the 'economist' group of countries (see Chapter 9), including the FRG and the Netherlands, maintained that before proceeding to monetary unification it was first necessary to reach a certain level of convergence of economic performance by setting common targets and co-ordinating economic policies. In contrast, the 'monetarist' countries (France, Belgium, Italy and Luxembourg) argued that the first step should be to narrow exchange rate fluctuations, as this would itself promote a certain degree of convergence.

A special study group was set up to examine EMU, and the results presented in 1970 are known as the Werner Report. This proposed a three-stage move to full EMU by 1980. The exchange rates of the EC member states would be irrevocably fixed and a single currency would eventually be adopted (though this was considered desirable, but not strictly necessary for the project).

The snake in the tunnel

In the event the proposals of the Werner Report were overtaken by the situation of international monetary turbulence.[1] To meet the heavy speculation against the dollar in 1971, the USA had to suspend dollar convertibility and introduce a 10 per cent surcharge on imports. A solution to the US dollar and balance-of-payments problem was reached with the 1971 Smithsonian Accords. These involved a devaluation of the dollar by 7.9 per cent against gold, an adjustment of the EC currencies against the dollar[2] and a return to fixed exchange rates with margins of fluctuation of +/–2.25 per cent around central rates. The US import surcharge was ended, and it was hoped that there would be an eventual return to dollar convertibility.

It was against this background that in 1972 the EC Six, together with the UK, Denmark, Ireland and Norway (who were expected to become the new EC members), decided to create what is known as 'the snake in the tunnel'.[3] For the EC currencies this entailed two margins of fluctuation:

1 +/–2.25 per cent against the dollar.

2 The maximum divergence between the strongest and the weakest EC currency was 2.25 per cent. Italy was allowed a wider margin of fluctuation of 6 per cent, and this was also offered to Ireland, though refused as a condition of more favourable credit.

However, speculation against currencies continued, and in 1972 the UK and Ireland were forced to float their currencies. Italy began to float in 1973, and France floated between 1974 and 1975, and again from 1976. By 1977 the snake members were Benelux, Germany, Denmark, Norway and (after 1973) Sweden, so the 'snake' had lost its EC character. In 1973 the 'tunnel' collapsed, and a 'joint float' of the snake against the dollar began.

---

[1] For a more detailed account of these events see Gros and Thygesen (1998), or Swann (2000).

[2] The D-mark and guilder were revalued, sterling and the French franc remained unchanged, and the lira was devalued by 1 per cent.

[3] The attempt has been made here to explain the jargon associated with the EU as far as possible, but if additional information is necessary see the Europa Glossary of the EU: http://europa.eu/scadplus/glossary, the site of the European Convention at keywords www. european-convention.eu.int/glossary or the website of Baldwin and Wyplosz (2006) at www.mcgraw-hill.co.uk/textbooks/baldwin

The launching of EMS

Far from reaching EMU by 1980, the Community was no nearer this objective in the late 1970s than it had been in 1969. Moreover, the volatility of exchange rates was threatening to undermine such progress as had been made in integration. Exchange rate uncertainty acts as a barrier to trade and posed difficulties for the CAP.[4]

Partly as a reaction to the years of 'Eurosclerosis', by the late 1970s there was growing support for the idea of setting up a regional system of exchange rates as a first step towards EMU. The initiative would also help to bolster EC countries from the negative consequences of the US policy of benign neglect in international monetary matters.

The origins of the EMS date from a speech by Roy Jenkins at the European University Institute in Florence in 1977, calling for efforts to relaunch monetary integration. With strong support from President Giscard d'Estaing and Chancellor Helmut Schmidt, the idea of creating a zone of monetary stability in Europe gained ground (Ludlow, 1982). For the French this offered the prospect of escape from US dominance and a renewed role for France in integration initiatives, while for Germany reduced speculative pressure on the D-mark should lower inflationary pressures.

In drawing up the EMS proposals, the other EC countries implicitly accepted the traditional German priority attached to combating inflation, and both France and Italy considered participation in the EMS part of an anti-inflation strategy. The members of the former snake were pleased to see the area of exchange rate stability extended. Ireland was in favour of external discipline of monetary policy, independence from the UK and the credits offered as part of the new system. The UK was wary of the political objectives of the EMS and feared its deflationary consequences, so only became a full member 11 years later.

The EMS mechanisms

The EMS was introduced in 1979 and its membership comprised all the then EC members, although the UK only participated in the provisions regarding exchange rates from 1990. The EMS built on the snake, but included new characteristics, namely:

- The exchange rate mechanism (ERM);
- The introduction of the European currency unit (ECU);
- A divergence indicator designed to ensure that adjustment was symmetrical;
- A system of monetary co-operation with very short-, short- and medium-term credits to defend fixed interest rates.

There are two systems that can be used to peg fixed exchange rates: a parity grid and a basket of currencies. A **parity grid** is based on bilateral exchange rates between all the participating countries.[5] A **basket of currencies** is a monetary unit made up of fixed quantities of the currencies of participating countries. For instance, the ECU[6] or European Currency Unit was composed of

---

[4] As discussed in Chapter 12, the operation of the agrimonetary system meant that at times during the 1970s the difference in agricultural price levels in the national currencies of EC countries was greater than it had been prior to introduction of the CAP.

[5] If n countries participate, each country will have n − 1 exchange rates against the other currencies. The total number of exchange rates among participating countries will be n(n − 1), but it is sufficient to know n − 1 rates to calculate them all.

[6] ECU indicates both the acronym in English and a coin formerly used in France.

given quantities of each of the EU currencies, including those (such as the UK up until 1990) that did not participate in the exchange rate mechanism. The ECU consisted of so many D-marks, so many francs, so many lira etc. The quantity of each currency in the basket was decided by some agreed criterion, and in the case of the ECU it roughly reflected the share of each member state in EC GDP and intra-EC trade. The central rates of each EC currency in ECU were used to establish a parity grid of cross rates between the participating currencies. This constituted the basis of the **exchange rate mechanism**.

The EMS was a system of fixed but adjustable exchange rates. Member countries participating in the ERM were obliged to maintain their exchange rate with each other within a target band of fluctuation around their central rates. Between 1979 and 1993 the band of fluctuation for most participating currencies was +/– 2.25 per cent. A wider band of +/– 6 per cent was allowed for Italy between 1979 and 1990, and for the countries that joined later: Spain (1989), the UK (1990) and Portugal (1992). As described below, Italy and the UK were forced to abandon the exchange rate mechanism in September 1992, and Greece remained out of the ERM because of its higher level of inflation. The bands of fluctuation for countries participating in the ERM were widened to +/– 15 per cent from August 1993, when only the exchange rate between the D-mark and Dutch guilder maintained the narrow +/– 2.25 per cent band.

The EMS was a hybrid system since the introduction of a currency basket, the ECU, is not strictly necessary for the operation of a parity grid. One of the main reasons for introduction of the ECU was its importance as a symbol, indicating commitment to the ultimate objective of EMU. Later the ECU provided the basis of what was to become the euro.

The ECU performed the following functions:

- It acted as the numeraire for defining the central rates of the parity grid.
- The ECU was the unit of account used for the EU budget, including all payments and credits granted by the Community.
- It was used as a means of payment, initially by the EC authorities, and subsequently also by member states, international organizations and for private use.[7]
- It provided the basis for a divergence indicator aimed at ensuring early and symmetrical intervention. When a country's currency was out of line, the divergence indicator was intended to act as an alarm bell and there was a 'presumption' (not obligation) that the country would take corrective action.

The aim of the **divergence indicator** was to signal the direction and extent of divergence of a currency from its central rate in ECU. It was hoped that the divergence threshold would require adjustment by both strong and weak currency countries equally. If one currency reached the trigger point against another, both countries were expected to intervene. If, however, policies to maintain an exchange rate were unsustainable, or the balance of payments indicated that a parity was out of line, then by mutual agreement exchange rates could be realigned.

Given the obligations to maintain currencies within the bands of fluctuation, if necessary through unlimited intervention on exchange markets, the EMS was accompanied by provisions to ensure **monetary co-operation** among the participating countries.[8] These operated through the European Monetary Co-operation Fund (EMCF) which was superseded by the European

---

[7] Following the 1985 Basle Agreement.

[8] The monetary co-operation for countries in difficulty consisted of credit provisions for the very short run (45 days, but extended to 60 days with the Basle–Nyborg Agreement of 1987), the short run (up to 75 days but renewable up to three months) and the medium term (2–5 years). With the Basle–Nyborg Agreement the use of the credit facilities was extended to intra-marginal intervention, and many of the restrictions on use of the ECU were removed.

Monetary Institute (EMI) in 1994. The central banks of EMS participants were required to pool 20 per cent of their gold and foreign exchange reserves with the EMCF in exchange for ECU. The EMI later provided the framework for what became the ECB.

The problem of asymmetry in the operation of the EMS

At the time of its inception, the EMS was envisaged as a symmetrical system, with the introduction of the divergence threshold aimed at ensuring intervention by both the authorities responsible for strong and weak currencies. However, given the dominant role of Germany, it soon became apparent that the system was operating in an asymmetrical way.

Germany provided the anchor for the system, using the money supply to control German inflation. The high inflation members of the ERM used their monetary policy to maintain their exchange rates with the D-mark with the aim of 'importing' low German inflation rates.[9]

The strong economic performance of Germany, and the implicit acceptance of German leadership after 1983, meant that other EMS members tended to co-ordinate their monetary policies with that of Germany. Increases in German interest rates aimed at domestic stabilization were generally followed by a rise in other European interest rates (including those of countries outside the ERM). At times countries such as Italy and France introduced controls on capital movements to secure a certain degree of autonomy in monetary policy, but with the liberalization of capital movements from 1990 this was no longer possible.

All the ERM currency realignments carried out between 1979 and 1987 involved revaluation of the D-mark against other EC currencies and only the guilder–D-mark exchange rate remained unchanged over the 1984–87 period. The Bundesbank was hostile to unlimited intervention to support weak currencies. The divergence indicator never functioned particularly well in practice, and even when the divergence threshold was triggered, the Bundesbank rarely carried out intramarginal intervention. Most of the burden of intervention and adjustment was borne by the weaker currency countries.

The weight of the FRG in the system, and the importance of the D-mark as a reserve currency, meant that the Bundesbank was largely responsible for exchange rate policy with regard to third currencies (chiefly the dollar and the yen), while the other central banks were mainly concerned with intervention for adjustment within the system.

The phases of operation of the EMS

The literature generally divides the operation of the EMS into four periods:[10]

1 1979–83;

2 1983–87;

3 1987–92; and

4 from the 1992 crisis until introduction of the euro in December 1999.

---

[9] Barro and Gordon (1983) developed the theoretical underpinning of this point. The cost in terms of output of an anti-inflationary policy depends on the ability of the authorities to convince the public that they will not renege on their policy commitments. If governments succeed in announcing a credible anti-inflationary policy, inflationary expectations will be lower. In this way a reduction in inflation can be achieved with a lower level of unemployment than would otherwise be possible.

[10] For a more complete discussion of the phases of EMS see Bladen-Hovell (2007).

1979 until 1983

The first period from March 1979 until 1983 was characterized by an unstable international monetary environment following the second oil crisis. The frequency (seven) and size of realignments during this period was unexpected. Differentials in inflation between the EC countries were high, but from 1983 France and other EC countries adopted more determined counter-inflationary measures (Artis and Healey, 1995).

The 1983–87 period

The second phase of EMS covers the 1983–87 period and was characterized by relatively few realignments, and when these occurred few currencies were involved and the changes in central rates tended to be small. During this period (which dates from the French decision from 1983 to use the exchange rate anchor to bring and keep inflation down, and to align monetary policy with that of the Bundesbank) empirical evidence suggests that the EMS had a stabilizing effect on exchange rates, and that there was a convergence towards lower inflation rates. The average level of inflation in countries participating in the ERM fell from 11.6 per cent in 1983 to 2.3 per cent in 1986.

There has been considerable debate as to how far the EMS was responsible for this reduction in inflation, which was also experienced by countries not participating in the EMS. There seem to be two ways in which the EMS contributed to downward price convergence:

1 Member states used the EMS as a scapegoat to justify unpopular policies to reduce inflation and to limit wage claims.

2 The increased importance attached to the anti-inflationary objective implied an acceptance of the traditional German priority by other EMS members.

The 1987–92 period

The third period (1987–92), known also as the 'hard' EMS, was characterized by great stability, if not rigidity of exchange rates. There was, however, a 'technical' realignment when Italy entered the narrow +/–2.25 per cent band of fluctuation in 1990.

During this period there was a gradual extension of the ERM membership, to Spain, the UK and Portugal, so that Greece was the only EC country not participating. The decision of these countries to join seems likely to have been influenced by a mixture of economic and political motives, including the desire of the Southern European countries to demonstrate their commitment to the European cause. In the case of the UK, a major factor was undoubtedly fear of remaining outside the system because of the speculative pressures against the currency.

The currency crisis of September 1992

The currency crisis of September 1992 led to the widening of most ERM margins to +/– 15 per cent in August 1993. Three events which contributed to the 1992/3 crisis are:

1 The liberalization of capital movements;

2 The early difficulties encountered by the Maastricht Treaty and the decision to move to economic and monetary union; and

3 German reunification.

Up until 1990 countries such as France and Italy were able to resort to capital controls to regain a certain degree of autonomy for monetary policy. The use of capital controls can limit the scale of a speculative attack on a weak currency and may help to isolate interest rates from fluctuations on international markets. This was especially important given the Bundesbank's objection to unlimited intervention to protect weak currencies. The liberalization of capital movements from 1990 removed this safety valve from the system.

In 1992 there was great uncertainty about the prospects for the Treaty of Maastricht and the EMU programme. In July 1992 the Danish voted against Maastricht in a referendum, though this decision was reversed in 1993. Then followed the *'petit oui'* in France in which only 51 per cent voted in favour of the Maastricht Treaty. One of the main reasons that there were no currency realignments during the 1988–92 period was to prepare the way for EMU. In 1992 EMU seemed at risk, calling into question the credibility of the EMS and encouraging currency speculation.

The operation of the EMS in the years before 1992 rested on the acceptance of German policy leadership by the other EC countries. German unification represented a shock, leading to a tightening of German monetary policy that other EMS members were unwilling to follow.

The collapse of the Berlin Wall in November 1989 was followed at breakneck speed by the monetary unification of Germany in July 1990, and political unification in October. The German government hugely underestimated the cost of reunification, which entailed transfers to East Germany of $79 billion in 1991 and $105 billion in 1992 (Nuti, 1994). As a result the public sector deficit deteriorated by more than 3 per cent of GDP. Inflation rose from 1.3 per cent in 1988 to 4.8 per cent in 1992. During the 1990 elections Kohl had promised that reunification would not lead to an increase in taxes, and the main strategy for combating inflation was through an increase in interest rates, which reached 9.75 per cent in 1992.

At the same time, fear of recession meant that in the USA the Fed reduced interest rates to 3 per cent, and the prospect of elections limited attempts to cut the deficit. The difference of 6.75 per cent between German and US interest rates led to huge capital inflows to the FRG, causing upward pressure on the D-mark and leading to widespread expectation that there would be an EMS realignment. Fear of deflation (in particular in France, the UK and Italy) meant that other countries were reluctant to raise their interest rates to German levels. However, they were no longer able to use capital controls to protect their currencies from speculation. Pressure against sterling and the lira forced them to be 'temporarily' withdrawn from the ERM in September 1992, and subsequently there was speculation against the currencies of Spain, Denmark, Ireland, Portugal and France.[11] When the French franc came under attack again in August 1993, it was decided to widen the bands of fluctuation to +/− 15 per cent (with the exception of the D-mark–guilder rate). At the time many thought such wide bands were not very different from floating, but in practice EMS exchange rates did not fluctuate much more than they had previously (Bladen-Hovell, 2007). The crisis appears to have increased the commitment of policy makers to EMU.

The impossible trinity

Padoa Schioppa (1987) refers to the 'contradictory quartet' that no international monetary arrangement has been able to reconcile simultaneously:

- Liberalized trade;
- Free capital movements;
- Fixed exchange rates; and
- Autonomy of monetary policy.

---

[11] The French franc was defended by massive intervention and by a joint statement by the French and German authorities concerning the importance of the franc/D-mark exchange rate to the EMS.

As liberalized trade became generally taken for granted, the later literature refers to the impossible or 'unholy' trinity of the remaining three items.

During the first period of the EMS (1979–83) participating countries maintained controls on capital movements and there were frequent realignments of exchange rates. After 1983 Italy and France managed to acquire exchange rate stability but only through losing autonomy for monetary policy and recourse to capital controls. The UK realized free capital movements during the 1980s, but only at the cost of exchange rate stability.

The combination of the Single Market and EMS implied a commitment to free trade and capital movement with fixed exchange rates.[12] This system could survive only as long as the other ERM countries were prepared to sacrifice monetary autonomy and accept German policy leadership. After reunification this was no longer the case and the system broke down. EC countries regained a degree of monetary autonomy but at the price of sacrificing fixed exchange rates from August 1993.

The way forward proposed by the Treaty of Maastricht was to combine free capital movements and the decision to give up the exchange rate mechanism with a common monetary policy for the euro area.

The 1980s and 1990s: back to EMU

During the late 1980s, the objective of EMU was revived with a renewed vigour for a number of reasons:

■ Exchange rate uncertainty between the EC currencies was another obstacle to trade that should be eliminated in order to complete the Internal Market. The increased trade and interdependence between the EC economies would render exchange rate adjustment less effective, and a common currency would confirm the reality of the Single Market.

■ The aim was to take the relatively successful experience of co-operating in the EMS one step further.

■ The boom of the late 1980s was beginning to flag, so methods of prolonging business confidence were being sought.

■ According to the neo-functionalist approach, EMU was viewed as a means of pushing the integration process further in the direction of political union, since greater Community responsibility for economic and monetary policies would require more effective democratic control.

■ The EC Commission, and Delors in particular, played an active role in relaunching the initiative, supported by the French and German governments (despite the hesitancy of the Bundesbank).

■ Following German unification, Kohl was anxious to demonstrate that an even more powerful Germany remained firmly anchored in Western Europe, and commitment to EMU provided a means of demonstrating that this was the case.

For once the role of the CAP and the need for exchange rate stability to ensure the effective functioning of the price support system played a relatively minor role. Similarly, compared with the 1960s and 1970s, the revived EMU initiative seemed less of a response to worries about

---

[12] As explained in Chapter 6, capital movements were only liberalized in 1992 for Ireland and Spain. Greece and Portugal had a derogation until 1996, but Portugal liberalized all capital controls in 1992.

the international monetary system.[13] As the process gained momentum, a further reason for its continuation was that it would have been increasingly costly to abandon the whole initiative: the result would have been speculation and currency instability, and the probable collapse of attempts at fiscal discipline, at least in some of the Southern European countries.

The EMU project was formally launched at the 1988 Hannover Summit, when it was decided to set up a committee for the study of EMU under the president of the Commission, Jacques Delors.[14] The Committee's results were presented as the Delors Report in 1989. The 1990 Commission document 'One Money, One Market', which contained the first articulated study of the costs and benefits of EMU, was prepared as input to the Delors Report. However, this approach was not taken up at that stage, partly because optimum currency area theory was still not sufficiently developed to be applied in practice, but also because events were moving so quickly after the collapse of Communism. The Delors Report makes use of the impossible trinity argument, maintaining that the Single Market required freedom of capital movement, and exchange rate stability to promote trade, so the loss of monetary autonomy implied by the single money project was a necessary consequence. Many of the conclusions were similar to those of the earlier Werner Report, which is not surprising as several of the members of the two committees were the same. The Delors Report differs from the Werner Report in its emphasis on the institutional changes implied by EMU, and the need for transfer of authority to the Community. In particular, the central bankers in the Delors Committee seemed concerned to draw the attention of politicians to the need for some constraints on fiscal policy. The Delors Report also appears to be based on the conviction that a very tight exchange rate commitment was simply not as robust as a single money.

During the debate at that time only the UK expressed doubts about the overall objective of EMU. France wanted to fix early dates for the introduction of EMU in order to ensure continuing German commitment to the project. Germany stressed the importance of stringent fiscal criteria and independent institutions mirroring so far as possible the German model. The poorer EC member states such as Ireland, Portugal and Greece called for a link between EMU and cohesion for the weaker regions and countries of the Community and wanted more flexible criteria as a condition for entering the final phase of EMU. The final compromise combines the stringency of the criteria and institutional arrangements requested by Germany with the early deadlines favoured by France.

The Maastricht Treaty

The Maastricht Treaty followed the main indications of the Delors Report and its main provisions with regard to EMU are:

- The Treaty set out convergence criteria to be met before a country could participate in EMU, though allowance was made for certain countries opting out.
- A timetable was fixed for the introduction of a single currency by 1 January 1999 'at the latest'. This was to occur in three stages, and the Treaty describes the objectives to be reached and fixes the dates for each of these stages.

---

[13] According to Tsoukalis (1997), this reflected a greater confidence on the part of the EC countries and, in particular, less fear that the EMS was vulnerable to fluctuations in the value of the dollar.

[14] This was composed of the governors of the central banks of the EC member states and a group of independent experts.

■ The Treaty indicates the main institutional features of EMU and, in particular, of the European Central Bank.

The convergence criteria

Any country wanting to participate fully in the final stage of EMU had to satisfy the Maastricht convergence criteria. These were introduced in an attempt to ensure that the constraints on policy implied by the EMU were acceptable to the country concerned. The aim is to avoid destabilizing the EMU by the premature admission of countries whose underlying economic performance is not yet compatible with permanently fixed exchange rates. As mentioned in Chapter 9, these are nominal convergence criteria, rather than the real criteria suggested by the optimum currency area theory.

The criteria entail that:

■ Successful candidates must have inflation rates no more than 1.5 per cent above the average of the three countries with the lowest inflation rate in the Community.

■ Long-term interest rates should be no more that 2 per cent above the average of that of the three lowest inflation countries. This is to ensure that inflation convergence is lasting, because otherwise higher than expected future inflation in a country would be reflected in higher long-term interest rates.

■ The exchange rate of the country should remain within the 'normal' band of the ERM without tension and without initiating depreciation for two years. At the time of the Maastricht Treaty the 'normal' band referred to the margins of +/–2.25 per cent, but from August 1993 it was taken to refer to +/–15 per cent.[15]

■ The public debt of the country must be less than 60 per cent of gross domestic product (GDP).

■ The national budget deficit must be less than 3 per cent of GDP.

The last two on the list are referred to as the 'fiscal' criteria and are subject to an escape clause. A country may be granted a waiver if the gap between the actual and reference situation is 'exceptional and temporary' or if the excess in public deficit or debt is declining 'continuously and substantially'. As will be described below, in practice there has been rather flexible interpretation of whether various countries have met the criteria.

The three stages in the introduction of EMU

The first stage: July 1990–December 1993

The first stage in the introduction of EMU covered the period July 1990–December 1993. The main objectives of that stage were to liberalize capital movements between EU members, to introduce long-run convergence programmes and to adopt multilateral monitoring of economic policies and performance through the Ecofin (Council of Economic and Finance Ministers).

---

[15]The new member states, which joined the EU in 2004 and 2007 had to respect the margin of +/–2.25 per cent.

The second stage: 1 January 1994 until December 1998

The second stage in the introduction of EMU was to cover the period from 1 January 1994 until December 1996 or 1998. In the event the later date was chosen, and the 1995 Madrid European Council announced that the third stage would be launched from 1999 and adopted the name 'euro' for the single currency (see Box 10.1).

Box 10.1: *Key dates in the EMU Programme*

Date	Event
1989	Delors Report on EMU.
1990	Beginning of stage 1 and abolition of capital controls in July for most member states.
1993	Maastricht Treaty.
1994	Stage 2 of EMU begins with the creation of the EMI.
1995	The Madrid European Council announced that the third stage would be launched from 1999, and adopted the name 'euro' for the single currency.
1996	Stability and Growth Pact agreed at the Dublin European Council.
1998	The European Council of May decided on the euro members, and fixed the exchange rates between the currencies of the participating countries irrevocably.
May/June 1998	The president and Executive Board of the ECB were chosen, and it came into operation from June.
1999	The ECU was converted into the euro, and the third stage of EMU began.
2001	Greece joined.
2002	Euro notes and currencies introduced, and national currencies withdrawn.
2007	Slovenia adopted the euro.
2008	Cyprus and Malta adopted the euro.

The main aims of the second phase were to encourage convergence and to prepare for the final stage in particular by putting in place the necessary institutions and deciding which countries were to participate in the final stage. Temporary derogations were to be granted for countries deemed not yet ready. States subject to derogation would be reconsidered every two years. The EMI was set up in Frankfurt as the forerunner of the ECB, which came into operation from June 1998.

The selection of the countries participating in the euro took place at the May 1998 European Council.[16] Contrary to earlier expectations, when it was considered that several member states would fail to meet the Maastricht convergence criteria, this was only the case for Greece.[17] All countries had made serious efforts to meet the criteria. None the less the generous final inter-

---

[16] This summit took place in Brussels since, rather ironically, the country holding the presidency at the time was the UK, who chose not to participate fully in stage 3 of EMU.

[17] In most of the participating countries certain 'cosmetic' measures were introduced to enable the Maastricht criteria to be met. These included a payment by French Télécom, a refundable 'eurotax' in Italy and an attempt by Germany to adjust the value of its gold reserves.

pretation of who was able to satisfy the criteria probably owes much to the then weakness of the German economy. Germany had insisted on introduction of the fiscal criteria and their strict interpretation, but following German unification could not meet them to the letter when the time came.

The argument that high inflation countries could benefit from the borrowed credibility of a common monetary policy and monetary institution (see Chapter 9) explains the motivation of such countries to join the euro, so the question became why countries such as Germany with credible monetary institutions and low inflation were prepared to share their monetary autonomy with high inflation countries. As Torres (2008) describes, a 1993 ruling of the German Federal Constitutional Court made it possible for Germany to withdraw from EMU if monetary stability were not delivered and Germany insisted on prior agreement to basic economic principles and guarantees of the independence and commitment to price stability of the ECB. It was probably also felt that limited participation in stage 3 of EMU might undermine the achievements so far attained in monetary co-operation, and with regard to the Single Market (if, for example, currency misalignments disrupted trade). Moreover, if some countries were left out of the third phase of EMU because perceived as laggards, it was considered likely to be more difficult for them to join later, in particular, if currency speculation distanced them still further from the Maastricht entry requirements.

It was agreed to grant the UK an 'opt-out' clause so that the decision to participate or not in the final stage would be left to future governments. Blair subsequently announced that when

---

Box 10.2: *Should the UK adopt the euro?*

When Gordon Brown was Chancellor of the Exchequer, an extensive cost–benefit analysis was carried out to assess whether the UK should join the euro. The decision was to be taken on the basis of five economic tests:

- **Convergence** Are business cycles and economic structures compatible so that the UK can live comfortably with common euroland interest rates on a permanent basis?
- **Flexibility** If problems emerge, is there sufficient flexibility to deal with them?
- **Investment** Would adopting the euro create better conditions for firms taking long-term decisions to invest in the UK?
- **The City of London** How would adopting the euro affect UK financial services?
- **Stability, growth and employment** Would adopting the euro help to promote higher growth, stability and a lasting increase in jobs?

The conclusions were presented in 2003 and were rather pessimistic. The convergence and flexibility conditions were not found to have been satisfied, the investment and financial services tests were met, and the growth, stability and employment condition was said to require fulfilment of the first two tests. Brown stated that structural reforms would be undertaken to enable Britain to join the euro in the future, and Tony Blair promised a referendum before Britain could join. An opinion poll carried out by Cetelem suggested that the share of British expressing misgivings about the euro rose from 48 per cent in 1999 to 65 per cent in 2003.*

* As reported in the *Financial Times* of 8 January 2004.

certain economic conditions for membership had been met, British participation would be decided in a referendum (see Box 10.2). Denmark secured a milder version of the 'opt-out', and in 2000 the Danish people voted against participation in the euro in a referendum. In 2007 the Danish Government announced that a further referendum would be held on all the Danish opt-outs, including that on EMU. In 1998 Sweden also decided to remain outside on technical grounds, and in a referendum of September 2003, 56 per cent of the Swedish people voted against adopting the euro.[18]

One of the negative consequences of remaining out of the euro is that a member state's influence over certain decisions of crucial importance to the future of the EU economy is likely to be reduced, in particular, as many important decisions are taken in the monthly informal meetings of the Eurogroup[19] which take place the evening before Ecofin meetings. After September 2003 the UK, Denmark and Sweden were no longer even able to send senior officials to help prepare Eurogroup meetings.

At the May 1998 European Council it was also decided to fix the exchange rates between the currencies of the participating countries irrevocably. Conversion rates into the euro had to wait until 31 December 1998, because the euro was to replace the ECU (with one euro being equal to one ECU) and the ECU included currencies that were not then being replaced by the euro (those of the UK, Denmark, Greece and Sweden). These decisions account for the rather awkward numbers for converting the various national currencies into the euro (see Box 10.3).

Box 10.3: *The conversion rates for the currencies participating in the euro*

(See text for an explanation of how the conversion rates were derived).
€1 (one euro) =

BEF	40.3399	DEM	1.95583	ESP	166.386	ELD	340.750
FRF	6.55957	IEP	0.787564	ITL	1936.27	SLT	239.640
LUF	40.3399	NLG	2.20371	ATS	13.7603	CYP	0.585274
PTE	200.482	FIM	5.94573			MTL	0.4293

The third stage of EMU: From 1 January 1999

The third stage of EMU began on 1 January 1999 and entailed a three-year transition period during which the currencies of the countries participating fully in EMU continued to exist but only as subdivisions of the euro.[20] Financial markets were encouraged to use the euro increasingly. It is perhaps a reflection of how strong the political commitment to EMU was during this period that the process proceeded smoothly and without strong speculative attacks against cur-

---

[18]In Sweden 42 per cent voted in favour of the euro. Three days before the referendum the Swedish Foreign Minister Anna Lindh was stabbed to death in a department store. She had been strongly in favour of the euro, but the expected surge in 'yes' votes as a reaction failed to take place. According to exit polls carried out at the time (and reported in the *Economist*, 20 September 2003), the Swedish people feared the loss of democracy, sovereignty, national control of interest rates and threats to their welfare state (in that order).

[19]The Eurogroup is composed only of economics and finance ministers from countries participating in the euro.

[20]From 1999 the euro began its existence as a largely virtual or non-cash currency appearing in accounting systems. In theory from this date banks were to exchange euro currencies, and in particular euros, into those currencies without a commission, but in practice commissions continued to be charged.

rencies. From 1 January 2002 euro notes and coins were introduced, and national banknotes and coins were withdrawn in the first two months of that year.[21]

Countries outside the Euro area

Even without participating fully in stage 3 of EMU, all EU countries are obliged to treat their economic policies as a matter of common interest and co-ordinate them in the Council (Art. 99 of the Treaty establishing the European Community (TEC)). This involves participation in the procedures to monitor economic performance in the EU and its member states. It also entails the co-ordination of economic policies through national convergence programmes, broad guidelines and multilateral surveillance to assess the consistency of the policies of the EU and its member states with the broad policy guidelines.

The new member states that joined the EU in 2004 and 2007 were not given the possibility of opt-outs and will have to join the euro when they meet the Maastricht criteria.

To cater for countries outside the euro area, since 1999 the ERM was replaced by with a new ERM II linking the currencies of non-euro member states to the euro. Many of the arrangements of ERM II are simply a continuation of the earlier ERM. Central rates were defined in terms of the euro and member states are obliged to keep their currencies within a +/- 15 per cent margin of their central rate. There was to be automatic intervention at the margins, and very short-term credit facilities were available. Unlike in the earlier EMS, there was no attempt to impose symmetry of intervention.

Denmark, which joined ERM II in January 1999, keeps its currency within a narrower band of +/- 2.25 per cent. Estonia, Lithuania and Slovenia joined in 2004, with Estonia and Lithuania maintaining currency boards. A currency board entails that the outstanding liabilities of the central bank are backed at least 100 per cent by its foreign currency reserves. Cyprus, Latvia, Malta and Slovakia joined in 2005, with Latvia maintaining a margin of +/-1 per cent, and Malta keeping its currency at the central rate.

The Maastricht criterion on exchange rates entails that a country should remain within the 'normal' band of the exchange rate mechanism (ERM II) without tension and without initiating depreciation for two years. For the new member states, this meant that full participation in the third stage of EMU had to wait for at least two years after joining the EU, and only Slovenia was deemed ready to join in 2007. Lithuania's inflation rate was slightly above the then benchmark of 2.6 per cent, but was predicted to rise to 3.5 per cent in the following year. The benchmark entails inflation not being more than 1.5 per cent above that of the three best performers in the EU. These were then Sweden, Finland and either the Netherlands or Poland, and the fact that the benchmark referred to at least one non-euro country was a matter of controversy. Cyprus and Malta joined from January 2008.

The Central and East European Member States could have difficulties meeting the Maastricht criteria on fiscal deficits and inflation. These countries face pressure for government spending from a number of sources including completing the implementation of the *acquis*; reform of pensions, social security, health care and education; and improvements in infrastructure and the environment.

When the formerly closed and inefficient centrally planned economies were opened up to market forces, a process of catching up occurred, with rapid gains in productivity. If the productivity gains are faster in the traded than in the non-traded sector, this can also generate inflation according to what is known as the Balassa-Samuelson effect. When a small economy

---

[21] Initially 1 July was indicated for the date when national notes and coins were to cease being national tender, but subsequently it was decided to shorten the time period for the changeover on practical grounds.

opens to international trade its export prices are set at the world level. If the country is on its production possibility frontier, increased productivity in traded goods leads to increased wages in the traded-goods sector. However, if wages are equalized between the traded and non-traded goods sectors, and the non-traded goods sector has lower productivity, inflation will result. If the Central and East European countries (CEECs) attempt to peg their exchange rate when inflation is higher than in their main trading partners this can lead to loss of competitiveness, and may result in currency crises. As explained below, ongoing higher inflation in these countries could also be a source of tension when they join the euro.

The Eurosystem and the European System of Central Banks

The European System of Central Banks (ESCB) is composed of the European Central Bank (ECB) and the national central banks (NCBs) of all EU member states. A different name, the 'Eurosystem' is the term used to refer to the ECB and NCBs of the countries that have adopted the euro. The NCBs of member states that do not participate in the euro area are members of the ESCB with a special status since they do not take part in decision-making with regard to the single monetary policy for the euro area.

The Governing Council is the main decision-making body of the Eurosystem, formulating monetary policies, taking decisions on interest rates, reserve requirements and the amount of liquidity in the system. The Governing Council is composed of the Executive Board and the governors of the NCBs of the euro area member states (see Figure 10.1). The Executive Board has 6 members (a president, vice-president and four other members).[22]

As the Governing Council is assumed to be independent of national interests and to reflect the interests of the Eurosystem as a whole, except on certain financial issues,[23] the Maastricht Treaty made no provision for weighting of votes by the size of country. The Governing Council can act by a simple majority of the votes cast by members who are present, but in practice voting seems an exception (De Grauwe, 2007).

The relationship between the ECB and the Eurosystem resembles the federal banking system of Germany or the USA, though in practice it seemed likely that there would be more decentralization. This was probable given the small initial size of the ECB, with a staff of less than 600 (though subsequently it began to expand) compared with the 60000 working in the national central banks of the euro countries.[24] The number of governors of national central banks also outnumber the Executive Board in the Governing Council. However, De Grauwe (2007) maintains that the Executive Board occupies a strategic position in the Governing Council, so its proposals are likely to prevail,[25] though with enlargement of the euro area to more of the new member states this situation could change. As argued above, as many of these countries have

---

[22] There was a difference of opinion over the appointment of the first president between the French who favoured their own candidate, Trichet, and the Germans who wanted Duisenberg from the Netherlands. A compromise was reached whereby Duisenberg was appointed but seemed to agree that he stand down after four years on grounds of age. Subsequently, differences arose over the interpretation of this deal, but in November 2003 Trichet became the second president of the ECB (after having been cleared in a court case on financial irregularities in France).

[23] See Scheller (2006) for a more detailed discussion of this question.

[24] Baldwin et al. (2001).

[25] According to the Taylor rule first elaborated by Taylor (1999), central banks will set interest rates on the basis of deviations of inflation and output from their desired levels. De Grauwe (2007) used this rule to illustrate how in 2003 the Executive Board was able to prevail in the choice of interest rates reflecting Eurozone aggregates, despite the fact that various smaller countries would have preferred higher interest rates.

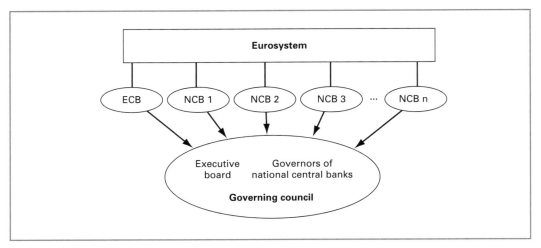

FIGURE 10.1 The decision-making process of the Eurosystem
Source: Figure 8.10 (p. 180) from *The Economics of Monetary Union* (2007) by De Grauwe, Paul. By permission of Oxford University Press.

higher inflationary pressures, so tensions in deciding the 'appropriate' interest rate could worsen. Reform of voting rights in the Governing Council as the number of euro area countries rises therefore becomes crucial.

In 2003 the European Council agreed a reform of the voting system. This entails that the number of NCB governors holding a voting right will be restricted to a maximum of 15. The 6 members of the Executive Board will maintain permanent voting rights, while the Governors of the NCBs will vote on the basis of a rotation system. Countries will be divided into tiers on the basis of the size of their GDP (on which five-sixths of their weighting would be based), and their share in the assets of the monetary financial institutions (determining one-sixth of their weighting). On the basis of the country rankings, larger member states would be entitled to vote more often.[26]

The tasks of the Eurosystem

The main tasks of the Eurosystem are:[27]

■ '*To maintain price stability*'. According to the EC Treaty, this is to be the '*primary objective*'. The ECB has adopted two policy guides to carry out this task: a reference value for monetary policy and an inflation target of 2 per cent or less over the medium term.

■ '*To support the general economic policies in the Community*'. This is a secondary function, only to be carried out without prejudice to price stability.

■ '*To define and implement the monetary policy of the Community*'. The Governing Council of the ECB was to set interest rates but not decide them unilaterally. The ECB would not nor-

---

[26]See Scheller (2006). For example, with 16 NCB governors those from the largest 5 countries would vote 100 per cent of the time, while those in the second group would vote 91 per cent of the time. With 22 countries there would be three tiers with the largest countries voting 80 per cent of the time, the middle tier 73 per cent and the smallest countries voting 50 per cent of the time.

[27]The reference is to Article 105 of the Treaty establishing the European Community.

mally engage in market operations, and the ESCB would be responsible for implementing monetary policy.

- *'To conduct foreign exchange operations'*. Decisions with regard to the exchange rate are to be taken by Ecofin but subject to consultation with the ECB, the European Parliament and the Commission in order to ensure accountability.

- *'To hold and manage the official foreign reserves of the member states'*.

- *'To promote the smooth operation of payments systems'* (which included the introduction of a euro-payments mechanism called TARGET).

- To contribute to *'the smooth conduct of policies pursued by the competent authorities relating to the prudential supervision of credit institutions, and the stability of the financial systems'* . However, the ECB is not to be responsible for supervision of banks and financial institutions.[28]

One of the criticisms of the interpretation of the ECB of its role in its early years was that it seemed to concentrate almost exclusively on the primary priority of price stability, and appeared to pay less attention to the secondary and less well-defined objective of supporting general economic policies, covering goals such as stabilization of the business cycle and financial stability.

The Maastricht Treaty failed to define the primary goal of price stability precisely. It was subsequently defined by the ECB as an annual growth in the harmonized consumer price index of a rate of below 2 per cent in the medium term. It was not clear whether all rates in this range were equally desirable. Various observers such as Fitoussi and Creel (2003) recommended moving to a more explicit inflation targeting procedure with a point target for inflation in the centre of a symmetric range. Inflation targeting involves announcing a target, publishing an inflation forecast for a specific time horizon (usually one or two years ahead) and adjusting the interest rate according to the difference between the forecast and the target. In 2003 the Governing Council of the ECB clarified that its aim was to maintain inflation below, but 'close to 2 per cent in the medium term'.

Initially the Eurosystem adopted a two-pillar strategy composed of a monetary pillar, defined as a 'prominent role for money' based on the evolution of monetary aggregates, and a second pillar, which entailed a 'broadly-based assessment' of all other factors influencing inflation. This approach came under considerable criticism partly because most central banks had abandoned the use of monetary aggregates as not being a reliable guide. Moreover, at the time inflation targeting was becoming popular.

Like the US Fed and the Central Bank of Japan, the Eurosystem rejected explicit inflation targeting. This was probably because it had adopted the money rule strategy of the Bundesbank, though in practice the Bundesbank had effectively abandoned this strategy since the mid-1990s (Wyplosz, 2006), but also to avoid the impression that the ECB acts mechanically. However, in practice the ECB has become what Wyplosz (2006) terms a 'closet' inflation targeter.

In 2003 the strategy of the Eurosystem was reformed with the order of the two pillars being swapped and their names changed. The Eurosystem also renounced its practice of reviewing its rules for monetary growth each year. The new pillars became:

- Economic analysis aimed at the short to medium run and including everything (such as growth, employment, prices, exchange rates and foreign conditions) apart from monetary aggregates; and

---

[28] This policy has been criticized in that the ECB is likely to obtain much information in carrying out its monetary policy operations, and this information will be wasted if it is not responsible for supervision. The narrow supervisory function of the ECB may reflect the German system in which the Bundesbank plays a limited role and supervision is carried out by a small number of large, private universal banks. However, the different institutional reality of the Community makes it likely that the system will be more open and deregulated.

■ Monetary analysis aimed at the medium to longer term and relying on monetary aggregates, in particular, M3.[29]

Like most other modern central banks the ECB implements this strategy essentially by the setting of one policy rate of interest, the 'Main Refinancing Rate', using the instruments of open market operations, standing facilities (credit lines) and minimum reserve requirements.[30]

The division of responsibility between the ECB, Ecofin, the Eurogroup and national governments is complex. The ECB is to define and implement monetary policy and hold foreign reserves. However, decisions with regard to the exchange rate are to be taken by Ecofin but subject to consultation with the ECB, the European Parliament and the Commission (despite the fact that the preference seem to have been for a policy of benign neglect, see below). National governments are to conduct fiscal policy, though, as discussed below, subject to the constraints of the Stability and Growth Pact .

The method of representing the euro countries on the international scene was decided at the Vienna European Council of December 1998. The president of the Ecofin was to participate in meetings of the G8, but if the president were from a non-euro state, representation would be by the president of the Eurogroup assisted by the Commission.

The independence and accountability of the European Central Bank

One of the main debates over the statute of the ECB centred on the issue of how far that bank should be independent and insulated from political pressure, or the extent to which it should be politically accountable.

France and some members of the UK government favoured the idea of a politically accountable bank that could act directly in the name of the EU countries and would be answerable to the governments of the member states. It was argued that certain functions of the ECB had important implications for the economic performance of the member states and, in particular, for politically sensitive issues such as unemployment. The activities of the bank should therefore be subject to adequate political control, and transparency was considered essential.

Germany, in contrast, wanted an independent bank modelled as far as possible on the Bundesbank. The theoretical justification for this type of institution draws on the economic literature on credibility (see Chapter 9), which takes the technical ability of a central bank to pursue an anti-inflationary policy for granted, and concentrates on the political will of governments to do so. It was feared that a political bank would be open to political pressure to reflate, and so would be 'soft' on inflation.

What institutional arrangements can be used to meet the credibility constraint while at the same time ensuring that the decision-making process is democratically accountable?

In a democracy politicians are elected on the basis of a certain mandate, but once in power have a certain independence to carry out policies. Ultimately, however, their accountability is ensured by having to face the electorate again. There may be a second phase in this process in that the politicians may delegate authority for a particular policy to a specialized agency. The politician will indicate the objectives and means of achieving them, but will have to monitor and oversee the activities of the agency to ensure that the objectives are realized. The Public Choice or New Political Economy literature sometimes makes use of the terms 'principal' and 'agent' to

---

[29]M3 includes cash in circulation, sight deposits, private-sector time deposits, and certificates of deposit.

[30]See Artis (2007), or De Grauwe (2007) for more detailed discussions of this issue.

analyse this relationship. The principal delegates responsibility to the agent, but ultimately has to ensure the accountability of the agent.

In the case of the ECB the initial principals were the national governments of member states operating through the European Council and Council of Ministers to decide on the objectives, rules and institutional arrangements of EMU. They delegated responsibility for monetary authority to an agent (the ECB) and to meet the credibility constraint institutional arrangements were introduced to ensure that the principal could not exert political pressure on the agent. In other words, according to Giavazzi and Pagano (1988), the 'hands of the principal were tied' to avoid political interference. A series of institutional arrangements also introduced to ensure the accountability and transparency of the agent, and the European parliament was given a key role in this process.

In order to meet the credibility constraint the Treaty Establishing the European Community attempts to ring-fence the independence of ECB by:[31]

- stipulating that the ECB shall not ' seek or take instructions from Community institutions or bodies, from any Member State or from any other body' (Article 108);

- forbidding the ECB to lend to 'national, regional, local or other public authorities or to Community institutions or bodies' (Article 101), though this implies that the ECB will not perform one of the functions usually attributed to central banks, namely, that of 'banker of the government';[32]

- requiring that members of its Executive Board be appointed for eight-year non-renewable terms by the heads of government of the euro area following consultation by the European Parliament and Governing Council (Article 112).

At least on paper the ECB appears one of the most independent central banks in the world, but in practice its track record has yet to be proven.

With regard to accountability, the President of the ECB has to present an annual report to the EP (Article 113(3) TEC); the EP can hold a debate on that basis, and relevant committees can hear the ECB Executive Board. The European Council has to consult the EP about nominations to the Executive Board. Torres (2006) argues that the ongoing process of negotiation and discussion both in setting up EMU and with regard to its operation has ensured a certain responsiveness of governance to the preferences of European citizens.[33] However, the effectiveness of control by the EP reflects the weakness of this institution, though, as explained in Chapter 3, its powers have been increasing over time. Moreover, while the US Congress can change the statutes of the Fed by a simple majority vote, in the case of the ECB this requires a revision of the treaties.

Accountability is also weakened by the fact that the task of the ECB 'to support the general economic policies in the Community' is not well defined, and the ECB tends to concentrate on its primary task of price stability. This was the basis of the attacks by the French President, Sarkozy, who maintained that the ECB should give more weight to other general economic policies such as employment and growth (see also Chapter 17). He also argued in favour of a more active exchange rate policy to keep the value of the euro down and promote the competitiveness of exporters.

---

[31] Reference is to Articles in the Nice Treaty.

[32] Though the ECB is forbidden to finance governments and local authorities, indirectly there would seem ample scope to do this through open market operations.

[33] As discussed in Chapter 9, in addition to credibility constraints (the temptation to deviate from initial plans), there are also political constraints or conflicts about what the final goals should be. Torres (2006) also argues the informal institution of continual interaction and multi-level dialogue also offers a framework for resolving political constraints and increasing the chances of reaching consensus with regards to ultimate goals.

Transparency can play an important role in ensuring accountability. Though detailed minutes of the meetings of the Governing Council are not made public, press conferences are held immediately after. The ECB has made a considerable effort to explain its decisions, and publishes widely about its positions (in, for instance, its Monthly Bulletin, see also Box 10.4).

Box 10.4: *Communication by the ECB*

During the early years of the ECB when Duisenberg was President the Bank was sometimes criticized for its haphazard communication style. Under President Trichet a traffic light system of code words signalling a rise in interest rates came into operation. Two months ahead of a rate rise President Trichet would announce that the ECB would 'monitor very carefully' inflation risks. The term 'strong vigilance' indicated a rate rise a month later. In 2007 Trichet made it clear 'monitor very carefully' would no longer be used, and an overhaul of the communication strategy of the ECB seemed likely. The use of such key words was considered useful during a phase of bringing interest rates up to a level in line with the pace of economic growth, but less so when that level had been reached.

The early record of the Eurosystem

The Eurosystem has been relatively successful in realizing its primary objective of price stability. Though at times inflation has been above the ceiling of 2 per cent, this is a target for the medium term. Moreover, in 2001 higher inflation (see Figure 10.2) was probably due to an increase in energy prices, worsened by depreciation of the euro.[34] Official inflation statistics probably over-estimate inflation as they fail to take full account of quality improvements. A low (rather than zero) level of inflation may permit more flexible adjustment of real wages.

Between 2001 and 2007 growth was relatively low, and worse than US performance (see Figure 10.3, and also Chapter 7 for a discussion of the relative improvement in EU performance since 2006), though some euro area countries such as Ireland, Luxembourg and Greece grew rapidly. The explanation probably lies largely in the structural weaknesses of the EU economy (see Chapter 7), and perhaps not surprisingly the ECB denied that the cause was an over-restrictive monetary policy stance.[35]

The movements of the euro in its early years defied the predictions of many observers, with an initial fall followed by a substantial rise against the dollar since 2002. The Eurosystem made it clear at the start that it would not take responsibility for the exchange rate, and that blind neglect was the best policy, but intervened in 2000 to support the euro. Since 2002 the Eurosystem was accused of allowing overvaluation of the euro to the detriment of EU exporters.

Various explanations of the initial weakness of the euro were given: the faster productivity increase and more flexible markets of the USA; a few untimely statements by the first ECB president, Duisenberg; capital outflows from the EU; and the untested and cumbersome nature of EMU institutions. Some observers have also argued that market nervousness about EU enlarge-

---

[34]See Chapter 9 for a description of the controversy over official inflation statistics after the introduction of the euro in Italy.

[35]See Artis (2007) for a discussion of this issue.

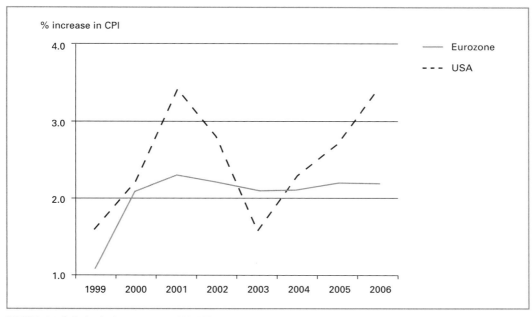

FIGURE 10.2 Inflation in the euro area 1999–2006
Source: Elaboration on the basis of Eurostat data, © European Communities, 2008.

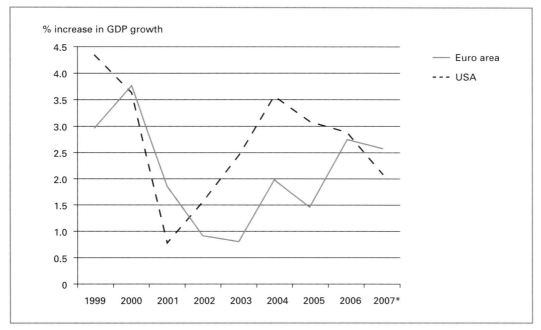

FIGURE 10.3 Growth in the Euro area and the USA 1999–2007
*forecast
Source: Elaboration on the basis of Eurostat data, © European Communities, 2008.

ment also contributed to the weakening of the euro. Subsequently the strength of the euro was said to reflect factors such as international portfolio adjustment (della Posta, 2006), relatively high interest rates in the euro zone and falling confidence in the dollar (spurred also by the large US current account and fiscal deficits).

Asymmetries

The theory suggests that for an optimum currency area member countries should experience similar ('symmetric') shocks and business cycles. If not the problem of 'one size fits all' will arise with the monetary policy likely to be inappropriate for at least some member states. How far is this likely to be the case for the euro area?

As Figures 10.4 and 10.5 suggest, there are still substantial differences in inflation and growth of the euro area countries. Baldwin and Wyplosz (2006) also indicate various reasons why it is likely there will be lasting inflation differentials between the euro countries:

■ The Balassa-Samuelson effect (see above), which implies that there will be higher inflation in countries that are catching up;

■ Some initial conversion rates of national currencies into the euro seem to have been wrong. The conversion rate of the D-mark was probably overvalued contributing to the relatively high German inflation rate in the early years of the euro. This could be a problem as membership of the euro is expanded;

■ Energy and food price rises may act as an asymmetric shock affecting countries differently;

■ Individual countries may give in to pressure for wage and price increases or introduce expansionary fiscal policies (see next section).

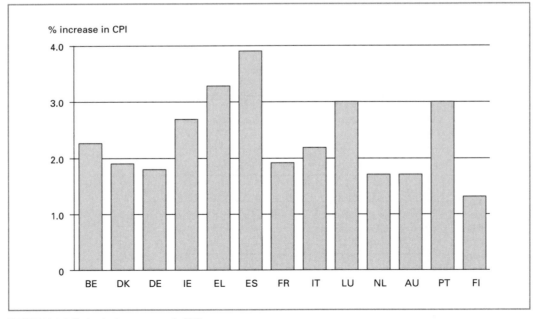

FIGURE 10.4 Inflation in the euro area in 2006
Source: Elaboration on the basis of Eurostat data, © European Communities, 2008.

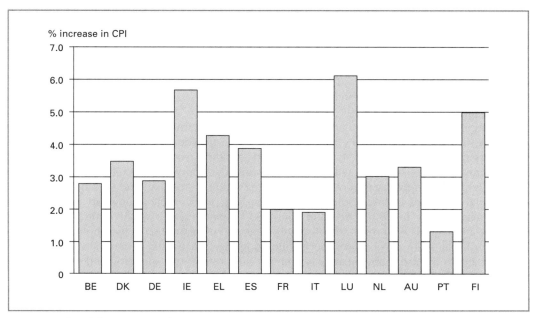

FIGURE 10.5 Growth in the euro area in 2006
Source: Elaboration on the basis of Eurostat data, European Communities, 2008.

Fiscal policy in a monetary union

In order to understand the role of fiscal policy in a monetary union it is useful to return to the example of the asymmetric shock described in Chapter 9.[36] With the wine scare there is a fall in output and an increase in unemployment in France. The opposite occurs in Germany. With a common federal budget, the tax contributions will fall and unemployment benefits will rise in France. The German tax contributions will rise and unemployment benefit payments will fall, so the net effect is a transfer to France through the federal budget.[37]

What, however, would occur if there were no federal budget? The lower taxes and higher benefit payments in France will lead to an increased government deficit that will have to be covered by borrowing. In Germany higher taxes and lower unemployment payments will reduce the deficit or increase the government surplus. With freedom of capital movement, the higher savings of Germany could cover the increased borrowing requirement of France. However, this implies an increased French external debt, which will have to be paid back by future generations.

The lessons of traditional optimal currency theory suggest either:

■ that it is preferable to have a large enough federal budget to compensate for the asymmetric shock; or, if this is impossible,

---

[36] The analysis can also be presented using the framework of aggregate supply and aggregate demand curves presented in the Appendix to Chapter 9. According to early versions of the theory, fiscal policy could be used to offset the shift in the aggregate demand curve.

[37] This account assumes either that the asymmetric shock is temporary, or if the shock is permanent the transfer should only be used in a temporary way to avoid hindering the necessary adjustment of wages and prices and/ or labour movement.

- that fiscal policy should be used in a flexible way to compensate for the asymmetric shock (in this case with an increased deficit in France.

However, in the example above the use of a government deficit by France to accommodate the negative demand shock will lead to an increase in indebtedness. This increase in debt will have to be serviced in future, and this will imply higher taxes or lower spending. Continued use of fiscal policy to accommodate negative shocks will therefore run into a problem of sustainability.

Distinction also has to be made between 'automatic stabilizers' and discretionary fiscal policy. As in the case described above, when there is a slowdown in the economy, automatic stabilizers come into play, with taxes falling and spending rising, increasing the government deficit. In this way fiscal policy will work in a countercyclical way. Discretionary fiscal policy involves explicit attempts by government to change the amount of taxes and spending. However, discretionary changes in fiscal policy run into the long and complex budgetary process, with compromises having to be reached and approved by parliament over the various changes in spending and taxes.[38] As a result, there may be lags and uncertainties in the application of discretionary fiscal policy.[39] Moreover, during the budgetary process the government is also likely to be subject to intense lobbying activity with pressure to increase spending and cut taxes.[40] In consequence the budgetary process generally entails a bias in favour of deficits.

What are the implications for fiscal policy in a monetary union? In general the literature justifies co-ordination of fiscal policy as being necessary in a monetary union to deal with interdependencies or spillovers. Baldwin and Wyplosz (2006) identify various forms of spillovers:[41]

- **Cyclical income spillovers**
  When a country is in an expansionary phase of the business cycle, it is likely to import more so this will have a knock-on effect of the country from which it is importing. The size of this spillover will be greater the larger the size of the importing country and the more tightly the two economies are integrated.[42]

- **Borrowing cost spillovers**
  An increased deficit requires higher government spending and this may increase interest rates. Against this, there seems little evidence that borrowing by one member country has increased interest rates in the euro area. However, the capital inflows associated with higher borrowing could lead to euro appreciation against third currencies.

- **Spillovers associated with excessive deficits**
  As argued above, persistent deficits can lead to a problem of sustainability of debt. If on international financial markets the public deficit of a member country is judged unsustain-

---

[38]See, for instance, Chapter 11 for a description of this process for the EU budget.

[39]As any Macroeconomic textbook explains, the debate about the effectiveness of fiscal policy is at the heart of the differences between Keynesian and New-Classical economists. There have been various challenges to the Keynesian view that an active fiscal policy can stabilize economic fluctuations. Barro (1974), for example, picked up an argument first noted by David Ricardo, which maintains that taxpayers may not spend debt-financed transfers as they expect higher taxation in the future to finance the debt.

[40]The New Political Economy Literature discussed in Chapter 4 provides insights into this lobbying process. See Mueller (2003) for a discussion of the political business cycle.

[41]See Beetsma et al. (2005) for an attempt to quantify these spillovers.

[42]Against this, in particular if the importing country is large, the income spillover might be offset by the fiscal expansion leading to a higher interest (and/or exchange) rate slowing the level of economic activity. However, as explained in the text, there seems little evidence so far of borrowing by a single country leading to a higher interest rate in the euro area.

able, this could lead to lack of confidence in the euro and capital outflows. There is also the risk of default by a country if its debt becomes unsustainable. This was recognized by the Maastricht Treaty, which contained a no-bail-out clause, expressly forbidding the ECB from bailing out a member state.

In addition to dealing with spillovers, a further argument in favour of some form of co-ordination of fiscal policy in a monetary union is that it might provide a scapegoat to contain the requests of lobbies that push in the direction of a deficit bias. This argument is likely to be particularly strong in countries with weak political institutions.

Against such views, co-ordination of fiscal policies may involve a sacrifice of sovereignty. Member states may argue that tax and spending decisions are better taken at the national level to reflect the preferences of citizens, and where understanding of the issues involved may also be better.[43] The principle of subsidiarity (see Chapter 1) may also require decisions to be taken at a more decentralized level.

Traditional open-economy Macroeconomic analysis as illustrated in the Appendix to this chapter also suggests that fiscal policy will be effective at the national level where the exchange rate is fixed, but ineffective at the EU level where the euro is floating against third currencies. For the monetary union as a whole the euro is floating and so monetary policy will be effective.

In the case of the euro area there has been much debate about whether and what form of co-ordination of fiscal policies is necessary or desirable.[44] The EU solution is for the member states to retain responsibility for fiscal policy, though subject to detailed rules and procedures, but even this solution has been challenged on various occasions by the member states as can be seen from the discussion on the Stability and Growth Pact.

The Stability and Growth Pact

In line with the logic of the convergence criteria for euro membership, Article 104 of the Maastricht Treaty required countries to avoid excessive deficits, and outlines an excessive deficit procedure. The details of the procedure were to be worked out later, and this took place when the Stability and Growth Pact was agreed at the Dublin Council of 1996 and confirmed at Amsterdam in 1997.

According to the initial version of the Pact, budget deficits would be limited to 3 per cent of GDP, except if the country experienced a fall in GDP of over 2 per cent. Countries were invited to strive for a 'close to balanced budget', so that the margin between 0 and –3 per cent could be used for counter-cyclical policies in times of economic downturn. The excessive deficit procedure was designed to ensure conformity with the Stability and Growth Pact. If the Council decides that a country has an excessive deficit and insufficient action has been taken, sanctions can be imposed.[45] European Union countries outside the eurozone must keep their

---

[43] See the discussion on fiscal federalism in Chapter 11, which deals with the problem of the 'appropriate' level (local, regional, national or EU) for taking decisions.

[44] See Torres et al. (2006) for a discussion of some of the main issues in this debate.

[45] The country in question would have to make a non-interest-bearing deposit of 0.2 per cent of GDP plus 0.1 per cent for each point of the excess deficit, up to a maximum deposit of 0.5 per cent of GDP. The deposit would be returned when the deficit falls below 3 per cent of GDP, but if the excess deficit lasts for over two years the deposit could become a fine. If a country deviates substantially from its path, the Council can issue a recommendation to bring the country back on track. The underlying assumption appears to be that excessive public borrowing could weaken a currency, drive up interest rates or give rise to moral hazard. However, the ECB is expressly forbidden to bail governments out.

deficits below 3 per cent, but they are not subject to disciplinary proceedings should they break the Pact.

The Stability and Growth Pact was largely introduced in response to German beliefs about the need to create a system that would ensure co-ordination of budgetary policies (Heipertz and Verdun, 2006). It was felt that the Pact could encourage consolidation of fiscal policy, would help to avoid possible negative effects of fiscal spillovers between increasingly interdependent countries and would prevent excessive deficits undermining the independence of the ECB (despite the no-bail-out clause).

With the slowdown of the EU economy from 2002, the Stability and Growth Pact came under attack for being excessively rigid, or 'stupid' in the words of the then Commission President Prodi.[46] By late 2002 the excessive deficit procedure had been initiated for Portugal, France and Germany. Portugal subsequently brought its deficit below the ceiling, but France and Germany were expected to break the Pact for the third year running in 2004. Germany announced measures to bring the deficit below 3 per cent, though the Commission considered these inadequate. The German finance minister, Eichel, maintained that Germany had followed the Commission's recommendations but only failed to respect the fiscal ceiling because of the sluggish economy. In November 2003 the EU finance ministers decided to suspend the sanctions mechanism of the Pact against France and Germany.

The ECB warned that suspension of the Pact could lead to 'serious dangers' including higher interest rates. Smaller countries that had introduced fiscal consolidation (notably Austria, Finland, the Netherlands, Sweden and Denmark) attacked the failure of the two larger member states to respect the fiscal constraints.

In 2004 Commissioner for Monetary Affairs Pedro Solbes took the member states to the Court of Justice for failure to respect the Pact. In July 2004 the Court ruled that the Council acted illegally in suspending the threat of sanctions against France and Germany. However, the Court maintained that 'responsibility for making the member states observe budgetary discipline lies essentially with the Council'. In other words, the Council can decide whether to back the Commission in its efforts to reduce budget deficits.

In 2005 the Ecofin agreed on a reform of the Stability and Growth Pact. The ceilings of 3 per cent for the budget deficit and 60 per cent for public debt were maintained, but the decision to declare a country in excessive deficit can now rely on a series of parameters including:

- the behaviour of the cyclically-adjusted budget;
- the level of debt;
- the duration of the slow growth period; and
- the possibility that the deficit is related to productivity-enhancing procedures.

The 2005 agreement overcame the crisis, but it remains to be seen how the reformed Pact operates in practice. Additional discretion has been introduced in interpreting the rules, but it is open to question how far this can be reconciled with ongoing commitments to sound financing in all member states.

The euro in the international financial system

There has been much speculation about future relations between the euro and the dollar, and whether the euro represents a challenge to the dollar in the international financial system. The role of the dollar in international trade and finance is far greater than its share of world trade and

---

[46]In a speech on 18 October 2002.

output might suggest. Given the economic weight of the EU, and the likely deepening and widening EU financial markets, the euro has been playing a growing international role. However, the extent to which the euro can challenge the dollar as an international currency will depend on how far the money and securities markets of the EU become effectively integrated and on confidence in the euro as a stable currency.

Textbooks traditionally indicate the functions of money as a medium of exchange, a unit of account and a store of value, and these may also be performed by a currency in its international role.

The international role of money as a medium of exchange means that it is used to invoice trade. In 1998 it was estimated that roughly half of total world export invoicing in the world was in dollars, while one-third was in the major EU currencies (IMF, 1998). According to ECB (2007), use of the euro as a settlement/invoicing currency in trade with non-EU countries has risen and reached 50 per cent of exports and 35 per cent of imports in 2006. None the less, widespread use of the dollar in invoicing seems likely to continue, in particular in oil and commodity markets.

With regard to money as a unit of account, transactions on international financial markets often take place in a vehicle currency to reduce the number of bilateral trades between currencies. According to ECB (2007) the average euro share in daily settlements of foreign exchange trades was 39 per cent in 2006. Several euro area neighbouring countries (including non-euro EU member states, candidate countries and Russia) continued to intervene on foreign exchange markets using the euro.

Money can be used as a store of value by foreign authorities or individuals. All central banks hold foreign exchange reserves to back their currency and, if necessary, intervene on foreign exchange markets. In 1997, 57 per cent of all official foreign exchange reserves were held in dollars, with a further 20 per cent being held in EU currencies and the ECU, and about 4.9 per cent in yen (IMF, 1998). The time horizon over which a shift into using the euro might occur is extremely uncertain as inertia is an important force, and, for example, the pound sterling continued to play an important role as a reserve currency long after the UK's decline as a hegemonic power.[47] According to ECB (2007), in December 2006 global international foreign exchange reserves amounted to $5028 billion, and the share of the euro was 25.8 per cent.

The ECB defines international debt securities as long-term securities such as notes and bonds, and short-term securities such as money market instruments.[48] According to ECB (2007), the total outstanding amount of these securities was $7857 billion in December 2006. ECB(2007) found that the euro share in the stock of international debt securities rose from 20 per cent in 1998 to 31.4 per cent in December 2006 (following a slight decline in 2006). The US share was 44 per cent, and that of Japan was 5.3 per cent in December 2006.

The euro also acts as an anchor to which other countries may tie their currency. In 2006 the IMF listed 100 countries with exchange rate regimes involving a reference currency or basket of currencies. Counting separately countries that are members of a currency union such as the Central African Economic and Monetary Community and the West African Economic and Monetary Union, according to ECB (2007), about 40 countries were using the euro as the point of reference for their exchange rate policies in 2006. The different arrangements adopted included:

- ERM II membership (see above);
- euro-based currency boards (Bulgaria, Bosnia and Herzegovina);

---

[47] See Kindleberger (1984) and Eichengreen (1989).

[48] See ECB (2007) for a definition of the various types of security.

- peg arrangements or managed floating based on the euro or currency baskets involving the euro (various countries including Hungary, the Czech Republic, Romania, Croatia, FYR Macedonia, Serbia, and the Russian Federation); and

- euroization (Montenegro,[49] Kosovo, the European microstates, and French territorial communities).

A foreign currency may sometimes be used as a parallel currency, operating alongside national money. In this case it performs all the functions of money (unit of account, means of exchange, and store of value). Though it is difficult to obtain reliable data, according to ECB (2007), the cumulative stock of euro banknotes shipped out in net terms by euro area monetary and financial institutions to destinations outside the euro area amounted to about €60 billion by December 2006.

As explained in Chapter 9, aside from the prestige, the financial gains of having an international currency are relatively small. About half of all dollars are held outside the USA but the benefit of these expatriate dollars to the USA is only about 3 per cent of GDP (Baldwin and Wyplosz, 2006).

Evaluation

Though the Treaty of Rome did not envisage economic and monetary union, the 1969 Hague Summit called for EMU by 1980. The unstable international monetary environment during the 1970s rendered this goal impossible, but the discussions of the time laid the basis for what was eventually to become the euro system. The launching of the EMS in 1979 provided a framework for ongoing monetary co-operation, created the ECU that evolved into the euro, and set up the EMCF that became the EMI and was subsequently transformed into the ECB.

Progress in implementing the three stages of EMU set out in the Maastricht Treaty proceeded surprisingly smoothly, though the number of countries fully participating in stage 3 was larger than initially foreseen. It was only subsequently that unresolved questions began to emerge. Did the priority given to price stability imply slower growth and higher unemployment? How likely were asymmetric shocks in the monetary union? Would the problem of asymmetries persist? What balance of power between the Ecofin, Eurogroup, ECB and Commission would emerge? Was co-ordination of fiscal policies necessary or desirable after giving up the autonomy of monetary policy? How would the reformed Stability and Growth Pact operate in practice? How effective would the decision-making process of the ECB prove, in particular after enlargement? How would the international role of the euro develop? The introduction of the euro was an ambitious and apparently irreversible initiative, but it is still too early to make judgements about its lasting consequences.

---

[49] In October 2007 Ecofin announced that unilateral euroization on the part of Montenegro was not compatible with the EC Treaty, which envisages eventual adoption of the euro as the endpoint of a convergence process in a multilateral framework.

Summary of Key Concepts

- **The 1969 Hague Summit** envisaged EMU by 1980, but the initiative failed in the face of the monetary instability of the 1970s.

- The '**snake in the tunnel**' was created in 1972, but by 1973 this had become a 'joint float' of currencies linked to the D-mark against the dollar.

- The **European Monetary System** was launched in 1979 and entailed: the exchange rate mechanism, introduction of the ECU, a divergence indicator and monetary co-operation. The ECU was the forerunner of the euro, and the European Monetary Institute provided the institutional basis on which to build the future European Central Bank.

- The operation of EMS can be divided into four periods: 1979–83, 1983–87, 1987–92 and the 1992 crisis and after. From August 1993, the bands of fluctuation were widened to +/– 15 per cent.

- According to the '**impossible trinity**', no international monetary arrangement has been able to reconcile simultaneously: free capital movements, fixed exchange rates and autonomy of monetary policy.

- The 1993 **Maastricht Treaty** set out the criteria for joining the single currency, the timetable for its introduction and the main institutional features of EMU.

- The **Maastricht criteria** entail that successful candidates must have: inflation rates no more than 1.5 per cent above the average of the three countries with the lowest inflation rate in the EU; long-term interest rates no more than 2 per cent above the average of the three lowest inflation countries; an exchange rate within the 'normal' band of the ERM without tension and without initiating depreciation for two years; a public debt of less than 60 per cent of GDP and a national budget deficit of less than 3 per cent of GDP.

- The decision about which countries could join the euro was made in May 1998 (though Greece joined later), and from that time no further exchange rate changes were made between their currencies. Britain, Sweden and Denmark remained outside the euro. The euro replaced the ECU from 1 January 1999. The European Central Bank began to operate from June 1998. Euro notes and coins were introduced from 1 January 2002. In January 2007 Slovenia joined, and Cyprus and Malta adopted the euro from January 2008.

- Even without participating fully in stage 3 of EMU, all EU countries are obliged to respect the **EMU** *acquis* and treat their economic policies as a matter of common interest and co-ordinate them in the Council. To cater for countries outside the euro area, since 1999 the ERM was replaced by with a new ERM II linking the currencies of non-euro member states to the euro.

- The new member states that joined the EU in 2004 and 2007 were not given the possibility of opt-outs and will have to join the euro when they meet the Maastricht criteria.

- The **European System of Central Banks** is composed of the European Central Bank and the national central banks of all EU member states. The '**Eurosystem**' is the term used to refer to the ECB and NCBs of the countries that have adopted the euro.

- The main priority of the Eurosystem is to maintain **price stability**. It is responsible for supporting general economic policies, defining and implementing monetary policy for the euro area and holding foreign reserves. It also has to ensure the smooth operation of the payments system and supervision by the relevant authorities. At least on paper the ECB appears one of the most independent central banks in the world, but the track record of the ECB has yet to be proven.

- The early years of the euro were associated with relatively low inflation (though the ceiling of two per cent was often exceeded), but rather sluggish growth. The value of the euro against the dollar first fell, and then rose substantially from 2002. It seems likely that there will be lasting differentials between inflation among euro member areas for some time.

- In the case of the euro area there has been much debate about whether and what form of co-ordination of **fiscal policies** is necessary or desirable. The EU solution is for the member states to retain responsibility for fiscal policy, though subject to detailed rules and procedures.

- According to the **Stability and Growth Pact**, budget deficits should generally be limited to a maximum of 3 per cent of GDP and countries should aim at balanced budgets in the medium term. The Pact was reformed in 2005 to take more account of the business cycle, the level of public debt, and the extent to which deficits promoted productivity-enhancing activities.

- The **international role of the euro** in the invoicing of trade, and in official reserves and private holdings of international financial assets has been increasing.

Questions for study and review

1 Why do you think that the objective of introducing EMU by 1980 failed?

2 What are the main features of the EMS?

3 In what ways did the EMS set the stage for introduction of the euro?

4 How does the idea of an 'impossible' trinity explain the main developments in each of the phases of EMS?

5 What were the motives for a return to the objective of EMU in the late 1980s?

6 Describe the main features of EMU as set out in the Maastricht Treaty.

7 What was the aim of the Maastricht criteria?

8 Describe the main steps in introducing the euro.

9 What are the chief functions of the European Central Bank, and what criticisms can be made of its operation?

10 Explain why there is a tension between independence and accountability of the ECB.

11 What are the arguments in favour or against co-ordination of fiscal policies in a monetary union?

12 How useful do you consider the Stability and Growth Pact?

13 How do you think the role of the euro in the world economy will change?

Appendix

The Mundell–Fleming model

The Mundell–Fleming model can be used to show the effects of monetary policy and fiscal policy with fixed and floating exchange rates and perfect capital mobility.[50]

Figure A10.1 presents the usual textbook version of IS and LM curves. The IS curve illustrates the various combinations of interest rates (i) and national income (y) that yield equilibrium in the goods market. It is negatively sloped, since lower interest rates are associated with higher levels of investment and income (and higher saving and imports) for the quantities of goods and services demanded and supplied to remain equal. The LM curve illustrates all the points at which the money market is in equilibrium. As can be seen from Figure A10.1, the curve is positively sloped. The derivation of the LM curve is based on the assumption that the money supply is fixed. Higher incomes imply higher transaction demand for money. Higher incomes will therefore have to be associated with higher interest rates to ensure lower demand for money for speculative purposes (the opportunity cost of holding speculative money balances is greater with high interest rates), and thereby ensure that the total amount of money demanded remains equal to the fixed amount of money supplied.

An expansionary monetary policy will shift the LM curve to the right (from LM to LM' in Figure A10.1) since at each level of interest rate the level of national income must be higher to absorb the increase in money supply. With perfect capital mobility, assume that the interest rate

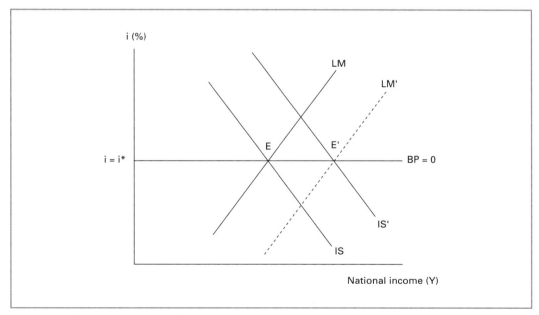

FIGURE A10.1 Monetary policy in the IS-LM model

[50] In a pure floating exchange rate regime the exchange rate is allowed to find its equilibrium level without central bank intervention in buying and selling foreign exchange reserves. In a fixed exchange rate regime the authorities are committed to maintaining a certain exchange rate. Dirty floating implies that there may be some intervention in the foreign exchange rate market to maintain the exchange rate in the short run, but that in the long run the exchange rate finds its equilibrium level through the market. For a more complete discussion of these issues see a macroeconomic textbook such as Begg et al. (2008).

prevailing on international markets is i*. Along the BP curve the balance of payments is in equilibrium, but this will only occur when the domestic interest rate i is equal to that prevailing on international markets. If, for example, the government attempts monetary expansion moving the LM curve to LM', at the intersection of IS and LM' the domestic interest rate is below i*. Perfect capital movement means that this will cause an outflow of capital. What happens depend on the exchange rate regime.

If the exchange rate is freely floating the balance of payments will be in deficit, and there will be pressure towards depreciation of the exchange rate. The improvement in competitiveness means increased exports and falling imports, raising demand for domestic products. This will push the IS curve to the right until it reaches IS' where i = i* and capital outflows stop. The new equilibrium will be E'. In the case of flexible exchange rates monetary policy will be effective.

If the exchange rate is fixed, the central bank will have to intervene on the foreign exchange market, selling foreign currency and buying national currency until the LM curve has moved back to its original position, LM. The new equilibrium will be E. According to the model, monetary policy is ineffective with fixed exchange rates and free capital movements.

The same figure can be used to illustrate the effects of fiscal policy, which involves changes in taxation or government spending. An increase in public spending or a cut in taxes will raise demand, causing a shift of the IS curve upwards to the right to IS', as shown in Figure A10.1. If there is no change in monetary policy the LM curve remains in the same place. At the new intersection of the IS' and LM curves both output and the interest rate have risen. The interest rate rises as the increase in the budget deficit means that government borrowing has risen, pushing up interest rates. In a small open economy with perfect capital movement, interest rates cannot prevail at levels above i*. What happens depends on the exchange rate regime.

If the exchange rate is fixed, capital inflows create pressure for an appreciation of the currency. The central bank must therefore intervene to sell domestic currency to counteract the capital inflows and this will increase the money supply, shifting the LM curve to the right. The process stops only when the domestic interest rate has returned to i* with the new curve LM'. The new equilibrium is E'.

If the exchange rate is freely floating, the capital inflows lead to an appreciation of the exchange rate. If prices are sticky, the nominal appreciation leads to a real appreciation, and there is a loss of competitiveness and deterioration of the domestic account. The IS curve will shift to the left returning to its initial position. The equilibrium is again E. In this case fiscal policy is ineffective.

These results are summarized in Table A10.1

	Fixed exchange rate	**Flexible exchange rate**
Monetary policy	ineffective	effective
Fiscal policy	effective	ineffective

TABLE A10.1 The effects of fiscal and monetary policy in different exchange rate regimes

References

Artis, M. (2007) 'The ECB's Monetary Policy' in Artis, M. and Nixson, F. (eds) *The Economics of the European Union. Policy and Analysis*, 4th edn, Oxford University Press, Oxford.

Artis, M. and Healey, N.M. (1995) 'The European Monetary System' in N.M. Healey (ed.) *The Economics of the New Europe*, Routledge, London and New York.

Baldwin, R., Berglöf, E., Giavazzi, G., Widgren, K. (2001) 'Preparing the ECB for enlargement', *CEPR Policy Paper*, No. 6, Centre for Economic Policy Research, London.

Baldwin, R. and Wyplosz, C. (2006) *The Economics of European Integration*, 2nd edn, McGraw-Hill Education, Maidenhead, UK.

Barro, R. (1974) 'Are Governments' bonds net wealth?', *Journal of Political Economy*, Vol. 82, pp. 1095–117.

Barro, R. and Gordon, D. (1983) 'Rules, discretion and reputation in a model of monetary policy', *Journal of Monetary Economics*, Vol. 12, pp. 101–21.

Begg, D., Fischer, S. and Dornbusch, R. (2008) *Economics*, 9th edn, McGraw Hill, Maidenhead.

Beetsma, R., Giuliodori, M. and Klaasen, F. (2005) *Trade Spillovers of Fiscal policy in the European Union: A Panel Analysis*, CEPR Discussion Paper No. 5222.

Bladen-Hovell, R. (2007) 'The creation of EMU', in Artis, M. and Nixson, F. (eds) *The Economics of the European Union. Policy and Analysis*, 4th edn, Oxford University Press, Oxford.

De Grauwe, P. (2007) *Economics of Monetary Union*, 7th edn, Oxford University Press, Oxford.

Della Posta, P. (2006) 'Fundamentals, international role of the euro and "framing" of expectations: What are the determinants of the dollar/euro exchange rate?', in Torres, F., Verdun, A. and Zimmermann, H. (eds) *EMU Rules: The Political and Economic Consequences of European Monetary Integration*, Nomos, Baden Baden.

Eichengreen, B.J. (1989) 'Hegemonic stability theories of the international monetary system', in Cooper, R.N., Eichengreen, B.J. and Henning, C.R. (eds) *Can Nations Agree? Issues in International Economic Co-operation*, The Brookings Institute, Washington DC.

ECB (European Central Bank) (2007) *Review of the International Role of the Euro*, June 2007, www.ecb.europa.eu

Fitoussi, J.-P. and Creel, J. (2003) *How to Reform the European Central Bank*, Centre for Economic Policy Reform, London.

Giavazzi, F. and Pagano, M. (1988) 'The advantage of tying one's hands: EMS discipline and central bank credibility', *European Economic Review*, Vol. 32, pp. 1055–75.

Gros, D. and Thygesen, N. (1998) *European Monetary Integration*, 2nd edn, Addison-Wesley Longman, Harlow, UK.

Heipertz, M. and Verdun, A. (2006) 'The dog that would bark but never bite? Origins, crisis and reform of Europe's stability and growth pact', in Torres, F., Verdun, A. and Zimmermann, H. (eds) *EMU Rules: The Political and Economic Consequences of European Monetary Integration*, Nomos, Baden Baden.

IMF (1998) *World Economic and Social Survey*, Washington DC.

Kindleberger, C. (1984) *A Financial History of Western Europe*, Allen & Unwin, London.

Ludlow, P. (1982) *The Making of the European Monetary System*, Butterworths, London.

Mueller, D.C. (2003) *Public Choice III*, Cambridge University Press, Cambridge.

Nuti, D.M. (1994) 'The impact of systematic transition on the European Community', in Martin, S. (ed.) *The Construction of Europe: Essays in Honour of Emil Noel*, Kluwer Academic Publishers, Dordrecht, the Netherlands.

Padoa Schioppa, T. (1987) *Efficiency, Equity and Stability*, Oxford University Press, Oxford.

Scheller, H.P. (2006) *The European Central Bank: History, Role and Functions*, 2nd edn, www.ecb.int

Swann, D. (2000) *The Economics of Europe: From Common Market to European Union*, 2nd edn, Penguin Business Library, London.

Taylor, J.B. (1999) 'An historical analysis of monetary policy rules', in Taylor, J.B. (ed.) *Monetary Policy Rules*, University of Chicago Press, Chicago.

Torres, F. (2006) 'On the efficiency-legitimacy trade-off in EMU', in Torres, F., Verdun, A. and Zimmermann, H. (eds) *EMU Rules: The Political and Economic Consequences of European Monetary Integration*, Nomos, Baden Baden.

Torres, F. (2008) 'The long road to EMU: The economic and political reasoning behind Maastricht' in Baroncelli, S., Spagnolo, C. and Talani, L.S. (eds) *After Maastricht: The Legacy of the Maastricht Treaty for European Integration*, Cambridge Scholars Publishers, Cambridge.

Torres, F., Verdun, A. and Zimmermann, H. (eds) (2006) *EMU Rules: The Political and Economic Consequences of European Monetary Integration*, Nomos, Baden Baden.

Tsoukalis, L. (1997) *The New European Economy Revisited*, 3rd edn, Oxford University Press, Oxford.

Wyplosz, C. (2006) 'European Monetary Union: the dark sides of a major success', *Economic Policy*, Vol. 21, No. 46, pp. 207–61.

Useful websites

The British Treasury has carried out extensive research into the issues of exchange rates and EMU, much of which is available on:
www.hm-treasury.gov.uk

The European Central Bank for statistics, reports and analysis:
www.ecb.int

The website on Economic and Monetary Affairs of the EU:
www.europa.eu/pol/emu

The EU and EC treaties available on:
www.europa.eu.scadplus/leg

The *Financial Times* publishes frequent articles on the euro, the ECB and the Stability and Growth Pact:
www.ft.com/centralbanks

The International Monetary Fund publishes statistics, theoretical research, and articles on the international financial architecture:
www.imf.org

CHAPTER 11

The EU Budget

❖ *LEARNING OBJECTIVES*

By the end of this chapter you should be able to understand:

❖ That although the Treaty of Rome envisaged the Community budget as having contributions and receipts roughly in balance, some member states have emerged as net beneficiaries and others as net losers;

❖ The main items of expenditure from the EC budget and how these have changed over the years;

❖ The basic principles of the Community budget;

❖ How the financing of the budget has changed over time;

❖ Why and when financial perspectives covering a number of years were introduced;

❖ The main features of the 2007–2013 Financial Perspective;

❖ The 2008/9 debate on the future of the EU budget.

Introduction

The changing nature of the EU with its widening and deepening processes has been reflected in the evolution of its budget. Budgetary considerations have played an important role in Community proceedings for much of the history of the EU, and the budgetary procedure is the outcome of many disputes and finely balanced compromises. There have been controversies about whether the Community should have its own resources, about the respective roles of the Community's institutions in the budgetary process and over the redistributive effects of the budget on different member states. The European Parliament, like most parliaments in history, has used its budgetary powers to increase its role and influence and to wrest concessions from the Commission and Council.[1]

---

[1] For instance, the 1999 institutional crisis described in Chapter 3 began with the European Parliament's refusal to approve the 1996 budget accounts.

The main features of the EU budget

In the early years of the Community some redistribution was expected to occur through the European Investment Bank, which was established with the main objective of encouraging development in the Italian South or Mezzogiorno. As can be seen from Figures 11.1 and 11.2, over the years some countries have emerged as net beneficiaries, others as net losers, and the respective shares have frequently been the subject of heated disputes.

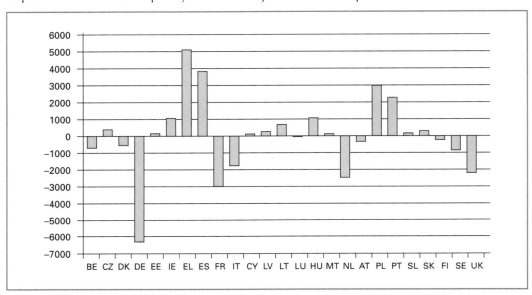

FIGURE 11.1 'Operating budgetary balances' 2006 (difference between allocated expenditure and national contributions after UK rebate), € million
Source: European Commission (2007a), © European Communities, 2007.

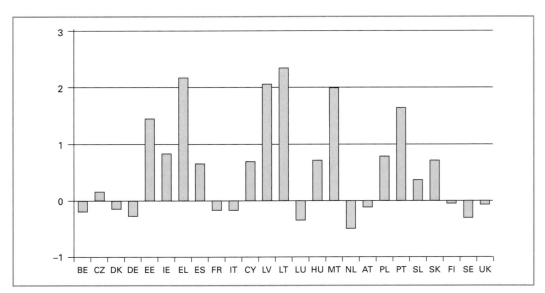

FIGURE 11.2 'Operating budgetary balances' 2006 (difference between allocated expenditure and national contributions after UK rebate) as a percentage of Gross National Income
Source: European Commission (2007a), © European Communities, 2007.

On the expenditure side, in the early years of the Community agriculture accounted for some 90 per cent of spending from the Community budget. The share remained as high as 73 per cent in 1985, and agriculture was allocated 45.6 per cent of spending in 2006. The share spent on structural operations steadily increased over the years, from 6 per cent in 1965 to 17.2 per cent in 1988, and should reach 35.7 per cent of the EU budget by 2013.[2]

From 2007 there was a change in the way in which the various budgetary headings for expenditure from the EU budget were classified (see Figures 11.3, 11.4 and 11.5), and five main categories were indicated:

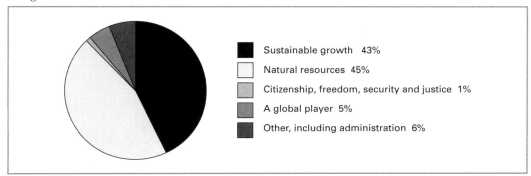

FIGURE 11.3 Expenditure from the 2007 budget (commitment appropriations)
Source: European Commission (2007d), © European Communities, 2007, www.ec.europa.eu/budget

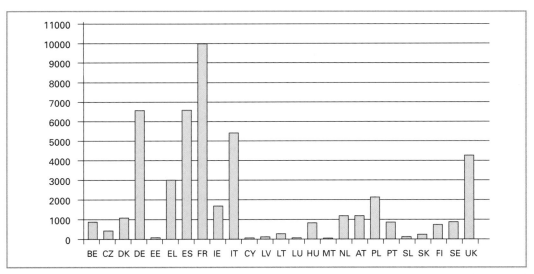

FIGURE 11.4 Expenditure on agriculture and rural development from the EU budget in 2006, by member state (million euro)
Source: European Commission (2007a), © European Communities, 2007, www.ec.europa.eu/budget

---

[2] European Commission (2007b). The term 'structural operations' covered spending on the Structural Funds (the European Social Fund; the European Regional Development Fund (ERDF); Guidance Section of the European Guidance and Guarantee Fund (for agriculture), and the Fisheries Guidance Instrument, and the Cohesion Fund. From 2007 the term 'cohesion policy' was adopted and the three financial instruments for cohesion became the European Social fund, the European Regional Development Fund and the Cohesion Fund (see Chapter 15).

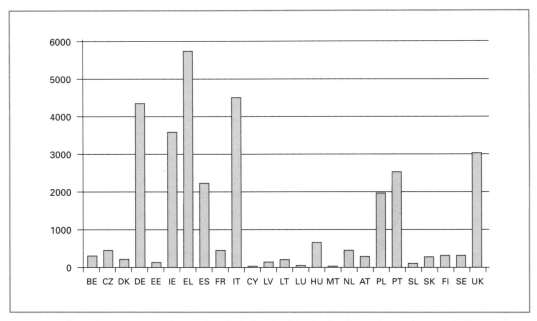

FIGURE 11.5 Expenditure on structural operations (including the Cohesion Fund) 2006, by member state (million euro)
Source: European Commission (2007a), © European Communities, 2007.

- **Competitiveness and cohesion for sustainable growth.** This reflects the priorities of the Lisbon Strategy,[3] and is broken down into two sub-headings: (i) investing in competitiveness for growth and employment, and (ii) cohesion for growth and employment. Spending on competitiveness includes the categories of: education and training, research, the information society, and energy and transport.[4] Spending on cohesion includes regional development, the Cohesion Fund and employment and social affairs so covers most of the former heading 'structural operations'.

- **Preservation and management of natural resources.** The previous heading of agriculture and rural development (including fisheries) was expanded to include environmental policy.

- **Citizenship, freedom, security and justice.** Spending on 'freedom, security and justice' also includes sectors like culture, the media, public health and consumer protection.

- **The EU as a global partner.** The heading 'global player' covers enlargement, relations with third countries and humanitarian aid.

- **Administration.** At 6 per cent of the budget this category absorbs less of the budget than the general public (as reflected in successive Eurobarometer opinion polls) often thinks.

Overall the scale of budgetary spending as a share of the GDP of the EU has remained small, increasing from 0.3 per cent in 1960 to 0.53 per cent in 1973, and being fixed as a ceiling of 1.05 per cent of Gross National Income (GNI) for the 2007–13 period (see below). Despite successive enlargements and extension of EU competences to new policy areas, the share of the EU

---

[3] See Chapter 7 for a discussion of the Lisbon Strategy.

[4] Most of these categories had previously been included under the heading 'internal policies'.

budget in GNI has actually fallen in recent years. By way of comparison, about 45 per cent of the Union's GNI goes to national, regional and local public expenditure in the Member States.[5]

The basic principles of the EU budget

Throughout its history the budget of the EU has been guided by certain basic principles:

Unity and universality

According to Article 268 of the EC Treaty, all revenues and expenditures have to be entered into the budget. Individual revenues must not be assigned to any particular expenditure, and all revenues and expenditure must be entered in full in the budget without any adjustment against each other.

In practice there have always been certain exceptions to this rule and, for example, the activities of the European Investment Bank are outside the budget. The European Development Fund (EDF; which provides financial aid to developing countries, see Chapter 19) is also not included in the budget.[6]

Equilibrium

According to Article 268 of the EC Treaty, the budget has to balance, i.e. estimated revenues for a financial year have to equal expenditure for that year.[7]

Annuality

The budget runs for a financial year from 1 January to 31 December (see Box 11.1). In 1984 and 1985 financial difficulties led to budgets covering only the 10 months up to October in order to satisfy the principle of equilibrium, with supplementary budgets being voted for the remaining period. The European Court of Justice ruled against this expedient as being contrary to the principle of annuality.

Specification

Although revenues cannot be earmarked for particular items of expenditure, all items of expenditure must be specified in the budget.

A common unit of account

All items of revenue and expenditure have to be indicated in a common unit of account rather than in national currencies. Since 1981 the unit of account used was the European currency unit (ECU), and this was replaced by the euro from 1 January 1999.

---

[5] The European Union Budget at a Glance, www.ec.europa.eu/budget_glance

[6] Though its inclusion in the EU budget was proposed from 2007, this was not agreed.

[7] This, together with the small size of the EU budget, limits the ability to correct for asymmetric shocks – see Chapter 9.

Box 11.1: *The budgetary procedure*

Since 1977 the annual budgetary procedure of the EU has generally entailed:

- Establishment of the preliminary draft budget by the Commission and transmission to the budgetary authority no later than 15 June.
- First reading of the preliminary draft by the Council before 31 July and transmission of the draft to the European Parliament in the first half of September.
- First reading by the Parliament in October.
- Second reading by the Council in the third week of November.
- Second reading by the Parliament and adoption of the budget.

Parallel to the debate on subsidiarity in the context of EU institutions, in the field of public finance a similar theoretical literature has emerged on what is referred to as 'fiscal federalism'. This literature deals with the criteria for deciding the appropriate level of government (European, national, regional or local) for decisions with regard to expenditure and revenue. A central concept of the literature is the idea of 'congruence', according to which each level of government has to have its own source of revenue to match its expenditure responsibilities.

Criteria for assigning functions to higher levels of government could include the presence of externalities (e.g. in fighting pollution), indivisibility or economies of scale (such as in research and development programmes) or ensuring minimum standards of services or of prosperity (as in the case of the Cohesion Fund). Criteria for assigning functions to lower levels of government could include the need for democratic control or to bring decisions closer to the citizens, flexibility, competition among units, or the aim of reflecting preferences more accurately given the greater political homogeneity that often characterizes smaller communities.

The financing of the Community up until 1980

The Treaty of Rome envisaged a transition period until 1970 during which financing of the Community was to consist essentially of contributions from the member states. The basic contribution of the three large members (France, Germany and Italy) was fixed at 28 per cent of total budget revenue, while that of the Netherlands and Belgium was 7.9 per cent, with 0.2 per cent for Luxembourg. However, the basic financing rule was adjusted according to the importance of the policy in question for each member state. For instance, Italy's contribution to the European Social Fund was reduced to 20 per cent, while those of France and Germany were raised to 32 per cent, Belgium to 8.8 per cent, with the Netherlands at 7 per cent and 0.2 per cent for Luxembourg. During the transitional period the system of financing was further complicated by the existence of separate institutions for the three Communities up until 1967.

According to Article 201 of the Treaty of Rome, a system of own resources (or self-financing) for the Community was to be introduced at the end of the transition period. Own resources consist of revenue allocated automatically to the Community without any need for further decisions by the member states.

The 1962 agreement on the basic principles of the Common Agricultural Policy (CAP) called for a decision on the rules for financing Community policies by 1965. The CAP was due to come into operation from 1967 and, backed by France and the Netherlands, the President of the Commission, Hallstein, was pushing for the new system of financing to begin operation at the same time.

The Commission's proposals for the Community Budget were presented in 1965 and, in line with the provisions of the Treaty of Rome and the logic of a customs union, the proposals entailed that the Community should be financed directly by proceeds from the common external tariff.

Federalists such as Hallstein, Monnet and Spinelli regarded the introduction of own resources as a step in the process of building a united Europe, in which the European Parliament would exercise powers of budgetary control. For example, Jean Monnet drew on his experience of international organizations and concluded that if such institutions relied on their members for financing, their powers tended to be more limited. This had been a major motive for his insistence on own resources for the European Coal and Steel Community. Altiero Spinelli used his knowledge of the history of the taxing power of the US federal government to argue that the power to tax directly was 'the essence of federal institutions'.[8]

However, the Commission's proposal to introduce own resources was opposed by France since it appeared to challenge De Gaulle's concept of national sovereignty. The budgetary issue was directly linked to the question of how Community institutions should evolve (and, in particular, the balance of power between the Commission and Council, parliamentary budgetary powers and the use of the qualified majority vote in the Council) and was at the heart of the 1965 'Empty Chair' Crisis.

It was only when de Gaulle resigned in 1969 and was replaced by Pompidou that the introduction of own resources could proceed as part of the 'completion' of the Community called for by the 1969 Hague Summit. The French government considered a solution to the budgetary question as being in its own interests as a means of ensuring adequate financing for the CAP.

Treaties on Community financing came into operation in 1970 and 1975,[9] though practical difficulties meant that the full system of EC self-financing had to be delayed until 1980. In the meantime a hybrid system was adopted, based partially on contributions from the member states, and partially on own resources.

By the time agreement was reached on own resources, the system of financing envisaged by the Treaty of Rome, based on tariffs and levies on agricultural imports from third countries, was clearly inadequate to meet the growing expenditure needs of the Community and, in particular, the already high and growing cost of the CAP. It was therefore decided to introduce a common system of turnover tax from 1967 based on the French tax, VAT, or value added tax. Value added tax is paid at each stage in the production process (including marketing) on the value added at each stage. A major reason for delaying full implementation of the system was that the VAT base varied from country to country, with differences in the products covered and the rates of VAT applied (see Chapter 6).

The own resources system, which was applied fully from 1980, consisted of three elements:

1 Tariffs on manufactured imports from third countries;[10]

---

[8] The initial federal system in the USA ran into difficulty because of the refusal of states to pay their contributions.

[9] Decisions on the budgetary powers of the European Parliament and the distinction between compulsory and non-compulsory expenditure were also taken in this context.

[10] Member states were granted a 10 per cent reimbursement on tariffs and agricultural levies to cover the administrative costs of collecting these resources.

2 Levies on agricultural imports from the rest of the world, and on sugar and isoglucose; and

3 A percentage of VAT, fixed at 1 per cent up until 1986.

The continuing difficulties of the Community budget during the 1980s

During the 1980s, primarily because of excess spending on the CAP but also because of its widening membership and extension into new policy areas, inadequate budgetary resources continually plagued the Community. In 1980 and again in 1985 the European Parliament rejected the proposed budget on the grounds of excessive growth in agricultural spending.

One of the most heated controversies over the EC budget was the so-called British budget question, which dragged on over several years. When Britain joined the Community a large share of its agricultural imports traditionally came from the rest of the world, in particular Commonwealth countries such as New Zealand. This together with its relatively small but efficient agricultural sector, meant that Britain would be a large net contributor to the EC budget. It was hoped that during the seven-year transition period following UK accession the weight of agriculture both in the Community budget and economy would decline, thereby reducing the bias against Britain. According to the terms of accession, if the situation remained unacceptable, an equitable solution would be negotiated.

An initial proposal to resolve the situation entailed establishing an ERDF that would provide transfers to the economically weaker areas of the Community, including the regions of industrial decline in the UK. However, the recession after the 1973 oil crises meant that funding for the ERDF was not forthcoming on the scale initially envisaged.[11] Following a not very successful attempt by the British Labour government to renegotiate the terms of accession, from 1979 there was a determined attempt by the prime minister, Margaret Thatcher, to get Britain's 'money back'.[12]

By 1984 an increase in the VAT ceiling was urgently needed to avoid bankruptcy of the EC budget and to provide the necessary financing to permit the accession of Spain and Portugal to the Community from 1986. Any change in the VAT ceiling required ratification by all the member states, and UK acquiescence was conditional on settlement of the British budget question. The outcome was the 1984 Fontainebleau Agreement that entailed:

- A refund of two-thirds of the UK's net contribution to the budget;[13]

- An increase in the VAT contribution to 1.4 per cent from 1986;

- A limit on the growth of agricultural spending which could not grow more than the increase in own resources;[14] and

- The introduction of quotas on the production of milk.

---

[11] Transfers through the ERDF amounted to only 300 million units of account in 1975 and 500 million units in 1976 and 1977.

[12] For a discussion of these issues see Pinder (1995).

[13] According to the Agreement, 'any member state sustaining a budgetary burden which is excessive in relation to its relative prosperity may benefit from a correction at the appropriate time'.

[14] This could be considered as a type of 'constitutional rule' to limit increases in government spending favoured by some members of the public choice school such as Buchanan and Tulloch (1962).

The evolution of the sources of revenue of the EU budget

The Fontainebleau Agreement failed to resolve the ongoing financial difficulties of the Community budget. On the expenditure side CAP spending continued to grow, and the three countries that joined the EC in the 1980s (Greece, Spain and Portugal) were all net beneficiaries from the budget. The poorer regions of the Community feared the additional competitive pressure expected to arise from the Single Market Programme and were pressing for compensation in the form of a substantial increase in the Structural Funds.

On the revenue side all three sources of EC budgetary financing had been subject to erosion. Successive GATT rounds had reduced the average level of tariffs, thereby reducing the tariff share in budget revenue as shown in Table 11.1. The growing level of EC self-sufficiency in agricultural products meant a falling share of levies on agricultural imports in budget resources.

	1975	1980	1987	2002	2007
Tariffs	52.5%	37.7%	25.0%	10.3%	13.2%
CAP levies and tariffs	11.0%	14.8%	8.7%	1.6%	1.7%
VAT contribution	36.5%	47.5%	65.7%	28.8%	15.4%
GNP/GNI**	—	—	—	59.1%	68.5%

TABLE 11.1 The share of difference resources in EC budget revenue*
*Totals may be less than 100 per cent because of correction for budgetary imbalances.
**The GNP/GNI resource was not used before 1988; see text for explanation.
Source: Website of the European Commission (2007a) © European Communities, 2008, www.ec.europa.eu/budget

Although, as Table 11.1 illustrates, the VAT share in budget revenue rose between 1975 and 1987, the VAT base (i.e. the goods and services on which VAT was levied) was not growing as rapidly as the overall economy. Savings and investment and spending on services such as health and education are not subject to VAT, and these are often higher in richer countries. The VAT contributions of different member states also depended on the level and number of VAT rates applied in each country (see Chapter 6).

By 1987 it was estimated that to balance the budget an increase in the VAT ceiling from 1.4 per cent to 1.9 per cent would be necessary. However, the regressive nature of VAT and the fact that increases in the VAT contributions of the member states failed to reflect their respective GDP performance led in 1988 to the decision to introduce a new resource, or additional form of financing for the EC budget.

Since 1988 the sources of revenue of the EU budget (see Figure 11.6) have been:

- Tariffs on imports of industrial products from third countries;

- Variable levies (which became tariffs from 1995) on imports of agricultural products from third countries, and the levies on sugar and isoglucose;[15]

- A percentage of the total VAT levied by the member states, fixed at 0.5 per cent from 2004;[16]

- The 'fourth resource', which was based on the difference between VAT levies and the GNP

[15]Minus a reimbursement to member states to cover the administrative costs of applying the levies, which was 10 per cent up until 1999 and 25 per cent subsequently.

[16]1.4 per cent from 1986 to 1987, 1 per cent from 1988 to 2000, and 0.75 per cent from 2001–2004.

of a member state and which can be levied up to a maximum percentage of the GNP of the Community if the budget financing from the other three resources proves inadequate. In 1995 the concept of GNP was replaced by the concept of GNI.[17] The ceiling was fixed at 1.27 per cent of GNI for the 2000–2006 period and 1.05 per cent for the 2007–2013 period.[18]

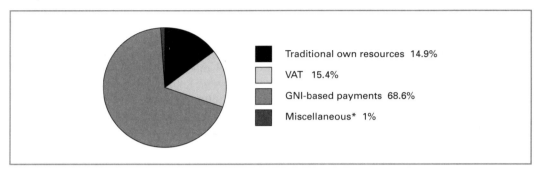

Traditional own resources 14.9%

VAT 15.4%

GNI-based payments 68.6%

Miscellaneous* 1%

FIGURE 11.6 Financing of the EU budget (2007)

*unspent amounts from previous years, contributions of EU staff, etc.

Source: European Commission (2007a).

Financial perspectives

The creation of the fourth resource formed part of the 'First Delors Package' or 'bill for the Single Market' agreed in 1988. The package established the precedent of setting out the financial perspective of the Community for several years to come, in this case the 1988–92 period. The financial perspective fixes the maximum amount and composition of EU expenditure over the next few years. The advantage of this approach was to ensure adequate financing for projects extending over several years and to establish objectives and priorities from the outset. Successive financial perspectives cover the periods:

1988–1992 the 'First Delors Package' or 'bill for the Single Market': With the 1988–1992 financial perspective the link between the Single Market and redistributive policies became explicit. The poorer regions and countries of the Community insisted on reform of the Structural Funds and a near doubling of their financing in order to assist their adjustment to the additional competitive pressures of a less fragmented market. The strategy for rendering the necessary financing available was twin pronged: creating new resources for the Community and re-dimensioning spending on the CAP.[19]

---

[17] Gross national product is the total income earned by domestic citizens regardless of the country where their factor services are applied, and is equal to GDP plus net property from abroad. Gross national income is GNP minus depreciation.

[18] This is the global level of commitment appropriations for the 2007–2013 period. Commitment appropriations are legal pledges to provide finance in a year, while payment appropriations are the actual transfer to the beneficiary and may include commitments from the current year and/or earlier years. The margin between appropriations for payments and for commitments allows for flexibility with multi-annual programmes.

[19] The 1988 budget package introduced the 'Stabilisers' (see Chapter 12), and placed a ceiling on the rate of increase in Guarantee spending of the European Agricultural Guidance and Guarantee Fund, which could not exceed 74 per cent of the growth of the GNP of the Community. The European Parliament was to be responsible for ensuring that this limit was not passed.

1993–1999 (Delors 2, or the bill for Maastricht): The main innovations of the second 'Delors Package' agreed in Edinburgh in 1992 included a further increase in spending on the Structural Funds and the creation of the Cohesion Fund to compensate the poorer areas and countries of the Community for the additional competition expected to result from introduction of the single currency. The British budget rebate was also continued. The relative importance of the VAT contributions and the fourth resource were also adjusted. With the reduction in the ceiling of the VAT contribution to 1 per cent and the gradual increase in the GNP ceiling of the budget to 1.27 per cent by 1999, it was hoped that resources paid by each of the member states to the EU budget would better reflect their overall economic performance.

2000–2006 (the Berlin Agreement on Agenda 2000): The financial perspective for the 2000–2006 period was decided at the Berlin European Council of March 1999. The package is also known as Agenda 2000 after the document of July 1997 setting out the Commission's proposals. A main priority of the package was to prepare the way for enlargement of the EU, and the deal included agreements on reform of the CAP and Structural Funds (see Chapters 12 and 15).

The Berlin Agreement on Agenda 2000 entailed a total budget commitment of 640 billion euro for the 2000–2006 period. At the insistence of the main contributor countries, and Germany in particular, the ceiling on budget spending as a percentage of GNI remained at 1.27 per cent. The VAT contribution was to be decreased from 1 per cent in 2000 to 0.75 per cent in 2001 and 0.5 per cent in 2004. This would again have the effect in increasing the share of the fourth resource in total revenue, with the intention of bringing the relative contributions of the different member states closer in line with their overall economic performance. The percentage of tariffs and agricultural levies to be retained by the member states in order to cover administrative costs was raised from 10 per cent to 25 per cent.

The British budget rebate was to continue (and was worth about 4 billion euro per year), but the UK agreed to forgo certain windfall gains that it would otherwise have received.[20] The other main contributors to the EU budget (Germany, the Netherlands, Austria and Sweden) also requested a reduction in their net contribution, but in the final compromise accepted simply that their contribution to the UK rebate would be reduced. It was, however, agreed that there would be a revision of budgetary procedures before the next financial perspective.

With regard to total spending on agriculture, the initial intention was to freeze annual expenditure in real terms at the 1999 level of 40.5 billion euro for the 2000-2006 period,[21] but in the event an additional 3 billion euro was agreed.

The Agenda 2000 package also entailed reform of the Structural Funds. The financial perspective earmarked some 195 billion euro for the Structural Funds for the 2000–2006 period, with a further 18 billion for the Cohesion Fund.

The 2000–2006 financial perspective allocated 3.14 billion euro per year in pre-accession assistance to the applicant countries. This was to consist of 1.56 billion euro each year in PHARE (Poland/Hungary Aid for Economic Reconstruction) assistance.[22] Initially PHARE was aimed primarily at facilitating economic and political transition, but increasingly it became

---

[20]These included: the benefits from reducing the VAT ceiling, which was expected to increase the relative contribution of Italy, Belgium, Denmark and France, and to decrease that of Germany and the UK; the increased reimbursement to member states to cover administrative costs on traditional financing (i.e. tariffs and agricultural levies) from 10 per cent to 25 per cent; and the expenditure on EU enlargement, which was excluded from calculation of the British rebate.

[21]Allowance was made for 2 per cent inflation each year.

[22]The PHARE programme began in 1989, and the acronym, Assistance for Economic Reconstruction in Poland and Hungary, soon became a misnomer as assistance was extended to other countries in Central and East Europe (see Chapter 20).

focused on preparing the applicant countries for EU accession. This entailed assistance for institution building, investment support, and economic and social cohesion (see Chapter 20). The pre-accession assistance also included an allocation of 1.04 billion euro for ISPA, or the Pre-Accession Structural Instrument, and a further 0.52 billion euro each year for SAPARD, or the Special Accession Programme for Agriculture and Rural Development.

The Berlin Agreement on Agenda 2000 agreement also fixed a budgetary allocation for new EU members, which was to rise from 4.14 billion euro in 2002 to 14.21 billion euro in 2006. The Berlin estimates were based on the assumption of the 6 'front-wave' candidates of the Luxembourg group joining in 2002,[23] even though by then accession negotiations had begun and such an early deadline was clearly unrealistic. Presumably, in confirming the hypothesis which had been set out in the initial 1997 Agenda 2000 document, the EU wished to leave a certain amount of room for manoeuvre, and avoid possible diplomatic incidents that might arise if the date were postponed.

The Copenhagen European Council of December 2002 agreed on a revised financial package for EU enlargement over the 2004–2006 period. This was based on the assumption that 10 countries would join in 2004, with Bulgaria and Romania joining in 2007. It was agreed that no new member state should be a net contributor (which might risk happening because of delays in spending) to the Community budget from 2004.

The aim of the Copenhagen agreement was to keep within the Berlin budgetary key. The annual budgetary allocation for enlarging to ten countries set out at Copenhagen was below the Berlin allocation for each year for only 6 new members. The total allocation for commitment appropriations for accession was 42 590 million in the 1999 financial perspective, and 37 468 million in the 2002 agreement.

The financial perspective for the 2007–2013 period

In 2004 the European Commission (2004a) presented proposals for the financial perspective for the 2007–2013 period. According to an Interinstitutional Agreement of 6 May 1999 if a new financial perspective could not be agreed, the existing spending framework would be extended mechanically. The new member states had transitional arrangements for 2004–2006 and had a strong interest in reaching agreement on a new financial perspective as it was likely to mean higher transfers from the EU budget. After an initial failure at the Luxembourg European Council in June 2005, Tony Blair was concerned to reach an agreement during the UK Presidency, and this was achieved with the December 2005 European Council. In May 2006 an Interinstitutional Agreement between the European Parliament, the Council and the Commission formalized the Financial Framework and the rules for its management.

The new Financial Framework had to resolve certain controversial questions:

- The resources for the EU budget and the budget ceiling;
- The British rebate;
- Spending priorities (CAP reform and the allocation of the Structural Funds).

The Commission initially proposed fixing the own resources ceiling at 1.24% of GNI for the 2007–2013 period. In December 2003 the six main contributors to the EU budget (Germany, Austria, France, the Netherlands, Sweden and the UK) published a letter calling for a ceiling of 1 per cent of GNI on expenditure from the EU budget. The Commission proposal was cut sig-

---

[23]Cyprus, the Czech Republic, Estonia, Hungary, Poland, and Slovenia (see Chapter 20).

nificantly by the European Council agreement of December 2005, but subsequently increased slightly (by €4 billion) by the Interinstitutional Agreement of May 2006 to reach €864 billion in 2004 prices for 2007–2013, or 1.05 of EU GNI.[24]

Over the 2007–2013 period a number of financial instruments are available outside the expenditure ceiling in order to face unforeseen events. They include:

■ The EU Solidarity Fund (maximum €1 a year) to allow rapid financial assistance in the event of natural disasters in a member state or candidate country;

■ The Instrument for Flexibility (maximum €200 million a year) to allow additional expenditure in defined circumstances;

■ The Emergency Aid Reserve (maximum €221 million a year) to allow a rapid response to specific unforeseen aid requirements of third countries.

In addition, the European Globalisation Adjustment Fund can mobilize unused appropriations from the previous year to provide additional support for workers who have suffered as a result of major structural changes in the pattern of world trade.

A key is published indicating how much each of the other member states must contribute each year to the British rebate, pitting the UK against all the other member states. The Commission proposed a possible general rebate from 2007, extended to other net contributors.[25] According to Commission (European Commission, 2004b), when the UK was granted the rebate it was one of the poorest EU countries with a GNI per capita of only 91 per cent of the EC average, but by 2003 this percentage had risen to 111 per cent, second only to Luxembourg. Without correction the UK rebate would have risen from €4.3 billion over the 1997–2003 period (when spending on enlargement was excluded) to €7.1 billion for the 2007–2013 period, and the new member states would also have had to pay part of the British rebate. Under the correction mechanism proposed by the Commission, Britain would have contributed 0.51 per cent of GDP to the EU budget, becoming the highest contributor in terms of share of GDP. Not surprisingly this proposal was strongly contested by the UK. In the event, at the December 2005 European Council Britain agreed to give up about one fifth of its rebate or a maximum of €10.5 billion attributable to Eastern enlargement.[26] Reduced VAT-based contributions were also agreed for all member states, with additional discounts for the other main contributors (Germany, the Netherlands, Sweden and Austria).

As shown in Table 11.2, despite the lip service paid to the Lisbon Strategy, the initial Commission proposal for spending on competitiveness was whittled away substantially in the budgetary decision-making process. The outcomes for spending on citizenship, freedom, security and justice, and the EU as a global actor were also less than initially proposed. In contrast cohesion (covering the former category of structural operations) and natural resources (covering the previous agriculture and rural development heading) were cut far less, suggesting some inertia in spending patterns of the EU budget.

---

[24]The financial framework may be revised in the event of unforeseen circumstances on a proposal of the Commission in compliance with ceilings defined in the own resource decision setting the maximum potential level of financing of the EU (1.24 per cent of GNI for payments and 1.31 per cent for commitments). Any revision requires unanimity in the Council.

[25]A generalized corrective mechanism could be used to implement the principle of 'juste retour' with each country getting back what it puts in.

[26]The rebate continues to apply on expenditures from the EU(15) and CAP, and part of the rural development funds for the new member states. The then UK Chancellor of the Exchequer, Gordon Brown, was consulted throughout the negotiations, but according to the Financial Times (26/6/06) was dismayed by the outcome, and later argued that the UK rebate should also apply on UK payments to compensate the reduced contributions of Austria, Germany, the Netherlands and Sweden.

	Commission Proposal	European Council Agreement	Interinstitutional Agreement
Competitiveness	121	72	74
Cohesion	336	308	308
Natural resources	400	362	371
Citizenship, freedom, security and justice	15	10	11
Global partner	62	50	49
Administration	58	50	50

TABLE 11.2 Changes in the proposed expenditure of the 2007–2013 Financial Perspective, €billion, 2004 prices
Source: Elaboration on the basis of Commission data, © European Communities, 2008.

At the June 2005 European Council Tony Blair linked the question of the UK budget rebate to reduced spending on agriculture, but France, in particular, opposed further CAP reform. At the Brussels European Council of October 2002 the French President, Chirac, (a former Minister of Agriculture) convinced Germany and the European Council to accept a limit of 1 per cent per year on the increase in nominal spending on the CAP from 2007 until 2013 (see Chapter 12). This limited the scope for cuts in CAP spending before 2013, but as part of the compromise on the 2007–2013 financial perspective it was agreed to carry out a comprehensive review of all expenditure and resources by 2008/9, including a review of the UK rebate and a 'health check' of the CAP.

Financial irregularities

In recent years there has been growing concern with financial irregularities in payments from the EU budget. According to Article 274 of the EC Treaty, the Commission is responsible for implementing the budget (see Box 11.2), but in practice the Commission has to rely on the member states to implement certain policies. It is estimated some 22 per cent of funds is managed centrally by the Commission, 76 per cent of funds is delegated to the member states by the Commission under 'shared management', while the rest is managed with international organizations or with third countries (European Commission, 2007b).

Box 11.2: *Control of implementation of the EU budget*

According to Community budgetary law, control of implementation is exercised by:

- Internal control by the authorizing officers of each institution and Commission supervision of the systems to combat fraud;
- External control by the Court of Auditors (see Chapter 3);
- Discharge from the European Parliament. The discharge procedure 'releases' the Commission from responsibility for management of a budget by marking the end of a budget's existence.

Following the scandal that led to resignation of the Commission in 1999 (see Chapter 3), the then president of the Commission, Romano Prodi, announced a policy of 'zero tolerance' of corruption and set up an anti-fraud office, OLAF, to look into cases of financial irregularity. However, as Box 11.3 suggests, the EU continued to suffer shortcomings in financial accountability.

Box 11.3: *Financial irregularities in the EU accounts*

January 2002 Marta Andriessen was appointed EU chief accountant.

March 2002 Andriessen argues with the Commission over a complete rehaul of the EU accounting system.

May 2002 Marta Andriessen is removed from her job and offered a post in the personnel department.

August 2002 Andriessen is suspended on full pay for going public to the press and European Parliament. She was also banned from Commission buildings. Following the suspension of Marta Andriessen, the then Commissioner responsible for the budget, Michele Schreyer, promised a vigorous programme of reform and a switch to the modern accrual system of accounting by 2005.

November 2002 The Court of Auditors strongly criticized the 2001 accounts, arguing that it could only certify that 5 per cent of spending was legal and regular.

June 2003 The chief internal auditor of the Commission, Jules Muis, attacked the Commission's 'rudimentary financial control systems', and announced that he would be leaving his job the following year. In a leaked paper, Muis accused the Directorate General for the budget as being 'a department haunted by a profound lack of qualified staff, a host of vacancies/absentees in crucial functions, a power ambience totally catered to the DG' (*Financial Times*, 10 March 2003).

Eurostat was also accused of financial irregularities. Complaints had been made about Eurostat by trade unions in 1997 and by internal Commission audits in 1999 and 2000.* In 2003 the EU anti-fraud office, OLAF, maintained that Eurostat had been responsible for a 'vast enterprise of looting', with false contracts and the channelling of EU funds into unofficial bank accounts in Luxembourg. OLAF accused Eurostat officials of rewarding contracts to companies they had set up and whose boards they sat on. The value of these contracts was said to be artificially inflated, for work that was sometimes fictitious. The director general, Yves Franchet, and a director, Daniel Byk, were required to resign, and a multi-disciplinary task force comprising OLAF and Commission officials was set up to further investigate Eurostat. The commissioner nominally in charge of Eurostat, Pedro Solbes, refused to be held responsible for things he 'didn't know about'.

*Financial Times, 17 July 2003.

Evaluation and outlook for the EU budget

The history of the EU budget seems essentially a process of lurching from one crisis to another. Generally compromises have been reached to resolve these crises, though often with substantial concessions and delays. The arrangements that emerge from these compromises frequently seem messy and not very transparent, and are often difficult to justify on 'rational' grounds.[27]

In line with the reform of the decision-making institutions, enlargement of the EU to 27 members or more also requires changes in the budget. For this reason in 2008/2009 the EU is to scrutinize the present system, taking into account topics such as CAP spending and the British rebate (or 'correction mechanism').

In September 2007 the Commission published a Consultation Paper with the aim of opening debate on the question of EU budget reform. The debate is not intended to provide numbers for the financial perspective from 2014, but to examine future spending priorities and the most effective ways of finding resources to finance them. The CAP is to undergo a 'health check', and the work of the Fourth Cohesion Report (European Commission 2007c) in evaluating cohesion policy to date and assessing ways of further reducing regional disparities is to be carried forward. On the expenditure side the aim is to look at questions such as the focus of EU funding (is a widespread approach preferable to more concentration?); ways of increasing transparency and accountability; the balance between stability and flexibility; the experiences and lessons to be learned from co-financing; and decisions concerning the levels of management (the degree of decentralization, and whether joint or shared mechanisms are more appropriate).

The sources and mechanisms of the EU budget are also to undergo review in order to meet principles such as 'economic efficiency, equity, stability, visibility and simplicity, administrative cost-effectiveness, financial autonomy and sufficiency' (European Commission, 2007b).

The aim of the debate is to ensure that the EU budget is more responsive to changing needs, and that policy priorities are more closely reflected in spending priorities. How far these objectives will be realized remains to be seen.

Summary of Key Concepts

- Over time some countries have emerged as **net beneficiaries to** and others as **net losers** from the EU budget.

- **The share of agriculture** in spending from the Community budget has been falling, while the **share of economic and social cohesion** (formerly called structural operations) in expenditure has been increasing steadily.

- Since 2007 the main items of **expenditure** from the EU budget are: competitiveness and cohesion for sustainable growth; preservation and management of natural resources; citizenship, freedom, security and justice; the EU as a global partner, and administration.

- Overall the scale of **budgetary spending as a share of the GDP** of the EU has remained small, increasing from 0.3 per cent in 1960 to a ceiling of 1.05 per cent of GNI for the 2007–13 period

- Throughout its history the budget of the EU has been guided by certain basic **principles:** unity and universality, equilibrium, annuality, specification and a common unit of account.

---

[27] As, for instance, the distinction between compulsory and non-compulsory expenditure, see Chapter 3.

- **Fiscal federalism** deals with the criteria for deciding the appropriate level of government (European, national, regional or local) for decisions with regard to expenditure and revenue.
- The Treaty of Rome envisaged a **transition period until 1970** during which financing of the Community was to consist essentially of contributions from the member states to be followed by the introduction of a system of own resources.
- During the 1980s, excess spending on the CAP, widening membership and extension into new policy areas meant that **inadequate budgetary resources** continually plagued the Community.
- Since 1984 Britain has had a budget refund or 'correction', but this has been increasingly contested by other member states.
- The **own resources** consist of: tariffs on manufactured imports from third countries; agricultural tariffs and levies; a percentage of VAT and the fourth resource based on GNP/GNI.
- Since 1988 the **financial perspective** of the Community has been set out for several years to come. This was the case for the 1988–92 period (Delors 1 or the bill for the Single Market), 1993–99 (Delors 2, or the bill for Maastricht), 2000–06 (the Berlin Agreement on Agenda 2000, which could also be termed the bill for enlargement), and 2007–13 (the bill for the Lisbon Strategy).
- In 2008/9 there is to be a fundamental debate on the future of the EU budget.

Questions for study and review

1 What are the main principles underlying the Community budget, and how far have they been respected in practice?

2 Describe how the concept of fiscal federalism could be applied in the EU context.

3 Explain why the Community budget ran into difficulties on both the expenditure and revenue sides.

4 Indicate the main changes in the Community budget over the years.

5 What changes do you expect to see in the Community budget as a result of enlargement?

6 What issues are likely to arise in the 2008/9 debate about the future of the EU budget?

References

Buchanan, J.M. and Tullock, G. (1962) *The Calculus of Consent*, University of Michigan Press, Ann Arbor.

European Commission (2004a) 'Building our common future. Policy challenges and budgetary means of the enlarged Union 2007–13', COM(2004)101 of 10 February 2004.

European Commission (2004b) 'Proposal for a Council decision on the system of the European Communities' own resources. COM(2004) 501 final, 14 July 2004.

European Commission (2007a) *EU Budget 2006 – Financial Report*, www.ec.europa.eu/budget

European Commission (2007b) *Reforming the Budget, Changing Europe. A Public Consultation Paper in View of the 2008/2009 Budget Review*, www.ec.europa.eu/budget

European Commission (2007c) *Fourth Report on Economic and Social Cohesion*, www.ec.europa.eu./regional_policy

European Commission (2007d) *General Budget of the European Union for the Financial Year 2007*, www.ec.europa.eu/budget

Pinder, J. (1995) *European Community: The Building of a Union*, 2nd edn, Oxford University Press, Oxford.

Useful websites

The European Commission:
www.ec.europa.eu/budget

The EU Court of Auditors:
www.eca.europa.eu

CHAPTER 12

The Common Agricultural Policy

❖ LEARNING OBJECTIVES

By the end of this chapter you should be able to understand:

- ❖ The reasons for public intervention in agriculture;

- ❖ The objectives of the Common Agricultural Policy (CAP) set out in the Treaty of Rome and how they changed over time;

- ❖ The three principles on which the CAP is based;

- ❖ The main mechanisms used by the CAP and their changes through the years;

- ❖ How the system of price support works;

- ❖ The pressures for reform of the CAP;

- ❖ Why a policy of high prices was adopted, and what were the negative consequences of that policy;

- ❖ Why policies to improve farm structures played such a minor role for so many years;

- ❖ The various attempts at CAP reform;

- ❖ The outlook for the CAP.

The reasons for public intervention in agriculture

Agriculture has always been one of the sectors most subject to state intervention, and this was also the case for the six founding members of the European Community.[1] There are various explanations for the scale of public intervention in agriculture. The dependence of agricultural production on biological cycles,[2] climate and natural phenomena (including epidemics) provide justification for government measures to stabilize farm prices and incomes. Empirical studies show that the elasticity of demand for food products is relatively low both with respect to price and income, meaning limited outlets for sales of foodstuffs over time, and rendering farmers

---

[1] For analysis using the New Political Economy Approach of why agriculture played (and continues to play) such an important role in the EU, and the reform resistance of the CAP see Senior Nello (1984 and 1997).

[2] According to the Cobweb theory, if the quantity supplied adjusts with a lag to the market price a cycle may result (with an explosive cycle when supply is more elastic than demand in absolute terms), and government intervention may be necessary to stabilize prices and incomes. Though the theory is based on extremely simplifying assumptions, there does appear to be empirical evidence for cycles in the production of certain agricultural products such as beef or pig meat.

more vulnerable to shocks on the supply side.[3] Difficulties may also arise for farmers because supply may be very inelastic in the short run. This may be because some output decisions (e.g. sowing a crop) may be impossible to reverse in a changed market situation.[4] Farms in the EU are often of a relatively small dimension, which renders it difficult to exploit economies of scale, and may place the farmer at a bargaining disadvantage *vis à vis* larger producers in the food processing or farm input sectors. The economic and social difficulties many farmers have in leaving the sector have meant that for protracted periods farm incomes and living conditions may compare unfavourably with those in the rest of the economy.[5]

Public intervention may also be justified to deal with cases of 'market failure' as for instance may occur when information is costly or difficult to obtain. It may be extremely hard for con-

---

Box 12.1: *BSE or the 'mad cow' crisis*

Identified for the first time in the UK in 1985, bovine spongiform encephalopathy (BSE) or the 'mad cow' disease causes the destruction of the animal's brain tissue, transforming it into sponge-like material. The disease is spread by simple proteins known as prions which are resistant to heat, radiation and antibiotics. In 1987 animal feed containing prions from infected animals was identified as a likely cause of the diffusion of BSE. The number of identified cases of BSE had risen to 183 716 in the EU by the end of 2002, of which 181 024 were in the UK, 958 were in Ireland, 654 were in Portugal and 601 were in France. *

At the same time as the outbreak of BSE a new variant of Creutzfeldt-Jakob disease (CJDv) appeared in humans, and the cause was soon attributed to eating infected meat. By 2001 there were 78 deaths out of 87 cases of CJDv in the UK and one death in Ireland.

Measures to contain the disease included a total EU block of imports of British beef from 1996 to 1999, a ban on eating parts of the animal at risk (the spinal cord, brain and even for a time steaks on the bone) and a prohibition on using animal waste (such as bone meal) in animal feedstuffs. European Union consumption of beef fell by 20 per cent in 2001. At the height of the crisis in February 2001 beef consumption in Italy had fallen by roughly 50 per cent compared with 2000 levels, and it was only in the week of Christmas and the New Year that there was a marked recovery to earlier levels.**

*Unless otherwise stated, the statistics in this section are taken from the UK Creutzfeldt-Jakob Disease Surveillance Unit: www.cjd.ed.ac.uk

**The data on Italy are taken from Marco Buoncristiani, 'La crisi della mucca pazza', unpublished student research, University of Siena, 2001.

---

[3] According to Engel's law, as incomes rise the share of foodstuffs in household expenditure falls. Numerous empirical studies over time and across countries find support for this 'law'.

[4] There are various explanations of the low short-run elasticity of supply in agriculture. Fixed costs tend to be relatively high and while these have to be considered when expanding production, only variable costs are taken into account in deciding when to stop production (the shutdown point). According to Johnson and Quance (1972), the difference in the prices of certain factors of production (such as farm machinery on the new and used markets) may help to explain inelasticity of supply in the short run. If the price of second-hand factors of production is very low, they will continue to be used even when their marginal productivity in terms of value falls very low. Nerlove (1956) shows how elasticity of supply tends to increase over the time period considered.

[5] This is frequently referred to as 'the farm problem'.

sumers to acquire adequate information about the nature and safety of a food product even after that good has been consumed as, for instance, emerged clearly during the BSE or 'mad cow' crisis (see Box 12.1). Public intervention may be required to ensure standards are met, to carry out certification and testing, and to provide information through labelling, trademarks and so on.

Public intervention may also be justified when there are externalities, i.e. when there is a difference between the costs and benefits to the individual and to the public. In other words, externalities are the positive or negative effects of the production or consumption by one individual on others, which are not reflected in prices (see Chapter 14 for an economic analysis of externalities). Negative externalities may arise, for example, from the impact of agriculture on the environment, with some forms of intensive production causing soil and water pollution, or the elimination of biodiversity. Positive externalities may occur when agriculture contributes to rural development, care of the landscape, protecting animal welfare or preservation of breeds in danger of extinction.

The activities of farm lobbies also help to explain the persistence and scale of state support for the farm sector.[6]

Agriculture in the Treaty of Rome

Given the tradition of intervention in agriculture in the founding members of the EC and the diversity of measures used, France, in particular, was adamant that the new Community policy could not simply be a collation of national policies and that some kind of common policy was necessary (see also Chapter 2).

Articles 38–47 of the Treaty of Rome deal with agriculture.[7] Article 39 is probably one of the most frequently quoted articles of the Treaty and sets out the objectives of the CAP:

1. (a) to increase agricultural productivity by promoting technical progress and by ensuring the rational development of agricultural production and the optimum utilization of factors of production, in particular, labour;
   (b) thus to ensure a fair standard of living for the agricultural community, in particular by increasing individual earnings of persons engaged in agriculture;
   (c) to stabilize markets;
   (d) to ensure availability of supplies;
   (e) to ensure that supplies reach consumers at reasonable prices.

2. In working out the common agricultural policy and the special methods for its application, account shall be taken of:
   (a) the particular nature of agricultural activity which results from the social structure of agriculture and from structural and natural disparities between the various agricultural regions;
   (b) the need to effect the appropriate adjustments by degrees;
   (c) the fact that in the Member States agriculture constitutes a sector closely linked with the economy as a whole.

---

[6] See Senior Nello (1984, 1989 and 1997) for more detailed descriptions of why farmers have been so successful in organizing pressure groups and how they manage to influence policy in their favour.

[7] Article 38 defines the field of action as 'plant, livestock and fish products, including those subject to the first stage of processing'. Articles 40–47 speak in very general terms about the policies to achieve these objectives, the institutions for agricultural decision-making and the arrangements for the transitional period. See Fennel (1997) for a discussion of agriculture in the Treaty of Rome.

Despite the importance that has always been attached to this statement of objectives, it is vague and lacking in precision on certain crucial points, and is not without contradictions. For instance, how is the increase in productivity mentioned in 39/1a to be achieved – by increases in output (which was the interpretation of the farm lobby at the time) or by reductions in the labour force? If, as turned out to be the case, support for agricultural prices is the main instrument used to achieve 'a fair standard of living' for farmers, how is this to be reconciled with 'reasonable prices' for consumers? The reference to the 'social structure of agriculture' can be interpreted as a commitment to the family farm (which has to be read in the context of the post-war collectivization in Central and Eastern Europe). However, given the small size of many farms at that time, the question of how to ensure their efficiency arises. The stress on availability of supplies reflects the post-war concern with shortages, even though surpluses had already emerged for certain Community agricultural products (such as grains, dairy products and sugar) by the late 1950s.

What is missing from the Treaty is a precise description of what form this CAP should take, and, in particular, there is little mention of the policy mechanisms to be used. These omissions from the Treaty reflect the ongoing differences among the member states about how a common policy should be constructed. After its earlier experiences of co-operation on agricultural policy matters with Luxembourg and Belgium, the Netherlands was anxious to ensure less restricted markets and effective guarantees against reintroducing restrictions on trade. In contrast, the French favoured a more interventionist approach in order to ensure adequate levels of support and protection.

The agreement on the CAP mechanisms

As many of the key questions were still unanswered, Article 43 of the Treaty of Rome called for a conference to work out the details of the future CAP. This led in 1958 to the Stresa Conference, generally recognized to be one of the milestones in the creation of the European Community. However, the conference failed to resolve many issues, and heated debate about the future form of the CAP continued. Agreement was not reached until 1962.

The second stage of the transition period was due to come into operation from January 1962, with deadlines for more dismantling of tariffs between the member states and further progress in the creation of the common external tariff. While Germany was anxious for progress on trade issues, France and the Netherlands threatened to block the move to the second stage of the transitional period (due to begin from January 1962) if sufficient progress were not made on agriculture. The issue of what mechanisms to adopt for the CAP was hammered out in the famous 23-day marathon of the Council of Ministers, and failure to meet the January deadline led to the expedient of 'stopping the clocks' until agreement was finally reached on 14 January 1962.

The package eventually agreed by the Council of Ministers included what subsequently became known as the three fundamental principles of the CAP:

1 Unity of markets

Trade would be progressively liberalized between the member states and common prices would be introduced for the main agricultural products throughout the Community.

2 Community preference

Barriers on trade between member states were to be removed, but common levies on imports of agricultural products from the rest of the world meant that EC producers would be at an advantage *vis-à-vis* those from third countries in selling their agricultural produce on Community markets.

3 Financial solidarity

A European Agricultural Guarantee and Guidance Fund (EAGGF or FEOGA after its French acronym) would finance agricultural policy measures. The Guarantee Section of the EAGGF would be responsible for market intervention and export refunds, while the Guidance Section would cover expenditure on structural measures.

Agreement was also reached on the market organization to use for cereals and the so-called cereal-based products: poultry and pig meat.[8] Similar mechanisms were subsequently extended to about three-quarters of all agricultural products. Figure 12.1 sets out the basic price support mechanism. Though not shown in the diagram, target prices for each year are agreed by the Council of Ministers as the basis for calculating all the other common prices. Initially target prices were calculated according to the 'objective method', which involved taking account of the evolution of costs and revenue in order to ensure that developments in farm incomes were in line with those in other sectors. This method was abandoned from the mid-1980s when a policy of price restraint for agricultural products had to be introduced.

Each year intervention prices, or minimum guaranteed prices, are also agreed. Intervention agencies have to stand ready to buy up the product to ensure that prices do not fall below this floor level.[9] The intervention agencies are organized on a national basis, with, for example, the AIMA (l'Azienda Italiana per i Mercati Agricoli) and subsequently the AGEA (Agenzia per le

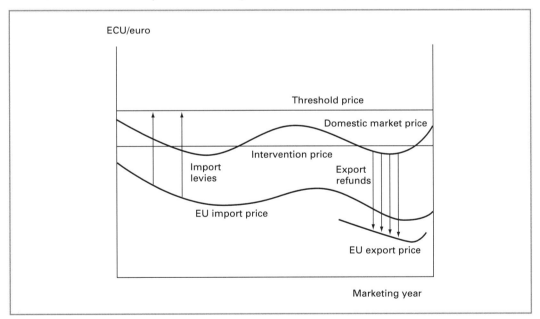

FIGURE 12.1 The basic price support mechanism for cereals
Source: Adapted from Tracy (1993).

---

[8] The introduction of the variable levy in mid-1962 on imports from the rest of the world led to the 'chicken war', or first trade dispute between the Community and the USA.

[9] Initially the intervention prices were calculated on the basis of the target price minus the cost of transport from the point of major production of grain (Ormès in France) to the point of main consumption in the Community (Duisburg in Germany), also taking into account margins of distribution, but subsequently the ratio of intervention price to the other common prices has become a matter for political compromise.

Erogazioni in Agricoltura) in Italy. The Intervention Board in Britain was replaced in 2001 by the Rural Payments Agency responsible for CAP payment schemes in England and for certain schemes throughout the UK.

The threshold price is a minimum entry price applied on imports from the rest of the world at the point of entry to the EU. In the first years of the CAP the threshold price was calculated as the target price minus the cost of transport from the main port of entry (Rotterdam) to the main consumption area (Duisburg), and was estimated at 10 per cent below the target price. In later years the ratio of threshold to other common prices also became subject to negotiation.

The level of Community preference, or advantage, that EU farmers have on Community markets over producers from the rest of the world is given by the difference between threshold and intervention price. In general the market price in the EU will oscillate between these two limits, but weakening of the intervention system in subsequent years (with, for example, disincentives and time and quality restrictions before intervention could take place) means that at times market prices could descend below intervention levels.

Variable import levies were applied on imports from the rest of the world in order to bring their prices up to the threshold price. If prices on world markets fell while Community prices remained unchanged, the variable levy would simply increase, and this was regarded by the USA, in particular, as a particularly insidious form of protection. In 1995 as a result of the 1994 General Agreement on Tariffs and Trade (GATT) Uruguay Round Agreement on Agriculture variable import levies were replaced with tariffs on imports of agricultural products from the rest of the world (see Chapter 18).

For exports, export refunds (also called restitutions) or subsidies generally cover the gap between domestic EU prices and prices on world markets. Each week management committees in the Commission calculate the difference between EU and world prices in order to set the level of export refunds, though there is a certain leeway to take account of market conditions. On numerous occasions the EU has been criticized for its 'generous' calculation of the level of export refunds.

The 1964 agreement on common price levels

The 1962 decision on the mechanisms of the CAP failed to give any indication of what the common levels of prices would be, and clearly the level of prices has crucial implications for the evolution of output and consumption in the Community.

Again the difficulties in reaching agreement reflected different national positions. At the time agricultural prices were relatively high in Germany, Luxembourg and Italy, and lower in France, Netherlands and Belgium. The solution of the EC Commission in document COM(60)105 was to propose that an average price be applied as the basis for the new common policy.

However, the national farm lobbies, and COPA (the Comité des Organisations des Producteurs Agricoles, the umbrella organization of national farm associations which had been established in September 1958) were strongly opposed to the Commission proposal. The Agricultural Committee of the European Parliament (composed mainly of farmers) also called for an increase in prices to the level of those in the main consumer country, i.e. Germany (Tracy, 1989).

In May 1964 the Kennedy Round of GATT negotiations opened formally, but France made progress on reaching a common Community position conditional on resolution of the question of grain prices.[10] In November 1964 Germany accepted a wheat price slightly below the German

---

[10] Tracy (1989), Fanfani (1998). See Chapter 17 for a discussion of the GATT/WTO.

level, but obtained agreement that the new prices would apply only from 1967/8; that prices for barley, maize and rye (of which Germany was a major producer) would be fixed relatively close to wheat and that there would be temporary, degressive payments to compensate for the agricultural price cuts in the high-price countries: Germany, Italy and Luxembourg.

The effects of EU price support policy

The effects of the traditional Community price support system can be analysed using a partial equilibrium framework similar to that used for tariffs in Chapter 4. The world supply curve of a particular product is assumed to be perfectly elastic at Pw in Figure 12.2. The demand and supply curves (assumed linear for simplicity) of the Community for the traded product are indicated by D and S in the diagram. Without price support, the domestic price of the product in the EC is assumed equal to the initial world price Pw. At the world price Pw the Community would produce Qs and demand Qd of the product, so the EC would import Qs – Qd (equivalent to the excess demand) of the product.

For simplicity, the EC threshold and intervention prices are assumed to be the same and are both Pd. At Pd the Community will import Q's – Q'd of the product. As can be seen from the figure, the level of EC prices is shown to be considerably higher than the world price level, as was generally the case for many products (grain prices, for instance, were often over twice as high as world levels).

The EU is assumed to be a large nation. As can be seen from the diagram, the application of EC price support reduces net imports from Qs – Qd to Q's – Q'd. *Ceteris paribus* in the case of a large nation, the fall in net imports would have the effect of reducing demand on world markets, causing the world price level to fall. Conversely, the reduction or elimination of price support would increase EU net imports causing the world price to rise. The gap between the new world price P'w and the EC minimum import (or threshold) price Pd was covered by a variable

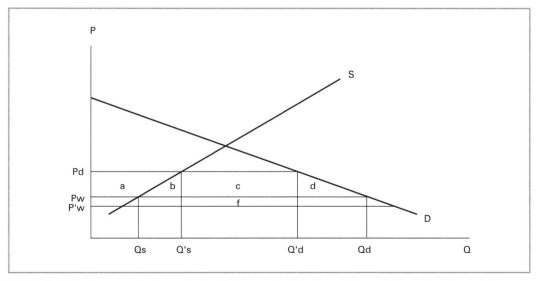

FIGURE 12.2 The price support system when the EC is assumed to be a large nation and net importer of a product

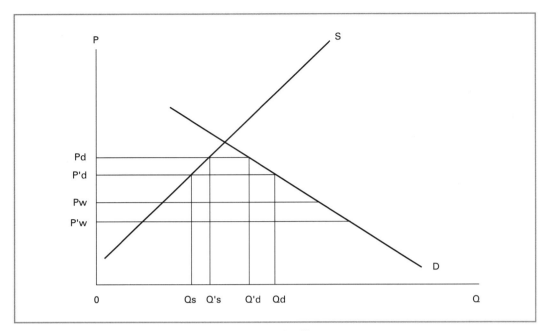

FIGURE 12.3 The difference between variable import levies and tariffs

import levy until 1995. Subsequently tariffs (the difference is explained below) were applied on EU agricultural imports.

The variable import levy or tariff is a source of revenue for a government budget.[11] The total revenue for the budget will be equal to the unit value of the variable import levy or tariff (Pd − P'w) multiplied by the quantity imported after introduction of the tariff (Q'd − Q's). In the diagram this corresponds to the area of the rectangles c and f, or (Pd − P'w) × (Q'd − Q's). If this revenue is used in a socially useful way, it represents a welfare benefit to a country. This benefit could be considered an increase in the income of taxpayers in that *ceteris paribus* in the absence of the tariff the government would have to charge higher taxes.[12]

With the introduction of price support producer surplus rises by area a, consumer surplus falls by a + b + c + d and the revenue for the budget is areas c + f. As the EC is assumed to be a net importer, the fall in world price from Pw to P'w as a result of the introduction of price support causes a transfer from producers in the rest of the world to consumers in the EU of area f (given by the quantity of imports Q'd − Q's times the fall in world price Pw − P'w). The net welfare effect for the EC of introducing price support is therefore area f minus areas b and d.

Figure 12.3 illustrates the difference between a variable import levy and a tariff. Again the EU is assumed to be a net importer of the product, and a large nation. Introduction of price support will reduce the world price from Pw to P'w. Under the traditional price support system of the EC the threshold price Pd was fixed for the year and did not change even if world prices fell (by Pw − P'w). All that happens is that the variable import levy increases to cover the gap between the new world price and the threshold price, so the unit value of the variable levy becomes Pd − P'w.

---

[11] See the discussion on the sources of revenue of the EU budget in Chapter 10.

[12] See Chapter 4 for a description of these effects.

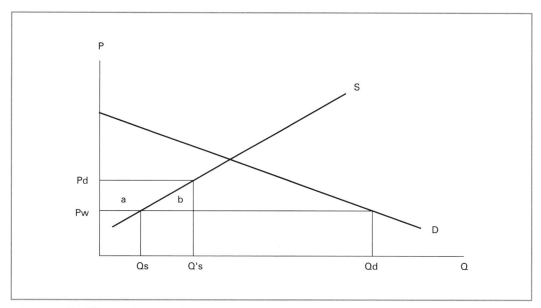

FIGURE 12.4 The difference between price support and producer subsidies

In contrast, with an *ad valorem* tariff following the fall in the world price, the internal EU price becomes P'd. With a tariff EU domestic prices are therefore more sensitive to movements in world price levels, and this was why the USA, in particular, criticized the Community's variable import levies. From 1995 EU variable import levies were converted into tariffs as a result of the 1994 GATT Uruguay Round Agreement on Agriculture.

The difference between the price support system and producer subsidies can be seen from Figure 12.4. In agriculture these producer subsidies are often also referred to as 'deficiency payments' after the system applied in Britain before joining the EC. The main difference between the EC price support system and producer subsidies is that the introduction of producer subsidies leaves the domestic price unchanged for consumers. As Figure 12.4 shows, with the producer subsidy the domestic price to producers rises to Pd, while the price paid by consumers remains Pw. Producer surplus rises by area a, the cost of the surplus to budget contributors is area a + b (i.e. the unit cost of the subsidy, Pd – Pw times the new quantity of output Q's). The net welfare loss is triangle b.

The impact of high and stable prices was to turn the EU from a net importer into a net exporter of many temperate agricultural products. As explained above, export subsidies or restitutions were used to cover the difference between the internal EU market price and the world price. Figure 12.5 shows the effect of EU export subsidies. D and S are the EU demand and supply curves for the product. With price support the internal EU price Pd is above the world price Pw, and the EU will export Q's – Q'd. The unit value of the export subsidy is Pd – Pw, and it is applied on the exports of the product Q's – Q'd. The export subsidy increases producer surplus by areas a, b and c, reduces consumer surplus by areas a and b and costs the budget areas b, c and d. The net welfare loss as a result of the export subsidy is equivalent to areas b and d. The Online Learning Centre for this textbook provides a numerical example of the effects of an export subsidy as an exercise.

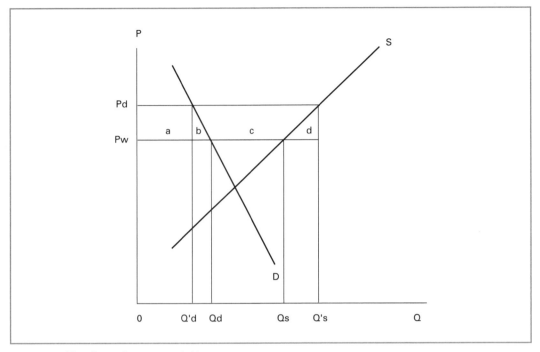

FIGURE 12.5 The effects of an export subsidy

The 1968 Mansholt Plan

The 1968 Mansholt Plan was probably one of the most controversial documents ever produced relating to the CAP. Published in December 1968 as Commission document COM(68)1000, the plan set out proposals to resolve the problems of surpluses and inadequate farm incomes over the following decade, so was also known as 'Agriculture 1980'.

The plan involved a dual approach, with price policy being used to achieve market balance, while structural measures (expected to account for about one-third of the agricultural budget) would be used to create large, efficient farms. A central concept of the plan was the 'modern farm enterprise' that could ensure farm incomes and working conditions (including working hours, holidays etc.) comparable with those in other sectors. A modern farm enterprise could be formed out of a single farm or by a group of farmers coming together. The plan also introduced the concept of production units, or the dimension of production required to ensure efficiency and the use of modern technology. The creation of co-operatives was to be encouraged in order to concentrate supply and render prices more stable.

The Mansholt Plan also aimed at the reduction of surpluses and the improvement of the structure of production by cutting the number of factors of production in the sector. The objective was to induce 5 million people to leave farming, 4 million of whom would be persuaded to retire, while a further 1 million would be found alternative jobs in other sectors.

It was expected that the reduction in the labour force would release 20 million hectares, most of which could be used to restructure farms. However, to cut surpluses some 5 million hectares would be withdrawn from agricultural production and used for forestry, recreational purposes, etc. To meet the problem of dairy surpluses, 3 million cows would also be put down.

The plan also encouraged the formation of co-operatives and producer associations to improve marketing. Account was to be taken of regional diversity (a proposal opposed by the member states) arising because farmers were operating under different natural conditions.

The reaction of the farming community to the plan was violent outrage. The proposals were thought to be too radical, and the dimension of farms proposed was considered too far removed from reality. The Commission was accused of being 'technocratic' and of attacking the family farm through back-door collectivization. Particular concern was expressed about the proposed reduction in the labour force, and about whether the means to ensure employment in other sectors would prove adequate.

In 1972 the Council finally agreed three Directives on structural measures, but these were far removed from the original Mansholt Plan.[13] The financial allocation for the Directives was extremely limited (and in general the Community contribution was only 25 per cent), and the extent to which they were taken up was far less than expected. The use of the Directives also seemed to depend more on the administrative capacity of the member state in question than structural needs. The whittling down of the Mansholt Plan is a major factor explaining the evolution of the CAP with its almost exclusive reliance on price support for many years. As late as 1983 Guarantee spending (on price support) accounted for 95 per cent of FEOGA (or EAGGF) spending, and in 1995 the share had only fallen to 92 per cent.[14]

The agrimonetary system

What was considered to be one of the early achievements of the CAP, the introduction of common prices, was soon undermined by changes in exchange rates between the member states. Common prices were set in units of account and had to be converted into national currencies. According to the neo-functionalist approach to integration, it was hoped that the introduction of common agricultural prices would spill over into economic and monetary union in order to avoid complications to the system as a result of exchange rate changes.

This optimism was soon to prove unfounded, and beginning with French devaluation and a German revaluation in 1969, changes between EC currencies became a frequent occurrence. Special 'green' exchange rates were introduced for agriculture. Changes in these green rates lagged behind those in the central rates of EC currencies, since in that way it was possible to delay adjustment of agricultural prices in national currencies. This meant that a system of taxes and subsidies had to be set up at the border between EC countries to avoid speculative trade flows, and as a result market unity was undermined.[15] The operation of this 'agrimonetary system' led at times to price divergences between member states in national currencies larger than before the CAP had been introduced. In 1976, for example, for a time the gap between prices in the UK and Germany was over 50 per cent. It was only with the introduction of the euro that these difficulties were finally resolved (at least for euro members).

---

[13] The three structural Directives of 1972 relate to modernization of farms (72/159), early retirement (72/160) and socio-economic advice to farmers whether to continue farming or not (72/161).

[14] EC Commission, 'The Agricultural Situation in the Community'. Various years.

[15] The system of subsidies and taxes at the borders were called monetary compensatory amounts (MCAs). See Senior Nello (1985) for a more complete account of the system and its effects.

The ongoing need for reform of the CAP

During the 1970s and 1980s, the CAP seemed increasingly to be transformed from the cornerstone to the stumbling block of the Community. The negative effects of what had begun as a high price policy were accentuated each year by substantial increases in prices for the main agricultural products (see Table 12.1). High and stable prices encouraged production leading to surpluses. Grain and butter mountains and wine lakes were the visible symbols of the malfunctioning of the CAP. According to the Commission (COM(91)100), between 1973 and 1988 EC agricultural production rose by 2 per cent per year, while consumption rose by only 0.5 per cent each year.

These surpluses either had to be held in public storage, or sold on world markets with the help of export subsidies. Public storage was expensive, unpopular and involved the deterioration of foodstuffs over time, while the use of export subsidies antagonized other agricultural exporters, and the USA in particular.

	Commission proposal (1)	Council decision (2)	Difference (2) – (1)	COPA proposal
Community of six				
1968–69		−1.3		
1969–70		0.0		
1970–71		0.5		
1971–72		4.0		
1972–73		4.7		
Community of nine				
1973–74	2.8	5.0	2.2	
1974–75	11.8	13.9	2.5	12.4
1975–76	9.2	9.6	0.4	15.0
1976–77	7.5	7.5	0.0	10.6
1977–78	3.0	3.9	0.9	7.4
1978–79	2.0	2.1	0.1	5.0
1979–80	0.0	1.3	1.3	4.0
1980–81	2.5	4.8	2.3	7.9
1981–82	7.8	9.2	1.4	15.3
Community of ten				
1982–83	8.4	10.4	2.0	16.3
1983–84	4.2	4.2	0.0	
1984–85	0.8	−0.5	−1.3	
1985–86	−0.1	0.1	0.2	
1986–87	−0.3	−0.3	0.0	
Community of twelve				
1987–88	−0.5	−0.2	0.3	
1988–89	0.0	−0.1	−0.1	
1989–90	−0.2	−0.2	0.0	
1990–91	−1.1			

TABLE 12.1 Average increase in Community agricultural prices (percentage variation)
Source: Fanfani (1998).

Although the successive reforms of the CAP described below attempted to address its various shortcomings, then as now the main criticisms of the CAP were:

■ the cost to the EU budget;

■ the burden on consumers;

■ tensions with third countries, and, in particular, agricultural exporters;

■ disparities in the level of support with a bias in favour of larger farmers and those in Northern Europe; and

■ adverse consequences for the environment.

The high and rising level of agricultural prices posed an excessive burden on the EC budget (see Chapter 11). FEOGA Guarantee spending rose from 4.5 billion ECU (European currency unit) in 1975 to 11.3 billion in 1980 and 31.5 billion in 1991. In 2005 FEOGA Guarantee spending still accounted for 42.5 per cent of the EU budget.

The CAP entails heavy costs to consumers as a result of the higher prices that have to be paid for food and agricultural products. Because the share of food in household expenditure is higher for less well-off households, price support hits the poorest disproportionately. As Marsh and Tarditi (2003) argue, although more than 70 per cent of consumer expenditure on food and beverages relates to processing, distribution etc.,[16] the burden of the CAP on consumers remains substantial and varies between products. According to the OECD between 1986 and 1988 the Consumer Support Estimate (CSE) or annual monetary value of gross transfers from consumers of agricultural commodities measured at the level of farm gate arising from policy measures that support agriculture was €68272 million or 37 per cent of the value of farm production in the EC. Even after the successive reforms of the CAP described below, according to the OECD in 2005 transfers from consumers to farmers in the EU(25) were an estimated €42050 million or 17 per cent of the value of the value of production at the farm gate.

As well as the CSE, the OECD publishes two other indicators annually, which can be used to compare support to agriculture in different countries: the Producer Support Estimate (PSE), and the sum of the most production- and trade- distorting forms of support. The PSE adds up the monetary value of government interventions that result in financial transfers from consumers and taxpayers to support agricultural producers. When expressed as a percentage of total farm receipts the PSE allows comparisons of support across countries and commodities (see Figure 12.6). Following the various CAP reforms the share of most distorting forms of support in total CAP support fell from 97 per cent in 1986–8 to 63 per cent in 2003–5.[17]

The growing EC self-sufficiency in the major foodstuffs lowered imports from the rest of the world and increased exports, thereby reducing prices of these products on world markets. Less-developed countries accused the Community of agricultural protectionism, increasing instability on world markets and lowering prices for their agricultural exports. Despite the various CAP reforms, as Table 12.2 shows, EU agricultural tariffs remain relatively high, also when compared with those of the USA (see also Chapter 18).

Linking support to prices meant that those farmers who produce more benefit most from the system. According to the European Commission (1991), it was estimated that between 1970 and 1990, 80 per cent of support from the EAGGF (or FEOGA) went to the 20 per cent of farmers with

---

[16] Data of Coldiretti, an Italian farmers' association, suggest that in 2004 the share going to farmers was 7 per cent for pasta, 9 per cent for tomato sauce, 27 per cent for wine and 40 per cent for beef.

[17] This consisted of market price support, plus payments based on input use, and payments based on output (www.oecd.org).

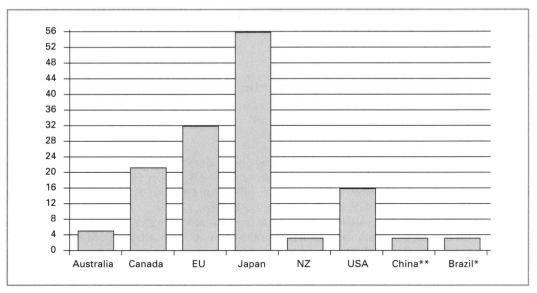

FIGURE 12.6 Producer Support Estimate by selected country

Transfers to farmers as a percentage of value of gross farm receipts, provisional data for 2005.

Note:

*2000

**2003

Source: OECD (2006).

the largest farms. As explained below, when price support was reduced, the largest farms were compensated most so the new system also failed to resolve the problem of income disparities.

The CAP also tended to favour Northern European producers rather than Mediterranean farmers. For instance, in 1986 dairy products, which are mainly produced in Northern Europe, accounted for 20 per cent of the value of production, but 27 per cent of CAP spending, while grains were 13 per cent of production and 16 per cent of spending (see also Figure 12.7). In contrast the equivalent figures for typical Mediterranean products were 6 per cent for production and 3 per cent of spending for wine and 15 per cent of production and 5 per cent of spending for

	Meat	Milk (processed)	Rice	Sugar	Wheat
Australia/New Zealand	0.0	0.9	0.0	2.1	0.0
Canada	7.9	103.2	0.0	3.7	1.7
EU 25	39.7	47.0	138.6	128.6	0.5
USA	1.7	18.8	4.9	34.9	2.4
Argentina	8.6	16.8	12.2	17.5	5.7
Brazil	6.0	19.7	14.5	17.5	4.6
China	9.9	11.4	1.0	19.8	1.0
India	24.2	51.4	72.8	59.5	7.7

TABLE 12.2 Average tariffs applied on selected major agricultural products (per cent), 2005

Source: Bouët (2006). MacMap-HS6 and author's calculation. Reproduced with permission from the International Food Policy Research Institute www.ifpri.org. The paper from which this table comes can be found online at http://www.ifpri.org/divs/mtid/dp/mtidp93.asp.

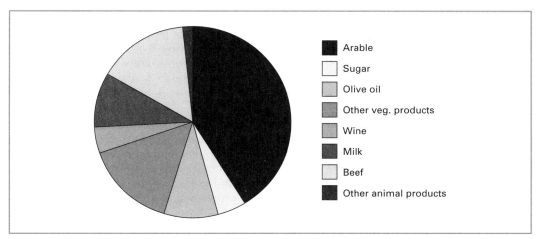

FIGURE 12.7 Breakdown of CAP spending by main product group, excluding rural development (2005)
Source: European Commission (2006), © European Communities, 2006.

fruit and vegetables. The exceptions were tobacco and olive oil, which were relatively expensive regimes.[18]

The almost exclusive reliance on price support encouraged specialization and intensive methods of production with negative implications for the environment and biodiversity. There has been growing public concern about water and soil pollution by fertilizers, pesticides and intensive livestock units, destruction of wildlife habitats and changes in the appearance of the countryside.

Attempts at reform in the 1970s and 1980s

During the early years of the 1970s reform of the CAP was still a taboo subject. It was thought that by undermining the progress achieved in the only functioning common policy, the whole fragile edifice of European integration might come tumbling down. Discussion documents of the Commission at this time refer to 'Improvement of the CAP' (1973) or 'Stocktaking of the CAP' (1975).

Over time it became increasingly difficult to deny the need for change, and there were early and not very successful attempts at price restraint during the late 1970s.[19] In addition there were various reform attempts to tackle the problems of surpluses and excessive budgetary expenditure and, in particular:

■ Co-responsibility levies;

■ Milk quotas;

■ Stabilizers, and the 1988 reform package.

---

[18]Tobacco accounted for 0.6 per cent of production and 3.7 per cent of spending in 1986, while olive oil was 1.6 per cent of production and 2.9 per cent of spending. These data are taken from European Commission, 'The Agricultural Situation in the European Community' (1987).

[19]Gundelach, the Agricultural Commissioner over the 1977–81period, favoured a prudent price policy.

The aim of the **co-responsibility levies** was to render farmers 'responsible' by involving them in bearing the cost of surpluses. Each year a certain level of production for an agricultural good would be fixed, and the cost of any excess production over that level would be totally or partially borne by farmers. Co-responsibility levies were introduced for milk from 1977 and cereals from 1986. In both cases the measures had a positive impact on the budget but failed to resolve the problem of surpluses largely because in practice their application became subject to negotiation.

The dairy sector was proving one of the most expensive CAP regimes, accounting for over 40 per cent of FEOGA Guarantee spending between 1976 and 1980. In 1983 the Commission document COM(83)500 called for reform of the sector, arguing that a price cut of 12 per cent would be necessary to restore market balance. The member states were reluctant to accept such a large price cut and agreed on a system of **milk quotas** as a lesser evil.

The aim of the quota system was to freeze milk production at 1981 levels (1983 for Italy which imported 40 per cent of its milk and for Ireland, which is a major exporter). The EC quota was then broken down by country, and the member states could decide on two methods of application. System A involved dividing the national quota by single farms. If a farm exceeded its quota, it would have to pay a fine of 75 per cent (100 per cent from 1987). According to system B quotas were granted to dairies and or other processors who paid a supplementary levy of 100 per cent if the quota was exceeded. From 1992 the two systems were fused, with quotas being allocated to farms and dairies being responsible for paying a levy of 115 per cent if quotas were exceeded. Initially quotas could only be transferred through the renting or sale of a farm, but from 1992 unused quotas could be reallocated to other producers.

Figure 12.8 uses a partial equilibrium approach to compare the welfare effects of production quotas and reductions in price support. The situation is shown for a net exporter, say the EU,

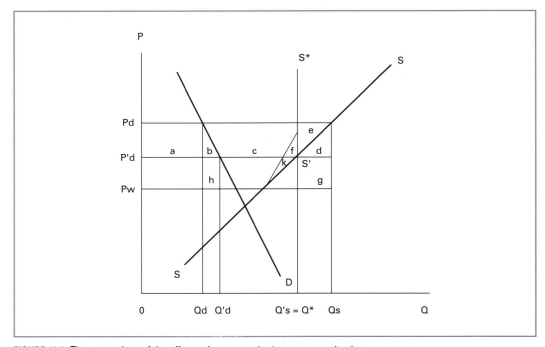

FIGURE 12.8 The comparison of the effects of quotas and price support reduction
Source: Burrell (1989).

even though certain member states (such as Italy) were net importers of dairy products. A reduction of support prices from Pd to P'd would have caused EU net exports of dairy products to fall from Qs – Qd to Q's – Q'd. The budgetary cost of export subsidies as a result of the reduction in price support would fall by the area b + c + f + e + d + h + g. Consumer surplus would rise by a + b, while producer surplus would fall by area a + b + c + f + e. The net improvement in welfare from reduction of price support would therefore be area b + d + h + g.

In contrast, assume that a quota of Q* for total production of milk in the EU was introduced. The EU supply curve would then become SS'S* because at Q* the EU supply curve would become perfectly inelastic. Consumers would continue to buy quantity Qd at prices well above

Box 12.2: *The Italian milk quotas*

The history of the Italian milk quotas is one of long delays in applying Community legislation, huge fines, fraudulent activity and violent farm protests. One of the main complaints of Italian milk producers was that it was difficult for honest farmers to operate in such an environment.

Italy was granted a quota of 9.9 million tonnes on the basis of national statistics, and in 1984 the Italian minister for agriculture argued that there was a discrepancy between the quota and actual production of 11.4 million tonnes. Disagreements over the actual level of production and number of producers were to continue for many years.

Since Italy imports 40 per cent of its milk requirement, in order to exploit the full national quota it was decided to treat the whole country as a single national entity for two years, and not allocate individual quotas. In 1985 Italy applied to adopt System A, but 'administrative problems' delayed its implementation. In 1988 in order to use the quota fully, it was decided to allocate the quota to producer associations who would act as a 'single producer' and Unalat was created for this purpose. Unalat decided to apply the legislation on a voluntary basis. Unofficially Unalat and the Ministry were encouraging farmers to exceed their quotas since Italy was a deficit country, and the exact level of production had not yet been established.

The non-application of the system meant that Italy was running up a fine of about 300 billion lira (roughly 150 million ECU) each year. In 1991 the European Court of Justice stopped 330 billion lira from payments to Italy through FEOGA, but by 1992 the fine had reached 4000 billion lira (2 billion ECU). Italy maintained that the quota was inadequate and requested a backdated increase. In 1994 a compromise was reached whereby the Italian quota was increased (not retroactively) and the fine was reduced to 3620 billion lira. In the logic of a supply-control measure, this fine should be paid by farmers, but in the face of protest by Italian farmers was passed on to taxpayers.

In 1993, nine years after the measure was introduced, a first attempt was made to collect data to establish quotas. Individual quotas were published, but their sum exceeded the national system. It was decided to rely on a system of *autocertificazione* whereby farmers provided their own data on production. Such a system was an invitation to irregular practices, with quotas representing herds of cows that only existed on paper. One famous case involved a herd of 1500 cattle based in Piazza Navona in the centre of Rome, which was said to have been rented out 12 times.

In a further moratorium in 2003, Italian dairy farmers were given 30 years to pay off the backlog of their fines.

world levels, and consumer surplus would remain unchanged. The loss in producer surplus from introduction of the quota would be area e.

Burrell (1989) has presented a more realistic version of the model with an initial loss of producer surplus of e + f + k. Area e is lost because the quota restricts output, but areas f and k are lost because of the way quotas are allocated to individual producers. If a transfer of a quota is permitted (as was the case from 1992), the purchase of quotas by low-cost producers from high-cost producers would enable k + f of producer surplus to be recovered.

Budgetary savings as a result of introduction of the quota amount to area e + d + g. The total welfare effect of introducing a quota when transferability of quotas is permitted is therefore only a welfare gain of d + g. The question then becomes: why were quotas introduced if the net welfare gain (d + g) would be less than that of a price cut (b + h + d + g)? The answer is that probably quotas were more politically acceptable to the farm lobby since, while restraining the budgetary cost of milk support, they entailed less dislocation to producers (Colman, 2007).

The quota system involves freezing the structure of production, so introducing an element of economic inefficiency (though this was somewhat attenuated by introducing the transferability of quotas in 1992). It tends to be costly to administer (see Box 12.2) and may enable cuts in milk prices to be deferred. The operation of quotas may also entail windfall gains for existing producers from the sale or rent of quotas. Moreover, the operation of quotas may exert upward pressure on land prices. However, the operation of milk quotas in the EU made a substantial contribution to reducing the problem of surpluses and slowing the rate of price increases.

The Green Paper of 1985 (COM(85)333), published by the EC Commission, marks the beginning of a change in priorities of the CAP. The document calls for a diversification of policy instruments in order to realize a number of objectives that cannot be reached through the almost exclusive reliance on price support. The Green Paper lists the priorities of the CAP as: reducing surpluses, promoting the quality and variety of agricultural production, improving the incomes of small family farms, supporting agriculture in areas where it is necessary for rural development, promoting awareness of farmers of environmental questions and assisting the processing industry.

The aims of the 1985 Green Paper were to some extent taken up by the package of reforms introduced in 1988. As explained in Chapter 11, these reforms were introduced in the context of the financial perspective for the 1988–92 period and involved reform of the Structural Funds, a ceiling on the growth of CAP spending and the introduction of the stabilizers and accompanying measures.

The **stabilizers** were intended to introduce an automatic check on agricultural spending. In general these entailed fixing a maximum guaranteed quantity (MGQ) for a product, and if that quantity were exceeded, the following year there would be a cut in prices or subsidies. The effectiveness of the stabilizers as a supply-control measure was undermined by the fact that the maximum guaranteed quantities tended to be set at relatively high levels.[20] In practice there was also a tendency to challenge the 'automatic' nature of the price or subsidy cut and its attempt to negotiate a compromise measure.[21]

With the benefit of hindsight, the most lasting and radical change for agriculture introduced by the 1988 package was that of the accompanying measures. These included incentives for early retirement, more extensive production methods, reforestation and set-aside.

---

[20]The maximum guaranteed quantity for cereals was fixed at 160 million tonnes in 1988 compared with a 1987 EC production of 154 million tonnes.

[21]Stabilizers had first been introduced for cereals in 1982 and should have brought about a 5 per cent cut in prices in 1985/6. A compromise was reached whereby prices were only cut by 1.8 per cent.

The set-aside scheme was voluntary and involved compensation for farms withdrawing at least 20 per cent of their arable land for at least five years. The land set aside could be left totally idle; used for forestry or non-food production (such as linen); included in a land rotation scheme or used for pasture or the production of selected crops such as chickpeas, lentils or vetches. It was hoped that set-aside would improve soil conservation and would contribute to the reduction of surpluses. However, the impact of set-aside on production is undermined by the phenomenon of 'slippage' whereby marginal land tends to be removed from production, and labour and capital tend to be used more intensively on the land that remains in production.

The 1992 MacSharry reform

The stabilizer package failed to resolve the problem of surpluses of the main CAP products, and by 1991 reform had again acquired a new urgency. The EC became increasingly aware that CAP reform was necessary to avoid collapse of the GATT Uruguay Round negotiations (see Chapter 18). A new financial perspective was due from 1993 and spending on agriculture would have to be re-dimensioned. Reform of the CAP was essential to permit eastward enlargement of the CAP (see below). The aim was to re-enforce the new priorities set out in the 1985 Green Paper, including rural development, environmental objectives and fairer distribution of support for farm incomes.

A central element of the reform was cuts in administered prices for certain key products, compensated by the introduction of direct payments to farmers. For cereals, the intervention price was to be cut by 29 per cent over three years, reaching 100 ECU/tonne in 1995/6.[22] The target price was to be reduced to 155 ECU/tonne, leaving a substantial Community preference. Farmers were to be compensated for the price cut by direct payments on a per hectare basis.[23] The compensation was calculated by multiplying a basic rate (45 ECU/tonne in 1995/6) by average yields in the past in each region. For farmers claiming compensation for an area producing less than 92 tonnes of cereals, compensation was available unconditionally in what was called the 'simplified scheme'. Farmers claiming a higher level of compensation through the 'general scheme' were required to set aside a certain percentage of their land. The percentage of land that had to be set aside varied with market conditions, and, for example, was 15 per cent in 1993/4.[24]

Oilseeds (such as soya, sunflower and colza) were at the centre of a protracted dispute between the USA and the EU. In the early years of the Community oilseed production was small, and in 1962 an EC–USA deal agreed duty-free access. Given the relatively high prices for grains in the Community, oilseeds had increasingly been replacing grains in animal foodstuffs, and production of pigmeat and poultry grew rapidly around the main ports where oilseeds were imported, such as Rotterdam, Bremen and Antwerp. The EC introduced relatively low tariffs on oilseed imports (maximum 15 per cent) and subsidies for 'crushers' to ensure domestic producers a return compatible with that from cereals (Tracy, 1993). The USA maintained that this system ran counter to the 1962 agreement, and two successive GATT panels ruled in their favour. In

---

[22] Common prices were then fixed in terms of ECU or the European currency unit, which, as explained in Chapter 11, was subsequently replaced by the euro. The intervention price was to be cut to 100 ECU/tonne in 1995/6. The target price was to be reduced to 155 ECU/tonne, leaving a substantial Community preference.

[23] The use of the hectare as the basis for calculating arable compensation led to an increase in land prices.

[24] The percentages of compulsory set-aside were: 12 per cent for 1994, 10 per cent for 1995, 17.5 per cent for 1996 and 5 per cent for 1997. Initially set-aside was to be rotational, but this obligation was dropped in 1996 (also because the administrative costs involved were substantial).

1992 the USA threatened to introduce prohibitive duties on imports worth $300 million from the EC (including pasta, white wine and so on) if the oilseed dispute were not resolved, and for a time the whole GATT Uruguay Round appeared threatened by this dispute (see Chapter 18). As a concession to the USA in the MacSharry Reform the EC fixed a separate base area for oilseeds, on which a minimum set-aside area of 10 per cent was to be levied.[25]

Since beef producers would benefit from the lower grain prices, the intervention price for beef was also to be cut by 15 per cent, and premia per head of cattle were introduced to encourage more extensive forms of production. The quota system was to remain for milk, and there was to be a cut of 5 per cent in the institutional price for butter. The tobacco regime (which was one of the most expensive common market organizations relative to the amount of production) was simplified and updated.[26]

The MacSharry Reform also included accompanying measures with a series of financial incentives for early retirement, reforestation and protection of the environment. The environmental measures were numerous, and included incentives to reduce the use of fertilizers and pesticides; to encourage extensive production methods and voluntary set-aside; to encourage the creation of natural parks, and to protect endangered species.

The MacSharry Reform represents a radical break with the past and sets a precedent for the shape of successive CAP reforms. From the point of view of economic efficiency, direct payments are preferable to price support (see Figure 12.4 above) and have the advantage of being more transparent. The reform recognizes the role of farmers in rural development and protection of the environment, but the funds allocated to these objectives were limited.

The reform was instrumental in permitting a successful outcome to the GATT Uruguay Round, though at the time the Commission was adamant that the reform was not introduced in response to US pressure. The 1992 reform failed to ease the pressure of agricultural spending on the Community budget, also because there was overcompensation for the price cuts. According to Buckwell et al. (1997, p. 30), the overcompensation for cereals between 1992 and 1996 was 16 per cent. This overcompensation amounted to ECU 2.0, 4.2 and 5.0 billion for the three years 1993–96.

Although the compensation for price cuts was initially intended to be temporary, a date for its elimination was never fixed. Over time it becomes increasingly difficult to justify continued compensation for a once-and-for-all cut in prices. One of the objectives of the reform was to correct the inequity in the distribution of CAP transfers. However, compensation was highest for those who produced most so the iniquity of the system was protracted.

The 1999 Berlin Agreement on Agenda 2000

The lengthy document, Agenda 2000, published by the Commission in July 1997 was intended to prepare the EU for enlargement, *inter alia* by setting out the financial perspective for the 2000–06 period and proposals for the reform of the CAP and Structural Funds.[27]

Agenda 2000 refers to new concepts in the agricultural policy debate, including 'multifunctionality' and the 'European model of agriculture'. **Multifunctionality** entails that farmers should not simply be considered producers of agricultural goods but account should be taken of the role

---

[25] The reform fixed the ratio of prices between cereals and oilseeds (1 to 2.1) as a basis for calculating per hectare compensatory payments for oilseeds.

[26] Intervention and export refunds were to be abolished. The number of varieties classified was reduced to eight, and each group was subject to a quota.

[27] See Chapter 15 for a discussion of the Structural Funds.

they can play in pursuing other objectives such as rural development, protecting the environment, safeguarding the countryside, guaranteeing the safety and quality of food and promoting animal welfare (see Box 12.3). **The European model of agriculture** requires social, historical and environmental considerations to be taken into account, and not just economic factors (and is sometimes seen by the USA as an excuse by the EU not to cut farm subsidies).

Box 12.3: *Animal welfare*

Problems for animal welfare may arise from intensive farming methods in view of the confinement and restricted movements imposed on animals, and the increased use of antibiotics. More integrated markets may subject animals to lengthy travel, with increased risk of spreading disease (as for example in the outbreak of foot and mouth disease in the UK in 2001). Many of the consequences of new developments such as genetically modified organisms and growth-producing hormones for animal health and biodiversity are still unknown.

The issue of animal welfare may have ethical, health, environmental and quality implications. EU Directive 98/58 of 20/6/98 fixes minimum animal welfare standards for all animals reared for food production. Member states are required to ensure that the conditions under which animals are kept and bred correspond to the needs of their species as well as their physiological and ethological needs. From January 2007, a new EU Regulation on the protection of animals during transport came into operation. These rules are based on European Convention for the Protection of Animals kept for Farming Purposes, a framework convention agreed by the Council of Europe in 1976.

However, implementation of legislation may be difficult in view of:

- The implications for trade and international trade agreements. It may be claimed that animal welfare measures are being used as a non-tariff barrier, and agreement on such issues may be difficult to reach at an international level.

- The additional costs of production (increased expenditure on feed, energy, housing, etc.), though at times this may be offset by technology and, at the level of overall welfare, may be compensated by the reduction in negative externalities.

- Detailed labelling and traceability may be costly.

In March 1999 the Berlin European Council reached agreement on the Agenda 2000 package (overruling an earlier agreement of the Council of Agricultural Ministers). The agricultural aspects of the final agreement included three main elements:

1 Reform of the common market organizations for products such as cereals, beef, milk and wine (see Box 12.4);

2 Increased flexibility for the member states in the use of funds through measures such as cross-compliance and modulation;

3 Rural development policy was to become the 'second pillar' of the CAP.

Box 12.4: *The main changes in common market organizations introduced by the 1999 reform*

- Cereal prices were to be cut by 15 per cent, with farmers being compensated with direct payments for 50 per cent of the price reduction. Compulsory set-aside of land for large farmers (i.e. those claiming direct payments on more than 92 tonnes of cereals) was to continue and was set at 10 per cent. Arable area payments on oilseeds and linseed were to be reduced and brought in line with those of cereals from 2002. Supplementary payments were to be made to Finland and Arctic regions of Sweden to compensate for extra drying costs.

- The milk price was to be cut by 15 per cent with direct aids compensating farmers for 65 per cent of the price cut. Milk quotas were to continue until 2006, with a 0.9 per cent increase in the size of the quota for Ireland, Northern Ireland, Italy, Spain and Greece from 2000, and a further 1.5 per cent increase in quotas for all member states from 2005.

- There was to be a 20 per cent reduction in beef prices, with 85 per cent compensation for farmers, and certain increases in the premia per head of cattle.

- For wine there was to be a block on planting new vines until 2010 with limited exceptions. Quality improvement was to be encouraged, and there was to be a grubbing programme. Voluntary distillation and 'crisis' distillation in times of surplus would be permitted.

Among the more innovative aspects of the reform were cross-compliance and modulation. **Cross-compliance** is a form of conditionality whereby farmers have to meet certain environmental requirements to receive their direct payments in full. **Modulation** entails reductions in the payments to a farm on the basis of total amount of aid paid to the holding, overall prosperity of the holding or overall employment on the farm. The funds saved in this way can be used for environmental and related measures. Use of cross-compliance and modulation after the 1999 reform was extremely limited. By 2001 only France, the UK and Portugal had implemented modulation.

The Berlin Agreement aimed at upgrading rural development policy (see also Box 12.5, p. 302), even though spending on such measures continued to account for only 10 per cent of the agricultural budget. Tighter conditions were imposed on member states in the administration of rural development schemes. Money not utilized the first year could not be carried forward. New legislation was introduced in order to promote environmentally friendly measures through the use of 'good farming practices' The definition of 'good farming practice' was flexible, but was to be based on the usual good farming practice in the area to which the measure applies.

The CAP and the enlargements of 2004 and 2007

Agriculture frequently threatened to prove a stumbling block in the enlargement process. As shown in Table 12.3, agriculture continues to play an important role in many of the new member states. With the 2004 enlargement the numbers employed in agriculture in the EU increased from about 7 to 11 million. At the same time the share of agriculture in employment rose from 4 per cent to 5.5 per cent, becoming 7.5 per cent with Bulgaria and Romania in 2007.

	Utilized agricultural area (m. ha) 2005	Gross value added in ag. € billion 2005	Agriculture as % GDP 2005	Employment in Agriculture Fishing and forestry(1000s) 2005	Ag. as % total employment 2005	Food expenditures % income 2004
Bulgaria	5.3	1.5	7.2	280	9.3	n/a
Czech Rep.	3.6	0.9	1.0	195	4.1	24.8
Slovakia	2.4	0.4	1.2	108	4.9	24.8
Hungary	5.9	2.4	2.7	187	4.8	26.1
Poland	18.4	6.1	2.5	2386	17.1	25.8
Romania	14.8	6.3	8.0	3048	32.8	n/a
Slovenia	0.5	0.5	1.8	83	8.9	20.2
Estonia	1.0	0.2	1.9	35	5.8	26.7
Latvia	2.5	0.2	2.2	130	12.6	29.4
Lithuania	3.5	0.6	2.9	218	14.8	35.2
Cyprus	.1	0.3	2.5	16	4.5	22.2
Malta	.01	0.05	1.3	3	1.7	20.6
EU(15)	130.3	131.2	1.3	6180	3.7	n/a

TABLE 12.3 Basic data on agriculture in the new member states
Source: European Commission DG Agriculture and Rural Development, © European Communities, 2006. www.ec.europa.eu/agriculture/agrista/2006

The new member states had the complex task of adapting to EU policies and standards (food and agricultural measures account for roughly half the *acquis communautaire*), while the EU wanted to ensure that enlargement did not result in excessive transfers from the Community budget.

There was considerable debate about extending direct income payments to farmers in countries joining the EU. At least initially, such payments were introduced as compensation for the reductions in price support. At first the Commission argued that farmers in applicant countries would not generally experience price cuts and so should not benefit from direct payments.[28]

According to the European Commission, prices for most agricultural products were below EU levels,[29] and it was argued that farmers in the Central and Eastern European countries (CEECs) would receive the benefit of higher prices when they joined the EU, so compensation in the form of direct payments was superfluous. However, this argument was somewhat undermined by rapid price increases for agricultural products in the CEECs. The proposed differential treatment between 'rich' Western farmers and their poorer counterparts in the CEECs was subject to fierce criticism in those countries.

In March 2002 the Commission published an extensive study of the impact of enlargement on agricultural markets and incomes,[30] confirming the view that immediate payment of 100 per cent direct payments on accession of the CEECs would lead to social distortions and inequalities. Moreover there would be non-rural beneficiaries who had generally become landowners as a

---

[28]See, for example, the Agricultural Strategy Paper (EC Commission, 1995), and Agenda 2000 (European Commission 2007). See also Tarditi et al. 1995 for a discussion of this issue.

[29]The EC Commission (1995) maintained that, depending on the product, CEEC prices were between 40 and 80 per cent of EU levels.

[30]European Commission (2002).

result of the privatization process that included restitution in most CEECs. The report took into account four different policy scenarios:

1 No enlargement;
2 Application of the 1999 CAP without direct payments;
3 Introduction of the CAP with full, immediate direct payments; and
4 Acceptance of the candidate countries' negotiating positions.

The working assumption of the analysis was accession of eight CEEC candidates from 2007 (Bulgaria and Romania were assumed to join later). According to the Commission report, even without direct payments the CEEC farmers would benefit on average from a 30 per cent increase in income as a result of EU market support. With the scenario of full application of direct payments in the new member states, the average expected income gain tripled, reaching a level of 89 per cent, while assuming that the applicant countries' negotiating positions were accepted, the predicted gain quadrupled to reach an estimated 123 per cent.

At the Copenhagen European Council of December 2002 it was agreed that direct aids for the new member states would be phased in gradually over 10 years. These countries would receive direct payments equivalent to 25 per cent of the existing system in 2004, 30 per cent in 2005 and 35 per cent in 2006, rising to 100 per cent only in 2013. The new member states were offered the possibility of topping up direct payments through national funds and their rural development funds to 55 per cent in 2004, 60 per cent in 2005 and 65 per cent in 2006.

In order to meet problems of administrative costs and fraud, the new member states could opt for simplified system of direct payments for three years, renewable for up to two more years. This would entail area payments per hectare on the whole of the agricultural area of the new member states. There would be no obligation for farmers to produce in order to receive these payments.

Difficulties also arose in deciding on production quotas for milk and sugar for the new member states. The EC Commission proposed taking 1995–99 as the reference period, but this was contested by some of the CEECs as not being representative. For instance, since milk production fell during these years due to the process of restructuring, countries such as Poland and the Czech Republic argued in favour of a quota based on production in the 1980s or some estimate of 'productive potential'. The Copenhagen European Council agreed on production quotas on the basis of 'the most recent historical reference periods for which data is available', though in fact some concessions were granted.

A further sensitive issue was whether the CEECs would be allowed a derogation on land ownership. Land prices were much lower in the CEECs, and though a general derogation of seven years, with the option of extending the derogation for a further three years, was eventually agreed (12 years for Poland), the initial requests were higher (18 years in the case of Poland).

The mid-term review or Fischler Reform

The Berlin Agreement envisaged a mid-term review of progress in implementing the 1999 reform. The debate over the mid-term review was often acrimonious, and the final compromise reached in 2003 is also called the Fischler Reform as the agreement owes much to the personal efforts of the then Commissioner for Agriculture. Some member states (and notably France under President Chirac) had insisted that the mid-term review should be limited to mere revision of policies and should not introduce substantial changes, but the Commission rightly called the agreement a 'fundamental reform' of the CAP.

The 2003 reform entailed the introduction of a Single Farm Payment (SFP) for most EU farmers, and the aim was to render this decoupled, or independent from the level of production. Decoupled support is considered to have the advantage of causing less distortion of international trade, but, as explained in Chapter 18, subsequently debate emerged as to how far the SFP was in effect 'decoupled' and modifications have been introduced to reduce the risk of challenge in the World Trade Organization (WTO). In its 'historical' form the SFP would be based on a reference amount of the annual average of the arable crop and meat direct payments that the farmer received during the 2000–2002 period. The farmer would receive the SFP regardless of whether land were used to produce anything (except fruit, vegetables or permanent crops apart from olives in the initial version of the reform), or were left idle (but maintained in good agronomic condition). Member states wanting to reduce the risks of abandonment of production could continue to pay limited per hectare payments for production of certain arable crops, and some premia per head of animal (partial decoupling). The aim of the reform is to render the system simpler and more transparent, and to allow market forces again to play a role in influencing what (or whether) farmers decide to produce.

The member states have the option of introducing a system of regionalization of the direct payments. Regions would be defined on the basis of homogeneous production conditions, and all farmers in the region would receive the same basic payment per hectare, regardless of what they received or produced during the 2000–02 period. The aim of regionalization is to reduce distortions between the single payments made to farmers, which might arise because of the different choices made in the base period. In the new member states a flat rate of per hectare payments was to be paid to all farmers.

The SFP is linked to respect of environmental, food safety, and animal health and welfare standards, and to the requirement to keep all farmland in good agricultural and environmental condition (cross-compliance). Failure to respect these objectives would entail reduction of the direct payments to farmers.

There were also revisions in the cereals, durum wheat, butter, rice, nuts and dry fodder sectors.[31] Subsequently similar reforms were introduced for sectors such as olive oil, tobacco, fruit and vegetables, wine, and, partly in response to disputes in the WTO framework, for cotton, sugar and bananas. In all cases support was to become at least partially decoupled and included in the Single Farm Payment system.

The 2003 reform strengthens rural development policy (the second pillar of the CAP) with increased EU financing, reshaping of all measures into a single Rural Development Regulation covering the 2007–2013 period (see Box 12.5), and new measures to promote the environment, quality, animal welfare, and to help farmers to meet EU production standards. European Union co-financing of agri-environmental measures was increased to 85 per cent in Objective 1 regions and 60 per cent elsewhere.

The 2003 package introduces a wide scope for choices to be made by member states in deciding how the reform is to be applied. It is hoped that this additional flexibility will allow the CAP to be adapted better to national and local conditions. The reform also introduces national envelopes that enable the member states to cut total direct aids and use the funds saved for specific objectives. Total direct aids can be cut by up to 10 per cent to finance additional spending on environmental objectives or measures to improve the quality of agricultural products. Alternatively total aids can be cut by 3 per cent to resolve 'particular situations' and allow certain categories of farmers also to receive single payments.

---

[31] Though the current intervention for cereals was to be maintained, monthly increments were to be cut by a half. The intervention price for butter was to be reduced by 25 per cent, which is 10 per cent more than the reduction envisaged by the Berlin Agreement.

Box 12.5: *Rural development measures 2007–2013*

Axis 1 **COMPETITIVENESS**
Human resources
vocational training, young farmers, early retirement, farm advisory services, setting up farm management services etc.
Physical capital
Farm/forestry investments, processing/marketing, co-operation for innovation, agriculture/forestry infrastructure, restoring agricultural production potential
Quality of agricultural production and products
Transitional measures
Semi-subsistence, setting up producer groups

Axis 2 **LAND MANAGEMENT**
Sustainable use of agricultural land
Sustainable use of forestry land

Axis 3 **Wider rural development**
Quality of life
Basic services for the rural economy, renovation and development of villages, protection and conservation of the rural heritage
Economic diversification
diversification to non-agricultural activities, support for micro enterprises, encouragement of tourism
Training skills and animation

Leader Axis
A Community Initiative involving a number of states and aimed at specific groups and targets. Local Action Groups draw up strategies for the sustainable development of local areas

Source: European Commission DG Agriculture and Rural Development, © European Communities, 2006. www.ec.europa.eu/agriculture

---

A mechanism for financial discipline is to be introduced to ensure that during the period 2007–13 the agricultural budget is not overshot. Excessive spending is to induce an automatic reduction in total spending on direct payments. Measures to stabilize markets and improve common market organizations are also to be introduced.

As part of the 1999 reform, the Commission had proposed a ceiling, whereby if the sum total of acreage and headage to a single holding exceeded €100 000, it would have been reduced. However, this was not accepted by the Council as larger farmers, in particular in Britain and East Germany, did not want limits on their transfers. The 2003 reform introduced compulsory modulation, with reductions in the direct payments to farmers of 3 per cent in 2005, 4 per cent in 2006, and 5 per cent from 2007 (the initial proposal of the Commission had been 20 per cent). The first €5000 received by a farm are exempt from this reduction. The funds released will be used to improve the environment, ensure the quality and safety of foodstuffs, or to protect animal welfare. A reduction of 5 per cent a year in direct payments will release an additional €1.2 billion a year to finance these objectives. The European Council subsequently agreed on

Size Class	Payment per farm	% of EU15 farms in size class	Number of farms in size class 1000	% of EU15 payments to size class
0 to 1.25	€ 366	62.76%	4359	4.9%
1.25 to 2	€ 1,588	6.71%	480	2.3%
2 to 5	€ 3,241	11.74%	815	8.1%
5 to 10	€ 7,083	7.46%	518	11.3%
10 to 20	€ 14,172	5.54%	384	16.8%
20 to 50	€ 30,535	4.15%	288	27.1%
50 to 100	€ 67,085	1.05%	73	15.1%
100 to 200	€132,596	0.25%	18	7.2%
200 to 300	€238,762	0.04%	3	2.3%
300 to 500	€379,769	0.02%	2	2.0%
over 500	€879,245	0.02%	1	2.9%
Average, All farms €4679				

TABLE 12.4 The inequity of direct payments in the EU(25), receipts of direct payments per farm by farm size, 2005
Source: European Commission DG Agriculture and Rural development, Indicative figures on the distribution of aid, © European Communities, 2006. www.ec.europa.eu/agriculture

voluntary modulation of 20 per cent, but there is debate about whether this should be rendered compulsory because different application in member states may cause distortions.[32]

As emerges also from European Commission statistics, there is a bias of direct payments in favour of larger farmers. In 2005 there were 670 farms of over 500 hectares that received on average €879 245 in direct payments. Half the farms in the EU were less than 1.25 hectares, but these only received 4.9 per cent of all direct payments, or €366 on average (see Table 12.4).

One solution has been to publish lists of the transfers received by farmers, while on various occasions the EU farm Commissioner, Mariann Fischer Boel, has proposed setting a ceiling on payments to individual farmers. The figure €300000 (also suggested by the previous Commissioner, Fischler) has been voiced.

Biofuels in the EU

In 2003 the EU agreed Directive 2003/30/EC to increase the use of energy from forestry, agriculture and waste materials, setting a 'reference value' of 5.75 per cent of transport fuel to be covered by biofuels and other renewable fuels by 31 December 2010. In 2006 the EU adopted a Strategy for Biofuels, and in 2007 the EU agreed a renewable energy roadmap, which sets binding targets of 20 per cent of EU energy requirements being met by renewable sources by 2020, with at least 10 per cent of transport fuel from bioenergy (compared with about 1 per cent in 2007).

Decisions on biofuels are likely to have a profound impact on the future of EU food and agricultural markets. In 2007 world prices of certain agricultural commodities such as corn

[32] The European Parliament twice rejected the Commission proposal on the grounds that it distorted competition and implied a re-nationalization of the CAP.

rose rapidly partly because of bad weather and increased imports by China and certain other emerging countries, but also due to the demand for biofuels. In 2008 the food price index of the Food and Agricultural Organisation (FAO) reached the highest level since it was launched in 1990, causing difficulties for the World Food Programme of the UN, a pasta boycott in Italy and food riots in Mexico.

The first-generation biofuels produced in the EU include ethanol from grain and sugarbeet, and biodiesel from oilseeds. These are relatively costly, in particular, when compared with Brazilian ethanol produced from sugar cane, and their impact on the environment has been questioned. The advantage of biofuels is said to be that carbon emissions from use of the fuel is balanced and reabsorbed by new plant growth. However, in practice biofuels are not carbon neutral as energy is needed to grow crops and process them into fuel. The production of crops for biofuels may lead to a reduction in biodiversity or, in some parts of the world (such as Indonesia or Malaysia), to deforestation.

Second-generation technologies, such as cellulosic ethanol made from plant waste, have a more positive effect on greenhouse gas emissions and lower costs of production, but most will not be ready for commercial production for some years. The OECD (2006) estimated that without imports of biofuels, 43 per cent of the land currently used for the production of cereals, oilseeds and sugar beet in the EU would be needed to meet 10 per cent of current transport needs.

The ongoing CAP reform process

At the Brussels European Council of October 2002 the French President, Chirac, (a former Minister of Agriculture) convinced Germany and the European Council to accept a limit of 1 per cent per year in nominal terms on the increase in CAP spending from 2007 until 2013.[33] Phasing in of the CAP in Bulgaria and Romania (who joined the EU in 2007) will also have to be covered by this budgetary guideline. Although some cuts in market support seem likely, reductions in SFPs (of possibly in the order of 3 per cent; Anania, 2007) will probably be necessary to release funds for CAP spending in the two new member states. Spending on rural development was excluded from the limit agreed in 2002.

At the June 2005 European Council Tony Blair linked the question of the UK budget rebate to reduced spending on agriculture, but France, in particular, opposed further CAP reform. By way of compromise in 2005 it was agreed that there would be a comprehensive review of all expenditure and resources of the EU Budget by 2008/9, including a review of spending on the CAP.

The Commission has stressed that the debate about the future of the CAP is characterized by 'one vision', but two steps. The first, according to the EU Commissioner for Agriculture and Rural Development, Mariann Fischer Boel, is a 'health check' of the CAP until 2013 and is said to be simply an adjustment and simplification of the CAP and not a 'new reform'. However, as can be seen from the description in the next section, some of the proposals raised in this context would seem to imply profound changes in the CAP. The second stage is to be a fundamental debate on the future of the CAP in the context of a Mid-Term Review to decide on the new financial

[33] '... total annual expenditure for market-related expenditure and direct payments in a Union of 25 cannot, in the period 2007–2013, exceed the amount in real terms of the ceiling of category 1A for 2006 agreed in Berlin for the EU(15) and the proposed corresponding expenditure ceiling for the new member states for the year 2006. The overall expenditure in nominal terms for market-related expenditure and direct payments for each year in the period 2007–2013 shall be kept below this 2006 figure increased by 1 per cent per year.' Conclusions of the Brussels European Council of October 2002 (Doc. 14702/02).

perspective from 2013. The Commissioner seemed determined to arrive at that debate with a more transparent, rational CAP that is easier to defend.

The 2008/9 health check of the CAP

In November 2007 the Commission presented proposals for the 2008/9 health check of the CAP.[34] Three main questions are addressed:

1 How to make the Single Farm Payment Scheme more effective and simpler;
2 How to make market support instruments, initially conceived for a Community of six, relevant today; and
3 How to meet new challenges.

With regard to the **SFP** scheme, proposals included:

- moving from the historical system (which becomes harder to defend over time) to a flatter-rate regional system;
- capping or placing upper limits on the SFP to individual farmers (though exceptions would be allowed for farms with multiple ownership providing relatively high levels of employment such as the co-operatives in East Germany);
- placing lower limits on the SFP (to exclude those who are not genuine farmers);
- prolonging the simplified single area payment scheme (which applies on the whole of the agricultural area) beyond 2010 in the new member states;
- improving the operation of cross compliance (in particular, to meet technical concerns about controls and sanctions);
- ending many of the exceptions from decoupling,
- harmonization of entitlements to SFPs.

With regard to **market support** the main proposals involved:

- eliminating export subsidies, regardless of what happens in the Doha Round (see Chapter 18);
- ensuring that intervention operates as a genuine safety net (in particular, given the rise in agricultural prices) by, for instance, limiting intervention for grains to bread-making wheat;
- abolishing set-aside, though rural development measures could be used to maintain its positive environmental effects; and
- providing a 'soft landing' for the abolition of milk quotas in 2015 by, for instance, increasing the size of quotas and using rural development measures if necessary for areas heavily dependent on milk production.

The Commission identified the **challenges** to be met as:

- risk management (with a role that to be played by risk prevention, insurance and disaster aid);
- climate change;

---

[34]European Commission (2007). See the Commission website for a discussion of these proposals (www. ec.europa/agriculture).

- biofuels;
- water management; and
- continuing to protect biodiversity.

In order to finance such measures the Commission proposed a strengthening of the second pillar of the CAP (rural development). As the CAP budget is fixed until 2013, the Commission proposed an increase in compulsory modulation.

Evaluation and outlook

Since the mid-1980s the CAP has changed fundamentally. One of the first indications of this change was the 1985 Green Paper published by the EC Commission. This document called for an end to the almost exclusive reliance on price support and listed among the priorities of the CAP: the reduction of surpluses, the promotion of the quality and variety of agricultural production, rural development and environmental objectives.

After a rather limited attempt to move the CAP in this direction with a package of reforms in 1988, radical changes followed with the 1992 MacSharry Reform, the 1999 Berlin Agreement and the Fischler Reform or Mid-term Review of the CAP of June 2003. By 2005 direct payments accounted for 69 per cent of CAP spending (see also Figure 12.9), rural development had become the second pillar of the CAP and the 'multifunctionality' of farmers was recognized as a central tenet of EU policy.

Three developments influenced (and continue to influence) the pace and shape of CAP reform:

1 the weight of agricultural spending in the Community budget, in particular in an enlarging EU;

2 GATT/WTO commitments; and

3 the concern of the public for safer food and more environmentally friendly agriculture.

In order to finance emerging EU policy areas (and notably the Internal Market and Single Money Projects, which were accompanied by increased spending on structural actions), the

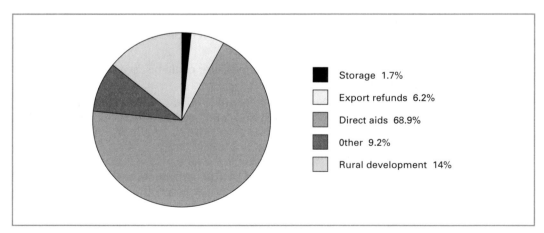

FIGURE 12.9 Breakdown of CAP expenditure by type (2005)
Source: European Commission (2006), European Communities, 2006.

CAP share of the EC budget had to be re-dimensioned, at least in relative terms. The October 2002 European Council agreed on an annual increase in nominal terms in CAP spending over the 2007–13 period, but the allocation now has to be shared among 27 countries. As explained above, agriculture continues to play an important role in some CEEC economies and the discrimination in treatment between old and new member states with regard to CAP payments will eventually have to be ended. Given the constraints of the EU budget ceiling, which seem likely to continue for the new financial perspective after 2013, a solution to this dilemma would be to move further in the direction of co-financing of agricultural policy by the member states. A constant aim in successive CAP reforms is to place higher priority on rural development measures. Community financing of such measures is only partial, so by strengthening the 'second pillar' of the CAP, national co-financing of the CAP would be increased, and also in this way it would be partially re-nationalized.

A second factor influencing CAP reform is the GATT/WTO framework (see Chapter 18). The 1992 MacSharry Reform has to be read against the background of fear of collapse of the Uruguay Round because of disputes on agriculture. The USA was pushing for larger cuts in domestic support and export subsidies, and easier market access than the EU was prepared to grant. When a compromise had to be reached, the EU solution was to transform price support into direct payments, reducing the need for export subsidies. It was also hoped that direct payments would be exonerated from the obligation to reduce domestic support (see Chapter 18). The 1999 Berlin Agreement and the 2003 CAP reform represent further steps in this direction, with the attempt to 'decouple' support from production, thus rendering it more compatible with GATT/WTO commitments. As explained in Chapter 18, even with a collapse of Doha Round negotiations, WTO dispute settlements and the growing proliferation of regional trade blocs that increasingly cover agriculture in a more systematic way will continue to stimulate the process of CAP reform.

The third factor behind reform is the growing public insistence on increased priority for rural development, environmental objectives and guaranteeing the safety and quality of food. The reform of 2003 to some extent meets these requests by rendering direct payments more conditional on furthering these objectives. Repeated public opinion surveys show that the general public have strong feelings about the health and safety of food, and about protection of the environment. For instance, in Eurobarometer (2007) respondents were presented with a list of policy aims and asked to choose a first priority before selecting a maximum of five others that should be prioritized. The aim of EU agricultural policy prioritized by the highest number of respondents was 'supplying the population with healthy and safe food' (41 per cent).[35] Ensuring a fair standard of living for farmers emerged as the second highest priority (37 per cent), while ensuring reasonable prices to consumers was the third priority (35 per cent). When asked to select one priority only 17 per cent chose 'ensuring a fair standard of living for farmers', followed by 'supplying the population with healthy and safe food' (12 per cent) and 'ensuring reasonable prices to consumers' (9 per cent). Successive Eurobarometer surveys also show that most EU consumers simply do not want genetically modified organisms (GMOs) (Loureiro, 2003).

It is unrealistic to expect that a CAP based more on these new priorities will cost less. Health and quality controls involve high administrative costs, in particular when associated with measures such as effective labelling, animal passports and the traceability of all stages of the production and distribution processes. Budgetary constraints are likely to become even tighter in an enlarged EU. The increased emphasis on rural development and environmental measures implies a shift towards measures that already tend to be partially co-financed by national governments. A partial re-nationalization of the CAP seems difficult to avoid.

---

[35] For the results of the survey see www.ec.europa.eu/public_opinion

Summary of Key Concepts

- The scale of **public intervention in agriculture** can be explained by: the dependence of agricultural production on biological cycles, climate and natural phenomena (including epidemics); low elasticity of demand with respect to price and income; the inelasticity of supply in the short run; the small size of many EU farms; the economic and social difficulties many farmers face in leaving the agricultural sector; the need to provide consumers with adequate information and guarantees about the quality and safety of food; and the role farmers may play in protecting the environment, safeguarding the countryside, ensuring animal welfare and promoting rural development.

- The activities of **farm lobbies** also help to explain the persistence and scale of state support for the farm sector.

- Article 39 of the Treaty of Rome set out the initial **objectives of the CAP**.

- In 1962 there was agreement on the **three fundamental principles of the CAP:** unity of markets, Community preference and financial solidarity. There was also agreement on the price support mechanisms.

- Until 1995 **variable import levies** were applied on imports from the rest of the world, but as a result of the 1994 GATT Uruguay Round most variable import levies were replaced with tariffs.

- Export refunds (also called restitutions) cover the gap between domestic EU prices and prices on world markets.

- The failure of the **1968 Mansholt Plan** meant that for many years structural measures played a very limited role in the EC.

- During the 1970s and 1980s, high and stable EC agricultural prices encouraged production leading to surpluses. The **criticisms of the CAP** are that it weighed excessively on the Community budget, caused tensions with other agricultural exporters, imposed a heavy burden on consumers, failed to improve the relative income situation of small farmers and encouraged intensive farming methods that had a negative impact on the environment.

- **Early attempts at CAP reform** included co-responsibility levies, milk quotas and stabilizers. The 1988 reform package introduced accompanying measures, which included incentives for early retirement, more extensive production methods, reforestation and set-aside.

- The **1992 MacSharry Reform** and the 1999 Berlin Agreement on Agenda 2000 cut prices for certain key products and introduced direct payments for farmers. The MacSharry Reform also introduced measures for early retirement, reforestation and protection of the environment. With the Berlin Agreement rural development policy became the second pillar of the CAP.

- Since the late 1990s EU agricultural policy has increasingly been based on the concepts of **multifunctionality and the 'European model of agriculture'.**

- **The Mid-term Review or Fischler Reform of 2003** introduced the Single Farm Payment aimed at rendering support more decoupled from production. Subsequently similar reforms were introduced for other sectors such as sugar, cotton, olive oil, tobacco and fruit and vegetables, while a new regime was proposed for wine. Rural development was again given a higher priority, with a single Rural Development Regulation covering the 2007–2013 period.

- The **'health check'** is aimed at adjusting and simplifying the operation of the CAP until 2013. In 2008/9 there is to be **a fundamental debate on the future of the CAP from 2013.**

Questions for study and review

1 Why has the CAP always played such a central role in the European Community?

2 What are the main defects of a price support policy?

3 Why did structural policy play such a minor role in the EC for so long?

4 What were the objectives of the CAP set out in the Treaty of Rome, and to what extent have they been realized? How have the objectives of the CAP changed over time?

5 Why has the CAP proved so resistant to reform over the years?

6 Describe the early attempts to reform the CAP.

7 The 1992 MacSharry Reform, the Berlin Agreement and the 2003 CAP reform changed the mechanisms used by the CAP. Describe the fundamental aspects of these reforms.

8 What does a rural development policy involve?

9 What are the advantages and disadvantages of 'decoupling' support from production? How far is the Single Farm Payment decoupled (see also chapter 18)?

10 Describe the main sources of pressure for further reform of the CAP.

11 What are the likely effects of increased use of biofuels?

12 Exercise on the introduction of an export subsidy in a large nation (see Chapter 4 and the Online Learning Centre to this textbook for examples of how to carry out the exercise):

Assume that in conditions of free trade with a world price Pw of 100 euros per tonne for a product, the quantity of that product demanded Qd by a country is 1500 t and the quantity supplied Qs is 2500 t. Assume that the price elasticity of demand for the product in that country is –0.4, and the price elasticity of supply is 0.3. The country then introduces an export subsidy of 20 euro/tonne which causes a change in world prices (i.e. the terms of trade of that country) of 3 euros/t. Calculate the effects of introducing the export subsidy on consumer expenditure, producer revenue, the trade balance and the total welfare of the country.

References

Anania, G. (2007) *Multilateral Negotiations, Preferential Trade Agreements and the CAP. What's Ahead?* TradeAg (Agricultural Trade Agreements) Working Paper 07/1, http:tradead.vitamib.com

Bouët, A. (2006) *What can the Poor Expect from Trade Liberalization? Opening the Black Box.* MTID Discussion Paper No. 93. IFPRI, Washington, DC.

Buckwell, A. et al. (1997) 'Towards a common agricultural and rural policy for Europe', *European Economy Reports and Studies*, No. 5.

Burrell, A. (1989) *Milk Quotas in the European Community*, CAB International, Wallingford.

Colman, D. (2007) 'The Common Agricultural Policy', in Artis, M. and Nixson, F. (eds) *The Economics of the European Union. Policy and Analysis*, 4th edn, Oxford University Press, Oxford.

EC Commission (1995) *The Agricultural Strategy Paper*, CSE(95)607.

EC Commission (various years) 'The agricultural situation in the European Union'.

Eurobarometer (2007) Europeans, Agriculture and the Common Agricultural Policy, Report 03/07, www. ec.europa.eu/public_opinion

European Commission (1991) 'The Development and Future of the CAP: Reflections Paper of the Commission', COM(91)100.

European Commission (2002) SEC(2002)95 *Enlargement and Agriculture: Successfully Integrating the New Member States into the CAP, Issues Paper*, Brussels, January.

European Commission (2006) '35th Financial Report on the European Guidance and Guarantee Fund', 2005 Financial Year COM (2006) 512 final.

European Commission (2007) 'Preparing for the "Health Check" of the CAP', COM(2007)722, www.ec.europa.eu/agriculture

Fanfani, R. (1998) *Lo Sviluppo della politica agricola comunitaria*, 2nd edn, Carocci, Roma.

Fennel, R. (1997) *The Common Agricultural Policy: Continuity and Change*, Oxford University Press, Oxford.

Johnson, G.L. and Quance, C.L. (1972*) The Overproduction Trap in US Agriculture*, Johns Hopkins University Press, Baltimore.

Loureiro, M.L. (2003) 'GMO food labelling in the EU: Tracing "the seeds of dispute"', *Eurochoices,* Vol. 2, No. 1.

Marsh, J. and Tarditi, S. (2003) *Cultivating a Crisis: The Global Impact of the Common Agricultural Policy*, Consumers International, London.

Nerlove, M. (1956) 'Estimates of the elasticities of supply of selected agricultural commodities', *Journal of Farm Economics*, No. 2.

OECD (2006) *Agricultural Market Impact of Future Growth in the Production of Biofuels*, OECD, Paris, www.oecd.org.

Senior Nello, S.M. (1985) 'Reform of the EC agrimonetary system: A public choice approach', *Journal of European Integration*, Vol. IX, pp. 55–79.

Senior Nello, S.M. (1989) 'European interest groups and the CAP', *Food Policy*, No. 2, May, pp. 101–6.

Senior Nello, S.M. (1997) 'Applying the new political economy approach to explain agricultural policy formation in the European Union', EUI Working Paper, RSC No. 97/21, Robert Schuman Centre, European University Institute, Florence, p. 46.

Tarditi, S., Marsh, J. and Senior Nello, S.M. (1995) *Agricultural Strategies for the Enlargement of the European Union to Central and Eastern Europe*, study prepared for DG–1 of the Commission, Siena.

Tracy, M. (1989) *Government and Agriculture in Western Europe 1880–1988*, Harvester Wheatsheaf, London.

Tracy, M. (1993) *Food and Agriculture in a Market Economy. An Introduction to Theory, Practice and Policy*, Agricultural Policy Studies, Genappe, Belgium.

Useful websites

The European Commission presents explanations of the functioning of the CAP, statistics, key documents on CAP reform, and news of recent developments:
www.ec.europa.eu./agriculture

The Food and Agriculture Organization publishes statistics and reports:
www.fao.org

The Organization for Economic Co-operation and Development provides data and analysis:
www.oecd.org

The World Trade Organization presents statistics and information on the Doha Round:
http://www.wto.org

Fisheries Policy

❖ LEARNING OBJECTIVES

By the end of this chapter you should be able to understand:

❖ The objectives of the Common Fisheries Policy (CFP);

❖ The economic basis for public intervention in fisheries;

❖ The main steps in the evolution of the CFP;

❖ The principal aspects of the 2003 reform;

❖ The main criticisms of the CFP.

Introduction: Objectives of the Common Fisheries Policy

The legal basis of the CFP in the treaties is the same as that of the Common Agricultural Policy (CAP). Article 38 of the Treaty of Rome (now Article 32 of the EC Treaty) referred to a common market extending also to products of fisheries and 'of first stage processing relating to those products'. The CFP therefore also shares the objectives of the CAP, but over the years there has been increased emphasis on conservation of stock and (as in the case of the CAP) the need to take account of environmental considerations. These additional objectives were defined in Council Regulation 3760/92, and again in the context of the debate on the December 2002 reform of the CFP, and entail:

- conservation of fish stocks;
- protection of the marine environment;
- ensuring the economic viability of the fleet; and
- respect for the interests of consumers.

The economic analysis of fisheries

Public intervention to control fisheries is generally justified on the grounds that the sea and the fish stock can be regarded as an example of common property. Analysis of the 'tragedy of the commons' owes much to the seminal work by Hardin (1968). The term 'common' tradition-

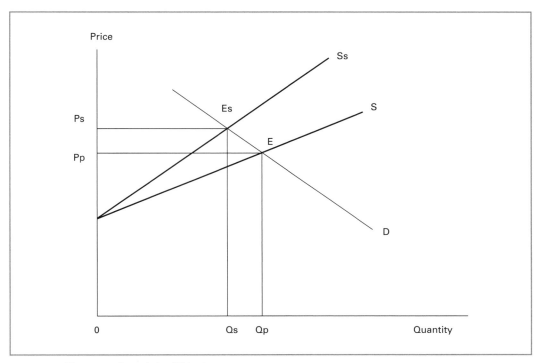

FIGURE 13.1 The economic analysis of fisheries

ally refers to a field in an English village whose use by the villagers is free and unrestricted. If the common were privately owned, animals would be grazed on the field until their marginal product equalled their cost. However, the marginal product of each animal will decline as the number of animals grazed on the field increases. If there is free access to the common, each villager will fail to take into account the fact that grazing his animal on the common will reduce the output of other animals grazed there (i.e. the social cost is ignored), and the common will be overused.

A simple framework can be used to show the divergence between private marginal cost and marginal social cost in the case of fisheries. Figure 13.1 illustrates the conventional demand curve D and the supply curve S of the EU member states for fish. Marginal social cost (as shown by the supply curve Ss in the diagram) is above private marginal cost, reflecting negative externalities. The equilibrium taking account of externalities occurs at Es with price Ps and quantity Qs. If only private marginal costs are taken into account, the market equilibrium is E and QpQs represents the quantity of over-fishing. If one country attempts unilaterally to regulate supply and limit fishing, other EU member states will simply fish more to meet demand. A common policy is therefore needed to prevent over-fishing and reach the social equilibrium Es.

If, however, the common policy provides subsidies to fishermen, price support and financial incentives to renew and improve the fleet and fisheries infrastructure, it will reduce costs, stimulate investment and encourage a situation of over-capacity.

Figure 13.2 shows how the problem of commons can be applied to the choice of size of the fishing fleet. Assume that the number of fish caught increases with the number of fishing boats, but less than proportionately, so the number of fish caught by each boat decreases as the number

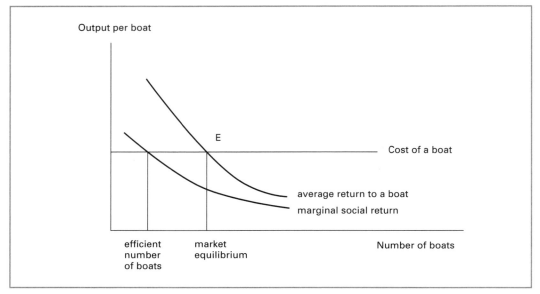

FIGURE 13.2 The problem of commons
Source: From *Economics of the Public Sector*, 3rd edn by Joseph Stiglitz. Copyright © 2002, 1998, 1986 by Joseph E. Stiglitz, the Trustee of Edward Hannaway Stiglitz Trust, the Trustee of Julia Hannaway Stiglitz Trust and the Trustee of the Trust or the Benefit of Joseph E. Stiglitz's children. Used by permission of W.W. Norton & Company Inc.

of boats increases. The marginal social benefit is therefore less than the marginal private benefit since some of the fish caught by an additional boat would have been caught by other boats. In deciding whether to buy a boat a fisherman will consider private marginal benefit, or average return, but as shown in Figure 13.2 this is greater than marginal social benefit, so market equilibrium E leads to an excess number of boats.

The historical evolution of the Common Fisheries Policy

Differences between the member states meant that the CFP was not set up until 1970, and only became fully operative from 1983. In 1970 two regulations established free and equal access to all EC fishing grounds for all EC fishermen subject to certain exceptions for sensitive coastal waters. Market support and structural measures were also introduced.

The 1973 enlargement substantially increased EC waters. The UK, Denmark and Ireland claimed that the EC principle of equal access conflicted with domestic preference and managed to obtain certain special reserved areas (6- to 12-mile zones) until 1983. In 1975 the UN Conference on the Law of the Sea failed to reach agreement on fishing rights, and subsequently various countries (including the Community) declared 200-mile zones reserved for exclusive fishing.

Following a protracted debate among EC countries over allowable catches, their allocation between the member states and access to coastal waters,[1] the revised CFP was finally introduced in 1983 and was a 20-year agreement lasting until 2002. The measures introduced included access arrangements that provide for national zones of up to 12 miles (19 kilometres) for member states with limited access for other EC countries, and a 200-mile exclusive Community zone.

---

[1] At times this led to clashes between fleets, with boats being protected by respective navies.

Quotas or total allowable catches (TACs) were established for each member state for about a hundred fish species. Market support measures were adopted, which entailed some support buying to maintain fish prices and stabilize incomes, but the burden to the EU budget was relatively limited as the EU imports about 60 per cent of its fish requirements. Structural policies were used to reduce overcapacity, restructure the fishing industry and increase competitiveness. Multi-Annual Guidance Plans (MAGPs) set the conditions for development of each country's fleet in terms of 'fishing capacity' (i.e. vessel tonnage and engine capacity). The aim was to manage the 'fishing effort', or maintain a balance between fishing capacity and the conservation of fish stocks.

The evolution of the CFP was shaped by the withdrawal of Greenland from the EC in 1985 and by the Mediterranean enlargement. The accession of Spain and Portugal to the Community doubled the number of fishermen and added 50 per cent to the size of the Community fleet. In principle these countries were granted mutual access; however, temporary limits were

	Number of coastal vessels 2005	Number of off-shore vessels 2005	Total employment in fisheries sector (including processing and aquaculture)# 2002/2003	Employment in fisheries as % total employment 2002/2003	Value of landings 2004 € million
Belgium	1	122	1743	0.0	86
Denmark	2531	877	14060	0.5	352
Germany	1743	415	16409	0.1	190
Estonia	843	201	6700	0.0	18
Ireland	961	464	10584	0.6	195
Greece	17284	1322	37701	0.9	291
Spain	9774	3731	92777	0.5	1850*
France	2374	92	64712	0.3	1000*
Italy	9511	5434	47957	0.2	1380
Cyprus	821	75	1175	0.4	:
Latvia	743	192	10580	1.1	19**
Lithuania	196	87	6565	0.4	52
Malta	1242	117	1441	1.0	11
Netherlands	244	613	9049	0.1	380
Poland	811	475	19923	0.1	40
Portugal	9379	953	33229	0.6	347
Slovenia	117	25	623	0.1	91
Finland	3171	173	2740	0.5	21
Sweden	1249	357	3955	0.1	91
UK	5649	1419	33534	0.1	740
Total	72302	18892	421318#		7053

TABLE 13.1 Data on fisheries in the EU
*assumed value to allow calculation of totals
**Baltic only, :not available, # EU (25)
##Taking into account processing and aquaculture, though not shown in the table, total employment in the fisheries sector amounts to 734 in Austria, 2267 in the Czech Republic, 1680 in Hungary and 1180 in the Slovak Republic.
Source: European Commission (2006), © European Communities, 2006.

introduced on allowable catches and access to the waters of certain other member states. The Mediterranean continental shelf is narrow and this influences the form of fisheries there. Most fishing is in the coastal band and involves a large number of small vessels. In addition, highly migratory species such as tuna are found offshore.[2] Most of the Mediterranean has been declared 'high sea', so the 200-mile limit was not applied.

According to the 1983 agreement, some elements of the CFP were subject to review before the end of 2002. The Commission used this opportunity to launch an extensive debate on the whole of the Common Fisheries Policy. In 2002 a Green Paper was published setting out objectives for a revised policy.[3] It was widely felt that the CFP was not meeting its objectives as too many fish were being taken from the sea, leaving too few adult fish to maintain stocks. Several important fish stocks, including cod, were on the verge of collapse. This also had a negative knock-on effect on the incomes of fishermen.

The Commission's proposals for reform of the CFP were subject to an intense lobbying activity.[4] Agreement was eventually reached and the new EU fisheries policy came into operation from January 2003.

Of the new member states, only Poland and the Baltic states had substantial fishing sectors, and in 2003 the combined fishing catch of the 12 new member states amounted to only about 7.2 per cent of the total EU catch (see also Table 13.1). Despite the 2004 enlargement of the EU, the number of EU vessels in January 2006 was slightly less than 90 000, which was 17 000 less than in 1995.[5]

The main instruments of the Common Fisheries Policy since the 2002 reform

Since the 2002 reform the main elements of the CFP are:

- **Conservation and limitation of the environmental impact of fishing aimed at protecting fish resources by regulating the amount of fish taken from the sea**. The annual fixation of TACs divided among member states had prevented fishermen planning ahead and failed to ensure the conservation of stocks. With the reform two types of multi-annual plans were to be introduced: recovery plans to help rebuild stocks in danger of collapse, and management plans to help maintain other stocks at safe biological levels. There would be tighter regulatory measures to reduce catches of younger fish, by-catches in mixed fisheries and discards. On the basis of these longer-term objectives catch limits in the form of TACs would continue to be set each year. Technical rules were introduced to limit the catching of small fish, including minimum mesh sizes, closing of certain areas, bans on some fishing gears, and measures to promote more selective fishing techniques. The Commission launched an Action Plan to try and ensure that environmental aspects are integrated into the CFP.

- **Structural policies for the fleet.** The member states are to have responsibility for matching capacity and fishing possibilities (or managing the 'fishing effort'). Public aid to renew or modernize fishing vessels was to be phased out, though assistance to improve safety

[2] Quotas for blue fin tuna were introduced from December 1997.

[3] European Commission (2001).

[4] An informal grouping, 'Les Amis de la Pêche', was formed between France, Italy, Portugal, Spain, Greece and Ireland.

[5] European Commission (2006).

and working conditions on board, and to ensure hygiene and the quality of fish products would continue. An entry–exit system was be established whereby the introduction of new fishing capacity without aid will have to be compensated by the withdrawal of at least as much capacity. Aid was to be given for the decommissioning of vessels and retraining of fishermen.

- **Market support measures.** The common organization of the market sets standards; encourages the creation of producers' organizations among fishermen to stabilize markets; continues the price support system with minimum prices below which fish cannot be sold; and sets rules for trade with non-EU countries.

- **Relations with the outside world.** Fisheries agreements became necessary when EU fishing vessels lost access to traditional grounds following the extension of zones for exclusive fishing. Fishing rights for such vessels were negotiated with various non-EU countries in return for compensation. With the 2002 reform access agreements were replaced by 'Partnership Agreements' aimed at responsible fishing by the parties concerned. The EU participates in various international fisheries conventions and organizations and in international attempts to limit illegal fishing.

- **Enforcement.** With the 2002 reform better application of the rules was to be ensured by increased co-operation between national enforcement authorities and the Commission. There was to be greater uniformity of controls and sanctions, with an agreed list of the most serious infringements. A compliance scoreboard showing the enforcement record of the member states was to be introduced. The powers of the Commission to monitor the enforcement activities of the member states was strengthened, and the use of a satellite vessel monitoring system was extended. A European Fisheries Control Agency with powers of inspection and surveillance of fishing activities was to be set up in Spain. Stakeholders' involvement was also to be increased through greater involvement of fishermen in the management of the CFP. In order to ensure more effective conservation of stocks seven Regional Advisory Councils (RACs) were to be set up to allow fishermen, scientists and other stakeholders to work together at the regional or local level. RACs were to cover areas under the responsibility of at least two member states, and to co-operate with the Commission and member states in the planning and implementation of CFP measures.

From 2007 the European Fisheries Fund (EFF) replaced the Financial Instrument for Fisheries Guidance (FIFG). Fisheries were allocated €0.9 billion in the 2008 EU budget (out of a total of €129.1 billion) and €4.3 billion for the 2007–2013 financial perspective.

An EU strategy has been adopted to strengthen the role of aquaculture in ways that limit damage to the environment and ensure safe and good quality products. The aim is to create between 8000 and 10 000 jobs over the 2003–2008 period. To meet demand for fish the Commission has estimated that acquaculture would have to double by 2030.

Criticisms of the Common Fisheries Policy

The 2001 Green Paper of the Commission carried out a detailed analysis of fisheries in the EU and indicated the main shortcomings of the CFP in conservation, economic and political terms.[6]

With regard to **conservation**, many stocks of fish are outside safe biological levels, and this situation has not been resolved by the 2002 reform. In 2007 a report by independent experts to

[6] European Commission 2001.

the Commission maintained that that 80 per cent of species in EU waters were over-fished compared with 25 per cent worldwide.[7] Over-capacity of the EU fleet, failure to stand up to special interests, and poor enforcement of decisions contributed to this situation.

The Council of Ministers systematically fixed quotas at levels higher than indicated by scientific advice. The main provider of information on marine biology to the EU, the International Council for the Exploration of the Seas (ICES), and the Scientific, Technical, Economic Committee on Fisheries (STECF) warned the European Commission of the risk of a complete collapse in cod stocks with no eventual recovery (as occurred for cod on Canada's Grand Banks off Newfoundland) and recommended a total ban on cod fishing. The Council of Ministers agreed a multi-annual recovery plan for cod, hake and plaice, which entailed lower annual catches, new restrictions on days at sea and tighter policing.[8] By 2007 the situation for North Sea cod had improved leading to an increase in the TAC by 11 per cent in 2008, though days at sea were to be cut by 10 per cent.

In *economic terms*, the EU fisheries sector has been characterized for many years by falling employment and rising costs. The 2002 reform aimed at ensuring that structural policies do not add to over-capacity (which had not always been the case in the past), but improved technology such as sonar has meant that the capacity to catch fish is rising more rapidly than their ability to reproduce. It is difficult to understand the economic rationale for continuing price support in a situation of over-capacity.

Politically the 2001 Green Paper criticized the CFP for shortcomings in enforcement and compliance, and even after the 2002 reform the situation seems little improved.[9] Member states are largely responsible for ensuring application of the CFP in their waters, and the stringency of monitoring and sanctions is generally low, but varies considerably among countries. Even when a member state was found not to be respecting its obligations, there was often a significant time lag before legal action was taken.[10] In 2007 the European Court of Auditors found that quotas were not been properly monitored, and illegal fishing was only lightly punished. The Auditors carried out spot checks in 6 countries with large fleets: the UK, Spain, France, Denmark, Italy and the Netherlands, and found that unreliable statistics on catches and discards were being supplied, while underreporting by up to a third was commonplace.[11] In 2007 the Commission launched legal proceedings against all the EU Mediterranean member states for exceeding blue fin tuna quotas, and maintains that the stock is close to collapse. In response the Council agreed a bluefin tuna recovery programme.

Political discontent with the CFP also arose from the allocation of quotas among member states and, in particular, from the practice of 'quota-hopping'. Taking advantage of the EU right to freedom of establishment, many vessel operators were able to purchase or reregister vessels and thereby acquire fishing rights in another member state. It is estimated that Spanish companies managed to acquire fishing rights over 100 UK, 28 Irish and 25 French vessels, while

---

[7] As reported in *Financial Times*, 27/9/2007.

[8] For instance the initial Commission proposal for 2003 entailed a reduction of 80 per cent in cod fishing mortality, but the final Council agreement entailed a cut in allowable catches of only 45 per cent.

[9] In 2007 the EU budget allocated about €46 million to enforcement compared with €837 million in aid to the fishing industry.

[10] For instance, the Court of Justice ruled against the UK in 1999 for infringements in 1985–88 and 1990 on the grounds of failure to carry out inspections and close fisheries once the catch quota had been taken. The Court simply declared that the UK had failed to respect its commitments and was required to pay court costs. Again in 2002 the Court dealt with UK infringements relating to the 1985–96 period (Valatin, 2001).

[11] It was estimated that Spain had caught 169 000 more tonnes of fish in 2005 that it had reported to the Commission.

Dutch companies accounted for 30 UK, 33 German, 11 Belgian, 1 French and 1 Danish vessel (Hoefnagel, 1998; see also Table 13.1 above).

Fishing generally accounts for less than 1 per cent of GDP in the member states, and employed about 229 702 fishermen in the EU(25),[12] with a further 1.5 million in associated industries. However, in certain regions, such as the Atlantic coast of Spain and the east coast of Italy and of Scotland, fishing accounts for about 10 per cent of employment. The fishing industry would have declined even without the CFP in many of those regions, but in some areas, notably the British ports, EU measures were blamed (in particular the policy of allowing access to fishermen from other countries, quotas, limits on days at sea, and the uneven application of rules), and there were calls for an opt-out of the CFP.

Effective monitoring and control is necessary to prevent over-fishing, but 'co-operation between national authorities', scoreboards and limited increases in EU surveillance as introduced by the 2002 reform seem rather weak instruments to resolve this question.

Evaluation

The December 2002 reform represents a step in the right direction, but so far does not seem to have resolved the shortcomings of the CFP. Even the substantial reduction in quotas and limitations on days at sea seem too little and too late to ensure conservation of certain fish stocks, in particular, as enforcement is weak. Over-capacity of the EU fleet has to be corrected, but this requires an integrated approach to the fishing-dependent regions of the EU, with active measures to reduce capacity and encourage employment in alternative occupations. Past experience illustrates the difficulties the EU is likely to encounter in agreeing effective measures with third countries to combat the depletion of fish stocks at a global level. Encouraging the development of aquaculture seems a promising development, but far more attention will have to be paid to the environmental implications. Even after the 2002 reform it seems likely that further efforts to improve the transparency, conservation, compliance and performance of the CFP will prove necessary.

Summary of Key Concepts

- Public intervention to control fisheries is generally justified on the grounds that the sea and the fish stock can be regarded as an example of **common property.**
- Differences between the member states meant that the Common Fisheries Policy was not set up until 1970, and only became fully operative from 1983.
- The **instruments of the CFP** agreed in 1983 were: access arrangements, quotas or total allowable catches (TACs), market support measures and structural policies.
- **The 2002 Reform of the Common Fisheries Polic**y involved: a long-term approach to ensure the conservation of stocks, a new policy for the fleet to reduce over-capacity, better application of the rules and increased involvement of shareholders.
- Among the **criticisms of the CFP** is its insufficiency to guarantee conservation since many stocks of fish are outside safe biological levels. In economic terms, the EU fisheries sector is characterized by over-capacity, low productivity and falling employment. Politically the CFP has experienced shortcomings in enforcement and compliance.

[12]European Commission (2007).

Questions for study and review

1 What do we mean by the problem of 'commons', and how does it apply to fisheries?

2 How has the Common Fisheries Policy evolved over the years?

3 What measures should be taken to ensure conservation of fish stocks?

4 What are the advantages and disadvantages of developing aquaculture?

References

European Commission (2001) 'Green Paper on the future of the Common Fisheries Policy', www. ec.europa.eu/fisheries

European Commission (2006) Employment in the fisheries sector: Current situation', www. ec.europa.eu/fisheries

European Commission (2007) Facts and Figures on the CFP. Basic data on the Common Fisheries Policy, 2007 Edition.

Hardin, G. (1968) 'The tragedy of the commons', *Science*, Vol. 162, pp. 1243–7.

Hoefnagel, E. (1998) 'Legal but controversial: Quota-hopping, the CFP and the Treaty of Rome', in Symes, D. (ed.) *Property Rights and Regulatory Systems in Fisheries*, Fishing News Books, Oxford.

Stiglitz, J.E. (2002) *Economics of the Public Sector*, 3rd edn, W.W. Norton & Co., London and New York.

Valatin, G. (2001) 'Solving the "tragedy" of the Common Fisheries Policy: What role for economic instruments?' Paper presented at the XIIIth Annual Conference of the European Association of Fisheries Economists, Salerno, Italy, 18–20 April.

Useful websites

The European Commission provides background information and documents relating to the key aspects of the CFP:

www.ec.europa.eu/fisheries

European Court of Auditors has published reports critical of the functioning of the CFP:

www.eca.europa.eu

The European Parliament regularly discusses fisheries issues:

www.europarl.europa.eu

The UK Department of the Environment, Food and Rural Affairs:

www.defra.gov.uk

The International Council for Exploration of the Sea:

www.ices.dk

The World Wildlife Fund:

www.wwf.org

CHAPTER 14

Environmental and Energy Policies

❖ *LEARNING OBJECTIVES*

By the end of this chapter you should be able to understand:

- ❖ The economic basis of environmental policy;

- ❖ The main instruments used in environmental policy;

- ❖ How EU measures have evolved over the years;

- ❖ The five principles of EU environmental policy;

- ❖ The role of the European Environmental Agency (EEA);

- ❖ The international dimension of EU environmental policy, in particular with regard to the Kyoto Protocol;

- ❖ The main features of the EU energy market;

- ❖ The evolution of EU energy policy.

Introduction

During the German Presidency of 2007 Angela Merkel singled out environmental policy as a way of re-launching the integration process, announcing that the EU was at the vanguard of the battle against climate change. The choice seemed strategic as a way of injecting new adrenaline into the EU fifty years after its foundation: environmental measures are widely favoured by the public, and action at the regional or national level is generally not considered effective. According to a Eurobarometer survey of June 2007,[1] 69 per cent of EU citizens would like to see protection of the environment dealt with at the EU level, while 88 per cent affirmed that the EU should deal with global warming as a matter of urgency. Eighty-nine per cent of the same poll unequivocally welcomed EU policies to reduce greenhouse gases by 20 per cent by 2020. European Union initiatives may act as an incentive to reaching agreement at a wider international level, and may also act as a way of increasing the weight of the EU as a global actor.

After a slow start, since the early 1970s the EU has developed a wide range of environmental

---

[1] Eurobarometer (2007). According to a survey carried out in Eurobarometer (2003), the causes of environmental degradation most worrying EU citizens were nuclear disasters (50 per cent) and industrial disasters (45 per cent). Air pollution, natural disasters, water pollution and the elimination of tropical rainforests were also high on the list of concerns and were quoted by between 41 per cent and 44 per cent of respondents.

policies. The main stepping stones in the development of EU environmental policy include the introduction of six Environmental Action Programmes (EAPs), successive Treaty changes increasing the EU role in environmental issues, and the creation of a European Environmental Agency in Copenhagen in 1994. The EU and its member states operate a common negotiating position on environmental issues at an international level.

Environmental and energy policies are closely linked, in particular, in the task of tackling climate change. Energy policy also returned to centre stage in the integration process in recent years, with a renewed effort to tackle national champions and complete the Internal Market in this sector. With the Lisbon Treaty for the first time the treaties would contain a section on energy. This sets out the objective of ensuring proper functioning of the energy market, including promotion of energy efficiency, increasing the security of energy supply and the development of new and renewable forms of energy.

This chapter first sets out the economic basis of public intervention and the various types of instrument used in environmental policy, before describing the various EU measures, with particular reference to the policies with regard to climate change. Then follows an analysis of the EU energy market, and a description of the evolution of EU energy policy, focusing on recent developments.

The economic basis of environmental policy

The economic basis of environmental policy can be explained with the help of Figure 14.1.[2] In the figure there are two horizontal axes. The higher axis indicates the level of output Q of a firm that pollutes. The lower axis shows the level of pollution or waste associated with each level of

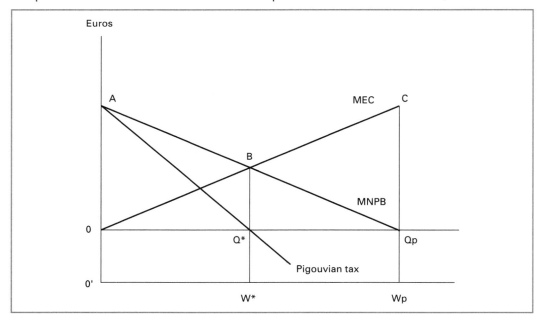

FIGURE 14.1 The optimum level of pollution

Source: Figure 9.1 (p. 217) from The Economics of the European Union 3/e (2003) by Artis, M. and Nixson, F., by permission of Oxford University Press.

[2] The explanation here is based on Pearce (2003).

output. It is assumed that as the level of output Q increases, so too does the level of pollution W. One of the main aims of environmental policy is to 'decouple' negative environmental effects from the level of economic activity.

The vertical axis indicates money units or euros. The line MNPB sloping downwards from A to Qp shows the marginal net private benefit to a firm, or the additional profit on an extra unit of output. As output increases, the marginal net private benefit is assumed to fall, finally reaching zero at Qp. The area under the MNPB line gives total profits, so at Qp the firm maximizes profits. Wp is the level of pollution associated with Qp, the profit-maximizing level of output for the firm.

The pollution causes externalities to third parties. An externality in production occurs when the activity of a firm has an unintended impact on the utility or production function of another individual or firm. The externality may be positive or negative. The diagram here illustrates the situation for negative externalities, such as the impact of the firm polluting water or the air on others. The marginal external cost line MEC shows the additional damage to third parties from each extra unit of pollution. The MEC line slopes up from O to C in the diagram because it is assumed that each extra unit of pollution will cause more damage (though in practice the line may take various shapes). The marginal external cost is also measured in money units, or euros.

The diagram can be used to show the optimum level of pollution from the point of view of society as a whole. If a firm aims at maximizing profits, and fails to take into account the effect of its pollution on others, it will produce at Qp with total profits of OAQp. However, at Qp the total external cost of the pollution on others is OCQp. The overall impact on society (i.e. taking into account the impact on the firm and on those suffering the pollution) will therefore be a net gain of OAB and a cost of BCQp[3] This is not an optimum, because it fails to maximize the gains to society as a whole.

The optimum level of output is at output Q* with a waste level W*, where the net gain to society OAB is at a maximum. At levels of output below Q*, the net marginal private benefit to the firm is greater than the marginal external cost (the MNPB line is above the MEC line), so the net social gain could be increased by expanding output. At levels of output above Q*, the MEC line is higher then the MNPB line, so the total gain to society could be increased by cutting output. It is important to note that the optimum level of pollution is not zero since society would forgo the gain OAB. The 'optimum' from the point of view of Economics may therefore differ from that of ecologists who set an intrinsic value on aspects of the environment such as biodiversity or continuation of the species even if no humans are involved.

The problem then becomes how to ensure that the firm will produce at level of output Q*, and this can be achieved in various ways:

■ Bargaining can occur between the firm and those suffering from pollution in situations where the firm is given the right to pollute.[4] As long as the marginal external cost to sufferers is greater than the net marginal benefit to the firm (i.e. the MEC line is above the MNPB line), those suffering from pollution will have an incentive to pay the firm to cut back pollution, and the firm will have an incentive to accept those payments. These payments will continue until the marginal external cost equals the marginal net private benefit (i.e. the MEC line intersects the MNPB line), which occurs at level of output Q*. In practice high transaction costs may prevent bargaining between sufferers and the firm reaching the optimal level of pollution. There may also be a tendency for individuals suffering from pol-

---

[3] From the point of view of society, the benefit of OBQp to the firm and the cost OBQp of pollution on others cancel out.

[4] The classic article by Coase (1960) provides the framework for this type of analysis.

lution to 'free ride' and not pay their contribution to stop the firm polluting, in particular if the sufferers are numerous. Individual sufferers assume that their non-payment to the firm will not be noticed and that others will bear the cost of inducing the firm to cut production and pollution.

■ In the absence of transaction costs, bargaining between the firm and those suffering from pollution will also lead to the optimum level of output Q* in situations where the firm is obliged to pay compensation for pollution. Starting from a level of output O, the firm will have an incentive to pay compensation to those suffering from pollution as long as the marginal net private benefit of the firm is higher than the marginal external cost (i.e. the MNPB line is above the MEC line), and this is the case up until level of output Q*.

■ The government may prohibit firms from emitting more than a certain level of pollution, or require them to use a particular technology, and impose sanctions (such as fines) on firms failing to comply with the legislation. This type of intervention is usually called 'command and control' (see below), though strictly the term entails the government fixing both the level of pollution and the means of achieving this goal as is usually the case in fixing technology requirements. To achieve the optimum level of pollution, the government would fix the level of pollution at W*.

■ The government may require the firm to pay a tax equal to the marginal external cost. This is called a 'Pigouvian tax' after the economist Alfred Pigou who first proposed this type of tax and is shown by the dotted line in Figure 14.1. At each level of output, the MNPB line of the firm is reduced by an amount equal to the MEC.[5] The firm will have an incentive to produce at Q*, because this is the level of output which maximizes output after tax.

In practice it is difficult to calculate the level of a Pigouvian tax, so they are not frequently used. However, other kinds of taxes and subsidies are often used to promote environmental objectives. For example, landfill taxes tax waste going to landfills to encourage more efficient means of waste disposal. These are forms of market-based instruments and offer firms financial incentives or penalties to encourage them to realize the objective.

Instruments of environmental policy

In general environmental measures may be divided into three broad categories, though in practice the distinction between these categories is not always absolutely clear:

1. 'Command and control' entails introducing legislation to fix norms and environmental standards that have to be complied with. These may take the form of the prohibition of certain products or substances, or emission standards combined with requirements to use certain types of technology. Strictly the term 'command and control' entails public intervention to fix both the level of pollution and the means of achieving this goal, but in practice the term is often used more widely. The Community relied heavily on 'command and control' in the early years of its environment policy, and an example of the approach was the strict standards for the quality of drinking water introduced in the 1970s and 1980s which included measures relating to the discharge of dangerous substances into rivers and seas.

2. Market-based instruments set standards (in theory on the basis of an analysis of the costs and benefits involved) and offer firms a financial incentive or penalty to encourage them to

---

[5] In other words, the vertical distance from the horizontal axis to the MEC line is subtracted from the vertical distance from the horizontal axis to the MNPB line.

realize the objectives. These instruments give a firm a choice of how to reduce pollution. Examples of market-based instruments include charges on emissions, products and users; environmentally related taxes (see below); subsidies to encourage environmentally friendly production methods (which, as described in Chapter 12, are widely used in the CAP), and tradable permits. Tradable or transferable permits involve the authority issuing a number of permits to pollute and allowing firms to trade these permits. Tradable permits are widely used in the USA. In the past the EU tended to rely more on environmental taxes and subsidies, but, as explained below, from 2005 an Emissions Trading Scheme was introduced.

3. Voluntary agreements (in general between some public authority and private enterprise) may be introduced to encourage environmentally friendly measures. An example of an EU measure of this type is the Environmental Management and Audit Scheme (EMAS).[6] According to this scheme a firm voluntarily chooses to introduce an environmental programme, which is subject to external audit and publication of the results. The firm may gain from increased competitiveness and an improved image with clients, suppliers and public institutions.

The evolution of EU environmental policy

The number and variety of instruments now used in EU environmental policy render their description difficult. However, in recent years there has been a growing tendency to use market-based instruments rather than the strategy of 'command and control'. Such instruments generally involve lower implementation costs than command and control.

There is no mention of a role for the Community in the Treaty of Rome, reflecting the rather low priority given to such questions at the time, and creating difficulties in finding a legal basis for Community initiatives for some years. Though some environmental measures were implemented at a national level by the member states, it was not until the early 1970s that environmental objectives appear on the Community agenda.

According to Pearce (2003), the 1972 study by the Club of Rome, 'Limits to growth', marks a growing international awareness of environmental questions. This study drew attention to the limits of natural resources and of the Earth to absorb waste. In the same year at the Paris Summit the EC member states called for environmental issues to be included in the Community agenda.

In 1973 the Community embarked on the first of what are now six EAPs. These are indicative programmes, even though many of their guidelines were subsequently translated into Community legislation.

The First EAP covered the period 1973–76 and set out the general principles and goals of environmental policy.[7] In order to achieve these objectives the First EAP attempted to increase awareness of environmental problems, conduct impact studies, reduce pollution and improve waste management (see Box 14.1).

The following three EAPs (1977–81, 1982–87 and 1987–92) were mainly concerned with consolidating the aims of the First EAP. Given the limited success of these programmes, the Fifth EAP (1993–2000) reflected a change in approach with a shift to emphasis on prevention rather than correction of the damage, and from the top-down 'command and control' approach

---

[6] Introduced in 1993 with Regulation 1836/93 and updated in 2001 with Regulation 761/2001.

[7] These included the first four of the five principles subsequently included in the Maastricht Treaty, as described below.

Box 14.1: *EU policy towards waste*

Each year the EU throws away roughly 1.3 billion tonnes of waste, 40 million tonnes of which is hazardous. According to European Environment Agency, this amounts to 3.5 tonnes per person. In addition there is a further 700 million tonnes of agricultural waste. EU municipal waste is burnt in incinerators (18 per cent), recycled or composted (33 per cent), or dumped in landfill sites (49 per cent). Landfilling occupies land space and discharges chemicals such as carbon dioxide and methane into the atmosphere, and chemicals and pesticides into the soil and groundwater. Landfills are becoming so difficult to site that the term 'NIMBY' or 'not in my back yard' has been coined.

The approach of the EU to waste management is based on three principles:

- **Prevention of waste** This includes improving production techniques and encouraging consumers to use more environmentally friendly goods and less packaging.

- **Recycling and reuse** EU Directives require member states to introduce legislation on waste collection, reuse and recycling.

- **Improving final disposal and monitoring** Where possible waste should be incinerated, and landfills should only be used as a last resort. The EU has introduced a Directive on landfill management, which bans certain types of waste such as used tyres.

The statistics in this box are taken from www.ec.europa.eu/environment/waste and wwweuropa.eu/scadplus/leg

based on regulatory legislation to a bottom-up approach based on a wider range of policies, in particular on market-based instruments involving a larger number of socioeconomic actors.

The Sixth EAP, 'Environment 2010: Our future, our choice', covers the 2001–10 period and aims at using a wide range of instruments to influence decisions made by 'business, consumers, policy-planners and citizens'.[8] This is to be achieved by:

- improving the implementation of existing legislation;
- integrating environmental concerns into other policies;
- working closer with the market;
- empowering people as private citizens and helping them to change behaviour; and
- taking account of the environment in land-use planning and management decisions.

The programme identifies four priority areas:

1. climate change;
2. nature and biodiversity;
3. environment and health (see Box 14.2); and
4. management of natural resources and waste.

It is difficult to imagine a wider agenda, and the European Commission has at times been criticized for being too ambitious in setting objectives.

---

[8] The Sixth EAP, 'Environment 2010: Our future, our choice', http://europa.eu.int/scadplus/leg/en/lvb/128027

Box 14.2: *The REACH legislation*

In 2006, after much controversy, Regulation 1907/2006 on REACH or Registration, Evaluation, Authorisation and Restriction of Chemical Substances was passed. This requires manufacturers and importers to gather information on chemicals used in their products, and to register some 30 000 substances in a central database of the European Chemicals Agency in Helsinki. The Agency will help in the better and earlier identification of the intrinsic properties of chemical substances, and in the co-ordination of in-depth analysis of potentially dangerous chemicals. The Regulation requires progressive substitution of the most dangerous chemicals when alternatives have been identified. The REACH legislation was drawn up on the basis of extensive consultation with stakeholders, and will be phased in over 11 years. As a result of intensive lobbying by industry, numerous exceptions were allowed, and the list of hazardous substances for which alternatives should be found was reduced to 1500–2000. According to the European Commission, the cost to industry of abiding by the Regulation could be in the order of €2.6–5.2 billion over 11 years, but by reducing exposure to hazardous materials savings in health care could be as much as €50 billion over the next 30 years.*

* As reported in *The Economist*, 26 November 2005

Environmental policy in the Treaties

The first explicit statutory mandate in the Treaties for Community environmental policy came in 1987 with the Single European Act. The Maastricht Treaty strengthened the role of the EU in environmental policy, and revised Article 2 of the Treaty of Rome, which sets out the objectives of the Community. The expression 'continuous and balanced expansion' was replaced with 'sustainable and non-inflationary growth respecting the environment'.

The Treaty of Amsterdam again changed the wording of Article 2 of the EC Treaty. The rather imprecise concept of 'sustainable growth respecting the environment' was replaced by 'sustainable development', though again the concept was not defined in the Treaty. The concept of sustainable development was raised in the UN Bruntland Report of 1987 and is generally interpreted to mean economic and social development that is sustained over time. As a result future generations will have more assets per capita than the present generation. The assets in question are capital (plant and machinery), human capital (the stock of knowledge and skills), natural capital (the environment yields flows of services over time) and social capital (relations between people and between people and institutions). If the total stock of these assets per capita increases over time, development is said to be sustainable, even though environmental damage may be increasing. In 2001 the European Council adopted the EU Sustainable Development Strategy, which has the long-run aim of combining a dynamic economy with social cohesion and high environmental standards.

Building on earlier Treaties, the Treaty of Nice confirmed:

- environmental mainstreaming, which requires environmental issues to be taken into account in defining and implementing all EU policies. The Cardiff Process (named after the European Council of 1998) implements Article 6 of the EC Treaty, by obliging the different Councils to integrate environmental considerations into their activities;
- the objectives of environmental policy;

- the principles of EU environmental policy; and
- the requisites the EU must take into account in developing environmental policy.

The objectives of EU environmental policy entail: preserving, protecting and improving the quality of the environment; protecting human health; prudent and rational utilization of resources, and promoting measures at international level to deal with regional or worldwide environmental problems.

The Maastricht Treaty confirmed the four principles of Community environmental policy that had been set out in the Single European Act and added a fifth, the precautionary principle, so that the principles of EU environmental policy became:

- **The principle of prevention.** Prevention is preferable to correction of damage.
- **The polluter pays principle.** The polluter should bear the cost of prevention and correction of the damage.
- **The principle of correction at source.** As a priority actions in one member state should not be allowed to affect the environment in another member state.
- **The principle of subsidiarity.**
- **The precautionary principle.** The precautionary principle implies that lack of scientific evidence linking cause and effect should not be deemed sufficient reason to take no action when there are considered to be significant risks.[9]

Assessment of environmental policy may be carried out on the basis of cost/benefit analysis. This entails a formal comparison of the costs and benefits of a policy (or investment). The assessment may, for example, consist of a formal appraisal of the expenditure involved in adapting to the legislation, an estimate of the risks associated with the pollution addressed and an analysis of how effective the measure is likely to prove in practice. A policy should only be introduced where the expected benefits exceed the costs and, where different policies are being compared, that producing the highest net benefits should be chosen. In assessing the effectiveness of environmental measures, account has not only to be taken of their impact on the environment, but also their economic and equity implications.

The Maastricht Treaty required EU environmental measures to take into account the potential benefits and costs of action or lack of action (Article 130R). Though this has been interpreted as not necessarily requiring a fully-fledged cost/benefit analysis before introducing EU measures, some form of assessment is necessary. It is only since the early 1990s that the Commission has begun to use cost/benefit analysis in a routine way. The Amsterdam Treaty required the Commission to prepare assessments of the environmental impact for policy proposals with significant environmental implications, and this involves taking account of:

- available scientific and technical data;
- environmental conditions in the various regions of the Community;
- the potential benefits and costs of action or lack of action;
- the economic and social development of the Community as a whole and the balanced development of its regions.

---

[9] The precautionary principle is taken up again in Chapter 18.

The European Environment Agency

Situated in Copenhagen, the EEA came into operation in 1994. The aim of the Agency is to support sustainable development and to help achieve a significant and measurable improvement in Europe's environment through the provision of information to policy-making agents and to the public. The EEA is at the centre of the European Environmental Information and Observation Network (Eionet). Eionet is composed of national institutes in Europe through which it collects and disseminates environment-related information and data. The EEA is a Community body open to other members, and in 2007 had 32 member states.

The international dimension

Since pollution is an international phenomenon, EU policy also has a wider dimension. The EU (the member states and European Commission acting collectively as a negotiating bloc) takes part in global attempts to tackle transnational environmental problems such as the ozone layer, climate change and the depletion of tropical rainforests.[10]

In 1987 the Community signed the Montreal Protocol aimed at reducing depletion of the ozone layer. Among the main causes of ozone depletion were CFCs (chlorofluorocarbons) which were used in refrigerators, spray cans and air conditioning (see Box 14.3). In 1985 a hole in the ozone layer had been noted over the Antarctic. A thinner ozone layer allows more UV-Bs to pass through, increasing the risks of skin cancer and premature ageing of skin. International compliance with the Montreal and subsequent CFC protocols succeeded in reducing the use of CFCs, also because relatively cheap substitutes were generally available. However, the process of halting ozone depletion is also slow because of the existing levels of ozone-depleting chemicals in the stratosphere.

Box 14.3: *Ozone depletion*

In the 1930s the Dupont Corporation, one of the oldest chemical firms in the USA, developed a new form of chemical refrigerant. This relied on simple chemicals containing chlorine, fluorine and carbon, hence the name CFCs. CFCs are non-toxic stable substances which functioned significantly better than earlier substances used as refrigerants such as ammonia.

CFCs (together with halons) are referred to as 'ozone-depleting' substances. They may accidentally escape and disperse into the troposphere, and because they are stable, they may persist in the troposphere long enough to escape into the stratosphere. In the stratosphere these substances may react with ozone under the influence of intense solar radiation.

Initially the Dupont Corporation denied that there was a scientific connection between CFCs and the ozone layer. In 1983 the US Academy of Sciences released a report illustrating that CFCs had contributed to ozone depletion. Based on the Report, Dupont agreed to reduce CFC production, and in 1987 announced its commitment to developing ozone-friendly substitutes for CFCs.

---

[10]The EU has also played an active role in noise abatement policies related to aircraft noise. The unilateral ban in the past on hush-kitted aircraft in the EU was a major source of tension with the USA.

In 1992 at the Earth Summit at Rio de Janeiro two international agreements were signed: the Convention on Biological Diversity and the United Nations Framework Convention on Climate Change (UNFCCC). In 1997 the Kyoto Protocol to the UNFCCC was agreed. Under the Kyoto Protocol countries are required to limit or reduce their emissions of six greenhouse gases (see Box 14.4).

Box 14.4: *Climate change*

Climate change refers not just to global warming but also to more extreme weather events such as more frequent storms, floods, droughts and heat waves. Possible effects include: changes in rainfall putting pressure on water resources in many regions and leading to desertification in southern European areas; melting snow and ice (with also glaciers in retreat) causing a rise in sea levels and creating difficulties for coastal areas, and geographical shifts in the occurrence of different species and/or the extinction of certain species.

Greenhouse gases such as carbon dioxide (CO_2), methane (CH_4), nitrous oxide (N_2O), hydrofluorocarbons (HFC), perfluorocarbons (PFC) and sulphur hexafluoride (SF_6) can contribute to global warming. When visible light is scattered and absorbed at the Earth's surface it changes into heat, part of which is trapped in the lower atmosphere by gases such as CO_2 and then reradiated back to the surface of the Earth. Carbon dioxide accounts for 55–60 per cent of present heat-trapping gases and is the main worry of policy makers. The quantity of CO_2 in the atmosphere has increased as a result of the combustion of oil, gas and coal, and also because of reduced absorption arising from deforestation, in particular in tropical areas.

The Intergovernmental Panel on Climate Control (IPCC) probably reflects the most authoritative global scientific consensus on climate change, and in 2007 won the Nobel Peace Prize together with Al Gore and his film 'An Inconvenient Truth'. The IPCC presented its Fourth Assessment Report in 2007. According to the Report, the Earth's average temperature has risen by 0.76 degrees Celsius since 1850, with Europe warming faster than average, by about one degree Celsius. Fifteen of the hottest years on record occurred in the last 20 years. Assuming that no further action is taken to reduce emissions, the average temperature could rise by between 1.8 and 4.0 degrees centigrade this century. Though it is difficult to isolate the effect of greenhouse gases from other factors having an impact on climate change, or the long-term natural variability of climate, there is growing consensus among the world's leading scientists that human activity has contributed to climate change. The IPCC Report suggests a 90 per cent probability that increased man-made emissions have caused most of the temperature rise since the mid-twentieth century. Even the lower end of the range predicted by the IPCC would take the temperature increase to above 2 degrees since pre-industrial times, the threshold beyond which strong scientific evidence indicates that the risk of irreversible and possibly catastrophic changes greatly increases. It is projected that global warming could cause a further rise in sea levels by between 18 and 59 mm this century, though this could be an underestimate as it fails to take full account of changes in ice flows.

One of the more controversial aspects of the climate change debate is that it might cost more for some countries (such as the USA or Japan) to cut carbon dioxide emissions than to adapt to climate change. Moreover, powerful lobbies are opposed to reduction in carbon dioxide emissions and the reduced energy consumption it implies. It is sometimes argued that certain countries such as Russia and Canada might benefit from global warning, but this view probably fails to take full account of the possibility of more extreme weather events.

The economic costs of climate change and the economic advantages of taking early preventative action were set out in the Stern Review (Stern, 2006), commissioned by the UK Government. According to the Review, without further action to limit emissions, climate change could reduce global GDP by between 5 and 20 per cent a year. The Review estimated that early action to stabilize greenhouse gas emissions to prevent climate change reaching dangerous proportions could cost about one per cent of GDP. The Stern Review was criticized on three main counts: overestimation of the economic costs of global warming; underestimation of the costs of mitigating action, and the discount rate used for comparing present costs of mitigating action to the long-term costs of continuing with present action was said to be wrong.* The debate over the Review confirmed the difficulty of evaluation of the losses from climate change, but added to the growing consensus on the need for present action.**

*See, for example, Nordhaus (2006) or Dasgupta (2006) on this debate.

**For dissenting views see Lomborg (2001) or Lawson (2008).

The Kyoto Protocol entered into force in February 2005. To come into effect the Protocol had to be ratified by developed countries emitting more than 55 per cent of greenhouse gases in the world, and with the ratification in 2004 by Russia (under EU pressure) that threshold was crossed. Emerging economies such as China and India were exempt from the Protocol, and it has not been ratified by the USA. The USA did, however, embark on a campaign to encourage research into improved technology such as carbon sequestration and began to sign bilateral international deals on climate change, but many observers criticized these moves as inadequate. Some individual states in the USA have started moving towards binding emission limits, and California is also considering the possibility of moving to an EU-style emissions trading system (see below). With the change in government Australia ratified the Protocol in December 2007.

The EU(15) countries that were member states at the time of ratification of the Kyoto Protocol in 2002 agreed to cut their emissions to 8 per cent below base year levels (generally 1990) between 2008 and 2012. The target set out under the Kyoto Protocol is for the EU as a whole, and the EU Burden Sharing Agreement allows some countries to increase emissions provided these are offset by reductions in other member states. The Community must ensure that the actions of the member states are consistent with the Protocol. If a party fails to meet its emissions target the Kyoto Protocol requires it to make up the difference in the second commitment period (after 2012), with an additional 30 per cent penalty. The Commission called for the development of a strategy in all sectors that produce pollution (energy, transport, agriculture, industry, etc.), and the introduction of an effective monitoring system.

Monitoring data suggests that the EU(15) member states that ratified the Protocol will meet their targets, though there are considerable differences in performance between countries (see Table 14.1). In the CEECs emissions fell after 1989, largely because of the decline in heavy industries. Cyprus and Malta do not have Kyoto targets, but the other new member states have individual reduction commitments of 6–8 per cent.

In 2012 Kyoto's targets expire and after that date a new initiative will be needed to limit global warming. In June 2007, as host of the G-8 summit, the German Chancellor, Angela Merkel, was instrumental in enabling the G-8 to pledge to begin discussions on a successor to the Kyoto Protocol after 2012 (see Box 14.5). In a speech of 2001 President Bush had questioned

	2005	target		2005	target
EU (25)	92.1	N/a	Netherlands	98.9	87.0
EU(15)	98.0	92.0	Austria	118.1	87.0
Belgium	97.9	92.5	Poland	68.0	94.0
Bulgaria	52.8	92.0	Portugal	140.4	127.0
Czech R.	74.2	92.0	Romania	54.4	92.0
Denmark	92.2	79.0	Slovenia	100.4	92.0
Germany	81.3	79.0	Slovakia	66.4	92.0
Estonia	48.0	92.0	Finland	97.4	100.0
Ireland	125.4	113.0	Sweden	92.6	104.0
Greece	125.4	125.0	UK	84.3	87.5
Spain	152.3	115.0			
France	98.1	100.0	Croatia	95.5	95.0
Italy	112.1	93.5	Turkey	184.0	N/a
Cyprus	163.7	N/a			
Latvia	42.0	92.0	USA	116.3	N/a
Lithuania	46.9	72.0	Japan	107.8	94.0
Luxembourg	100.4	72.0			
Hungary	65.5	94.0			
Malta	154.8	N/a			

TABLE 14.1 Greenhouse gas emissions, 2005

In general the base year is 1990 for the non-fluorinated gases (carbon dioxide (CO_2) methane (CH_4), nitrous oxide (N_2O),) and 1995 for the fluorinated gases (HFC, PFC and SF_6). Data exclude emissions due to land use change and forestry.

N/a: not applicable.

Source: Eurostat 'Total greenhouse gas emissions', © European Communities, 2008, http://eurostat.ec.europa.ec

the science of global warming, and had subsequently blocked proposals to begin negotiating on a Kyoto successor. At the G-8 Summit President Bush promised that the USA would 'be actively involved, if not taking the lead, in a post-Kyoto framework, post-Kyoto agreement'. In October 2007 he acknowledged climate change as 'one of the greatest challenges of our time' and called for long-term goals to cut emissions (though no timescale was given, and opposition to an emissions trading scheme was expressed).[11]

In December 2007 at the UN climate change conference in Bali a timetable was agreed to complete the negotiations of a post-2012 global climate change agreement in Copenhagen in December 2009. At Bali a roadmap setting out the key areas to be addressed in the negotiations was also agreed. The conference also decided to launch a UN fund to help poor countries adapt to the effects of climate change such as droughts and flooding.

[11] *Financial Times*, 2 October 2007.

Box 14.5: *Key Dates In The Debate On Climate Change*

1988 The UN forms the International Panel on Climate Change (IPCC).

1992 At the Earth Summit at Rio de Janeiro the United Nations Framework Convention on Climate Change (UNFCCC) was signed.

1997 The Kyoto Protocol to the UNFCCC was signed.

2005 The Kyoto Protocol came into effect.

2005–2007 The first phase of the Emission Trading Scheme of the EU.

2007 The IPCC presented its Fourth Assessment Report warning of the consequences of climate change unless emissions peak in 2015–2020.

March 2007 Under the German Presidency the European Council agrees to cut emissions by 20 per cent by 2020 compared to 1990 levels.

June 2007 The G-8 (including the USA) pledge to begin discussions on a successor to the Kyoto Protocol after 2012.

2007 Following the change in government Australia decides to ratify the Kyoto Protocol.

December 2007 The UN climate change conference in Bali agreed a timetable to complete the negotiations of a post-2012 global climate change agreement in Copenhagen in December 2009.

2008–2012 The second phase of the Emission Trading Scheme of the EU.

The EU Emissions Trading Scheme

A core element of the EU's efforts to meet its Kyoto objectives is the Community Emissions Trading Scheme (ETS or 'carbon trading'), which was introduced from 2005. This was the first and to date largest emissions trading scheme in the world, and applies in the 27 member states and in the three countries of the European Economic Area: Norway, Iceland and Liechtenstein.

At present under this 'cap and trade' system member states set a national allocation plan or 'cap' on carbon dioxide emissions from what are now over 10 000 energy-intensive plants (power plants, steel factories, oil refineries, paper mills, glass and cement producers and so on) responsible for close to half the EU's emissions of CO_2 and 40 per cent of its other greenhouse gas emissions.[12] Discussions are underway to extend the scheme to the aviation sector from 2011 or 2012.

Under the present system each member state grants permission to individual companies to emit a certain amount of carbon dioxide each year within the limits of the national cap. Companies that expect to more than meet their target can trade the right to carbon dioxide emissions with those who cannot meet their target. The idea is that for climate, it does not matter who emits the carbon dioxide. If company A can cut its carbon dioxide emissions at a lower

---

[12] European Commission (2008b) Questions and answers on the Commission's proposal to revise the EU emissions trading system, www.europa.eu/rapid/pressReleasesAction

cost than company B, from the point of view of economic efficiency there is an advantage in company A cutting its emission more, and company B cutting less. Companies motivated by the profit they can make by selling their excess emission allowances will be encouraged to develop and use clean technologies.

The first phase of the ETS (2005–2007) ran into difficulties when it emerged that companies had been issued with more permits than they needed. Member states had overestimated the need for emissions, and as a result the price of carbon fell. The scheme failed in its aim of forcing companies either to reduce emissions or buy permits from cleaner companies.

In the second phase of the Scheme from 2008 to 2012 the European Commission wanted to ensure that projections of future emissions were more accurate, and that there was more transparency to check that member states are on track to meet their targets. In the initial phase companies were generally given permits free of charge, but in the second phase there would be more auctioning of permits. The need for more harmonization of the scheme throughout the EU became evident.

In January 2008 the Commission presented proposals for a reform of the ETS[13], which would entail:

- One EU-wide cap on the number of emissions allowed rather than the 27 national caps. The Commission proposes reducing the permits by 21 per cent from 2.1 billion tonnes of CO_2 in 2005 to 1.7 billion tonnes in 2020. The idea of setting caps by sector rather than by country was also to reduce discrepancies;

- A larger share of permits auctioned rather than granted free of charge. Auctions of permits could raise up to €75 billion a year or 0.5 per cent of EU GDP by 2020; [14]

- Part of the rights to auction allowances would be redistributed from member states with high per capita income to poorer countries (in particular the new CEEC member states) to strengthen the capacity of the latter to invest in climate-friendly technologies;

- Other industries (such as aluminium and ammonia producers) and new gases (nitrous oxide and perfluorocarbons) would be included in the scheme;

- Industrial sectors vulnerable to non-EU competition (such as iron, steel, cement, aluminium, paper and chemicals) would be given free emissions trading permits. Auctioning of permits would be phased in gradually from 2013 to 2020 and full auctioning would be used from 2020. The system would be subject to review in 2011;

- The power section would face full auctioning of permits from 2013 onwards;

- Member states will be allowed to exclude small installations from the system, provided they are subject to similar emission reduction measures;

- Importers might be required to buy the same carbon emissions allowances for non-EU goods as EU manufacturers themselves have to purchase.

Environmentalists maintained that the proposals had been watered down in the face of industrial lobbies (with, for instance, a deferral of the date on which firms would have to start paying for their emissions permits), but business groups in sectors such as iron and steel argued that the measures would undermine their global competitiveness. There were fears that the proposal to force importers to pay the same emission charges as domestic producers could provoke a trade war, with retaliation and/or litigation in the WTO.

---

[13] European Commission (2008c).

Other aspects of the European Climate Change Programme

To assist in meeting its Kyoto obligations in 2000 the EU launched the European Climate Change Programme (ECCP). The ECCP entailed the introduction of a wide range of measures, such as initiatives to promote renewable energy sources, expand the use of biofuels in transport (see chapter 12), and promote the energy performance of buildings, as well as the introduction of the Emissions Trading Scheme.

A second European Climate Change Programme began in 2005 with the aim of identifying further cost-effective ways of reducing emissions (see also Box 14.5). This led to various new measures, including proposals by the Commission for the inclusion of aviation in the ETS, and the strategy of using legislation to reduce carbon dioxide emissions from new cars.

Box 14.6: *A proposal to save energy*

As part of the fight against climate change in July 2007 there was a proposal to allow the 11 700 male eurocrats working in the European Commission to come to work without ties. It was hoped that tie-less officials would be better able to tolerate heat in July and August and so reduce the need for air conditioning in the 64 offices of the Commission across Brussels.*

*Financial Times, 9 July 2007

At the centre of EU policy towards climate change is the commitment to keep temperature increase to a maximum of 2 degrees above the pre-industrial level, the threshold beyond which scientific evidence suggests there is increased risk of irreversible and possible catastrophic changes (see Box 14.3 above). According to the European Commission, this would require global emissions to fall by almost 50 per cent compared with 1990 levels by 2050, which implied a cut by 60–8 per cent by developed countries and a gradual but significant effort by developing countries.[14] To meet these objectives, the European Council of March 2007 agreed:

- A unilateral cut in its greenhouse gas emissions by 20 per cent by 2020 compared to 1990 levels.

- If developed countries committed to cutting their emissions by about 30 per cent by 2020 as part of a comprehensive international agreement, the European Council would ensure a 30 per cent cut in EU emissions by 2020.

With this in mind an action plan on energy for the 2007–2012 period was agreed (see below). The European Commission (2008c) presented the results of an impact assessment of various measures to meet the targets, which led in January 2008 to a proposal for a Climate Action and Renewable Energy (CARE) Package.[15] The aim is to pass the necessary EU-level legislation by March 2009 (before elections to the European Parliament and the UN climate change conference in December 2009 in Copenhagen). The main proposals are:

- Reform of the Emissions Trading Scheme (as described above);

- Twenty per cent of energy use should be from renewables by 2020 including a 10 per cent

[14] European Commission (2007a).

[15] European Commission (2008a).

biofuels target. If a country meets its renewables target it could make a contribution by supporting the development of renewable energy in another member state. As in the case of carbon reduction, renewable energy targets would be set for each of the member states on the basis that wealthier countries should bear more of the burden than the new CEEC member states.

■ Sharing of efforts to meet the EU's independent greenhouse gas reduction commitment in sectors not covered by the ETS (such as transport, buildings, services, smaller industrial installations, agriculture and waste). Emissions in these sectors were to be cut by 10 per cent of 2005 levels by 2020, and it was proposed that member states contributed to this target according to their relative income.

■ Promotion and safe use of carbon storage, or a series of technologies that allow carbon dioxide emitted by industrial processes to be captured and stored underground where it cannot contribute to global warming. Revised guidelines for state aids will permit more government support for this type of initiative.

In presenting the package, Commission President Barroso acknowledged that the EU(27) would face costs of an estimated €60 billion a year or 0.45 per cent of GDP as a result of implementing the measures, but argued that the cost of inaction (as indicated by the Stern Report) would be much higher.

Evaluation of EU environmental policy

For many years environmental issues lacked the status of a fully-fledged Community policy, and even now in practice the various measures do not always appear to be co-ordinated into a single approach. Successive treaties have attempted to raise the priority given to environmental issues in the EU, requiring the Community to introduce environmental mainstreaming and to take account of sustainable development, not always with complete success. Over the years there has been a shift away from the 'command and control' approach in favour of market-based instruments, which tend to have lower implementation costs.

At the EU level tensions frequently arise between environmental objectives and the Single Market, and northern member states often express fears that their higher environmental standards might be undermined in a 'race to the bottom'.

During the German presidency of 2007, the German Chancellor, Angela Merkel, presented EU initiatives in environmental policy and mitigation of the effects of climate change as a way of reinventing the integration process 50 years on. The public, and increasingly business, supports EU initiatives despite fears that more regulation might render the EU less competitive compared with countries with less restrictions (leading to a risk of environmental dumping and/or a 'race to the bottom'). The EU seems intent on inventing a role for itself in promoting global initiatives with respect to the environment (and seems to have more success in reaching common positions than in foreign policy or defence issues). The proposed Climate Action and Renewable Energy Package of 2008 represents a landmark in this direction. However, the success of international agreements depends on other key actors such as the USA, China and India whose commitment is not always forthcoming.

The evolution of the EU energy market

During the first 15 years of the Community growth led to increased energy consumption, and the relatively low world prices for oil caused the gradual substitution of oil for coal. As a result the EC became increasingly dependent on imports of energy and of oil in particular. In 1950 coal accounted for two-thirds of energy consumption and oil for 10 per cent in what were the original six EC countries, but by 1973 oil covered 67 per cent of consumption (Kengyel and Palankai, 2003). In 1960 domestic production accounted for 60 per cent of EC energy requirements (with coal being produced mainly in Germany, France and Belgium), but by 1973 this proportion had fallen to 37 per cent.[16]

When the OPEC (Organization of Petroleum Exporting Countries) cartel increased oil prices by 475 per cent in 1973 and a further 134 per cent in 1979, the Community was therefore very vulnerable. Despite a certain lack of co-ordination, the reaction of the Community was to introduce measures to reduce dependence on oil imports, encourage the development of alternative energy sources (such as nuclear, wind, solar, water, geothermal, bioenergy, etc.), hold minimum stocks against emergencies and introduce energy-saving measures. Western industrialized countries (except France) joined the IEA (International Energy Agency), formed under the auspices of the OECD in 1974.

The policy of developing domestic energy sources and cutting consumption met with some success. North Sea oil production began in 1976, and the UK became a net exporter of oil. However, production met less than a quarter of EC requirements and was relatively costly. The Netherlands became an important producer of natural gas, but again extraction costs were relatively high. Renewable energy sources were slow to develop, and the public in many member states increasingly opposed the use of nuclear power plants. Table 14.3 shows the gross inland consumption by energy source of the member states, and the difference in choices about nuclear energy emerges clearly from the table.[17] Coal production continues to be important in countries such as Spain, Germany, Poland and the Czech Republic. See Figures 14.2 and Tables 14.2 and 14.3 for breakdowns on energy consumption in the EU (27) by type of fuel.

	Solids	Oil	Gas	Nuclear	Hydro	Biomass
EU (25)	17.9	37.3	23.9	14.5	1.5	4.1
USA	23.4	40.7	22.1	9.1	1.0	3.0
Japan	21.8	47.8	13.2	13.8	1.5	1.3
Russia	16.2	20.4	54.0	5.9	2.4	1.1
China*	61.4	19.6	2.7	0.8	1.9	13.6
India	34.1	22.2	4.1	0.8	1.3	37.4
World	25.1	34.3	20.9	6.5	2.2	10.6

TABLE 14.2 Fuel shares in per cent, 2005
*Includes Hong Kong
Source: European Commission (2007b), © European Communities, 2007.
www.europa.eu.int.comm/energy_transport

[16] Kengyel and Palankai (2003).

[17] The European Atomic Energy Community (Euratom) Treaty aimed at establishing the basic installations necessary for the development of nuclear energy in the Community, and ensuring that all users in the Community received a regular and equitable supply of ores and nuclear fuels. The Euratom Supply Agency, operative since 1960 and with a renewed statute since 2008, is the body established by the Euratom Treaty to ensure this supply by means of a common supply policy. The Euratom Supply Agency acts under the supervision of the European Commissioner responsible for energy.

	All fuels	Solid fuels	Oil	Natural gas	Nuclear	Renewables	Other
EU (27)	1816.1	320.0	669.8	445.4	257.4	120.8	2.8
	100%	17.6%	36.9%	24.5%	14.2%	6.6%	0.2%
BE	59.0	5.4	24.6	14.1	12.3	1.9	0.6
BG	19.9	6.9	4.8	2.8	4.8	1.1	−0.6
CZ	44.8	20.1	9.7	7.7	6.4	1.8	−1.0
DK	19.5	3.7	8.1	4.4		3.2	0.1
DE	345.5	82.8	123.4	80.9	42.1	16.7	−0.4
EE	5.6	3.2	1.1	0.8		0.6	−0.1
IE	15.1	2.7	8.4	3.5		0.4	0.2
EL	31.2	9.0	18.0	2.4		1.6	0.3
ES	143.5	20.7	69.5	29.8	14.8	8.7	−0.1
FR	275.6	14.4	92.1	41.0	116.5	16.8	−5.2
IT	186.8	16.5	83.2	70.7		12.1	4.3
CY	2.5	0.0	2.4			0.1	0.0
LV	4.7	0.1	1.4	1.4		1.7	0.2
LT	8.6	0.2	2.7	2.5	2.7	0.8	-0.3
LU	4.7	0.1	3.1	1.2		0.1	0.3
HU	27.9	3.1	7.4	12.1	3.6	1.2	0.6
MT	1.0		1.0				
NL	81.0	8.2	32.0	35.3	1.0	2.8	1.6
AT	34.1	4.0	14.3	8.2		7.0	0.6
PL	93.9	55.2	22.5	12.2		4.5	−0.5
PT	26.7	3.3	15.4	3.8		3.6	0.6
RO	39.1	8.8	10.2	13.9	1.4	5.0	−0.2
SL	7.3	1.5	2.6	0.9	1.5	0.8	0.0
SK	19.4	4.3	4.0	5.9	4.6	0.8	−0.2
FI	34.5	4.9	10.5	3.6	6.0	8.0	1.5
SE	51.6	2.6	14.6	0.8	18.7	15.4	−0.6
UK	232.7	38.2	82.7	85.6	21.1	4.1	1.1

TABLE 14.3 Gross inland consumption by type of energy in the member states in 2005 (million tonnes)
Source: European Commission (2007b), © European Communities, 2007, www.europa.eu.int.comm/energy_transport.
Note: Gaps indicate zero or insignificant amounts.

In 2005 the EU(27) continued to rely on imports for 52.4 per cent of its energy requirements (82.3 per cent in the case of oil but 57.6 per cent for natural gas). The main sources of supply are shown in Table 14.4. The heavy dependency of the EU on Russia for oil and gas imports is at times a source of concern (see below). French import dependency fell from 79 per cent in 1980 to 51.6 per cent in 2005 (thanks also to its nuclear power programme). However, as can be seen from Table 14.5, even in 2005 the import dependency of other EC member states such as Luxembourg (98.0 per cent), Portugal (88.2 per cent), Ireland (89.5 per cent), and Italy (84.4 per cent) remained high. Apart from Malta (100 per cent in 2004) and Cyprus (100.7 per cent in 2005) energy import dependency in the new member states was lower at, for example, 18.0 per cent for Poland and 27.4 per cent for the Czech Republic in 2005, also due to the production of coal in these two countries.

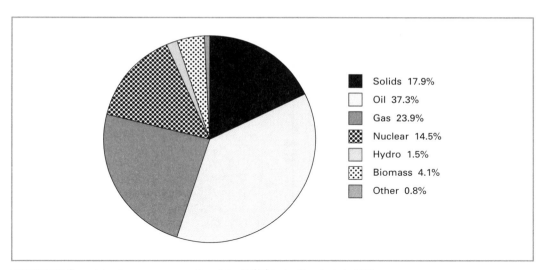

FIGURE 14.2 Gross inland energy consumption of the EU(15) by fuel/products in 2005

Source: European Commission (2007b), © European Communities, 2007.

www.europa.eu.int.comm/energy_transport

Main non-EU suppliers of oil to the EU (per cent of EU imports)	Million tonnes		Main non-EU suppliers of natural gas to the EU (per cent of EU imports)	
Russia	29.9	188.0	Russia	45.1
Norway	15.5	97.5	Norway	24.1
Saudi Arabia	9.7	60.7	Algeria	20.6
Libya	8.0	50.6	Nigeria	4.0
Iran	4.8	335.4	Libya	1.9
Middle East not specified	4.8	30.0		

TABLE 14.4 The main sources of EU(27) energy imports in 2005

Source: European Commission (2007b), © European Communities, 2007. www.europa.eu.int.comm/energy_transport

	All fuels	Solid fuels	Oil	Gas
EU (27)	52.4	39.6	82.3	57.6
BE	79.6	101.1	100.8	100.6
BG	47.1	37.0	102.6	87.7
CZ	27.4	-17.4	97.4	97.8
DK	−51.6	94.7	−104.8	−113.9
DE	61.6	32.4	97.1	81.3
EE	25.8	0.9	71.8	100.0
IE	89.5	73.3	99.7	86.7
EL	68.5	4.1	97.7	99.1
ES	81.2	69.7	101.2	101.4
FR	51.6	94.7	99.6	99.3
IT	84.4	99.3	91.8	84.7
CY	100.7	120.8	102.3	
LV	56.1	94.7	99.6	105.6
LT	58.4	94.6	92.7	100.6
LU	98.0	100.0	99.4	100.0
HU	62.9	43.4	79.2	81.1
NL	37.8	101.5	97.1	−59.3
AT	71.8	97.7	92.2	88.1
PL	18.0	−22.6	96.0	69.7
PT	88.2	96.3	102.2	103.8
RO	27.4	33.1	38.1	30.1
SL	52.2	21.0	101.1	99.6
SK	64.6	88.5	81.9	97.2
FI	54.7	67.8	98.8	100.0
SE	37.2	93.8	103.9	100.0
UK	13.8	71.9	−2.6	7.0

TABLE 14.5 Import dependency by type of energy as a percentage
Definition: Import Dependency = Net Imports / (Bunkers+Gross Inland Consumption)
Data for Malta was not available.
Source: European Commission (2007b), © European Commission, 2007, www.europa.eu.int.comm/energy_transport

The evolution of EU energy policy

Two of the initial Communities were set up to deal with energy. The European Coal and Steel Community was responsible for coal, and Euratom covered nuclear energy. Oil, gas and electricity fell within the scope of the EEC, though the Treaty of Rome did not list energy policy among the specific competences of the Community. Defence of national companies, differences in dependence on energy imports of the various member states and in the mix of energy sources used, have acted as obstacles to the development of a common policy.

In 1964 a Protocol on Agreement on Energy represented a first attempt at co-ordination of the energy policy of the member states. This set out as common objectives: fair competition between different sources of energy, security of supply, low prices, freedom of choice for consumers and co-ordination of state aids to coal, and for coal and coke consumption by the steel industry. Introduction of a common policy was again attempted in 1968 when the three Communities were merged, but with few practical results (Hitiris, 2003).

After 1978 the Community tried to co-ordinate the national measures of the member states, set energy targets and fix a collective target for the rationalization of production, consumption and imports.

The Single Market Programme aimed at the liberalization of energy (which in the case of gas and electricity was generally controlled by national monopolies) and the promotion of investment in infrastructure and networks. The objective was to reduce segmentation of the market, increase competitiveness and ensure awareness of the environmental implications of energy policy. As explained below, progress in realizing these objectives was slow, and over a decade later the Commission was still presenting proposals to liberalize the EU energy market.

The Maastricht Treaty confirmed the legal basis for Community measures in the sphere of energy (TEU, Article 3t) and called for joint efforts in the creation of trans-European networks (TENs) in energy infrastructure.[18] Community action for the development of TEN-Energy relates to the main transportation and transmission networks for electricity and natural gas. Priority measures for the electricity sector include the connection of isolated electricity networks and the development of interconnections between member states and with third countries. TEN-Energy gas priorities include the introduction of natural gas into new regions, the interconnection of isolated networks and increased capabilities for storage and transport. After the 2004 and 2007 enlargements, emphasis was placed on integrating the new member states into priorities and projects.

As with environmental policy the debate about energy in the EU acquired a greater urgency in the new century. Green Papers (European Commission, 2001, 2005 and 2006a) stimulated a lively debate and led to the publication of an 'Energy Package' in January 2007, and a further package of legislative proposals in September 2007.[19] From this debate certain central, but interlinked concerns of EU energy policy emerge:

- The problem of ensuring security of supply, in particular, given the dependence of the EU on imports from Russia;
- The need to reduce consumption, increase efficiency in the use of energy and promote renewable forms of energy;
- The environmental and social implications of energy policy;
- The need to complete the internal market for energy in order to increase competitiveness. Interconnections between countries may be necessary to increase efficiency and cut costs.

According to the European Commission (2001) the EU continues to rely heavily on fossil fuels (oil, coal and natural gas) which make up four-fifths of its total energy consumption, almost two-thirds of which are imported. Without a change in policy, EU imports could rise to 70 per cent of requirements (90 per cent in the case of oil) by 2030. According to the IEA (International Energy Agency, 2007), world energy needs will be 50 per cent higher in 2030 than today, with China and India alone accounting for 45 per cent of the increase in demand. As shown in Table 14.3 a large share of EU oil and gas imports come from Russia. The EU has had difficulty in agreeing on an energy strategy with Moscow, and Russia continues to sign bilateral agreements with individual member states, and has created various difficulties for EU companies operating energy projects in Siberia.

The EU has relatively little room to manoeuvre with regard to energy supplies because of its low or less competitive (e.g. coal and North Sea oil) energy resources, so the strategy proposed

---

[18]TEC Treaty, 129b, which became Article 154 in the Nice Treaty.

[19]See Energising Europe: A real market with secure supply, September 19, 2007, www.europa.eu/rapid/pressReleases

by the Commission relies heavily on demand management and the promotion of renewable energy. The European Council in March 2007 took up much of this proposal, and agreed on an action plan for energy policy containing the following elements:

■ To improve energy efficiency to save 20 per cent of the energy consumption of the EU compared with forecasts for 2020;

■ To raise the share of renewable energy to 20 per cent of EU overall energy consumption by 2020; and

■ To raise the share of biofuels to at least 10 per cent of total petrol and diesel consumption for transport in the EU by 2020.

The CARE Package of January 2008 confirmed these objectives, and proposed national renewable energy targets for each member state. The package also set out sustainability criteria to ensure that biofuels deliver real environmental benefits (see also Chapter 12).

The attempt at 'unbundling' of the EU energy sector

The characteristics of certain industries are influenced by the technologies used. For electricity supply is based on generation, transmission, distribution and retailing, and the situation is similar for gas. The existence of expensive infrastructure such as gas pipelines and an electricity grid is often advanced as a case of natural monopolies (see Chapters 4 and 17). Historically in the EU the provision of electricity and gas services has tended to be organized on the basis of vertical integration, with regional or national monopolists, and often public ownership.

According to the European Commission, structural failings (and, in particular, excessive vertical integration) of the EU gas and electrical industries led to high prices for consumers, and discrimination against new users of the network in favour of incumbent production and supply companies. The European Commission (2007c) estimated that between 1998 and 2006 in EU countries where the electricity networks were owned by the supply and generating companies, prices rose by 29 per cent compared with a price rise of 6 per cent where the networks were independent. There was also said to be insufficient investment in infrastructure, and a tendency to restrict capacity to protect parent companies. The idea was to open the energy sector making it easier for smaller firms to operate in the hopes that this would lower prices and that independent network companies might be more prepared to upgrade facilities by, for example, improving cross-border links.

In January 2007 as part of the Energy Package, the European Commission, therefore, set out proposals for 'unbundling' or separation of companies responsible for transmission (the networks of pipes and wires) from those dealing with distribution (supply of gas and electricity). The proposal met with heated opposition from about half the EU member states and, in particular, from large power groups such as Eon and RWE in Germany and Gas de France and Electricité de France.

In the face of such opposition in September 2007 the Commission presented a revised proposal with an opt-out clause. Countries not wanting to split up their large energy companies could choose to set up 'independent system operators', which are separate companies controlling access to, and investment in, networks that would still be owned by suppliers. In addition there would be more co-operation between national transmission operators backed by a new EU network, increased powers and independence for national regulators, and a new EU Agency for the co-operation of Energy Regulators to facilitate cross-border energy trade. Non-EU firms would only be able to control energy networks in the EU if they met certain stringent conditions, and this was interpreted in some circles as a move to ensure reciprocal access to the Russian energy market for EU companies.

Even the watered-down proposal, together with the increased emphasis on transparency, could still imply substantial pressure on large groups to break up voluntarily. Not surprisingly, there was heated opposition from member states such as Germany, France, Austria, Latvia, Bulgaria, Greece, Luxembourg and Slovakia. It was claimed that the EU needed power giants to stand up to large suppliers such as those in Russia and Algeria. In contrast countries such as the UK, the Netherlands, Italy, Spain and Poland were more in favour of liberalization.

Parallel to its legislative proposals the European Commission also carried out anti-trust actions (see Chapter 17) against large energy companies. This led in 2008 to a deal with the German group Eon, which agreed to sell its electricity grid and 20 per cent of its power plant capacity (though Eon denied that this was as a result of the Commission's enquiry).[20] Electricité de France, Belgium's Electrabel and Germany's RWE were also under investigation by the European Commission.

At the same time a series of mergers and acquisitions were changing the structure of the EU energy sector. The Belgian-French group, Suez is due to merge with Gas de France, while the Italian ENEL was successful in bids for shares in Electricité de France and Spanish Endesa.

Evaluation of EU energy policy

The EU is frequently criticized for its slowness in developing an energy policy, but defence of large national firms, differences in the import dependency of the member states and in the structure of energy sources used to meet consumption, render it difficult to reach common positions.

In the early years of the Community oil gradually replaced coal as the main source of energy, leading to increased import dependency. The EC member states were therefore vulnerable to the oil crises of the 1970s and reacted by attempting to reduce import dependency, develop alternative sources of domestic supply and reduce energy consumption.

Security of energy supply remains a key priority for the EU, and the present strategy relies heavily on the introduction of energy-saving measures and incentives to develop renewable energy sources. Commission proposals to harmonize taxation and liberalize energy markets in the EU have met with limited success, but in recent years there has been a growing consensus enabling measures to tackle climate change to be introduced. In contrast, attempts to liberalize EU gas and electricity markets by 'unbundling' transmission and distribution networks have encountered opposition from large national companies, often backed by national governments such as those in France and Germany.

---

[20] *Financial Times*, 1–2 March 2008.

Summary of Key Concepts

■ **The evolution of EU environmental measures has encountered tensions** because of differing environmental standards in the EU member states; the fuzzy boundary between EU and national policies; difficulties in implementing policies; the persistence of environmental problems; difficulties in reconciling environmental measures with other EU policies and disagreements about how to share the financial burden for measures.

■ **Environmental measures fall into three broad categories**: 'command and control', market-based instruments and voluntary agreements. In recent years there has been a growing tendency in the EU to use market-based instruments rather than the strategy of 'command and control'.

■ There is no mention of a role for the Community in the Treaty of Rome. In 1973 the Community embarked on the first of what are now six Environmental Action Programmes.

■ The **principles of EU environmental policy** are: the principle of prevention; the 'polluter pays' principle; the principle of correction at source; the principle of subsidiarity and the precautionary principle.

■ **'Environmental mainstreaming'** requires that environmental issues should be taken into account in deciding all EU policies.

■ The European **Environment Agency** came into operation in 1994.

■ The EU takes part in global attempts to tackle transnational environmental problems such as the ozone layer (the **Montreal Protocol** of 1987 and subsequent agreements), climate change (the 1997 **Kyoto Protocol**) and the depletion of tropical rainforests.

■ The EU introduced an **Emissions Trading Scheme** (or 'carbon trading') in 2005, but difficulties arose during the first phase (2005–2007) as too many permits were issued.

■ In the early years of the Community oil gradually replaced coal as the main source of energy, leading to increased import dependency.

■ The EU is frequently criticized for its **slowness in developing an energy policy**, but large national firms, and differences in the import dependency of the member states and in the structure of energy sources used to meet consumption, render it difficult to reach common positions.

■ **Security of energy supply** remains a key priority for the EU, and the present strategy relies heavily on the introduction of energy-saving measures and incentives to develop renewable energy sources.

Questions for study and review

1 What were the obstacles to developing an EU environmental policy?

2 Describe main types of instrument used in environmental policy.

3 Describe how EU environmental policy has evolved over time.

4 What difficulties arise in applying the principles of EU environmental policy?

5 What is sustainable development? How can it be ensured in practice?

6 What role has the EU played at an international level in deciding on environmental questions?

7 What are the limitations of the Kyoto Protocol? What aspects should a successor agreement to Kyoto have?

8 Describe the Emissions Trading Scheme of the EU. What improvements could be made to this Scheme?

9 Why do most countries introduce an energy policy?

10 Describe the different sources of energy the EU uses to meet its requirements. How have these changed over time?

12 Describe the evolution of EU energy policy.

12 What strategies is the EU adopting to ensure security of energy supplies?

References

Artis, M. and Nixson, F. (2003) *The Economics of the European Union*, Oxford University Press, Oxford.

Coase, R. (1960) 'The problem of social cost', *Journal of Law and Economics*, October, pp. 1–44.

Dasgupta, P. (2006) *Comments on the Stern Review's Economics of Climate Change*, www.econ.cam.ac.uk/faculty/dagupta/STERN.pdf

Eurobarometer (2003) *Public Opinion in the EU*, No. 60, Autumn, www.ec.europa.eu/public_opinion

Eurobarometer (2007) *Public Opinion in the EU*, No. 67, Spring, www.ec.europa.eu/public_opinion

European Commission (2001) 'Towards a European Union strategy for the security of energy supply', http://europa.eu/scadplus/leg

European Commission (2005) *Energy Efficiency or Doing More with Less*, COM (2005)265, www.ec.europa.eu/energy_transport

European Commission (2007a) *Limiting Global Climate Change to 2 degrees Celsius: The Way Ahead for 2020 and Beyond,* www.europa.eu/scadplus/leg

European Commission (2007b) *European Union Energy and Transport in Figures 2007*, www.ec.europa.eu./energy_transport

European Commission (2007c) *An Energy Policy for Europe*, Communication from the Commission to the European Council and the European Parliament, COM (2007)1, final, http://europa.eu/scadplus/leg

European Commission (2008a) 'Proposal for a decision of the European Parliament and of the Council on the effort of the member states to reduce their greenhouse gas emissions to meet the Community's gas emission reduction commitments up to 2020', COM (2008)30 final.

European Commission (2008b) Questions and answers on the Commission's proposal to revise the EU emissions trading system, www.europa.eu/rapid/pressReleasesAction

European Commission (2008c) 'Impact Assessment. Document accompanying the package of implementation measures for the EU's objectives on climate change and renewable energy for 2020', SEC(2008)85/3.

Hitiris, T. (2003) *European Community Economics*, 5th edn, Prentice Hall, Hemel Hempstead, UK.

International Energy Agency (2007) *World Energy Outlook*, www.iea.org

Kengyel, A. and Palankai, T. (2003) 'Structural policy roles and directions' in Palankai, T. (ed.) *Economics of European Integration*, Akadémiai Kaido', Budapest.

Lawson, N. (2008) *An Appeal to Reason: A Cool Look at Global Warming*, George Duckworth, London.

Lomborg, B. (2001) *The Sceptical Environmentalist. Measuring the Real State of the World*, Cambridge University Press, Cambridge.

Nordhaus, W. (2006) *The Stern Review on the Economics of Climate Change*, Working Paper 12741, www.nber.org

Pearce, D. (2003) 'Environmental policy', in Artis, M. and Nixson, F. (eds) *The Economics of the European Union. Policy and Analysis*, 3rd edn, Oxford University Press, Oxford.

Stern, N. (2006)*The Economics of Climate Change*, www.hm-treasury.gov.uk.

Useful websites

Statistics, a description of environmental policies and key documents are available from the European Commission:
www.ec.europa.eu//environment
http://europa.eu/scadplus/leg

The European Environment Agency provides reports and statistics on various environmental issues:
www.eea.eu.int

Various international organizations provide information on environmental questions:
Greenpeace:
www. greenpeace.org

The International Energy Agency:
www.iea.org

The International Panel on Climate Control:
www.ipcc.ch

IUCN–World Conservation Union:
http://www.iucn.org/

Convention for Biodiversity:
http://www.biodiv.org/default.aspx
WWF International:
http://www.panda.org

For US environmental policy see:
US Environmental Protection Agency:
www.epa.gov

The OECD provides statistics and analysis of both environmental and energy questions:
www.oecd.org

For a description of EU energy policy, statistics and key documents, see European
Commission:
www.ec.europa.eu./energy_transport

Statistics on energy are available from *BP Statistical Review of World Energy*:
www.bpamoco.com/worldenergy/

Regional Policy

15

❖ **LEARNING OBJECTIVES**

By the end of this chapter you should be able to understand:

❖ Various views about the link between integration and regional disparities;

❖ The problem of regional disparities in the EU;

❖ What the main funds used by the EU for regional and cohesion policy are;

❖ The main stages in the evolution of EU regional policy;

❖ How EU regional and cohesion policy operates over the 2007–2013 period;

❖ The extent to which there has been convergence between EU regions and countries;

❖ How effective EU regional policy has been;

❖ The ways in which regional policy might be rendered more effective.

Introduction

Regional problems are the disparities in levels of income, in rates of growth of output and employment, and generally in levels of economic inequality between different regions. Public intervention may be considered necessary to reduce these disparities through redistribution. Over the years the EU has gradually evolved an active policy of redistribution between different regions and countries of the Community (the regional dimension), and different sections of the population (the social dimension, see Chapter 16).

The aims of EU regional policy figure among the objectives set out in Article 2 of the EC Treaty:

■ To promote a harmonious, balanced and sustainable development of economic activities;

■ Convergence of economic performance;

■ Economic and social cohesion and solidarity between member states.

Articles 158–62 of the Treaty establishing the European Community lay down that the EU should promote harmonious development and strengthen social and economic cohesion by encouraging convergence. Convergence involves a process of catching up by less favoured regions so that the disparities are narrowed. While there is no clear definition of cohesion, it can be understood as 'the degree to which disparities in social and economic welfare between different regions or groups within the Community are politically and socially acceptable' (Molle, 2006, p. 287).

Regional policies are often advocated on grounds of efficiency since they may help to remove bottlenecks and obstacles to development. For instance, public investment in infrastructure may encourage firms to move to a less favoured region, or programmes for retraining may help workers to find jobs. Regional policy may help to ease the problems of overcongestion or overheating in areas where economic activity is concentrated. The concept of social and economic cohesion also suggests a justification for redistributive policies on equity grounds: regional policies may be required to guarantee certain minimum levels of services, while social policy may ensure certain minimum incomes or living standards.

Various indicators can be taken into account in assessing the degree of disparity between different regions or countries:

- Income per capita (which is the indicator generally used by the EU);
- Labour productivity;
- The availability and accessibility of jobs;
- The standard of living, which involves also taking into account the environment, the health service, cultural infrastructure, leisure activities, etc.

A major, and still unresolved controversy is whether economic integration leads to greater or less convergence between different regions. The first part of this chapter will review some of the main theories advanced on either side of the argument. Then follows a survey of the instruments of EU regional policy and how they evolved over the years. The final part of the chapter addresses the question of whether there has been convergence in the EU. This is complicated by the fact that convergence may take place both within and between countries. A further difficulty arises in attributing the causes of convergence (or lack of it).To what extent was convergence due to integration, and what was the role of EU regional policy? The last part of the chapter will attempt to identify elements that make for a successful regional policy.

The view that integration leads to less income disparity

The view that integration will lead to greater convergence is generally based on faith in markets. Integration allows free operation of the market forces and sets in motion a process by which the return to labour and capital in different regions will tend to converge. The mechanisms by which this convergence comes about are:

- **Free trade**, which permits regions to specialize on the basis of comparative advantage (see Chapter 4). A region with surplus labour will specialize in labour-intensive goods causing incomes to rise and unemployment to fall. The Heckscher–Ohlin–Samuelson theorem described in Chapter 4 provides an explanation of how the removal of barriers to trade may lead to the convergence of incomes in different regions. The limitation of this explanation arises from the restrictive assumptions on which the theorem is based.
- **Labour migration and capital mobility**. Labour will tend to leave regions with lower wage levels and move to regions where wages are higher, bringing about a process of wage equalization, as described in Chapter 8. A similar mechanism to that in Figure 8.2 can be used to explain capital movements by simply reversing the position of capital

and labour.[1] Capital will be attracted to the regions where wages are lower and returns on capital are higher, setting in motion a process that leads to equalization of returns on capital in different regions.

- **Capital accumulation**. According to orthodox neo-classical growth theory (see the description of the Solow model in Chapter 5), in regions with higher productivity and per capita incomes, growth will prove more difficult as capital accumulation runs into diminishing returns.

The view that integration leads to greater regional disparity

Various theories are also advanced to explain why integration may lead to divergence or greater disparities between regions:

- **Modern growth theory,** which was briefly described in Chapter 5, may explain why more prosperous areas can enjoy ongoing long-term growth. Important factors in explaining growth are market access, human capital, investment in R&D, technological change, economies of scale, institutional efficiency, etc., and these may be encouraged by integration. Some countries master good combinations and grow, others fail to do so and fall behind.

- **Technology diffusion**. According to evolutionary economic theory, knowledge and innovation tend to concentrate in certain areas.

  Evolutionary economics owes much to the pioneering work of Nelson and Winter (1982) and adds new insights into the role of knowledge and innovation.[2] According to the Schumpeterian view, the evolution of the economy is constantly being 'disrupted' by technological change in a process of 'creative destruction'. Learning and evolution are seen as a disequilibrium process, and dynamic selection and mutation lead to superior responses. Structural change and growth are the result of the irruption of new technologies in the economic system which provide opportunities for investment and the opening of new sectors. Drawing on Kondratiev's concept of waves of economic activity, Schumpeter argued that radical innovations tend to be concentrated in certain periods.

  Knowledge is a key concept in this framework, and evolutionary economics makes the distinction between codified and tacit knowledge. Codified knowledge is formalized and can be stored and transmitted easily, while tacit knowledge is obtained through experience, requiring a process of learning-by-doing in order to be passed on.

  According to evolutionary economics a large part of knowledge needed for innovation is tacit, so contacts between people are important, and location therefore counts. There will tend to be an agglomeration of innovation in geographic clusters. In contrast codified knowledge can be transmitted easily so activities based on this knowledge can be moved to low-cost locations. According to the view that integration encourages economic concentration, by reducing barriers to the location of industry, integration will render it easier for firms to move to areas where there is an agglomeration of innovation.

- **The New Economic Geography approach** developed by Krugman and Venables.[3] This approach involves a kind of circular causality. The possibility of exploiting scale economies is an incitement to the concentration of industry, while trade costs are reduced if firms

---

[1] See Baldwin and Wyplosz (2006) for an example of how this approach is applied to capital movement.

[2] This account is based on Navarro (2003).

[3] Krugman and Venables (1990) and Krugman (1991).

locate close to large markets.[4] Where firms are concentrated, there will be large markets and large markets provide an incentive for firms to locate. The combination of opportunity to exploit economies of scale and reduce trade costs makes for this circular causality.

Supporters of the New Economic Geography approach argue that it explains the existence of centripetal forces in the EU. The central core area is said to lie in a so-called pentagon stretching from London, across to Hamburg, down to Munich, across to Milan and up to Paris.[5]

According to the view that integration encourages economic concentration, by freeing trade, creating a Single Market and introducing a common currency, the integration process will help remove various obstacles that could hinder the agglomeration process.

However, even when considering the various 'stages' of integration, different views emerge as to whether integration leads to more or less convergence. The customs union frees trade, creating opportunities for exploiting comparative advantage, but there may be rigidities in the process, and where adjustment takes place it may involve costs. These costs may be concentrated in certain sectors or regions. A common market introduces the four freedoms, enabling labour to move from less favoured regions, but in practice capital tends to move faster and may concentrate in faster-growing regions. Economic and monetary union removes the possibility of using exchange rate and monetary policies for adjustment between countries. However, disparities also arise within countries, and with higher levels of integration the effectiveness of the exchange rate instrument has been challenged, and it has been argued that exchange rate changes may even be a source of shocks (see Chapter 9).

EU instruments for cohesion and regional policy

EU implementation of regional and social policy operates chiefly though what were traditionally called the Structural Funds and related instruments, though clearly other policies (such as the CAP) will have distributional implications.

Up until 2006 the term 'Structural Funds' referred to the European Social Fund (ESF), the European Regional Development Fund (ERDF), the Guidance Section of EAGGF (or the European Agricultural Guidance and Guarantee Fund, often known by its French, or Italian, acronym, FEOGA, as the English equivalent is unpronounceable),[6] and the Financial Instrument for Fisheries Guidance (FIFG).[7] Related instruments are the European Cohesion Fund and the European Investment Bank (EIB).

The system was reformed for the 2007–2013 period, with a reduction in the number of financial instruments for economic and social cohesion to three:

---

[4] Trade costs include transport costs but also the more general costs of adapting to the local market which depend on information, culture, distance, etc.

[5] The earlier literature refers to a golden triangle in North-West Europe running from Paris to London and including most of Belgium and the Netherlands (Harrop, 2000), and a so-called 'blue banana' in the shape of a banana that runs from the golden triangle through West German cities such as Bonn and Frankfurt, parts of Austria and Switzerland to Milan (Williams, 1996).

[6] The Guidance Section of FEOGA was established as a result of the 1962 agreement on CAP mechanisms (see Chapter 12) and traditionally financed measures to adapt and improve farm structures and the marketing of agricultural products and to develop rural infrastructure.

[7] The FIFG was created in 1993 in order to modernize the EU fleet, safeguard certain marine areas and improve the structures for processing and marketing of fish in the EU (see Chapter 13).

1 The ESF;

2 The ERDF;

3 The Cohesion Fund.

The EAGGF (or FEOGA) and the FIFG were transformed into a new European Agricultural Fund for Rural Development (EAFRD) and a European Fund for Fisheries (EFF).

The ESF

Created in 1960, according to the Treaty of Rome, the aim of the ESF was to increase employment opportunities and contribute to the improvement of living standards. The strategy for realizing this aim is dual: through creating jobs and assisting training.

During the 1960s the activities of the ESF were mainly concerned with increasing the geographical and occupational mobility of workers. During the 1970s the chief objectives became the fight against long-term and youth unemployment. The ESF is now implemented in conjunction with the European Employment Strategy (see Chapter 16) and is focused on four key areas:

1 Increasing adaptability of workers and enterprises;

2 Enhancing access to employment and participation in the labour market;

3 Reinforcing social inclusion by combating discrimination and facilitating access to the labour market for disadvantaged people; and

4 Promoting partnership for reform in the fields of employment and inclusion.

The ERDF

The ERDF is the largest of the financial instruments for cohesion. Created in 1975, the aim of the fund is to reduce disparities between various regions in the Community through the promotion of public and private investments. Following the 1973 enlargement and the entry of Britain with its difficulties in Northern Ireland, Scotland, Wales and the North of England (see Chapter 2), the ERDF was initially conceived as a means of assistance to regions facing industrial decline.

Box 15.1: *Examples of projects supported by EU cohesion policy**

EU cohesion policy supported the extension of the Faculty of Mathematics and Computer Science of the Nicolas Copernicus University in Torun, Poland. With financing from the ERDF the centre was extended in a way consistent with the original 1930s architecture. The new wing consists of a lecture hall with capacity for 350 people, a conference room, 10 computer laboratories, and 40 rooms for academic staff.

Near Porto in Northern Portugal the Sousa Valley is famous for its Romanesque architecture. In 2003 a project was set up with support from the ERDF to restore buildings, highlight their cultural significance, and promote the area as an important tourist attraction. In 2006 promotional and marketing activities were launched to establish this 'Romanesque art road' as a principal tourist attraction in Portugal.

*source: Inforegio of December 2006, © European Communities, 2008, www.ec.europa.eu/ regional_policy

Over the 2007–2013 period the ERDF will provide financing for programmes addressing general infrastructure, innovation and investments. The ERDF finances projects in areas such as (see Box 15.1):

- research and innovation;
- infrastructure projects (for transport, telecommunications, energy and water supply);
- information society;
- environmental protection;
- risk prevention;
- education and professional training;
- health services;
- tourism;
- culture.

The Cohesion Fund

Introduced as part of the Maastricht package, the Cohesion Fund provides assistance to those member states that fear that they will not be able to meet the additional competitive pressures resulting from economic and monetary union. The criterion for eligibility is that the country has a GDP per capita that is less than 90 per cent of the Community average. The countries receiving assistance through the Cohesion Fund are the new member states, Greece and Portugal. Spain is subject to a transitional phasing-out arrangement as it met the 90 per cent threshold for an EU of 15, but not EU(25) and indeed a number of Spanish regions were well above the threshold in an EU of 25 or 27. Ireland was also initially a cohesion country, but no longer qualifies, so aid has been phased out. Countries benefiting from the Cohesion Fund are obliged to adopt economic policies conducive to convergence. In return they receive financial assistance for projects in favour of the environment and trans-European networks to improve transport infrastructure. The contribution of the Fund may amount to up to 85 per cent of total financing of the project (see Table 15.1).

Criteria	Member states, regions	ERDF, ESF	Cohesion Fund
(1) Member States whose average per capita/ GDP was below 85% between 2001-03	CZ, EE, GR, CY, LV, LT, HU, MT, PL, PT, SL, SK, BG, RO	85%	85%
(2) Member States other than those under (1) eligible to the Cohesion Fund	ES	80%/50%*	85%
(3) Member States other than those under (1) and (2)	AT, BE, DK, DE, FR, IE, IT, LU, NL, SE, FI, UK	75%/50%*	–
(4) Outermost regions referred to in Article 299 (2) of the Treaty	regions in ES, FR, PT	85%	85%**

TABLE 15.1 EU co-financing rates for the 2007-2013 period
* The first rate concerns regions eligible under the 'Convergence' objective; the second one those under the 'Regional Competitiveness and Employment' objective
** If applicable
Source: Website of the European Commission, Regional Policy Inforegio www.ec.europa.eu/regional_policy

The EIB

The Treaty of Rome (Articles 129–30) envisaged the creation of the EIB. The EIB helps to finance projects in the member states and in certain third countries (such as those in the Mediterranean area, in Central and Eastern Europe and in the ACP group). The EIB raises funds on financial markets using its name as a guarantee, and provides subsidized loans to finance projects carried out by public authorities and private firms. In recent years the EIB has been involved in supporting the Lisbon Strategy with, for example, loans for investment in education, health care and high-technology sectors.

The European Union Solidarity Fund

Following the intense flooding in the EU in August 2002 it was decided to set up the European Union Solidarity Fund (EUSF). This is not one of the structural instruments, but member states and countries negotiating accession can request assistance from this Fund in the event of a major disaster.

Actions were taken in response to the 2002 flooding in Germany, Austria, the Czech Republic and France. Other intervention was for the 'Prestige' oil spill in Spain, earthquakes in Molise and Poulles, the eruption of Etna and forest fires in Portugal in 2003.

The historical evolution of EU regional policy

The 1958–75 period

During the 1958–75 period regional measures were widely implemented at a national level in the member states, but there was no real Community policy. The original six member states were a relatively homogeneous economic group, with the exception of the Mezzogiorno of Italy. The European Investment Bank was set up principally with the aim of resolving the problems of Southern Italy, but in practice its activities were on a relatively limited scale. It was hoped that measures to promote labour movement in the Community would also have the effect of reducing unemployment in the Mezzogiorno. It was also considered that the CAP could play a redistributive role since farm incomes were generally below those in other sectors.

The 1975–88 period

The second phase of EC regional policy covers the 1975–88 period and was characterized by the introduction of new measures, the wider use of existing instruments and a gradual increase in the funds available for redistributive measures (Tsoukalis, 1997).

The ERDF was created in 1975 largely at British request. With a tradition of importing food from the rest of the world, and a small but efficient agricultural sector, the UK was expected to be a large net contributor to the EC budget (see Chapter 11). The ERDF was considered a mechanism for correcting this imbalance, though following the 1973 oil crisis its operation was on a far smaller scale than initially foreseen. The funds available for the ERDF increased over the years, but it was criticized for poor co-ordination, insufficient flexibility in the choice of project and of being used simply to replace funding by national authorities.

In 1978 a 'Mediterranean package' was introduced as a response to criticisms that the CAP had traditionally favoured northern farmers and fear that the Mediterranean enlargement would add to competitive pressures. Requested by France and Italy, the measures were also extended to Greece from 1981, and entailed increased price and market support for certain Mediterranean products, assistance for irrigation, the infrastructure and reforestation. From 1981 similar 'integrated development programmes' were introduced for other less favoured areas such as Lozère in France, Southern Belgium and the Northwest islands of Scotland.

Building on these initiatives, and with a view to preparing for Spanish and Portuguese accession, in 1985 the Community introduced 'Integrated Mediterranean Programmes'. These marked the beginning of a new strategy aimed at overcoming some of the shortcomings of earlier redistributive measures. There was to be more co-ordination both between the then three Structural Funds (the ESF, FEOGA Guidance and the ERDF) and with the EIB. Decentralization was to increase with more involvement of local and regional authorities. The measures were directed chiefly at rural areas, but it was argued that assistance should not simply be to agriculture in these regions but should take account of the wider economic and social environment. Between 1985 and 1992, 4.1 billion ECU was allocated to these programmes, but the change in approach was probably more important than the increase in funding available.

Since 1988

During the period since 1988 the current instruments of EU economic and social policy were gradually evolved. In 1985 the new President of the European Commission, Delors, announced his programme for the completion of the Internal Market. The less favoured peripheral regions and countries feared that they would not be able to meet the additional competitive pressures in the Single Market. Increased disparities in the Community following the accession of Greece, Spain and Portugal were also expected, and the limited results achieved by the separate operation of the various Structural Funds and the need to increase their effectiveness was recognized. Reform of the Structural Funds was therefore agreed in 1988.

In 1987, the Single European Act introduced the concept of economic and social cohesion and called for harmonious development, the reduction of regional disparities, and the co-ordination and rationalization of the Structural Funds (Articles 130A–130E).

The 1988 reform covered the 1989–93 period, and its underlying philosophy was confirmed and strengthened in the subsequent cycles of the Structural Funds covering the periods 1994–99 and 2000–06. The main aspects of the reform were:

- A doubling of the Structural Funds from 7 billion ECU in 1989 to 14 billion in 1993;
- The creation of so-called Community Initiatives which involve a number of member states;
- The introduction of a series of principles of operation;
- The concentration of the Funds on priority objectives.

The aim of Community Initiatives was to encourage co-operation between different member states on matters of common interest. Community Initiatives accounted for about 10 per cent of spending under the Structural Funds. During the 1989–93 and 1994–99 periods there were a number of Community Initiatives aimed at specific groups and targets, but for the 2000–06 period they were reduced to four:[8]

1 LEADER + (rural development);
2 INTERREG II (cross-border, transnational and interregional co-operation);
3 URBAN (economic and social regeneration of cities and urban neighbourhoods);

---

[8] These were incorporated into the new objectives for the 2007–2013 period, with URBAN II and Equal being integrated into the Convergence and Regional Competitiveness and Employment Objectives, and INTERREG providing a basis for the European Territorial Integration Objective (see below).

4 EQUAL (transnational co-operation to combat all kinds of discrimination and inequalities in the labour market).

The 1988 reform introduced four principles for implementing cohesion policy, and these have applied ever since:

1. **Concentration.** Measures were to be concentrated on priority objectives to ensure close co-ordination of policies (see Box 15.1). Concentration is also intended to ensure that the effectiveness of measures is not undermined by resources being spread too thinly either geographically or by policy measure, but it does not always succeed in this aim.

2. **Partnership.** This implies close co-operation between the European Commission and the appropriate national, regional and local authorities at all stages. This requires horizontal co-operation between organizations at the regional and local levels, and the development of vertical aspects of multi-level governance and the interplay between different tiers of government. Partnership may help to disseminate information and to take a broader range of views into account in assessing needs and evaluating projects. The disadvantage of this approach is that procedures may be complex and heavily bureaucratic. Because allocation decisions are made primarily at the level of member states and their regional and local authorities (in line with the principle of subsidiarity) this appears to have changed little over the years despite efforts made to streamline the objectives and protocols for submitting proposals.

3. **Programming.** The Structural Funds would be implemented through structured programmes lasting a number of years (1989–93, 1994–99, 2000–06 and 2007–13). The cycles generally coincide with successive financial prospectives. Programming is intended to encourage longer-term, more strategic planning, but at times difficulties are encountered with the length of time taken to approve programming documents and with their complexity.

4. **Additionality.** This aims at ensuring that allocations are additional to national financing, and do not simply replace national measures. The aim is to stimulate an increase in finance (both public and private) available, and at least in Objective 1 regions this objective appears to have been realized.[9]

The main changes introduced in the Structural Funds for the 1994–99 period were:

- The creation of the Cohesion Fund;
- An increase in financing through the Structural Funds;
- A change in the objectives (see Box 15.2);
- The introduction of the Financial Instrument for Fisheries Guidance;
- A simplification of procedures;
- An increased role for regional and local authorities.

Despite the aims of this reform, the criticisms of complex procedures, lack of co-ordination and insufficient decentralization continued to be levelled at the Structural Funds during this period.

At the Berlin European Council of 1999 agreement was reached on reform of the Structural Funds for the 2000–06 period, also with a view to EU enlargement (see Chapter 20). The reform aimed at simplification of the instruments, by reducing the number of regulations, objectives and sources of financing. The procedures of programming and financial management were also to be rendered less complex, and the instruments of control, monitoring and evaluation were to be

---

[9] European Commission (2004).

Box 15.2: *The evolution of the objectives of the Structural Funds between 1989 and 2006*

First period 1989–93	Second period 1994–99	Third period 2000–06
Objective 1: the less well-developed areas of the Community, which are defined as those whose GDP per capita is less than 75% of the EU average in the previous three years.	*Objective 1*: the less well-developed areas of the Community, which are defined as those whose GDP per capita is less than 75% of the EU average in the previous three years.	*Objective 1*: the less well-developed areas of the Community, which are defined as those whose GDP per capita is less than 75% of the EU average.
Objective 2: regions affected by the decline of traditional industries.	*Objective 2*: the conversion of regions seriously affected by industrial decline.	*Objective 2*: the economic and social conversion of regions that were facing natural difficulties, including declining rural areas and those dependent on fishing.
Objective 3: the fight against long-term unemployment.	*Objective 3*: combating long-term unemployment (more than 12 months) and facilitating the integration into work of young people (under 25 years of age), women and persons exposed to exclusion from the labour market.	*Objective 3*: improvement of human capital by promoting employment, education and professional training.
Objective 4: integration into working life of young people.	*Objective 4*: facilitating the adaptation of workers to industrial change and changes in production systems.	
Objective 5a: assisting the structural adjustment of agriculture and fisheries. *Objective 5b*: aid to rural areas.	*Objective 5a*: assisting the structural adjustment of agriculture and fisheries. *Objective 5b*: aid to rural areas.	Rural development became the second pillar of the CAP.
	Objective 6: regions with a low density of population in the extreme north of Finland and Sweden.	

Note: With the 1993 reform the previous objectives 3 and 4 were integrated into a revised objective 3, and new objectives 4 and 6 were created. With the 1999 reform the old objectives 1 and 6 were incorporated into the new objective 1, the old objectives 2 and 5a were included in the new objective 2 and objective 5b was transformed into rural development, which became the second pillar of the CAP.

reinforced. Subsidiarity was to be strengthened, with increased decentralization to regional and local authorities. The objectives of the Structural Funds were to be reduced to three:

1 Objective 1 regions where GDP per capita was less than 75 per cent of the EU average. These were to receive 69.7 per cent of all spending.

2 A further 12.3 per cent of Structural Funds was earmarked to assist the economic and social conversion of Objective 2 regions which were facing change in industrial and service sectors or urban difficulties, declining rural areas and depressed regions dependent on fishing.

3 The remaining funds were allocated to Objective 3, which is a so-called horizontal measure in the sense it applies throughout the EU. Its aim is to improve human capital by promoting employment, education and professional training. Objective 3 schemes must promote equal opportunities between men and women.

It was hoped that by adopting these three objectives, priorities would be fixed, and the use of funds would be rendered more effective.

The European Council in Berlin agreed €195 billion for the Structural Funds and €18 billion for the Cohesion Fund for the 2000–06 period. Each year €1.04 billion would be earmarked over the 2000–06 period for ISPA (the Pre-Accession Structural Instrument) for the CEECs, and the financial perspective contained a budgetary heading for Structural Funds for the new member states.

EU cohesion and regional policy over the 2007–2013 period

For the 2007–2013 period the term 'cohesion policy' replaced the earlier expression 'structural actions' and various changes were introduced:

- Thirty-six per cent of spending from the EU budget over the 2007–2013 period or €308 billion is to be allocated to cohesion policy (see Figure 15.1 for the division of this allocation by member state);

- A reduction in the number of financial instruments used for cohesion policy to three (the ESF, the ERDF and the Cohesion Fund, see above);

- Continuation of the principles of concentration, partnership, programming and additionality (see above);

- A tighter and more explicit linking of cohesion policy to the Lisbon Strategy,[10] including

---

[10] See Chapter 7 for an account of the Lisbon Strategy.

'earmarking' of resources to support specific priorities of the Strategy and so ensure an adequate financial contribution for promoting growth and employment;

■ New objectives for social and economic cohesion;

■ Changes in operating procedures, with increased concentration and simplification of measures;

■ A wider delegation of responsibility to member states and regions;

■ The introduction of new measures (such as JASPERS for investment programmes and technical assistance, JESSICA to encourage sustainable development in urban areas, and JEREMIE, by which the EIB and Commission can provide repayable types of assistance to micro-to-medium firms).

Cohesion policy was to support the Lisbon Agenda by:

■ making countries more attractive for investments;

■ encouraging innovation, entrepreneurship, and the knowledge economy; and

■ creating more and better jobs.

There were to be three new priority objectives for structural actions in the 2007–13 period (see Table 15.2):

1 convergence;

2 competitiveness and employment co-operation;

3 the European Territorial Co-operation Objective.

The aim of the first objective is to speed up the economic convergence of less developed regions. The Convergence Objective will concern regions whose per capita gross domestic product (GDP) is less than 75 per cent of the average for the EU(25).[11] In the EU(27) this objective covers 84 regions with a total population of 154 million in 17 member states (see Figure 15.2).[12] This objective will receive 81.6 per cent of contributions for cohesion actions (or €283 billion) over the 2007–2013 period compared with the 75 per cent for the previous Objective 1 over the 2000–2006 period.

The average GDP per capita was reduced with the enlargements of 2004 and 2007. As a result, if the criterion for Objective 1 regions of being under 75 per cent of average EU GDP remained unchanged, some regions that previously qualified for Objective 1 status would no longer do so in an enlarged EU. A phasing-out system (see Figure 15.2) was therefore adopted

objectives	Financial instruments		
Convergence	**ERDF**	**ESF**	**Cohesion Fund**
Regional Competitiveness and Employment	ERDF	ESF	
European Territorial Co-operation	ERDF		

TABLE 15.2 Financing the different cohesion policy Objectives 2007–2013
Source: European Commission, © European Communities, 2008, www.ec.europa.eu/regional_policy

[11] Bulgaria and Romania were not yet member states when agreement was reached in 2006 on cohesion policy for the 2007–2013 period.

[12] The statistics in this section are taken from www.ec.europa.eu/regional_policy

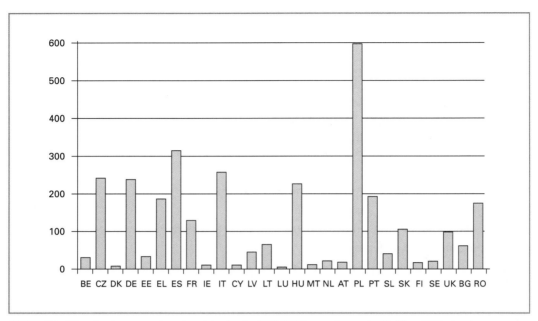

FIGURE 15.1 Allocation for economic and social cohesion 2007-2013 by member states (€million, 2004 prices)

Source: Elaboration on the basis of data taken from European Commission, website, © European Communities, 2008, www.ec.europa.eu/regional_policy

for regions that would have been eligible for funding if the threshold had been calculated for EU(15) rather than EU(25).

The Regional Competitiveness and Employment Objective is to receive 15.9 per cent of resources for cohesion actions. It applies in 168 regions representing 314 million inhabitants. The aim of the objective is to implement regional development programmes to strengthen regional competitiveness and attractiveness by anticipating economic and social change and supporting innovation, the knowledge society, entrepreneurship, protection of the environment, accessibility and risk prevention. The new Objective 2 also envisages programmes financed by the ESF to help workers and companies on the basis of the European Employment Strategy. Some regions are to be covered by a 'phasing-in' arrangement (see Figure 15.2) as they were covered by the former Objective 1 for the 2000–2006 period, but their GDP now exceeds 75 per cent of the average GDP of the EU(15).

The European Territorial Co-operation Objective accounts for 2.5 per cent of the total allocation for cohesion over the 2007–2013 period. The purpose of this objective is to strengthen co-operation at three levels:

1 cross-border co-operation through joint programmes;

2 co-operation between transnational zones;

3 networks for co-operation and the exchange of experiences throughout the EU.

A European Grouping for Territorial Co-operation (EGTC) has been set up as a legal entity to promote cross-border, transnational and regional co-operation.

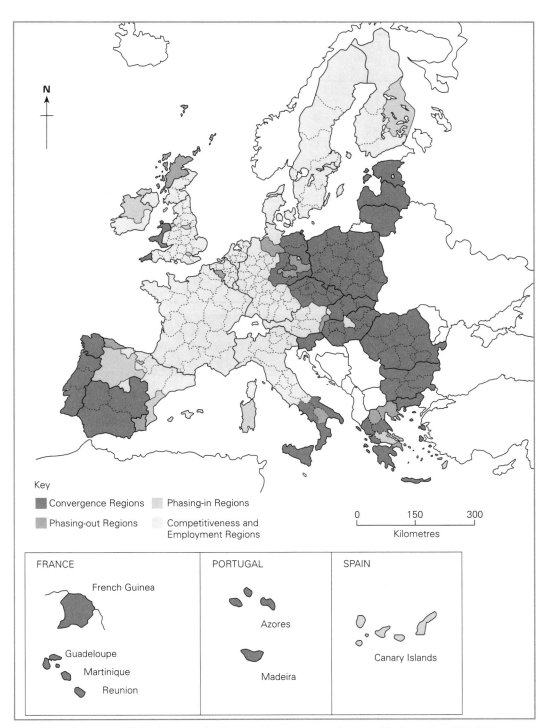

FIGURE 15.2 Convergence Objective and regional competitiveness and employment objective regions 2007–2013

Source: European Commission, © European Communities, 2008, www.europea.eu/regional_policy

	1950 (euros)	1990 (euros)	2000 (euros)	Average GDP growth 1996–2000	Real GDP Growth in 2006	1997 (PPS) EU(27)=100	2006 (PPS) EU(27)=100
Germany	93	125	111	1.8	2.9	124.9	113.6
France	136	111	106	2.7	2.0	115.2	112.8
Italy	71	101	89	1.9	1.9	119.6	103.7
Netherlands	100	100	111	3.7	3.0	127.6	131.2
Belgium	166	104	106	2.7	2.8	126.2	123.2
Luxembourg	201	149	191	7.1	6.1	215.7	278.6
UK	140	89	113	3.1	2.8	116.7	119.1
Denmark	153	132	142	2.7	3.5	133.8	126.6
Ireland	81	71	112	9.8	5.7	115.4	142.8
Spain	35	69	67	4.2	3.9	93.7	102.4
Portugal	35	37	49	3.9	1.3	76.5	74.5
Greece	30	43	52	3.4	4.3	85.0	96.9
Austria	58	109	112	2.7	3.3	133.2	128.7
Sweden	170	142	122	3.2	4.1	122.6	120.3
Finland	114	143	110	4.7	5.0	111.2	118.4
EU15	100	100	100	2.7	2.8	115.5	112.1

TABLE 15.3 GDP per capita and growth in the EU(15)

Source: European Commission, www.europa.eu.int/comm/regional, and elaborations based on Eurostat data, © European Communities, 2008.

PPS = purchasing power standards.

For the implementation of policy the Commission consults with the member states and draws up Community Strategic Guidelines on cohesion. Each member state then prepares a National Strategic Programme Reference Framework. The Commission validates the parts of these Frameworks, which require a decision as well as the Operating Programmes. The Operating Programmes present the priorities and methods of programming of the member states and/or regions.

Has there been convergence in the EU?

The disparities in GDP per capita and in employment among EU countries have narrowed over the past decade (though, as explained below, it is difficult to assess how far this was due to cohesion policy).[13] With the exception of Portugal, growth in the countries that benefited most from the Cohesion Fund (Greece, Portugal, Ireland and Spain) over the 1995–2006 period was well above the average for the EU (15) and this translated into higher rates of GDP per capita relative to the rest of the EU (see Table 15.3 and Figure 15.3). Between 1997 and 2006 GDP per capita in terms of purchasing power parity rose from 85 per cent to 96.9 per cent for Greece; from 93.7 to 102.4 per cent for Spain and from 115.4 to 142.8 per cent for Ireland (see Box 15.3 below), but fell from 76.5 per cent to 74.5 per cent for Portugal.

---

[13] European Commission (2007).

	Growth in 2000	Growth in 2005	Growth in 2006	Labour productivity increase 2004	Labour productivity per person employed 2006 EU(27)=100
Bulgaria	5.4	6.2	6.1	N/a	35.3
Cyprus	5.0	4.0	3.8	1	85.8
Czech Rep.	3.6	6.4	6.4	3.7	71.2
Estonia	10.8	10.2	11.2	7.5	63.7
Hungary	5.2	4.1	3.9	5.6	74.8
Latvia	6.9	10.6	11.9	10.5	52.9
Lithuania	4.1	7.9	7.7	6	58.6
Malta	N/a	4.1	3.9	0.3	88.2
Poland	4.3	3.6	6.1	4	61.5
Romania	2.1	4.1	7.7	N7a	38.3
Slovakia	1.4	4.1	5.7	3.6	71.4
Slovenia	4.1	6.6	8.5	6.3	84.7
EU(15)	3.8	1.6	2.8	1.5	110.4

TABLE 15.4 Growth of Real GDP and labour productivity in the new member states
Source: Eurosta, © European Communities, 2008.

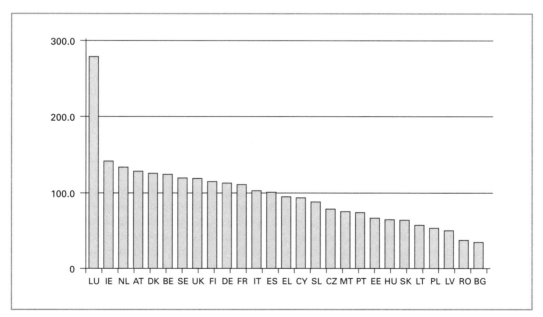

FIGURE 15.3 GDP per capita in the EU in 2006 in Purchasing Power Standards (PPS) (EU(27)=100)
Source: European Commission, © European Communities, 2008, www.ec.europa.eu/regional_policy

Box 15.3: *A case study of the catching-up process in the EU: the Celtic Tiger*

From the early 1990s the Irish economy experienced consistently high growth both compared with the USA and average EU performances, leading to the term 'Celtic Tiger'. Irish GDP per capita increased from 64 per cent of the Community average in 1973 when Ireland joined, to 71 per cent in 1990 and 143 per cent in 2006 (see Table 15.5). Various explanations have been advanced for this exceptional performance. In general, attention is drawn to the strategy to reduce unemployment adopted by successive Irish governments since the 1960s, which entails attempts to attract foreign direct investment and promote export-led growth. A favourable regime combining low corporation tax, and financial incentives, was used to encourage investment by foreign companies. Active intervention by, for example, the IDA Ireland (the Industrial Development Agency Ireland) was used to select investment in what were considered sectors with a global growth potential (such as electronics and the pharmaceutical industries). The FDI strategy also encouraged upstream linkages between foreign and indigenous companies, the creation of industrial clusters and the location of industry in the less developed areas of the country such as the West. The stability offered by EU membership and the advantage of an English-speaking labour force helped to attract foreign investors. An important role was also played by a policy of improving education and human capital from the 1960s and by the introduction of appropriate macroeconomic policies and a restrained wage-setting environment in the 1980s. A key component of the latter was the development of a social partnership, which enabled wage demands to be stabilized and allowed Ireland to gain competitiveness (Sweeney, 2008).

Substantial financing through the EU Structural Funds (see Tables 15.1, 15.2 and 15.4) contributed to the financing of regional investments and incentives at a time when the Irish economy could not have provided these resources without undermining its corrective macroeconomic policies (Braunerhjelm et al., 2000). A relatively efficient administration also favoured the successful implementation of measures financed with the EU Structural Funds.

The main shortcoming was insufficient attention paid to developing infrastructure, in particular, transport.

There has also been faster growth and more rapid catching up in the new member states (see Table 15.4). The GDP of the three Baltic states almost doubled in the decade between 1995 and 2005, while Poland, Hungary and Slovakia also had rapid growth rates during that period. However, given the low initial level of GDP per capita and assuming present growth rates continue, it is estimated that it will take at least 15 years for Poland, and more for Romania and Bulgaria to reach a GDP per capita of 75 per cent of the EU(27) average.[14]

Also at a regional level there has been a catching-up process, with relatively strong growth in regions with a low GDP per capita over the past decade, leading to overall convergence. The number of regions with GDP per capita below 75 per cent of the EU average fell from 78 to 70 between 1995 and 2004, while the number of those below 50 per cent fell from 39 to 32.[15] The regions that received most support from the Structural Funds over the 2000–2006 period

[14]European Commission (2007).

[15]The statistics in this section are taken from European Commission (2007).

Labour productivity increase	1996–2000	2004	Labour productivity per person employed 2006 EU(27)=100
Greece	2.5	3.0	116.9 f
Spain	0.7	0.7	100.3
Ireland	3.9	1.4	132.1
Portugal	1.8	0.1	68.3
Belgium	1.4	3.6	134.9
Germany	1.1	0.7	106.4
France	1.5	1.6	125.3
Italy	1.1	0.6	109.5
Lux.	2.8	3.7	183.3
NL	1.2	3.5	114.4
Austria	1.9	1.9	121.1
Finland	2.4	2.8	111.5
Denmark	1.6	1.9	108.4
Sweden	2.5	3.3	110.1
UK	1.6	2.4	110.3
EU(15)	1.3	1.5	110.4

TABLE 15.5 Percentage increase in labour productivity in the EU(15) f: forecast
Source: European Commission, © European Communities, 2008, www.ec.europa.eu/regional_policy

also showed a substantial increase in GDP per capita compared with the rest of the EU. In 1995 regions with a population of 71 million had a GDP per capita below 75 per cent of the EU average. By 2004 one in four of these regions (covering a population of almost 10 million) had risen above the 75 per cent threshold.

However, despite this progress large disparities remain within the EU, in particular, after enlargement. Much of the convergence that has taken place in the EU is the result of low-income countries catching up rather than regions as such. Within member states there has been convergence in some countries (such as Austria), but increasing disparities in others (such as the UK, Sweden, the Netherlands and Portugal). Disparities widened over the 1995–2004 period in the Czech Republic, Romania, Bulgaria and, to a lesser extent, in Slovakia. In Poland and Hungary disparities grew between 1995 and 2000, but subsequently remained largely unchanged. A major cause of disparity is the concentration of economic activity around capital cities. For instance, London and Paris account for about 30 per cent of national GDP. In parts of the EU there is still outward migration from rural areas, such as those in Southern Italy, the North of Finland, Sweden, Scotland, East Germany and eastern Poland.

The level of GDP per capita of a country or region can be attributed to the output of each person working (labour productivity), and the number of people working. Labour productivity has been growing rapidly in the new member states (see Tables 15.4 and 15.5). Between 1995 and 2004 productivity in the three Baltic States and parts of Poland grew four times faster than the EU average, though starting from low levels in some cases (European Commission, 2007).

As discussed in the context of the Lisbon Strategy in Chapter 7, in 1995 GDP per person employed in the EU was only 3 per cent lower than in the USA, but the gap had widened to 12 per cent in 2004. Much of the difference is due to the longer hours worked and shorter holidays in the USA, and in terms of GDP per hour worked the gap virtually disappears. However, growth in productivity over the 1995–2004 period was higher in the USA than in the EU(15).

	1998	2006
EU(15)	61.4	66.0
Greece	56.0	61.0
Spain	51.3	64.8
Ireland	60.6	68.6
Portugal	66.8	67.9
Bulgaria	50.4**	58.6
Czech Republic	67.3	65.3
Estonia	64.6	68.1
Cyprus	65.7**	69.6
Latvia	59.9	66.3
Lithuania	62.3	63.6
Hungary	53.7	57.3
Malta	54.1**	54.8
Poland	59.0	54.5
Romania	64.2	58.8
Slovenia	62.8	66.6
Slovakia	56.8	59.4

TABLE 15.6 Employment rates in the Cohesion Fund countries (per cent)*

*including Ireland, which was a former cohesion country, and Spain, which has transitional arrangements for the 2007–2013 period.
**2000
Source: Eurostat, © European Communities, 2008.

Only in Ireland, Greece and Sweden was productivity growth higher that that of the USA over the 1995–2004 period (data are not available for the new member states before 2000), though it was similar in Finland, Portugal and the UK.

Regional employment rates converged in the EU between 2000 and 2005, but in 2005 employment rates in the lagging regions were about 11 points lower than in the rest of the EU (European Commission, 2007). Some countries experienced an increase in employment over the 2000–2005 period (Spain, Cyprus, the three Baltic States, Greece, Italy and Bulgaria), while in others (Romania, Poland, Portugal, Germany, Malta, the Czech Republic, Denmark and Sweden) it declined (see Table 15.6).

Empirical studies such as those by Brülhart and Traeger (2003) and Midelfart-Knarvik and Overman (2002) suggest that over time within EU countries the internal concentration of manufacturing in certain geographical areas has increased. Variations in results may arise because different time periods, regions and indicators of regional disparities are taken into account.

The role of cohesion policy

It is extremely difficult to assess the effectiveness of cohesion policy on a number of counts, and the following list does not pretend to be exhaustive:

- The impact of many projects and programmes (e.g. infrastructure) can only be assessed in the long run.
- Problems arise in isolating the effects of regional policies from other factors (including other EU policies with regional implications such as the CAP).

■ It is difficult to separate the impact of national and EU regional policies.

■ Recipients tend to overestimate the impact of regional measures.

The European Commission and member states carry out regular in-depth assessment of cohesion policy. European Union member states are responsible for ex-ante evaluation, while the Commission carries out ex-post assessment. Many of the results of the studies carried out by the Commission are presented in the Reports on Economic and Social Cohesion. The econometric research carried out by the European Commission using three different macroeconomic models presented in the most recent of these Reports suggests that cohesion policy in the EU has had a significantly positive effect.[16]

According to simulations using the Hermin model, GDP in absolute terms was about 5–10 per cent higher in the new member states than it would have been without intervention. About half the increase in GDP was attributable to supply-side effects such as increases in physical and human capital, and R&D. The simulation also suggests that cohesion policy would create a predicted additional 2 million jobs by 2015.

The largest estimated percentage gains on GDP and employment in 2006 as a result of cohesion policy between 2000 and 2006 were for Greece, Portugal, the Baltic States, the Czech Republic and the Italian Mezzogiorno. The predicted gains in GDP in 2015 from cohesion policy between 2000 and 2013 were highest for the Baltic States, the Czech Republic and Romania, while the largest gains in employment were expected for the Baltic States, the Czech Republic, Malta and Slovakia. Differences between countries were attributed to the scale of funding, and differences in the structure of the economy, such as the sectoral structure of the economy, openness to productivity growth driven by technological advance, trade openness and wage flexibility.

According to an alternative model, EcoMod, cohesion policy is again predicted to have a positive impact in all 15 cohesion countries, in particular, in the new member states. In Slovakia, Lithuania, Latvia and Bulgaria, GDP is predicted to be about 15 per cent higher in 2020 as a result of cohesion policy. Employment increases were predicted to account for 40–50 per cent of GDP growth in most cases, with the remainder coming from productivity growth.

The QUEST model assumes that policy intervention will have strong crowding-out effects so estimates a limited impact on demand. In contrast a slow improvement on the supply side is predicted largely in the form of productivity gains. Most of the gains are expected to occur in the long period, after the programming period and funding come to an end.

The results of simulations carried out with the three models differ, partly reflecting the different features of the models, but all three point to a significant effect of cohesion policy boosting GDP in the lagging regions of the EU.[17]

The need to select an appropriate development strategy

Though there is much debate about the role of structural measures (redistribution, resource allocation policy or *juste retour*; see, for example, Hardy et al., 1995), there seems widespread consensus that a low level of economic development should not be a sufficient condition for receiving transfers. Instead an effective policy should be based on a development strategy.

In evolving that strategy there are differences of opinion about whether industrial districts or clusters are preferable to more evenly spread growth. What emerges from the experience of EU

---

[16] See European Commission (2007) for a description of these models and the simulations.

[17] Bottom-up surveys carried out by the Commission confirm that cohesion policy has added to job creation (see European Commission, 2007).

member states and, in particular the Irish example, is the importance of paying adequate attention to the interaction of regional measures and the wider framework of macroeconomic policies (see Box 15.2).

The objectives of regional policy are strongly linked to the Lisbon Strategy. At a regional level various factors determine competitiveness and hence potential for economic growth and employment creation. According to the Fourth Report on Economic and Social Cohesion (European Commission, 2007) these include:

- A sound macroeconomic framework with price stability and balanced budgets, permitting low interest rates that can stimulate investment and capital accumulation. It also helps to increase the rate and diffusion of innovation and reduce the cost of capital;
- An efficient administrative framework providing sufficient institutional support;
- An adequate endowment of infrastructure of various types: physical (in the form of transport, energy and telecommunications networks); human (in the form of skills and know-how of the work force) and social (in the form of care and other support service);
- Capacity for innovation, which encompasses human resource endowment, but also the resources devoted to R&D and the effectiveness with which they are used;
- A development path that is sustainable in order to protect the environment.

It is also essential to develop an appropriate system for selecting projects and programmes, for setting out clear objectives and targets and for carrying out effective evaluation and monitoring. There are also substantial differences in the ability to implement structural measures among existing EU member states. Experience suggests that the extent to which a member state can derive benefits from the resources it receives depends not only on the level of financing but also on administrative capacity and the efficient use of national and Community resources (Bollen et al., 2000). The system should also be able to withstand pressure from politicians and pressure groups.

In short, it is necessary to develop a strategy for ensuring the effectiveness of regional policy, and this is likely to include the following elements:

- Evolving an overall strategy to regional and national development to avoid the risk of piece-meal, unco-ordinated measures;
- Ensuring stable macroeconomic policies;
- Adopting robust selection procedures and effective monitoring of programmes; and
- Developing an effective institutional framework for planning and implementing measures.

Evaluation

With EU enlargement in 2004 and 2007 income disparities in the EU increased substantially. Disparities between regions in the new member states were similar to those in the EU(15), but at a lower level of income. The aim of EU cohesion policies is to reduce these regional income disparities throughout the EU, and according to various studies carried out by the European Commission, intervention has had positive effects on GDP per capita and employment.

For the 2007–2013 period 36 per cent of EU spending has been allocated for cohesion policy, and the aim is to link cohesion policy to the objectives of the Lisbon Strategy. The objectives include encouraging investment, innovation and the knowledge society, and creating more jobs. Nobody denies the validity of such aims, but often in practice inadequate funds are allocated for their realization, both at the national and EU level. The EU budget is little more than

1 per cent of GDP, but even here, as described in Chapter 11, cuts in the initial Commission proposals for cohesion spending were made.

The principles of partnership and subsidiarity imply decentralization of decision-making with the involvement of national, regional and local authorities. At times this has the disadvantage of complex and bureaucratic procedures. Despite efforts to streamline the objectives and protocols for submitting proposals over the years, this shortcoming has proved rather intractable. Differences in administrative capacity of regions and/or member states appears to be a major factor in determining the effectiveness of measures

Summary of Key Concepts

- Regional problems are the disparities in levels of income, in rates of growth of output and employment, and in general in levels of economic inequality between different regions.

- The view that integration will lead to greater convergence assumes effective functioning of the market. Convergence is said to occur through free trade, labour migration, capital mobility and diminishing returns to capital accumulation.

- Theories explaining why integration may lead to divergence or greater disparities between regions include modern growth theories, the evolutionary economics view of knowledge diffusion and the New Economic Geography approach.

- For the 2007–2013 period the three funds for regional and cohesion policy are: the European Social Fund, the European Fund for Regional Development and the Cohesion Fund. Related instruments are the European Investment Bank and the European Union Solidarity Fund.

- The historical evolution of EU regional policy up until 2007 can be divided into three main stages: 1959–75 (mainly national measures), 1975–88 (new EC initiatives were launched) and since 1988 (the development of regional policy with the reforms of 1988, 1993, 1999 and 2007).

- The four principles of operation of the Structural Funds are: concentration, partnership, programming and additionality.

- The reform of cohesion policy for the 2007–2013 period is tightly integrated to the objectives of the Lisbon Strategy; allocates 36 per cent of the EU budget to cohesion measures; changes the objectives of cohesion policy; aims at improving implementation and monitoring; and introduces new instruments.

- The objectives of cohesion policy have changed over the years. Since 2007 there have been three objectives. Objective 1 covers the convergence regions, which are defined as those whose GDP per capita is less than 75 per cent of the EU average. Objective 2 concerns Regional Competitiveness and Employment, while Objective 3 promotes Regional Territorial Co-operation.

- There appears to have been convergence between EU countries and regions though large disparities remain.

- It is extremely difficult to assess the effectiveness of structural measures because the impact of many projects can only be assessed in the long run; problems arise in isolating the effects of regional policies from other factors; and recipients tend to overestimate the impact of regional measures.

- To render regional policy effective, it is necessary to develop an overall strategy to regional and national development; to ensure stable macroeconomic policies; and to develop an effective institutional framework for planning and implementing measures.

Questions for study and review

1 Do you think that integration leads to more or less income disparity?

2 Describe the various financial instruments used to implement EU cohesion policy.

3 What are the main stages in the evolution of EU regional and cohesion policy?

4 How well do you consider that the four principles for implementing cohesion policy function?

5 Has there been convergence between EU countries and regions?

6 How effective was the cohesion policy of the EU ? Why is it so difficult to provide an assessment of its effectiveness?

7 What strategies can be used to render regional and cohesion policy more effective?

References

Baldwin, R. and Wyplosz, C. (2006) *The Economics of European Integration*, 2nd edn., McGraw-Hill Education, Maidenhead, UK.

Bollen, F., Hartwig, I. and Nicolaides, P. (2000) *EU Structural Funds beyond Agenda 2000: Reform and Implications for the Current and Future Member States*, European Institute of Public Administration (EIPA), Maastricht.

Braunerhjelm, P., Faini, R., Norman, V., Ruane, F., and Seabright, P. (2000) *Integration and the Regions of Europe: How the Right Policies Can Prevent Polarization*, Monitoring European Integration 10, CEPR, London.

Brülhart, M. and Traeger, R. (2003) 'An account of geographic concentration patterns in Europe', Cahiers de Recherches Economiques du Département d'Econometrie e d'Economie Politique (DEEP), Université de Lausanne, www.hec.unil.ch/deep/publications-english

European Commission (2004) 'Third Report on Economic and Social Cohesion', www.ec.europa.eu/regional_policy

European Commission (2007) 'Growing Regions, Growing Europe. Fourth Report on Economic and Social Cohesion,' www.ec.europa.eu/regional_policy

Hardy, S., Hart, M., Albrechts, L. and Katos, A. (1995) *An Enlarged EU: Regions in Competition?* Jessica Kingsley Publishers, London and Bristol, PA.

Harrop, J. (2000) *The Political Economy of Integration in the European Union*, 3rd edn, Edward Elgar, Cheltenham.

Krugman, P.R. (1991) *Geography and Trade*, Leuven University Press, Leuven and The MIT Press, Cambridge, MA.

Krugman, P.R. and Venables, A. (1990) 'Integration and the competitiveness of peripheral industry' in Bliss, C.J. and Braga de Macedo, J. (eds) *Unity with Diversity in the European Economy: The Communities' Southern Frontier*, Cambridge University Press, Cambridge.

Midelfart-Knarvik, K-H. and Overman, H. (2002) 'Delocation and European integration: Is structural spending justified?', *Economic Policy*, Vol. 17.

Molle, W. (2006) *The Economics of European Integration. Theory, Practice, Policy*, 5th edn, Ashgate, Aldershot.

Navarro, L. (2003) 'Industrial policy in the economic literature: Recent theoretical developments and implications for EU policy', Enterprise papers No. 12, www.europa.eu.int/comm/enterprise

Nelson, R.R. and Winter, S.G. (1982) *An Evolutionary Theory of Economic Change*, Harvard University Press, Cambridge.

Sweeney, P. (ed.) (2008) *Ireland's Economic Success – Reasons and Lessons*, New Island, Dublin.

Tsoukalis, L. (1997) *The New European Economy Revisited*, 3rd edn, Oxford University Press, Oxford.

Williams, R.H. (1996) *European Union Spatial Policy and Planning*, Paul Chapman, London.

Useful websites

European Commission Directorate-General for Regional Policy is one of the better websites of the Commission:
www.ec.europa.eu/regional_policy

The Committee on Regional Development of the European Parliament:
www.europarl.europa.eu/committees/regi_home_en.htm

The Committee of the Regions:
www.cor.europa.eu

Eurostat for regional statistics:
www.epp.eurostat.ec.europa.eu

Social and Employment Policies

Introduction

The term 'social policy' covers a wide range of issues whose boundaries are at times indistinct. Social policies include the various measures to regulate the labour market but also measures to combat poverty and social exclusion, and to improve education, training, housing and health care.[1] One of the main ways in which social policy may reduce disparities is by improving access to employment. Social policy and the fight against unemployment are therefore intrinsically linked.

As described below, the EES was launched in 1997 to combat unemployment through preventive methods and active policies to promote employability. In 2003 the EES was streamlined and revised with the aim of better realizing the Lisbon Strategy in an enlarged EU (see Chapter 7).

European social policy includes the social policies of the member states and EU, and so has to be distinguished from EU social policy. EU social policy covers a relatively limited range of issues and amounts to just a small fraction of welfare expenditure by the member states, tending simply to complement national measures.

The aims and actions of EU social policy have evolved over the years, and since the 1990s increased priority has been given to:

■ Employment policies and working conditions;

---

[1] European Commission (1993a) defines European social policy as the 'full range of policies in the social sphere, including labour market policies'.

- Social exclusion, or the fight against poverty;
- Equality between men and women;
- The involvement of the so-called social partners (trade unions and employers) in the legislative process;
- The participation of workers in the decision-making of the firm.

Differences in the level of social protection between the member states may also give rise to fears of social dumping. Firms may have an incentive to locate in countries where wages and the cost of social protection is lower (usually the poorer member states). To counter this tendency countries with higher social standards may be forced to reduce social standards, giving rise to the risk of a 'race to the bottom'. One way of tackling the risk of social dumping is by setting certain minimum standards for working conditions, health and safety in all member states.

Despite the increasing role of the Community in the social sphere, there remain several obstacles to developing a fully-fledged EU social policy:

- Differences in the demographic and socio-economic conditions of the member states;
- The contentious nature of social policy issues, with strong ideological differences about what the role of the state should be;
- The diversity of national social policy regimes;
- The reluctance of member states to give up control of social policy;
- The scale of budgetary transfers necessary for an extensive EU social policy; and
- The even greater diversity of social policy requirements and regimes after the 2004 and 2007 enlargements.

The evolution of EU social policy

The origins of EU social policy are to be found in all three of the original treaties founding the European Communities. Article 46 of the Treaty of Paris establishing the European Coal and Steel Community refers to the improvement of the living and working standards of workers in the coal and steel industries. The Euratom Treaty sets out provisions for the health and safety of workers in the civilian atomic energy industry. By far the most extensive treatment of social policy is to be found in the Treaty of Rome, which refers to:

- Free movement of workers (Articles 48–51);
- Improvement in working conditions and in standards of living (Articles 117–28);
- Equal opportunities for men and women (see Box 16.1) (Article 119); and
- The creation of the European Social Fund (Article 123).

However, there was a dichotomy between the very ambitious objectives set out in the Treaty of Rome and the very limited means to achieve these aims. The commitments set out in the Treaty were far from being precise, and there was no fixed timetable for action. For instance, it was envisaged that improved working standards and conditions of work would be realized through operation of the common market.

The evolution of EU social policy can be divided into four main periods: 1958–73, 1974–85, 1985–92 and since 1993.

Box 16.1: *Gender equality in the EU*

Article 119 of the Treaty of Rome (now Article 141 of the EC Treaty) guarantees equal pay for men and women. As some member states were failing to comply with Article 119, the Community introduced Directives on equal pay (1975), equal treatment (1976) and the elimination of discrimination in pension schemes (1986). The Court of Justice also reinforced EU gender policy in judgments such as Defrenne vs. Sabena on equal pay (1976), and the Marschall Judgment of 1997, which allowed priority to be given to the woman in the event of male and female candidates possessing the same qualifications.

In 1996 the Commission adopted the gender mainstreaming approach that involves 'incorporating equal opportunities for women and men into all Community policies and activities' (COM(96)67 final). The European Social Fund is used to promote gender equality. Over the 2000–2006 period the Community Initiative, EQUAL, aimed at ensuring equality of opportunity for everyone. Since 2007 the Community Programme for Social Solidarity, PROGRESS (see below), has also provided funding for gender equality.

Under the Amsterdam and Nice Treaties co-decision and qualified majority voting are to be used on matters relating to equal pay for equal work or for 'work of the same value' (Article 141, EC Treaty). Article 2 includes a general objective to promote 'equality between men and women' which is reiterated in Article 3 that sets out the instruments to be used. Article 13 provides a legal basis to prevent discrimination on grounds of sex.

The EES provides the member states with guidelines on how to attract more women into the labour force and narrow the gap between men and women with regard to pay, employment and unemployment.

Figure 16.2 (p. 381) shows the member states that in 2006 met the Lisbon target of a 60 per cent employment rate for women, but in Greece, Italy, Poland and, in particular, Malta, participation of women in the EU labour force remained lower.[2] The gender pay gap (measuring the difference in average gross hourly earnings) has narrowed only marginally since 2000. In 2000 women had on average 16 per cent lower earnings than men, with a gap of less than 10 per cent in Portugal and Italy, but 20 per cent or more in Austria, Germany, the Netherlands and the UK. In 2005 women's earnings were 15 per cent below those of men, with a gap of still 20 per cent or more in Germany and the UK. The number of member states where the gap was below 10 per cent had increased, and included Belgium, Ireland and Greece in 2005.

In June 2003 news that the Commission was proposing legislation to prevent sexism in advertising, the media and financial services caused consternation in some of the British and German popular newspapers and Italian television.

1 The 1958–73 period

The social policy of the Community maintained a low profile during this period, and its principal aim was to promote the free movement of labour.[2] This entailed co-ordinating the national social security systems of member states in order to guarantee the rights of emigrant workers. Progress in recognizing qualifications obtained in other member states was slow, so movement of labour was mainly confined to young or unskilled workers (Tsoukalis, 1997).

---

[2] See also Chapter 7.

2 The 1974–85 period

Following the 1973 oil crisis the economic situation in the Community degenerated rapidly, with increasing unemployment and stagnating growth. The deteriorating conditions led the Community to introduce the first Social Action Programme in 1974 aimed at:

- The attainment of full and better employment;
- The improvement and upward harmonization of living standards;
- Greater involvement of employer and employee organizations in the economic and social decisions of the Community and of workers in the life of their firms.

Despite its good intentions the programme led to few concrete actions, though it served as a frame of reference for later programmes. At the time unemployment was soaring, funds were limited and the member states were reluctant to transfer responsibility for social matters to the Community. European Community intervention tended to be piecemeal, but a few successes were registered (Tsoukalis, 1997). Directives were introduced to improve work standards and safety, to promote equality between men and women and to regulate the conditions for collective dismissals.

During this period EC social policy was still mainly concentrated on the co-ordination of national social security systems to permit the freedom of movement of labour and the operation of the European Social Fund (ESF). The ESF became more directed towards the fight against youth and long-term unemployment, in particular by promoting training schemes. However, EC policy was characterized by a lack of flexibility in selecting programmes and a tendency to rubber-stamp decisions already taken at the national level. Moreover, in many cases it seems likely that EC measures simply replaced national financing (the so-called additionality problem; see Chapter 15).

3 The 1985–92 period

Given the limited success of earlier measures, many of the social policy objectives of the Treaty of Rome still had not been realized when the Single Market Programme was introduced. Although social policy was not mentioned in the White Paper of 1985, debate about a 'social dimension' to the Single Market was soon to emerge. Proponents of a more active EC role in social policy argued that this was necessary because the adjustment implied by the Single Market Project could lead to higher unemployment and that deregulation could lead to a risk of social dumping.

Though the debate about EC social policy was linked to the Single Market Project, its ideological basis was wider, reflecting different views of the role of the state in the economy. The case for an increased role for the Community was generally based on a fundamental belief that the workings of the market had to be corrected on grounds of equity and consensus. Social cohesion was necessary to correct the possible negative impact of increased competition on the weaker and more vulnerable regions and sections of the population. Minimum social standards had to be introduced to prevent the risk of social dumping. Increased participation of the workers in the decisions of firms, and of the so-called social partners (employers and trade unions) in EC decision-making, were ways of achieving consensus.

Those in favour of this type of approach included the Socialist President of the Commission, Delors, centre-left members of the European Parliament and the Socialist governments in France and some of the Southern EC countries (Tsoukalis, 1997). Most Christian Democratic parties were then in favour of legislation to protect welfare and employment. In Germany there was a long tradition of worker participation in the decisions of the firm and attempts to find consensus between the social partners.

Perhaps the main opposition in the ideological debate was to be found in the British Conservative Party, and Margaret Thatcher, in particular. Increased government regulation of working conditions was considered to add to labour market rigidities, reducing competitiveness and increasing unemployment. The poor British performance when the Conservatives took office was interpreted as being largely the result of excessive trade union influence. Worse still, the attempt to strengthen the Community role in this area was considered an attack on national sovereignty and a violation of the principle of subsidiarity. The British government found support for this position among EC employers' federations and its own businessmen.[3]

Delors was among the main proponents of a more active EC social policy, or 'European Social Space', and four aspects of this position can be distinguished:[4]

- **Social dialogue, or the involvement of the social partners in the EC decision-making process**. In 1985 Delors arranged a meeting of associations at the Belgian château of Val Duchesse to promote social dialogue between the Commission, employers and employees. This subsequently became known as the 'Val Duchesse Process' and was institutionalized by the Single European Act (Article 118b) and the Maastricht Treaty (Article 3 of the Social Protocol). An institution that has played a growing role in social dialogue is the European Economic and Social Committee or EESC (see Chapter 3), which has evolved from a mere consultative body into an important institutional forum for social partners to engage in key discussions of different aspects of integration that affect the lives of EU consumers and citizens.

- **The Social Charter, or Community Charter of the Fundamental Social Rights of Workers**. This was drawn up as a non-binding declaration of intent at the request of the Commission, European Parliament and EESC. It builds on the Social Charter of the Council of Europe and similar documents of the International Labour Office. An action programme accompanied the Charter with specific measures designed to assist realization of the objectives. As can be seen from Box 16.2, the objectives are couched in very general terms, but some were still the subject of heated controversy. For instance, the aim of achieving an 'equitable wage' was interpreted in certain quarters as implying the introduction of a minimum wage. Measures to protect seasonal, temporary and part-time workers were seen as an attempt to extend full social protection to such forms of atypical work, so adding to labour market rigidities. Although amended to take account of British objections, the Charter was not accepted by the UK, but it was adopted by the other 11 member states in 1989.

- **The creation of a 'Europe of the citizens'**, aimed at reducing the democratic deficit and bringing the Community closer to the people (see Chapter 2).

- **The introduction of an EC company statute** that would ensure the participation of workers in the decisions of the firm along the lines of the German and Dutch models. In December 2000 the Council agreed on the introduction of a European Company Statute which would enable a company with a European dimension to set up as a single company under EU law with a unified set of rules, management and reporting system, and provisions for safeguarding workers' rights.

---

[3] Tsoukalis, 1997.

[4] Delors presented his vision of a European Social Space, *inter alia*, at the European Trades Union Conference (ETUC) of 1988.

Box 16.2: *The Social Charter*

- The improvement of living and working conditions;
- The right to freedom of movement;
- The right to employment with adequate remuneration;
- The right to social protection;
- The right to freedom and collective bargaining;
- The right to vocational training;
- The right of men and women to equal treatment;
- The right to information, consultation and worker participation;
- The right to health protection and safety at the workplace;
- The protection of children and adolescents;
- The protection of elderly persons;
- Specific measures for disabled people.

Though the Single European Act contained relatively few increases in the EC role in social policy, reference was first made to the need for economic and social cohesion, social dialogue (Article 118b) and improvements in health and safety at the workplace (Article 118a).

4 Since 1993

The Social Charter was subsequently to form the basis of the Social Chapter of the Treaty of Maastricht, which covers issues such as minimum hours of work, social security, health and safety requirements and consultation of the social partners.

Following its earlier refusal to sign the Social Charter, the UK also opted out of the Maastricht Social Chapter during the 1993–97 period, and only under the Blair government was policy reversed. The Social Chapter was therefore added to the Maastricht Treaty as a separate Protocol, and was only incorporated into the Community pillar under the Amsterdam Treaty. However, certain other aspects of social policy (such as protection of public health) were included in the Maastricht Treaty and were applicable in all member states. As can be seen from Chapter 3, some elements of the Social Charter and Maastricht Social Chapter were similar to the Charter of Fundamental Human Rights approved at Nice in 2000.

The Amsterdam Treaty added three new objectives to EU social policy (Articles 136 and 137):

1 Proper social protection;
2 Social dialogue between management and labour; and
3 The development of human resources with a view to lasting high employment and combating forms of economic and social exclusion.

In 2005 the EU agreed the Social Agenda covering the 2005–2010 period, which aims at providing jobs, fighting poverty and promoting equal opportunities for all, including for workers who move around so that they have the same social security and pension rights throughout the EU. The Social Agenda involves national, regional and local authorities, the social partners (i.e. representatives of employers and workers) and non-governmental organizations. It supports member states in their efforts to reform pension and health care systems, tackle poverty, meet the demographic challenge, and foster equal opportunities.

With regard to financial assistance from the EU, the European Social Fund has €77 billion for the 2007–2013 period to increase the adaptability of workers and enterprises, enhance access to the labour market, combat discrimination, improve education and training systems, and improve institutional capacity in disadvantaged regions. The European Globalisation Adjustment Fund provides €500 each year for workers made redundant as a result of trade liberalization.

The European Employment Strategy

At the time of the Treaty of Rome unemployment was relatively low in the Community, so the Treaty contained few provisions on employment. The Commission published White Papers in 1993 and 1994 aimed at promoting employment, competitiveness and growth without compromising social protection. However, it was not until the Amsterdam Treaty that the legal basis of employment as a major area of EU policy was established.

The key elements of the Treaty of Amsterdam with regard to EU employment policy are as follows:

- The development of a co-ordinated strategy of the member states toward unemployment;
- The commitment to achieving a high level of employment is recognized as one of the key objectives of the EU;
- Employment is a matter of common concern;
- Member states and the EU were obliged to work together in developing a co-ordinated strategy towards employment;
- The 'mainstreaming' of employment policy, which must be taken into account in the formulation of all EU policies and strategies;
- Multilateral surveillance;
- The Council, on a Commission proposal, may issue recommendations to member states for urgent action;
- Establishment of an Employment Committee to play a part in these processes and serve as a forum for debate;
- Decisions on employment policy are to be taken by a qualified majority.

The employment strategy was based on what are known as 'active labour market policies' to enable people to take up employment opportunities, increase skills and keep the unemployed in touch with the labour market. The EU adopted a dual approach to achieve these aims: setting the policy framework and guidelines, and providing financing for programmes through the Structural Funds. However, the Treaty again stressed the need to 'take account of the diverse forms of national practices in particular in the field of contractual relations', and EU social and employment policy remains very much a complement to national measures.

Given persistent high levels of unemployment during the early 1990s, which were attributed to structural problems in labour markets, in November 1997 an Extraordinary European Council on Employment was held. It was agreed that it was necessary to act collectively at the EU level to find solutions through more co-ordination and convergence of policies. This marks the beginning of the Luxembourg Process to launch the EES. The strategy is organized around four pillars:

1 Improving 'employability' (through active labour-market policy such as training schemes for the young and long-term unemployed; see Box 16.3);

2 Encouraging the adaptability of businesses and their employees (through union-negotiated work reorganization). As described in Chapter 7, this should also help in meeting the challenges of globalization;

3 Strengthening policies for equal opportunities (between men and women, and also increasing job possibilities for the disabled, see also Box 16.4);

4 Developing entrepreneurship (in particular through deregulation and simplification of market access for small firms).

Box 16.3: *An example of a project to combat long-term unemployment financed by the European Social Fund*

A French project, CREATIVE, co-ordinated by the National Employment Agency, was established to encourage the long-term unemployed to find work or set up small businesses of their own. Operating through seven employment agencies, the project involved a micro-finance organization for individuals with a business idea but without the financial guarantees necessary to get a loan through a traditional bank. The loans offered were less than €5 000 in value, but in 2003, they helped 75 participants to set up their own business. The project also helps those with few qualifications to get a driver's licence as an additional skill for the job market. Successful participants, accompanied by a trainer, provide services to the community by giving lifts to people who have mobility problems. A further initiative teaches skills to jobseekers by running courses giving practical training in arts and crafts. One course resulted in the successful transformation of a hallway in a residential building of a deprived area. Total funding for the project was €1 380 thousand, of which €450 thousand came from the ESF.

Various arrangements provide for country surveillance. On the basis of proposals from the Commission, the Council sets yearly Employment Guidelines, some also having detailed quantitative targets with the aim of rendering monitoring easier. Member states are asked to set out annual National Action Plans indicating labour market targets and their implementation. A yearly Joint Employment Report established by the Commission and the Council examines the employment policies of the member states. In addition to monitoring, the European Commission may propose, and the Council adopt, recommendations to individual member states.

Box 16.4: EU measures for the disabled

The EU has developed policies for the disabled, though also here the primary responsibility remains with the member states. The EU provides support for access to jobs for the disabled through the ESF and, over the 2000–2006 period, through the Community Initiative, EQUAL. Support for disabled persons has also been mainstreamed into the other employment policies of the EU. The National Action Plans of the member states include measures such as training, counselling and placements to encourage access of the disabled to employment. The EU co-ordinates national measures, and provided a budget of €12 million in 2003 for the European Year for the Disabled.

Employment Incentive Measures are proposed by the Commission and help member states to meet the objective of a high level of employment by promoting a co-ordinated approach, supporting initiatives to be carried out, financing evaluation and exchanging knowledge of good practice with regard to employment policy. In 2007 the Employment Incentive Measure was adapted and included under PROGRESS (the Community Programme for Employment and Social Solidarity). This has a budget of €743 million for the 2007–2013 period and finances measures in five main fields of action: employment, social protection and inclusion, working conditions, anti-discrimination and diversity, and gender equality.

The EES is closely linked to the Lisbon Strategy. The aims of the Lisbon Strategy include achieving higher employment rates (rather than lower unemployment rates), increasing the rate of participation in the labour force to 70 per cent by 2010 (60 per cent for women and 50 per cent for older persons aged 55–64). The interim target was 67 per cent for total employment and 57 per cent for women in 2005.[5] The Lisbon Strategy also aimed at addressing skill shortages and improving the quality of work, increased mobility and lifelong learning.

With the 2004 and 2007 enlargements, the new member states had to take on the employment and social policy *acquis* at a time when the budgets in many of these countries were overstrained (see Chapter 20) and their welfare systems (health care, pensions, education, etc.) required urgent reform. To prepare these countries for joining the EES, the Commission published 'Joint Assessment Papers' that analyse the labour market situation and trends, and identify proposals for reform.

The first five years of the EES were evaluated in 2002, and the Strategy was reinforced and streamlined in 2003 to underpin the Lisbon process in an enlarged EU. In 2005 as explained in Chapter 7, the Lisbon Strategy was revised, and this included setting out Guidelines for Growth and Jobs for the 2005–2008 period with three main priorities:[6]

1 Attracting and retaining more people in employment, and making work an option for all (through more active labour market policies and targeting disadvantaged groups);

2 Increased adaptability of workers and enterprises;

3 More investment in human capital.

To further these objectives various initiatives were introduced: the Mutual Learning Programme (to exchange knowledge of good practice); the European Employment Observatory (to exchange information and statistics on employment and labour market policies and to carry out research); Territorial Employment pacts (to encourage the more active involvement of regional and local actors); and Flexicurity (to combine flexibility and security in the labour market).

Assessment of the European Employment Strategy

Assessing the effects of the EES encounters the usual difficulty of isolating the impact of EU policies from other factors (such as growth) influencing employment levels.[7] The question is further complicated in that national employment policies may not always be co-ordinated with those

---

[5] As shown in Chapter 7 and below in 2006 the employment rates were still below these levels.

[6] With regard to employment, the Strategy took on board the recommendations of the European Employment Taskforce, which had been set up in 2003 under the former Prime Minister of the Netherlands, Wim Kok. The report of the Taskforce was published in 2003 as 'Jobs, Jobs, Jobs – Creating More Employment in Europe'.

[7] See Chapter 2 for statistics on growth and unemployment in the member states.

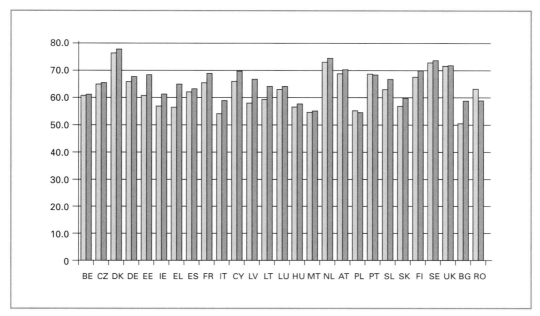

FIGURE 16.1 Employment in the EU Member States in 2000 and 2006 (percentage)
Source: Elaboration on the basis of Eurostat data, © European Communities, 2008.

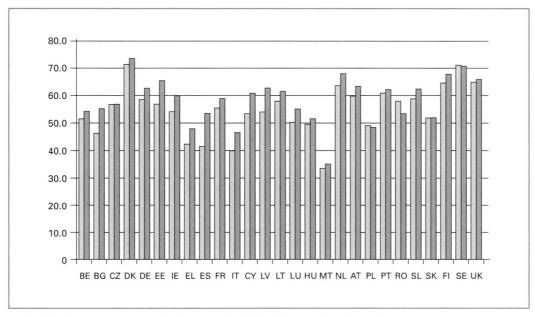

FIGURE 16.2 Employment of women in the EU Member States in 2000 and 2006 (percentage)
Source: Elaboration on the basis of Eurostat data, © European Communities, 2008.

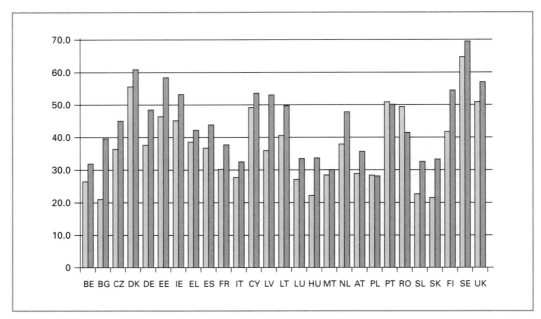

FIGURE 16.3 Employment of older workers (aged between 55 and 64) in the EU Member States in 2000 and 2006 (percentage)
Source: Elaboration on the basis of Eurostat data, © European Communities, 2008.

of the EU though, as described above, over time there have been various initiatives to reduce such disparities.

As discussed in Chapter 7, the EU has not met the various targets with regard to employment set out in the Lisbon Strategy (see also Figures 16.1 to 16.3). Eurostat calculates the employment rate by dividing the number of persons aged 15 to 64 by employment in the total population of the same age group. Total employment for the EU (27) rose from 62.2 per cent in 2000 to a predicted 64.4 per cent in 2006 (see also Figure 16.1), but is still well below the target of 70 per cent for 2010. The equivalent figures for the EU(15) were 63.4 per cent in 2000 and a predicted 66.0 per cent in 2006. In the Central East European countries (CEECs), following the collapse of Communism in 1989 there was a transitional recession, accompanied with a collapse in output and employment, a trend reversed in Poland and others of these countries from 1992/3. As can be seen from Figure 16.1, in Romania employment fell between 2000 and 2006. At times one of the consequences of the migration from the CEEC new member states (see Chapter 8) to the EU(15) was shortages of skilled labour at home.

Employment of women in the EU(27) rose from 53.7 per cent in 2000 to 57.3 per cent in 2006, just above the Lisbon target of 57 per cent for 2005, but still below the Lisbon target of 60 per cent for 2010. Employment of older workers (between 55 and 64) was 36.9 per cent in 2000 and 43.5 per cent in 2006 compared with the 2010 target of 50 per cent.

Fighting poverty and social exclusion in the EU

'Social exclusion' is the term used by the Commission for poverty and marginalization. The definition of poverty adopted by the EU is having a disposable income less than 60 per cent of mean income in the country concerned (see Table 16.1).[8] Despite having some of the most developed social protection systems, some 64 million people remain at risk of poverty in the EU.[9] In general countries spending more on social protection have lower poverty rates, as in the case of the Scandinavian countries (see Table 16.1). In the difficult economic transition process in some of the new member states, an effective social protection system can pay a key role in keeping the level of poverty low, and the experience of the Czech Republic is noteworthy.

The risk of poverty is slightly higher for women, and is greater for children, young people, single parents and the elderly (see also Box 16.5).[10] Being unemployed significantly increases the risk of being below the poverty line. The proportion of those unemployed for more than six months below the poverty line in 2004 ranged from 26 per cent in Denmark and Sweden (five times higher than the equivalent percentage of those employed for most of the time) to about 60 per cent in the three Baltic States (where it was six times higher than for those mainly employed). In contrast, in Greece, Spain and Portugal the difference in the risk of poverty between being employed or unemployed is significantly lower than elsewhere. This is mainly due to a large

Country	Before social %	After social transfers %	Country transfers	Before social transfers %	After social transfers %
Belgium	27	15	Bulgaria	17	14
Denmark	28	12	Czech Republic	22	10
Germany	26	13	Estonia	25	18
Greece	23	21	Hungary	30	16
Spain	24	20	Lithuania	27	20
France	25	13	Poland	29	19
Ireland	33	18	Romania	24	19
Italy	24	20	Latvia	28	23
Luxembourg	24	14	Slovakia	20	12
Netherlands	21	10	Malta	22	14
Austria	25	13	Cyprus	22	16
Portugal	25	18	Slovenia	24	12
Finland	29	13			
Sweden	29	12	EU(25)	26	16
UK	30	19	EU(15)	26	16

TABLE 16.1 Population at risk of poverty 2006*
*Less than 60 per cent of mean income in the country concerned.
Source: Eurostat, © European Communities, 2008, www.epp.eurostat.ec.europa.eu

[8] Those at risk of poverty are defined as having an 'equivalized' income (which takes into account the household size and composition) below 60 per cent of the national median level. Retirement and survivor's pensions are counted as income before transfers and not as social transfers.

[9] European Commission Directorate-General for Employment, Social Affairs and Equal Opportunities, www.ec.europa.eu/employment_social

[10] European Commission (2007a).

number of the unemployed living in households where somebody is employed, rather than a reflection of the level of employment benefits.[11]

Box 16.5: *The ageing of the EU population*

According to Eurostat projections based on assumptions about future trends in fertility, mortality and immigration, the total population of the EU is still growing, but is expected to start falling from about 2023.[11] The total population of the EU(27) is projected to shrink from 486.3 million in 2004 to 472.2 million in 2050 (European Commission, 2007b). According to the baseline projection, the median age in the EU is expected to rise from 39 years in 2004 to 49 years in 2050. The number of young people (aged 0 to 14) is expected to decline from about 100 million in 1975 to roughly 66 million in 2050. The population aged 65 and over is expected to increase from about 86 million in 2004 to 141 million by 2050. The old-age dependency rate is expected to rise from about 25 per cent in 2004 to 51 per cent in 2050. In other words, the EU will move from having about 4 people of working age (between 15 and 64) in 2004 to roughly 2 people in 2050 for every person above 65.

Measures used to offset the effects of ageing of the population in the EU include immigration policies (see Chapter 8), raising the retirement age and encouraging continued participation in the labour force by women and older workers.

Though between 1975 and 1994 the Community introduced three 'poverty' programmes, EU financing of such measures has always been limited, mainly because the richer member states insist that this is primarily a policy area for national competences.

In 2000 when European Council agreed on the Lisbon Strategy, it was also decided to set up a Social Inclusion Process to fight against poverty and social exclusion over the 2000–10 period. Since then the EU has provided a framework for the development of national strategies to fight poverty and social exclusion, and has been responsible for policy co-ordination through the 'Open Method of Co-ordination'. The key elements of this Process are:

- Common objectives;
- National Action Plans against poverty and social exclusion;
- Joint reports and regular monitoring on social inclusion;
- Common indicators;
- A Community Action Programme to encourage co-operation between member states to combat social exclusion.

The common objectives of the Open Method of Co-ordination cover four main themes:

1 Facilitating participation in employment and access by all to resources, rights, goods and services;
2 Protecting against the risk of exclusion;
3 Helping the most vulnerable;
4 Mobilizing all the relevant bodies.

---

[11] European Commission (2007a).

According to the European Commission, the Social Inclusion Process has increased awareness of poverty and social exclusion, created more consensus about what needs to be done, and encouraged EU member states to place these challenges higher in the political agenda.[12] However, the role of the EU still appears to rely more on co-ordination than EU financial support. A more effective policy would need more funding from national governments and an increased allocation in the EU budget.

Evaluation of EU social and employment policies

Until the mid-1980s EU social measures were mainly concerned with providing the legislative framework to facilitate freedom of labour movement. The announcement of the Single Market Programme in 1985 sparked a heated ideological debate about the role of the state in social policy and the role of the Community in particular. At the EC level the question was complicated by considerations of subsidiarity and the reluctance of member states to give up their sovereignty. With the 1990s priorities shifted, and the fight to promote employment gradually became a main policy concern of the EU. However, EU employment and social policy remained very much a complement to national measures, and expenditure amounted to only a small fraction of that of the member states.

Differences in national welfare systems, the socio-economic conditions of the member states, ideological conceptions concerning the role of the state in the economy and views about the appropriate balance of power make it unlikely that the EU will ever develop a fully fledged social policy.

Since the 1990s the EU has launched various strategies to combat unemployment and increase employment. Though at times the rhetoric and statements of intent and solidarity seem to exceed the results, there has been a slight reduction in unemployment and increase in participation in the labour force since the EES was launched in 1997. The EU approach relies heavily on active labour market measures (such as training and the creation of job opportunities), but financing is limited, and the effectiveness of this type of approach has sometimes been called into question. At least formal EU frameworks for the formulation, development and review of strategies to combat unemployment have been set in place, but progress remains slow in realizing the Luxembourg and Lisbon objectives.

---

[12] European Commission Directorate-General for Employment, Social Affairs and Equal Opportunities, www. ec.europa.eu/employment_social

Summary of Key Concepts

- **EU social policy** has evolved over the years, but includes measures for: employment and working conditions; social exclusion, or the fight against poverty; equality between men and women; the involvement of the so-called social partners (trade unions and employers) in the legislative process; and the participation of workers in the decision-making of a firm.

- **Obstacles to developing a fully fledged EU social policy** include: differences in the conditions of the member states; the contentious, ideological nature of social policy issues; the diversity of national social policy regimes; the reluctance of member states to give up control of social policy; the scale of budgetary transfers necessary for EU social policy; and the even greater diversity of social policy requirements after enlargement.

- **The evolution of EU social policy** can be divided into four main periods: 1958–73 (a low profile for the Community), 1974–85 (piecemeal intervention), 1985–92 (the evolution of policy) and since 1993.

- **The Luxembourg Process to launch the European Employment Strategy (EES)** is organized around four pillars: improving 'employability'; encouraging the adaptability of businesses and their employees; strengthening policies for equal opportunities; and developing entrepreneurship.

- The Lisbon European Council of 2000 aimed at **higher employment rates** (rather than lower unemployment rates) by increasing the rate of participation in the labour force.

Questions for study and review

1 What do we mean by the term 'social policy'?

2 What do we mean by 'social dumping'? To what extent do you think that it poses the risk of a 'race to the bottom'?

3 What are the obstacles to developing a fully fledged EU social policy?

4 How has EU social policy evolved over the years?

5 What do we mean by the 'social dimension' of the Single Market Programme?

6 Indicate the main features of EU employment policy. What do the Luxembourg and Lisbon processes entail?

7 What policies do you think the EU should use to increase employment?

8 What policies do you think the EU should use to reduce poverty?

References

European Commission (1993a) 'Green Paper on European social policy – A way forward for the Union', COM(93)551.

European Commission (2007a) 'Growing Regions, Growing Europe. Fourth Report on Economic and Social Cohesion,' www.ec.europa.eu/regional_policy

European Commission (2007b) 'Europe's demographic future: Facts and figures,' www.ec.europa.eu/employment_social

Tsoukalis, L. (1997) *The New European Economy Revisited*, 3rd edn, Oxford University Press, Oxford.

Useful websites

European Commission Directorate-General for Employment, Social Affairs and Equal Opportunities:
www.ec.europa.eu/employment_social

International Labour Office provides data and analysis:
www.ilo.org

EURES – the European Job Mobility Portal:
www.ec.europa.eu/eures

Committee on Employment and Social Affairs of the European Parliament:
www.europarl.europa.eu/committees/empl_home_en.htm

The European Social Fund:
ec.europa.eu/employment_social/esf/index_en.htm

CHAPTER 17

Competition and Industrial Policies

❖ *LEARNING OBJECTIVES*

By the end of this chapter you should be able to understand:

❖ The ways in which distortions in competition may undermine the integration process;

❖ The main features of Community antitrust policy;

❖ How merger control operates in the EU;

❖ What measures are used by the EU to prevent abuse of state aids on the part of national governments;

❖ The criticisms made of the role of the European Commission in competition policy;

❖ The ways in which EU competition policy could be rendered more effective;

❖ The reasons for industrial policy;

❖ How EU industrial policy has evolved over the years;

❖ The main aspects of research and development (R&D) policy in the EU;

❖ The revived debate about supporting national and EU champions.

Introduction: EU competition policy

Competition policy was envisaged as an essential part of the integration process both in the Treaty of Paris establishing the European Coal and Steel Community (ECSC) and in the Treaty of Rome. Competition policy is aimed at preventing distortions in competition caused either by private firms, or by government actions. EU competition policy is complementary to national measures, but in cases of conflict EC competition law prevails.

Central to the analysis of the likely benefits of integration are the cost and price reductions that were expected to accrue.[1] However, there is a risk that restrictive practices between otherwise independent firms, or the behaviour of dominant (or monopoly) firms, might prevent

---

[1] For a discussion of the link between competition policy and integration see Bongardt (2005). See also European Commission (2007a) for a user-friendly guide to EU competition policy, and European Commission (2004a) for an explanation of strategy.

these price reductions from being realized. Integration is also expected to lead to increased competition, and to meet these additional pressures firms might be induced to form cartels or undertake mergers in order to reach dominant market positions. National governments may be tempted to help their firms face the additional competitive pressures by granting them state aids.

To prevent such developments undermining competition, and as a necessary complement to the four freedoms, EU policy therefore covers:

- Antitrust measures, or the fight against cartels and restrictive practices (Article 81) and against dominant position (Article 82);[2]
- Mergers (Reg. 4064/89 of 1989 and 139/2004 of 2004); and
- State aids and regulated industries (Articles 86–88).

To prepare for EU enlargement, the EU introduced new rules on competition policy from 1 May 2004. Before discussing the various aspects of EU competition policy and its reform, it is useful to present the theoretical basis for introducing competition policy, and a description of the institutions involved in EU competition policy.

The theoretical basis for competition policy

Though a complete analysis of different forms of behaviour by firms is beyond the present scope, the aim of this section is to compare the outcome of certain non-competitive models with a situation of perfect competition. Even these simple models can be used to show why competition policy may be necessary. Students familiar with models of monopoly and collusion can skip this section.

The simplest model of the non-competitive behaviour of a firm is that of monopoly. A monopoly entails that there is only a single seller of the product, so the firm does not have to take into account the behaviour of other suppliers. Perfect competition occurs where there are a large number of buyers and sellers, a homogeneous product, free entry of firms to the market and perfect information.

Since the monopoly is the only seller of the product, the demand curve of the firm and the demand curve of the industry are the same. The industry demand curve faced by the monopolist will slope downwards. The monopolist is a price maker. If the monopolist sets a higher price, less will be sold. For simplicity it is assumed that the aim of the monopolist is to maximize profits. In order to decide what quantity of output to produce in order to maximize profits, the monopolist will have to take into account the different revenues and costs associated with each level of output.

Marginal revenue (MR) can be defined as the change in total revenue when output is changed by one unit. When the demand curve slopes downward, MR will be less than price. This can be seen from Figure 17.1. When the price is €6 the firm can sell 2 units and total revenue is €12. To sell 3 units, the firm must reduce its price to €5 and total revenue becomes €15. When the firm increases its sales from 2 to 3 units, the first two units are sold for €5, and total revenue decreases by area a, which is equal to €2. At the same time total revenue increases by area b, which indicates the addition to revenue from selling the third unit at €5. Area b is equal to the price of the product €5. When increasing output from 2 to 3 units, total revenue rises by area b

---

[2] The references here are to Articles in the EC Treaty.

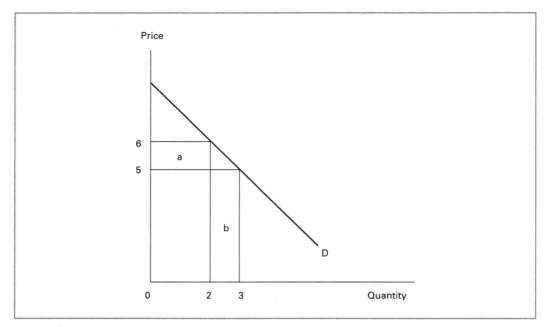

FIGURE 17.1 The demand curve of the monopolist

minus area a. This increase in total revenue for a one-unit change in output is marginal revenue. Marginal revenue is therefore less than price.[3]

In order to maximize profits the monopolist will also have to take costs into account. Marginal cost (MC) is defined as the change in total costs of production when output is varied by one unit. The monopolist will maximize profits at the level of output where MC equals MR. At lower levels of output MR exceeds MC, so the monopolist can increase profits by producing more. Equilibrium occurs where MC and MR intersect at point Em in Figure 17.2, where the level of output is Qm.[4] The price Pm charged for level of output Qm is given by point C on the demand curve directly above Em.

The aim is now to show how the quantities produced and prices charged differ under conditions of monopoly and perfect competition. In order to render comparison simpler, a few additional assumptions are now introduced:[5]

- An industry is initially assumed to be operating under perfect competition and then a monopoly is introduced.

- The industry demand is assumed to be the same for the monopoly and the competitive industry.

---

[3] Another way of explaining this concept is to recall that the demand curve represents average revenue (AR). Average revenue is the total revenue divided by number of units sold. If the demand curve is negatively sloped, AR is falling, so MR must lie below the average.

[4] The same type of graphical analysis can be used for long- or short-term analysis, using long-term cost curves or short-term cost curves respectively. The difference between long and short run arises because in the short run a firm is not able to vary the quantities of all the inputs it uses.

[5] The analysis here follows Browning and Browning (1992).

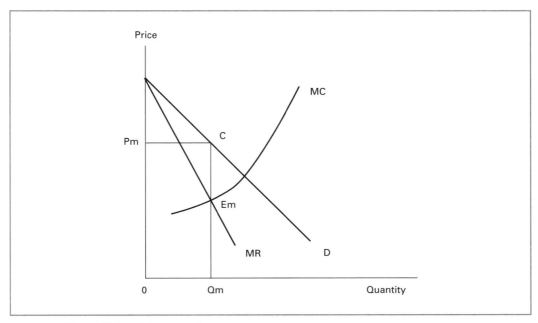

FIGURE 17.2 The equilibrium of the monopolist

- The long run is considered when firms have adjusted fully to each price.
- The industry is assumed to operate under constant costs. Average costs are defined as the total costs of producing a given number of units output divided by the number of units of output. In a constant-cost industry, the long-run MC and AC curves will coincide. The assumption of constant costs implies that input costs will be the same under perfect competition and monopoly.
- All competitive firms are equally efficient.

The demand curve of the industry is D in Figure 17.3. With monopoly the demand curve of the industry is the demand curve of the firm. In contrast under perfect competition the two are different. Under perfect competition the firm is a price taker, and the demand curve of the individual firm is a horizontal straight line at the going price. Price will therefore equal MR for the competitive firm. In the short run the perfectly competitive firm will maximize profits when MC equals price and MR.[6]

In the long run for the competitive industry to be in equilibrium, each firm must make zero profits, so there is no incentive for firms to enter or leave the industry.[7] The firm will earn zero profits if and only if the price for the product is equal to long-run MC and long-run AC.[8] The long-run competitive supply curve LS of the competitive industry will be a horizontal line as shown in Figure 17.3. In a constant-cost industry an increase in industry output will not raise

---

[6] For a review of this topic see, for example, Varian (1999) or Begg et al. (2000).

[7] All competitive firms are assumed to be equally efficient.

[8] The condition for long-run equilibrium is:
Pc = MR=LMC=LAC where Pc is price, MR is marginal revenue, LMC is long-run marginal cost, and LAC is long-run average cost.

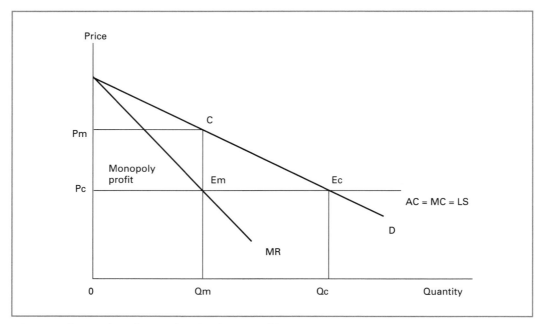

FIGURE 17.3 A comparison of monopoly and perfect competition
Source: Browming and Browming (1992), Figure 11.6, p. 369 © Harper Collins.

factor prices. If industry output increases, the cost curves of firms do not change, and the expansion of industry output takes place at the same cost as new firms enter the market. Under perfect competition long-run equilibrium occurs where the industry demand curve intersects LS the long-run supply curve. In Figure 17.3 this occurs at Ec, where output is Qc and price is Pc.

Assume now that the industry becomes a monopoly. In order to maximize profits the monopolist will produce quantity Qm, at which MC equals MR and the price charged will be Pm. At the level of output Qm, the difference between price Pm (or average revenue) and AC gives the average profit per unit of output. The total profit of the monopolist is given by average profit multiplied by the quantity of output Qm, or the rectangle PcEmCPm shown in Figure 17.3.

Since it is assumed that the monopolist faces the same costs in its different plants as did competitive firms, the long-run competitive supply curve LS is also the long-run MC curve of the monopolist. The assumption that the industry operates under constant costs means that the long-run MC curve and the long-run AC curve of the monopolist coincide, and both are equal to LS in Figure 15.3. At equilibrium the monopoly produces Qm at price Pm.When the industry was competitive, quantity Qc was produced and sold at price Pc. Under monopoly there is therefore a lower quantity of output and higher prices than in a competitive situation.

Figure 17.3 can also be used to illustrate the welfare costs of introducing a monopoly. The monopoly reduces output from Qc to Qm. The fall in output releases resources and these can be used to create other products. In competitive markets the resources released can be used to produce output worth rectangle QmQcEcEm. The increase in price under monopoly causes a fall in consumer surplus of PmCEcPc. Rectangle PcEmCPm showing the monopoly profit is simply a transfer from consumers to producers so does not represent a net welfare loss to society. The net welfare loss to society is indicated by triangle CEcEm.

As explained below, one of the main aims of EU competition policy is to avoid abuse of monopoly power by firms in a dominant position. The simplified analysis here shows that com-

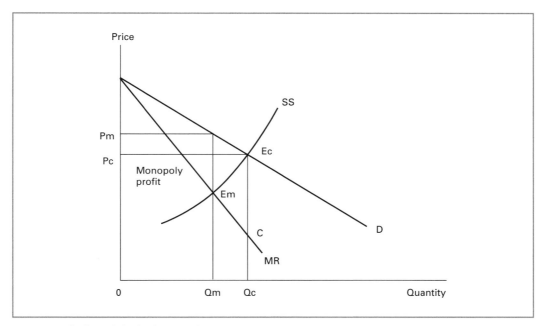

FIGURE 17.4 Profit maximization by a cartel

petition policy may be aimed at reducing or avoiding the net welfare loss to society as a whole that results from the reduction in output and the rise in price, and limiting or eliminating (generally on equity grounds) the transfer from consumers to the producer represented by monopoly profit.

Monopoly is an extreme case, and in practice firms generally face some form of competition. Though beyond the present scope, most texts on microeconomic theory deal with situations of duopoly, oligopoly and monopolistic competition[9] and consider how outcomes vary according to the different market structure and assumptions about the behaviour of the firm – in particular, attitudes towards competitors. Here the discussion is limited to a model of collusion or cartel. As explained below, cartels are forbidden in the USA, but subject to heavy regulation in the EU.

The aim of collusion or the formation of a cartel by firms in a competitive industry is to co-ordinate their activities in order to earn monopoly profits. Figure 17.4 shows the downward sloping industry demand curve D for the product, and the marginal revenue curve MR. SS is the short-run supply curve of the industry, that is the sum of the short-run marginal cost curves of all the firms. Under conditions of perfect competition, industry equilibrium occurs at Ec, with price Pc and quantity of output Qc.

Assume that the firms then form a cartel and agree to restrict output in order to raise prices. The firms will behave like a monopolist and will maximize their combined profits at Em, where the SS curve intersects the marginal revenue curve MR, with a combined output of Qm and a monopoly price of Pm. This outcome is the same as if a single monopoly controlled all the firms making up the cartel (see, for analogy, Figure 17.2 above).

---

[9] A duopoly consists of an industry with two firms, while in an oligopoly a few firms produce all or most of the output of the industry. Monopolistic competition occurs where entry and exit to the industry are unrestricted but firms produce differentiated products.

Area EcEmC indicates the increase in total profits for all the firms in the cartel. By reducing the quantity produced from Qc to Qm, the firms eliminate all output for which their combined marginal costs exceed MR, and in this way the firms in the cartel can increase their combined profit.

However, as explained in Chapter 4, there are inherent economic reasons that cartels are unstable and tend to break down. As Figure 17.3 shows, the cartel can restrict output to raise prices, but at the higher prices each firm has an incentive to cheat since the individual firm could increase its profits by expanding output. Members of the cartel may find it difficult to reach agreement over price, output and profit sharing. Moreover, the monopoly profits earned by a cartel may encourage other firms to enter the industry.

The institutions responsible for EU competition policy

The Commission plays a central role in the implementation of EU competition policy. It may investigate rules at its own initiative, or upon the receipt of a complaint from an individual, company or member state. It can force firms to hand over documents and carry out raids on firms without prior warning (known as 'dawn raids' by the media). Decisions are prepared by the Directorate-General for Competition (DG COMP), which is responsible to the Commissioner for Competition, Neelie Kroes since 2004, and Mario Monti in the two preceding Commissions. If a case of infringement is found, the Commission will generally attempt to convince the company or government in question to bring practices in line with EU competition law voluntarily. If this is not possible, the Commission can order enforcement or, in some cases, impose a fine.

The European Court of Justice was responsible for appeals, but subsequently this role was taken over by the Court of First Instance. The role of the Council of Ministers is limited to deciding on Regulations and Directives in the Community decision-making process. As explained below, with the reform of 2004 national courts and national competition authorities are to assume a more active role in competition policy in the EU.

Antitrust enforcement

Antitrust measures cover cartels and restrictive practices, and abuses of dominant position. Article 81 of the EC Treaty prohibits as 'incompatible with the Common Market' all agreements that affect trade between the member states and have the intention or effect of preventing, distorting or restricting competition. Fines of up to 10 per cent of their annual worldwide turnover may be imposed on the guilty parties (see Box 17.1). Collusive behaviour (or concerted action having the same effect as collusion) is considered contrary to consumer interests when it entails agreements to:[10]

- Raise prices;
- Restrict output, markets, technical development or investment;
- Share markets or sources of supply;
- Apply dissimilar conditions to equivalent transactions with other trading parties;
- Make the conclusion of contracts subject to supplementary obligations.

---

[10] Article 81(1).

Box 17.1: *The ten largest fines imposed by the Commission in cartel cases*

Firm	Fine (euros)
ThyssenKrupp	479 669 850
Hoffmann-La Roche AG	462 000 000
Siemens AG	396 562 500
ENI SpA	272 250 000
Lafarge SA	249 600 000
BASF AG	236 845 000
Otis	224 932 950
Heineken NV	219 275 000
Arkema	219 131 250
Solvay	167 062 000

Source: Competition: Commission acts against cartels – Questions and answers, European Communities, 2008, europa.eu/rapid/pressReleasesAction

One of the major difficulties in implementing EU policy with respect to Article 81 is that in practice it may be difficult to establish that collusive behaviour has taken place. In the Franco-Japanese ball bearings case of 1972, representatives of firms and trade associations from the two countries met in Paris and wrote minutes recording their agreement to fix prices.[11] The minutes ended in the hands of the European Commission competition authorities, but rarely is such information readily available.

The task of proving that collusive behaviour has taken place is further complicated by the fact that, for example, in a situation of oligopoly the outcome may appear collusive (with lower output and higher prices) without the firms actually having to collude in a legal sense.[12]

Horizontal co-operation involves firms at the same stage in the production process, and is generally found to violate EU competition policy when it can be established that there are agreements to set prices, impose entry barriers or reserve particular geographical areas for certain firms.

Vertical co-operation is between firms at different stages in the production process. The 1999 Regulation on vertical restraints forbids agreements on:[13]

---

[11] Official Journal 343 of 21/12/74.

[12] This was evident in the wood pulp case of 1993 described in Martin (2007). The EU was supplied largely by firms in Northern Europe and North America, which tended to adjust prices by similar amounts at about the same time. Most of these firms met regularly at a trade association in Switzerland. The Commission maintained that there was collusion but was overruled by the Court of Justice on the basis of insufficient evidence. According to the Court, the parallel pricing might be based on collusion, but it might simply be the consequence of transparent prices in an oligopoly market.

[13] Official Journal 336 of 29 December 1999.

- Exclusive purchasing;
- Resale price maintenance (the distributor agrees to sell at or above the price indicated by the manufacturer).

These types of vertical restraint typically infringe EU competition policy by fragmenting the Single Market and/or by introducing price discrimination. A frequently cited example is that of the car distribution system in the EU which for many years allowed car manufacturers to sell through designated dealers in specific territories.[14]

Box 17.2: *The Microsoft decision and other technology cases*

In 2004 the European Commission ruled against Microsoft for abusing its near-monopoly in the PC market (Windows is the operating system on more than 90 per cent of PCs) to extend its market power in two adjacent markets. According to the Commission, Microsoft had deliberately restricted interoperability between Windows PCs and non-Microsoft work group servers, and had tied sales of its Media Player to sales of the Windows operating system. As a result, the Commission claimed that Microsoft had used its PC market strength to acquire a dominant position in the work group server operating systems market and had significantly weakened competition in the Media Player market. The Commission decided to fine Microsoft €437 million and required Microsoft to take remedial action. The latter included disclosing information to competitors about interfaces allowing non-Microsoft work group servers to interoperate with Windows PCs and offering a version of Windows client PC operating system without Media Player in the EU. The Commission stated that the fine was calculated on the basis of EU sales and not on worldwide sales in deference to the USA.

The Commission turned down an offer of settlement by Microsoft. Microsoft decided to appeal against the Commission's decision, arguing that it had invested substantially in developing Windows and that its corporate strategy was to increase the sales of Windows. Microsoft stated that being forced to disclose interface information for servers runs against this strategy and would act as a disincentive to innovation. The company also maintained that Windows might not be able to function properly without Media Player.

In September 2007 the Court of First Instance confirmed the Commission decision, maintaining that withholding information that is needed for servers and PCs to work together can constitute an abuse of dominant position if it prevents rival firms developing alternative software for which there is potential consumer demand.

In February 2008 the Commission fined Microsoft a record €899 million for failure to comply with its decision. The fine came days after Microsoft announced that it would open parts of its software to rival companies, but the Commission expressed scepticism about Microsoft's promise to make its Windows operating system and other software open and more transparent.

---

[14]See Martin (2007) for a more complete description. The justification given was the repair and maintenance that cars require. Manufacturers were, however, obliged to allow dealers to sell cars to customers who were not resident in the designated sales area. On various occasions the Commission fined EU firms (VW in 1995 and 1999, and the Dutch General Motors in 2000) for attempting to block dealers from selling in other territories. In October 2002 a new car distribution regulation came into operation which offers distributors greater freedom to operate multi-brand dealerships (Regulation (EC) No.1400 of 31 July 2002).

Although collusion is forbidden, Article 81(3) of the EC Treaty envisages exemptions and permits other forms of cooperation between firms, which improve the production or distribution of goods, promote technical progress and allow consumers a fair share of the resulting benefit.

In the early years of competition policy, the Commission itself was responsible for granting exemptions, but the huge workload that this entailed meant that alternatives had to be developed. These include the block exemption system, 'comfort letters' from the Commission, which indicated whether a firm was considered likely to qualify for an exemption or not (though, according to the Court of Justice, these letters were not legally binding). As explained below, the 2004 reform reinforced the trend towards a growing role for national competition authorities and courts.

Article 82 of the EC Treaty prohibits abuse of dominant position by one or more firms.Types of behaviour that are found to constitute such abuse are:[15]

- Restriction of output;
- Price discrimination;
- Applying dissimilar conditions to equivalent transactions with other trading parties;
- Making the conclusion of contracts subject to supplementary obligations.

There are no exemptions to Article 82. Examples of decisions by the Commission against abuse of a dominant position were those against Microsoft (see Box 17.2) and Unilever and the ice-cream distribution market. Unilever provided freezer cabinets free to Irish distributors on condition they stocked only Unilever ice cream. This was found to limit the choice of Irish consumers.

The 2004 reform

From 1 May 2004 a 'modernization package' of EU competition policy came into operation, including a new EU enforcement regime on restrictive practices and dominant position. Routine 'notification of agreements and practices to the Commission for clearance' is no longer required. Instead, companies will make their own assessment. All agreements considered to have a net positive effect on the internal market are automatically valid. This will free the competition authorities to tackle serious violations, in particular the cases affecting cross-border trade. The fear was that with enlargement extension of the previous notification system to 25 or 27 member states would have led to a paralysis of enforcement activities.

The reform applies the notion of 'safe harbours' for firms. If a company is below a certain market share threshold, it can benefit from a 'safe harbour' and does not have to worry about the compatibility of agreements with EU competition law. At the same time guidelines will help to define 'hardcore restrictions' relating to practices that are prohibited because they have a negative impact on the common market (such as agreements to fix prices, limit output or share markets or consumers).

In order to ensure a more effective division of tasks, the Commission, national competition authorities and national courts are to share responsibility for enforcing EU antitrust rules. The Commission will focus on the infringements presenting the greatest risk of distortion at the EU level. To facilitate co-ordination between the various authorities a European Competition Network (ECN) has been set up. This is composed of the Commission and competition authorities of all the member states. The role of the ECN is to establish principles for the allocation of

---

[15]EC Treaty Article 82.

cases among the various authorities, exchange information, provide mutual assistance in investigations and co-ordinate the final decisions taken.

Merger control

While measures relating to restrictive practices and dominant position were already envisaged by the Treaty of Rome, the addition of merger control to EC competition policy came only in 1989. This was partly because the idea of promoting EC champions was popular in the 1970s and early 1980s, and, as explained below, there may be a tension between industrial policy and competition policy. However, it was also because the level of merger activity in the Community remained relatively low until the mid-1980s. During this period most mergers were between firms in the same country and were aimed chiefly at increasing market share on the domestic market.

The announcement of the Single Market Programme was accompanied by a spectacular increase in the number of mergers in the Community, which rose from 200 in 1985 to 2000 in 1989 (Tsoukalis, 1997). Mergers were increasingly cross-frontier and also involved firms from outside the EU in an attempt to strengthen positions on world markets. The composition of mergers also altered, with a growing number of mergers in service sectors (such as banking, insurance and the retail trade).

The 1989 Merger Control Regulation (Reg. 4064/89) gave the European Commission the authority to control mergers that met a specified size and multi-nationality conditions, including mergers between non-EU businesses with substantial sales in the EU.[16] The number of notifications was growing by about 30 per cent annually, and reached about 300 each year in the late 1990s (European Commission, 2000b). The aim of the Regulation was to provide a 'one-stop shop' where firms could request clearance for the mergers and acquisitions in the whole EU, thereby reducing the costs, legal uncertainty and bureaucracy associated with multiple filings.

According to the 1989 Regulation, a merger should be blocked if it led to a potentially abusive dominant position and, therefore, was likely to result in higher prices, more limited choice for consumers and less innovation. The Commission and European Courts interpreted this concept as applying also to collective dominance (as in the cases of Gencor/Lonrho and Airtours/First Choice). This is different from the US concept of 'avoiding a lessening of competition'. The Commission's use of the notion of 'collective dominance' was frequently challenged as offering a blank cheque to veto mergers.

During the 1989–95 period the approach of the Commission to merger control was sometimes criticized as being too cautious and bland (Tsoukalis, 1997). Of 398 mergers considered during this period, only 4 were blocked. Over the 1990–2007 period the Commission examined 3668 mergers and 20 were stopped.[17] In 2007 a record 402 mergers were notified to the Commission, in-depth proceedings were initiated in 15 cases, and one case was prohibited.

In 2002 the Court of First Instance upheld three high profile cases of appeal against the Commission's merger decisions (Airtours/First Choice, Schneider/Legrand and Tetra Laval/Sidel), giving rise to heated debate about the powers and procedures of the Commission (see Box 17.3).

---

[16] The worldwide threshold based on the turnover of the companies involved amounted to €5 billion, and the Communitywide threshold to €250 million. Below these thresholds, the national authorities in the member states carried out merger control. Above the threshold the Commission had to be notified of the proposed merger.

[17] www.ec.europa.eu/comm/competition/mergers/statistics/pdf

Box 17.3: *Examples of EU merger cases*

In the case of the British Airtours proposed takeover of First Choice, the 1999 decision of the Commission argued that the merger would reduce the number of tour operators in the UK to three, and that their UK collective dominance could impede competition. In June 2002 the Court of First Instance overruled the decision, arguing that it was not clear that there were significant barriers to other (foreign) operators entering the market or that smaller operators would not have access to favourably priced seats. According to the Court, the Commission had not proved its case and the decision was based on factual errors so the Court annulled the decision of the Commission.

In 2003 the European Commission blocked a deal to merge two French electrical equipment companies, Schneider and Legrand, maintaining that the deal would have a negative impact on competition. The Court of First Instance overturned the decision in 2002, maintaining that there were also serious procedural errors, and in 2007 awarded damages to Schneider for some of the losses incurred as a result of the decision of the Commission. The compensation was to cover the losses from having to file a second merger case and sell Legrand later than would otherwise have been the case. According to the Court the Commission showed 'grave and manifest disregard' for the limits of its powers of assessment.

In October 2002 the merger between Tetra Laval and Sidel was blocked because the Commission argued that Tetra Laval was carrying out leverage, i.e. using its dominant position in the packaging sector to obtain a dominant position in another sector, that of machinery for making plastic (PET) bottles. While the Court did not rule out the underlying theoretical argument, it maintained that so far there had been no evidence of this type of behaviour.

To address these reversals, in May 2004 the 'modernization package' of EU competition policy included a new merger control regulation and internal reform of the DG for Competition in the Commission (with the introduction of the post of Chief Economist, and a system of internal review by an independent panel before decisions are confirmed). The new merger regulation entailed:

- Reinforcing the one-stop shop concept to avoid the problem of multiple filings for authorization (i.e. notification of the same operation having to be made to several competition authorities in the EU);[18]

- Continuing the application of merger control to mergers having a 'Community dimension', including firms from third countries with a large presence in the EU;

- Extending the authority of the Commission to investigate all types of harmful scenarios resulting from a merger and not just cases of market dominance. With the new merger rules the 'substantive test' of whether a merger should be challenged or not has been modified. Now any merger that will 'significantly impede effective competition in the common market or in a substantial part of it' is to be blocked. Dominance will remain a major concept, but the test will now extend to oligopolistic markets where the merged company may not

---

[18]The new legislation maintains the same turnover thresholds for exclusive jurisdiction of the Commission. According to the new merger rules, companies can ask to benefit from the one-stop shop if they are required to notify in three or more member states. If none of the authorities in the competent member states object within 15 working days, the merger case is subject to examination by the Commission.

be dominant. The central question becomes whether there is competition to provide consumers sufficient choice;

- Adding some flexibility to the investigation timeframes;[19]
- Providing guidelines for the assessment of mergers between competing firms;[20]
- Adopting a set of best practices on the conduct of merger investigations.

The 2004 reforms aim at improving the system of referral between EU and national jurisdictions, clarify the concept of dominance and improve the internal working of the Commission.

Liberalization and state aid

Whereas Articles 81 and 82 and the 1989 Merger Control Regulation relate to the behaviour of firms, Articles 86–88 of the EC Treaty attempt to prevent competition being undermined by government intervention.

Article 86 covers the monopoly rights granted by member states to private or public undertakings to perform services in sectors such as the postal service, energy, telecommunications and transport. However, the Commission argues that these special rights should not go beyond what is necessary to provide the service, otherwise competition could be restricted. Many of these services require expensive infrastructure, and the Commission makes the distinction between infrastructure and services. While monopoly of the infrastructure is permitted, the monopolist must allow access to other competitors to provide the services. The European Commission has been instrumental in opening up such markets to competition (also known as liberalization).

An example of an Article 86 ruling is that by the Commission against Spain in 1997 over the liberalization of the mobile phone market. A private company, Airtel Móvil, was charged €510 million to operate, while the state firm Telefónica could enter the market without payment. The Spanish government was required to introduce corrective measures.[21]

Article 87 prohibits state aids to business if they distort competition, or intra-community trade. State aid is defined as an advantage conferred on a selective basis to firms by national authorities, and may take various forms, including subsidies, capital investment, tax breaks and sales of assets at favourable prices. General measures applying to all firms regardless of size and location such as tax measures or employment legislation are not regarded as state aid.

Article 87 (2) and (3) of the Treaty indicate that exceptions are allowed for state aid. Article 88 requires member states to give prior notification of state aid,[22] and gives the Commission

---

[19]Under the 1989 Regulation after an initial scrutiny period of one month, the Commission would decide whether to authorize the merger (90 per cent of cases) or to continue with a four-month investigation. At the end of this period the Commission could authorize the merger conditionally or unconditionally, or prohibit it. With the reform the initial scrutiny period is fixed at 25 working days with the possibility of extension to 35 working days. The investigation period is 90 workings days extendible by 15 working days if companies offer remedies, or 20 working days if the Commission or notifying parties so request. Under the new legislation it will be possible to notify a transaction prior to conclusion of a binding agreement provided there is evidence of good faith to enter into that agreement.

[20]The Guidelines aim at providing indications to companies and the legal community about which mergers are likely to be challenged. As part of the assessment the Commission will also take into account possible increases in efficiency arising from a merger. For instance, mergers may allow firms to reorganize their activities or bring together complementary capabilities that allow them to compete better.

[21]In 2007 Telefónica again came into the limelight of EU competition policy when it was fined by the European Commission for keeping rivals out of the broadband market.

[22]There are exceptions to the notification requirement such as aid to encourage training, employment, small and medium enterprises (SMEs) and R&D.

control over the enforcement of rules preventing undue granting of state aid. Over the years the Commission has developed a framework for types of state aid that are allowed, and these include so-called 'horizontal' measures for developing disadvantaged regions, promoting small and medium enterprises (SMEs), R&D, the protection of the environment, training, employment and culture. In contrast controversial types of aid, which are subject to investigation by the Commission, include rescue and restructuring aid (see the theoretical analysis of industrial policy below) and financial aid to sensitive sectors such as steel, shipbuilding and motor vehicles. The Commission maintains that large enterprises should make a substantial contribution to the financing of restructuring (see also Box 17.4).

Box 17.4: *The Alstrom case*

In August 2003 France informed the European Commission about a package of measures in favour of the Alstrom engineering group, which (among other things) produces high-speed trains. The package included a commitment by the French state to subscribe irrevocably half of a capital increase worth €600 million. The package was to be put immediately into effect without waiting for clearance from the Commission and so, according to the Commission, violated the obligation of prior notification of aid.

In September 2003 the Commission began its investigation and considered introducing an injunction to suspend the participation in the capital increase because of its irreversible structural effects. In the event the Commission gave France five days to renounce the measure, and France agreed to introduce debt instruments instead, which would not have irreversible structural effects on the market. France also agreed to subject the envisaged entry into Alstrom's equity to prior authorization by the Commission.

The Commission then began its analysis of whether the package was in line with the rescue and restructuring guidelines and, in particular, whether the restructuring plan would restore Alstrom's viability and if compensatory measures were necessary to counterbalance the distortions of competition.

In 2004 (when Nicolas Sarkozy was involved in the negotiations as Finance Minister) the Commission agreed to a package of €3.2 billion government aid to Alstrom including an €800 million debt-for-equity swap on condition that Alstrom disposed of businesses accounting for 10 per cent of revenues worth about €1.5 billion. The Commission argued that industrial partnerships were necessary to ensure the viability of Alstrom and compensate for the distortions in competition caused by state aid.

State aid has proved a particularly sensitive issue in the new member states of Central and Eastern Europe, which needed to restructure their economies and to prepare for EU membership. Following enlargement the European Commission launched a State Aid Action Plan in 2005.[23] The aim was also to ensure that state aid rules could contribute to the Lisbon Strategy by increasing EU competitiveness and creating sustainable jobs. The Plan builds on the objectives decided at the Barcelona European Council when the member states called for 'less and better state aid'. 'Better aid' is interpreted to mean the horizontal measures to correct market failures.

---

[23] COM(2005) 107 final.

Since 2005 a number of new regulatory texts have been adopted (such as the new regional aid guidelines) and others are under revision with the aim of completing the process by 2009.

The Commission publishes regular state aid scoreboards to monitor the amount and nature of state aid, and these suggest that member states are respecting the commitment to use less and better targeted aid. With the exception of Hungary and Malta over the 2001–2007 period the EU member states have reoriented their aid towards objectives such as regional development, R&D, SMEs and protecting the environment.

Evaluation of EU competition policy

According to a survey carried out in June 2007 by the Global Competition Review, EU competition authorities were considered one of the three best anti-trust enforcement agencies in the world (together with those of the UK and USA).[24] The survey was based on questionnaires sent to business groups, academics, legal departments and competition authorities. The Commission was praised for its record in cracking down on cartels since Neelie Kroes became Commissioner for Competition in 2004. The work of the Commission in merger control and inquiries into sectors such as energy and financial services was also praised. However, the survey criticized the slow pace of EU investigations (on average over 35 months and among the slowest examined), and insufficient use of economic reasoning in some cases of investigation into alleged abuse of dominant position.

It is still too early to assess how the 2004 reforms will prove in practice. One of the initial aims of vesting so much power in the Commission was to limit the opportunities for political pressure and lobbying over decisions (in particular on state aid). Now responsibility is to be decentralized with a greater role for national authorities, many of which have limited experience in applying competition law. Decentralization could lead to many merger decisions being referred back to member states, increasing uncertainty as rules and substantive tests still differ among member states.

In recent years there have been increased efforts to co-operate on competition policy and investigations with major trading partners such as the USA, Japan and Canada. However, relations with the USA were strained by the Commission rulings over General Electric's proposed takeover of Honeywell in 2001 and the Microsoft case (see Box 17.2 above). United States authorities had approved the General Electric–Honeywell merger, and though the Commission attempted to co-operate with US antitrust authorities over the Microsoft case, the USA maintained that its own settlement with Microsoft was the appropriate framework for dealing with the case. US politicians also criticized the Commission's ruling on Microsoft, arguing that it would lead to loss of jobs.

Industrial policy: Introduction

One of the difficulties in discussing industrial policy is that of separating industrial policy from all the other measures having an impact on industry. The European Commission defines industrial policy as relating to manufacturing industry, but in the literature a wider concept is sometimes used which includes agriculture and certain services. Most industrial policy is carried out by the member states rather than at the EU level.

---

[24]www.globalcompetitionreview.com

In general the aim of industrial policy is to increase competitiveness. The Commission defines competitiveness as the ability of an economy to provide its population with high and rising standards of living, and high rates of employment on a sustainable basis.[25] There are very different views of how this is best achieved, depending on differing opinions about the effectiveness of the market mechanism. At the risk of oversimplification, it is useful to distinguish certain main tendencies.

According to the market-orientated approach to industrial policy, the most effective way of promoting competition and efficiency is by allowing the market mechanism to operate as fully as possible. The removal of trade barriers and the creation of a common market will intensify international competition. The role of policy is to allow the market to operate by preventing abuse of monopoly power and ensuring that state aids do not distort competition. The role of industrial policy is therefore 'negative' in the sense that it is mainly concerned with eliminating distortions to competition.

At the other end of the scale, a selective, interventionist industrial policy may be used to favour certain firms or industries (see next section). An active industrial policy is sometimes advocated in order to support declining industries and avoid loss of jobs. For instance, if a declining industry is important in a particular region, allowing it to fail could lead to a high level of long-term unemployment in that region, with a heavy social cost. However, in many cases it seems likely that a subsidy to the declining industry will simply postpone unemployment.

An active industrial policy may also be seen as a means of promoting key or strategic industries, such as the aerospace industry, telecommunications and the audiovisual industry, in an effort to create national or EU champions. This is very similar to the strategic trade theory and infant industry arguments described in Chapter 4. According to this approach, public intervention may be used to create a competitive advantage for firms. However, there are numerous objections to these arguments on theoretical grounds. These include the negative implications of protection, insufficient information and the difficulty of picking winners, and the risk of retaliation by other countries.

Measures to encourage R&D and innovation are generally a central component of industrial policy. The traditional economic justification for such measures is in terms of externality. The social return on R&D and innovation is higher than the private return, so public intervention is justified to favour such activities.

An alternative justification for measures to promote R&D and innovation can be found on the basis of evolutionary economics. As described in Chapter 15, evolutionary economics makes the distinction between codified and tacit knowledge. Codified knowledge is formalized and can be stored and transmitted easily, while tacit knowledge is obtained through experience, so requires a process of learning-by-doing in order to be transferred. According to evolutionary economics a large part of knowledge needed for innovation is tacit, so contacts between people are important. As innovation depends on interaction between people, public intervention can be used to encourage that interaction. Measures may be introduced to encourage networking and co-operation on research and technological development between public authorities, firms, research institutions and universities. There may also be a case for favouring the creation of economic clusters, or networks of production of strongly interdependent firms. Highly skilled labour is often relatively mobile and may help to transmit tacit knowledge, so there may be a role for public intervention in attempts to attract highly qualified people to an area.

The instruments of industrial policy are various and include: financial assistance, tax breaks, aid for R&D, public contracts, trade barriers, export assistance and measures to encourage technology diffusion.

---

[25] European Commission (2007b).

The theoretical basis of interventionist industrial policy

A simple framework can be used to explain the link between interventionist industrial policy and integration. The first step is to assume imperfect competition and a closed economy. As explained above, in the absence of perfect competition firms will charge a price that is above their marginal cost in order to maximize profit. Figure 17.2 above illustrates the equilibrium position for a monopolist and the difference between prices and marginal cost or mark-up of the monopolist. If there are more firms in the market, competition will lower the mark-up that each firm can charge. In Figure 17.5 the competition curve showing the relationship between the number of firms and mark-up each firm can charge is therefore assumed to slope down to the right.[26]

With imperfect competition and increasing returns to scale only a given number of firms can survive in a market. The higher the mark-up (or gap between prices and marginal cost) the more firms can survive. The break-even curve (or zero profit curve) shows how many firms can break even at each level of mark-up. Intuitively, more firms can survive when the mark-up is high, so the break-even curve is assumed to slope up to the right.[27] In the short run firms will not always be on the break-even curve, but in the long term firms can enter and leave the sector, so being on the curve will be a condition for equilibrium. Firms will be on the competition curve as they can adjust prices quickly in response to changes in the number of firms. The intersection of the competition and break-even curves indicates the equilibrium mark-up m-u and long run number of firms n as shown in Figure 17.5.

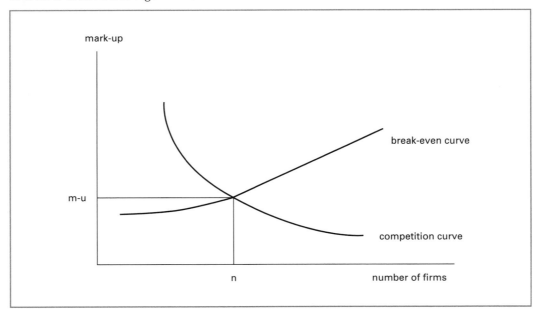

FIGURE 17.5 The competition and break-even curves
Source: Baldwin and Wyplosz (2006).

---

[26] The discussion in this section follows Baldwin and Wyplosz (2006). The downward slope of the competition curve is intuitive, but for an analysis of the theoretical basis of this curve see these authors.

[27] Again, see Baldwin and Wyplosz (2006) for the theoretical derivation of this curve.

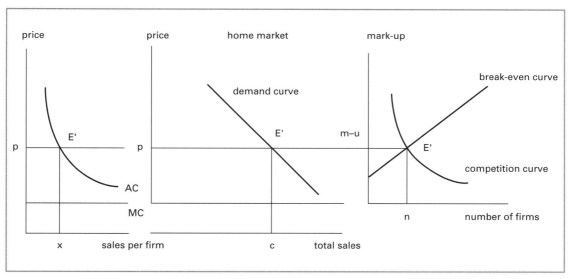

FIGURE 17.6 Prices, output and equilibrium firm size in a closed economy
Source: Baldwin and Wyplosz (2006).

Figure 17.6 uses this result to establish the equilibrium price and firm size in a closed economy. The right-hand panel indicates that at equilibrium n firms would charge m-u mark-up. By definition, the equilibrium price p is MC plus the equilibrium mark-up (i.e. MC plus m-u). The left-hand panel in Figure 17.6 introduces the marginal and average cost curves of a typical firm in the sector. The equilibrium price is p, where price equals average cost. At p total revenue equals total costs and profit is zero (as required by equilibrium). As shown in the left-hand part of Figure 17.6, at equilibrium, price is p and the size of the firm is x.

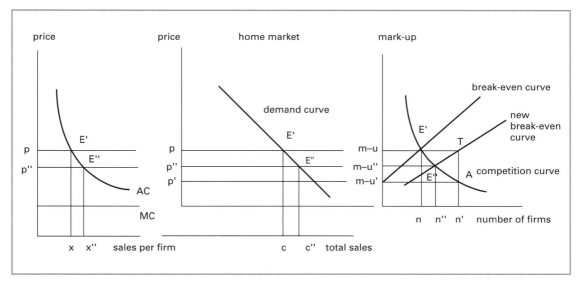

FIGURE 17.7 Prices, output and equilibrium firm size with integration
Source: Baldwin and Wyplosz (2006).

The middle diagram shows the demand curve, which indicates that at price p total sales of the sector will equal c.

The framework can be used to analyse the effects of integration. For simplicity it is assumed that integration leads to trade liberalization between two countries: home and foreign. The impact of the trade liberalization implied by integration is to increase the size of the market leading to more competition. Increased competition means that the typical firm will have to cut its mark-up. At the same time the larger market means that more firms can survive. This is because the larger market creates opportunities for higher sales, so with a given mark-up a larger number of firms can survive. As shown in figure 17.7, this has the effect of shifting the break-even curve to the right.

The size of the shift of the break-even curve will depend on the number of firms in the integrated market. Assume that the number of firms increases to n', so the break even curve passes through point T. The competition curve in Figure 17.7 indicates that n' firms will charge m-u' mark-up, and the price will be p'. However, point A is below the break-even curve, so there will be an incentive for firms to leave the sector. This will occur until the new long-term equilibrium of E'' with n'' firms is reached. At the long-term equilibrium price will be p'', total sales are c'',[28] and sales per firm are x''. The increase in competition means that price-cost margins are m-u'', and so lower than in the pre-integration situation. The left-hand part of Figure 17.7 illustrates that the typical firm increases its sales and efficiency as average cost is lower at E''. The integration effect therefore has two components, a short-term move from E' to A and a long-term move from A to E''.

The move to the long-term equilibrium after integration therefore increases competition and forces many firms to leave the sector, while remaining firms increase their size and become more efficient. This restructuring process involves adjustment costs, and is likely to involve to unemployment. Firms (and trade unions) may attempt to resist this pressure either by collusion (see Figure 17.4 above) or by exerting pressure on governments for subsidies.

In terms of Figure 17.6, at the limit these subsidies (or state aid as it is called in the EU context, see above in the context of competition policy) could avoid the move from A to E'' and would enable n' firms to stay in business by receiving subsidies that cover their losses (the difference between m-u and m-u').

Applying this framework to the EU, the subsidies to maintain loss-making firms in business and slow down the restructuring process could be given by the EU to firms from all member states. Alternatively, it might simply be given by one member state to its domestic firms. In this case the restructuring process will be forced on firms from other member states that do not subsidize giving rise to claims of unfair competition. It is for this reason, as explained above, the EU has rules on state aid.

The evolution of EU industrial policy

Industrial policy in the treaties

Two of the original Communities, the European Steel and Coal Community (ESCC) and Euratom, covered key industrial sectors, and the approach used was essentially *dirigiste*, with an active role envisaged for public intervention. At the time, this type of approach was also deemed appropriate for sectors such as agriculture and transport, which were subject to intensive state

---

[28]The centre panel shows the demand for the home country, but demand for the foreign partner is assumed to be identical so is left out.

intervention. It was considered easier to introduce a common policy for these sectors rather than attempt to harmonize the diverse national approaches.

The Treaty of Rome failed to make any mention of industrial policy, though a legal basis for industrial policy can be found in various articles. With the exception of the sectors mentioned above, the Treaty seems to be based on a market-orientated approach. The removal of trade barriers was seen as the means of promoting competition and efficiency, and the role of public intervention was to eliminate obstacles to the functioning of the market. Many of the articles in the Treaty of Rome considered most relevant for industrial policy were therefore those setting out competition policy. As discussed above, these articles dealt with cartels and restrictive practices, abuse of dominant position and state aids. Other articles were also intrinsically linked to industrial policy, such as those on the movement of capital and labour, the right of establishment and the creation of the common market. Industrial policy measures could also be justified on the basis of general treaty objectives set out in Article 235 (now Article 308 of the EC Treaty).

The early years: a market-orientated approach to industrial policy

In the 1960s the market-orientated view of the role of the Community continued to prevail, and industrial policy consisted mainly in removing barriers to operation of the common market. In 1967 the Directorate-General for Industry (DG III) was set up to promote cross-border co-operation. However, the industry of the member states seemed to encounter difficulty in adapting to the enlarged market and was less active than US and Japanese firms in setting up FDI in the Community (Hitiris, 2003).

At the time there were considerable differences in prevailing ideologies with regard to industrial policy in the member states, with Germany favouring a neo-liberal approach, while France and Italy were traditionally more in favour of intervention. Under the *laissez-faire* approach of the Commission, national industrial policies of the member states failed to converge.

As the market-orientated approach to Community industrial policy was not realizing the expected results, in 1970 the Commission published a Memorandum on Industrial Policy, also known as the Colonna Report. This called for a Community industrial policy aimed at economic expansion and technological development. However, the differing ideologies in the member states meant that there was little consensus on what Community industrial policy should be, and a change in approach failed to materialize.

In 1972, with the prospect of enlargement, the Paris Summit called for the establishment of 'a single industrial base for the Community as a whole'. In December 1973 the Commission published the Spinelli Memorandum proposing a competition-orientated Community policy based on harmonization of national regulations, company law and capital markets, the opening of public procurement and measures to encourage the creation of EC-wide firms. Again the consensus necessary to implement the measures was not forthcoming.

Towards a more active Community industrial policy

As described in Chapter 6, the 1973 oil crisis was followed by the years of Europessimism, with stagflation and growing fragmentation of the Community market as member states attempted to assist their own industries. Many of the interventionist policies were taken over, at times reluctantly, by the Community in order to co-ordinate assistance and render it more transparent. Community industrial policy during these years was mainly characterized by crisis management for specific sectors such as steel, shipbuilding and textiles. These are 'problem' industries with excess supply at a world level, and/or competition from lower-cost producers abroad.

Etienne Davignon, Commission vice-president with responsibility for industry from 1981 to 1985, attempted to 'build Europe' by increasing the competitiveness of Community firms and gained the support of industrialists for cross-border collaboration on technology. At the Copenhagen European Council of 1982 agreement was reached on strengthening the Single Market, increasing research related to industry and providing more funding for investment in industry, technology and energy. While interventionist measures for declining industries continued,[29] from about 1985 there was a shift in emphasis in Community policy away from saving declining industries towards promoting high-technology industries.

Despite the obvious advantages of pooling R&D, the Treaty of Rome made no mention of a common Community R&D effort. During the early 1980s the first Community research and development programmes were launched. The European Strategic Programme for Research and Development in Information Technology (ESPRIT) came into operation from 1984 in response to lobbying by prominent firms active in the information technology sector. ESPRIT was a joint Community and private sector programme to promote co-operation in research with potential industrial applications. The emphasis was on 'pre-competitive' or basic research in order to ensure compatibility with Community competition law. The private sector was required to make a substantial contribution to the financing of projects to ensure their commitment and avoid accusations, in particular on the part of the USA, that the Community was subsidising industry.

Firms in other sectors soon became aware of Community financial support for information technology and began lobbying the Commission for similar measures in their favour. The Community responded by introducing the First Framework Programme covering the 1984–87 period. This aimed at proving coherence and continuity by incorporating all Community aid for R&D into a single instrument and by extending the programme over a number of years.

Programmes for other industries were also introduced including JET (Joint European Torus on thermonuclear fusion), BRITE/EURAM (Basic Research in Industrial Technology for Europe/Advanced Materials for Europe) and RACE (Research and Development in Advanced Communications Technology in Europe). RACE was subsequently replaced by ACTS (Advanced Communications Technology and Services), whose aims include the development of broadband technology.

In 1985 Eureka (European Research Co-ordination Agency) was set up partly as a response to Reagan's Star Wars initiative. It was established as a French initiative to reduce the fragmentation of European industry. Eureka is pan-European, including members such as Turkey, and involves public support for firms to launch new high-technology products and increase competitiveness in key areas for the future.

The early R&D programmes of the Community probably had a fairly limited impact on competitiveness, but they established the tradition of firms working with the Commission, and laid the basis for the Single Market. If the Commission were encouraging co-operation between firms and financing R&D to overcome the fragmentation of EC industry, why not tackle the causes of fragmentation directly?

This was the aim of the Single European Act, which also called for measures to promote research and technological development, to assist small and medium enterprises and to encourage co-operation between firms from different regions of the Community.

Not only did the prospect of the Single Market provoke the spate of cross-border mergers and acquisitions described in Chapter 6, but these changes in European industry in turn led to a reassessment of Community industrial policy. An intense debate ensued, with lobbying from

---

[29]Davignon sponsored 'crisis cartels' for problem industries such as steel. In order to avoid chaotic price-cutting, there were common scrapping programmes that entailed common and binding floor prices, or public intervention to fix prices.

industries in difficulty, such as electronics firms, and some member states (notably France) for Community support in favour of certain industries.

The Bangemann Memorandum and after

In contrast, the Commission view was that effective competition was the best means of ensuring the success of industry, and this position was set out in the Bangemann Memorandum of 1990,[30] named after the then Commissioner responsible for industry. The report established the broad principles on which EU industrial policy has been based ever since. According to the Memorandum, the main role of the Community was not to provide selective intervention for individual firms or industries but rather to adopt a 'horizontal' approach aimed at:

- Maintaining a competitive environment;
- Providing catalysts for structural adjustment, including completion of the Single Market; and
- Developing instruments to accelerate structural adjustment.

According to the Memorandum, a competitive position could be best be ensured by measures to control state aids, avoid abuse of dominant position and eliminate barriers to international trade. The main responsibility for structural adjustment was said to lie with economic operators, but the Community could help to provide the necessary prerequisites for adjustment, including a high level of educational attainment, social cohesion and environmental protection. Community assistance was therefore to be aimed at ensuring a 'level playing field' through an appropriate combination of the Single Market and trade, competition, regional, social and environmental policies. In order to accelerate the process of structural adjustment, measures could be introduced to promote research and technology, encourage a better use of human resources, ensure the conditions for the development of business services and favour SMEs.

This view of the role of the Community also permeates the Maastricht Treaty, where the Community received explicit responsibility for industrial policy for the first time. Article 130 of the Maastricht Treaty called on the EU and its member states 'to ensure that the conditions needed to make the Community competitive are met in a system of open and competitive markets'. However, unanimity voting was required in the Council, limiting the possibilities for the Community to extend its role.

In the years following the 1990 Bangemann Memorandum, the 'horizontal' approach continued to characterize Community industrial policy. The EU moved away from selective industrial policy, but still continued to take measures aimed at the specific requirements of several sectors including: steel (see Box 17.5), textiles and clothing, shipbuilding, the automobile industry, and advanced technology industries such as aerospace, communications, biotechnology, and information technologies and so on. The EU attempted to avoid direct intervention, instead relying on measures to:

- Reduce capacity;
- Limit the use of state aids;
- Avoid cartels;
- Promote technology;
- Assist regional and social adjustment;
- Promote environmental objectives;
- Control competing imports.

---

[30] European Commission (1990).

Box 17.5: *Measures to assist the EU steel industry*

Concern with the steel industry was one of the reasons for creating the ECSC in 1951. During the 1950s and 1960s the problem was adjusting to meet growing demand, but during the 1970s the steel industry became characterized by overcapacity at a world level. Since 1974 output and employment in the Community's steel industry have been falling. The situation was worsened by falling demand for steel products with the development of substitutes and the emergence of new competitors on world markets such as Japan, South Korea and Brazil. The Community implemented a series of restructuring plans in the 1970s (such as the Simonet Plan and the Davignon Plan) aimed at modernization and reductions in capacity, but state aids and resistance to capacity cuts at a national level continued. Following the second oil price increase in 1979, the Community was forced to declare the steel industry in 'manifest crisis'. The Commission responded with mandatory production quotas on firms and restrictions on imports. The effort to restructure the industry and cut excess capacity continued, but one of the effects was to reinforce the oligopolistic structure of the sector.

Difficulties continued into the 1990s with falling employment in the sector and rising EU trade deficits, in particular, after the 1992–93 recession. The Community responded with financial incentives to cover some of the costs of restructuring, and foreign trade measures aimed at stabilizing the EU steel market. As these measures initially proved insufficient, the Commission tightened the application of state aids and controls on cartels in the steel sector. State aids were only to be tolerated if accompanied by capacity reductions. Social measures were introduced to assist workers who lose or change jobs, support was given to R&D and to measures to reduce regional disparities, improve the environment, modernize economic and social infrastructure, and develop alternative economic activities.

After a long and costly adjustment, according to the Commission the EU emerged with a modern and competitive steel sector.* Over a 20-year period the EU closed down 50 million tonnes of excess capacity and reduced manpower from 900 000 to 250 000. The EU enlargement of 2004 increased the steelmaking capacity by 40 million tonnes to 240 million tonnes, and since the mid-1990s there has been significant restructuring of the steel industry also in the new member states.

www.ec.europa.eu/enterprise

The Nice Treaty: Promoting competitiveness

Article 157 of the Nice Treaty replaced Article 130 of the Maastricht Treaty, and states that the Community and its member states should 'ensure that the conditions necessary for the competitiveness of the Community's industry exist'. To achieve this objective, action is to be aimed at:

- 'Speeding up the adjustment of industry to structural changes;
- Encouraging an environment favourable to initiative and to the development of undertakings throughout the Community, particularly small and medium-sized undertakings;
- Encouraging an environment favourable to co-operation between undertakings;
- Fostering better exploitation of the industrial potential of policies of innovation, research and technological development.'

Promoting small and medium enterprises is considered a high priority, and by 2007 it was estimated that there were 23 million SMEs accounting for 75 million jobs and 99 per cent of all enterprises in the EU.[31] In line with the European Charter for Small Enterprises adopted at the Fiera European Council of 2000, the Commission called for a business environment conducive to SMEs, improved entrepreneurship and skills, measures to encourage consultation and dialogue, improved access to markets and increased growth potential (through better R&D capacity).

Under the Barroso Commission there was commitment to reducing the regulatory burden on business, in particular SMEs by 25 per cent by 2012. It was estimated that this could add about 1 per cent or about €150 billion to the GDP of the EU.

R&D policy in the EU

The Barcelona European Council agreed the objective of increasing EU research spending to 3 per cent of GDP by 2010 (see also Chapter 7 on the Lisbon Strategy). In 2005 R&D investment as a share of GDP was 1.84 per cent in the EU.[32] This was lower than the previous year, and is a lower than in the US, Japan or South Korea. On current trends, China will close its gap with EU R&D spending by 2009. Lower spending on R&D by the private sector is a major reason for the low EU percentage. Business financing of R&D accounts for only 1 per cent of GDP in the EU, compared with 1.7 per cent in the US and 2.4 per cent in Japan.

EU funding of research continued to be covered by Framework Agreements, and the Seventh Framework Programme was introduced for the 2007–2013 period. The budget amounted to €50.5 billion, an increase of 40 per cent compared with the Sixth Framework. An additional €3.6 billion was allocated to the Competitiveness and Innovation Programme over the same period. The aim is to create a European Research Area (ERA) with integrated cross-border and multi-disciplinary research programmes in order to overcome the fragmentation of research efforts in the EU.

Four priority areas for research were chosen:

1 **Co-operation**: collaborative research in health, food, agriculture, fisheries, biotechnology, information and communication technologies, nano-sciences, nanotechnologies, materials and new production technologies, energy, environment (including climate change), transport (including aeronautics), socio-economic sciences and the humanities, space and security. This is allocated €32.4 billion for the 2007–2013 period.

2 **Ideas**: including the establishment of the European Research Council (ERC) to support research at the frontiers of science (€7.5 billion);

3 **People**: human resources, which has an allocation of €4.75 billion to be spent on training, research and so on (and so is linked to the European Employment Strategy, see Chapter 16).

4 **Capacities**: research infrastructures, development of the potential research capacity of SME's, developing knowledge and science clusters in Europe's regions (see also Chapter 15), and promoting science in society as a whole (€4.1 billion).

The EU normally pays for 50 per cent of the research, but SMEs can receive grants of up to 75 per cent, while research at the frontiers of knowledge can be fully funded. Plans to create a European

---

[31] The statistics are taken from the Directorate-General for Enterprise www.ec.europa.eu/enterprise and the overview of enterprise activities at www.europa.eu/pol/enterprise

[32] The statistics in this section are taken from the Directorate-General for research and Innovation, www.ec.europa.eu/research and from the overview of EU policy presented at www.europa.eu/pol/rd

Institute of Technology or EIT (similar to the MIT or Massachusetts Institute of Technology in the USA), which were much favoured by Commission President, Barroso, were eventually agreed in 2007.

The outlook and evaluation of EU industrial policy

As described in Chapter 7, the EU is experiencing considerable difficulty in moving towards the Lisbon goal of making the EU 'the most competitive and dynamic knowledge-based economy in the world, capable of sustainable growth with more and better jobs and greater social cohesion'. Productivity, in particular in high-technology sectors, remains lower than in the USA. The EU seems unlikely to meet the Barcelona Council objective of R&D spending at 3 per cent of GDP by 2010, with shortfalls in private sector spending well below the levels to realize the target. Slow growth and the increasing strength of emerging competitors at a world level, such as China and India, led to questioning of the 'horizontal' approach to industrial policy adopted by the EU since 1990.

In this context the old debate about promoting national and European champions re-emerged, in what the Commissioner then responsible for the then Internal Market, Frits Bolkenstein, called a 'time warp' reverting to the 1970s.[33] In May 2004 French President Jacques Chirac and German Chancellor Gerhard Schroeder called a meeting to discuss encouraging 'the creation of the industrial champions of the Europe of tomorrow, of which France and Germany could build a certain number'.[34]

President Nicolas Sarkozy continued in this direction, supporting French firms and becoming known as a 'liberal Colbertian'.[35] Jean-Baptiste Colbert was finance minister under Louis XIV in the seventeenth century. Colbert aimed at making France economically self-sufficient with active involvement of the state in industrial policy, and protectionism in order to maximize exports and minimize imports. Colbertism suggests less competition and more economic nationalism. In a speech to the European Parliament in November 2007 Sarkozy maintained that 'Europe should not be alone in the world in making competition a religion'. He famously persuaded the European Council to drop the refrence to 'free and undistorted competition' in Article 2 of the Lisbon Treaty, and challenged the independence of the European Central Bank calling for less emphasis on inflation and an exchange rate policy geared towards more promotion of EU exports. The French Government has also been active in support for national champions, though the emphasis seems more on nationality rather than state ownership (hence the description as a 'liberal' Colbertian). For instance the Government supported the creation of a power giant through the merger of state-owned Gaz de France and Suez to ward off foreign takeovers. Government support was also given to the state-owned Arena to ensure its dominance of the French market (and avoid a merger with the German firm Siemens). The Government was also examining the possibility of a merger between Thales and Safron to create a French champion in the defence sector. France also resisted EU efforts to open up its railways and postal market (see Chapter 6).

France was not alone in this economic nationalism. Italy, Poland and Germany resisted foreign takeovers in the banking sector. For a long time the Italian Government opposed foreign

---

[33] *Financial Times*, 14 June 2004.

[34] *Financial Times*, 19 May 2004.

[35] A phrase used by Mario Monti, former Commissioner for Competition, as reported in the *Financial Times*, 9 May 2007. Monti and Sarkozy were involved in negotiating the Alstrom case described in Box 17.3 above.

control of Alitalia and of its motorways, while Spain seemed determined to keep its electric companies in national hands.

Revival of the debate on an activist industrial policy also found echo at the EU level. The 2003 Brussels European Council expressed concern that the EU was undergoing a process of deindustrialization, and maintained that EU industry was having increasing difficulties in the face of competition, which it perceived as 'unbeatable and sometimes unfair'. The Council called for a Commission inquiry into the question in order to identify appropriate remedies if necessary.

The solutions proposed by the Commission included the usual call for higher priority to be given to innovation, research, training, competition and the better functioning of markets.[36] The most surprising aspect of the 2004 Commission document is the call for development of a sectoral policy. The Commission argues that 'this does not indicate a return to the interventionist policies of the past' but consists in adapting the horizontal approach to the specific needs of certain sectors. However, this change in orientation has to be read against the revival of interventionist policies in some of the member states. Such policies tend to breed rent-seeking activities and politicization of decisions; can lead to unfair competition; and, as explained above, are difficult to justify on the grounds of economic theory.

Concentrating on the more tradition prescription of the Commission of promoting research and innovation, investing in human capital, favouring SMEs and improving the functioning of markets would seem a more promising way forwards, but the main difficulty here that words have generally failed to be matched by actions.

Summary of Key Concepts

- **Competition policy** is aimed at preventing distortions in competition caused either by private firms or by government actions.
- Article 81 of the EC Treaty prohibits as 'incompatible with the Common Market' all agreements that affect trade between the member states and have the intention or effect of preventing, distorting or restricting competition. Although **collusive behaviour** is forbidden, the EC Treaty permits other forms of co-operation between firms that are not considered to threaten consumers.
- Article 82 of the EC Treaty prohibits abuse of **dominant position** by one or more firms.
- The announcement of the Single Market Programme was accompanied by a spectacular increase in the number of mergers in the Community. The 1989 Merger Control Regulation (Reg. 4064/89) gives the European Commission the authority to control mergers that meet a specified size and multi-nationality conditions.
- Article 86 covers the **monopoly rights** granted by member states to private or public undertakings to perform public services, but these rights should not go beyond what is necessary to provide the service, otherwise competition could be restricted.
- Article 87 prohibits **state aids** to business, which have the effect of distorting competition. Exceptions are allowed for certain types of aid.
- A reform of competition policy was introduced in May 2004. Companies will no longer be subject to the obligation of routine notification to the Commission for antitrust clearance. National competition authorities and national courts are to share responsi-

---

[36] European Commission (2004b).

bility for enforcing EU antitrust rules. New merger rules alter procedures and extend the authority of the Commission to investigate all types of harmful scenarios resulting from a merger and not just market dominance. The state aid reform aims at simplification and acceleration of procedures, and encouraging member states to use a more economic approach in assessing state aids.

- A **market-orientated industrial policy** aims at removing the barriers to the operation of competition.

- Selective, **interventionist industrial policy** involves support for declining industries to avoid loss of jobs and the promotion of industries considered 'key' or strategic.

- During the 1960s Community industrial policy was based on a market-orientated approach, but in the 1970s and 1980s more selective intervention was used in favour of specific sectors.

- Following the 1990 **Bangemann Memorandum**, the Community adopted a 'horizontal' approach to industrial policy.

- In recent years the debate about supporting **national and EU champions** has revived.

Questions for study and review

1 Explain how the integration process may be undermined by distortions in competition.

2 Describe the role of the various EU institutions with regard to competition policy.

3 What criticisms can be made, and what reforms could be introduced?

4 Explain the difficulties in establishing whether collusive behaviour between firms has taken place.

5 Describe what kinds of behaviour by firms are considered evidence of abuse of dominant position. Explain why market definition may pose difficulties in this context.

6 How has EU merger control changed over the years?

7 How successful do you think that EU policy with regard to state aids has been?

8 Describe the different forms industrial policy may take.

9 How successful has Community industrial policy proved?

10 What difficulties arise in the promotion of national and EU champions? Give some examples.

References

Baldwin, R. and Wyplosz, C. (2006) *The Economics of European Integration*, 2nd edn, McGraw-Hill Education, Maidenhead, UK.

Begg, D., Fischer, S. and Dornbusch, R. (2000) *Economics*, 6th edn, McGraw-Hill Education, Maidenhead, UK.

Bongardt, A. (ed.) (2005) *Competition in the European Union: Experiences and Challenges Ahead*, National Institute of Administration, Oeiras, Portugal.

Browning, E.K. and Browning, J.M. (1992) *Microeconomic Theory and Applications*, 4th edn, Harper Collins Publishers Inc., New York.

European Commission (1990) 'Industrial policy in an open and competitive environment: Guidelines for a Community Approach', COM(90) 556.

European Commission (2002) 'Productivity: The key to competitiveness of European economies and enterprises', COM(2002) 262 final.

European Commission (2004a) 'A pro-active competition policy for a competitive Europe: Communication from the Commission', COM(2004) 293 final, 20 April 2004.

European Commission (2004b) 'Fostering structural change: An industrial policy for an enlarged Europe', COM(2004) 274 final.

European Commission (2007a) 'Competition Policy and the European Consumer', www.ec.europa.eu/comm/competition

Hitiris, T. (2003) *European Union Economics*, 5th edn, Prentice Hall, Harlow, UK.

Martin, S. (2007) 'Competition policy', in Artis, M. and Nixson, F. (eds) *The Economics of the European Union: Policy and Analysis*, 4th edn, Oxford University Press, Oxford.

Tsoukalis, L. (1997) *The New European Economy Revisited*, 3rd edn, Oxford University Press, Oxford.

Varian, H.R. (1999) *Intermediate Microeconomics: A Modern Approach*, 5th edn, W.W. Norton & Co., London and New York.

Useful websites

The website on competition is one of the best organized of the European Commission's websites, with explanations of policy and transcripts of speeches explaining recent reforms and cases:
www.ec.europa.eu/comm/competition

For industrial policy see the website of the Directorate-general for Enterprise of the Commission:
www.ec.europa.eu/enterprise

For R&D see the Directorate-General for research and Innovation:
www.ec.europa.eu/research

For a description of issues in competition policy at a wider international level see:
Global Competition Review:
www.globalcompetitionreview.com

International Competition Network:
www.internationalcompetitionnetwork.org

CHAPTER 18

The EU and the GATT/WTO

❖ LEARNING OBJECTIVES

By the end of this chapter you should be able to understand:

❖ The importance of the GATT/WTO for the EU;

❖ The main functions of the GATT/WTO;

❖ Who negotiates for the EU in the WTO;

❖ The most important results of the GATT Uruguay Round;

❖ The difficulties encountered in launching a new round of multilateral trade negotiations;

❖ The EU position in the Doha Round;

❖ The reasons for collapse of the Doha Development Agenda;

❖ Some consequences of a collapse in the Doha Round;

❖ The move from multilateral trade liberalization to regionalism and litigation;

❖ The links between trade negotiations and environmental, health and safety issues.

Introduction

The EU is the world's largest trader, accounting for about 17 per cent of global exports and imports in 2006 (see Chapter 1). Not surprisingly then, EU relations with the main organization regulating international trade – the WTO (World Trade Organization) and its predecessor the GATT (General Agreement on Tariffs and Trade) – are of paramount importance.

As will be shown, the Common Commercial Policy means that the EU represents member states and negotiates trade agreements for them. As explained in Chapter 2, the need to present a common front in GATT negotiations was instrumental in driving forward the early integration process, in particular, with regard to trade policy and agriculture. Subsequently, the commitments made (or expected to be made in the future) in the GATT/WTO shaped key aspects of EU policy, and notably the CAP (see Chapter 12) and external relations (Chapter 19).

At the same time, given its importance in world trade, the EU is one of the main actors in trade negotiations and trade disputes taking place in the GATT/WTO framework[1].

The aim of this chapter is to explain the links between the EU and the GATT/WTO and the

---

[1] See Chapter 19 and the Online Learning Centre for this book for descriptions of some of these disputes.

ongoing attempts to liberalize world trade. The chapter can, therefore, be considered as a complement to the theoretical analysis of trade and integration carried out in Chapters 4 and 5, and as a precursor to the description of EU relations with major trading partners and regional trade blocs in the next chapter.

After a brief description of the GATT and WTO and of the representation of the EU in this framework, the world trade negotiations are presented, and the EU position is indicated. Some possible consequences of a collapse in these negotiations are discussed before considering the links between trade and environmental and health considerations.

The GATT/WTO

The GATT came into operation in 1948 with the aim of providing a framework for international trade negotiations, and attempts to regulate world trade. The original intention after the Second World War was to create an International Trade Organization, (ITO) but difficulties in ratification (in particular, by the US Congress) led to the ITO Convention being abandoned. In its place the 'temporary' GATT arrangement was adopted. The WTO replaced the GATT from 1995, and its framework was reinforced.

The GATT/WTO has three main functions:

1 Setting out regulations governing the conduct of international trade;

2 Making provisions for the settlements of disputes and retaliatory actions;

3 Providing the framework for multilateral negotiations to liberalize world trade.

The GATT system has traditionally been based on three principles: tariff reductions, reciprocity and non-discrimination. Tariffs were preferred to other barriers on trade since they were considered the most transparent form of protection. Reciprocity implies that the concessions made by the parties should be more or less balanced. This generally involves matching tariff concession with tariff concession. When a country joined the GATT, it received the benefit of trade concessions already negotiated within that framework on the basis of the most favoured nation (MFN) principle.[2] The MFN clause was conceived as a means of ensuring non-discrimination.

Among the GATT rules with particular implications for the EC was Article XXIV dealing with regional groupings. By its nature a customs union is regional and the trade preferences involved are not extended to all GATT members, and this seems to run counter to the principle of non-discrimination.[3] To meet this difficulty Article XXIV sets out certain conditions for the creation of regional groupings. In particular, the Article requires that the move to implementation must take place within a reasonable time (defined by the WTO as a period that should exceed 10 years only in exceptional cases), and that such arrangements should cover *'substantially all'* trade.

---

[2] In return the principle of reciprocity meant that the country had to offer 'equivalent' concessions.

[3] Further controversy arose concerning the trade preferences granted by the Community under the Association System. The preferences given by France, Italy, Belgium and the Netherlands to former dependencies were acceptable to the GATT because they had been granted before 1947. However, the GATT opposed the extension of these preferences so that all EC members could grant them. The question was examined in a working party with GATT and EC representatives, and it was decided that the EC should take mitigating action if damage to third parties were proved.

In 2007 the WTO waiver that allows the EU to grant unilateral preferences to the ACP countries (African, Caribbean and Pacific countries covered by the Lomé Conventions and the Cotonou Convention) under the Cotonou Agreement expires. Since 2002 the EU has been negotiating Economic Partnership Agreements (EPA) with 6 regional groupings of ACP countries to come into operation from 2008, which would entail reciprocal preferences, and extend to 'substantially all trade' (see Chapter 19).

The *'general incidence of duties and other regulations of commerce'* should also be no higher than before creation of the regional trade arrangement. The underlying assumption of the GATT therefore seemed to be that regional integration arrangements were a building block rather than a stumbling block to global liberalization of trade.[4]

Typically the liberalization of world trade proceeds in series of successive 'rounds' of negotiations. To date eight such rounds have been completed (see Box 18.1). Following the failed attempt to launch a new Round at Seattle in 1999, in November 2001 the Doha Development Agenda (DDA) began, but negotiations were suspended in 2006. Despite subsequent attempts to revive the Round, a successful conclusion in the near future seems unlikely.

Box 18.1: *GATT/WTO Rounds*

Name of the Round	Year	Topic of negotiation
Geneva	1947	Tariffs
Annecy	1949	Tariffs
Torquay	1951	Tariffs
Geneva	1956	Tariffs
Dillon Round	1960–62	Tariffs
Kennedy Round	1964–67	Tariffs and anti-dumping
Tokyo Round	1973–79	Tariffs, non-tariff barriers, multilateral agreements
Uruguay Round	1986–94	Tariffs, creation of the WTO, agriculture, textiles, services, TRIMs, TRIPs and VERs*
Doha Round	2001–?	

*See text and Box 18.2 for a more detailed explanation.

The World Trade Organization

The WTO replaced the GATT in 1995, and by 2008 it had 153 members. It was considered that much of the future reputation of the WTO would depend on the performance of the new Disputes Settlement Mechanism (DSM). This established procedures for consultations, the setting up of panels, the presentation of panel reports and the possibility of appellate review, with precise deadlines for each. The consensus was now to be *against* the establishment of panels, or the adoption of panel reports for decisions not to be made, and so represented a reversal of the GATT condition. Moreover, the possibility of appeal against a decision was now introduced. The WTO may authorize sanctions if a member state is found to be in contradiction of the rules.

Who represents the EU in the WTO framework?

The legal basis of the Common Commercial Policy of the EU is Article 133 of the Treaty Establishing the European Community.[5] According to this provision, the European Commission

---

[4] Bhagwati first used these expressions (see, for example, Bhagwati, 1994). Chapter 5 takes up this debate.

[5] This section is based on 'The EU and the WTO', www.ec.europa.eu/trade/issues/newround/index_en.htm

negotiates trade agreements on behalf of the member states, in consultation with a special committee known as the 133 Committee. The 133 Committee is made up of representatives of all the member states, and the European Commission. It meets on a weekly basis to discuss all trade policy issues affecting the EU, from WTO negotiations, to trade problems with specific products, or trade implications of other EU policies. The Commission requests endorsement of policies on trade policy issues in this Committee, and the major formal decisions are then confirmed by the Council of Ministers. The Council takes the ultimate decision on trade agreements by qualified majority vote (see Chapter 3). The Commission has to keep the European Parliament informed of all developments and maintains dialogue with civil society. Agreements involving services or intellectual property rights require a unanimous vote in the Council, after consulting the European Parliament. The assent of major treaty ratifications covering more than trade requires assent by the European Parliament.

For instance, in the Doha Development Round (see below) the Commission sets out the positions and priorities of the EU in line with the guidelines established by the Council of Ministers. Officials from the Directorate General for Trade under the responsibility of the Commissioner (Peter Mandelson in the 2004–2009 Commission) conduct negotiations and speak on behalf of the EU as a whole. Co-ordination with the member states is assured through the 133 Committee, and the Commission informs the European Parliament. An eventual agreement would require formal approval by the Council.[6]

The Uruguay Round

The Uruguay Round, launched in 1986 at Punta del Este, was far more ambitious than earlier GATT trade negotiations, which had been almost exclusively concerned with tariff reductions. The aim of the Uruguay Round was to further the process of tariff reduction, but also to extend fair trade disciplines to areas that hitherto had been largely exempt from GATT rules and regulations, including agriculture, textiles, services (through the GATS or General Agreement on Trade in Services), trade-related investment measures (TRIMs) and trade-related intellectual property rights (TRIPs). Despite initial US reluctance, it was also agreed to replace the GATT with the WTO.

The Uruguay Round was protracted well beyond all initial deadlines, and during the seven tortuous years of negotiations the Round seemed near to breaking down on various occasions, usually over the question of agriculture. Though falling short of many expectations, the results were substantial and are presented in Box 18.2.

From Seattle to the Doha Development Agenda

A new 'Millennium Round' of multilateral trade negotiations was to be launched at Seattle in December 1999 with the aim of furthering the achievements of the Uruguay Round, both in terms of trade liberalization and extension of the coverage of the WTO. The backlash of criticism and the violence of the demonstrations outside were unexpected, and Seattle marks a milestone in the history of globalization. The failure to launch the Round at Seattle was partly due to poor organization but was also due to heated differences between:

---

[6] At times the member states have challenged the authority of the Commission over such issues. This was the case for the 1992 first Blair House agreement of the Uruguay Round (see below), when France argued that the Commission had exceeded its mandate, and in the attempts in the 1970s to extend Community authority to trade relations with the Soviet Union and central and east European countries (see Senior Nello, 1985).

Box 18.2: *The main results of the Uruguay Round Agreement*

- A detailed timetable was agreed for tariff cuts of about 40 per cent on average, which is well beyond the initial objective of 30 per cent.

- Despite initial US reluctance, it was agreed to replace the GATT with the WTO.

- Agriculture was incorporated in the GATT framework, and some agricultural trade liberalization was achieved, with commitments to improve market access, cut domestic support and reduce export subsidies (see Senior Nello, 2005).

- Textiles had remained largely outside the GATT framework and were covered by the Multifibre Agreement (MFA) of 1974, subsequently renewed in 1977, 1981 and 1986. The MFA permitted industrial countries or groups of countries to impose restrictions on imports from over 30 countries, but it also imposed obligations on the industrial countries. However, if a country pleaded threat of market disruption, bilateral agreements were allowed with the exporting country and these could contain departures from the obligations. In practice market disruption was so widely invoked that the MFA became far less important than the bilateral agreements introduced under its aegis. The Uruguay Round Agreement entailed progressive liberalization of international trade in clothing and textiles over the 10 years to 2005. During the 10 transitional years bilateral quotas would remain, but measures were introduced to ensure more rapid growth of the ceilings fixed by quantitative restrictions. However, even after the Uruguay Round, tariff rates on clothing and textile imports remain high. A surge in Chinese textile and clothing exports from 2005 led to other countries (including the EU) introducing anti-dumping measures.

- For the first time in the GATT framework the Uruguay Round included a GATS. It is estimated that services account for about two-thirds of world GDP, while the share of manufacturing is only about a third. In developed countries the share of manufacturing is even lower, accounting for only about a fifth of the US GDP or a quarter of that of the EU.

  The term 'services' covers a wide range of activities, and the GATT classification covers seven categories: distribution, education, communication, health, transport, tourism and professional activities (such as architecture, engineering, legal services, accounting, etc.). One of the main reasons that services remained largely outside the GATT is that it is difficult to provide rules for such diverse phenomena, and in the event the Uruguay Agreement on GATS was extremely limited.

  The Agreement on GATS comprised three main elements:

  (a) That GATT members open up service industries listed in a schedule of commitments. However, countries were left discretion in drawing up these schedules, so the outcome depends heavily on what each country wished to include in its schedule and the number of exemptions to the MFN clause invoked.

  (b) Signatories to the Uruguay Round have to subscribe to certain general principles, including the agreement to prohibit practices such as limitations on the number of suppliers, the volume of output or transactions and on the percentage of foreign capital.

  (c) GATS negotiations were to resume in 2000.

■ Though much energy was devoted to discussing trade-related investment measures (TRIMs) during the Uruguay Round, in the final act it is one of the shortest texts. The main element of the Uruguay Round Agreement on TRIMs is a list of measures inconsistent with GATT requirements (such as local content obligations, limits on imported inputs, trade balancing requirements or limits on the percentage of production which may be exported).

■ The Uruguay Round also included an agreement on TRIPs. Growing difficulties in enforcing respect for copyright, patents and trademarks, in particular in newly developed countries, led to increasing demands (also on the part of business) for multilateral rules. The Uruguay Round Agreement on TRIPs was rather limited, calling simply for increased transparency, inclusion of TRIPs under the Dispute Settlement Procedure and a general commitment to reducing disparities in national legislation in this area.

■ Voluntary export restraints (VERs) were phased out over 10 years (see Chapter 4).

■ developed countries, in particular between the USA, EU and Japan;

■ developed and developing countries;

■ non-governmental organizations (NGOs) including environmentalists, consumer groups, trade unions, etc. who criticized both the WTO and official government positions.

Differences among developed countries arose even over the agenda for the negotiations:

■ The USA was in favour of a relatively narrow, 'manageable' agenda based on a core of Uruguay Round 'leftovers', with a few additional issues such as the further liberalization of e-commerce and the linking of trade concerns to environmental questions and labour rights. The EU (backed by Japan) favoured a wider agenda that would include subjects like investment and competition (antitrust) policy, but the USA accused the EU of attempting to widen the agenda in order to talk about 'anything but agriculture'. On agriculture the USA pushed for more liberalization than the EU or Japan were prepared to concede.

■ The US was reluctant to include TRIMs in the discussions as earlier attempts to tackle this issue had achieved so little. A central concept with regard to TRIMs is that of 'equal treatment' for nationals and foreigners. In its strongest form this implies binding commitments with regard to opening markets, providing adequate guarantees for repatriation of assets and profits and a multilateral surveillance system. In practice regulations relating to foreign direct investment raise sensitive issues relating to ownership and national sovereignty, helping to explain the difficulties encountered by developing countries, in particular.

■ The USA preferred to leave competition policy off the agenda since countries such as Japan, South Korea and others tended to use this as a pretext for introducing criticisms of US anti-dumping measures (in particular on steel) into the discussion. The argument for linking competition policy to trade issues is that otherwise the effects of trade liberalization may be undermined by restrictive practices by firms that, for example, may collude to divide markets. Differences in national antitrust policies may also distort international competition and influence the decisions of firms on where to locate.

The less developed countries argued that the Uruguay Round Agreement was biased against them, and that multilateral discussions failed to take adequate account of their needs on a number of grounds:

- They had difficulty in meeting the Uruguay Round commitments on TRIPs, TRIMs, subsidies and anti-dumping, and wanted their obligations reduced in these areas.

- They argued that the benefits of the Uruguay Round in sectors of interest to them were less than expected. The EU was criticized for continuing high levels of agricultural protection, while the USA was said to have backloaded its liberalization of textile imports, so that most of the increased access would occur towards 2005.

- The developing countries interpreted the proposals to liberalize e-commerce, TRIMs and services such as telecommunications as an attempt by developed countries to further extend the markets of their multinationals and hinder the creation of indigenous least developed countries' (LDC) industries.

- Though there was general agreement that WTO procedures should be subject to 'review, reform and repair', and that developing countries should be given more say in procedures, there was no common view of how this should take place.

- Finally the US proposal to include environmental issues on the agenda, and to link core labour standards[7] to trade, was regarded as a pretext for higher protectionism on the part of industrialized countries.

Box 18.3: *The Mandate of the Doha Development Agenda*

- Strengthening of WTO rules, and 'improvements and clarifications' to the dispute settlement procedure;

- Increasing the role of developing countries in the global trading system and stronger provisions for Special and Differential Treatment (SDT) of poorer members;

- Agreeing a declaration on international drugs patents and access to medicines (which was one of the TRIP reforms requested by developing nations);

- Liberalization of trade in industrial goods and services;

- Liberalization of agricultural trade;

- Negotiations on investment and competition rules following two years of preparatory work;

- Negotiations on trade facilitation (customs procedures, etc.) and transparency in government procurement;

- Negotiations on 'clarifying and improving disciplines' on anti-dumping and anti-subsidy rules;

- Further work on e-commerce;

- Further work on environmental matters, but no commitment to negotiations;

- On labour issues note was taken of the work on the social dimensions of globalization by the International Labour Organization.

---

[7] The effectiveness of insisting on trade measures to push for core labour standards in developing countries has been the subject of much debate. If, for example, children are forced out of work in such countries, there may be a risk that they become simply poorer. It is argued that child labour is a development, not a trade issue, and should be treated as such.

Before the event the scale of participation of NGOs and individual protesters at the Seattle negotiations was hugely underestimated.[8] In 1998 about 1200 NGOs signed a statement calling for reform of the WTO, and many of them sent activists to Seattle.[9] Non-governmental organizations differ considerably in size and vary from huge agencies such as Greenpeace to tiny fringe groups. Their interests are also extremely diverse, ranging from issues such as the environment and agriculture to labour unions expressing fears that trade liberalization could lead to widening wage disparities or higher unemployment (see the discussion on globalization in Chapter 4).

Agreement was finally reached on launching the Doha Development Agenda in November 2001 in Qatar. The phrasing of the mandate for the Round was often vague, trying to accommodate very different positions (see Box 18.3).

The EU position in the Doha Round

Though it changed over time it is useful to outline the main features of the EU position in the DDA. As agriculture played such a crucial role in the Round (as in the Uruguay Round before), the EU position is first presented on the three pillars of agricultural trade negotiations: export subsidies, tariffs and domestic support, before moving on to other issues.

During the DDA at Hong Kong in December 2005 the EU agreed to complete elimination of agricultural **export subsidies** by 2013. Subsequently, the EC reiterated its commitment to abolishing export subsidies regardless of the outcome of the Doha Round (see Chapter 12).

On **agricultural tariffs** in 2006 the EU Commissioner for Trade, Peter Mandelson, stated that the EU was prepared to improve on its earlier formal offer of an average reduction of 39 per cent and that the member states had given him a licence to offer a larger tariff cut (51 per cent was mentioned unofficially). Certain member states, and notably France, subsequently denied this. For instance, at the St Petersburg G-8 Summit of July 2006 the President of the European Commission, Barroso, promised to hand EU negotiators a stronger bargaining mandate, but President Chirac maintained that Barroso had no power to dictate the terms of the WTO talks.[10]

On **domestic support**, the EU offer to cut trade-distorting domestic farm subsidies by more than 70 per cent was based on the view prevalent at the time of the 2003 reform that the Single Farm Payment (SFP) of the CAP (see Chapter 12) was sufficiently decoupled to fall into the green box category of policies (see Box 18.4), which were exonerated from the obligation to reduce domestic support.[11] Cross-compliance may create problems as in certain circumstances it requires that some form of production be maintained. Swinbank and Tranter (2006) also point out that cross-compliance requires that SFPs are tied to land that is 'maintained in good agricultural and environmental condition' and this could create difficulty with the criterion that

---

[8] Clinton initially called on such groups to come and express their opinions in Seattle, undoubtedly not anticipating the havoc this would create.

[9] *The Economist*, 10 November 1999.

[10] Dow Jones Newswires of 23/7/2006.

[11] Farmers could initially claim the SFP on land only provided it was not used for fruit, vegetable or permanent crops other than olives. This was a similar condition to that applied on payments for US cotton (as land used to produce fruit and vegetables could not be enrolled in the programme), which was found contrary to WTO rules also on this ground. With the reform of the fruit and vegetable sector agreed in 2007 this condition for receipt of the SFP was dropped, and the sector was integrated into the Single Payment Scheme.

Swinbank and Tranter (2006) argue that difficulties remain with the partially decoupled schemes permitted in some cases by the reform, but the elimination of such schemes has been proposed by the EU.

payments should not be 'related to or based on, the factors of production employed in any year after the base period' (Uruguay Round Agreement on Agriculture, URAA, Article 6/d, see Box 18.4). Moreover, the single farm payment changes the uncertainty distribution of total farm income, and in doing so affects the production decisions of farmers. The rules for classification of a policy in the green box are imprecise.

Box 18.4: *The WTO classification of domestic support for agriculture*

The WTO classification of policies follows a traffic-light analogy: red measures must be stopped (but no agricultural policies are included in this category), amber box policies should slow down (by means of reduction), while green measures can go ahead.

The **amber box** covers policies considered to distort production and trade, which are permitted within the limits agreed in international negotiations. They are defined in Article 6 of the Uruguay Round Agreement on Agriculture (URAA) as all domestic supports except those in the blue and green boxes.

The **blue box** is the amber box with conditions, and covers support under 'production-limiting schemes'. It was initially designed to cover the EU direct payments to farmers following the 1992 CAP reform and the US deficiency payments.

Green box measures must meet the 'fundamental requirement that they have no or at most minimal trade-distorting effects or effects on production', are provided through government funding, and do not have the effect of providing price support (URAA, Annex 2, Article 1). In addition there are programme-specific requirements such as that 'the amount of such payments in any given year shall not be related to, or based on, the type or volume of production ... [or] ... the factors of production employed in any year after the base year' (URAA, Annex 2, Article 6).

On **market access for industrial goods** the EU was in favour of eliminating high tariffs and tariff peaks through a reduction of all tariff lines ensuring a similar level of tariff reduction across the board. This would apply also in north–south and south–south trade.

The EU wanted further **market access negotiations on services**, but was committed to defending the right of WTO members to protect cultural diversity, and did not seek general deregulation or privatization of sectors where principles of public interest were at stake.

The EU stressed the importance of **sustainable development** and, in particular, social development and consumer concerns, and increased coherence between trade and the environment.

The EU also maintained that it wanted to find workable solutions for **developing countries** with regard to their concerns about implementing existing WTO commitments, and their proposals for SDT.

The difficulties encountered by the Doha Round

In 2003 at Cancún in Mexico negotiations on the Doha Round were suspended. Though there were differences over agriculture, the reason for the deadlock was differences over the so-called Singapore Issues (investment rules, competition, trade facilitation, and transparency in government procurement).

The EU supported Singapore issues though they were a fairly low priority for EU business and member states. Again the EU was accused of a Machiavellian attempt to broaden the agenda, and so reduce the pressure for agricultural trade liberalization. Many developing countries refused to negotiate on all four Singapore issues, maintaining that they neither had the resources to negotiate nor to implement them. The EU offered to drop the two most controversial issues (competition and investment) at the last moment, but Japan and Korea were unprepared for the change in position by the EU and stood their ground. The Mexican chairman, Derbez, concluded the debate, arguing that 'despite considerable movement in consultations, members remained entrenched, particularly on the Singapore issues'.

At Cancún there was antagonism between developing and developed countries, and though the former have differing interests, they remained relatively united in their attacks on developed countries. The issue of the African cotton growers (see Box 18.5) became emblematic of Cancún.

Box 18.5: *The African cotton-producing countries*

Benin, Burkina Faso, Chad and Mali had been encouraged by the World Bank to produce their high-quality cotton, but argued that they encountered difficulties due to falling prices and the expansion of exports from developed countries, from the USA in particular. For 10 million people in Central and West Africa cotton is the main cash crop. According to Eurostat data, in 1999/2000 the share of cotton in exports was 79 per cent for Mali, 65 per cent for Benin and 56 per cent for Chad.

US subsidies to its 25 000 cotton farmers amount to $3–4 billion a year, which is more than the GDP of Burkina Faso, and three times the US aid budget for Africa (*Financial Times*, 16 September 2003). The USA agreed to help build up Africa's textile industry, diversify from cotton production and address market distortions but was only prepared to discuss cotton subsidies in the general context of agricultural negotiations. The African countries did not consider such proposals adequate.

In 2004 the EU introduced a reform of its cotton regime that decoupled 65 per cent of support from production (see Chapter 12) and introduced limits on the areas that could produce cotton in Spain, Greece and Portugal. The EU also announced that it was prepared to eliminate exports subsidies on cotton to the LDCs and allow duty and quota-free access for cotton from these countries. The African cotton-producing countries expressed disappointment since they had hoped that the EU would completely decouple its support for cotton.

After Cancún formal negotiations were 'discontinued' for a few months, but in July 2004 consensus was reached on a framework agreement for continuing negotiations. At Hong Kong in December 2005 a further attempt was made to narrow differences, and a timetable was set with the goal of completing negotiations by the end of 2006.

However, as in the Uruguay Round, the main stumbling block in the DDA was to prove agriculture, and it was generally considered that without an agreement on agriculture it would be impossible to continue negotiations on other topics such as improvements to non-agricultural market access (NAMA).

The EU, backed by countries such as Japan and South Korea, had been arguing that the agricultural negotiations should take account of the 'multifunctional' role of farmers in protecting the environment and countryside, and in promoting food quality and safety, rural development and animal welfare, and in the Doha Round it was agreed to take note of such 'non-trade concerns'.

Difficulties also arose on the question of geographical indications. The EU wanted world-wide protection for geographical indications, not only on wines and spirits (such as champagne, or Scotch whisky) but also on a wide range of products such as Parma ham, Roquefort cheese, Darjeeling tea and so on, reflecting the high percentage of processed foods and beverages in EU agricultural and food exports. The EU argued that quality guarantees were necessary to compensate for the liberalization of agricultural markets. The proposal was opposed by countries such as the USA, Australia, Canada and South Africa who maintain that well-known geographical indications have either become generic terms, or have been registered by a trademark in their country.

In the event in 2006 the Round broke down over agriculture. In June 2006 with a view to reaching agreement the Director General of the WTO, Pascal Lamy, launched the famous slogan 20/20/20. This called for the USA to cap its subsidies to agriculture at $20 billion, for emerging countries such as India and Brazil to place a ceiling of 20 per cent on industrial tariffs, and for the EU to accept the proposal of the G-20 with regards to reductions in agricultural tariffs (an average cut in tariffs by 54 per cent). Crawford Falconer, who chaired the farm negotiations, presented a draft proposal for a potential agreement, but the 74-page document contained 760 square brackets indicating the wide range of points on which consensus had not yet been reached. In April 2007 a revised paper indicated the points that could act as a 'centre of gravity' for agreement, but there were no major changes in the positions of parties, which might suggest that a settlement could be reached.

The reasons for collapse of the Doha Round

In July 2006 negotiations on the DDA were suspended, and again in 2008 (too late to discuss in this book but see the OLC for updating). Although for a long time the main obstacle to reaching agreement appeared to be the reluctance of the EU to improve its offer on market access for agricultural products, many agree that the major cause for the collapse of negotiations in July 2006 was US resistance to cuts in its farm subsidies.[12] Large emerging countries such as India and Brazil pushed for reductions in farm tariffs and subsidies in developed countries, but failed to meet the corresponding requests for improved access to their markets.

In 2003 when Pascal Lamy was European Trade Commissioner, he referred to the WTO as a medieval organization whose rules did not support the weight of its tasks. Agreement in the Doha Round requires consensus among the 153 WTO members. In 1994 when the GATT had 117 members it had proved possible to reach agreement on the Uruguay Round. What had changed in the meantime?

Key to the success of the Uruguay Round was the provisional Blair House Agreement on agriculture of November 1992 between the EU and USA.[13] A further year was needed to extend the agreement to other GATT members, and to overcome opposition by France (a position

---

[12] Subsequently in 2007 the USA was to improve its offer, with high grain prices as a result of demand for ethanol offering scope for reductions in subsidies. However, 58 senators from both parties had written to Bush asking him not to reduce domestic support if there were not signs of an improved offer on market access from other WTO members. It was claimed that an excessively generous special and sensitive treatment would render proposals on tariffs empty of content (Listorti, 2007).

[13] See Senior Nello (2005) for a description of the Uruguay Round Agreement on Agriculture.

influenced by the strength of the French farm lobby, and the 1993 elections), who maintained that the Commission had gone beyond its negotiating mandate. The USA was not prepared to renegotiate the deal, and encouraged by industrial lobbies, countries such as Germany, the UK and the Netherlands were pushing for a successful conclusion to the Uruguay Round. French resistance was eventually overcome by a series of concessions, including more favourable

Box 18.6: *The actors in the Doha Round: some of the main groups of countries*

Group	Membership	Description
G6	The EU, USA, Australia, India, Brazil and Japan.	Some of the leading industrialized and emerging economies.
The Non-G6	Canada, Chile, Indonesia, Kenya, New Zealand and Norway.	Formed in 2006 as part of 'quiet diplomacy' they represent many of the major negotiating groups in the WTO.
G20	Emerging countries such as Brazil, India, China and South Africa (though the membership has fluctuated).	Created in 2003 with the aim of ensuring that negotiations do not simply reflect the narrow concerns of the EU and USA.
G33	Now over 40 countries, under the co-ordination of Indonesia.	Set up in 2003 in order to use the concepts of a Special Safeguards Mechanism and Special Products to ensure food security and protect rural livelihoods in developing countries.
G90	An alliance of developing countries receiving preferential treatment, including the ACP countries at the centre of the development policy of the EU.	The G90 are concerned to avoid erosion of their preferences by ensuring that they receive SDT.
The Cairns Group	18 agricultural exporting countries	Formed in 1986 during the Uruguay Round.
Cotton-producing countries	Chad, Mali, Benin and Burkina Faso.	Joined together in 2003 to attack the high level of subsidies by developed countries (and, in particular, the USA and EU) to cotton.
G10	Countries with a high level of support to agriculture such as Japan, Korea, Norway and Switzerland.	

treatment of French regions benefiting from the Structural Funds and increased aid for durum wheat. The treatment of the Uruguay Round as a 'single undertaking' with cross-linking of issues meant that others with a stake in a successful outcome, such as the industrial lobby, were able to exert pressure. Also in the Doha Round there were attempts by the International Chamber of Commerce and various business leaders to push for continuation of negotiations,[14] but with less success.

A major constraint on the Doha Round was that Fast Track, or the Trade Promotion Authority of President Bush expired in June 2007. Fast Track binds Congress to voting on trade agreements without amendment, and is considered necessary to prevent the agreement becoming unravelled subsequently. Fast track is needed for the approval of an agreement, not for the continuation of negotiations, but other players could interpret its absence as a lack of commitment by the USA to the Round. Events such as the French elections in 2007, the need to pass a new US Farm Bill, and US Presidential elections in 2008 also reduced the leeway for manoeuvre of key players.

The Doha Round differed from the Uruguay Round in the more active participation of developing countries, and the emergence of various more-or-less formal alliances of groups of countries.[15] These groups reflect the differing interests and vulnerabilities of WTO members (see Box 18.6). The likely future entry of Russia into the WTO could further complicate the pattern of international trade relations.

Developing countries were vehement in criticizing the developed countries in the WTO negotiations, but slower to present viable initiatives, common positions or concessions. After Cancún the then US trade representative, Zoellick, complained of the transformation of the WTO into a 'forum for the politics of protest'. Various parties accused certain NGOs of inflammatory behaviour and attempting to radicalize the issues.[16]

Some consequences of the collapse of the Doha Round

There are various surveys of the impact of the liberalization of world trade and of a successful conclusion to the Doha Round (see, for instance, those by Bouët, 2006a and 2006b; Tangermann and Ash, 2006; and FAO, 2006). Despite difficulties in comparison, and though a full discussion is beyond the present scope,[17] certain general observations can be derived from these studies:

- All the studies point to an overall increase in welfare as a result of world trade liberalization.

- Tariffs and subsidies are often higher in agriculture than other sectors, so all studies indicate liberalization of agricultural trade as a major contributor to the global welfare gains from overall trade liberalization.

- The largest absolute gains from agricultural trade liberalization would go to developed countries (such as those of the EU) where markets are most distorted (FAO, 2006), with consumers (in particular, those in less well-off families, Tarditi, 2006) and, possibly, taxpayers in such countries benefiting. However, most studies show that world trade liberalization would be development-friendly with the share of gain to developing countries being well above their percentage of global GDP (Anderson and Martin, 2005).

---

[14]See, for instance, the letter to the *Financial Times* of 1/3/2007.

[15]For lists of the members of these various groups see the WTO website, www.wto.org

[16]See, for example the letter of Commissioner Fischler to the *Financial Times* of 20/9/2003.

[17]For a discussion of these results see Bouët (2006a) or Senior Nello (2007).

■ World agricultural trade liberalization entails the elimination of tariffs and of production and export subsidies. This removes distortions and leads to an improvement in the global allocation of resources. At the same time it reduces supply and increases the demand for agricultural products so raising world agricultural prices for many products. Net food importing countries would experience a loss if the higher price for imports were not matched by an increase in their export prices. The picture is complicated by the fact that even within the agricultural sector distortions vary considerably according to product.[18] According to Bouët (2006b), some Middle East and North African countries, Mexico, Bangladesh and China would experience negative terms-of-trade effects.

■ Most studies suggest that tariffs are more harmful than agricultural subsidies for developing countries (see, for example, Tangermann and Ash, 2006) but the erosion of preferences means that tariff reduction would not benefit some of the poorest countries. Many of these have preferential access to the EU through the Cotonou Agreement and the Everything-but-Arms (EBA) initiative (see Chapter 19), and to the USA through the AGOA (Africa Growth and Opportunity Act) and the Caribbean Basin Initiative. Bouët (2006b) finds that with multilateral trade liberalization preferences would be eroded for part of Sub-Saharan Africa, Mexico, Tunisia and Bangladesh, and that countries such as Australia or Brazil would be able to replace the preferential exports of Africa, the Caribbean or Andean countries.

■ The benefit of eliminating agricultural export subsidies for developing countries may also be overestimated. According to Gallezot and Bernard (2004), EU export subsidies vary by product and destination and tend to be aimed at countries that are dependent on imports and represent a benefit to consumers in those countries. Some NGOs stress the impact of unfair competition for LDC producers, but, as Bureau et al. (2005) argue, empirical studies suggest this is limited to certain products such as sugar, beef (for West Africa) and milk (India and Jamaica).

■ Liberalization can involve adjustment costs and increase short-term risk owing to competition from imports and reallocation of production factors. In developed countries safety nets are largely in place to compensate such developments, and care must be take not to slow down the adjustment process excessively. In developing countries additional mechanisms may be necessary to compensate the losers. However, wide-scale recourse to SDT with high levels of protection for special products does not seem an answer as all studies indicate that a large share of the benefits would come from the liberalization of developing-country markets (Anderson and Martin, 2005).

■ According to many authors (see, for example, Bureau et al., 2005) the main reason for the poor agricultural trade performance of developing countries (see Chapter 19) is not so much tariffs and the agricultural subsidies of developed countries, but rather sanitary and phytosanitary standards (see below), and poor infrastructure. For instance, the tightening of EU regulations with regard to traceability, responsibility, and tighter hygiene procedures (see Chapter 12) could render exporting from developing countries more difficult. Foreign direct investment may represent a means of improving food safety and quality, but is often not attracted to LDCs. The 'Aid for Trade', and trade facilitation initiatives announced in the WTO and EU frameworks could play a role here.[19]

■ A breakdown in WTO negotiations could lead to an increase in regionalism (see Chapter 5) and litigation (see Box 18.7). Given the difficulties of WTO negotiations, it seems likely that

---

[18]World price rises from agricultural trade liberalization are expected to be highest for wheat, meat, rice and sugar (Bouët, 2006b), and dairy products (Tangermann and Ash, 2006).

[19]See, for example, the recommendations of the WTO task force of 27 July 2006.

more countries will switch to legal challenge in an attempt to force change in the policies of key players such as the EU and USA. Moreover, the collapse of attempts at multilateral trade liberalization seems likely to reinforce the proliferation of regional and bilateral arrangements.

Box 18.7: *WTO litigation as a catalyst for reform of the CAP*

Many of the WTO disputes involve agricultural products, and in some cases litigation has resulted in change of the CAP. For instance, the EU has introduced reform of its sugar and banana regimes following decisions in the WTO. However, the EU preferred to face sanctions rather than accept the WTO ruling that imports on beef with growth-promoting hormones from the USA and Canada should be allowed. In 2008 a WTO panel ruled against these sanctions, but maintained that scientific risk assessment carried out by the EU was still insufficient to demonstrate that such hormone-treated meat presents unacceptable risks. If the WTO rules against the EU on genetically modified organisms (GMOs) a similar decision to 'live with sanctions' might also result. This probably reflects the strong preferences of EU consumers with regard to food safety and scepticism about the effectiveness of food authorities.

Other aspects of food and agricultural policies would seem vulnerable to litigation after the demise of the 'Peace Clause' from January 1 2004. The Peace Clause was set out in Article 13 of the URAA and precluded most WTO dispute settlement challenges against a country that was complying with the liberalization commitments of the URAA.

Two aspects of the CAP would appear especially vulnerable to challenge in the WTO: the SFP (as described above in the text) and export subsidies on processed foods incorporating primary products. GATT Article XVI permitted the use of export subsidies on primary goods under certain conditions, but not those on non-primary products, though it was never resolved whether export subsidies could be paid on primary agricultural products incorporated into processed goods such as pasta. The URAA appeared to legitimize the EU practice of paying export subsidies on incorporated products, but with the expiry of the Peace Clause it is open to question whether GATT Article XVI has any residual force (Swinbank, 2006).

GATT/WTO rules and disciplines are often ambiguous and imprecise, lending themselves to conflicting interpretations, and different provisions are not always consistent with each other. As a result the outcome of WTO litigation is rendered more complex and less certain for potential complainants.

* See http://trade.ec.europa.eu/doclib/html/134652.htm or www.wto.org for a list of these disputes. Some of these disputes (such as those over the EU banana regime, beef hormones, and GMOs) are discussed in more detail on the OLC for this book, see www.mcgraw-hill.co.uk/textbooks/senior.

The GATT/WTO and environmental, health and safety issues

One of the most controversial areas in international trade negotiations is the link between trade liberalization and environmental protection. Conflicts may arise from trade-offs between different policy objectives and the different priorities of countries. Countries with higher standards are concerned that the liberalization of international trade, or more specifically, WTO rulings, may lead to a 'race to the bottom' with legislation on environmental, safety or health issues being relaxed or undermined. It has also been argued that there may be a tendency towards the concentration of the most polluting industries in developing countries where environmental regulations are less strict. There is also a fear that increased trade and travel could encourage the spread of epidemics, and threaten biodiversity.

GATT/WTO rules have always allowed countries to impose restrictions for environmental or health or safety motives, and, according to Article XX of the WTO, these are defined as measures necessary 'to protect human, animal or plant life or health'. Under WTO agreements subsidies are also permitted for environmental protection, and environmental objectives are recognized in agreements dealing with product standards, food safety and intellectual property protection. Otherwise 'like products' have to be treated identically, and this has led to some extremely controversial rulings (see Box 18.8).

Box 18.8: *GATT/WTO rulings on certain environmental issues*

In 1991 Mexico brought a case against a US embargo of imports of tuna from Mexico under the Marine Mammals Protection Act because the Mexican fishing techniques resulted in a higher level of accidental deaths of dolphins than the Act permitted. The embargo was also extended to other countries that could not prove that the tuna had not come from Mexico. Mexico's case was upheld since it was argued that in this case other GATT rules should not override the basic prohibition of import restrictions. In the event, the controversy was resolved by Mexico and the USA agreeing to improve fishing methods.

In a similar case the WTO Appellate Body upheld a complaint by five Asian countries (India, Malaysia, Pakistan, Thailand and the Philippines) over restrictions on imports imposed by the USA because their shrimps were caught by methods that incidentally caught sea turtles, an endangered species. According to the WTO, members could take measures relating to the conservation of exhaustible natural resources, including turtles, but these measures should not be applied in a way that is arbitrary or unjustifiable, or which constitutes a disguised restriction on international trade. The justification given for the ruling against the USA was that it had treated some WTO members less favourably than others, failed to recognize that the sea turtle protection programmes of other countries were equivalent to that of the USA, who banned imports of shrimps, even if the country complied with US regulations but the country of origin had not been certified under the US regulation. Moreover the USA had given only four months' notice to these countries to adopt US-type legislation on turtle-excluding devices.

Two aspects of the 1994 GATT Uruguay Round Agreement deal specifically with health and safety matters. The Agreement on Sanitary and Phytosanitary measures (SPS) sets out certain basic rules concerning the setting of standards for food safety and animal and plant health. The

Agreement on Technical Barriers to Trade deals with other standards, such as those establishing safety requirements for cars and electrical equipment, and labelling requirements.

The reference standard of the SPS Agreement is based on the food standards established by the Codex Alimentaris, which is a joint body of two international organizations, the World Health Organization (WHO) and the Food and Agriculture Organization (FAO). Sanitary and Phytosanitary measures also have to be based on an appropriate assessment of risks, taking into account available scientific evidence and other relevant factors such as testing and inspection methods, or potential damage from spread of disease.

In discussions of such issues, certain countries, and the EU in particular, have placed increasing emphasis on the 'precautionary principle', also known as being 'better safe than sorry'. Faced with incomplete knowledge, and uncertainty regarding the possible consequences of some actions, the principle allows regulators to intervene, though the measures taken should only be proportionate to suspected risks. A justification sometimes given for the precautionary principle is that in such uncharted territory if disaster occurs it may be irreversible.

According to the SPS agreement, in the absence of sufficient scientific evidence, a country is permitted to take a provisional measure on the basis of information available. If a country takes such a measure, it is obliged to seek further information and review the measure in this light. However, in practice trying to evolve policy guidelines on the basis of the precautionary principle proves extremely complex.

Evaluation

The Uruguay Round took seven long years of negotiations, with talks threatening to collapse over the question of agriculture on numerous occasions. After the false start in Seattle in 1999, the Doha Round was launched in November 2001, but was suspended in 2003 at Cancún over the Singapore issues. Despite attempts to revive negotiations, they again broke down in July 2006. This time the main obstacles seemed to be US reluctance to cut its domestic subsidies to agriculture, EU market access for agricultural goods, and the unwillingness of emerging countries such as India and Brazil to improve access to their markets. Fast Track authority in the US lapsed in June 2007, and it is unlikely that an agreement will be reached in the near future.

The WTO reaches agreement by consensus, and this seems increasingly difficult to reach among its growing membership, in particular, with the more active role of emerging and developing countries.

It seems likely that with the reduced effectiveness of the negotiating capacity of the WTO, there will be more resort to its role in dispute settlement to force change in the policies of its members. For instance, this has occurred for the EU sugar and banana regimes. In some cases, such as beef with growth-promoting hormones, strong consumer preferences with regard to food safety has meant that the EU has preferred to live with sanctions rather than comply with WTO decisions. However, GATT/WTO rules are not always open to precise interpretation, and there may be contradictions between different provisions rendering the outcome of litigation uncertain. The collapse in WTO negotiations also seems likely to reinforce the growing trend towards regionalism.

GATT/WTO rules have always allowed countries to impose restrictions for environmental or health or safety motives, but also here have led to some extremely controversial rulings. The process of trade liberalization, or, more generally, globalization, with more movement of goods (including plants and animals) and people also seems likely to have important implications for the environment and biodiversity.

Summary of Key Concepts

- The **GATT** came into operation in 1948. The GATT was replaced by the **WTO** in 1995.

- **The functions of the GATT and subsequently the WTO** are: to set out regulations governing the conduct of international trade; to make provisions for the settlements of disputes and retaliatory actions and to provide the framework for multilateral negotiations to liberalize world trade.

- The GATT/WTO system has traditionally been based on **three principles**: tariff reductions, reciprocity and non-discrimination.

- The liberalization of world trade proceeds by **'rounds'** of negotiations, the last of which to be completed was the Uruguay Round (1986–94).

- The aim of the **Uruguay Round** was to further the process of tariff reduction but also to extend fair trade disciplines to areas that hitherto had been largely exempt from GATT rules and regulations, including agriculture, textiles, services, trade-related investment measures and trade-related intellectual property rights. It was also agreed to replace the GATT with the WTO.

- Following the failure to launch a trade round at Seattle, the **Doha Development Agenda** eventually began in November 2001.

- At **Cancún** in September 2003 negotiations broke down on the Singapore issues (competition, investment, trade facilitation and transparency in government procurement).

- **The DDA again broke down in July 2006** over US domestic subsidies to agriculture, EU market access for agricultural goods, and market access to countries such as India and Brazil.

- **Fast Track authority** in the US lapsed in June 2007, making it unlikely that an agreement in the DDA will be reached in the near future.

- The WTO reaches agreement by **consensus**, and this seems increasingly difficult with its growing membership, in particular, with the more active role of emerging and developing countries.

- The **consequences of a breakdown of multilateral negotiations** seem likely to be lower world welfare and increased use of the WTO Dispute Settlement Procedure, and regionalism.

- GATT/WTO rules have always allowed countries to impose **restrictions for environmental or health or safety motives**, but otherwise 'like products' have to be treated identically, and this has led to some extremely controversial rulings.

Questions for study and review

1 *What were the main functions of the GATT, and how effective was it in meeting its objectives?*

2 *How is the WTO different from the GATT?*

3 *How has the GATT/WTO influenced the EU?*

4 *Describe the EU position in the DDA.*

5 *What are the reasons for the collapse of the DDA?*

6 *What are the likely consequences of increased regionalism and resort to litigation in the WTO?*

7 *What are the tensions between trade liberalization and environmental considerations? How has the GATT/WTO attempted to reconcile these objectives?*

References

Anderson, K. and Martin. W. (eds) (2005) *Agricultural Trade Reform and the Doha Development Agenda*, Washington, DC, OUTP and the World Bank.

Bhagwati, J. (1994) 'Regionalism and multilateralism: An overview', in de Melo, I. and Panagariya, A. (eds) *New Dimensions in Regional Integration,* Cambridge University Press, Cambridge.

Bouët, A. (2006a) *How Much Will Trade Liberalization Help the Poor? Comparing Global Trade Models*, International Food Policy Research Institute IFPRI Research Paper 5, www.ifpri.org

Bouët, A. (2006b) *What can the Poor Expect from Trade Liberalization? Opening the Black Box.* MTID Discussion Paper No. 93, IFPRI, Washington, DC.FAO.

Bureau, J.C., Jean, S. and Matthews, A. (2005) *Agricultural Trade Liberalisation: Assessing the Consequences for the Developing Countries*, paper presented at the XIth European Association of Agricultural Economists, Copenhagen, Denmark, August 24–7.

FAO (Food and Agriculture Organization) (2006) *The State of Food and Agriculture 2005*, FAO, Rome, www.fao.org

Gallezot, J. and Bernard, F. (2004) *EU Export Subsidies on Agricultural and Agri-food Products to Africa*, The World Bank, www.worldbank.org

Listorti, G. (various issues) *Finestra sul WTO*, www.agriregioni.it

Senior Nello, S.M. (1985) *EC-East European Relations: Cooperation at the Government and Firm Levels*, European University Institute (EUI) Working Paper No.85/183, Florence, p. 49.

Senior Nello, S.M. (2005) *The European Union: Economics, Policies and History*, McGraw Hill, Maidenhead, UK, and the related website at: www.mcgraw-hill.co.uk/textbooks/senior

Senior Nello, S.M. (2007) Winners and Losers from World Agricultural Trade Liberalisation, EUI Working Papers RSCAS 2007/18, Robert Schuman Centre for Advanced Studies, European University Institute, Florence.

Swinbank, A. (2006) 'The EU's export refunds on processed foods: Legitimate in the EU?', *The Estey Centre Journal of International Law and Trade Policy*, Vol. 7, No. 2.

Swinbank, A. and Tranter, R. (2006) 'Decoupling EU farm support: Does the new Single Payment

Scheme fit in the green box?', *The Estey Centre Journal of International Law and Trade Policy*, Vol. 6, No. 1.

Tangermann, S. and Ash, K. (2006) *Agricultural Policy and Trade Reform. Potential Effects at Global, National and Household Levels*, OECD, Paris, www.oecd.org

Tarditi, S. (2006) 'Politica agricola e accordi internazionali: gli interessi dei cittadini europei', *Consumatori, Diritti e Mercato*, 2-2006, www.Tarditi_2006_03_CDM

Useful websites

The European Commission explains the EU position and provides statistics and key reports: www.ec.europa.eu.

The Institute for International Economics in the USA publishes various studies of trade and international monetary economics: www.iie.com

The Organization for Economic Co-operation and Development publishes reports and statistics on international trade: www.oecd.org

Oxfam provides a critical view of international economic relations: www.oxfam.org.uk

The United Nations publishes international trade statistics, though with a certain delay: www.un.org

The US position is presented by:
The US Department of Commerce, International Trade Administration: www.ita.doc.gov

The US Trade Representative: www.ustr.gov

The US International Trade Commission: www.usitc.gov

The World Bank provides statistics and analysis, in particular of the developing countries' prospective: www.worldbank.org

The World Trade Organization provides statistics, explanations and key documents on the Doha Round: www.wto.org

EU Trade and Aid Policies

By the end of this chapter you should be able to understand:

❖ What we mean by the 'hierarchy' of trade preferences of the EU;

❖ What we mean by the General System of Preferences (GSP);

❖ What trade and aid measures the EU uses for developing countries;

❖ The trade and investment relations between the EU and the USA;

❖ What the institutional framework for the transatlantic dialogue involves;

❖ Some possible explanations of the conflictual co-operation between the EU and the USA;

❖ What are the main features of the European Neighbourhood Policy (ENP); the Mediterranean Partnership, and EU relations with Russia, Asia and Latin America.

Introduction

Although the EU has primarily been concerned with promoting integration internally, it has also had to develop a trade policy towards the rest of the world. The Common Commercial Policy (CCP) of the EU was based on Article 113 of the Treaty of Rome, which required a common Community tariff regime and common trade agreements with third countries. European Union trade policy is intrinsically linked to other policy areas, and notably the Common Agricultural Policy (CAP), the Single Market and the Common Foreign and Security Policy (CFSP). The EC represents the Community in multilateral trade negotiations. Table 19.1 indicates the main trading partners of the EU.[1]

At times the gradual extension of EU responsibility into questions of external relations not strictly related to trade has been hotly contested by the member states. The external aid policy of the EU has been influenced by historic and strategic considerations, with former French and British colonies receiving particularly favourable treatment, and continuation of this historical bias in policies has at times been challenged.

---

[1] In 2006 total EU(25) imports of merchandise trade amounted to €1350 billion excluding intra-EU trade and €2358 billion including intra-EU trade. In the same year total EU(25) exports of merchandise trade amounted to €1161 billion excluding intra-EU trade and €2430 billion including intra-EU trade.

Partner	Share of EU imports from	Million euro	Partner	Share of EU exports to	Million euro
China	14.2	191.3	USA	23.0	267.7
USA	13.0	175.8	Switzerland	7.4	86.4
Russia	10.1	136.8	Russia	6.2	71.8
Norway	5.9	79.0	China	5.4	63.2
Japan	5.6	75.6	Turkey	4.0	46.3
Switzerland	5.2	70.8	Japan	3.8	44.6
Turkey	2.8	38.5	Norway	3.3	38.1
Korea	2.8	38.1	Romania	2.3	27.2
Brazil	1.9	25.7	Canada	2.3	26.5
Taiwan	1.9	26.1	United Arab Emirates	2.1	24.7
			India	2.1	24.7

TABLE 19.1 The major EU (25) import and export partners n extra- EU merchandise trade (value percentage), 2006
Source: Eurostat.

Over time the EU has developed a patchwork of preferential agreements with other countries or groups of countries (see Box 19.1). Reference is frequently made to the 'hierarchy of EU preferences' or the 'pyramid of privileges'. In practice it is no longer possible (if it ever was) to discern a clear hierarchical pattern since the system is complex, in flux, the concessions are generally riddled with exceptions and the agreements rarely refer exclusively to trade issues.

The aim of this chapter is to describe certain of these arrangements and, in particular, those with developing countries, the USA, eastern and southern neighbours, Russia, Asia and Latin America.[2] Table 19.2 sets out EU relations with certain other trade blocs (some of which are discussed in the text). Countries involved in the EU enlargement process are discussed in the following chapter.

The Generalized System of Preferences

As trade is generally considered one of the most effective tools in fostering development, in 1968 the UNCTAD (United Nations Committee on Trade and Development) called for a Generalized System of Preferences under which industrialized countries would grant preferences to all developing countries.[3] In 1971 the Community established a Generalized System of Preferences (GSP). Under the GSP the EU imports products either duty free, or with a tariff reduction, depending on the arrangement with the beneficiary country.[4] The GSP system of the EU is based on guidelines covering ten-year cycles. In 2004 the guidelines for the 2006–2015 period were agreed, and on the basis of these, a new GSP system came into operation for the

---

[2] For a further discussion of these issues see, for instance, Victor et al. (2007).

[3] In order to implement the system, a waiver was required from Article 1 of the GATT, which prohibits discrimination. This waiver was granted in 1971 and originally for a period of ten years, but was renewed in 1979, for an indefinite period of time. According to the clause, preferential treatment under the GSP has to be non-discriminatory, non-reciprocal and autonomous. While discrimination in favour of developing countries is allowed, there should be no discrimination between them, except for the benefit of least developed countries.

[4] Up until 1995 the GSP system adopted quotas and ceilings for individual countries and products.

Box 19.1: *The trade arrangements of the EU*

- The European Economic Area with Norway, Iceland and Liechtenstein (see Chapter 2);

- Customs unions with Turkey, Andorra and San Marino;

- Free trade agreements with the Faroe Islands, Switzerland, Macedonia, Croatia and Albania;

- The Cotonou Convention covering relations with African, Caribbean and Pacific (ACP) countries. This is to be replaced by Economic Partnership Agreements (EPAs) expected to come into operation from 2008. These are agreements between the EU and groups of neighbouring ACP countries. The objective is to build free trade areas in different ACP regions (see text);

- The GSP that entails the elimination or reduction of tariffs on imports from developing countries on a non-reciprocal basis;

- The 'Everything-but-Arms' (EBA) initiative for least developed countries by which all other imports (with a few exceptions such as delayed implementation for bananas, sugar and rice) from these countries enter the EU duty free;

- The Euro-Mediterranean Partnership, which involves Euro Mediterranean Agreements aimed at introducing a free trade area for the Mediterranean by 2010;

- Wider Europe or the ENP with EU eastern and southern neighbours;

- Stabilization and Association Agreements (SAAs) with South-Eastern European countries;

- Trade and Co-operation Agreements, and Co-operation and Partnership Agreements with Russia and other ex-Soviet Republics;

- Free trade agreements with countries such as Mexico, Chile and South Africa, and Certain Overseas Countries and Territories (OCT/PTOM II);

- MFN (most favoured nation by which trade concessions already negotiated in the WTO framework are extended to all member states) treatment for countries such as the US, Japan and Australia;

- Negotiations have started (or are due to begin) on a free trade area with Mercosur and the Gulf Co-operation Council (GCC), and with Korea, ASEAN, India, and the Central American and Andean countries. *

* See text for descriptions of these regional blocs.

Source: Eurostat, © European Communities, 2008.

Integration bloc	Current membership	Characteristics/ weaknesses of bloc	Links with EU
ASEAN (Association of South-East Asian countries) created in 1967.	10 countries: Indonesia, Malaysia, Philippines, Singapore, Thailand, Brunei, Vietnam, Laos, Myanmar and Cambodia.	Differences between the countries meant that for many years it was difficult to move beyond co-operation to integration. The six more developed countries agreed to create the Asian Free Trade Area, and the four less developed members (Cambodia, Laos, Myanmar and Vietnam) are to reduce tariffs more slowly. The consensus-based approach to decision-making has helped to resolve political differences but has meant slow progress in integration.	In 2006 the EU accounted for 11.7 per cent of ASEAN's trade. The EU has regular ministerial meetings with ASEAN. Dialogue is based on a 1980 Co-operation Agreement. The EU has difficulties extending the Agreement to Myanmar (Burma).
SAARC (the South Asian Association for Regional Co-operation) set up in 1985.	Afghanistan, Bangladesh, Bhutan, India, the Maldives, Nepal, Pakistan and Sri Lanka. China and Japan have observer status.	There is an asymmetry between India (with about 76 per cent of the population and 77 per cent of regional GDP in 2006 (www.ec.europa.eu/external_relations) and the other members. Slow and cumbersome procedures, and tensions between members have limited the effectiveness of this bloc.	The EU maintains this bloc could play a useful role in encouraging regional co-operation.
Mercosur (EL Mercado del Sur) set up in 1991.	Argentina, Brazil, Paraguay and Uruguay. Venezuela signed in 2006 and is to become a full member from 2010. Chile, Bolivia and Peru, Colombia and Equador are associate members.	After some success in promoting trade liberalization and export growth during the 1990s, economic crises first in Brazil and then in Argentina acted as a setback to further attempts at integration. With a gradual improvement in the economic situation, the governments of Kirchner in Argentina and Lula in Brazil expressed a new determination to revive Mercosur, and create a real common market. This was also considered a way of strengthening their bargaining position in negotiations to create the Free Trade Area of the Americas, and in developing tighter links with the EU.	In 1995 the Madrid Treaty marked the beginning of negotiations to set up a free trade area between the Mercosur and the European Union, but the treaty was too generic in its means and goals. Actual negotiations began in 1999 but stalled as fallout from the economic crisis undermined the internal cohesion of Mercosur. In 2004 negotiations for an Association Agreement between the two blocs began, eased by the reform of the CAP of June 2003 and the willingness of the EU to grant more generous agricultural trade concessions to Mercosur. In return the EU requested Mercosur to lower industrial trade barriers, liberalize investment and open services and government procurement to EU firms.

TABLE 19.2 EU relations with certain integration blocs

Integration bloc	Current membership	Characteristics/ weaknesses of bloc	Links with EU
In 1969 the Cartagena Agreement established the Andean Pact, which in 1996 became the Andean Community, replacing the Caribbean Free Trade association (CARIFTA) that had been established in 1968.	Bolivia, Colombia, Ecuador, and Peru.	It is considered that regional integration could increase regulatory stability and create a market of sufficient size to attract trade and development. The EU maintains that tighter regional integration is a pre-condition for signing a free trade agreement with the bloc.	Trade with the Andean Community accounted for about 0.8 per cent of EU trade and EU trade amounted to 15.5 per cent of that of the Andean Community in 2006. In 1998 a Framework Co-operation Agreement came into force between the EU and Andean Community. One of the highest priorities is the fight against drugs. A new Political Dialogue and Co-operation Agreement was signed in 2003 and aims at reinforcing the political dialogue also to include conflict prevention, good governance, migration and counter-terrorism. In 2007 negotiations of an Association Agreement between the two blocs were launched.
Caricom (the Caribbean Community and Common Market) was formed in 1973.	Caricom consists of Antigua and Barbuda, The Bahamas, Barbados, Belize, Dominica, Grenada, Guyana, Haiti, Jamaica, St Kitts and Nevis, St Lucia, St Vincent and the Grenadines, Antilles and Turks and Caicos Islands.	Cariforum is the forum of the EU and ACP Caribbean states, which includes the Caribbean Community and Common Market (Caricom) and Haiti, Surinam and the Dominican Republic. Cariforum aims at better co-ordination of support from the EU and improved regional co-operation and integration.	In 1984 the EU and Central American countries set up the San José dialogue to promote democratization, peace and closer economic ties. A co-operation programme was established to address the socio-economic causes of unrest in Central America, and reduction of vulnerability to natural disasters. In 2006 the EU decided to launch negotiations of an Association Agreement between the EU and Central America, including a free trade area.
SICA (Central American Integration System)	Costa Rica, Guatemala, Honduras, Nicaragua, and El Salvador, with Panama having observer status. Costa Rica has opted out of initiative to create a monetary union, allow free labour movement and further political integration	The intra-regional freeing of trade has proved beneficial, but the bloc has both failed to avoid disputes between members (such as Nicaragua and Honduras), and to enable the countries to present a common front in wider fora such as the FTAA.	The EU participates in a specialized dialogue with SICA.

TABLE 19.2 continued

2006–2008 period.[5] This increases the number of products on which preferences are granted to about 7200, a rise of about 300, many of which are agricultural and fisheries products. The new system covered 178 countries and the number of GSP arrangements is reduced to three:

1 General arrangements;
2 The special incentive arrangement for sustainable development and good governance (the 'GSP +') provides additional benefits for countries implementing certain international standards in human and labour rights, environmental protection, the fight against drugs, and good governance;[6]
3 Special arrangements for the least developed countries (LDCs), also known as EBA.

Under the general arrangements products classed as 'non-sensitive' enter the EU duty-free, while 'sensitive' products are subject to tariff reductions. The classification of products by sensitivity largely depends on the market situation of the product in the EU.

The special incentive arrangements for the protection of labour rights, the environment (in particular, those relating to tropical forests) and so on entail additional tariff reductions on sensitive goods for countries respecting core requirements. This arrangement is limited to lower-income economies, land-locked countries, small island countries, and those that can demonstrate that their economies are poorly diversified.[7]

The UN identifies 50 LDCs on the basis of their low GDP per capita, weak human assets and economic vulnerability. In 2001 the EU launched its EBA initiative for these countries. This implies that apart from arms and ammunition all imports from these countries enter the EU duty-free and quota-free. The removal of import duties was delayed until 2006 for bananas, and 2009 for sugar and rice.

The GSP system has been criticized on a number of counts. The preferences given are relatively low, and concessions are often minimal on the products of most interest to the developing countries. In particular, this is the case for agricultural products, and though the 2006 reform increased their GSP coverage, even under the EBA, bananas, sugar and rice were treated as exceptions with delayed implementation. The system involves administrative costs and rules of origin, and often producers in developing countries consider that it is not worthwhile applying for preferences. The GSP scheme of the EU also envisages 'graduation' of more competitive countries (defined since the 2006 reform on the basis of the share of those countries in the exports of all GSP countries). Although the EU justifies this on the grounds of targeting preferences to those most in need, it also relieves the competitive pressures on EU producers.

The EU and developing countries

In 2000 the international community agreed on the Millennium Development Goals (MDGs) up to the year 2015. These entail:

■ eradicating extreme poverty and hunger by halving between 1990 and 2015 the proportion of people whose income is less than US$1 a day ;

---

[5] Through Council Regulation No. 980/2005.

[6] The list of countries receiving GSP+ is set out in Commission Decision 2005/924/EC.

[7] The list of countries is to ensure that the EU meets the WTO ruling that equal treatment should be given to all similarly situated GSP beneficiaries. India had raised a WTO complaint against the earlier EU scheme, which entailed trade preferences initially designed to discourage drug production in the Andes being extended to other countries including Pakistan.

- achieving universal primary education;
- promoting gender equality and empowering women;
- reducing child mortality by cutting the mortality rate of under fives by two-thirds between 1990 and 2015;
- improving maternal health;
- combating HIV/AIDS, malaria and other diseases;
- ensuring environmental sustainability;
- developing a global partnership for development.

The EU worked with member states and other international organizations such as the OECD, the World Bank and the UNDP (United Nations Development Programme) to develop a core set of indicators to assess progress in meeting the MDGs. According to the World Development Indicators,[8] the number of people living on less than US$1 a day fell by more than 260 million over the 1990–2004 period, thanks in particular to poverty reduction in China. In contrast the number of people living on less than $1 a day in Subsaharan Africa rose by 60 million, from 47 per cent of the population in 1990 to 41 per cent in 2004. Child mortality has declined since 1990, but only 35 countries are on track to meet the MDG of reducing under-5 mortality by two-thirds by 2015. Countries in Africa and South Asia are lagging behind with regards to the goals to improve maternal health and education.

In order to reach the MDGs, in 2002 at the Barcelona European Council member states agreed to increase their ODA (official development aid). In 2005 the EU adopted a timetable for the member states to reach the UN target of ODA equal to 0.7 per cent of gross national income (GNI) considered necessary to meet the MDGs. At the G-8 summit in Gleneagles in 2005, the UK prime Minister, Tony Blair, obtained a commitment from the heads of government of the 8 industrial countries present to spend $50 billion more each year on aid, with half the increase going to sub-Saharan Africa.

In 2006 the EU was the major source of development aid in the world, providing €46.9 billion in 2006 or 56.6 per cent of total ODA reported to the Development Assistance Committee (DAC) of the OECD (European Commission, 2007). The external aid managed by the European Commission amounted to €12.1 billion in 2006, of which 9.8 billion is classified as ODA. Table 19.3 presents the ODA of EU countries that were members of DAC, and the only countries to meet the UN target of 0.7 per cent of GNI were Denmark, Luxembourg, the Netherlands and Sweden.

EU development assistance is a shared competence between the EU and its member states. At the EU level development policy is implemented through instruments such as trade preferences, development finance and humanitarian aid. European Union development policy is centred on the 79 ACP countries, many of which are former colonies of EU member states. However, aid is also given to other countries, such as those in the Mediterranean area, the former Eastern bloc, Latin America, Asia and Africa.

In the EC the responsibility for policy and programming of aid is divided among the ACP countries (Directorate-General, DG Development), the non-ACP countries (DG External Relations) and the candidate countries and potential future EU members (DG Enlargement). Since 2001 Europe Aid has carried out the implementation of measures, while humanitarian aid for emergency and distress assistance is managed by a separate agency, ECHO (European Community Humanitarian Office).

As much aid is organized on a geographical basis, historically it was disbursed through a number of different financial instruments, such as the European Development Fund (EDF) for

---

[8] The data in this paragraph are taken from World Development Indicators 2007, www.worldbank.org

	% gross national income	US$ million		% gross national income	US$ million
Austria	0.47	1498	Portugal	0.21	396
Belgium	0.50	1978	Spain	0.32	3814
Denmark	0.80	2236	Sweden	1.02	3955
Finland	0.40	834	UK	0.51	12459
France	0.47	10601			
Germany	0.36	10435	USA	0.18	23532
Greece	0.17	424	Japan	0.25	11187
Ireland	0.54	1022	Canada	0.29	3684
Italy	0.20	3641	Norway	0.89	2954
Lux.	0.89	291	Switzerland	0.39	1646
Netherlands	0.81	5452	New Zealand	0.27	259

TABLE 19.3 Official development aid of the EU member states that belong to the Development Assistance Committee of the OECD, 2006
Source: www.oecd.org/dac/stats

ACP countries; Community Assistance for Reconstruction, Development and Stability (CARDs) for the Balkans (see Chapter 20); MEDA for Mediterranean countries; Technical Assistance for the Commonwealth of Independent States (TACIS) for former Soviet Republics, and so on. The EDF is not funded from the general Community budget but from direct contributions from the member states. The funding from a member state is partly based on GDP and partly on their historic links with the ACP country concerned. The EDF allocates €22 682 million at current prices for the 2008–2018 period, but the EDC will remain outside the EU budget despite a Commission proposal for its inclusion.

The 2007–2013 financial perspective attempts to simplify and rationalize the way in which EU external co-operation is financed through the EU budget. Nine financing instruments will replace the existing range of funds. Six instruments support policies with a geographic or thematic focus:

1 Instrument for pre-accession;
2 European Neighbourhood and Partnership Instrument;
3 Development Co-operation Instrument;
4 The Instrument for Co-operation with Industrialized Countries;
5 The European Instrument for Democracy and Human Rights;
6 The Instrument for Nuclear safety Co-operation.

Three instruments will address crisis situations:

1 The Instrument for Stability;
2 Existing humanitarian aid, which will incorporate emergency food aid;
3 Macro-financial assistance instruments.

The funds available for the Development Co-operation Instrument for the 2007–2018 period amount to €10.1 billion for developing countries from Latin America, Asia, the Middle East and South Africa.

The evolution of EU policy towards the ACP countries

The evolution of EU development policy has been influenced by changes within the EU itself but also by the political, strategic and economic changes on the international scene, decolonialization, changing views of economic and social development, the ending of the Cold War and globalization.

Community development policy dates from the Treaty of Rome when France wanted to maintain its links with its colonial territories but share some of the financial costs with other Community members (see Box 19.2). For this purpose in 1958 the EDF was set up, and financed social and economic infrastructure projects mainly in French-speaking Overseas Countries and Territories. Subsequently the EDF financed aid to the ACP countries.

Box 19.2: *The evolution of EU Policy towards the ACP countries*

Articles 131 and 136 of the Treaty of Rome provide for the association of non-European countries and territories with which the EEC states had particular relations.

1958: The EDF was established.

1963 Yaoundé I: trade concessions and financial aid to African ex-colonies.

1969 Yaoundé II.

1975 Lomé I: non-reciprocal trade preferences to ACP countries, equality of partners and introduction of Stabex.

1980 Lomé II: no major changes apart from the introduction of Sysmin.

1985 Lomé III: attention was shifted from the promotion of industrial development to self-reliant development on the basis of self-sufficiency and food security.

1990 Lomé IV (revised in 1995): covered a 10-year period and gave more emphasis to the promotion of human rights, democracy, good governance, the situation of women, protection of the environment (including forests), decentralization of co-operation and increased regional co-operation.

2000 Cotonou: intended to cover a 20-year period using an approach based on politics, trade and development to tackle poverty, but is to be replaced by EPAs.

During the 1960s many of the overseas territories gained independence, and a new framework of assistance was provided with the Yaoundé agreement of 1963 (renewed in 1969) covering trade and aid arrangements between the EC and former French colonies in Africa. The entry of the UK into the Community in 1973 led to a reappraisal of development policy, resulting in the first Lomé Convention of 1975. Subsequent Conventions followed in 1980, 1985 and 1990 (which covered a 10-year period) and the Cotonou Agreement of 2000.

In line with the then widely discussed objective of creating a New International Economic Order (NIEO), the initial ambitious aim of the Lomé conventions was to create a 'partnership of equals'. The main instruments adopted were non-reciprocal and included:

- tariff preferences;
- preferences for agricultural products;
- financial aid; and
- stabex arrangements (subsequently also Sysmin for mining sectors), which are funds to stabilize export earnings.[9]

However, the global economic instability following the oil shocks of 1973 and 1979 hit Sub-Saharan economies particularly hard and the ACP countries were disappointed with the Lomé Conventions. The Conventions were criticized for poor use of aid since projects were often badly designed and hindered by a hostile policy environment, and for weak management on the part of donors, with slow and cumbersome disbursement procedures and accusations of political interference.[10]

Although under the preferential system the ACP countries faced lower (often zero) tariffs than other developing countries, this failed to stem their decline in EU trade. The ACP share in extra-EU imports fell from 6.7 per cent in 1976 to 2.8 per cent in 1999, rising slightly to 4.5 per cent of EU(25) imports in 2005. Of these, roughly one-third is imports from South Africa, and about a quarter is energy from Nigeria. The poor infrastructure, fractured markets and difficulties in meeting EU standards and technical restrictions of many of the ACP countries limit the impact of tariff reductions. Too often trade promotion was regarded as an end in itself, rather than as a means of promoting development.

The need to tackle poverty, instability and political conflict led to a renewed debate on EU development policy in the late 1990s. To facilitate discussion the Commission published a Green Paper in 1996 and a discussion paper in 1997 setting out its proposals for a post-Lomé agreement.[11] Negotiations began in 1998, and in 2000 the Cotonou Agreement was signed between the EU and the ACP countries. This was to cover a period of 20 years. It is based on a perspective that combines politics, trade and development. The central objective of the agreement was the reduction and eventual eradication of poverty, and for that purpose five interdependent pillars were indicated:

1 A comprehensive political dimension;
2 Participatory approaches;
3 Strengthening the focus on poverty reduction;
4 A new framework for trade and co-operation; and
5 A reform of financial co-operation.

The Cotonou Agreement envisages a five-year review procedure, and the first revision of the Agreement took place in 2005.[12] The revised version of the Agreement entailed further emphasis on political dialogue, references to the fight against terrorism, co-operation in countering the proliferation of weapons of mass destruction and tighter relations with the International Criminal Court. The 2005 revision also takes participation under the second pillar (the CFSP) further by encouraging more involvement of non-state actors and local authorities.

The increased EU stress on the political dimension, and the need to promote respect for human rights, democratic institutions, the rule of law and avoidance of corruption is shared by

---

[9] Stabex applied on over 40 agricultural raw materials and guaranteed compensation for a fall in income from sales subject to maximum rates, and provided certain conditions were met.

[10] See Stevens (1990) for an early criticism of these agreements.

[11] European Commission (1996 and 1997).

[12] Council Decision of 21 June 2005, published in Official Journal L 209 of 11.8.2005.

other international organizations such as the World Bank and European Bank for Reconstruction and Development (EBRD).[13] Democratic elections and freedom of the media render politicians more answerable for their choices. Effective rule of law ensures that contracts are enforceable and, if necessary, redress is possible through the courts. Corruption and criminal activity may impede the establishment of new firms, and disrupt the activities of existing ones. Protection of property rights is necessary to ensure the efficient allocation of resources, and to encourage innovation and investment. Participation is aimed at encouraging ownership of policies and implies the involvement of civil society and a wide range of economic and social actors in development co-operation.

Poverty is not defined simply as lack of income or financial resources, but encompasses the notion of vulnerability and factors such as lack of access to adequate food supplies, education, healthy drinking water, employment, and political involvement. The focus on poverty reduction requires measures to support: economic development (including private sector development and investment, macroeconomic and structural policies and reforms, and sectoral policies); social and human development; and regional co-operation and integration. At the same time three horizontal themes are to be taken into account in all areas of co-operation (in accordance with the principle of 'mainstreaming'): gender equality; environmental sustainability; and institutional development and capacity building.

The aim is also to ensure 'the three Cs': coherence, co-ordination and complementarity in development policy. Coherence and co-ordination are necessary to render aid more effective, while coherence requires an integrated approach to external relations, security, economic and development policies.

The EPAs and the debate about the effectiveness of EU development policy

The special preferences granted by the EU to ACP countries were against WTO rules, which require reciprocal arrangements covering 'substantially all trade' and non-discrimination between similarly situated countries (see above). The EU preferences to the ACP countries came under sustained attack during the banana dispute.[14] The EU obtained a five-year waiver for its ACP treatment, but this came to an end on 31 December 2007. The EU was against seeking further waivers, and decided to introduce WTO-compatible arrangements in the form of EPAs or reciprocal free trade areas with groups of ACP countries.

Negotiations on the EPAs began in 2002, and they were expected to come into operation from January 2008. The EU proposed EPAs with six groups of neighbouring ACP countries. The aim was to liberalize trade among the ACP members of the regional grouping and gradually (in some cases over as long as 25 years) lower trade barriers against the EU. In return the EU would offer enhanced or almost free access to its market and simplification of procedures, including those relating to rules of origin.

In practice the EU was forced to modify its proposal for the EPAs radically. Initially the EU wanted to include services and foreign investment rules (two of the so-called 'Singapore Issues' that caused so much conflict in WTO negotiations, see Chapter 18), but was forced to drop these from the Agenda. The only region to sign a comprehensive EPA by the 2008 deadline was the Caribbean, though about half the ACP countries had signed interim agreements

---

[13] See, for example, EBRD *Transition Report*, 2003.

[14] See the OLC accompanying this textbook for a description of the banana dispute.

with the EU and pledged to continue negotiations during 2008. Many signed individually or as small groups of countries rather than the comprehensive regional EPA groupings initially envisaged.[15]

There was a heated debate about whether the EPAs would benefit the ACPs, or whether, as claimed in some quarters, the EU was acting mainly in the interests of its own exporters and forcing ACP countries into premature liberalization. In addition to trying to place services and investment on the agenda, the EU also maintained that by the MFN clause the ACP countries could not have higher tariffs with other trading partners than with the EU.

Various academic studies suggested that the EPAs would lead to trade diversion. For instance, Bouët et al. (2007) of the IFPRI (International Food Policy Research Institute) found that EPAs would lead to tariff and income losses for ACP countries, and would lead to an increase in EU exports to the ACPs by $14.7 billion by 2018, compared with a fall of $3 billion for exports from the rest of the world.

Messerlin and Delpeuch (2007) suggested that the ACP countries should be allowed to make a counter-proposal in place of the EPAs, offering more limited trade liberalization for the EU in return for maintaining their preferential access to the EU market.

Other observers maintained that the impact of the EPAs would be limited, pointing to the relatively small level of tariff cuts involved, and the long time scale for implementation.[16] Others objected to EU brinkmanship in trying to force the ACP countries to accept EPAs by the tight 2008 deadline, or be subject to GSP treatment (though the Commissioner for Trade, Peter Mandelson maintained that the EU had no choice under WTO rules). The EU Development Commissioner, Louis Michel, also offered the ACP countries compensation for eventual loss of tariff revenue and more development assistance, leading to accusations of bribery.

The debate extended to the more general issue of the effectiveness of EU development policy. Difficulties have been encountered in introducing common, simplified procedures and ensuring co-ordination and the complementarity of different aid measures and the activities of donors. Insufficient progress has also been made in realizing coherence with other EU policies, and ongoing attention is necessary to ensure that decisions in areas such as trade and agriculture are compatible with development co-operation.

The organizational structure of EU policy is complex, and there would seem a case for bringing all measures under one Directorate-General. There also seems a case for including the EDF under the EU budget.

Economic development is a complex process depending on a whole series of factors including the internal situation of the recipient countries, the international economic environment, globalization, the evolution of EU policies (such as the CAP or CFSP) and the outcome of the Doha Round. As the quantity of ODA seems likely to remain limited, it is essential to ensure its quality (House of Lords, 2004). Candidates for ensuring the quality of aid include the following:

- Emphasis on promoting economic growth;
- Focusing on essential priorities such as poverty reduction and fighting disease;
- Building democratic institutions that can ensure the rule of law and respect for minorities, the reduction of corruption and guarantees of property rights;
- Applying conditionality so that building democratic institutions, rule of law and respect for human rights are consistently applied as conditions for receiving aid;

[15] See the Special Edition of Trade Negotiation Insights (2008).

[16] See Christopher Stevens as quoted in the *Financial Times* of 13 December 2007.

■ Promoting sustainable development;

■ Simplifying the procedures and ensuring better co-ordination of aid programmes.

EU–US trade and investment

Trade relations between the EU and the USA have at times been tense, degenerating into surprisingly acrimonious disputes over issues as varied as bananas, beef, genetically modified organisms (GMOs) and subsidies to aircraft. At the same time there have been various initiatives to construct an institutional framework for transatlantic co-operation. The aim here is to describe and attempt to provide explanations of this conflictual co-operation.

In terms of economic dimension, the EU and the USA are roughly compatible. In 2006 the EU(27) had a population of 495 million, while that of the USA was 297 million.[17] The land area of the USA was considerably greater at 9.6 million square kilometres, compared with the 4.3 million of the EU(25). In 2006, compared with a GDP in purchasing power standards of the EU(27) of 100, that of the USA was a forecasted 154.5 per cent.

The EU and the USA are the world's most important traders, with the EU accounting for 17.1 per cent of world trade in 2006, followed by the USA with 15.6 per cent. The two account for about 57 per cent of world GDP. In 2006 the USA was the main destination of EU exports receiving 23.3 per cent of all extra-EU exports, and was second only to China in supplying 13.2 per cent of EU imports.

They are also each other's most important source and destination of FDI (foreign direct investment). In 2005 the total amount of two-way investment was over €1600 billion. In 2004 the EU held an estimated total of 709 billion in FDI in the USA, while the USA held €804 billion of investment stocks in the EU. In other words, these transatlantic foreign direct investments accounted for about two-thirds of the total foreign investments of EU and US companies. About one-quarter of all EU-US trade consists of transactions within firms based on their investments either side of the Atlantic.

The institutional framework for transatlantic co-operation

During the post-Second World War period, the USA demonstrated unequivocal support for the integration process in Europe. Marshall Aid was conditional on regional co-operation of the recipient countries and led to the creation of the OEEC.[18] The early European federalists hoped this would become a supranational institution, but in the event the Organization for European Economic Co-operation (OEEC) and its successor, the OECD, were firmly based on intergovernmental co-operation (thanks largely to Britain and the Scandinavian countries, see Chapter 2). The USA also expressed strong support for the creation of the European Community and was disappointed when the West European integration split into two blocs with the establishment of the European Free Trade Association (EFTA) in 1960.

An ongoing feature is the rhetorical character of statements made about EU–US relations (even when they are conflictual).[19] This, for instance, is typified in Kennedy's 'Declaration of

---

[17] Unless otherwise stated all the statistics in this chapter are taken from Eurostat.

[18] For a description of US attitudes towards European integration in the 1950s, see Chapter 2 of Guay (1999).

[19] On the negative side, in 2000 at the beginning of his term of office the then EU Commissioner for trade, Pascal Lamy, referred to the need to replace megaphone with telephone diplomacy.

Interdependence', or 'Grand Design', announced at Independence Hall, Philadelphia, on 4 July 1962. The aim was to create a concrete Atlantic partnership based on a declaration of interdependence with a united Europe.[20] The EC was viewed as an ally that could be induced to assist in the fight against communism (both at an international level and internally in countries such as Greece and Italy) and to bear part of the bill for international security.

Recent years have been characterized by several concrete attempts to promote EU–US co-operation, as summarized in Box 19.3.

Box 19.3: *Recent landmarks in EU–US relations**

1990 the Transatlantic Declaration

1995 the New Transatlantic Agenda (NTA)

1998 the Transatlantic Economic Partnership (TEP)

1999 Bonn Declaration

2002 Positive Economic Agenda (PEA)

2004 Dromoland Summit in Ireland

2007 the Framework for Advancing Transatlantic Economic Integration between the USA and EU

*See text for a description of these initiatives.

In 1990 the **Transatlantic Declaration** institutionalized a framework for consultation and co-operation, and led to the 1995 **NTA**, which entailed joint action in four areas:

1 Promoting peace, stability, democracy and development around the world;

2 Responding to global challenges;

3 Contributing to the expansion of world trade and closer economic relations;

4 Building bridges across the Atlantic (which implies promoting contacts at the level of individual citizens).

The institutional structure of the NTA entails twice-yearly meetings between the US president and the presidents of the EU Council and Commission, and an Action Plan to implement the above objectives. The NTA led to a number of bilateral agreements, covering, for example, co-operation and mutual assistance on customs matters (1997), science and technology (1997), competition laws (1998) and veterinary equivalence (1999).

In 1997 the Mutual Recognition Agreement was signed to meet complaints about customs formalities that often involve requests for additional documentation and information, and lengthy sampling and inspection procedures. Regulatory barriers are now the main obstacles to transatlantic business, and the agreement is a move towards reciprocal recognition of standards and technical regulations.

The NTA also established the Transatlantic Business Dialogue (TABD) that came into operation from 1995. The TABD involves top business people in a forum to discuss ways of reducing

---

[20]For a more detailed description see Guay (1999), p. 32.

barriers to trade and investment. Annual meetings take place alternately in the EU and the USA, and business people have been called on to make recommendations relating to the evolution of common standards, the reduction of tariffs and the implementation of anti-corruption measures. Governments have subsequently endorsed many of the recommendations.

Under the aegis of the NTA, in 1998 it was proposed to create a New Transatlantic Marketplace in order to eliminate barriers to the flow of goods, services and investment between the EU and USA by 2010. The EC approved the New Transatlantic Marketplace, but France subsequently blocked it over concerns that that audio-visual services (which had sensitive cultural implications) and agriculture would not receive adequate special treatment.

Following this failure, in 1998 a **TEP** was agreed. The TEP aimed at creating an open and more accessible world trading system, and improving economic relations between the EU and the USA. This involves tackling trade issues, and, in particular, regulatory barriers. The aim of the TEP is also to integrate labour, business, and environmental and consumer interests into the process.

In 1999 an EU–US summit resulted in the **Bonn Declaration** which aimed at developing an effective warning system to identify problems at an early stage and avoid the risk of conflicts undermining EU–US relations.

In 2002 the **PEA** was set up to enhance bilateral co-operation between the EU and the USA. It provides a framework for setting up new objectives, starting negotiations or increasing the momentum of existing dialogues. The PEA entails bilateral projects, with reports each year to the EU/US Summit in order to take stock of progress.

In 2004 at the Dromoland Summit in Ireland, agreement was reached on a new commitment to furthering transatlantic integration. In 2007 a **Framework for Advancing Transatlantic Economic Integration between the USA and EU** was signed. This involved the establishment of a work programme, and the creation of a **Transatlantic Economic Council** to oversee and accelerate implementation of the work programme.

Trade disputes between the EU and the USA

In addition to differences in the Uruguay Round and Doha Round negotiations (see Chapter 18), there have been numerous trade disputes between the EU and the USA. However, despite their high profile, according to the European Commission disputes only touched about 2 per cent of trade.

Between 1960 and 1985 the USA initiated 17 legal cases against the EC in the GATT, 13 of which (or 76 per cent) concerned agriculture and fisheries (Hudec, 1993).[21] More recent disputes cover a wide range of issues including:

- genetically modified organisms;
- beef with growth-promoting hormones;
- geographical indications
- the EU banana regime, which discriminated in favour of ACP countries;
- the UN ban on imports of beef from the USA and Canada containing growth-promoting hormones;
- the US use of foreign sales corporations to reduce the taxes of US firms exporting abroad;

---

[21] The first dispute, the 1962 US/EU 'Chicken War', was the direct result of the 1962 EC agreement creating the CAP. The USA objected to the system of variable levies used by the EC on its imports of agricultural products from the rest of the world; the level of EC domestic support to agriculture and the use of export subsidies on agricultural products. See Chapter 12 for a more detailed discussion of these questions.

- the EU failure to authorize additional genetically modified organisms;
- US public procurement (the Massachusetts–Burma case raised by the EC in 1997);[22]
- US use of trade defence instruments (such as anti-dumping and safeguards);
- EU protection of trademarks and geographical indications for agricultural products and foodstuffs; and
- preferential loans for the development of a flight management system by the French government to Airbus, and the 2004 Airbus-Boeing case (see Box 19.4).[23]

Box 19.4: *The Airbus-Boeing Dispute*

In October 2004 the EU and USA launched the biggest dispute to date in the WTO over subsidies to the civil aircraft makers Airbus and Boeing. After unsuccessful attempts to reach a bilateral agreement, the US lodged a complaint that Airbus had received illegal subsidies from the EU and a 'reimbursable launch investment' from France, Germany, Spain and the UK. It was said that as a result Airbus was able to overtake Boeing, accounting for 54 per cent of the world market of large aircraft.* The USA unilaterally abrogated a 1992 agreement with the EU to limit subsidies for aircraft manufacturers, maintaining that the EU had not respected the agreement. The 1992 Agreement was somewhat ambiguous as to what forms of state aid were permitted (and the EU argued that it allowed the launch aid for Airbus). Boeing expressed support for the US complaint, though earlier it had indicated fears that a WTO case might alienate passengers. The US complaint was lodged a month before the Presidential elections.

In return, the EU filed a counter-complaint, maintaining that Boeing had received about $23.7 billion in US Federal, State and local subsidies in the two decades to 2004. The European Commission argued that this violated the 1992 Agreement and that the subsidies were not consistent with WTO rules. The EU also filed a complaint over tax breaks worth $3.2 billion from Washington State to Boeing to finance the new 7E7 Dreamliner jet.

Differences over Airbus and Boeing had been dragging on for years and many observers questioned the decision to take the dispute to the WTO. As a result, peaceful settlement of other differences might become more difficult and if the WTO rules against the subsidies, huge trade sanctions could be allowed.

* *Financial Times*, 7 October, 2004

The increasing number of disputes may simply reflect the interdependence and the higher level of international trade and FDI between the EU and the USA. It may also be an indication that countries are more willing to refer their conflicts to a multilateral forum, since the WTO is considered to be more effective in settling disputes than its predecessor, the GATT.

---

[22] The Commonwealth of Massachusetts forbade business with anyone having official relations with Burma (Myanmar). The EU maintained that subnational action violated international trade agreements signed by national governments. See www.wto.org:wto/dispute/bulletin.htm

[23] Other EU-US disputes (such as those over the EU banana regime, beef hormones, foreign sales corporations and GMOs) are taken up as case studies and discussed in more detail on the OLC for this book. See also the WTO website (www.wto.org).

The increase in EU–US trade disputes may also reflect the changed international environment since 1989 with the end of the Cold War. Earlier reliance of West European countries on the US nuclear umbrella constrained the extent to which they could provoke the USA with bitter trade wars.

According to international relations theory, the increased strength and changing role of the EU could imply a decline in the hegemonic stability of the USA. The basic hypothesis of this type of approach is that the existence of a single hegemonic nation will lend stability to the international economic and political system, but if rival countries emerge to challenge the hegemony, the system may become unstable. The picture that emerges varies considerably according to the policy area considered. Few would contest the continued hegemonic role of the USA with regard to international security. In the international monetary sphere there has been much speculation as to whether the euro would challenge the dollar, both as a reserve currency, and in the invoicing of international trade (see Chapter 10.) However, it is in the area of international trade that the real discussion about possible decline of US hegemony emerges.

Domestic pressures, and, in particular interest groups, and big business have generally played a role in the disputes. The USA challenged the EU banana regime, though bananas are not produced in the USA. However, the US government appeared subject to pressure from large multinationals, Chiquita and Dole, while in the EU the firms controlling banana licences had a vested interest in not reforming the regime. The banana lobby was also strong in some of the ACP countries. The GMO market is controlled by large multinationals, and in most cases producer lobbies (such as the National Cattlemen's Beef Association in the beef hormone case) were active in claiming compensation for their losses.

In certain cases sanctions were applied (as in the banana and beef hormone cases), and these took the form of tariffs on a certain value of imports. These sanctions hit consumers, but the general public may have been unaware of these effects. Alternatively, in the beef hormone case, EU authorities may have considered sanctions a worthwhile price to pay in view of the strong preferences of consumers with regard to possible health risks. It seems likely that other lobbies quite unconnected to the case in question influenced the choice of products on which to apply sanctions.

Disputes may arise from different regulatory approaches that reflect economic, social, historical and cultural diversity, or different sensitivities and societal values with regard to health, consumer and environmental protection. For instance, the EU public seems to have less confidence in the ability of food safety authorities to guarantee safe and healthy food. The increasing complexity of the issues renders it difficult to draw up clear and unambiguous rules, in particular when there may be conflicts between policy objectives, such as between free trade and the environment (see also Chapter 18).

The EU has frequently complained about US attempts to apply extra-territoriality and unilateralism in trade policy. The EU objects to extra-territorial application of US domestic legislation when it requires individuals or companies in the EU to comply with US laws or policies. In general the EU and the USA also have different views about the effectiveness of linking strategic and commercial objectives. While the USA sees trade as a useful diplomatic weapon in dealing with rogue countries, the EU is more sceptical about the effectiveness of sanctions and tends to favour a policy of engagement.

Wider Europe: The European Neighbourhood Policy

In March 2003 the European Commission published the Communication on Wider Europe, setting out the ENP to deal with relations between an enlarged EU and its eastern and southern neighbours.[24] The aim is to prevent new dividing lines emerging between the EU and its neighbours and to enhance security and narrow the prosperity gap on the new external borders of the EU.

The ENP is for countries with no immediate prospect of EU membership, covering countries such as the western NIS (newly independent states) and Southern Mediterranean countries, but not South East Europe (see Chapter 20).

The approach is based on mutual commitment to common values such as the rule of law, good governance, respect for human rights, including minority rights, the promotion of a market economy, sustainable development and certain foreign policy goals. The Neighbourhood Policy aims at establishing a pan-European integrated market, functioning on the basis of rules that are similar or harmonized with those of the EU.

Central to the policy are bilateral ENP Action Plans negotiated between the EU and individual partners, covering areas such as:

- Political dialogue, including measures against terrorism and to prevent the spread of weapons of mass destruction and the encouragement of regional co-operation;
- Economic and social development policy, offering partner countries a stake in the EU Internal Market based on regulatory and legislative convergence, participation in certain EU programmes (such as education, training, research and innovation) and improved interconnections and physical links with the EU (in transport, energy, the environment and telecommunications);
- The promotion of trade, including convergence with EU standards;
- Co-operation on issues such as border management, migration, the fight against terrorism, organized crime, trafficking in human beings, the drugs trade and so on.

From 2007 the European Neighbourhood and Partnership Instrument replaced the TACIS, MEDA and other assistance instruments used by the EU in these countries.

While it seems a positive move to avoid new divisions with neighbouring countries, it is difficult to see how a single policy can be applied to countries with such different characteristics and needs, even with a differentiated approach. Moreover, EU geographical co-operation programmes (see next section) already apply in many of the countries. The use of benchmarks in applying the ENP Action Plans seems to imply that the EU is attempting to introduce some form of conditionality, but as the experience of the former Yugoslav Republics of South-East Europe and other countries (including those of the Mediterranean Area) has shown, conditionality is a very blunt weapon without the prospect of EU membership. The idea that European Neighbourhood Policy is extended to countries with no immediate prospect of EU membership might also be interpreted as a 'cold shoulder' by some of them.[25]

---

[24]European Commission (2003).

[25]See Chilosi (2007) for a critical account of the ENP.

The Mediterranean region

In 1995 what is known as the Mediterranean Partnership, or Barcelona Process, began. This provides a framework for co-operation between the 15 EU members and Mediterranean countries: Algeria, Egypt, Israel, Jordan, Lebanon, Morocco, the Palestinian Authority, Syria, Tunisia and Turkey. Turkey is a candidate country for EU membership, but (as was the case for Cyprus and Malta) can participate in Euro-Mediterranean regional co-operation until accession. Libya currently has observer status.

The Euro-Mediterranean Partnership is composed of bilateral and regional relations.

At a bilateral level the EU carries out activities with individual countries, including those implemented through Euro-Mediterranean Association Agreements.[26] The Euro-Mediterranean Agreements differ between countries, but their main features include:

- Respect for human rights and democratic principles. To further this aim common political dialogue is to occur at regular intervals and at various levels;
- Free trade is to be established, with dismantling of tariffs by the Mediterranean countries over a transitional period of up to 12 years (EU tariffs on industrial goods have already been eliminated). Trade in agriculture and services is to be 'gradually liberalized';
- Provisions relating to intellectual property rights, public procurement, competition rules, state aids and monopolies;
- Financial assistance from the Community (except to Israel);
- Co-operation on economic and cultural matters;
- CFSP themes;
- Co-operation on workers' rights and social policy, and the possibility of re-admission of illegal immigrants (though the terms vary between countries).

At regional level the aim is to promote activities in all three domains of the Barcelona Declaration:

1 The political and security dimension;
2 The economic and financial dimension;
3 The social, cultural and human dimension.

Within the political and security dimension emphasis is placed on creating a zone of peace and stability. The aim is also to encourage 'horizontal' or 'South–South' integration through the creation of free trade areas among the Mediterranean Partners themselves. In 2001 the Agadir Initiative entailed agreement to set up a free trade area between Egypt, Jordan, Morocco and Tunisia. However, to date the Partnership resembles more of a hub-and-spoke arrangement with the EU.

The MEDA Programme was the main financial instrument of the EU for the implementation of the Euro-Mediterranean Programme (replaced by the European Neighbourhood and Partnership Instrument from 2007), and was allocated €5 350 million for the 2000–06 period. By 2008 the European Investment Bank had also spent some €14 billion for developing activities with Euro-Mediterranean partners.

In July 2003 the Palermo Action Plan was launched to facilitate the free movement of industrial goods. This involved trade facilitation and the simplifying of customs procedures, and the

---

[26]Agreements have been signed with all partners except Syria. The agreement with Syria was initialled in 2004, but the EU member states deemed that the political situation was not yet ready.

incorporation of provisions into the Association Agreements of provisions for the creation of a common pan-Euro-Mediterranean origin protocol.

The main weakness of the Euro-Mediterranean Partnership is that the aspiration of creating an area of peace, prosperity and progress around the Mediterranean is constantly threatened by the ongoing unsettled international situation, in particular in the Middle East. Despite the Mediterranean Partnership, the income gap between the Northern and Southern Mediterranean has been widening. The Mediterranean partners criticize the EU for limited concessions in the sectors that interest them most, namely agriculture and textiles and clothing. Co-operation over immigration is inadequate, and attempts to insist on improvements in human rights are hampered by limited EU leverage when there is no prospect of EU membership.

The Russian Federation

Russia is the third trading partner of the EU after the USA and China, while the EU is Russia's main trading partner. Energy products account for more than 60 per cent of Russian exports to the EU.[27] Sixty per cent of all Russian oil exports are to the EU, and account for over 25 per cent of total EU oil consumption. Fifty per cent of Russian natural gas exports go to the EU and amount to over 25 per cent of total EU consumption of natural gas. Russia is also an important exporter of nuclear fuels to the EU. The exports of the EU to Russia are diversified and include machinery and transport equipment (46 per cent in 2006), chemicals, manufactured goods, and food and live animals.

The EU dependence on Russian energy conditions its attitude, but what has emerged since the early 1990s is a growing gap between what appears on paper as an extensive institutional framework for co-operation, and increasing tensions in practice between Russia on the one hand, and the EU and various of its member states on the other.

The legal basis for EU relations with Russia is the Partnership and Co-operation Agreement (PCA), which came into operation in 1997. The Agreement covered a 10-year period, but Poland blocked negotiation of a new replacement agreement (probably over fears that the EU failed to present a sufficiently united front in the face of Russia). It was therefore decided to extend the existing agreement annually and it entails:

- Trade and economic co-operation. Trade liberalization is to entail MFN treatment, the elimination of quantitative restrictions and legal harmonization. There are also provisions on the establishment of companies, capital movement and competition and intellectual property rights. Both sides are committed to creating a free trade area as soon as circumstances permit;

- Co-operation in sectors including science and technology, energy, the environment transport, space and so on;

- Political dialogue, which also includes democratization and respect for human rights;

- Justice and Home Affairs, which entails co-operation to combat illegal activities, drug trafficking, money laundering and organized crime.

The PCA was extended to the new member states after EU enlargement, and also establishes an institutional framework for consultations.

Bilateral trade agreements between the EU and Russia cover sectors such as steel and textiles, and entail the progressive removal of restrictions on EU imports. Negotiations are being carried

---

[27]Unless otherwise stated all the statistics in this chapter are taken from Eurostat.

out for an agreement on trade in nuclear materials. An Energy Dialogue was established in 2000 as a forum for discussion and co-operation on energy issues.

Since 1991 the EU has provided technical assistance to Russia through the TACIS Programme. By 2008 a total of €2.6 billion had been given through TACIS, and the EU was the main provider of economic and technical aid to Russia.

In 2003 the Final Declaration of the EU–Russian Summit in St Petersburg defined four 'common spaces' or areas for co-operation within the framework of the PCA:

1 The economy;

2 Liberty, security and justice;

3 Research, education and culture;

4 External security.

Since enlargement part of the Russian Federation, Kaliningrad, is surrounded by EU member states. This raised the sensitive question of how to guarantee transit between Kaliningrad and the rest of Russia. In 2002 at the Brussels Summit, agreement was reached on a package of measures addressing this problem, which included:

- a facilitated transit document;

- assessing the feasibility of a non-stop, high-speed train;

- discussions on the long-term goal of visa-free travel between the EU and Russia; and

- full use of existing international conventions to simplify transit of goods, including energy.

The implementation of these arrangements has led to high increases in transit figures. The EU also provides substantial financial assistance for the development of the Kaliningrad region.

Despite the institutional framework for co-operation, there have been numerous tensions between Russia and the EU and its member states. The worsening of relations was exacerbated by enlargement, with various countries formerly in the Soviet sphere of influence joining the EU. Disputes covered a wide range of issues including a ban on Polish meat exports, a blockade of Lithuanian oil imports, a row with Estonia over moving a Soviet War memorial, and criticism of Czech and Polish plans to host a US anti-missile system. However, there were also differences with the EU(15) over energy security, trade (Sweden and Italy) and a Russian spying scandal with Spain. Following the killing of Alexander Litvinenko and the dispute over British Council activities, relations between the UK and Russia seemed redolent of the cold war. The EU was also concerned about human rights restrictions and violations of democracy in Russia, including the detention of former chess champion, Gary Kasparov. Kosovo was a major source of tension, with Russia backing Serbia and threatening to block the proposal of UN envoy, Martti Ahtisaari, for gradual independence of Kosovo. Russia also backed separatist enclaves in Georgia and Moldova, and there were also differences over Ukrainian moves to draw closer to the EU.

Following the era characterized by the Russophile tendencies of Chirac, Berlusconi and Schroeder, a new realism seems likely in EU attitudes towards its eastern neighbour. In June 2007 under the German Presidency both the German Chancellor, Angela Merkel, and Commission President, Barroso, stressed that it was important for Russia to realize that the EU was based on solidarity, so the difficulties of countries such as Poland, Lithuania or Estonia with Russia were also EU problems.

EU relations with Asia

Trade between the EU and Asia has been growing rapidly, and now accounts for about a third of total EU trade flows. European Union FDI in Asia has been increasing and now amounts to about a third of EU FDI abroad. Strengthening relations with Asia has therefore become one of the highest priorities of EU foreign relations.

The Asia–Europe Meeting (ASEM) was set up in 1996 to encourage dialogue and co-operation between the EU and now 13 Asian countries. It involves summits (which have taken place every two years), ministerial meetings and conferences and seminars at expert level to discuss political, economic and cultural issues. Action Plans have been drawn up to facilitate trade and investment. There are also meetings on a regular basis of civil society and of the private and public sectors in the Asia–Europe Business Forum. The Asia–Europe Foundation was set up in 1997 in Singapore in order to promote cultural and intellectual meetings between the two regions. The dialogue encouraged by the ASEM process has recently concentrated more on political issues such as the fight against terrorism and transnational crime, and the management of international migration.

The EU also has relations with sub-regional Asian groupings such as ASEAN, and the South Asian Association for Regional Co-operation (SAARC), as described in Table 19.2 above. The EU also has bilateral relations with individual Asian countries, such as China, Japan and India.

Trade between the EU and China has been growing rapidly, and in 2006 China was the second trading partner of the EU and displaced the USA as the largest source of EU imports. According to official Chinese statistics, the EU was the main trading partner of China, ahead of Japan and the USA. In 2006 Chinese exports to the EU totalled about €191 billion, an annual increase of about 21 per cent. European Union exports to China increased by about 22.5 per cent in 2006, amounting to roughly €63 billion. Whereas the EU(15) had a surplus with China at the beginning of the 1980s, the EU deficit of128 billion with China in 2006 was the largest bilateral deficit of the EU.

The EU supported China's World Trade Organization (WTO) membership (achieved in December 2001) and is now concerned to ensure implementation of China's WTO commitments, in particular with regard to market access and intellectual property rights. In 2004 a major EU–China Co-operation Programme was launched to support the integration of China into the world trading system.

The 1984 EC–China Trade and Co-operation Agreement (replacing an earlier agreement of 1978) is the main legal framework covering bilateral relations. It was complemented in 1994 and 2002 by exchanges of letters establishing broad political dialogue. In January 2007 negotiations of a more comprehensive Partnership and Co-operation Agreement were launched. The EU and China also have sectoral agreements in areas such as customs co-operation, tourism, science and technology and maritime transport.

European Union relations with Japan are covered by the 1991 Political Declaration, which set out common principles and shared objectives in the political, economic, co-operation and cultural areas, and established a consultation framework for annual summits between the EU and Japan. In 2001 an Action Plan ('Shaping Our Common Future') was established, covering EU–Japanese relations for a ten-year period to 2011. The Action Plan has four basic objectives: promoting peace and security (through measures such as arms control, non-proliferation, conflict prevention); strengthening the economic and trade partnership; coping with global and societal change; and bringing together people and cultures. The EU and Japan have also attempted to co-ordinate their positions in international organizations such as the UN and the WTO.

Between 1980 and 2002 EU imports from Japan grew by 7 per cent on average a year, and EU exports by 10 per cent. Historically Japan has had a large trade surplus with the EU, but since the 1990s trade with Japan has become more balanced. In 2006 Japan was the fifth trading partner of the EU, with total two-way trade valuing €116.9 billion. In 2006 the EU was the largest foreign investor in Japan investing 4.5 billion, and the EU was the main destination for Japanese FDI, attracting €7.8 billion in 2005, bringing the total investment stock to €78 billion.

In the past EU relations with Japan tended to be dominated by trade disputes, and the EU continues to complain of difficulties in market access. Since the 1990s there has been increased Japanese willingness to meet EU requests for structural reforms and deregulation. Since 1994 the Regulatory Reform Dialogue has provided a forum for reciprocal requests for reducing the number of unnecessary regulations that may obstruct trade. In 2002 an EU–Japan Mutual Recognition Agreement entered into force, and in 2003 an Agreement on Co-operation on Anti-Competitive Activities was adopted. In 2004 a Co-operation Framework for two-way investment promotion was agreed.

European Union–India trade has been growing rapidly from €4.4 billion in 1980 to over €46 billion in 2006. Trade with the EU amounts to about 20 per cent of the exports and imports of India, but India accounted for just 1.8 per cent of EU trade and 1.3 per cent of EU FDI in 2006.

European Union–India relations date from the 1960s, and agreements were signed in 1973 and 1981. The current Co-operation Agreement, which dates from 1994, extends beyond trade and co-operation. In 2004 it was agreed to launch a Strategic Partnership between the EU and India, to be implemented through an Action Plan.

EU–Latin American relations

With the entry of Spain and Portugal into the Community, relations with Latin America acquired a higher priority. Trade between the EU and Latin America more than doubled between 1990 and 2005. The EU is Latin America's second trading partner after the USA, with imports to the EU from Latin America and the Caribbean amounting to €67.4 billion, and exports to the region to 58.2 billion in 2005. The main exports of these countries to the EU are agricultural products, transport equipment and energy, while capital goods, transport equipment and chemicals are the main EU exports. The EU is the second foreign investor and major source of foreign aid. In 2005 net FDI flows from the EU to Latin America and the Caribbean amounted to US$71 billion. The EU is concerned that Latin America should maintain a balanced relationship between its two principal partners, also in view of the proposed Free Trade Area of the Americas (FTAA). This would involve an extension of the North American Free Trade Association (NAFTA), but since 2005 this initiative appears stalled.

The EU has developed a parallel set of ties with Latin America and the Caribbean, and relations are carried out simultaneously at regional, sub-regional and bilateral levels. At a regional (sub-continent) level, in 1986 six Latin American countries set up the Rio Group in order to discuss matters of common interest. Membership of this group has gradually expanded, and it now includes all the Latin American countries and representatives of Caribbean countries. Meetings are held between the EU and Rio Group every two years.

In 1999 at the Rio Summit it was decided to develop a strategic partnership between the EU and Latin America and the Caribbean (EU–LAC) in order to develop political, economic and cultural understanding between the partners. Emphasis was traditionally placed on developing democracy, the rule of law, human rights, pluralism, peace and security and political stability. Over time, however, more priority has been given to international challenges affecting the region such as the environment, new technologies and WTO negotiations.

At a sub-regional level, as shown in Table 19.3, the EU has relationships with the three main integration blocs in Latin America: Mercosur ('El Mercado del Sur'), the Andean Community, and Central America (the SICA or Central American Integration System). The EU encourages regional integration as a means of ensuring economic development and security.

The EU also has bilateral links with individual countries and, in particular, Mexico and Chile, which are not members of Latin American integration blocs. In 2005 an Association Agreement between the EU and Chile came into force and covers political and trade relations and co-operation. An Economic Partnership, Political Co-operation and Co-operation Agreement (Global Agreement) was signed between the EU and Mexico in 1997. This envisages the creation of a free trade area in goods and services, the mutual opening of the procurement markets, the liberalization of capital movements and payments, and the adoption of disciplines in the fields of competition and intellectual property rights.

Evaluation

The EU seems to have become more willing to take a more active role in promoting initiatives to tighten links with its main trading partners and encourage the efforts of other regional integration blocs. Through the GSP (and, in particular, the EBA) initiative the EU offers trade concessions to developing countries, but the impact of these in promoting development seems to have been minimal. The foreign aid of the EU and its member states is still below the levels required to reach the Millennium Development Goals, and the decision to render trade relations with ACP countries WTO-compatible through the introduction of EPAs led to contention over the risk of trade diversion, and pressure on developing countries to open their markets, opening a wide debate about the style and effectiveness of EU development policy. In relations with Russia, despite the extensive institutional framework for co-operation, dealings have been tense, and though relations with other major trade partners are better, at times there have been conflicts, such as in the various WTO disputes with the USA and the limitations on Chinese imports of textiles and clothing. In part these difficulties might simply reflect the consequences of globalization (see Chapter 7) and an awareness of the increased weight of an enlarged EU in the world and of the need to present a counterweight to other major actors and, in particular, the USA and China.

Summary of Key Concepts

- The **Common Commercial Policy** of the EU is based on Article 113 of the Treaty of Rome and entails a common Community tariff regime and common trade agreements with third countries. Over time the EU has developed a patchwork of preferential agreements with other countries or groups of countries.

- In 1971 the Community established a **Generalized System of Preferences**. This entails a list of products negotiated each year on which tariffs are reduced by an amount that depends on the 'sensitivity' of the product and degree of development of the exporting countries.

- **EU development policy** is centred on the now 79 ACP countries, most of which are former colonies of EU member states. However, policies to reduce world poverty have met with limited success.

- Following the four Lomé Conventions, the 2000 **Cotonou Agreement** between the EU and ACP countries aims at poverty reduction and covers a 20-year period. It places a new emphasis on the political dimension (respect for human rights, democracy and rule of law) and on improved implementation.

- The proposed **Economic Partnership Agreements** uniting the EU with regional groupings of ACP countries with the aim of eventually creating free trade areas have proved extremely controversial.

- In terms of economic dimension, the **EU and the USA** are roughly compatible. The USA and the EU are each other's largest trading partner and most important source and destination of FDI.

- During the post-Second World War period, the USA demonstrated unequivocal support for the integration process in Europe. Marshall Aid was conditional on regional co-operation of the recipient countries and led to the creation of the OEEC.

- Recent years have been characterized by several concrete attempts to promote EU–US co-operation, but there have been numerous trade disputes between the EU and the USA on issues such as: subsidies to Airbus and Boeing, bananas, meat containing growth-promoting hormones, foreign sales corporations and genetically modified food.

- In March 2003 the European Commission launched the **European Neighbourhood Policy** to deal with relations between an enlarged EU and its eastern and southern neighbours.

- What is known as the **Mediterranean Partnership**, or Barcelona Process, began in 1995. This provides a framework for co-operation between the EU members and 10 Mediterranean countries.

- The Partnership and Co-operation Agreement is the legal basis for **EU–Russian relations**. In 2003 Russia and the EU agreed on a framework for creating 'common spaces', but in practice relations have been tense.

- The document, 'Towards a new Asia strategy' sets out the framework of **EU policy towards all Asian countries**. The Asia–Europe Meeting was set up in 1996 to encourage dialogue and co-operation between the EU and 10 Asian countries. The EU also has bilateral links with ASEAN and SAARC, and individual countries such as China, Japan and India.

- **EU relations with Latin America** are carried out simultaneously at regional, sub-regional and bilateral levels. The EU is concerned that Latin American countries maintain a balance in their links with major partners if and when the Free Trade Area of the Americas is set up.

Questions for study and review

1 *What are the main features of EU trade policy?*

2 *What are the main criticisms of EU development policy? How successful do you think that the Cotonou Agreement was in overcoming these shortcomings?*

3 *What is the link between economic development and democracy?*

4 *What strategies should be used to ensure the effectiveness of development policies?*

5 *Indicate the main features of EU–US economic relations.*

6 *Describe the main attempts at EU–US co-operation. How successful do you consider these initiatives?*

7 *Describe some of the main trade disputes between the USA and the EU (see the OLC website for this book and the WTO website).*

8 *How can we account for the increase in trade disputes between the EU and the USA in recent years?*

9 *How successful do you consider the WTO in resolving these disputes?*

10 *How do you envisage the future of EU–US relations?*

11 *Do you think that the European Neighbourhood Policy will prove successful?*

12 *What criticisms can be made of the Euro-Mediterranean Partnership?*

13 *How could the EU reduce tensions in its relationship with Russia?*

14 *How could Europe–Asia relations be strengthened?*

15 *Describe EU and US rivalry in Latin and Central America.*

16 *Do you think that the EU is right to promote efforts at regional integration in other areas?*

References

Bouët; A. Laborde, D. and Mevel, S. (2007) 'Searching for an alternative to economic partnership agreements', IFPRI (International Food Policy Research Institute), www.ifpiri.org

Chilosi, A. (2007) 'The European Union and its neighbours: "Everything but Institutions"?', *European Journal of Comparative Economics*, Vol. 4, No. 1, pp. 25–38.

European Bank for Reconstruction and Development (various years) *Transition Report* and *Transition Update*, London.

European Commission (1996) 'Green Paper on the relations between the European Union and the ACP countries on the eve of the 21st century – Challenges and options for a new partnership', COM(96)570, 20 November.

European Commission (1997) 'Guidelines for the negotiation of new co-operation agreements with the African, Caribbean and Pacific countries', COM(97)537, 29 October.

European Commission (2003) 'Wider Europe – neighbourhood: A new framework for our relations with our eastern and southern neighbours', COM(2003)104final.

European Commission (2007) 'The Annual Report on the European Community's development policy and on the implementation of external assistance in 2006', www.ec.europa.eu

Guay, T.R. (1999) *The United States and the European Union: The Political Economy of a Relationship*, Sheffield Academic Press, Sheffield.

House of Lords (2004) 'EU development aid in transition', www.parliament.uk/parliamentary_committees/lords_s_comm

Hudec, R.E. (1993) *Enforcing International Trade Law: The Evolution of the Modern GATT Legal System*, Butterworth Legal Publishers, Salem, NY.

Messerlin, P. and Delpeuch, C. (2007) EPAs: A Plan A+, Groupe d'Economie Mondiale, Sciences Politiques, www.gem.sciences-po.fr

Stevens, C. (1990) 'The Lomé Convention', in Kiljunen, K. (ed.) *Region-to-Region Co-operation between the Developed and Developing Countries: The Potential for Mini NIEO*, Avebury, Aldershot.

Trade Negotiation Insights (2008) *Special Edition, December 2007 and January 2008*, Vol. 6, No. 8, www.ictsd.org/tni

Victor, J.C, Raisson, V. and Tétart, F. (2007) *Le Dessous des Cartes: Atlas d'un Monde qui Change, Volume 2*, Editions Tallandier, Paris.

Useful websites

The European Commission for information on EU development policy and external relations:
www.ec.europa.eu

The Food and Agricultural Organization for data and analysis on world food and agricultural issues:
www.fao.org

The Organization for Economic Co-operation and Development for statistics and country reviews:
www.oecd.org

Oxfam for a less orthodox view on trade and development questions:
www.oxfam.org.uk

For data and analysis of development issues see: United Nations Development Programme (UNDP):
www.undp.org

United Nations Educational, Scientific and Cultural Organization (UNESCO):
www.unesco.org

UNICEF:
www.unicef.org

The World Bank:
www.worldbank.org

For the US position, see US Trade Representative:
www.ustr.gov

The World Trade Organization is useful for statistics and reports on international economic relations and accounts of trade disputes:
http://www.wto.org

CHAPTER

20

EU Enlargement

❖ **LEARNING OBJECTIVES**

By the end of this chapter you should be able to understand:

❖ Where we are in the EU enlargement process;

❖ How the theory of clubs has been used to analyse the question of EU enlargement;

❖ What measures were introduced by Western countries to assist the transition process in Central and Eastern European countries (CEECs) and with what success;

❖ The differences between aid for transition and the Marshall Plan;

❖ The difficulties encountered in trying to apply the Copenhagen criteria;

❖ The main steps involved in the pre-accession strategy;

❖ EU policy towards South-Eastern Europe;

❖ EU relations with the three candidate countries: Croatia, the Former Yugoslav Republic of Macedonia and Turkey.

Introduction

In May 2004 10 new countries joined the EU, and Bulgaria and Romania became members in 2007. Croatia, Turkey and the Former Yugoslav Republic of Macedonia are candidate countries. The EU is considering the possibility of further enlargements to countries in the Western Balkans, which could eventually include Bosnia and Herzegovina, Serbia, Kosovo, Montenegro and Albania.

The ongoing EU enlargement process raises fundamental questions about the future of the Union. Will, for instance, expanding membership lead to a change in identity of the EU? Is widening on this scale compatible with deepening? Will the EU be condemned to endless arguing about the relative size of contributions to and receipts from the Community budget? Will an expanded membership require fundamental changes in EU economic and cohesion policy and the Common Agricultural Policy (CAP) after 2013 (when a new financial perspective begins)? Will the Lisbon Treaty be ratified, and will it provide the EU with an institutional framework that enables it to avoid deadlock in decision-making, and at the same time increase its transparency and democratic accountability? The EU is committed to further enlargements, but where should its borders end?

In order to address these questions, this chapter will first provide some theoretical background. The main features of the 2004 and 2007 enlargements are described, also because these might provide insights into future enlargements. The present state of play of the enlargement process is then discussed before drawing conclusions about the future of the EU.

The theory of clubs

The EU enlargement process is frequently analysed using the economic theory of clubs.[1] Clubs are assumed to pursue a well-defined common interest. The problem is to determine the optimal number of members or size of the club, and this will entail defining the costs and benefits of increasing membership. For simplicity here it is assumed that clubs provide goods and services for their members, which are intermediate between private and public goods in that the clubs supply a product that is excludable (like a private good) but non-rival (as in the case of a public good). However, it is debatable how far each of the various common EU policies is non-rival (see, for example, discussion of the common fisheries policy in Chapter 13) or even in some cases excludable (for example, non-EU members have been able to share in the benefits of adopting common standards).

The members of the club are assumed to be identical, so the marginal costs and marginal benefits of an additional member to existing members can be depicted in a single diagram as seen in Figure 20.1. If every member is different a separate axis for the marginal costs and benefits of each member is necessary.

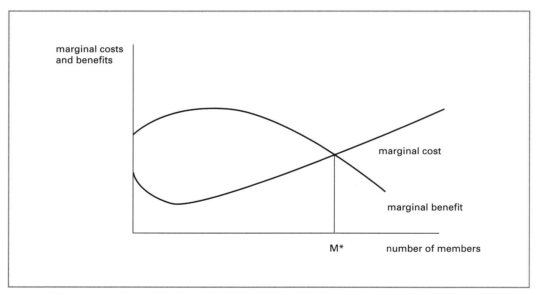

FIGURE 20.1 Costs and benefits to existing club members of expanding membership

---

[1] See Mueller (2001) for a discussion of this theory, which was initially elaborated by Buchanan (1965). For an application to EU enlargement see Gros and Steinherr (2004), De Benedictis and Padoan (1994), or Alesina and Spolaore (2003). For the latter authors, benefits may come from economies of scale and costs from increasing heterogeneity of preferences. Though the application of the theory is less developed, it is not without parallels to the theory of the Optimal Currency Area discussed in Chapter 9.

In the case of the EU the benefits of membership include, for instance, the right to be a member of the EU and to participate in common policies such as the single market, economic and monetary union (EMU), economic and social cohesion and the CAP. Starting with a small number of members the benefits to incumbents are assumed to rise initially as membership increases, but eventually decline as congestion grows (implying a decline in the benefits both to new and existing members), causing the marginal benefit curve to take the form shown in Figure 20.1.

For simplicity it is assumed that the total cost of providing these policies is fixed, that the members are identical, and costs are shared equally. As the number of members increases, each new member will bear a share of the total cost, but the share will gradually decrease as more members are added. The cost to existing members also declines initially as membership increases, but will eventually rise. The increase in marginal costs is also the result of congestion and the greater difficulty of reaching agreement among more numerous members with more heterogeneous preferences, and of sacrificing sovereignty.

The optimal number of members of the club M* occurs where the curves indicating marginal costs and marginal benefits to existing members (who are also responsible for deciding on the admission of new members) intersect. Changes in EU institutions and policies can be introduced to alter both the marginal costs and benefits. For example, increased use of qualified majority could shift the marginal cost curve down so optimal size of the club increases.

As applied to EU enlargement the theory of clubs raises interesting questions, but is difficult to apply in practice. For instance, it suggests that the net advantages of membership are greatest for the early members of the Community, but fell as more members were added. The framework can also be used to illustrate how reforms in areas such as EU decision-making, the CAP or the EU budget could be used to shift the marginal cost and benefit curves, and increase the optimal size of EU membership. However, it is difficult to identify the various costs and benefits as a result of EU enlargement, or to give weights to them, and the shape and position of the marginal cost and benefits curves are not known with any precision. The members and potential members are clearly not identical, so separate analyses would have to be carried out for individual member states and potential candidates.

A brief chronology of the enlargement process

Before dealing with the main aspects of enlargement in more detail, it is useful to provide a brief chronology of the main steps in the process (see also the OLC to this book for a list of key events).

As soon as the central planning system collapsed in 1989, many of the smaller CEECs were anxious for tighter links with, or membership of, the European Community. The Community responded with a series of trade and aid measures, but a strategy with regard to enlargement emerged only gradually.

It was as late as 1993 that the Copenhagen European Council set out the conditions applicant countries have to fulfil in order to join the EU. The 1994 Essen Summit established a 'pre-accession strategy' to help prepare the candidate countries for eventual membership. As described below, this entailed the PHARE Programme of assistance (Poland, Hungary Aid for Economic Reconstruction), the Europe or Association Agreements and a 'structured dialogue', bringing together the EU and candidate countries to discuss questions of common interest.

On the basis of the accession criteria, in July 1997 the EC Commission published 'Opinions' on the readiness of the applicant countries to join the EU. These Opinions were included in the document, Agenda 2000, which represents a milestone in the enlargement process. Agenda 2000 analysed the necessary steps to prepare both the EU and accession countries for enlargement and set out the Commission's proposals for the 2000–06 financial perspective.

Following the decision of the Luxembourg European Council in December 1999, accession negotiations started with Cyprus and with five of the 10 Central and East European countries in March 1998.[2] Each year the EC published Regular Reports on the progress made by applicant countries in preparing for EU membership. At the 1999 Helsinki European Summit it was decided to extend negotiations to a further six countries.[3] Malta's application lapsed in 1993 but was subsequently resumed in 1998, and Malta was included in the Helsinki group.

Turkey applied for EU membership in 1987. In December 1997 it was decided to establish the European Conference that would entail an annual meeting of the EU member states and the 'European states aspiring to accede to it and sharing its values and internal and external objectives'.[4] The aim was to reassure those countries not included in the first wave of negotiations and, in particular, Turkey. However, Turkey was offended by the fact that it had been overtaken by so many countries in the accession queue, and refused to attend the first two meetings of the European Conference. At the Helsinki Summit of 1999 Turkey was declared a candidate, and Turkey began to participate in a reinforced pre-accession strategy similar to that of the other candidate countries.

	Population in 2007 (millions)	Exports to EU(27) as share of total exports	Imports from EU(27) as share of total imports	Inflation 2006	Unemployment 2006	GDP per capita as % of EU (27) average (PPP) 2007 (f)	GDP growth in 2006 (%)
FYR Macedonia	2.0	61.2%	52.9%	3.2	36	28 (f)	3.1
Turkey	73.4	51.6%	39.3%	7.1	9.1	30	6.1
Croatia	4.4	64%	70%	3.3*	12.7	52	4.8 (f)
EU(27)	497.1			2.2**	8.1	100	3.0

TABLE 20.1 Basic data on the candidate countries

f: forecast

* 2005

**EU(25)

Source: Eurostat, © European Communities, 2008.

---

[2] The Czech Republic, Estonia, Hungary, Poland and Slovenia. See Senior Nello and Smith (1998) for a discussion of this process.

[3] Bulgaria, Latvia, Lithuania, Romania, Slovakia and Malta.

[4] Conclusions of the European Council, Luxembourg, December 1997, where the decision to establish the European Conference was taken.

At the Berlin European Council of March 1999 agreement was reached on the Agenda 2000 package, including the financial perspective for the 2000–06 period and reform of the CAP and Structural Funds.[5] Following the rather disappointing results of the Amsterdam and Nice treaties, the Lisbon Treaty set out further proposals for reform of EU decision-making, also with a view to enlargement.

In May 2004 ten new countries joined the EU, with the date being chosen so they could participate in the elections to the European Parliament of June 2004. In a referendum on 24 April the Greek Cypriots voted against a UN proposal for settlement and, as a result, in May 2004 only the Greek Cypriot part of the island joined the EU. Bulgaria and Romania joined in 2007.

In October 2005 the EU decided to begin negotiations for membership with Croatia and Turkey (see Table 20.1). The negotiations with Turkey are likely to prove lengthy, with 2015 being mentioned as the earliest expected date for accession. In December 2005 the Former Yugoslav Republic of Macedonia was declared a candidate country.

The EU is considering the possibility of further enlargements to countries in the Western Balkans, which could eventually include Bosnia and Herzegovina, Serbia, Kosovo, Montenegro and Albania, but these are not expected to take place before 2013.

Trade and aid arrangements between the EU and CEECs before enlargement

The 'First Generation' Trade And Co-operation Agreements

After a long history of stormy relations between the European Community and the Eastern integration bloc, the CMEA (Council for Mutual Economic Assistance), in June 1988 a Joint Declaration of Mutual Recognition was signed.[6] This opened the way for tighter links between the EC and individual Central-East European countries.

In September 1988 Hungary signed a trade and co-operation agreement with the Community, and similar 'first generation agreements' with the other CEECs and the USSR soon followed. The agreements related to trade and to commercial and economic co-operation. The first-generation agreements were soon overtaken by events, but remain important as a milestone in EC–CEEC relations.

Aid measures for the CEECs prior to accession

The question of whether to aid transition was decided in July 1989 when, encouraged by President Bush, the EC Commission chaired a meeting of the then 24 Organization for Economic Co-operation and Development (OECD) countries (the G–24) to seek ways of facilitating the process of moving towards democracy and market-orientated economies. Also involved in the programme were the EIB (European Investment Bank), the World Bank, the International Monetary Fund (IMF) and the OECD.

---

[5] The financial package for the new member states was subsequently amended at the 2002 Copenhagen European Council.

[6] Also known as the Comecon, the CMEA was founded in 1949 and formally dissolved in 1991. It was composed of the USSR, Bulgaria, Czechoslovakia, East Germany, Hungary, Poland, Romania, Cuba, Mongolia and Vietnam. Angola, Ethiopia, Laos and North Korea had observer status, while Yugoslavia only participated with regard to certain sectors. For a more detailed account of EC–CMEA relations up until 1988 and a description of the CMEA and its activities, see Senior Nello (1991).

The main argument advanced in favour of giving aid to the CEECs and former Soviet Republics was Western self-interest. Despite the low levels of East–West trade at the end of the 1980s, and the difficulties of transition, the CMEA countries represented a potential market of some 450 million consumers. For generations the objective of ensuring Western security *vis-à-vis* the Eastern bloc had entailed huge defence budgets, and now a different type of effort was needed to further peace and prosperity. If transition failed, the West could risk experiencing external costs in the form of migratory pressures and/or spillover of ethnic and nationalistic tensions.

The term PHARE (Economic Reconstruction Aid for Poland and Hungary) was adopted for the Community's programme, though this soon became something of a misnomer as aid was soon extended to the other CEECs. After a heated debate on possible political and economic consequences, assistance was also extended to the Soviet Union and, subsequently, to former Soviet Republics through the TACIS Programme (Technical Assistance for the Commonwealth of Independent States).

The PHARE Programme came into operation from 1990 and was initially demand-driven and based on the requests of the recipient countries. The measures included:

- Food aid to Poland, Romania, Bulgaria and the USSR;
- Agricultural assistance;
- Training and human resources;
- Energy and the environment;
- Improved market access;
- Assistance for privatization and restructuring (for small and medium enterprises, the financial system, technical assistance, investment guarantees, etc.);
- Medical aid.

In addition loans were granted for stabilization and to cover balance-of-payments difficulties, and debt relief was extended to countries such as Poland and Bulgaria.

The European Bank for Reconstruction and Development (EBRD) was established in 1991 to encourage investment in transition countries and reduce financial risks. From 1993 PHARE became more concerned with preparing CEECs for accession. Increasingly PHARE used the procedures of the Structural Funds in order to familiarize the CEECs so they could use the Structural Funds more efficiently upon accession.

One of the main mechanisms used in the task of institution building was 'twinning'. Twinning brings administrations and semi-public organizations in the EU and candidate countries together to work on common projects related to the *acquis*. Typically twinning involves secondment of civil servants from the EU member states working on Community policies to a candidate country for a certain period of time.

The 1999 Berlin Council established PHARE as one of the three pre-accession instruments for the 2000–06 period to help prepare the candidate countries for membership. The three pre-accession instruments were:

1 PHARE, which had an allocation of €1.56 billion per year, 30 per cent of which was earmarked for institution building, 35 per cent is for the regulatory infrastructure required for implementation of the *acquis*, and 35 per cent for economic and social cohesion;

2 ISPA (Instrument for Structural Policies Pre-Accession), which was allocated €1.04 billion per year for assistance for the environment and transport infrastructure;

3 SAPARD (the Special Accession Programme for Agriculture and Regional Development), which received an allocation of €0.52 billion per year. Measures include improving quality,

applying veterinary and plant controls, setting up producer groups and creating land registers.

There was much debate about whether Western assistance to the transition countries could be construed as a new Marshall Plan. However, there were substantial differences from the Marshall Plan:[7]

- Post-war reconstruction is very different from transition.

- Most of Marshall Aid came from one donor, so the co-ordination problems were fewer.

- The scale of financing, and the share of grants (80 per cent compared with 15 per cent, according to Mayhew, 1998) were higher under the Marshall Plan.

According to some observers,[8] the financial assistance under the Marshall Plan was probably less important than the conditionality imposed. In order to receive aid West European countries were encouraged to opt for market economies, liberalized trade and regional co-operation.

Western measures to assist the transition process were also conditional. For instance PHARE aid to Romania was suspended on human rights grounds in 1990 and was not extended to Albania until 1991. However, as a growing literature demonstrates, it is the prospect of EU membership that ultimately renders the conditionality effective.[9]

Regional co-operation was also a condition of EU assistance, and this was a major factor leading to the creation of arrangements such as the Central European Free Trade Area (CEFTA) in 1992[10] and the South-East Europe Co-operation Initiative of 1996.[11] However, a major shortcoming of these initiatives among transition countries was that they were generally more interested in co-operation with the EU than with each other.

Given the size and number of post-communist economies and the cost of transition, it was inevitable that the role played by external financial assistance would be relatively modest.[12] Much aid was in the form of loans, and much consisted of export credits, which also benefit Western firms. However, occasionally aid may arrive at a crucial, vulnerable time. The policy advice and training given was often criticized as being contradictory, inconsistent and not always tailored to the needs of the recipient country. Another complaint was that the main beneficiaries were often Western consultants. There was also criticism of the insufficient co-ordination and excessive bureaucracy in giving aid. With the benefit of hindsight, trade liberalization, FDI and the prospect of EU membership were probably more important catalysts in encouraging transition.

The 'Second-Generation' Europe Agreements

Between 1991 and 1996 the EU signed second-generation 'Europe Agreements' with 10 CEECs deemed to have made sufficient progress in economic and political transition (these were the

---

[7] As reported in Mayhew (1998).

[8] De Long and Eichengreen (1993).

[9] Grabbe (2002), Smith (2001),Vachudova (2001), and Smith (2003).

[10]CEFTA was composed of the Czech Republic, Hungary Poland and Slovakia; Bulgaria, Romania and Slovenia subsequently joined.

[11]This was composed of Albania, Bosnia and Herzegovina, Bulgaria, FYR of Macedonia, Hungary, Romania, Moldova and Turkey, with Croatia as an observer.

[12]However, the EU and international financial institutions (IFIs) have played an important role in attracting additional financing from official sources, including debt relief through the Paris Club.They have been rather less successful in attracting complementary private financing or private (London Club) debt relief.

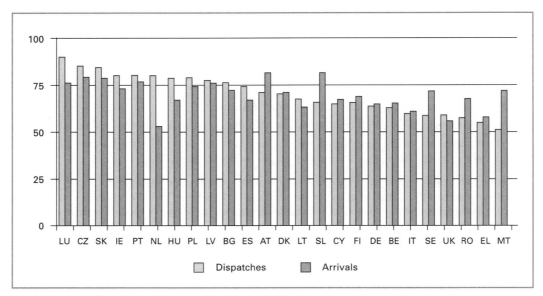

FIGURE 20.2 Intra-EU trade as a proportion of total trade 2004 (percentage)
Source: Eurostat Key Figures on Europe, Statistical Pocketbook 2006, © European Communities, 2007, www.ec.europa.eu/eurostat

same 10 that were subsequently the first to start accession negotiations).[13] The Europe Agreements were the basic legal instruments covering the relationship between the EU and the CEEC(10).[14] The Agreements covered trade-related issues, political dialogue, legal approximation, 'phased introduction' of the four freedoms (though the EC failed to grant any access to workers beyond what was guaranteed by its member state) and co-operation in other areas, including industry, environment, transport and customs (Mayhew, 1998).

The Europe Agreements created a free trade area between the EU and associated CEECs. Because the CEEC partners needed more time to become competitive, the tariff cuts were asymmetric, with the Community proceeding more rapidly. The removal of tariffs on certain sensitive sectors such as steel, and textiles and clothing was to be phased over several years, but by 1998 most restrictions on industrial products had been removed.[15] The concessions granted on agricultural trade were less favourable than in other sectors, and it was only in 2003 that agricultural trade with the new member states was liberalized for products meeting EU standards.

As a result of the provisions of the Europe Agreements, a free trade area was in place before enlargement. For the CEECs, joining the EU meant moving from a free trade area to a customs union (by adopting the Common Commercial Policy with its 'hierarchy' of trade preferences) and the Single Market.[16]

---

[13] From 1992 negotiation began leading to the signing of less far-reaching 'trade and partnership' agreements with various former Soviet Republics, including Russia, Belarus, Ukraine, Kazakhstan, Georgia and Kyrgyzstan.

[14] See Senior Nello (1991) for a more detailed description of these agreements.

[15] See Mayhew (1998) or Senior Nello (2002) for descriptions of the timing of trade liberalization for various groups of products.

[16] In contrast, many empirical studies of integration effects are based on the assumption of a move from free trade to a customs union (see Chapter 5).

	2005	2006
Outward flows to extra EU(25)	186.1	202.2
From EU(15)	182.0	196.9
From new member states	4.1	5.3
Inward flows from extra EU(25)	94.3	145.0
To EU(15)	90.5	139.4
To new member states	3.8	5.6
Intra-EU(25) flows	422.4	396.2
From EU(15) to new member states	25.3	45.8
From new member states to EU(15)	12.0	-0.4
Between EU(15) members	389.3	355.3

TABLE 20.2 EU(25) FDI Flows (billion euro)
Source: Eurostat, © European Communities, 2008.

What is significant about the level of trade between the EU and CEECs is the speed of its reorientation from Eastern to Western markets, also thanks to the Europe Agreements.[17] In 2006 the share of intra-EU trade in total trade of the new member states was similar to that of the EU(15), as shown in Figure 20.2. EU(15) investment flows to the new member states reached almost €46 billion in 2006, rising from 6 per cent of total intra EU(25) investment flows in 2005 to 11 per cent in 2006 (see Table 20.2).

The Copenhagen Criteria

In 1993 the Copenhagen European Council agreed that 'accession will take place as soon as the applicant country is able to assume the obligations of membership by satisfying the economic and political conditions required'. The conditions were first drawn up for the CEEC countries, but were subsequently extended to apply to all candidate countries and entail that:

- The applicant state must have a functioning market economy with the capacity to cope with competitive pressures and market forces within the Community;
- The applicant state must have achieved stability of institutions, guaranteeing democracy, the rule of law, human rights and respect for and protection of minorities;
- The applicant state must be able to take on the obligations of membership, including adherence to the aims of political, and economic and monetary union.

At the Copenhagen Summit it was also stipulated that enlargement is subject to the condition that the EU is able to absorb new members and maintain the momentum of integration.

The criteria are generally divided into political criteria, economic criteria, and ability to take on the *acquis communautaire* and to establish the administrative and judicial capacity to ensure its effective implementation.

There are three political criteria:

1 Stability of institutions guaranteeing democracy, the rule of law, human rights and respect for and protection of minorities;

---

[17] See Senior Nello (2002) for a discussion of this issue.

2 Adherence to the objective of political union; and

3 Maintaining the momentum of integration.

The economic criteria are similarly divided into three:

1 The existence of a functioning market economy;

2 Capacity to cope with competitive pressures and market forces within the Community; and

3 Adherence to the aim of economic and monetary union.

The accession criteria are presumably intended to provide some kind of objective basis for selecting countries ready to join the EU, as well as indicating to the applicant countries the tasks they are expected to perform. The introduction of the Copenhagen criteria would therefore seem aimed at replicating the experience of the Maastricht criteria but in a different field, that of enlargement.

However, although there is a certain flexibility and political leeway in deciding whether the Maastricht criteria have been met, this is far more the case for the accession criteria. This arises from the number of criteria and, in some cases, from the vague and imprecise nature of the concepts involved. This is the case, for instance, in deciding whether a country has a 'a functioning market economy' or the 'capacity to cope with competitive pressures'. There are different models of market economies, and no indication is given as to which model is appropriate, or how to assess when an economy has 'arrived'. In deciding whether a country is ready to cope with competitive pressures in an enlarged EU, a detailed analysis of its economy is necessary, together with predictions about which sectors will be able to cope in the internal EU market.

For other criteria, such as the obligation to take on the objective of political union, or the requirement that the momentum of integration can be maintained (which presumably requires some form of enhanced co-operation or flexibility, see Chapter 3) the objective in question has yet to be defined fully.

The simple rule 'when a country meets the accession criteria, it can join the EU' is misleading given the degree of discretion in deciding whether the accession criteria have been met. In the end choice of who joins when becomes a political issue.

Though at the time of the Copenhagen European Council no indication was given with regard to the weights of the different criteria, subsequently the European Commission indicated that predominance was to be given to the political criteria, so a country must fulfil these before joining and must be making substantial progress towards meeting the economic criteria. Agenda 2000 stresses that 'the effective functioning of democracy is a primordial question in assessing the application of a country for membership of the Union'.[18] Political criteria were also introduced into the Amsterdam Treaty and Article 6 states: 'the Union is founded on the principles of liberty, democracy, respect for human rights and fundamental freedoms, and the rule of law, principles which are common to the member states'. According to Article 49, any country that respects these principles may apply to become a member of the Union. It is mainly on the basis of the political criteria (including treatment of minorities) that the European Commission continues to express misgivings about Turkey (see below).

Also in this context the European Commission has emphasized the need for regional co-operation and good neighbourly relations before accession,[19] and applicant countries have generally taken this condition seriously. The Commission has repeatedly stressed that this is also a condition for the former Yugoslav Republics of South-Eastern Europe.

---

[18] Agenda 2000, p. 40.

[19] See Smith (2003) for a more detailed discussion of this point.

The pre-accession strategy

The Essen European Council of 1994 set out a pre-accession strategy to help the candidate countries prepare for EU membership, and an enhanced pre-accession strategy was launched from 1998. In addition to the Europe Agreements and pre-accession assistance (through PHARE, ISPA and SAPARD), the enhanced strategy included Accession Partnerships and National Programmes for the Adoption of the *Acquis* (NPAA), the opening of Community programmes and agencies, and a review procedure.

The Accession Partnerships set out the main priorities for each of the candidate countries in preparing for EU membership and provided a single framework for co-ordinating the various forms of EU assistance. Each of the candidate countries drew up an NPAA that indicated in detail how the country aimed to meet the priorities of the Accession Partnership. The Commission also prepared Action Plans with the negotiating countries to reinforce their administrative and judicial capacity.

The opening of Community programmes and agencies was aimed at promoting co-operation between the member states and applicant countries in areas such as public health, the environment, energy, research, small and medium enterprises, culture, vocational training and support for student and youth exchanges (such as Socrates). In this way it was hoped that the new member states could be familiarized with the way in which EU policies and instruments are put into practice.

Following the Opinions on the applications of the candidate countries for accession, each year in order to assess progress in preparing for membership the Commission submitted Regular Reports to the Council. Progress Reports continue to be published for each of the present candidate countries (usually in October/November), together with a Composite or Enlargement Strategy Paper. While useful as a source of information, often the style of these publications is not far removed from school reports, though the comments 'could try harder', or 'could do better' were usually expressed in slightly more diplomatic terms.

The accession negotiations

A first step in preparing for the accession negotiations is the 'screening' of the *acquis*. In the case of the CEECs screening began in March 1998 with all the candidate countries, whether negotiations had been opened or not. The purpose of the exercise is to identify issues likely to arise in the negotiations. It consists of a detailed presentation by Commission experts on the application of all the chapters of the *acquis* to the applicant countries. At the time of the screening of the CEECs the *acquis* consisted of 31 chapters but it has subsequently been somewhat reorganized and increased to 35 chapters (see Table 20.3). Though the Commission stressed that political criteria remained primordial, in the case of the CEECs the 'screening' of the candidate countries to assess their progress in taking on the 'obligations of membership' encouraged a shift of emphasis away from the other Copenhagen criteria. The speed and progress of accession negotiations appeared to depend heavily on the ability of a country to adopt the *acquis* and its administrative and judicial capacity to implement the *acquis*.

Following the screening process, negotiations were opened with the candidate countries, chapter by chapter. A chapter was considered 'provisionally closed' with a candidate country when the EU considered that further negotiation was not required on the chapter, and the candidate concerned accepted the EU common position. The EU reserved the right to return to the chapter at a later stage during the negotiation if new *acquis* were adopted, or if the candidate

1. Free movement of goods	26. Education and training
2. Freedom of movement for workers	27. Environment
	28. Consumer and health protection
3. Right of establishment and freedom to provide services	29. customs union
	30. External relations
4. Free movement of capital	31. Foreign and security and defence policy
5. Public procurement	
6. Company law	32. Financial control
7. Intellectual property law	33. Financial and budgetary provisions
8. Competition policy	
9. Financial services	34. Institutions
10. Information services and the media	35. Other
11. Agriculture and rural development	
12. Food safety, veterinary and phytosanitary policy	
13. Fisheries	
14. Transport policy	
15. Energy	
16. Taxation	
17. Economic and monetary union	
18. Statistics	
19. Social policy and employment	
20. Enterprise and industrial policy	
21 Trans-European networks	
22. Regional policy and co-ordination of structural instruments	
25. Science and research	

TABLE 20.3 Chapters of the *acquis*

country concerned failed to implement the commitments it had taken on the chapter. As a result, though chapters could be 'provisionally closed', the Commission's negotiating stance was based on the principle that 'nothing is agreed until everything is agreed' and that a final overall compromise deal was necessary to conclude negotiations.

For the areas linked to the functioning of the Single Market, according to the Commission, any transition periods were to be few and short (though there were exceptions to this general rule as, for instance, the derogation on movement of people requested by existing member states). For areas where considerable adaptations were necessary, and which required substantial effort (including large monetary outlays) such as the environment, energy and infrastructure, transition periods involving 'temporary derogations' were to be granted, but in some areas (nuclear safety, the fight against crime) the new members were expected to go 'beyond the *acquis*'.

The new member states criticized the Commission's attitude to the adoption of the *acquis* on a number of counts:

- The asymmetry of treatment compared with existing EU members (e.g. the Nice or Lisbon Treaties do not require respect for minorities, while the Copenhagen criteria do);

- The CEECs were given little opportunity to voice objections to the conditions, and their preferences seemed to be marginalized at times (while the EU(15) have on occasion challenged the overriding nature of the *acquis*);
- Taking on the *acquis* does not always further transition;
- The *acquis* is constantly evolving;
- The insistence on taking on all the *acquis* might divert attention from the need for a hierarchy of priorities.

Extending EU policies to the new member states

As explained in the relevant chapters, the EU enlargements of 2004 and 2007 posed particular challenges for the EU budget, economic and social cohesion, the CAP, EMU and labour movement.

Despite the recognition that enlargement would require additional transfers from the EU budget, the main contributors to the budget (and Germany, in particular, after having to meet the bill for German unification) were reluctant to raise the ceiling of the financial perspective, which was fixed at 1.05 per cent of GNI for the 2007–2013 period. As explained in Chapter 11, the main casualty of this financial stringency was the Lisbon Agenda. Although they have been growing faster than the EU(15) since the mid-1990s (see also Chapter 15), Table 20.4 shows that in all the CEECs the per capita income in terms of purchasing power standards

	Growth	GDP per capita in PPS# 2006	Population 2007 million	Agriculture as % GDP 2005	Employment in Agriculture, Fishing and Forestry (1000s) 2005	Ag. as % total employment 2005	Un-employ-ment	Inflation
BG	6.1	37	7.7	7.2	280	9.3	9.0	7.4
CZ	6.4	79	10.2	1.0	195	4.1	7.1	2.1
EE	11.2	68	13.4	1.9	35	5.8	5.9	4.4
CY	3.8	93	0.8	2.5	16	4.5	4.6	2.2
LT	11.9	56	2.3	2.2	130	12.6	6.8	6.6
LI	7.7	58	3.4	2.9	218	14.8	5.6	3.8
HU	3.9	65	10.1	2.7	187	4.8	7.5	4.0
MA	3.2	76	0.4	1.3	3	1.7	7.3	2.6
PL	6.1	53	38.1	2.5	2386	17.1	13.8	1.3
RO	7.7	38	21.7	8.0	3048	32.8	7.3	6.6
SL	5.7	89	2.0	1.8	83	8.9	6.0	2.5
SK	8.5	64	5.4	1.2	108	4.9	13.4	4.3
EU(15)	2.8	112	391.7	1.3	6180	3.7	7.7	2.2**

TABLE 20.4 Selected economic indicators for 2006 (unless otherwise indicated) for the member states that joined the EU in 2004 and 2007 (percentage)
*EU(25)
** EU(27)
# purchasing power standards EU(27) = 100
f = forecast
Source: Eurostat, © European Communities, 2008, www.epp.eurostat.ec.europa.eu

(PPS) is well below the EU average. Following enlargement the gap between the most and the least prosperous member states widened. The average GDP per capita was reduced with the increase in the number of member states from 15 to 27. As a result, if the criterion (GDP less than 75 per cent of the EU average) for Objective 1 had remained unchanged, some regions that previously qualified for Objective 1 status would no longer do so in an enlarged EU. This was the case for four regions in Eastern Germany, four in the UK, four in Spain, and one each in Greece, Italy and Portugal. It is estimated that some 19 million people in the EU(15) lived in such regions. Certain of the EU(15) member states were concerned about a reduction in their transfers for economic and social cohesion as a result of this 'statistical effect' of enlargement. To meet these fears a phasing-out system (see Chapter 15) was therefore adopted for regions that would have been eligible for funding if the threshold had been calculated for EU(15) rather than EU(25).

The new member states were allocated 50.5 per cent of total spending on economic and social cohesion for the 2007–2013 period. This represents a substantial increase both compared with the pre-accession assistance and the temporary arrangements for the 2004–2006 period reflecting the fact that in deciding the financial allocation for 2007–2013, ten of the new member states had voting power in the Council of Ministers.

Agriculture frequently threatened to prove a stumbling block in the enlargement process. Agriculture continues to play an important role in many of the CEECs, both in terms of share in employment and contribution to GDP (see Table 20.4). At the same time, the CAP continues to absorb just under half of the Community budget, while food and agricultural measures account for roughly half the *acquis communautaire*. The new member states had the complex task of adapting to EU policies and standards, while the EU(15) wanted to ensure that enlargement did not result in excessive transfers from the Community budget.

As described in Chapter 12, the 1992 MacSharry Reform, the 1999 Berlin Agreement and the June 2003 reform entailed cuts in support prices for some of the main Community products. The impact of these price cuts for farmers in the EU(15) was (more or less, see Chapter 12) offset by direct income payments. Direct aids accounted for over 69 per cent of the CAP budget in 2005. As explained in Chapter 12, the European Commission maintained that full, immediate payment of direct income support in the CEECs would have inequitable income effects. The solution was to phase in direct payments gradually so that full application of the system would not take place until 2013. Even partial payments of EU direct income support has led to substantial increases in farm incomes in some of these countries.

As land prices were lower in many CEEC countries, a general derogation on land ownership of seven years, with the option of extending the derogation for a further three years, was also agreed for the CEECs (12 years for Poland).

As described in Chapter 10, enlargement will further complicate the already cumbersome decision-making institutions of the European Central Bank (ECB) and add to the complexity of the division of responsibility between the ECB, Ecofin, the Eurogroup and national governments.

The Maastricht criterion on exchange rates entails that a country should remain within the 'normal' band of the exchange rate mechanism (ERM 2) without tension and without initiating depreciation for two years. For the new member states, this meant that full participation in the third stage of EMU had to wait for two years after joining the EU since they were not allowed to join the ERM 2 before they become EU members. Slovenia adopted the euro in 2007 and Cyprus and Malta joined in 2008. However, pressure for reducing government spending and relatively high inflation has meant that other new member states (such as Hungary and the Czech Republic) have had to postpone their plans for joining the euro. Even without participating fully in the third stage of EMU, with enlargement the new member states will have to accept the EMU *acquis*, which includes respect of the Stability and Growth Pact; treatment of the exchange rate and of other economic policies as a matter of 'common concern'; liberalization of capital movements; and independence of the central bank.

As explained in Chapter 8, although labour movement from the new member states was predicted to be on a manageable scale, after the 2004 and 2007 enlargements the EU applied transition periods of two plus three years, renewable for a further two on workers coming from the new CEEC member states. During this time the EC member states continue to apply their differing policies with regard to access to their labour markets for workers from the CEEC member states.

According the European Commission, since enlargement the efforts to tackle crime and corruption in Bulgaria and Romania have proved insufficient. As a condition for membership the two countries had to accept a system under which the Commission monitored efforts of the public sector and the judiciary to eliminate crime and corruption. In February 2008 the Commission maintained that progress was too slow, but so far the EU has not exercised the right granted until December 2008 to impose punitive measures such as withholding funds for agriculture or social and economic cohesion.

There have at times been tensions between 'old' and 'new' member states as, for instance, over the Service Directive and that on Posted Workers (see Chapter 6), the derogations for labour movement (see Chapter 8), the interpretation of the Maastricht inflation criterion for Lithuania in 2007 (Chapter 10), and the bargaining tactics over the Lisbon Treaty of the Polish Government (Chapter 3).

EU policy towards the Western Balkans

The EU generally uses the term 'Western Balkans' to refer to Croatia and FYR Macedonia (which are candidates for EU accession), and other countries with potential candidate status: Albania, Bosnia/Herzegovina, Montenegro, Serbia and Kosovo. South-Eastern Europe (SEE) is generally taken to refer to the Western Balkan countries and the two EU member states, Bulgaria and Romania.

The poor long-term economic performance of the Western Balkans has been compounded by the series of wars that resulted from the disintegration of Yugoslavia. The instability in the Western Balkans also imposes costs on the EU in terms of military intervention, migration, trade disruption, ecological damage and the need for humanitarian and other aid. Between 1991 and 1999 EU assistance (including EBRD measures) to the five Western Balkan countries amounted to €8.2 billion, of which roughly half was humanitarian aid (Uvalic, 2002).

Initially the EU underestimated the political problems arising from the collapse of Yugoslavia and failed to develop a long-term strategy towards the area, relying instead on *ad hoc* measures and 'day after' actions. It was only after the Dayton Peace Agreement of 1995 that the EU began to evolve a regional approach to SEE. In 1995 the EU launched the Royaumont Process aimed at promoting stability and good neighbourly relations in SEE. In 1996 the Regional Approach of the EU was introduced, but it was not well defined, had limited financial resources, arrived late, and failed to offer the SEE counties any incentive for compliance.

In 1999 the EU attempted to bring an end to its crisis-by-crisis approach by introducing the Stability Pact, which aimed at fostering peace, democracy, human rights and economic prosperity as a means of bringing stability to the region. Importantly, the EU attempted to reinforce its leverage in SEE by offering the prospect of eventual EU membership. The EU insisted that its approach would be differentiated according with the compliance of a country to the relevant conditions, including increased emphasis on regional co-operation.[20] Central to the approach was the Stabilization and Association Process that offered eligible West Balkan countries the possibility of signing Stabilization and Association Agreements (SAAs).

The Thessaloniki European Council and the Summit between the EU and Balkan countries of 2003 set out the 'Thessaloniki Approach', which entailed extending some of the more successful instruments of the pre-accession process to the SEE countries. In particular, European Partnerships were introduced to set out the short- and medium-term priorities these countries need to address. Over time it was expected that these Partnerships would be increasingly geared to the task of taking on the *acquis*. Annual Progress Reports monitor progress in these countries and the European Commission also publishes an annual Enlargement Strategy paper.

European Union assistance to the Western Balkans was provided mainly through the CARDS (Community Assistance for Reconstruction, Development and Stabilization) Programme over the 2000–06 period, and about €5 billion was earmarked for this purpose. From 2007 all pre-accession support was unified into a single instrument, the IPA or Instrument for Pre-Accession Assistance (see Table 20.5). This covers both the candidate countries and countries with potential candidate status. The IPA covers: transition assistance and institution building; cross-border co-operation; regional development; human resources development and rural development.

Turning to individual countries, Albania signed an SAA with the EU in 2006. The 2007 Progress Report called for a strengthening of democratic culture and constructive dialogue between parties, and further efforts in the fight against corruption. The economy was considered to suffer from shortcomings in infrastructure (in particular for energy), shortages in skilled labour and a widening external deficit.

For many years as an autonomous province within Serbia and as part of the former Yugoslavia, Kosovo enjoyed a considerable degree of autonomy, but this was ended by the Milosevic regime in 1989. After years of mainly non-violent protest, conflict erupted in 1998/9. In 1999 NATO intervened on humanitarian grounds to end ethnic cleansing of Albanian Kosovars and wide-scale displacement of the civilian population. Institutional arrangements in Kosovo are covered by United Nations Security Resolution (UNSCR) 1244, which established an interim civilian administration United Nations Mission in Kosovo (UNMIK). The constitutional framework divided responsibilities between UNMIK and the provisional institutions of self-government pending a final settlement.

United States Special envoy, Martti Ahtisaari, spent a year trying to negotiate a settlement, but Serbia was determined to reassert sovereignty over Kosovo, while the 90 per cent Albanian Kosovars insisted on independence. In March 2007 Ahtisaari presented a comprehensive proposal to the UN Security Council, maintaining that 'supervised independence' was the only viable option. The Security Council began considering a draft resolution, which would endorse this proposal, but Russia backed Serbia and threatened a Security Council veto. The Albanian Kosovar Government announced that it would declare independence even without a UN resolution. This would involve inviting the peace-keeping forces of NATO to stay on, and asking the EU to send a supervisory mission, as proposed by the Ahtisaari plan. Russia warned that a declaration of independence not backed by a UN resolution set a dangerous precedent for international law. Russia did, however, allay fears that there would be consequences for breakaway regions in the former Soviet Union, such as Abkhazia, South Ossetia and Transdnestr. While the

---

[20]Regional co-operation has led to the creation of Regional Co-operation Council, based in Sarajevo, the Transport Observatory in Belgrade, the Sava River Commission in Zagreb, and the Regional Centre of the Migration, Asylum, and Refugees Regional Initiative, in Skopje. Other initiatives include the Black Sea Economic Co-operation, (BSEC), including Russia and Turkey, the Adriatic-Ionian Initiative (AII) with the participation of all seven countries bordering these seas, and the South-East Europe Co-operation Process (SEECP).

Pre-accession assistance € million	2007	2008	2009	2010	2011	2007–2011
Albania	61.0	70.7	81.2	93.2	95.0	401.1
Bosnia/Herzegovina	62.1	74.8	89.1	106.0	108.1	440.1
Montenegro	31.4	32.6	33.3	34.0	34.7	166.0
Serbia	189.7	190.9	194.8	198.7	202.7	976.8
Kosovo	68.3	124.7	66.1	67.3	68.7	395.1
Total	412.5	493.7	464.5	499.2	509.2	2379.1

TABLE 20.5 EU Financial Assistance under the Instrument for Pre-Accession Assistance (IPA) for Potential Candidate Countries
Source: Website of European Commission DG Enlargement, © European Communities, 2008, www.ec.europa.eu/enlargement

USA and many EU member states were prepared to recognize an independent Kosovo, others such as Cyprus, Spain, Romania and Slovakia feared knock-on effects for unilateral separatist movements.

In February 2008 the EU agreed the financial and legal apparatus for a mission in which 1800 policemen, judges, prosecutors and customs officials would be sent to bolster stability in Kosovo after independence. The initiative was attacked by Russia on the grounds that any changes to the presence of the international community required a UN Security Council mandate. On February 18 2008 Kosovo declared independence. Serbs (including those in Kosovo) protested against this unilateral declaration of independence of what was traditionally an integral part of Serbia, maintaining that it ran counter to international law, and that they were being punished for the acts of Milosovic.

The conclusion of an SAA with Serbia is conditional on co-operation with the International Criminal Tribunal on the former Yugoslavia (ICTY), including the transfer of all remaining fugitives (including Ratko Mladic, the Bosnian Serb former commander accused of ordering the 1995 Srebrenica massacre) to The Hague. The 2007 Progress Report of the Commission noted the new Constitution of 2006, and parliamentary elections, but criticized the slow pace of judicial reform, corruption, the need to enforce human rights and reduce ethnic tensions, and differences with the EU over Kosovo. Following the election of the pro-EU Boris Tadic in 2008, the EU offered a more limited co-operation agreement, but tensions over Kosovo led to doubts whether this would be signed.

In 1995 the Dayton Peace Agreement brought an end to the 1992–1995 war in Bosnia and Herzegovina. The Agreement created two entities within the state of Bosnia and Herzegovina: the Bosniak/Croat Federation of Bosnia and Herzegovina, and the Bosnian Serb-led Republica Srpska. In accordance with the Dayton Peace Agreement, a UN-mandated office of the High Representative, who was also EU Special Representative, was created in order to restore peace in Bosnia and oversee implementation of civilian aspects of the Agreement. According to the EU, the authorities of Bosnia and Herzegovina have not demonstrated the capacity to take further political ownership and responsibility from the High Representative/EU Special Representative so closure of this office was postponed until June 2008 and is to be reviewed in 2008. The EU also provided aid and a peacekeeping force. Negotiations on an SAA with Bosnia and Herzegovina began in 2005, but its conclusion depends on the fulfilment of four conditions: police reform, full co-operation with the ICTY, and reform of public broadcasting and of public administration. According to the European Commission, further economic reform was necessary, in particular, to reduce the role of the public sector; overcome rigidities in the labour market and strengthen consensus on the fundamentals of economic policy. There were fears that the declaration of independence of Kosovo could cause tensions or even the disintegration of Bosnia and Herzegovina.

In May 2006, in line with the provisions of Article 60 of the Constitutional Charter of Serbia and Montenegro, Montenegro held a referendum on independence. Fifty-five and a half per cent of voters were in favour of independence, which was declared in June 2006. Montenegro signed an SAA with the EU in 2007. According to the 2007 Progress report, despite a certain success in establishing the necessary legal framework and institutions after independence, further progress was necessary in judicial and administrative reform, in fighting corruption and in dealing with the conditions of refugees and displaced persons, including the Roma.

Croatia

Croatia formally applied for EU membership in February 2003, and following a favourable Opinion by the European Commission, Croatia was granted candidate status by the European Council in June 2004. Screening began in October 2005, and formal accession negotiations began in June 2006.

In 2001 an SAA was signed and entered into force in February 2005. It is the legal framework for relations between the EU and Croatia during the pre-accession period and covers areas such as: political dialogue; regional co-operation; the four freedoms, with the creation of a free trade area by 2007 for industrial products and most agricultural products; approximation of Croatian legislation to the community *acquis*; and wide-ranging co-operation in all areas of Community policies. It is hoped that implementation of the SAA will help Croatia fulfil the Copenhagen criteria for EU membership. In December 2002 Croatia adopted the first 'National Programme for the Integration of the Republic of Croatia' as a roadmap for legal harmonization and this became the main co-ordinating instrument in preparing for EU membership.

In the case of Croatia, the political conditions for EU membership cover issues such as: facilitating the return of refugees, human rights (including minority rights), reform of the judiciary, the fight against crime and corruption, public administration reform, co-operation with the International Criminal Tribunal on the former Yugoslavia (ICTY), and regional co-operation with other countries in the Western Balkans region.[21] The economic criteria for EU membership do not seem to have posed particular problems for Croatia though, for instance, in 2007 the Regular Report of the European Commission noted the risk of rising external imbalances and slow progress in structural reforms of industries such as shipbuilding and steel.[22]

In contrast the political criteria have at times created difficulties. Issues such as refugee return and human rights and respect for democratic institutions meant that the EU was unwilling to negotiate the SAA with Croatia under the Croatian Democratic Union led by President Tudjman, and negotiations began only after he left office. The EU also interpreted Croatia's failure to deliver General Ante Gotovina to the Hague Tribunal as failure to respect the Copenhagen political criteria, and the European Council of March 2005 decided to postpone the start of accession negotiations. These negotiations only began in October 2005 after General Gotovina had been handed over to the ICTY, and during the course of 2005 support for EU membership as measured in opinion polls of the Croatian population fell substantially.[23] Croatia is also concerned that the

---

[21] This conditionality was also applied in the negotiation of the SAA.

[22] European Commission (2007a).

[23] See, for instance, Eurobarometer surveys of Croatia.

	2007	**2008**	**2009**	**2010**	**2011**	**Total 2007-2011**
Croatia	141.2	146.0	151.2	154.2	157.2	749.8
FYR Macedonia	58.5	70.2	81.8	92.3	98.7	401.5
Turkey	497.2	538.7	566.4	653.7	781.9	3037.9
Total	696.9	754.9	799.4	900.2	1037.8	4189.2

TABLE 20.6 EU Financial Assistance under the Instrument for Pre-Accession Assistance (IPA) for the Candidate Countries

Source: Website of European Commission DG Enlargement, © European Communities, 2008, www.ec.europa.eu/enlargement

pace of its accession negotiations will not be linked to those of Turkey, but is the only country expected to join the EU before 2013.

As a candidate country Croatia benefited from the three pre-accession instruments – PHARE, ISPA and SAPARD – and from the CARDS regional programme up until 2006, but from 2007 the IPA replaced these instruments (see Table 20.6).

The former Yugoslav Republic of Macedonia

The Former Yugoslav Republic of Macedonia applied for EU membership in 2004, received a favourable Opinion from the Commission in November 2005, and obtained candidate status in December 2005. An SAA was signed in 2001 and entered into force in 2004. The Ohrid Framework Agreement of 2001 aims at contributing to the consolidation of democracy and the rule of law, in particular, by ensuring equitable representation of the country's ethnic communities in public administration, and transferring more responsibility to local communities.

According to the 2007 Regular Report,[24] some progress has been made in the implementation of the Ohrid Agreement, and in judicial reform and the fight against corruption. However, political tensions were said to be delaying reforms. The Report called for dialogue between parties in the Parliament to be conducted in a more constructive manner, with all political stakeholders playing the role envisaged by the Constitution. This is considered necessary to further essential progress in areas such as the police, judiciary, consolidation of the rule of law, respect for minorities and fight against corruption. The economy was said to be moving towards fulfilment of the Copenhagen criteria, though unemployment was high, and institutional weakness was hampering the functioning of a market economy. According to the 2007 Report, the judiciary was unable to guarantee legal certainty, and labour markets were functioning poorly.

Turkey

A brief chronology of relations between the EU and Turkey is provided as Appendix 1 to this Chapter, but it is useful to recall certain events in the enlargement process here; then the prin-

---

[24]European Commission (2007b).

cipal arguments put forward in favour and against Turkish membership of the EU will then be discussed.[25] A short account of the Cyprus issue is provided in Appendix 2 to this Chapter.

At the Brussels European Council of December 2004 it was agreed that Turkey could start accession negotiations with the EU from 3 October 2005. The negotiations are likely to prove lengthy with 2015 being mentioned as the earliest expected date for accession. The Conclusions of the European Council also refer to the possibility of long transition periods, derogations, and specific arrangements or safeguard clauses. These could cover areas such as freedom of movement of persons, economic and social cohesion and agriculture.

The European Council reiterated the 1999 Helsinki conclusions that Turkey was a candidate destined to join the EU on the basis of the same criteria applied to other countries. However, it called for more progress in political and economic reforms. As a condition for opening negotiations Turkey was required to introduce six pieces of legislation enhancing human rights and the functioning of the judiciary, and sign the Adaptation Protocol extending its existing SAA with the EU to all new Member States, including the Republic of Cyprus. This created difficulties as Turkey recognizes only the Turkish Republic of Northern Cyprus (TRNC). The compromise eventually agreed was a verbal declaration that Turkey would extend its SAA with the EU to all new member states, including the Republic of Cyprus before beginning accession negotiations.

At the December 2004 European Council, the Greek Cypriots were isolated and were persuaded not to veto the possibility of Turkish accession. However, the President of the Republic of Cyprus, Tassos Papadopoulos, announced that he had 64 opportunities to veto Turkish accession: at the beginning and end of the accession negotiation process and before opening or closing each of the then 31 chapters of the *acquis*. Austria announced that it would hold a referendum on Turkish EU membership, and France would probably also do so.

In June 2006 Turkish accession negotiations began. However, the November 2006 Regular Report criticized Turkey for letting the pace of reforms slow and Turkey was given a month to open its ports and airports to Greek Cypriots. Turkey argued this should be part of a package with the EU fulfilling its promise to help end the isolation of northern Cyprus (see Appendix 2 to this Chapter). Under the Finnish Presidency there was an attempt to broker a deal,[26] but agreement was not reached and in December 2006 EU foreign ministers decided to suspend negotiations on 8 out of 35 chapters of the *acquis*. The suspended chapters related to the failure to recognize the Republic of Cyprus (the customs union, free movement of goods, transport, agriculture, fishing, external relations, and financial services). In practice the Greek Cypriots had effectively blocked negotiations since June 2006. Olli Rehn, the Enlargement Commissioner, maintained that a 'train crash' had been avoided, and negotiations on other chapters of the *acquis* continued. In 2007 six new chapters were opened.

The 2007 Regular Report on Turkey called for further progress in protecting the rights of non-Muslim religious communities and freedom of expression.[27] Article 301 of the criminal code

---

[25] See the Regular Reports of the European Commission on Turkey, and Hughes (2004) for more detailed discussions of these issues.

[26] According to the Finnish proposal, the port of Famagusta in the North would come under EU management and be opened for trade with the rest of the EU; the UN would take charge of the ghost tourist town of Varosha in the North, and access for the original Greek owners would be allowed; Turkey would have to include the Republic of Cyprus in its customs union and open ports. In response the Turkish government sent an informal transcript offering to open one major port and one airport provisionally for a year as part of a package in which the EU would back the goals of reaching a comprehensive settlement and reduce the isolation of northern Cyprus. However, the office of the then Turkish President, Sezer, said that it had not been informed of the offer and the army complained about it. The EU rejected the Turkish offer as inadequate (too vague and conditional).

[27] European Commission (2007c).

relating to 'denigration of Turkishness, the Republic and state organs and institutions' has been used against journalists and writers (such as Orhan Pamuk, the Nobel prize winner) for mentioning sensitive topics such as the Armenian massacres and the Kurdish question. The Regular Report also noted an increase in terrorist attacks by the PKK (Kurdistan Workers' Party), called for improvements in the fight against corruption, the judicial system, trade union rights, the rights of women and children, cultural rights and civilian oversight of the military.

As shown in Table 20.5 above, from 2007 EU pre-accession instruments to assist Turkey were replaced with the IPA.

One of the main reasons in favour of Turkish EU membership is that Turkey formally applied for EC membership in 1987, and was put off for a long time, so a further refusal could create disillusion with the EU, and might jeopardize the reform process in Turkey. Encouraged by the prospect of EU membership, Turkey has introduced a series of packages of radical political reforms, including:

- increased civilian control over the army;
- reform of the judiciary;
- attempts at more respect for human and minority rights;
- attempts to eliminate torture and ill-treatment in prisons;
- abolition of the death penalty;
- greater protection of freedom of expression, association and the media;
- improved treatment of the Kurdish minority.

The statesman, Mustafa Kemal Atatürk (1880–1938) left Turkey with the tradition of a modern secular state. Many members of the establishment see EU membership as a means of extending this goal. However, others, including certain elements of the military and nationalists, object to the extent of EU leverage over what are considered internal Turkish matters. Although the Turkish Government had pushed for a settlement to the Cyprus issue, the fact that it was being placed under pressure to recognize the Greek Cypriot Republic of Cyprus also caused resentment in some circles. Member of the secular élites were used to being those associated with the reform process and many remain sceptical of the Islamic leanings of the governing AKP party. A 'no' to EU membership could place the Erdogan Government with its record for delivering reforms at risk.

Turkish accession could increase security in an unstable part of the world. Turkey has borders with countries such as Syria, Iraq, Iran, Armenia and Georgia. With its large Muslim population, and tradition of a secular state, there are strong geostrategic reasons for encouraging the political and economic stability of Turkey. Turkey is a long-standing NATO member, so there may be an interest in including Turkey in EU initiatives relating to defence and foreign policy.

Against this, the principal reasons given against EU membership are that Turkey is too big in terms of population (see Table 20.1, p. 466), too poor and agricultural, still has to make much progress in political and economic reform, is too Muslim and would fundamentally change the nature of the EU and undermine the momentum of the integration process. Concerns are also expressed about the treatment of the Kurdish minority.

According to forecasts of the UN World Population Division, Turkey would have a population of 82 million in 2015, but this would rise to 87 million by 2025, making Turkey the largest member of the EU. The fears associated with having such a large new member state in terms of population relate to the possibility of labour migration (though a derogation would probably be applied), the weight of Turkey in EU decision-making, and the change in nature of the EU. However, the fast-growing Turkish population (with about half the population under 25) could help to resolve the problem of ageing in the EU.

Evaluation and outlook for an enlarging EU

Though the EU was slow to respond to the requests of the CEECs for membership, there were few illusions that transition and preparing for accession could prove other than lengthy and complex. Many aspects of transition (such as those relating to infrastructure, energy, the environment, human capital, social capital and institution building) will have to continue long after enlargement.

Though an enlargement on the scale of that of 2004 has never been attempted, it seems set to become simply one in an ongoing process. In addition to the accession of Bulgaria and Romania in 2007, Croatia and Macedonia and Turkey are candidate countries, though only Croatia is expected to join in the near future. As part of the Stability and Association Process, other countries of the Western Balkans have been granted potential candidate status. The Wider Europe or European Neighbourhood Policy foresees tighter links with eastern and southern neighbours, and even if the prospect of enlargement has been ruled out for the present, eventual enlargement or at least some kind of privileged relationship cannot be indefinitely excluded for at least some of these countries.

In 2008, largely at the instigation of French President, Sarkozy, a reflection group of independent experts (or wise men's committee) was set up under the former Spanish Prime Minister, Gonzales, to study the future of the EU until as far ahead as 2020–2030, but the group was not given an explicit mandate to decide where the ultimate borders of the EU should be as this was considered too divisive.

With regard to EU widening, the case of Turkey is undoubtedly the most contentious, sparking intense differences in opinion. It is difficult to pretend that accession will not pose difficulties for the EU, given the size of the Turkish population, the overwhelmingly Muslim population, the level of GDP per capita and the share of agriculture in the economy. Against this, the urgent need to provide security in such an unstable corner of the globe could prove overriding. The prospect of EU membership has encouraged the Turkish government to undertake an active policy of democratization, and there are strong reasons for continuing this process. Similar arguments apply for many of the countries in South-Eastern Europe, though at least in some cases the relatively smaller size of these countries means that fewer problems are posed for the EU. With previous enlargements (and those of 1973 and with the Mediterranean countries, in particular) there were fears that larger membership would profoundly change the nature of the Community. Is this still the case, and what kind of changes can be expected?

The fear of deadlock of decision-making with enlargement has led to the main energies and efforts of the EU being absorbed by the debate on institutional reform for many years. First the inconclusive Amsterdam and Nice Treaties, and then the long process of evolution of first the Constitutional Treaty, and later the Lisbon Treaty, have been at the centre of the debate on the future of the EU for some time. The Lisbon Treaty still requires ratification, but most countries (with the notable exception of Ireland, whose Constitution requires a referendum) have opted for the supposedly smoother path of ratification by national parliaments.

It seems likely that, despite the Irish 'no' vote in 2008, some version, or at least certain aspects of the Lisbon Treaty will eventually come into force, but how much difference will it make? To date decisions in the EU have generally been taken on the basis of consensus, and this seems to be the case even after the 2004 and 2007 enlargements. Even on issues where qualified majority voting is foreseen in the Council, votes are rarely taken and efforts are made to find a compromise. In a larger EU confrontational politics will probably be more difficult to avoid, and efforts to find a compromise could lead to a slowing of the integration process. There may be a shift to more application of the QMV rule, but even after the Nice or Lisbon Treaty, various sensitive policy areas remain subject to unanimity. Confrontational tactics could lead to a return to situations like the Empty Chair Crisis of 1965 or the eurosclerosis of the 1970s.

However, eurosclerosis 30 years later would be a different animal. The *acquis* has grown, and achievements like the Single Market and the euro seem irreversible, though less stringent application of, for example, competition or industrial policy (which is possible with the growing tendency to promote national champions) could erode some of the advantages. The tasks of the ECB have become more complex with the turbulence of financial markets following the US sub-prime mortgage crisis. In particular, differing traditions of regulation in the member states have rendered the task of strengthening financial supervision difficult.

Member states will continue to benefit from the advantages of a larger market with more price transparency, but the aim of the Lisbon Strategy is to move beyond this and create a knowledge-based economy of world quality reference by 2010. The date 2010 is drawing closer, and we do not seem much nearer this aim. Part of the difficulty is that the Lisbon goals are disparate and also rely on the efforts of national governments and private business for their realization. Insufficient resources are still devoted to education and research, and to reaching the goals of the European Employment Strategy, which include increasing employment, the improving the quality of work and more social cohesion.

One of the main aims of the 2007–13 financial perspective was to give these goals a higher priority. However, the member states that are net contributors to the EU budget opposed any increase in spending (and, indeed, its share of GNI was reduced for the 2007–2013 period). The Lisbon Strategy was the main casualty of tighter EU budgetary stringency.

The October 2002 European Council precluded the possibility of releasing substantial resources from the CAP for other spending before 2013. There have been calls for radical cuts, if not the elimination of the CAP, from some quarters. However, as argued in Chapter 12, there are well-founded reasons for public intervention in agriculture. The public has repeatedly expressed a strong preference for safe and high-quality food and a healthy environment. Though there is still space for improvement in gearing policy to these objectives, the CAP has been radically transformed by the 1992, 1999 and 2003 reforms. Goals such as food safety and protection of the environment are not achieved cheaply, but there may be an argument for shifting more of the burden to national governments, with a partial renationalization of the CAP.

Since the scope for increased spending on economic and social cohesion is also limited, the emphasis will have to be on increasing the effectiveness of measures. Many of the new member states would like to repeat the Irish experience, which, as argued in Chapter 15, was partly due to the Structural Funds. However, when Ireland joined it was the only poor member state, and now there are many.

One of the main challenges for the EU remains establishing its democratic legitimacy. When consulted in referenda or opinion polls the people of Europe have frequently expressed negative opinions of the integration process (as, for instance, the Danish and Swedish votes against the euro; the Irish vote on the Nice and Lisbon Treaties, or the French and Dutch votes on the Constitutional Treaty). Even if the Lisbon Treaty is ratified, as anyone who has attempted to consult it can verify, the proposed Treaty has severe limits as an attempt to 'sell Europe' to its citizens. As Siedentop (2000, p. 1) argues, ongoing debate about the future of the EU is the only way to convince Europeans that 'what is happening in Europe today is not merely the result of inexorable market forces or the machinations of élites, which have escaped from democratic control'.

New forms of privileged relationships with neighbouring countries will probably be set up. Given the energy dependency of the EU a better working relationship will have to be evolved with its increasingly prickly neighbour, Russia. The conflictual co-operation with the USA seems likely to continue, but more dialogue and an improved institutional framework could help to reduce the scope for disputes. The EU will also have to intensify its efforts if the Millennium Goals are to be met.

Clearly prescriptions concerning the future of the EU are beyond the present scope, but further forms of flexibility, or enhanced co-operation, will have to emerge. They will probably do so in the time-honoured, piecemeal EU method of reaching compromises and allowing exceptions. Grand designs for Europe invariably have to be whittled down and adjusted so that one size is stretched into shape to fit all.

Summary of Key Concepts

- In May 2004 10 countries joined the EU: Cyprus, the Czech Republic, Estonia, Hungary, Latvia, Lithuania, Malta, Poland, Slovakia and Slovenia. Bulgaria and Romania joined in 2007, and Turkey, Croatia and the former Yugoslav Republic of Macedonia are candidate countries. The EU is considering the possibility of further enlargements to countries in the Western Balkans, which could eventually include Bosnia and Herzegovina, Serbia, Kosovo, Montenegro and Albania.

- According to the **theory of clubs**, the optimal size of membership occurs when marginal costs and marginal benefits to incumbent members are equal. The theory yields insights, but in practice is difficult to apply to the EU.

- The PHARE Programme that came into operation from 1990 was initially demand-driven, and based on the requests of the recipient countries. From 1993 PHARE became increasing concerned with preparing CEECs for accession. PHARE was one of the three **pre-accession instruments** for the 2000–2006 period. The other two instruments were ISPA and SAPARD. These were replaced in the 2007–2013 period by the IPA or Instrument for Pre-Accession Assistance.

- Western assistance to the transition countries was different from the Marshall Plan. Post-war reconstruction is very different from transition, while the co-ordination problems were fewer, the scale of financing was higher and the conditionality was tighter under the Marshall Plan.

- The **Copenhagen criteria** for accession set out in 1993 are: a functioning market economy with the capacity to cope with competitive pressures and market forces within the Community; stability of institutions guaranteeing democracy, the rule of law, human rights and respect for and protection of minorities; and ability to take on the obligations of membership, including adherence to the aims of political, and economic and monetary union. It was also stipulated that enlargement is subject to the condition that the EU is able to absorb new members and maintain the momentum of integration.

- Difficulties arise in applying the Copenhagen criteria because of the number of criteria and, in some cases, the vague and imprecise nature of the concepts involved.

- European Union policy towards the **Western Balkans** covers countries with potential candidate status: Albania, Bosnia/Herzegovina, Montenegro, Serbia and Kosovo. In 1999 the EU introduced the Stabilization and Association process, which offered eligible West Balkan countries the possibility of signing Stabilization and Association Agreements and eventual EU membership.

- **Croatia** is the only country expected to join the EU in the near future.

- **The former Yugoslav Republic (FYR) of Macedonia** obtained candidate status in December 2005.

- **Turkey** started accession negotiations with the EU in October 2005, but the negotiations are likely to prove lengthy with 2015 being mentioned as the earliest expected date for accession. Even with membership, long transition periods, derogations and specific arrangements are likely for areas such as freedom of movement of persons, economic and social cohesion and agriculture.

- One of the main reasons in favour of Turkish EU membership is that Turkey formally applied for EC membership in 1987, and was put off for a long time, so a further refusal could create disillusion with the EU, and might jeopardize the reform process in Turkey. Turkish accession could also increase security in an unstable part of the world.

- The principal reasons given against EU membership are that Turkey is too big in terms of population, too poor and agricultural, still has to make much progress in political and economic reform, is too Muslim and would fundamentally change the nature of the EU and undermine the momentum of the integration process. Concerns are also expressed about the treatment of the Kurdish minority.

Questions for study and review

1 What criticisms can be made of Western measures to assist transition?

2 How far can Western measures to facilitate transition be considered a new Marshall Plan?

3 Discuss the conditionality applied by the EU in its dealings with the CEECs.

4 Describe the main features of the Europe agreements.

5 When the CEECs joined the EU, they passed from a free trade area to membership of the Single Market. What does this imply?

6 What criticisms can be made of the Copenhagen criteria?

7 Describe the main features and limitations of the policy of the EU towards the Western Balkans.

8 Why did the accession of Cyprus to the EU create difficulties (see Appendix 2)?

9 What are the arguments advanced in favour of and against Turkey joining the EU?

10 Where do you consider that the boundaries of the EU should end?

11 What is your view of the future of an enlarged EU?

Appendix 1

EU–Turkish Relations

Turkey became a member of the OECD in 1948, the Council of Europe in 1949 and NATO in 1952. It applied for Associate Membership of the EEC in 1959 (a few days after Greece), but following the coup in 1960, talks were suspended for two years.

In 1963 Turkey signed an Association Agreement, the Ankara Treaty, with the Community. Since being European is one of the conditions of Community membership, in 1963 the then President of the European Commission, Hallstein, ruled in favour of Turkey, announcing that it was 'part of Europe'. However, debate about the dual European and Muslim identities of Turkey and the implications for EU membership continues.

An Additional Protocol modified the Association Agreement in 1970 and called for the creation of a customs union by 1995. However, during the 1970s tensions arose over the 1974 Cyprus crisis and the Greek application of 1975 for full membership. In 1978 Turkey requested participation in European Political Co-operation (EPC) in order to prevent Greece using its position to hinder the development of tighter Turkish–EC relations. This request was rejected, and in 1978 Turkey issued a unilateral declaration freezing its relations with the EC. The military took over in Turkey in 1980, and relations with the EU remained suspended. Relations were resumed in 1986, leading to a reactivation of the Association Agreement from 1988.

Turkey presented a formal request for EU membership in 1987, and received a negative reply two years later. The official reason given by the Commission was the need to complete the Single Market Programme. In 1990 the EC implemented a package to improve relations with Turkey, which included financial and technical assistance and the creation of a customs union by 1995.

At the Luxembourg European Council of December 1997 Turkey was not even included among the slow-track countries being considered for EU accession. The Council decided to establish the European Conference, but Turkey refused to attend its first two meetings. In 1999 meetings were suspended, but were resumed with Turkish participation after the 1999 Helsinki European Council. At the 1999 Helsinki European Council Turkey was declared a candidate. The 2002 Copenhagen Summit agreed that a decision on whether Turkey was ready to join the EU would be taken in December 2004, and if so that negotiations would begin 'without delay'.

Appendix 2

The EU and Cyprus

Since 1974 the island of Cyprus has been divided into the Greek Republic of Cyprus and what in 1983 was declared the Turkish Republic of Northern Cyprus (TRNC), recognized only by Turkey.

Cyprus obtained its independence from Great Britain in 1960, and the Treaty of Guarantee placed the independence, territorial integrity and security of the island under the joint guarantee of Greece, Turkey and the UK. The Treaty envisaged a complex power-sharing arrangement and a bi-communal structure. The Turkish Cypriots claimed that representation in municipal authorities and the army failed to conform to planned ethnic proportions and began to exercise their veto rights. In 1963 President Makarios proposed constitutional amendments to reduce the opportunities for the Turkish Cypriots to block legislation, and there was a political crisis.

Intercommunal violence broke out, Turkish Cypriots moved into enclaves and withdrew from the common institutions.

In 1964 the UNFICYP (United Nations Peacekeeping Force in Cyprus) was established to prevent a recurrence of fighting and to contribute to the maintenance of law and order.

In 1974 the Greek junta staged a coup against President Archbishop Makarios and claimed annexation of Cyprus to Greece. Also committed to the protection of Cypriot independence, Turkey intervened on 20 July 1974. Two conferences were held in Geneva between Greece, Turkey and the UK, with the second also attended by Greek and Turkish Cypriots. The talks were inconclusive, and on 14 August the Turkish army launched a second offensive. According to the Greek Cypriots, this second invasion was not justified by the Treaty of Guarantee since the constitutional order had already been restored.

In 1974 Cyprus was divided by a 'Green Line', with the Turkish Cypriots holding almost 37 per cent of the island. In 1974 some 140 000–160 000 Greek Cypriots moved to the South, while an estimated 30 000–40 000 Turkish Cypriots fled to the North (Brewen, 2000). It is estimated that some 50 000 Turkish Cypriots left the island, while between 85 000 and 115 000 settlers (in particular from Anatolia) came over from the Turkish mainland, though the statistics are controversial.[28] A large Turkish force (estimated at 35 000) remained in Northern Cyprus.

The division of Cyprus left scars that are enduringly difficult to eradicate. Any proposed settlement of the Cyprus issue has a long list of questions to resolve, and these include:[29]

- The institutions of the federal state;
- The adjustments to the map of Cyprus;
- Movement of people after the adjustments to the map of Cyprus;
- Return of property or compensation payments;
- Resolution of the problem of people missing during the 1963–74 period;
- Progressive de-militarization, while at the same time guaranteeing the security of both communities on the island;
- The duration and shape of peacekeeping forces; and
- Improvement of trust and personal links across communities.

In 1990 the Republic of Cyprus applied for EC membership. In 1993 the EC Commission published its Opinion on application for EC membership, which appeared to make accession conditional on internal political settlement.

In 1994 Greece threatened to veto negotiations for a customs union between the EU and Turkey if Cyprus were not included in the next EU enlargement process, and at the 1997 Luxembourg European Council it was agreed to include Cyprus among the first-wave countries.

The EU continued to push for a settlement, but the Presidency Conclusions of the 1999 Helsinki European Council announced that 'if no settlement has been reached by the completion of accession negotiations, the Council's decision will be made without the above being a pre-condition'.

There have been numerous attempts by the UN to resolve the Cyprus issue. The most recent was that of November 2002 when the UN Secretary General, Kofi Annan, presented a detailed proposal to set up a Swiss-type confederation between the two parts of the island, which would also permit Northern Cyprus to join the EU. On 24 April 2004 a referendum was held in the

---

[28] The data here are taken from www.un.int/cyprus/cyissue.htm

[29] For a more detailed discussion of these issues see Senior Nello (2004).

two parts of the island over a revised version of the UN proposal. Had agreement been reached, the European Commission stated that the whole island could have acceded without any further need to renegotiate the terms of membership. However, although 65 per cent of Turkish Cypriots voted in favour of the proposal, it was rejected by 75.83 per cent of the Greek Cypriots. As a result, only the Greek Cypriot part of the island joined the EU in May 2004.

As their EU membership was assured, the Greek Cypriots were free to express their dissatisfaction with various aspects of the UN proposal or Annan Plan. Aside from resentment at a settlement being opposed from 'outside', the Greek Cypriots were concerned about security and the costs of reunification. They objected to the continued presence of what they considered too many Turkish troops and settlers in the North. The arrangements with regard to territorial adjustment and property were thought inadequate, and possibly many hoped for more favourable treatment by appealing to the European Court of Human Rights in Strasbourg. The Greek Cypriots also criticized the limits on their right to residence in the North.

Though the Turkish Cypriots also had misgivings about the Annan Plan, these were evidently overcome by the economic prosperity, end to isolation and stability EU accession promised.

The whole of the island is now considered to be part of the EU, but in the North EU legislation is suspended in line with protocol 10 of the Accession Treaty. These areas are therefore outside the customs and fiscal territory of the EU, though the personal rights of Turkish Cypriots as EU citizens are not affected.

In reaction to the referendum result, a General Affairs Council of April 26 2004 announced that measures would be introduced to end the isolation of the Turkish Cypriots. A Green Line Resolution was passed with the aim of making the Green Line as flexible as possible, with more border crossings being opened.

The Commission was also in favour of resuming direct flights to Northern Cyprus. Regulations on aid and direct trade were proposed. Goods certified by the Turkish Cypriot Chamber of Commerce were to be recognized and a wide variety of goods (including commodities, agricultural goods and fish) were to enter the South duty free. When the Republic of Cyprus became an EU member it blocked such measures, though eventually in 2006 the aid regulation was passed. The Greek Cypriots have resisted pressures to allow direct trade between North and South Cyprus on the pretext that if the Turkish Cypriots became more prosperous they would be less inclined to accept a settlement.

Following elections in 2008, the new President of the Republic of Cyprus, Demetris Christofias, agreed to meet his Turkish Cypriot counterpart, Mehmet Ali Talat for fully-fledged negotiations under the UN auspices, offering a new spiral of hope.

References

Alesina, A. and Spolaore, E. (2003) *The Size of Nations*, MIT Press, Cambridge, MA.

Brewen, C. (2000) *The European Union and Cyprus*, Eothen Press, Huntingdon, UK.

Buchanan, J.M. (1965) 'An economic theory of clubs', *Economica*, Vol. 32, February, pp. 1–14.

De Benedictis, L. and Padoan, P.L. (1994) 'The integration of Eastern Europe into the EC: A club-theory interest groups approach', in Lombardini, S. and Padoan, P.L. (eds) *Europe between East and South*, Kluwer Academic, Dordrecht.

De Long, B. and Eichengreen, B. (1993) 'The Marshall Plan: History's most successful structural adjustment programme', in Dornbusch, R., Nölling, W. and Layard, R. (eds) *Postwar Economic Reconstruction and Lessons for the East Today*, MIT Press, Cambridge, MA.

European Commission (2007a) 'Croatia Progress Report' COM(2007)663 final, www.europa.eu/enlargement

European Commission (2007b) 'The Former Yugoslav Republic of Macedonia Progress Report' COM(2007)663 final, www.europa.eu/enlargement

European Commission (2007c) 'Turkey Progress Report' COM(2007)663 final, www.europa.eu/enlargement

Grabbe, H. (2002) 'EU conditionality and the *acquis communautaire*', *International Political Science Review*, Vol. 23, No. 3, July.

Gros, D. and Steinherr, A. (2004) *Economic Transition in Central and Eastern Europe: Planting the Seeds*, Cambridge University Press, Cambridge.

Hughes, K. (2004) *Turkey and the European Union: Just Another Enlargement?* Friends of Europe Working Paper, June 2004.

Mayhew, A. (1998) *Recreating Europe. The European Union's Policy towards Central and Eastern Europe*, Cambridge University Press, Cambridge.

Mueller, D.C. (2001) *Public Choice III*, Cambridge University Press, Cambridge.

Senior Nello, S.M. (1991) *The New Europe: Changing Economic Relations between East and West*, Harvester Wheatsheaf, Hemel Hempstead.

Senior Nello, S.M. (2002) 'Preparing for enlargement in the European Union: The tensions between economic and political integration', *International Political Science Review*, Vol. 23, No. 3, July.

Senior Nello, S.M. (2004) 'Cyprus and EU accession' in Landuyt, A. (ed.) *Lo spazio politico nell'integrazione europea*. Gli allargamenti della CEE/UE dal 1961 al 2002, Il Mulino, Bologna.

Senior Nello, S.M. and Smith, K.E. (1998) *The Consequences of Eastern Enlargement of the European Union in Stages*, Ashgate Publishers Ltd, Aldershot, UK.

Siedentop, L. (2000) *Democracy in Europe*, Penguin Books, London.

Smith, K.E. (2001) 'Western actors and the promotion of democracy', in Zielonka, J. and Pravda, A. (eds) *Democratic Consolidation in Eastern Europe*, Vol. 2, International and Transnational Factors, Oxford University Press, Oxford.

Smith, K.E. (2003) 'The evolution and application of EU membership conditionality', in Cremona, M. (ed.) *The Enlargement of the European Union*, Oxford University Press, Oxford.

Uvalic, M. (2002) 'The economies of South-Eastern Europe – From international assistance to self-sustainable growth', Bertlesmann Foundation Risk Reporting 2001/2002 South-Eastern Europe Economics and Reform Assistance Strategy Report, Gütersloh, Germany, www.stiftung.bertlesmann.de

Vachudova, M.A. (2001) 'The leverage of international institutions on democratizing states: Eastern Europe and the European Union', EUI Working Paper RSC No. 2001/33, Florence, Italy.

Useful websites

European Commission provides data, description of policies and key documents:
www.ec.europa.eu/enlargement
www.ec.europa.eu/external_relations

The Countdown site of the Wiener Institut für Internationale Wirtschaftvergleiche provides an extensive bibliography, abstracts of publications and debate on key issues in transition:
http://wiiwsv.wsr.ac.at/Countdown/f_liter.htlm

European Bank for Reconstruction and Development presents statistics, country reports and analyses of key issues in transition countries:
www.ebrd.org

The Council of Europe provides analyses of democratic consolidation and human rights in transition countries:
www.coe.int

Data on FDI is available from the United Nations Conference on Trade and Development (UNCTAD):
www.unctad.org

Index